COLONIAL INTERNATIONALISM AND THE GOVERNMENTALITY OF EMPIRE, 1893–1982

In 1893, a group of colonial officials from thirteen countries abandoned their imperial rivalry and established the International Colonial Institute (ICI), which became the world's most important colonial think tank of the twentieth century. Through the lens of the ICI, Florian Wagner argues that this international cooperation reshaped colonialism as a transimperial and governmental policy. The book demonstrates that the ICI's strategy of using indigenous institutions and customary laws to encourage colonial development served to maintain colonial rule even beyond the official end of empires. By selectively choosing loyalists among the colonized to participate in the ICI, it increased their autonomy while equally delegitimizing more radical claims for independence. The book presents a detailed study of the ICI's creation, the transcolonial activities of its prominent members, its interactions with the League of Nations and fascist governments, and its role in laying the groundwork for the structural and discursive dependence of the Global South after 1945.

FLORIAN WAGNER is Assistant Professor of History at the University of Erfurt.

Global and International History

Series Editors
Erez Manela, *Harvard University*
Heather Streets-Salter, *Northeastern University*

The Global and International History series seeks to highlight and explore the convergences between the new International History and the new World History. Its editors are interested in approaches that mix traditional units of analysis such as civilizations, nations and states with other concepts such as transnationalism, diasporas, and international institutions.

Titles in the Series

Agnieszka Sobocinska, *Saving the World? Western Volunteers and the Rise of the Humanitarian-Development Complex*

Kirwin R. Shaffer, *Anarchists of the Caribbean: Countercultural Politics and Transnational Networks in the Age of US Expansion*

Stephen J. Macekura and Erez Manela, *The Development Century: A Global History*

Amanda Kay McVety, *The Rinderpest Campaigns: A Virus, Its Vaccines, and Global Development in the Twentieth Century*

Michele L. Louro, *Comrades against Imperialism*

Antoine Acker, *Volkswagen in the Amazon: The Tragedy of Global Development in Modern Brazil*

Christopher R. W. Dietrich, *Oil Revolution: Anti-Colonial Elites, Sovereign Rights, and the Economic Culture of Decolonization*

Nathan J. Citino, *Envisioning the Arab Future: Modernization in U.S.-Arab Relations, 1945–1967*

Stefan Rinke, *Latin America and the First World War*

Timothy Nunan, *Humanitarian Invasion: Global Development in Cold War Afghanistan*

Michael Goebel, *Anti-Imperial Metropolis: Interwar Paris and the Seeds of Third World Nationalism*

Stephen J. Macekura, *Of Limits and Growth: The Rise of Global Sustainable Development in the Twentieth Century*

COLONIAL INTERNATIONALISM AND THE GOVERNMENTALITY OF EMPIRE, 1893–1982

FLORIAN WAGNER
University of Erfurt

Shaftesbury Road, Cambridge CB2 8EA, United Kingdom

One Liberty Plaza, 20th Floor, New York, NY 10006, USA

477 Williamstown Road, Port Melbourne, VIC 3207, Australia

314–321, 3rd Floor, Plot 3, Splendor Forum, Jasola District Centre, New Delhi – 110025, India

103 Penang Road, #05–06/07, Visioncrest Commercial, Singapore 238467

Cambridge University Press is part of Cambridge University Press & Assessment, a department of the University of Cambridge.

We share the University's mission to contribute to society through the pursuit of education, learning and research at the highest international levels of excellence.

www.cambridge.org
Information on this title: www.cambridge.org/9781009069311

DOI: 10.1017/9781009072229

© Florian Wagner 2022

This publication is in copyright. Subject to statutory exception and to the provisions of relevant collective licensing agreements, no reproduction of any part may take place without the written permission of Cambridge University Press & Assessment.

First published 2022
First paperback edition 2024

A catalogue record for this publication is available from the British Library

ISBN 978-1-316-51283-8 Hardback
ISBN 978-1-009-06931-1 Paperback

Cambridge University Press & Assessment has no responsibility for the persistence or accuracy of URLs for external or third-party internet websites referred to in this publication and does not guarantee that any content on such websites is, or will remain, accurate or appropriate.

This book is dedicated to Levi Valentin Wagner.

CONTENTS

List of Figures viii
Acknowledgments ix
List of Abbreviations xi

Introduction 1

1 "More Beautiful than the Nationalist Thought"? Colonialist Fraternization and the Birth of Transnational Cooperation 24

2 A Transcolonial Governmentality Sui Generis: The Invention of Emulative Development 64

3 Politics of Comparison: The Dutch Model and the Reform of Colonial Training Schools 110

4 Cultivating the Myth of Transcolonial Progress: The ICI and the Global Career of Buitenzorg's Agronomic Laboratory 149

5 The Adatization of Islamic Law and Muslim Codes of Development 173

6 Creating an "Anti-Geneva Bloc" and the Question of Representivity 209

7 Inventing Fascist Eurafrica at the Volta Congress 257

8 False Authenticity: The Fokon'olona and the Cooperative World Commonwealth 281

9 "That Has Been Our Program for Fifty Years": Sustained Development and Loyal Emancipation after 1945 315

Conclusion 349

Bibliography 357
Index 409

FIGURES

1.1 Meeting of the INCIDI (former ICI) at Lisbon in 1957   62
3.1 German colonial officer and Dutch telegraph operator playing chess in Yap (Caroline Islands)   121
4.1 French Governor-General of Indochina Pierre Pasquier visits Java, dinner in the garden, around 1929   171
7.1 Italian fascists visiting the Nazi-Reichskolonialbund around 1938   265
9.1 Opening meeting of the INCIDI's session in Palermo in 1963   345

ACKNOWLEDGMENTS

The production of this book has put me in the debt of innumerable individuals and institutions. The dissertation that is at the origin of this book was made possible by the German Academic Exchange Service and the European University Institute in Florence. I thank Jörn Leonhard and Ulrike von Hirschhausen for employing me as an assistant lecturer at Freiburg and Rostock, where I made preliminary considerations of the dissertation. A fellowship at the German Historical Institute in Paris gave me the opportunity to conduct extensive research in archives in Paris, Aix-en-Provence, and Brussels. I made final revisions at the University of California, Berkeley, during a fellowship provided by the German Historical Institute (West) and the Institute for European Studies. Jürgen Zimmerer and Christiane Kuller allowed me to finish the book at the universities of Hamburg and Erfurt.

To an even greater extent, the book benefited from the exchange of ideas with many knowledgeable historians and admirable colleagues and friends. I would like to thank all those who commented on my dissertation or gave me the opportunity to discuss aspects and chapters in a formal or informal way. Among them are Catherine Atlan, Bruce Hall, Benedikt Stuchtey, Geert Castryck, Remco Raben, Cornel Zwierlein, Anne Kwaschik, Katja Naumann, Lorenzo Veracini, Frank Schumacher, Xosé Manoel Núñez Seixas, Volker Barth, Roland Cvetkovski, Ulrike Lindner, Florian Greiner, Frank Bösch, Heinz-Gerhard Haupt, Mathias Häussler, Brett Bennett, Ulrike Kirchberger, Jan Eckel, Riccardo Bavaj, Martina Steber, Dieter Langewiesche, Bartolomé Yun-Casalilla, Mareike König, Jakob Vogel, Ángel Alcalde, Haakon Ikonomou, Karen Gram-Skjoldager, Christian Methfessel, Iris Schröder, Ned Richardson-Little, Maria Framke, Jeroen Dewulf, Andrea Westermann, Sören Urbansky, Omar Kamil, Bernhard Schär, Sheer Ganor, and the members of "Der Kreis" at Berkeley. Pierre Singaravélou and Emmanuelle Sibeud allowed me to attend the inspiring "Séminaire Empires. Histoire des Colonisations" in Paris. In an equal measure, I benefited from various seminars at the École des hautes études en sciences sociales (EHESS) during my stay in Paris.

Frederick Cooper provided me with the most fruitful feedback and help. He always made time for my questions and concerns, be it in German beer gardens or on Tuscan terraces. His brilliant and comprehensive analyses of colonial empires were a starting point for my research. I owe particular debt to A. Dirk Moses, who introduced me to the American way of writing and guided me in developing a consistent argument. His immediate and parental advice made him the most valuable Doktorvater. I am equally grateful to Jörn Leonhard, whose dedication to scientific accuracy and scholarly excellence remain unmatched. His constant support and advice were indispensable. I thank Ann Thomson for her kind encouragement and rigorous feedback on French and British colonialism.

Erez Manela and Heather Streets-Salter accepted the book for the International History Series, and Lucy Rhymer and Rachel Blaifeder helped me to get it quickly and safely through the publishing process. I owe particular thanks to two anonymous reviewers, whose comments significantly improved the book.

Outstanding historians and good friends from Florence and Berkeley have used their precious time to read and comment on my chapters. Among them are Dónal Hassett, Per Tiedtke, Diana Natermann, Brandon Shanahan, Trevor Jackson, Stephanie Lämmert, Julia Wambach, and Angelo Matteo Caglioti. Nick Underwood and Katherine Meier have done the final grammar proofreading in an unobtrusive and thoughtful way. I would like to thank all of them.

My greatest debt and most fervent thanks I owe to my family. My nephew taught me a lesson about what really matters. Nothing compares to the role of Julia whose tolerance and patience was so exceptional, and without whom this volume would never have been written.

ABBREVIATIONS

AA	Auswaertiges Amt, Berlin (German Foreign Ministry)
AGRB	Archives Générales du Royaume Belge, Brussels (Belgian National Archives)
AMAEB	Archives du Ministère des Affaires Étrangères Belges/Archives Africaines, Brussels (Archives of the Belgian Foreign Ministry/ African Archives)
AMEAF	Archives du Ministère des Affaires Étrangères, La Corneuve, Paris (Archives of the French Foreign Ministry)
ANOM	Archives Nationales D'Outre-Mer, Aix-en-Provence (National Overseas Archives, France)
AOF	Afrique Occidentale Française (French West Africa)
BArch	Bundesarchiv, Berlin (German Federal Archives)
BNF	Bibliothèque Nationale de France, Paris (French National Library)
CFS	État Indépendant du Congo (Congo Free State)
CGTT	Confédération générale des travailleurs tunisiens (General Confederation of Tunisian Workers)
CO	Colonial Office Archives, in National Archives, Kew
CSMSA	*Convegno di Scienze Morali e Storiche 1938, Tema: Africa*, Rome: RAI, 1938 (Congress of the Moral and Historical Sciences on Africa, 1938)
ECOSOC	United Nations Economic and Social Council
HZA	Hohenlohe Zentralarchiv, Neuenstein (Hohenlohe Central Archives)
ICI	Institut Colonial International (International Colonial Institute)
IfL	Archives Institut für Länderkunde, Leipzig (Archives of the Institute for Regional Geography)
ILO	International Labour Organization
INCIDI	Institut International des Civilisations Différentes (International Institute of Differing Civilizations)
IVVR	Internationale Vereinigung für Vergleichende Rechtswissenschaft und Volkswirtschaftslehre (International Association for Comparative Law and Political Economy)
KNPA	Kilimanjaro Native Planters' Association

LIST OF ABBREVIATIONS

LoN	Archives League of Nations, Palais des Nations, Geneva
PMC	Permanent Mandates Commission, League of Nations
RAI	Reale Accademia d'Italia
RAI, *CSMSA*	Reale Accademia d'Italia, ed., *Convegno di Scienze Morali e Storiche 1938, Tema: Africa*, Rome: RAI, 1938
RKA	Reichskolonialamt (German Colonial Ministry)
StaHa	Staatsarchiv Hamburg (Hamburg State Archives)
UCL	Archives de l'Université Catholique de Louvain, Louvain-la-Neuve (Archives of the Catholic University of Leuven)
ULCSH	Universiteitsarchieven, Leiden (Leiden University Archives), Collection Snouck Hurgronje
UN	United Nations
UNESCO	United Nations Educational, Scientific and Cultural Organization

Introduction

In 1905, Mohandas Gandhi paid homage to Joseph Chailley, the founding father of the International Colonial Institute. Gandhi's appreciation for Chailley exposed the complex interconnectedness of the colonial world around 1900. The *Indian Opinion*, a journal Gandhi published in South Africa, bestowed honor upon the Frenchman Chailley, who had recently spent several months in the Dutch Indies and was about to coauthor a book with British colonial administrators. To give the imperial interconnectedness an institution, Chailley had established the International Colonial Institute (ICI) in Brussels, as early as 1893. By 1905, this institute had grown to become the most important think tank for colonial rule, continuing with 136 (white) members. As it styled itself as reformist, this institute raised hopes among colonial subjects around the world. Gandhi's *Indian Opinion* saw in Chailley's writings on India "an unbiased testimony of a stranger," and an adequate description of British colonial mismanagement: "He finds himself in a vast agricultural country, where there is great poverty and where commerce and trade are entirely local and therefore without real importance. He notices an absence of industrial activity, he discovers some people, perhaps owning fortunes, but – there is no capital."[1] Fighting against the underdevelopment of colonies was the declared aim of the ICI. Its members claimed to develop colonies through cooperation among international experts who would get the most out of the colonized population and the colonial economy. Gandhi was not alone in falling for this delusion, which actually served to legitimize and perpetuate colonial domination.[2]

Fifteen years later, Asians and Africans had rather mixed feelings about the cross-border schemes that the ICI designed. In 1919, Chailley initiated an Anglo-French economic conference on West Africa. The newspaper *The Gold Coast Nation*, which gave the Ghanaian coastal elite a voice, reported on this "four day conference of most authoritative Anglo-French Colonial officials": the conference intended to coordinate the activities of European shipping

---

[1] *Indian Opinion* (October 6, 1905), 5.
[2] On Indian internationalism in the empire, see Gorman, *The Emergence*, 109–148.

lines, standardize bills of lading, and align customs regulations. On top of that, it had contemplated building an "inter-colonial railway system" across Africa. Among West African entrepreneurs, these initiatives instilled little hope and raised much fear.

The *Gold Coast Nation* expected the practical cooperation between colonizers to be part of a revived international agreement to partition Africa, by which the "Acts of Berlin and Brussels may be renewed."[3] The Acts of Berlin (1885) and Brussels (1890) had sealed the deal between European powers to colonize Africa. They indeed became the legal basis for a renewed partition of Africa under the auspices of the League of Nations in 1919.[4] Thus, while observing the imperial atavism of the new League of Nations, the colonized populations equally monitored the activities of the ICI. The *Gold Coast Nation* expected immediate effects not only through the diplomats who met in Paris in 1919 but also by more hands-on members of the ICI, which dated from 1893.

Among Asians and Africans under colonial rule, the question emerged, whether the ICI represented the interests of the European metropoles or whether it might be a third actor in the dualist drama between colonizers and colonized. In 1921, the *Nigerian Pioneer* reported that the institute's secretary-general, Camille Janssen, presented more precise plans of cooperation across colonies:

> At a Congress of the International Colonial Institute ... M. Janssen submitted a report on railway construction in Africa. He said it devolved on the Institute to fix the great African trunk lines and dwelt especially on the Trans-Soudan and the Trans-Equatorial railways, which might connect the Belgian and French Congo. He contended that Beira and Lourenco Marques should be linked up with Lobito Bay and Mossamedes. The French railway system should be joined up to the South African system via the Belgian Congo.

The *Nigerian Pioneer* was a paper published by African entrepreneurs loyal to the British rulers in Nigeria. The economic cross-border schemes of the ICI attracted their interest.[5] They asked themselves whether these "transcolonial" projects might alter the relation between colonizers and colonized.

This book is about the internationalist colonial lobby that rallied around the International Colonial Institute and laid the groundwork for the structural and discursive dependence of the colonial world in the twentieth century. The enormous influence of the around 700 colonial internationalists who joined the ICI between 1893 and 1982 is still unknown today.[6] Gandhi and the West

---

[3] *The Gold Coast Nation* (July 6, 1919), 3.
[4] Pedersen, *The Guardians*, 108.
[5] *The Nigerian Pioneer* (June 3, 1921), 6.
[6] UCL Fonds Wigny Carrière C4, Report Voyage aux États-Unis, Speech Manuscript INCIDI, 3.

African journalists knew at least two by name: Joseph Chailley, a Frenchman, who had established the ICI in 1893, and the Belgian Camille Janssen, who became the ICI's long-serving secretary-general. Together with six other founders, Chailley and Janssen turned the ICI into the most important international organization and the biggest think tank for colonial policy prior to World War I. In 1913, the ICI listed 136 members from twelve countries. Among them figured colonialist icons such as the German colonial minister Bernhard Dernburg, the French general-resident in Morocco Hubert Lyautey, the British governor-general of Nigeria Frederick Lugard, the Belgian railway-builder Albert Thys, the governor-general of the Dutch East Indies Dirk Fock, and the Spanish colonial reformer Antonio Fabié. During the 1920s, the ICI supplied the League of Nations with colonial experts.[7] In the 1930s, its members joined hands with fascists to design a new Eurafrican empire. In 1949, the ICI changed its name to Institute of Differing Civilizations (INCIDI), and accepted the membership of non-Europeans. Under this name, it continued to exist until 1982.[8]

I argue in this book that colonial internationalists reshaped colonial policy by designing it as a transnational and governmental project. Transnationalism and governmentality were two sides of the same coin. They belittled the importance of the (nation-)state and its direct administration for colonial rule. We can define transnationalism as practices not primarily driven by nationalism and that go beyond the nation-state without necessarily overcoming it. Governmentality, as Foucault construed it, is government with the help of expert knowledge, attributions, categorizations, discourses, definitions, and, most importantly, the active cooperation of those who are governed.[9] Although Foucault found governmentality predominantly within liberal societies whose members voluntarily governed themselves, the colonized might equally have been autonomous individuals, even if the threat of violence frequently forced them to participate in the system of colonial governmentality.[10]

State government and unofficial transnational governmentality were not mutually exclusive, and their combination was indeed an attribute of empire.

---

[7] On the League between nationalism and internationalism, see Gram-Skjoldager and Ikonomou, "Making Sense of the League," 420–444.

[8] Pétit, "Éditorial," 7–8.

[9] Foucault, "Governmentality," 87–104. Among the early studies applying Foucault to colonial contexts, see Comaroff, *Revelation and Revolution*; Dimier, *Le gouvernement*, 75–108. On discourses, see Stoler, *Race and the Education of Desire*, esp. 1–18. For a discussion of the merits of the Foucauldian perspectives, see Mitchell, *Rule of Experts*, esp. 3–9.

[10] Cooper, "Conflict and Connection," 1533–1535; Seth, "Foucault in India," 43–57; Pesek, "Foucault Hardly Came to Africa," 41–59. See also Comaroff, "Governmentality, Materiality, Legality, Modernity," 107–134.

Unlike nation-states, empire-states made it easier for nongovernmental agencies such as the ICI to govern, especially in "transnational" spaces and remote colonial territories that partly escaped the control of nation-states.[11] Thus, ICI members operated both within conventional state structures and in transnational spaces of governmentality. Governmentality, as historians of the Subaltern Studies Group remarked, could be highly concrete and express itself in state intervention and police surveillance. More frequently, however, it took indirect and transnational forms such as in medical discourses about deficient indigenous hygiene that helped to legitimize colonial domination.[12] Colonial experts established the ICI in 1893 to develop such transnational technologies of governmentality.[13]

The ICI was unique because its members developed their own notion of transnational governmentality long before Foucault gave it a name. Hence, this book does not take governmentality at face value but analyzes the way colonial experts themselves imagined, used, and designed schemes of transnational governmentality in the colonies. Ruling through international experts who appropriated and manipulated indigenous discourses for their own cause, the ICI suggested, would be more efficient than involving naive bureaucrats from the metropole.[14] While racial bias led ICI members to believe that indirect governmentality was too abstract to be noticed among the colonized population, the latter actually understood the hypocritical shift to transnational governmentality very well. After all, the ICI promoted transnational governmentality to obscure the violent nature and brutal excesses of colonial rule. The colonized population saw through allegedly hidden power structures and contested them. Partha Chatterjee remarked that anti-colonialists of the twentieth century rejected participative governmentality and requested sovereignty, which promised full independence instead of restricted self-determination.[15] Nevertheless, members of the ICI developed technologies of transnational governmentality during their annual meetings and often implemented them in colonies. Going under the name of functional governance, the ICI's transnational governmentality would make a career in the League of Nations and the UN development agencies after World War II.[16]

The term "transnational governmentality" describes all forms of unofficial government without or outside the material and ideological infrastructure of

---

[11] Mann, *From Empires to NGOs*, 2.
[12] Arnold, "Touching the Body," 55–90.
[13] For the most nuanced analysis regarding cooperation in colonial hygiene after 1945, see Pearson, *The Colonial Politics of Global Health*, 67.
[14] The scale of colonial governmentality was unheard of, even though strategies of ruling through discourses existed in the nineteenth century. See Kalpagam, "Colonial Governmentality and the Public Sphere in India," 418–440.
[15] Chatterjee, "Governmentality in the East."
[16] Mazower, *Governing the World*; Karns and Mingst, *International Organizations*, 40–41.

the nation-state. The absence of nation-states in schemes of the ICI's transnational governmentality does not mean they were irrelevant. The ICI was far from systematically rejecting the nation-state or launching a transnational conspiracy to overcome it. On the contrary, transnational processes are so interesting because they were exceptional. Nation-states, manifesting themselves in collective participation, a bureaucratic apparatus, and a strong narrative of homogeneity, shaped the mindsets and activities of ICI members between 1890 and 1960 and few of them could afford to renounce its advantages. One core question of this book, therefore, is when, why, and to what extent self-declared *colonial* internationalists were able and willing to renounce their nation-state.

What did it mean to be a colonial internationalist? Declaring oneself an internationalist allowed ICI members to remain good patriots, since nationalism and inter-nationalism were complementary and not mutually exclusive.[17] Yet that did not necessarily make internationalists diplomats, thinking of themselves as intergovernmental brokers. Rather, declaring oneself internationalist was a conscious choice through which an individual or a group became part of a progressive movement.[18] In the 1890s, internationalism was indeed a label political or scholarly groups used to declare themselves progressive, be they socialists, liberals, utilitarians, colonialists, or medical experts. Since internationalism was rarely an end in itself, it mostly served as a means to make activities such as colonialism sound worldly.[19] For its declarative character, the term "international" must raise suspicions. ICI members used internationalism to portray colonialism as progressive and reformable, a claim that this book disproves.

While internationalism was a theoretical construct and a political choice, "transnational" describes the social and economic practice of "unpolitical" but not unintentional interaction across borders.[20] Contemporaries did not use the word "transnational," which gives us the opportunity to turn it into an analytical concept that describes interaction across state borders and national systems, mostly happening below the diplomatic level without a predominantly politicized purpose.[21] Unlike internationalism, transnationalism can be more than the sum of its parts and transcend nationalism and the nation-state or even make it irrelevant. Both internationalism and

---

[17] Sluga, *Internationalism*, 12.
[18] Also called utopia by some. See Clavin and Sluga, *Rethinking the History*, 8; Gorman, *The Emergence*, 3.
[19] Herren, *Hintertüren*, 169–173; Mazower, *No Entchanted Palace*, 31.
[20] There are, however, political projects of a transnational civil society: Iriye, *Global Community*, 7.
[21] Irye, *Global and Transnational History*, 9; Budde et al., *Transnationale Geschichte*. See also the definition in Paulmann and Geyer, *The Mechanics of Internationalism*, 3; Clavin and Sluga, *Rethinking*, 4.

transnationalism used to be Eurocentric, though, and therefore difficult to apply to the colonized world.[22]

To be sure, between 1890 and 1960, nation-states were equally empires and the expression "transimperial governmentality" would have had its merits.[23] Yet ICI members avoided the words empire and imperial between 1890 and 1960 because they were not regarded as progressive. They preferred to label themselves colonialists instead of imperialists. What is more, prior to World War II, empire-state infrastructure in the colonies was highly deficient.[24] It would thus make little sense to analyze transimperial governmentality and ask why colonial internationalists did not use the official imperial state infrastructure that did not even exist. No doubt, "empire" provides us with a powerful notion of a space linking up colonies and metropoles to produce inequality and restricted agency alike. The transimperial has lately become all-encompassing, applying to continental empires and colonial empires, imperial formations and formal empires, Non-European and European empires, and so on.[25] What is more, the term "transimperial" increasingly designates the cross-border activities among subaltern groups and anti-imperialists. Since the colonized had been denied participation in the international community for ages, their activity has now been labeled transimperial.[26] While this book is about empires and touches on all those transimperial processes, it looks more specifically at colonial and transcolonial processes.

A more promising analysis has to include the self-perceptions of colonial internationalists who used different networks and labels in different situations. They potentially labeled themselves internationalists, nationalists, "pure" colonialists, utilitarians, reformers, functionalists, and Eurafricanists, always depending on the context. Often, they used the infrastructure of their own nation-states, but equally networks and funding of other nations and international organizations and companies, while establishing their own "transcolonial" infrastructure.

By establishing the ICI, colonial internationalists intended to build a purely "colonial" and "transcolonial" infrastructure that emancipated itself from the metropoles' focus on state and nation. By denying the importance of nation-states for good practices of colonization, the ICI members designed such an autonomous colonial sphere.[27] "Transcolonial" referred predominantly to

---

[22] Clavin, "Defining Transnationalism," 431; Conrad and Osterhammel, *Kaiserreich*, 14.
[23] Ross, *Ecology and Power*, 256; Gissibl, *The Nature*, 15–16.
[24] Greenwood, *Beyond the State*, 9.
[25] Hedinger, "Transimperial History"; Stoler et al., *Imperial Formations*; Burbank and Cooper, *Empires*.
[26] Manela, *The Wilsonian Moment*; Goebel, *Anti-Imperial Metropolis*; Weiss, *Framing a Radical African Atlantic*. On their reclaimed internationalism, see Goswami, "Imaginary Futures"; Salter, *World War One*.
[27] Stockwell, *The British End*, 5–6; Van Laak, *Imperiale Infrastruktur*, 34.

knowledge circulation and technology transfers between different colonies, to which the state in the metropole were irrelevant and often an impediment.

Again, ICI members did not use the term "transcolonial" and spoke only sporadically about "inter-colonial" activities. Yet they developed an explicit esprit de corps and claimed to work in a transcolonial sphere "sui generis" (Chapter 2). Observing this autonomy, the British Colonial Office doubted whether "the title 'international'" applied to the ICI at all, because "its members are [exclusively] chosen from the countries which have colonies."[28] But the ICI was not a mere broker between colonies, empires, and nations. The ICI was involved in a transcolonial practice. It is one purpose of this book to uncover this transcolonial dimension and evaluate its autonomy from the nationalist history. It is important to know that transnational governmentality was not necessarily the precondition for the emergence of a transcolonial sphere. Both were mutually constitutive but also existed separately from each other.

Members of the ICI believed that transcolonial autonomy gave them access to the colonized to use them as tools for transcolonial governmentality, whereas the colonized themselves became important protagonists and experts who used transcolonial networks for their own purposes. Both sides contributed to developing technologies of colonial governmentality. Among those technologies were transcolonial development schemes, cooperation in sanitation policies, technology transfers between colonies, the use of pseudo-authentic indigenous concepts and laws to motivate them for work, stimuli for self-discipline by introducing salaries and credit banks, incentives for labor migration across colonial borders, internationalization of the colonial administration, the use of indigenous administrators and their representation on the local and international level, cooperative welfare schemes, and the partnership with local farmers and craft guilds. The chapters in this book take a closer look at what effect these technologies of transcolonial governmentality had.

Hence, four analytical concepts are necessary to think through colonial internationalism: the international, the transnational, the intercolonial, and the transcolonial. Internationalism is the label our protagonists chose for themselves and describes the *ideal* of cooperation among nationals from different countries.[29] Transnationalism is a word they did not know or use but provides us with an unencumbered analytical term to describe the social *practice* of cooperation and transfers across borders in the Global North.

---

[28] CO 323 984 7: Colonial Office to Foreign Office, [1931].
[29] Ideally, the cooperation among the "civilized" world. See Mazower, *No Enchanted Palace*, 28–65; Koskenniemi, *The Gentle Civilizer of Nations*, 98–177; Anghie, *Imperialism, Sovereignty, and the Making of International Law*, 32–195; Bell, *Victorian Visions of Global Order*, 10. See also Clavin and Sluga, *Internationalisms*, 8–10, Armitage, *Modern International Thought*, 41–44.

While both of these concepts refer to the nation, the protagonists occasionally described their collaboration overseas as "intercolonial," with no reference to the nation or the empire at all. Thus, they imagined an autonomous colonial sphere in which the nation was absent, if not irrelevant. In parallel to the discrimination between the international ideal and the transnational practice, we can distinguish between the *ideal* of intercolonial cooperation and the social *practice* of transcolonial transfers.[30] Thus, the four concepts under discussion are the contemporary ideals of international and intercolonial cooperation and today's analytical terms of transnational and transcolonial transfers, which allow us to frame the practice of transfers.

The ICI's ideal of internationalism was certainly compatible with the metropole's national sovereignty, as was the practice of transcolonial transfers with imperial integrity. Most imperial governments believed that transcolonial transfers made their own empire even stronger and more competitive. While representatives of small nations with large empires such as Belgium displayed particular interest in the ICI, governments of great powers equally hoped to benefit from its denationalized knowledge production.[31] All of the colonial powers ultimately funded the ICI and supported its schemes of colonial autonomy because it promised a universally applicable best practice of colonial governmentality. The ICI styled itself a learned society dedicated to a denationalized and colonial science, and its members thought of colonial science as an applied method rather than an armchair theory. Comparison and transfer were the most important operators of this method. While transcolonial emulation and technology transfers were ultimately less successful than imperial governments imagined, it mattered that they thought of them as progressive. Thus, the idea that transnational and transcolonial cooperation was more progressive than nationalist insularity was born.

This book assumes that the label internationalism was more important than nationalism for the longevity of colonial projects, because only transnational cooperation held out the prospect of profitability and legitimacy against allegations of inefficiency and illegitimacy. When Chailley established the ICI in 1893, he was responding to colonies being unprofitable for both the colonizers and the colonized. Indeed, in the 1890s, the enthusiasm of conquest gave way to increased criticism from European governments and colonial subjects alike. The ICI's promise to reform colonial administration convinced the critics that the inherent contradictions and poor results of colonialism could be overcome by a transnational, systematic, scientific, and governmental

---

[30] On intercolonial cooperation, see Streets-Salter, *World War One*, 11. Most historians seem to assume that transnational history is a new perspective on Western history. See Patel, "An Emperor," 3–5. Only rarely, they explicitly apply the term to North-South relationships. See, for example, Lorcin and Shepard, *French Mediterraneans*, 1–3.

[31] On "small nations," see Schayegh, "The Expanding Overlap," 782–802.

effort to improve colonial administration. Along these lines, Chailley's critical report on British India cited by Gandhi's *Indian Opinion* made believe that the ICI was a reformist institution, and its members were progressive experts.[32] Chailley proclaimed that colonies would only pay off if these experts cooperated with each other and with the colonized population. This book reveals how conservative their reforming zeal was.

Against this background, the combination of internationalism and reformism – representing the spatial and the temporal side of progress – provided the ICI with a narrative to justify colonial domination. This book challenges this narrative of progress, which portrayed colonialism as a cybernetic system able to cure itself of nationalism through reformist internationalization. As we will see, ICI members suggested that internationalism was more humane than nationalism and benefited the colonized population. They confined excesses to the era of colonial conquest, when overly emotionalized nationalists had violently occupied land without any rational purpose. Internationalists, instead, claimed to govern colonies based on principles of rationality, mutuality, and humanity. In this narrative, nationalist colonialism seemed to benefit the honor of the metropole, while internationalist colonialism seemed to benefit humankind. By establishing this narrative, propagandists of colonial internationalism added a temporal axis to the spatial one: over time, colonialism allegedly emancipated itself from its nationalist origins and became internationalist and benevolent.

Among historians, the debate concerning whether internationalizing colonial rule in 1919 perpetuated prewar colonialism or anticipated independence remained inconclusive.[33] Scholars who believe progress ruled the world often embraced the narrative of improvement through internationalization.[34] Some concluded that the violent conquests of the 1880s gave way to a more humane and liberal atmosphere in 1919, when the League of Nations internationalized former German and Ottoman colonies, reformed their administration, and granted their inhabitants a say. Historians were unaware, however, that ICI members had infiltrated the League of Nations' Permanent Mandate Commission and used their position to silence the inhabitants of the mandates, which actually differed little from traditional prewar colonies.[35] The analysis of the ICI between the 1890s and the 1950s reveals that internationalism and reformism, as well as humanitarianism, were inherent to colonialism from the beginning of imperial expansion and not a progressive element at all.[36] The year

---

[32] Mentioned in the footnotes in Wilder, *The French Imperial Nation-State*, 316.
[33] Martin and Toye, *Arguing about Empire*, 16–18; Pedersen, *The Guardians*, 4.
[34] Daughton, "Behind the Imperial Curtain," 506–507; Laqua, *Internationalism*; Richard, "Between the League of Nations and Europe," 97–116.
[35] Bandeira Jerónimo, "A League of Empires," 87–126.
[36] Hoffmann, *Human Rights*, 7–8.

1919 certainly became a "moment" of raised expectations among the colonized for more autonomy and their own nation-states.[37] By that date, however, the ICI had long designed strategies of autonomy and self-government to delegitimize those who asked for immediate independence. Therefore, judging by the ICI's persistent schemes of reformist governmentality, the world wars were not necessarily a significant stage in a linear history of progress toward independence.

A critical analysis of the ICI's long-term history reveals how little historical change mattered in modifying its members' colonial configurations: colonial internationalism existed long before 1919 and continued to shape the postindependence era after the 1950s.[38] Analyzing the ICI between the 1890s and the 1960s shows that the allegedly different consecutive epochs of colonialism resembled each other. The liberal imperialism of free trade of the nineteenth century was compatible with seemingly protectionist development projects of the early twentieth century.[39] The League of Nations' "humanitarian" colonialism of the 1920s unresistingly merged into the fascist project of a Eurafrican empire in the 1930s. At an international colonial congress organized by ICI members and Italian fascists in 1938, the participants promoted the liberal and progressive anthropology of Bronislaw Malinowski, which had the reputation of overcoming racist stereotypes. After 1945, ICI members perpetuated elements of governmental systems developed by the free traders who founded the ICI in 1893 and by fascist colonial internationalists. Analyzing the ICI helps us to understand that governmental strategies hardly changed, no matter whether republicans, liberals, nationalists, internationalists, or fascists ruled the colonial world.[40]

In equal measure, the ICI stood for the persistence of transnational governmentality from the period of conquest to the independence era. The ICI's transnational governmentality partly assumed the shape of functional governance, an allegedly depoliticized government through an international technocracy. Theories of functional governance stated that public international agencies and private companies should join forces to solve social and economic "world problems" through transnational cooperation, without relying too much on selfish states who were ineffectual in tackling problems of the Global South, for example. The main theorist of functional governance, David Mitrany, had learned his trade in Hamburg's Colonial Institute, a training school for colonial administrators established by ICI members in

---

[37] Manela, *Wilsonian Moment*, 6.
[38] Fogarty, *Race and War in France*, 10–14; Gerwarth and Manela, *Empires at War*, 1–16; Leonhard, *Der Überforderte Frieden*, 1275–1277.
[39] They were interventionist free traders as described by Slobodian, *Globalists*, 1–26.
[40] Hetherington and Sluga, "Liberal and Illiberal Internationalisms," 2; Fitzpatrick, *Liberal Imperialism in Europe*, 1–24; Alcalde, "Transnational Consensus," 243–252.

1908 and using transcolonial curricula designed by ICI members. In the interwar period, Mitrany helped to conceptualize the League of Nations' transnational governance before rising to fame among UN employees and international development agencies after World War II. The ICI held close ties with Hamburg's Colonial Institute, the League, and the UN development agencies, as well as with Unilever, a multinational company that Mitrany advised on international affairs and functional governance.[41]

Since the ICI's experts facilitated those governmental colonial structures largely without the metropole, the ICI was well prepared to endorse formal independence after 1945. By then, ICI members had specialized in pursuing colonial aims without the infrastructure of the empire–nation-state and with the help of indigenous institutions, be it Islamic law, customary law, representative councils, craft guilds, or cooperative schemes of mutual help. Members of the ICI promised to achieve the classical goals of colonialism through schemes of "indigenous" self-government, self-development, self-legislation, self-help, and mutual welfare. Thus, when the American President Harry S. Truman came up with similar ideas in his Point Four development program in 1949, ICI members disgruntledly remarked that these development schemes "had been our program for fifty years."[42]

What is more, the ICI's use of indigenous institutions had a postcolonial afterlife and partly continued to exist in the independence era. For example, ICI members redefined Islamic law as customary *adat* law to expropriate fertile lands from pious Islamic endowments. *Adat* law became the legal code of independent Indonesia and shaped notions of Islamic law in North Africa. In Chapter 8, I discuss how a cooperative scheme of agriculture and mutual help from Madagascar, called *fokon'olona*, enabled colonizers to maintain and legitimize forced labor, while simultaneously claiming to have abolished it. The *fokon'olona* schemes of cooperative economy were still in use following the decolonization period, when the International Labor Organization and the UNESCO recommended them as a tool of sustained economic development for the entire "Third World."[43]

We can follow Aimé Césaire in naming and blaming the hypocrisy of colonial internationalism. In 1950, the poet and pioneer of black empowerment from Martinique published his groundbreaking *Discourse on Colonialism* to expose the "cynicism" of a united "*Europe colonisatrice*" and

---

[41] Anderson, "David Mitrany," 577–592; Karns and Mingst, *International Organizations*, 40–41.
[42] UCL Fonds Wigny C4, Voyage aux États-Unis, Manuscript Belgian Colonial Policy, 5.
[43] On internationalism and development after 1945, see Macekura and Manela, *The Development Century*. For development before 1945, see Lorenzini, *Development*; Unger, *International Development*, 5–11; Cooper and Packard, *International Development*, 6–7.

its narrative about a progressive and enlightened colonialism. Césaire explained that European colonizers styled themselves as "honest bourgeois" and tried to "legitimize a posteriori the *action colonisatrice*" by focusing exclusively on "material progress." He admitted that "material progress ... has been achieved in certain fields under the colonial regime" but that it concealed the continued violence.[44] As an example of European hypocrisy, he cited one of the ICI's heroes, the Belgian Placide Tempels. Like many ICI members, Tempels had styled himself as a progressive *indigenophile*. He admired Bantu culture in Central Africa and published his famous book on Bantu philosophy in 1945.[45] It seemed that Tempels took the intellectual contribution of Central Africa to philosophy seriously. Césaire, however, pointed out that Tempels was a missionary who had invented Bantu philosophy to prove that "Bantus" from Central Africa were in favor of European colonization. Members of the ICI shared Tempels' strategy to advance "indigenous" arguments in favor of colonial domination.[46]

In so doing, Césaire blamed the colonial internationalists for obscuring the excessive violence of colonialism. Indeed, in 107 volumes that the ICI members published between 1893 and 1950 about colonial policy, violent repression and warfare was strikingly absent. Neither the destruction of the Herero-Nama in German South-West Africa (1904–1907), nor the mass murders during forced rubber collections in the Congo (1890s), nor the Italian chemical war to conquer Ethiopia (1935) appear directly in the ICI's publications.[47] Instead, the narrative of progressive colonial governmentality prevailed. This total absence of violence in Europe's transcolonial discourse led Césaire to conclude that Europeans were not imperial rivals who criticized each other but a sworn community that imposed their delusive narrative of liberality and governmentality. While Europeans blamed Hitler after 1945 for having broken the oath and abandoning a policy of liberal governmentality in favor of total destruction, Césaire exposed how European powers continued their equally racist and violent exploitation of the colonies. In the initiatives of the 1950s to (re)unify Europe and co-opt African colonies, Césaire identified an attempt to hide colonial violence and to reestablish the dissimulating narrative of progress. He warned that behind the new "Europe of Adenauer, Schuman, Bidault and others, there is Hitler."[48] Although this was a very unspecific suggestion of continuities, these founding fathers of a unified Europe stood for a persistence of colonial structures in the European project,

---

[44] Césaire, *Discourse on Colonialism*, 45.
[45] Fabian, *Philosophie Bantoue*.
[46] Ibid., 58.
[47] Zimmerer and Zeller. *Genocide*; Vanthemsche, *Belgium and the Congo*, 21–24.
[48] Césaire, *Discourse on Colonialism*, 37.

as exposed by Véronique Dimier and others.[49] Adenauer's past as a leading member of colonial lobby groups was indeed well known. When he became chancellor of Germany, Adenauer continued to send greetings to the ICI's meetings. Schuman initiated a paternalist and purely economic Eurafrica without democratic representation for Africans, a strategy that the ICI had used for decades.[50] Bidault, a former member of the French Résistance, had joined French settlers to fight against Algeria's independence and used his position as a foreign minister to take drastic measures in the Indochina war.[51]

The ICI stood for these dubious origins of the new Europe after 1945: fascist members of the ICI, who had designed a Eurafrican empire in the 1930s, continued promoting Africa as Europe's semi-colonial hinterland in the 1950s and evoked the Africans' "obligation" to supply Europe with its resources.[52] Superficially concealing this continuity, the ICI renamed itself Institute of Differing Civilizations (INCIDI) when it reestablished itself in 1949.[53] When empires turned into Eurasian and Eurafrican federations after 1945, the INCIDI recommended organizing these federations along functionalist principles. Functionalism highlighted the productive interconnectedness of economic, social, individual, and political relations within these federations and on a global scale, without providing a strategy for political participation and democratization. A functionalist system also worked very well beyond independence.

As soon as the processes of Europeanization and decolonization took off in the 1950s, the INCIDI kept "extremist" independence leaders at bay and tried to "emancipate" the colonies "loyally." Moderate anti-colonialists such as the Senegalese Léopold Sédar Senghor joined the INCIDI and publicly pledged allegiance to the European cause. Assured by their loyalty, INCIDI leaders went as far as proposing to invite African leaders to become representatives in the Council of Europe but without granting them real power.[54]

Fully aware of this hypocrisy, this book focuses on the ICI's techniques of governmentality developed between 1890 and 1945, which are key for understanding these continuities. Using comparison and transcolonial transfers as a method, ICI members tried to identify the most efficient methods of colonial administration and development. Their main concern was to abandon

---

[49] Hansen and Jonsson, *Eurafrica*, 118-119; Martin, *The French Colonial Mind*, 233; Dimier, *The Invention*, 11, 44, and 57. On Adenauer, see Schilling, *Postcolonial Germany*, 92.

[50] INCIDI, *Compte Rendu 1960*, 644; Patel, *Project Europe*, 244.

[51] Evans, *Algeria*, 285 and 307.

[52] Ageron, "L'idée d'Eurafrique," 446-475.

[53] UCL Fonds Wigny, M1, vols. 1-4, 1959, Conversation with Dulles, October 8, 1958, 4; vol. 5, 1959; Wigny: "L'Eurafrique," October 22, 1959.

[54] INCIDI, *Compte Rendu 1961*, 149.

North-South transfers from the metropole to the colonies. Instead, ICI members brought about South-South transfers between the colonies and favored "inter-colonial learning" among autonomous colonial experts. To achieve this, the ICI published a book series that established a new field of transcolonial and comparative colonial science, the *Bibliothèque Coloniale Internationale*. Transcolonial knowledge exchange helped experts to find a best practice of colonial rule and efficient development.[55] The purpose of South-South transfers was to develop colonial techniques that secured colonial self-sufficiency and colonial exploitation "on the cheap." For that purpose, the ICI held twenty-four plenary meetings and several smaller ones prior to World War II. In addition to hundreds of case studies published by its members, the ICI produced thirty-two volumes of records of those meetings, thirty-two volumes of compared legislation, and thirty-eight year books.[56]

The present book uses not only the above-mentioned publications to reconstruct the history of colonial internationalism but also relies on archival research in six countries. As only fragments of the ICI's original archives have survived in the African Archives in Brussels, I used hitherto unknown material from over twenty public and private archives in Belgium, France, Great Britain, the Netherlands, Germany, and Switzerland. A history of the ICI based on archival material reveals that this history of colonial internationalism was much more influential than historians have suggested.

Research in these archives has revealed that the minor role colonial internationalists play in the historiography does not do justice to their impact. Mainly for reasons of methodological nationalism, the ICI has received little historiographical attention.[57] A few historians have used the ICI's official publications to illustrate the transnational nature of colonial science.[58] However, no study has used archival material to consider the effects of the ICI's governmental program in the colonies. While the ICI's publications contributed to the establishment of area studies in Europe, it remains unclear to what extent ICI members made indigenous knowledge a pillar of colonial theory and praxis.[59] The ICI's effect on practical colonial policy is thus obscure, although studies on colonial labor policy, customary law, indigenous education, anthropological research, and development

---

[55] Schröder, *Wissen*; Kamissek and Kreienbaum, *An Imperial Cloud?*, 164–182.
[56] UCL Fonds Wigny C4, Voyage aux États-Unis, Manuscript INCIDI, 3.
[57] Two articles are rather tentative. See De Jong, "Kolonialisme op een Koopje," 45–72; Böttger, "Internationalismus und Kolonialismus," 165–172. Most importantly, see Poncelet, *L'Invention des Sciences Coloniales*; Wagner, "Private Colonialism and International Co-operation," 57–78; and Lindner, "New Forms of Knowledge Exchange," 36–57.
[58] Singaravélou, "Les Stratégies d'Internationalisation," 135–157.
[59] Kwaschik, *Der Griff nach dem Weltwissen*, 1–27.

schemes occasionally point toward the ICI's outstanding significance for the colonized world.[60]

Occasionally and superficially addressed in colonial studies, the ICI is strikingly absent in standard accounts about international organizations. Some authors have hinted at the ICI's influence on the International Labor Organization, but nothing is known about its important ties with the League of Nations and the fascist internationalism of the 1930s.[61] Historians who have analyzed development policies after 1945 acknowledge the ICI's significance while privileging UN institutions and financially more powerful private initiatives such as the Rockefeller Foundation. Such ignorance has led to misunderstandings. Some historians have declared the ICI a Belgian institution, although it was a transnational institution and held meetings in different cities all over Europe.[62] Others have confused the ICI with the Institute of International Law (1873), a consequence of the ICI's strong involvement with colonial law.[63] The absence of the ICI from the historiography of colonialism and internationalism is remarkable, if understandable, given that its archives are lost and sources multilingual.

Unlike anti-colonial internationalism, colonial internationalism remains understudied.[64] Although Frederick Cooper and Ann-Laura Stoler made the case for studying transfers between empires as early as 1997, the old tradition of comparing empires often persisted.[65] Comparison has frequently led to a typology of empires that contrasted, for example, repressive (Spanish) and liberal (British) empires, ordered imperial spaces according to distance (continental vs. blue water empires), and distinguished between degrees of indigenous integration (assimilation vs. indirect rule) or settler presence (settler vs. native policy).[66] Postcolonial thinkers such as Aimé Césaire had

---

[60] Daviron, "Mobilizing Labour in African Agriculture," 479–501; Bandeira Jerónimo, The "Civilizing Mission," 190–193; Schayegh, "The Expanding Overlap," 782–802; Gorman, International Cooperation, 117; Saada, "Penser le Fait Colonial," 106; Bertrand, "Histoire d'une 'Réforme Morale,'" 109–110.

[61] Van Daele, "Industrial States." The ICI is absent in Paulmann and Geyer, The Mechanics of Internationalism; Herren, Internationale Organisationen; Koskenniemi, The Gentle Civilizer; Sluga, Internationalism; Laqua, The Age of Internationalism.

[62] Called "Institut Colonial International belge" by Sibeud, Une Science Impériale, 67.

[63] Rousseaux, "Introduction," 8–9.

[64] Two monographs, however, address colonial internationalism. See Brückenhaus, Policing Transnational Protest; Streets-Salter, World War One. On anti-colonial internationalism before World War II, see Manela, The Wilsonian Moment; Goebel, Anti-Imperial Metropolis; Weiss, Framing a Radical African Atlantic; Goswami, "Imaginary Futures."

[65] Cooper and Stoler, Tensions of Empire, 13.

[66] Other studies also take mutual influences into account. See Cooper, Decolonization and African Society; Shipway, Decolonization and Its Impact; Bayly, The Birth of the Modern World; Leonhard and Hirschhausen, Comparing Empires; Eckert and Randeira, Vom Imperialismus; Lindner, Koloniale Begegnungen; Methfessel, Kontroverse Gewalt.

long urged the abandonment of such comparative approaches because comparison suggests that there were differences and gradations among European empires. From his postcolonial viewpoint, the colonialist and racist culture shaped all Western societies in equal measure and manifested itself in their violent claim to power. Half a century later, historians of empire tended to avoid over-generalizing political comparisons between empires and paid greater attention to regional and temporal specificities within empires.[67] Comparison was still employed but served to identify similarities between empires instead of contrasting them. Among the similarities was the observation that "intermediaries" and "indigenous elites" played a crucial role in building empires and that the powerful had at least to respond to the initiatives of the "weak." Based on this assumption, historians have defined empires as multiethnic and supranational states that managed inequality in addition to producing it and were characterized by fluctuating relations between center and periphery and not by fixed borders.[68] Since all "imperial formations" and their colonial culture preconfigured power relations in human encounters, Geoff Eley suggested that empire might even become the analytical lens through which historians have to study human interaction: "the concept of 'empire' seems even to acquire analytical, or, perhaps, epistemological equivalence with the older category of 'society.'"[69] To understand the ICI and its significance for asymmetric encounters within empires, however, we need to combine cultural and social history approaches, instead of pitting empire and society against each other.

This book does not compare empires but considers the way colonial internationalists themselves used comparisons. By historicizing their comparison of colonial policies, we can access their "politics of comparison," which enabled them to portray colonial internationalism as progressive.[70] The "political" purpose of the ICI's comparative approach was to emulate successfully tested technologies of colonial government and to transfer them to their own colonies. The cultural meaning was to portray this cross-fertilization among colonies as progressive.[71] However, like comparisons, transfers were vehicles of racial and cultural stereotyping and often stood in the way of progress. Assuming that social conditions and indigenous attitudes toward work were similar in Indonesia and East Africa, for example, made colonial

---

[67] Stoler, "Tense and Tender Ties," 847; Dimier, *Le gouvernement*; Dimier, "The Mandates Commission," 213–227; Singaravélou, "Les stratégies," 135–157.
[68] MacKenzie, *European Empires*; Leonhard and Hirschhausen, *Empires und Nationalstaaten*, 10; Maier, *Among Empires*, 31.
[69] Eley, "Empire by Land or Sea," 25; Wilder, *The French Imperial Nation-State*; Stoler, *Carnal Knowledge*.
[70] Stoler, "Tense and Tender Ties," 829–865.
[71] Tilley, *Africa as a Living Laboratory*; Headrick, *The Tentacles of Progress*.

internationalists believe that technology transfers between those colonies would lead to success – such as for establishing a colonial agriculture. More than once, ICI members' overgeneralization about the character of the colonized caused them to fail and they spread concepts of racial prejudice rather than a more productive agriculture.[72] Nevertheless, the ICI also learned to distinguish between regional peculiarities and partially replaced transcolonial transfers with transregional transfers.

The way colonial technocrats used comparison and transfers to impose governmental schemes of colonial development is well known, but historians often forgot that such technocrats were driven by their material interests rather than by their will to bring about progress.[73] Since colonial administrations increasingly believed in the progressive nature of transnational epistemic communities, colonial experts established the ICI.[74] For these experts, declaring themselves internationalists became a way to moralize their colonial careers and to raise funds. Around 1900, professionals, be they doctors, lawyers, engineers, or agronomists, flocked to the colonies in great numbers, describing their journey from Europe to Africa as a trip from ideology to professional pragmatism. However, their professionalism went hand in hand with their careerism. When professionals journeyed to the colonies, they envisioned a high salary before envisioning colonial progress.

The combination of money and scholarly ambition added up the much-cited "colonial career."[75] The Ghanaian Joseph Ephraim Casely Hayford, one of the most stimulating intellectuals of the early twentieth century, observed in 1903 that the colonial administration entirely relied on those professionals, who "seek not the making of history, but that of their own ephemeral fame" through a colonial career.[76] These professionals' career prospects often explain their inclination toward colonial internationalism and governmentality – and their dissociation from it if the national system lured them with money away from internationalism. Members of the ICI, for example, betrayed their internationalism when they tried to secure higher salaries, health insurance, and old-age pensions for themselves. The purpose was to draw benefits from the state, similar to those of civil servants in the metropole. Tellingly, ICI members used their transnational knowledge and comparisons with other countries to urge their own governments to increase their salaries. Using

---

[72] Zimmerman, *Alabama in Africa*; Beckert, *Empire of Cotton*.
[73] On experts in general, see MacLeod, *Government and Expertise*; Hodge, *Triumph of the Expert*.
[74] Rodogno, Struck, and Vogel, *Shaping the Transnational Sphere*; Neill, *Networks in Tropical Medicine*; Wagner, "Inventing Colonial Agronomy," 103–128.
[75] Hodge, *Triumph of the Expert*. On "imperial careering" in the British case, see Lambert and Lester, *Colonial Lives*.
[76] Casely Hayford, *Gold Coast Native Institutions*, 11.

internationalist arguments and the infrastructure of nation-states, they made the most of their colonial careers. Hence, their individual career interests often shaped the history of colonial (inter)nationalism more than abstract ideals.

To be sure, experts were neither exclusively male nor exclusively white. ICI members owed a lot to experts from the Global South, who provided them with knowledge about local agriculture, tropical medicine, customary and Islamic law, cooperative economy, and strategic governmentality. These experts were more than informants who helped the ICI to stuff ethnographic museums in Europe with knowledge about lost traditions and "primitive" communities. They designed progressive plans for dynamic societies and provided answers to complex problems. The most famous among them was probably Raden Adjeng Kartini from Java. An offspring of a high-ranking Javanese official, she was fluent in Dutch and an excellent writer, educator, and feminist. Although only twenty years old, ICI members viewed her with admiration. They traveled to Java to visit her and collected, published, and translated her writings. Kartini introduced schools for girls to Dutch Indonesia, which became known as Kartini Schools, but she also analyzed the colonial situation and its shortcomings.[77] Her impact on the ICI will appear here and there in this book.

Less directly, an important number of individuals and groups from the Global South influenced the ICI by building important transcolonial networks.[78] Apart from labor migrants, Lebanese merchants and Afro-American "returnees," both of whom shaped the economic and political life of West Africa, were important transcolonial networkers.[79] In the interwar period, politicized internationalisms emerged among Asians and Africans who often used transimperial spaces to voice anticolonial concerns.[80] While they appropriated the term "international" for their empowerment, the ICI remained highly skeptical toward transcolonial anticolonialism. Only in the 1960s, the ICI tried to reappropriate anticolonial internationalism by styling itself a "Second Bandung."

Generally, the ICI co-opted only loyal or moderately critical agents of the colonized world but rejected outright anti-colonialists, especially those "Westernized" elites whom they regarded as alienated and radicalized. While this book is not about anti-colonial internationalism, it will show here and there how "moderate" protagonists from the Global South used the ICI's schemes of governmentality to assert themselves. Moderates such as Raden Adjeng Kartini did so unofficially from the 1890s onwards but they became official members only after 1945. Thus, even though they had cooperated with

---

[77] Kartini, *Letters*, xi–xvii.
[78] Nugent, *Smugglers*; Fischer-Tiné, *Empires and Boundaries*, 1–22.
[79] Desbordes, *L'immigration*.
[80] Louro et al., *The League*, 16–51.

the ICI long before 1945, their names only became visible after World War II. To be sure, they were hardly representative of the colonized world. Yet they illustrate how the ICI's schemes of governmentality developed with their involvement. Regarding European protagonists, the book equally goes far beyond providing an institutional history of the ICI by revealing the far-reaching impact of colonial internationalists on colonial societies. Tracing their biographies shows that all of them claimed to be internationalists and reformers. No doubt, colonial reformers existed outside and before the ICI, but most of them joined the ICI eventually and made it the germ cell of colonial reform. Among them were men who reshaped colonial policies, such as the Dutch Isaäc Dignus Fransen van de Putte, the French Hubert Lyautey, the British Frederick Lugard and William Malcom Hailey, the German Bernhard Dernburg, and the Belgian Pierre Ryckmans. Asking whether the ICI or the reform movement existed first would be entering into an unproductive chicken-and-egg logic. What is more important here is to examine in greater depth the apologetic function of the ICI's reformism for the colonial project as a whole.

Historians have often regarded reformism as manifesting itself in the cost-intensive development programs that Britain and France launched in 1940 and 1946.[81] Unlike the centralized programs of the late colonial era, which half-heartedly imposed the Western "linear" path to "modernity" on the colonized populations, ICI members had designed decentralized and cheap schemes for softer development in the 1890s. Around 1900, ICI members started to combine elements of the social market economy, welfare schemes, workers' protection, cooperative schemes of mutual aid, and savings banks and micro credits to introduce a soft version of capitalism to the colonies.[82] These reformist development plans resembled the small-scale schemes of self-improvement of the 1970s rather than the planned economy of the 1940s and 1950s.[83] The paternalistic use of indigenous institutions for these self-supporting development schemes, however, often disguised the continued exploitation of resources and the continued use of forced labor. Moreover, they frequently failed to bring about development.

Although they embraced cultural relativism in the 1890s and cooperated with UNESCO after 1945, ICI members were no preservationists who intended to shield authentic native culture completely against capitalism and Westernization. Instead, the ICI members preferred sociological methods to understand the interactions between colonizing and colonized societies, an approach they had already proposed at the International Congress for Colonial Sociology in 1900. They were aware that only the knowledge of concrete colonial situations, rather than clichés about indigenous culture

---

[81] Cooper and Packard, *International Development*, 64–92.
[82] Unger, *International Development*, 23–48.
[83] Macekura, *Of Limits and Growth*, 137–171.

produced in Europe would enable colonial experts to govern more efficiently and to make development a success. Between the 1930s and the 1950s, progressive social anthropologists Bronislaw Malinowski and Georges Balandier became famous for similar sociological approaches. They argued that colonized societies did not consist of static and passive groups, as often imagined in Europe. Instead, the colonized constantly modified their behavior, adjusted their cultural predispositions, and acted rationally to take advantage of the new situation. In 1951, Balandier made his famous plea to analyze "societies *as they are now*" in the "colonial situation."[84] Since their approach resembled the ICI's agenda, Malinowski cooperated closely with the ICI and Balandier became a member.

In Balandier's view, the "colonial situation" was "the *mise en rapport* of two social beings, through which two civilizations are confronted with each other."[85] However, in the late 1940s, it was unclear whether this colonial situation would endure. Members of the ICI were among the first to react to this uncertainty. In 1949, the ICI sacrificed the label "colonial" and changed its name to International Institute of Differing Civilizations. By that time, some INCIDI members tried to save political dependence in the form of a Eurafrican union that even accepted African representatives to the Council of Europe (1949). Léopold Sédar Senghor, who had been a member of the Council of Europe for the French Union since 1949, for example, joined the INCIDI in 1954.[86] However, the INCIDI's belief in the differing nature of "civilizations" ultimately led to its members acknowledging political independence – while maintaining economic and administrative ties. Advocating formal independence was not a major change for them since the ICI's schemes of governmentality had always resembled informal colonialism rather than formal colonial rule with direct government. The transition allowed the INCIDI to style itself retrospectively as a successor of the Bandung conference.[87]

At the dawn of the independence era, the INCIDI extended its schemes of colonial governmentality to the entire "underdeveloped world," including Latin America and independent countries in Asia. Balandier, in particular, widely used the INCIDI's comparative studies to reframe the relationship between developed and "less developed or backward" countries.[88] Balandier and the INCIDI agreed that a less formal dependence shaped this relationship.[89] Adjusting to the lines of UN development agencies, the

---

[84] Mann, *From Empires to NGOs*, 25.
[85] Balandier, "La Situation Coloniale," 44–79.
[86] INCIDI, *Compte Rendu 1954*, 38.
[87] INCIDI, *Compte Rendu 1963*, 13–14.
[88] Balandier, *Anthropologie Appliquée aux Problèmes des Pays Sous-Developpés*, 18, 187.
[89] Balandier, "Contribution à une Sociologie de la Dépendance," 49.

INCIDI and Balandier avoided speaking of the colonial world and renamed it the "Third World."

In the eyes of the INCIDI members, the colonized countries were not only underdeveloped but also "underadministrated." To remedy these deficiencies, the INCIDI leaders invited representatives of the newly independent countries to join their ranks in 1949. To be sure, most members from the Global South had long participated in the ICI's scheme of colonial governmentality. Despite the new names, little changed in the traditional program of transnational governmentality, which the ICI had inaugurated some sixty years before the era of decolonization. This book is about the ICI's long history of transnational governmentality that emerged in 1893 and partly lived on in the neocolonial development schemes of the INCIDI, which existed until 1982. Therefore, the full meaning of the ICI's program of colonial governmentality is only apparent when we consider it from its end.

Nine chapters trace the ups and downs of the ICI's transnational and transcolonial governmentality from 1893 to the 1960s, when it merged in the UN's program of functional governance.

Chapter 1 reveals how the ICI rose to prominence between 1893 and 1914 by marginalizing the nationalist branches of the colonial movements in Europe and by institutionalizing transnational cooperation between colonial experts. Evoking internationalist ideals and transcolonial necessities alike, ICI members successfully delayed a war between imperial powers, especially during the conflict over the partition of Morocco.

Chapter 2 discusses the ICI's invention of transcolonial development schemes in the 1890s. For different reasons, tropical hygienists, free-trade capitalists, Social Christians, and experts on colonial law in the ICI embraced the idea that only the intrinsic motivation of Africans and Asians themselves could make colonial development a success. The ICI's notion of development differed from outright exploitation and abrupt industrialization because it claimed to respect indigenous culture and included notions of social welfare. By creating needs through the careful introduction of a capitalist reward system and by aligning colonial law with the needs of the colonial economy, the ICI claimed to bring about sustained development.

Chapter 3 reveals that the ICI initiated a transnational process to train a small elite of well-prepared Europeans who would promote sustained development in the colonies that left local cultural structures intact. Using comparison to derive the best method to prepare expert-administrators, the ICI members professionalized the training of colonial administrators, increased their salaries, and secured old-age pensions for them. In so doing, they excluded African and Asian administrators and experts from the benefits of health insurance and pensions.

In Chapter 4, I discuss how a group of colonial experts from around the world assembled at the transcolonial agronomic research station of Buitenzorg in Dutch Java shaped the myth that transcolonial technology transfers in agronomy and agricultural management led to the reform of global colonial agriculture. Buitenzorg indeed provided genetically engineered plants for the colonized world and fostered the participation of indigenous farmers in small-scale cash crop production.[90] Although Buitenzorg's colonial agronomists pretended to replace the "American" model of neo-slavery plantations with Buitenzorg's more liberal "East Indian" smallholder model, they continued to promote enforced cultivation.

The ICI's transcolonial initiative to codify customary and Islamic law, I argue in Chapter 5, provided experts with a "governmental" tool to expropriate fertile land and to blight democratic initiatives. Using a strategy that we can call the "adatization" of Islamic law, ICI members mixed and drafted new legal codes for Indonesia and Muslim Africa. These codes became more compliant to European necessities by strategically combining elements from customary law and from the four legal schools of Islam. Perfecting this strategy of legal manipulation, ICI members also used Islamic craft guild legislation in North Africa to promote a "Muslim code of labor" and a corporatist artisanal economy that allegedly shielded the colonized from the penetration of socialist and anti-colonial ideas.

On the international stage, Chapter 6 shows, the ICI equally silenced calls for reforms in the colonies. The ICI responded to the anti-colonial requests for self-determination in the interwar period by shifting the debate from sovereignty to representativity. While ICI members established (pseudo-) representative councils in the colonies, focus on representativity enabled the ICI to claim that no group genuinely represented the allegedly fragmented colonized population, a fact that allegedly rendered self-determination impossible. Arguing along these lines, ICI members delegitimized the complaints that Africans and Asians sent to the League of Nations' Permanent Mandates Commission.

Chapter 7 equally highlights the anti-democratic and corporatist attitude of ICI members who co-organized the transnational and predominantly fascist Volta Congress on Africa, which was held in Rome in 1938. At the Volta Congress, colonial internationalists synthesized liberal and fascist colonial ideas into a revived Roman Empire, which they called Eurafrica. Endorsing totalitarian policies, the Volta Congress did not want democratic representation in its Eurafrican Empire and favored a corporatist representation through the different branches of the economy.

Corporatist schemes reappear again in Chapter 8, which reveals how ICI members used transcolonial knowledge transfers to establish a colonial welfare

---

[90] Bloembergen and Kuitenbrouwer, "A New Dutch Imperial History"; Boomgaard, *Empire and Science*; Bosma, *Sugar Plantation*.

state at low cost, based on indigenous associations of mutuality and self-help. In practice, colonial administrations used and manipulated "indigenous" cooperatives such as the *fokon'olona* association to perpetuate coercive labor, a practice that persisted well into the postcolonial era.

The book concludes with a consideration in Chapter 9 of how the ICI (renamed the INCIDI in 1949) perpetuated its transnational and transcolonial governmentality in the form of modern functional governance in the 1950s and 1960s, which included coercive schemes of development and consulting for "under-administrated" independent countries. By selectively accepting members from the newly independent states, INCIDI members intended to control the middle classes of the entire "Third World." Appropriating and manipulating the concepts of decolonization, multiple civilizations, sustained development, and even anti-racism, the INCIDI disguised its ongoing program of colonial governmentality. The INCIDI went as far as styling itself as a "second Bandung," claiming to represent the moderate anti-colonialism of the emerging states. However, since fascist and racist thinking still shaped the INCIDI's designs of a postwar Eurafrica, this was yet another example of the ICI's hypocrisy, which is the topic of this book.

1

"More Beautiful than the Nationalist Thought"?

Colonialist Fraternization and the Birth of Transnational Cooperation

It was well into the night – after a convivial dinner held at the Dutch colonial minister's house in 1893 – when the general secretary of the French Colonial Union, Joseph Chailley, and the head of the Dutch Colonial Association, Pieter Antonie van der Lith, decided to found the International Colonial Institute (ICI).[1] This "after-dinner," one Dutch participant recalled, "was as gracious as it was spiritual" and appeased the nationalist passions of the banquet's international guests.[2] Under the impulse of this high-spirited moment, Chailley and van der Lith suggested setting up an international institution, in which experts could share colonial knowledge and work out best practices for colonial governance. Initially, their plan met with disapproval among many colonial experts who attended the dinner. However, the skepticism of the majority succumbed to the enthusiasm of the few. As the Belgian Albert Thys admitted a few years later, the founders had no clear idea as to the shape of such an institute, but nonetheless, everybody was "full of honor to be part of it."[3]

The vinous founding act stood in sharp contrast to the sober development that the ICI would take in the years to come. In 1894, the institute held its first meeting and invited delegates from thirteen countries to join their cause. Twenty years later, in 1914, the ICI listed 136 members from Great Britain, France, the Netherlands, Germany, Russia, Portugal, Spain, Italy, the United States, Latin America, Denmark, and Austria-Hungary. By that date, it had developed into the most powerful nongovernmental think tank of colonial rule and exploitation. Among its members figured colonial ministers, overseas governors, directors of colonial companies, the heads of colonial lobby groups, and experts in colonial science. They styled the ICI as a scientific institution that captured, shared, recorded, and distributed colonial knowledge.[4] Its aim, however, was not to develop another metatheory of

---

[1] ICI, *Compte Rendu 1897*, 50.
[2] ICI, *Compte Rendu 1901*, 47–48.
[3] ICI, *Compte Rendu 1897*, 82.
[4] Ibid., 50.

colonial science but to develop efficient methods of colonial governmentality that were universally applicable.[5]

On paper, the ICI's agenda was to transform colonialism from a nationalist to a transnational and scientific project. After all, the statutes banned "political debates" and nationalist rivalry from its meetings and writings.[6] The implicit message of this transformation to a transnational science was that colonialism was a progressive force that led humanity to a prosperous future and not a destructive force of rivaling nationalisms.

This chapter shows that the ICI gradually became transnational, mainly because transnationalism better served the individual interests of its members and internationalism the purpose of legitimizing colonial domination. Looking below the varnish of internationalist legitimating narratives about scientific exploration, the civilizing mission, and humanitarian intervention, the early history of the ICI can tell us a much more profane story about individual ambitions and competition for funding. The ICI membership boosted the reputation of its members as independent colonial specialists and increased the probability of funding. Thus, their reasons for joining the ICI were neither purely nationalist nor purely transnationalist but also individualistic.

Early private colonial initiatives illustrate that internationalism was a manipulable concept used in diplomatic theory, whereas transnational practice was seen as social, economic, and cultural interaction across borders that did not necessarily need the nation-state as a category of reference. Internationalist projects were not automatically transnational. In 1875, the Belgian King Léopold II – not the first colonial internationalist but the first to advertise his colonial internationalism – declared his private enterprise of conquering the Congo basin an international mission. Acting as a private person and not as a head of state, his International African Association (1876) put the project into practice. In return for opening up the Congo to the international community of colonizing states, the Berlin Conference acknowledged Léopold's international Congo Free State (CFS) in 1884/5. Yet Léopold failed to turn the CFS into a truly transnational project. In an individualistic move, he excluded foreign companies and monopolized the CFS' resources to line his own pockets.[7]

Around 1890, the CFS was nominally still an international state but ceased to be a transnational project. Léopold's protectionism left many colonial experts and private interest groups in Europe disappointed, since they had helped to bring about the CFS by investments, propaganda, and civil service in the Congo. Feeling betrayed, this chapter shows, even his Belgian compatriots

---

[5] Sluga, *Internationalism*, 7 and 150–160.
[6] "Article 12 of the Statutes," in ICI, *Compte Rendu 1909*, 30; ICI, *Notice Institut Colonial International* (Brussels, 1937), 24.
[7] Wagner, "Private Colonialism," 79–106.

turned their back on Léopold and established the ICI. Labeled equally "international," it was unclear in 1893 if it would turn out to be truly "transnational." Key to understanding whether the ICI was transnational or not is the analysis of the reasons why people joined the ICI and remained in it.

The history of the early ICI members is Eurocentric by nature, since only male Europeans and Americans joined, be it for individualistic, nationalist, or internationalist reasons. For a long time, historians assumed that either nationalism or capitalism made European men colonialists and imperialists. Occasionally, the annalists of imperial history also advanced individual ambition, (civilizing) missions, and philanthropism as potentially "internationalist." But pure internationalism as a driving force behind colonialism immediately raised suspicions of being dishonest. Historians were right to remark that internationalism and nationalism are not mutually exclusive and that internationalism is probably fake. This is certainly true for most ICI members but fails to explain why and when they abandoned nationalism and hypocritical internationalism to turn into transnational actors. Thus, transnationalism as a social practice needs explanation. Private and individual colonial initiatives examined in this chapter can provide that explanation.

As we will see, states did not become completely irrelevant through transnational practice. Transnational practice could emancipate itself from nationalist thought and establish an autonomous sphere in which colonial experts interacted. But states provided funding, armies, administrators, and imperial infrastructures. At the same time, states often failed in colonial expansion and administration. In the 1880s, it needed private initiatives and lobby groups were required to make nation-states colonizing states. George Goldie's Royal Niger Company and Hamburg's overseas merchants colonized independently of their states, and representatives of both merchant groups joined the ICI sooner (Hamburg) or later (successors of the Royal Niger Company). While states were monolithic and strong in the metropole, they were often weak and sometimes absent in the colonies.

States did not stand in the way of transnational activities, and state employees were often members in the ICI. By 1890, only two European nations had a proper colonial ministry (see Chapter 3). Apart from lacking colonial competence, they had to coordinate colonial rule between parliaments, foreign ministries, secretaries of state, the army and the navy, companies, settlers, and colonial lobby groups. Being not monolithic, states liked to outsource governmental tasks to private initiatives and transnational experts. Even in the well-organized British Empire, colonial servants were "semi-independent" and have to be seen as "distinct from the British state" with the "ability to negotiate a changing overseas landscape."[8] Around 1908, Germany and Belgium had

---

[8] Stockwell, *The British End*, 5–6.

semi-official Colonial Councils and France had a strong *Groupe Colonial* in the National Assembly. Memberships overlapped with the ICI. Dutch, Belgian, German, and other colonial ministers were members of the ICI. Thus, state representatives were often ICI members and inspired more by the ICI than by domestic bureaucracy. To explain their contribution to colonial history, it is all the more important to look at their reasons for joining the ICI, be they individualistic, nationalist, or transnational.

The combination of these three variables changed over time, and analyzing their specific constellation unveils the role of individual ambition for the shift from nationalism to transnationalism. The period between 1880 and 1914, habitually but inadequately labeled a phase of imperial rivalry, provided the context for this shift.

1.1 The Appeal of Internationalism: What Made Individuals Turn Away from Nationalism

When Western states developed an increased imperial conscience between 1870 and 1914, their role overseas blurred the traditional order between strong and weak nations in Europe. In 1893 – a few days after the convivial dinner in Amsterdam – the French Joseph Chailley and the Dutch Pieter Antonie van der Lith chose Brussels to hold the first session of the ICI and appealed to representatives of all colonizing nations to join them there. Members of "small nations," such as Belgium and the Netherlands, responded promptly to their rallying cry, mainly because their extensive colonial empires boosted their nations' importance in Europe. An international organization that ranked colonial grandeur over national strength increased their standing within Europe.[9] At the same time, the ICI's initiators made an effort to win powerful states such as France and Great Britain for their cause. Adhering to a Darwinist view of competing nation-states, the ICI's initiators claimed that all nations had to prove their fitness anew on colonial terrain, which differed widely from the European competitive society. The ICI was the institution that set the new standards.

Yet it was individuals, and not nations, who established the ICI. These individuals were colonial experts who often spoke for their nation but never fully represented it. The founding session of the ICI assembled five renowned colonial experts from France, Great Britain, Belgium, and the Netherlands. The railway entrepreneur Albert Thys, who made a fortune in the Congo, and the first governor-general of Léopold's Congo Free State, Camille Janssen, came from Belgium.[10] A former governor of Bombay, Donald Mackay, the

---

[9] Wesseling, "The Giant," 58–70; Sluga, *Internationalism*, 7 and 150–160; Koekkoek et al., "Visions of Dutch Empire," 79–96.
[10] Louwers, "Camille Janssen," 437–440.

eleventh Lord Reay, was the only British member at the inaugural session. He was Dutch-born but had become a British citizen in 1876. Moreover, the founders recruited two emblematic "figureheads" for the ICI: Léon Say, the famous French liberal economist and grandson of free trade ideologist Jean-Baptiste Say, and the Dutch colonial reformer Isaäc Dignus Fransen van de Putte, an ex-colonial minister who had become widely known as a reformer of the Dutch colonial administration in the 1860s. Those seven founding fathers would shape the ICI's policies for the next decade, with an omnipresent Joseph Chailley and a devoted manager, Camille Janssen. The latter became secretary general of the ICI and remained in place until the interwar period. While a permanent head office opened in Brussels, the ICI members met biennially or annually in different European cities. Prior to the World War I they held more than thirty official meetings to elect members and to debate and design the future of colonial administration.

Officially, the founding members advanced nationalistic reasons for joining the ICI, but a microhistory of their motivations unveils a mix of nationalist, transnational, and individual intentions. Joseph Chailley was no stranger to colonial internationalism when he initiated the ICI in 1893. After spending a few months in French Indochina, he had attended the first International Colonial Congress in Paris in 1889. The French foreign ministry had organized the congress to win the sympathy of Spanish, Portuguese, and Dutch colonial experts.[11] The congress was rather a promotional event for French colonialism but also a test for more holistic colonial events in the future. More importantly, Chailley had been a member of Léopold II's International African Association and its successor society, the Société du Haut Congo. These two international organizations had helped the Belgian King Léopold to secure the Congo basin as his private colony in 1885 and to found the CFS. This is why Chailley frequently participated in international banquets held in Belgium with administrators of the CFS.[12]

The reasons for Chailley's internationalist attitude, however, were homemade. A protégé of his father-in-law, the governor of Indochina Paul Bert, Chailley was ready to enter domestic colonial politics in the late 1880s. He made no secret of his *indigenophile* attitude, which he had inherited from Paul Bert. His pro-native stance, however, opposed him to the godfather of French colonialism in Algeria, the Oran deputy Eugène Étienne. Étienne intrigued against Chailley and denied him a colonial career in France.[13] Not acknowledging defeat, Chailley decided to turn the tables and publicly attacked the French-Algerian colonial establishment – headed by Étienne and the governor of Algeria, Charles Jonnart. To assert himself, he accused

---

[11] *Congrès Colonial International de Paris*, 3–6.
[12] "Joseph Chailley-Bert," *Biographie Coloniale Belge*, vol. 4, 154–155.
[13] Cohen, *Rulers of Empire*, 37.

1.1 THE APPEAL OF INTERNATIONALISM

the "Algerians" Étienne and Jonnart of being responsible for a general colonial mismanagement of Algeria that cost the French taxpayer an estimated 50 billion francs.[14] According to Chailley, the Algerian model of settler colonialism was dated and would give way to a new and less expensive way of colonizing that he himself would design.

The conflict that emerged between Étienne and Chailley in the late 1880s anticipated the clash of assimilationist and associationist attitudes in French fin de siècle colonialism. Chailley hoped that the internationalization of the conflict would substantiate his own position. Instead of conquering and settling Algeria, he argued that the French should have followed the Dutch and British example in the East Indies. Those countries did not try to "assimilate" the colonized, let alone "Frenchify" them, as the French had allegedly attempted in Algeria. Instead, the British and the Dutch used the indigenous population to establish a colonial economy, which had ultimately rendered the overseas possessions profitable. "Those colonies," Chailley claimed, "are not *colonies*, like we like to call them and there is no question of colonizing [*peupler*] them; they are *possessions*, inhabited by natives who occupy a big part of it ... seen from Britain and the Netherlands, the colonists are much less interesting than the natives, who produce [goods] and who pay taxes."[15] In 1893, Chailley established the French Colonial Union and the journal *La Quinzaine Coloniale* to promote his associationist philosophy and combat the assimilationists.[16] The French Colonial Union became a powerful think tank and an instrument to pressure the French government. To substantiate his claims to "learn from the Dutch and the British," Chailley founded the ICI.[17] His associationism also became programmatic for the ICI. It explains why he recruited former Dutch and British administrators first, before turning to less associationist countries.

To appease Chailley's zeal, Étienne – serving as a colonial undersecretary – officially dispatched Chailley on several missions abroad.[18] The outcome of his first official mission to the Netherlands in 1892 was the foundation of the ICI. Three other expeditions to Dutch and British India (1897–1898 to Java; 1900–1901 and 1904–1905 to British India) earned Chailley global fame. Each of his research trips lasted several months and received support from

---

[14] "Le Maroc et l'Opinion Publique," *Bulletin du Comité de l'Afrique Française* (January 1908), 10.

[15] Chailley-Bert, *Dix Années*, 36–40.

[16] Betts, *Assimilation and Association*. However, Betts did not elaborate the international dimension. For a more nuanced view, see Chafer and Sackur, *Promoting the Colonial Idea*. On decolonization, see Shepard, *The Invention of Decolonization*; Lorcin, *Imperial Identities*.

[17] Chailley, *Java et ses Habitants*, x.

[18] ANOM FM MIS/63/bis, Dossier 1 Chailley-Bert Mission aux Pays-Bas, recrutement des fonctionnaires coloniaux, Étienne to Chailley, January 20, 1892.

the French government as well as from private companies in Europe.[19] On his trips, he met with Dutch and British administrators along with experts on colonial law, tropical hygiene, and overseas agronomy. These encounters resulted in two extensive memoirs on British India and Dutch Java, which became global bestsellers and were translated into English.[20] They also inspired colonial officials around the world to revise their policy. In 1902, for example, the *Swakopmunder Zeitung*, a German newspaper in South West Africa, celebrated Chailley's approach to "reorganize the relationship between [the colonial administration] and the natives whom they govern by common sense rather than emotions." The newspaper particularly highlighted Chailley's plan to oblige the "natives" to contribute to the colonial economy, which the Dutch had done in Java between 1830 and 1870. If Chailley brought the Dutch model to France, the paper concluded, "Germany will surely follow the French."[21]

At home in France, Chailley's studies of Dutch and British colonial methods inaugurated a new era of colonial policy that claimed to co-opt and respect the indigenous population. Eminent colonial reformers such as Joseph Gallieni and Hubert Lyautey developed their doctrines on the basis of Chailley's writings and the ICI's comparative studies of the 1890s.[22] The architect of the French protectorate over Morocco, Hubert Lyautey, would appropriate the ICI's ideas in his younger years, long before his paternalistic colonial policy in the Sultanate earned him the reputation of being progressive. While Lyautey carefully forged his own myth as the founder of the *indigenophile* "Moroccan School," he confidentially admitted his indebtedness to the ICI and Chailley, whose books he devoured: "especially the book on Java" that he had read "with the pencil in my hand" and which he recommended to all his employees.[23] Lyautey regarded Chailley as his "master" and confessed to him that "nobody more than you has influenced my colonial doctrine. Since my beginnings in Tonkin, I found elaborated in your writings what my daily experience suggested to me."[24] Before World War I, Lyautey and Chailley cooperated confidentially to promote the ICI's developmental colonialism in France.[25]

---

[19] ANOM FP 100 APOM/93-98, Union Coloniale, Chailley Mission aux Indes Anglaises 1900–1901, Chailley to Ministère de l'instruction publique, July 29, 1900; Ministère des Colonies to Chailley, August 29, 1900.

[20] ANOM FP 100 APOM/93-98, Union Coloniale, Chailley, Projet de Mission aux Indes Anglaises et en Indochine: *The Times* September 22, 1896; Chailley to Constable [India Office], December 9, 1896.

[21] "Eine Wichtige Frage," *Swakopmunder Zeitung* (August 1, 1902), 2.

[22] Finch, *A Progressive Occupation*.

[23] Lyautey to Chailley, May 21, 1903, in Le Révérand, *Un Lyautey Inconnu*, 229–230; and Le Révérand, *Lyautey*, 162 and 203.

[24] Le Révérand, *Un Lyautey Inconnu*, 229–230.

[25] ANOM, FP 100APOM/321, Chailley à Lyautey; Union Coloniale, Section du Maroc, Correspondance avec Lyautey 1913–1915: Chailley to Lyautey, March 17, 1913.

Lyautey joined the ICI in 1903. He modeled his policies on Dutch and British examples, especially when establishing a system of indirect rule with Moroccan administrators and judges.[26] The governor of French Madagascar, Joseph Gallieni, also followed Chailley's missions to Java closely. The island became the model for his colonial administration in Madagascar. Guided by Chailley's reports, Gallieni officially abolished the corvée system in 1901 and introduced indirect and governmental measures of coercion (see Chapter 8).[27] Chailley, Lyautey, and Gallieni managed to establish an "anti-Algerian" model of indirect rule, which became the new paradigm of French colonial policy. Ultimately, even the assimilationist Eugène Étienne could not resist the new trend they set and joined the ICI in 1904.

Chailley's conflict with colonialists in Algeria strained the ICI's relations with settlers for decades but did not completely ruin them. Chailley persistently teased settlers in Algeria, for example, by publicly exposing how they disobeyed instructions from Paris in the name of democracy and Republicanism. The settler paper *L'Algérie Française* replied by calling Chailley an "insulter" and claimed that his report was "full of errors ... errors that a tighter documentation could have easily set right."[28] While settlers from British territories rarely referred to the French-speaking ICI, German and Dutch settlers did, mostly not to miss out on the latest insights in the best practice of colonization. Like the *Swakopmunder Zeitung* cited above, settlers thought the ICI's emphasis on native policy particularly useful in establishing a segregated society in which European and native policy were separated. Their interpretation of native policy became a basis for apartheid regimes, especially but not exclusively in South Africa (see Chapter 7).

ICI members from the Netherlands, whose policy received so much attention in France, showed an equally strong inclination toward transnational exchange. They had successfully made use of international know-how, labor, and capital in their own colonies since the times of the Dutch East India Company. At times, up to 70 percent of the company's employees were foreigners. Many of them stayed on after service and established a long-standing tradition of Dutch colonial internationalism. By 1815, the Dutch had a colonial army that enlisted 7,000 Germans, who made up around 20 percent of the colonial troops. Overall, 21,000 Germans – along with

---

[26] Ibid. Maroc Situation Politique 1917–1918: Notes on Cours 1917–1918: Le Maroc et les Grands Problèmes.

[27] ANOM 100APOM 95, Gallieni to Depincé (Comité de Madagascar), January 12, 1901. The official abolition of "prestation" had various reasons, continued to exist unofficially, and was reintroduced shortly after Gallieni resigned: Fremigacci, *État, Économie et Société*, 148–150.

[28] "Pour la Mémoire d'Édouard Cat," *L'Algérie Française* (March 7, 1909); *L'Algérie Française* (July 13, 1909).

smaller contingents of Belgians, Swiss, and French nationals – came to Dutch Java during the nineteenth century.[29] As we will see in Chapter 4, German physicians and European agronomists also joined them, as did British and American planters. Given the Dutch tradition of colonial internationalism, Chailley found a fellow traveler in the lawyer and ethnologist Pieter Antonie Van der Lith, whom he met in 1893 at the above-mentioned dinner in Amsterdam.

Van der Lith had been responsible for the first explicit manifestations of colonial internationalism. He had founded the *Revue Coloniale Internationale* in 1885 to give the colonialist "republic of letters" a forum. The *Revue* was the outcome of the International Colonial and Export Exhibition, held in Amsterdam in 1883. Published in the name of the Dutch Colonial Association (Nederlandsche Koloniale Vereenigung), the *Revue Coloniale Internationale* had styled itself as holistic and supposedly refrained from "embracing exclusively the Dutch interests in remote territories or the extension of the Dutch colonies." Instead, it wanted to "maintain the relations established among the representatives of colonial science and give a permanent character to the lively interest in general colonial questions." The *Revue* thus claimed to be the "first international organ of the colonial sciences" that united the "civilized nations of the two worlds."[30] Abroad, the *Revue* earned itself much admiration. The German *Colonial Gazette* regarded it as truly neutral: "This international journal provides precious material, especially to the reader of the German Colonial Gazette; the objective observer has to acknowledge the achievements of the *Revue* that lives up to its promising program."[31] Indeed, in the 1880s, colonial publicists from all the colonizing countries wrote for the *Revue*. Among them were the pioneer of the German colonial movement, Friedrich Fabri, the French colonial theorist and associationist, Louis Vignon, and the British governor of the Bengal presidency, Richard Temple. In addition, American and Russian contributors used the journal to promote the benefits of frontier colonialism in their countries.

While other Europeans regarded the *Revue Coloniale Internationale* as a truly transnational project, Van der Lith hid its nationalist agenda of competitive emulation in the fine print. For him, the *Revue* also aimed at "revealing the secrets" about colonial commerce, law, geography, and ethnography to serve Dutch "practical colonial interests."[32] By inviting international experts to write for the *Revue*, Van der Lith hoped to profit from the knowledge produced in bigger colonizing countries with a more developed scientific infrastructure. At the same time, the *Revue* gave him the opportunity to promote colonial

---

[29] Bossenbroek, "Dickköpfe und Leichtfüße," 48.
[30] "Introduction," *Revue Coloniale Internationale*, 1 (1885), I–II.
[31] "Die Revue Coloniale Internationale," *Deutsche Kolonialzeitung* 4, no. 4 (1887), 124–125.
[32] *Revue Coloniale Internationale* 1 (1885), IV and IX.

investments in the Dutch Indies. At the end of the day, the *Revue Coloniale Internationale* was an accumulative rather than a synthesizing expert journal. For want of funding, the different articles stood side by side in a seemingly disorganized way. The *Revue* ceased to exist in 1887 and gave way to the ICI's more organized attempt to synthesize knowledge about colonization.

The Dutch stood for the interest of smaller nations in cooperation and exchange, but the Belgian case shows that internationalism was not all about small nations' colonialism. After the international Congo conference of 1885 had entrusted King Léopold of Belgium with the government of the CFS in Central Africa, the territory became famous for its internationalized status. The Belgians Albert Thys and Camille Janssen, two of the ICI's founding members, had been instrumental in putting Léopold's CFS in place during the 1880s. Janssen became its first governor, after he had served as a judge at the international tribunals created in Egypt during the construction of the Suez Canal. In Egypt, Janssen had turned into an enthusiastic internationalist. In 1885, he agreed to govern the CFS because the European powers had declared it an international colony. Janssen's attitude came closest to an "uninterested" colonial internationalism. Albert Thys' internationalism was more materialistic, as he directed the construction of a railway line in the Congo. A railway entrepreneur, he desperately tried to attract international funding for building the track from the coast (Matadí) to the interior (Léopoldville).

Both Janssen and Thys were left disappointed when Léopold announced the sealing off of the CFS from international influence in 1890 and introduced a protectionist colonial policy. Janssen and Thys then turned to the ICI's international networks that held up internationalism and free trade. When Léopold abolished free trade in the CFS in the early 1890s, Janssen resigned from his post as its governor.[33] The engineer-entrepreneur Albert Thys, whose success in building the Congo-Matadí railway depended on international capital influx, equally criticized Léopold for introducing a protectionist concession system, which put an end to the open door policy in the CFS.[34]

In 1893, the ICI succeeded the CFS as the institution that preserved the internationalist ideal. For both Janssen and Thys, the ICI's internationalism was a compensatory internationalism that allowed them to preserve their autonomy in the face of Léopold's new protectionist policy. Throughout the 1890s, Léopold himself would try to use the ICI for his own purposes. He hosted banquets for its members in the belief that they supplied him with useful information and expertise.[35] Yet, his take-over was not successful and he never became an official member. Those Belgians who became ICI members instead adhered to transnational ideals and rejected Léopold's

---

[33] Louwers, "Camille Janssen," 437–440.
[34] Frankema and Buelens, *Colonial Exploitation and Economic Development*.
[35] BArch, R 1001/6186/5-7 *Indépendance Belge* (January 9, 1894).

protectionist policy. The ICI played a similar role as a refuge for internationalists in Germany.

In Germany, the ICI loomed large in pushing back the nationalist Pan-German branch of the colonial movement, which benefited the more cosmopolitan colonizers. It is well known that Germany's colonial tradition was highly nationalist and originated in an aggressive Pan-Germanism that developed into an expansive *Weltpolitik* during the 1890s. Such vigorous countries seemed to be less likely to engage with the ICI. Yet the ICI made German colonial experts succumb to the internationalist temptation. The relentless efforts of the ICI's founders to draw the Reich's colonialists from Pan-German nationalism unfolded in a tedious campaign. A detailed account of this recruitment effort gives proof of the ICI's deep commitment to win the favor of all colonizing countries.

At the University of Leiden, Van der Lith had made the acquaintance of the Heidelberg professor of colonial law Georg Meyer. Meyer was a member of the German Colonial Society and a deputy for the German National Liberal Party.[36] He was close to the founder of the German Colonial Society, the liberal Friedrich Hammacher, and acquainted with its first president, Hermann zu Hohenlohe-Langenburg. Using these networks of liberal-minded colonialists, Meyer approached Hohenlohe, asking him to become a member of a "scientific Institut Colonial International" and to attend its first session in January 1894.[37] Hohenlohe showed interest in the ICI mainly because of its founders' notoriety. He wrote to the government in Berlin that these prominent figures "did not allow Germany to stay away from such a new international association for colonial purposes, which is purely scientific."[38] However, he doubted the success of such an "experiment" and feared "political confrontations."[39] He refused to join the ICI himself and searched for a leading member of the German Colonial Society who took his place. In 1893, however, no leading member was able or willing to travel to Brussels to attend the ICI's inaugural meeting.[40]

Meanwhile, the ICI refused to accept members randomly chosen from the German Colonial Society, fearing that they might be too nationalistic. Invoking their solidarity as aristocrats, Lord Reay wrote to Hohenlohe: "The idea behind the institute was that the members join as individuals who

---

[36] G. Jellinek, "Georg Meyer," *Deutsche Juristen-Zeitung* 5 (1900), 130–131; Meyer, *Die staatsrechtliche Stellung*.

[37] HZA, La 140 Bü 246 "Gründung des Institut Colonial International in Brüssel," Meyer to Hohenlohe-Langenburg, December 18, 1893.

[38] BArch, R 1001, 6186: Akten betreffend das ICI vom Januar 1894 bis 31 Dezember 1906; Nr. 9: Präsident der DKG Hohenlohe to [Underscretary of Colonies?], March 24, 1894.

[39] HZA, La 140 Bü 246, Von der Heydt to Hohenlohe-Langenburg, April 28, 1894.

[40] HZA La 140 Bü 246, Vohsen to Hohenlohe-Langenburg, December 31, 1893; January 2, 1894 and January 5, 1894.

only present their individual opinions and do not have to consult with anybody but their own convictions." The ICI had invited Hohenlohe, he argued, because of his authority and his personal expertise in the colonial field. "The aim was not to invite the German Colonial Society, even though the Institute would be very glad to welcome the Society as an honorary member." To make the membership more tempting for Hohenlohe, Reay added that at the next meeting, "his majesty the king Léopold II of Belgium will give a dinner for the members of the Institute."[41] However, the royal argument did not have the intended effect. Hohenlohe pleaded that business affairs did not allow him to go to Brussels.

Impatient, the ICI's secretary general Camille Janssen postponed the ICI's first session and traveled to Stuttgart to personally meet Hohenlohe. The encounter took place in early March 1894 and finally secured Hohenlohe's membership in the ICI.[42] As its member, he became responsible for the recruitment of other Germans. Looking for suitable candidates, he turned to the director of the colonial division in the German foreign ministry, Paul Kayser, whom Pan-Germans attacked frequently because of his Jewish faith. Kayser proposed to send out members of the semi-official German Colonial Council, among them the explorer Georg Schweinfurth, who had been close to Belgian King Léopold II and his internationalist Congo project. Kayser added, "we could also send a member of parliament who has dealt with colonial issues, unless he is a member of the Pan-Germans."[43]

Kayser's advice against sending members of the Pan-German movement to Brussels originated in a split in the German colonial movement. The early 1890s had seen the separation of the Pan-Germans from the German Colonial Society. While the Pan-German breakaway faction was openly nationalist and racist, the German Colonial Society regarded itself as a more moderate association of colonial experts. Strangely, Kayser's remark seemed to inspire Hohenlohe in a way that nobody would have expected. Hohenlohe proposed the leading Pan-Germans Karl von der Heydt, Carl Peters, and Friedrich Ratzel as candidates for the ICI in Brussels.[44] All of them were affiliated with the Pan-German League and, moreover, were controversial figures within the German colonial movement.[45] Carl Peters, in particular, was notorious for his blunt racism and aggressive nationalism.[46] Although he had founded the

---

[41] HZA, La 140 Bü 246, Reay to Hohenlohe-Langenburg, January 1893.
[42] HZA, La 140 Bü 246, Janssen to Hohenlohe-Langenburg, March 3, 1894.
[43] HZA, La 140 Bü 246, Kayser to Hohenlohe-Langenburg, March 31, 1894.
[44] HZA, La 140 Bü 246, Von der Heydt to Hohenlohe-Langenburg, April 28, 1894 and May 31, 1894; Peters to Hohenlohe-Langenburg, July 20, 1894; Kayser to Hohenlohe-Langenburg, August 1, 1894.
[45] Eley, *Reshaping the German Right*, 49.
[46] Ciarlo, *Advertising Empire*, 41–43.

German East Africa Company which had acquired the colony of German East Africa (1885), the majority of the liberal and moderate members of the Colonial Society had turned against him. Long before the German government charged Peters with disobedience and murder, they regarded him as unrepresentative of the German colonial movement.

Why did Hohenlohe propose Pan-Germans as candidates for an international organization? It is possible that he hoped to shunt troublemakers like Peters out of the way, or at least to neutralize their fervent nationalist and racist views by placing them in a new internationalist environment in Brussels. Hohenlohe's correspondence with the German colonial authorities reveals his true intentions. He sent the Pan-Germans to Brussels to test if the ICI was indeed an apolitical and purely scientific institution. The Pan-Germans were his *agents provocateurs* who could provoke nationalist confrontations to see if the ICI members engaged in those discussions. After the first session had passed without any significant conflicts based on nationalist rivalry, Hohenlohe informed the German Colonial authorities, "I was not sure if it is a good idea to participate in an association whose purpose was unclear. Von der Heydt now informed me that the ICI really seems to pursue scientific goals. If that be true, [our] participation is important for the German influence." The ICI had delivered the proof that its agenda was transnational. Hohenlohe therefore recommended dispatching representatives of the highest colonial authority, the colonial division in the foreign ministry.[47]

In the 1890s, the ICI would manage to neutralize its Pan-German members during and even beyond its sessions. While Ratzel actually never joined the ICI, Peters participated solely in the first meeting.[48] During this session, Peters rose only twice to speak. In his first appearance, he asked for an international convention to protect animal wildlife in the colonies. As this was not the priority of the members in the ICI's early days, his remarks passed without comment. However, he caused an outrage when he spoke in favor of the enslavement and corporal punishment of African plantation workers.[49] Since many ICI members were also active in the international anti-slavery movement, they at least paid lip service to free labor in the colonies. Carl Peter's illiberal intransigence, and the fact that the German government prosecuted

---

[47] BArch R 1001, 6186: Akten betreffend das ICI, Nr. 15: Hohenlohe to Kolonialabtheilung, June 1, 1894.

[48] Ratzel accepted membership but is missing on the list after 1894: BArch R 1001, 6186: Akten betreffend das ICI 1894 bis1906, Nr. 32: Ratzel to Kolonialabtheilung, July 30, 1894.

[49] Peters considered African workers slaves and demanded severe punishment if they left their employer. This caused a long discussion in the ICI's meeting in 1895, in which most members argued against Peters and in favor of free labor: ICI, *Compte-Rendu 1895*, 253–254.

him for murdering two Africans, caused his disappearance from the ICI's membership list after the first meeting.

Unlike Carl Peters, Karl von der Heydt remained in the ICI and converted from Pan-German to internationalist positions. A rich banker based in Berlin, von der Heydt had been one of the Pan-German leaders.[50] In 1893, as he joined the ICI, he resigned as the director of the Pan-German League and assumed a more critical stance toward it. While his first petition in the ICI was still Pan-German – he urged to add German (as well as Italian and Spanish) to the official languages of the ICI – he took a more cosmopolitan stance in his later contributions.[51] Despite the failure of his Germanization initiative, he became a long-lasting and very active member of the ICI.

From the mid-1890s onwards, rather cosmopolitan Germans joined. They became one of the most active groups in the ICI. Adolph Woermann, the famous owner of the Hamburg shipping line, represented the Hanseatic merchants. He had spent a year in Dutch Batavia and in British Ceylon studying the production and trade of coffee, tea, and sugar. In the 1890s, his company would dominate trade in the whole of West Africa.[52] The most eminent German internationalist was Prince Franz von Arenberg, a Catholic internationalist born in Belgium and often residing in Brussels. He was a member of the Reichstag and had become vice-president of the German Colonial Society in 1892.[53] Oswald von Richthofen represented the colonial division of the foreign ministry, and Wilhelm zu Wied was a member of the German anti-slavery committee. Compared to the Pan-Germans, they belonged to the "liberal" and internationalist branch of the Colonial Society, which soon gained the upper hand in Germany. After the turn of the century, the reformist colonial minister Bernhard Dernburg also became a member of the ICI. The number of German members in the ICI grew steadily and reached a height of twenty-nine in 1913. They acquired a liking for the ICI's comparative approach and Hohenlohe ultimately celebrated it for "giving Germany the excellent possibility to profit from the rich experience that other colonial powers have made."[54] The colonial division of the foreign ministry regularly bought the ICI's publications and distributed copies among the governments in the colonies, as well was among consuls, navy, and state libraries in the Reich.[55]

---

[50] Barth, Die deutsche Hochfinanz, 59, 62–64.
[51] HZA La 140 Bü 246, Von der Heydt to Hohenlohe-Langenburg, April 28, 1894.
[52] Bohner, Die Woermanns, 61 and 118.
[53] "Franz Ludwig von Arenberg," in Meyers Großes Konversations-Lexikon, vol. 1. (Leipzig 1905), 735.
[54] BArch, R 1001, 6186: Akten betreffend das ICI, Nr. 15: Hohenlohe to Kolonialabtheilung, June 1, 1894.
[55] BArch R1001 6188 Nr. 141: Note; Nr. 44: Kolonialabtheilung April 13, 1896; Nr. 61: ICI (Janssen) to Kolonialabtheilung (Richthofen), March 18, 1897; Nr. 116: Königliche Bibliothek to Kolonialabtheilung, November 28, 1898.

British colonial experts were even more reluctant to join the ICI than the Germans, maintaining a sort of splendid isolation with regard to French-led continental internationalism. Initially, only the Dutch-born Lord Reay was committed to its cause. He was a cosmopolitan by birth. Descended from a Scottish noble family, he was naturalized British in 1876. From 1865 to 1869, he worked for the Dutch colonial ministry and earned himself a reputation as an expert in international law. Entering the public life of his adopted country, he was made a peer of the United Kingdom, with a seat in the House of Lords, and became governor of Bombay in 1885. After his return to England in 1890, he engaged in considerable activity as a member in several learned societies. He was secretary of the Royal Geographical Society and presided over the Social Science Congress, the Asiatic Society, the Franco- Scottish Society, and the British Academy while reforming the University of St. Andrews as its Lord Rector.[56]

Among the early British members was also Sir Alfred Lyall, who was less cosmopolitan than Reay but represented the remarkable interest of administrators from India in the ICI. Lyall had entered the Bengali Civil Service in 1855, took part in the suppression of the Indian rebellion of 1857, and afterwards held numerous posts in the administration of India. He had a mind of his own and occasionally got into conflict with his superiors in London. As a district officer at Hoshungabad in the central provinces, for example, he refused to grow cotton for export and promoted wheat production instead. Sympathetic to local needs, he was "very glad to see the honest rustic of Hoshungabad return to wheat crops" under his auspices.[57] In addition, he published a book on the *Rise of British Dominion in India* that celebrated Britain's grandeur but also pleaded for a cooperation with France and Russia to create a Western empire in Asia.[58] Lyall appreciated the social aspects of the ICI and used the meetings as opportunities to visit friends on the continent and to travel around Europe.[59] Only Reay and Lyall participated regularly in the earlier sessions. Two more British members, George Curzon and Robert Herbert, were never seen at the ICI's annual reunions, though they kept track of its publications.

Before 1900, most efforts to recruit more British members failed. In 1897, Chailley lost his temper and castigated those countries "who, up to now, have not participated at all, particularly England, a country of an enormous colonial affluence." Hence, the ICI referred to a recruitment strategy that had proven successful in Germany: "if the men of these countries do not come to us, we

---

[56] Baty, "Lord Reay," 9–10.
[57] Ross, *Ecology and Power*, 34.
[58] Lyall, *The Rise of the British Dominion*, 279–280.
[59] Durand, *The Life*, 406–408.

have to go and meet them."⁶⁰ Therefore, the general secretary, Janssen, traveled to England several times, at his own expense. As his attempts were unsuccessful, the ICI decided to hold its 1903 meeting in London. What was meant to be a recruitment event turned into a weekend escape for continental Europeans who wanted to know more about British India. The British showed little interest in the ICI's meeting in their own country. Even ICI member Lyall complained in a private letter that "next week we have here in London a meeting of the Institut Colonial International where representatives of various countries are to discuss colonial questions. But I think that, except among Hollanders and Englishmen, there is very little colonial experience or practical knowledge worth ventilating. The Germans are colonists, but they have no colonies. The French have colonies, but they are not colonists."⁶¹

Unlike the British in the metropole, however, the administrators from India showed great interest in the ICI. The ICI's *spiritus rector*, Joseph Chailley, spent eighteen months in British India, where he met with numerous British and Indian administrators and listened to their complaints. Upon his return, the Frenchman published an impressive volume of 500 pages about the shortcomings of British policy in the crown colony. The editor of the *Imperial Gazetteer of India* and secretary in India's Financial Department, Sir William Meyer, translated Chailley's book under the title *Administrative Problems of British India* (1910). Chailley's criticism was remarkable as it reproached the British for failing to implement indirect rule, a colonial method they claimed to have invented and perfected. It also accused the British administration of lavish spending while tolerating corruption and usury.⁶² Unexpectedly, the translation of Chailley's book, to which Meyer added his own critique of British mismanagement, became a bestseller among British colonial administrators and received praise from the whole empire.⁶³

Curiously, Indian nationalists and British administrators in India alike referred to Chailley's book to argue in favor of India's autonomy from the motherland. While Indians such as Gandhi used Chailley's critique to blame the British of underdeveloping India, British administrators equally referred to it when urging London to invest more capital in the colony. Their purpose was to increase their own scope of action and to become more autonomous in financial and administrative matters. Thus, although involving a good deal of self-criticism, administrators used Chailley's critique to impose their own individual interests on London as overseas administrators. Indeed, William Meyer, who had translated and popularized Chailley's book, frequently disobeyed London's directives and worked hard to provide British officers in

---

⁶⁰ ICI, *Compte Rendu 1897*, 89.
⁶¹ Durand, *Alfred Comyn Lyall*, 397.
⁶² Chailley-Bert, *L'Inde Britannique*, 106–107.
⁶³ *Indian Opinion* (October 6, 1905), 15.

India with more independent structures. In 1907, he joined the decentralization committee to give more power and financial autonomy to administrators in India, whom he thought to be better acquainted with local conditions.[64] When India finally received a more autonomous and decentralized status in 1919, Meyer became high commissioner of the subcontinent. The rise of the reformer Meyer in the autonomous Indian administration signaled an increased interest of the British administrators in the ICI and its schemes to empower the agency of the colonies.

It was therefore not until World War I that British experts from the metropole fully embraced the idea that mutual learning might be a way to enhance colonial domination and exploitation. By 1913, the number of British members in the ICI reached nine, whereas there had been only five up to that date. The Great War then reconciled the British and French colonial ambitions and facilitated a colonial rapprochement in international institutions like the ICI. In 1915, the Royal Colonial Institute in London edited a volume on comparative colonialism inspired by the ICI's comparative studies. The volume praised colonial comparison as a useful method "not only to understand thoroughly the methods of other nations, but to benefit from their experiences."[65] Even in the British Empire, the authors added, "we have something to learn from foreign nations." They particularly admired "French methods in West Africa, especially in the opening of the Sudan and the Sahara" and the French native policy. The Dutch, for their part, appeared to excel in colonial administration and the Belgians in scientific colonization.[66] Moreover, the authors believed that they owed to the Germans "great additions to our knowledge" of African fauna, flora, ethnology, scientific agronomy, tropical hygiene, and indigenous languages. This 1915 volume published by the Royal Colonial Institute – which had sent three delegates to the ICI – marked the beginning of increased British interest in the ICI's transnational project.[67]

Unlike the international "latecomer" Great Britain, colonial newcomers like Italy and the United States seemed more inclined to knowledge transfers through the ICI. Yet this was only partly true. Only three Italians joined in the 1890s and they kept a low profile. Italy's defeat in Adwa against Ethiopian troops in 1896 might have played a role in their reticence, but contemporaries came up with a more plausible explanation. Italy, explained a British agronomist from India, "has the advantage of a climate at home which enables them to do a great deal more in the way of preliminary work" and to test colonial

---

[64] Hobhouse et al., *Report of the Royal Commission*, 3.
[65] Royal Colonial Institute, *A Select Bibliography*, 3–5.
[66] Ibid.
[67] Those were George Baden-Powell, Francis de Winton, and Robert Herbert; Craggs, "Situating the Imperial Archive," 48–67.

methods at home before applying them in Africa.[68] Hence, he argued, the Italians learned from the internal colonization of the Italian South and did not need to refer to the colonial experience that others shared in the ICI. Indeed, colonial internationalists traveled to Italy to study sanitation measures against malaria. What is more, Northern Italians regarded Southern Italians as inferior, and the Mezzogiorno closer to Africa than to Europe.[69] It was not until the 1920s, however, that the Italians would become one of the most active groups in the ICI.

While Italians relied on their domestic experience, the US delegates in the ICI epitomized the colonial curiosity of a newcomer.[70] Although the four US members rarely embarked on a journey across the Atlantic to participate in the ICI's annual meetings, they studied its conference proceedings and publications thoroughly. In 1903, the ICI member and head of Washington's statistics bureau Oscar Phelps Austin drafted the most comprehensive official report on colonial policies ever published by the US government.[71] The report analyzed colonial history from 1800 to 1900 from a comparative perspective to work out a best practice of colonization. Austin used the ICI's publications as sources and cited its members to substantiate his claims. ICI members, he explained, were the "most distinguished and thoughtful of the world's students of colonial matters in other countries" who were aware of the "grave duties and responsibilities which rest upon those who have assumed the government of 500,000,000 people – one third of the earth's population." Austin's report provided the US government with "methods of government and development" for Cuba, the Philippines, and Puerto Rico, which it had conquered five years earlier from Spain.[72]

Through his report, Austin tried to prevent the US government from applying its own colonial experience – the internal colonization with European settlers – to the new tropical colonies.[73] Influenced by the ICI's emphasis on colonial governmentality and indigenous cooperation, he dismissed settler colonization as an adequate model for the new possessions conquered from Spain in 1898. According to Austin, the new tropical colonies needed to be governed in a completely different way, namely, through indirect rule developed in Dutch and British India. Based on the ICI's studies of colonies in the Indies, his report was supposed to be "the world's best

---

[68] *Proceedings of the Third International Congress of Tropical Agriculture*, 71.
[69] Finaldi, *A History of Italian Colonialism*.
[70] On American internationalism, see Ninkovich, *Global Dawn*.
[71] Curiously, this report is absent in Hopkins, *American Empire*. Little information may be found in Fergusson, *Colossus*; and Maier, *Among Empires*; More information is available in Kramer, *The Blood of Government*.
[72] US Dept. of the Treasury, *Colonial Administration*, 2692.
[73] This was also the purpose of the Taft Commission on the Philippines. See Ferguson, *Colossus*, 50.

judgement of to-day's requirement in the government of a people differing in race characteristics and climatic environment from that of the governing people and occupying noncontiguous territory."[74] He also discarded the Spanish colonial methods that had failed in "developing" the Philippines, Cuba, and Puerto Rico. While Austin was beating a dead horse by blaming Spain for their colonial mismanagement, he failed to mention that Spanish ICI members were equally about to realign their colonial agenda to the ICI's guidelines.[75]

Membership in the ICI put a new generation of Spanish and Portuguese colonial reformers in a position to ward off the accusations that they had exploited their empires without developing them.[76] By 1890, both the Spanish and the Portuguese empires in Latin America had become symbols of repressive and old-fashioned despotism built on a slave economy. Post-Portuguese Brazil had nominally abolished slavery as late as 1888, almost a century after France and Britain. Spain had led brutal wars against its colonial subjects and its Latin American empire gradually fell into the hands of the United States between 1890 and 1898, which seemed to confirm its decadence. Against this trend, Spanish ICI members tried to redefine and modernize Spanish colonialism. Even before 1898, when Spain lost all its colonies to the United States, progressive Spanish intellectuals who called themselves *regeneracionistas* undertook the task of reinventing the country's political identity. They portrayed Spain as a lost son to the European family who had enjoyed an opulent life in the Americas and returned to the European family after wasting his fortune.[77]

The *regeneracionistas* intended to prove Spain's "Europeanness" by taking part in supposedly modern and rational colonial projects in Africa, which also compensated the loss of the American possessions. One of the *regeneracionistas* was the reformer Joaquín Costa. He established the Spanish Society of Africanists and Colonialists in 1883, which lobbied for Spanish expansion in Morocco. Costa became the most eminent promoter of a reformed Spanish colonialism in Africa. Colonizing in a European and "modern" way, he argued, would strip Spain of its discredited "anachronistic" empire and rehabilitate it as a progressive nation.[78] Membership in the ICI was a great opportunity for Spanish reformers to substantiate their narrative of regeneration.

While Costa himself did not join the ICI, his reformist compatriots did. The most important was Antonio Maria Fabié, who became Spanish overseas

---

[74] US Dept. of the Treasury, *Colonial Administration*, 2559.
[75] Spain even became a model. See Beredo, *Import of the Archive*; Schumacher, "Kulturtransfer und Empire," 306–327.
[76] Bandeira Jerónimo, *The "Civilizing Mission,"* 109.
[77] Pedraz Marcos, "El Pensamiento Africanista," 31–48.
[78] Costa, *Reconstitución y Europeización*; Mateos y de Cabo, *El Pensamiento Político*.

minister in 1890 and was equally president of the Council of the Philippines and the Gulf of Guinea Possessions between 1891 and 1894. As such, he inaugurated administrative reforms in the Spanish colonies and rehabilitated Bartolomé de las Casas as founding father of empire critique and humanitarian colonialism.[79] Another member of the ICI was the liberal Fernando de Léon y Castillo, who had launched development projects as overseas minister in the 1880s and became a famous reformer– although he had used these development projects to enrich his own family. He would represent Spain at the Algeciras Conference in 1906, where he realized Costa's dreams of Spain returning to the international community as a modern colonial power. At Algeciras, he secured parts of Morocco for Spain.[80] A slightly different character was the publicist Wenceslao Retana, who specialized in Filipino culture and literature. While Retana was a fierce advocate of the Spanish Empire when he joined the ICI in 1893, he assumed a more critical attitude later in the decade, when he made himself the spokesman of the Filipino population. He became the first Spaniard to promote Tagalog as the national language of the Philippines and wrote a biography of the Filipino national hero José Rizal.[81] Like the German case – where the ICI contributed to making Pan-Germans more internationalist – the ICI inspired Retana to change his views and show more sympathy toward the colonized population. The internationalization of Spanish colonialism seemed to pay off when Madrid received parts of Morocco in 1911. The partition of Morocco among several colonial powers was also the result of diplomatic efforts by ICI members.

1.2 Colonialist Fraternization and the Prevention of an Imperial War

Even though the ICI might have served nationalist purposes in its early days, ICI members turned to a holistic transnational cooperation from 1900 onwards to prevent the outbreak of a European war. To avoid a war based on imperial rivalry, they launched press campaigns and engaged in secret diplomacy. Their activity reached a new level during the Moroccan crisis that peaked between 1906 and 1911, when Germany, France, and Spain laid claim on Morocco. Unlike European governments, who seemed to be willing to risk a conflict over the Sultanate, the ICI, and the leaders of moderate colonial interest groups attached to it, worked toward a peaceful partition. German and French colonial experts, whose nations had become the main competitors after the

---

[79] Fabié, *Don Fray Bartolomé*.
[80] Morales Lezcano, *El Colonialismo Hispanofrancés*, 21–22 and 25.
[81] Jiménez "W. E. Retana," introduction.

British had received compensation in Egypt in 1904, especially called for cooperation. In 1907, the French ICI member Albert de Pouvourville wrote in the German Colonial Gazette:

> We, the friends of colonial expansion in Germany and in France, shall cherish one ideal that we found on the journeys we have made at the remote places we have seen and during the strenuous and adventurous lives we have led. We should cherish that ideal among all people and in all the different climes. This ideal is certainly not more beautiful than the nationalist thought, but it complements it in the most useful and human way: it is the European ideal.[82]

Pouvourville's appeal echoed the close cooperation between German and French colonialists that had indeed resulted in a veritable friendship by the turn of the century. Inspired by the ICI's success, French and German colonial experts visited each other frequently and engaged in a lively activity of transnational exchange of knowledge.[83] This was remarkable given that the Franco-Prussian War lingered on in the collective memory of both nations and while a fresh conflict arose in Morocco. Nevertheless, both sides advocated colonial cooperation to overcome political rivalry on the continent.

When the French deputy Lucien Hubert gave a speech to members of the German Colonial Society in March 1907 to promote a "Franco-German rapprochement over colonial matters," the ICI member Johann Albrecht von Mecklenburg introduced him, claiming that "the recent events delivered the proof of the unifying force of the colonial idea" that might lead to "a similarly successful rapprochement between Germany and France." Lucien Hubert was less sentimental about colonial "friendship" but explained that the *force des choses* left Germany and France no other choice than to cooperate. He was struck by the warm welcome he received in Berlin and felt the "respect of the people he met" for the "French colonial methods." Therefore, he wanted to see France and Germany "associated, like noble rivals in the *grand oeuvre* of human progress."[84] The urge to bring about a peaceful solution went far beyond well-meant declarations.

Both in France and in Germany, colonial lobby groups close to the ICI launched press campaigns against nationalist media that favored an armed confrontation over Morocco. The influential Committee of French Africa even turned against the French foreign minister, Théophile Delcassé, who

---

[82] De Pouvourville, "Deutschlands Beteiligung am Französischen Kolonialkongreß 1907," *Deutsche Kolonialzeitung*, 33 (February 17, 1907), 329.

[83] "Deutsch-Französische Beziehungen," *Deutsche Kolonialzeitung* 29 (June 22, 1905), 301–302.

[84] BArch, R 1001, 6131 Internationales Ethnographisches Büro, Nr. 48-55: Hubert, "Le rapprochement franco-allemand sur le terrain colonial," *La Grande Revue* 11, no. 10 (July 10, 1907), 427–441.

advocated an Anglo-French rapprochement and a confrontation with Germany.[85] The German Colonial Society in turn criticized the *Staatssekretär* in Berlin's foreign ministry, Alfred von Kiderlen-Wächter, and his attempt to instigate Pan-German journals against France. Representatives of these colonial interest groups and ICI members confirmed each other's right to get a fair share of Morocco.[86]

The private correspondence between ICI members and other colonial internationalists confirms that they saw colonial wars as highly damaging to their own colonial interests. High colonial officials such as ICI member Alfred Zimmermann complained bitterly about the German kaiser who had provoked an international crisis by supporting the Moroccan sultan against the French and by openly insulting their diplomats during his journey to Tangiers in 1906.[87] While the crisis was underway, Zimmermann and Alexander von Danckelmann – two ICI members employed in the German colonial ministry – unofficially met with the head of the African Bureau in the French colonial ministry in a hotel in Germany.[88] Their aim was to prevent an armed conflict by downplaying the role of Pan-German enthusiasm about war. At the meeting, Danckelmann, a time-honored colonial internationalist who had been involved in establishing the Congo Free State, condemned Germany's "naval armament" and promised to his French counterpart that he worked hard "to prevent a war." At the same time, he explained that Pan-German "inflammatory pamphlets," did not represent the attitude of German colonial experts.[89] His efforts for appeasement fell on fertile ground in France.

In 1907, the leader of the French colonial party, Eugène Étienne, who had joined the ICI in 1904, traveled to Germany, presented himself to Kaiser Wilhelm II, and met with several leading politicians. He urged them to find a peaceful solution for the Moroccan conflict and offered to divide the Sultanate among the interested powers. While he gained Wilhelm's goodwill, the predominantly Anglophile government in Paris rebuked him for his impertinence.[90] Étienne was a member of the French parliament but had not been an official delegate of the government. Shortly after Étienne's diplomatic advance, a journey with similar intentions led the French general Hubert

---

[85] "Chambre, Séances du 19 Avril," *Bulletin du Comité de l'Afrique Française* (April 1905), 163–164.

[86] "Marokko," *Deutsche Kolonialzeitung* 28 (July 15, 1905), 287; "Deutschland und Frankreich," *Deutsche Kolonialzeitung* 51 (December 21, 1907), 531; BArch, R 1001, 6131 "Lucien Hubert," 434.

[87] BArch N2345/28, Nr. 3: Notizen Zimmermann über Holstein, October 3, [1906?].

[88] BArch N 2345/18, Nr. 34: Duchène (Ministère des Colonies) to Zimmermann, March 29, 1908.

[89] BArch N2345/15, Nr. 124: Danckelmann to Zimmermann, December 14, 1912; and Nr. 184: Danckelmann to Zimmermann, November 29, 1914.

[90] Grupp, "Eugène Etienne," 303–311.

Lyautey, the first resident general of French Morocco, to Spain. Lyautey, who was a member of the ICI, met with the Spanish king to coordinate colonial policies in Morocco.[91] Paris admonished both Étienne and Lyautey for their unauthorized diplomatic missions.

Ignoring the official position of their government, French colonialists continued to cooperate with like-minded Germans and Spaniards. Lucien Hubert and others came to Berlin while members of the Hamburg-based Colonial Institute visited the French Colonial Union. Relations with Spain were equally good. Hubert contributed to the organs of Spanish colonial lobby groups, such as the Boletín de la Sociedad Geográfica de Madrid, emphasizing the entente cordiale between the "Latin countries" in colonial matters. Already before the turn of the century, a member of the Spanish Geographical Society, Saturnino Jiménez, had used the German Colonial Gazette to press for a German-Spanish agreement on Morocco.[92] The early years of the twentieth century abounded with declarations of mutual friendship between colonial lobbyists and they contemplated organizing a European Colonial Congress to do away with all conflicts.[93]

Between 1905 and 1912, the ICI's diplomatic efforts seemed to be crowned with success. In 1905, the French minister of foreign affairs Delcassé, who had been ready to risk a war between France and Germany in Morocco, backed down under pressure from colonial interest groups and resigned from his post. Delcassé's demission finally opened the way for the agreements over Morocco in 1906 and 1911.[94] Pouvourville's "European ideal" seemed to become reality and the colonial entente a model for international conventions in general. When the French Hubert met with the German colonial minister and ICI member Dernburg in Berlin, the latter announced: "colonial problems can only be solved internationally." A journal from Frankfurt that reported on the meeting concluded that international conflicts in general, be they colonial or not, might be solved on a neutral terrain – the colonial terrain.[95]

Not without reason, the ICI's transnational fraternization during the Morocco crisis caused fear to arise among more nationalist-minded Europeans that the ICI might bring an aristocratic transnationalism back to life. Aristocrats were overrepresented in the ICI and their internationalism evoked the transnational phalanx of conservatives that had prevented the rise of democratic nations during the Vienna Congress in 1815. Indeed, noble ICI

---

[91] IdF, Fonds Terrier, MS 5955, Voyage Lyautey en Espagne.
[92] Nogué and Villanova, "Spanish Colonialism," 15.
[93] "Koloniale Vorlesung des französischen Deputierten L. Hubert," *Deutsche Kolonialzeitung*, 10 (March 9, 1907), 93.
[94] Andrew, *Théophile Delcassé*. For German-French cooperation, see Grupp, "Eugène Etienne," 306–309.
[95] BArch, R 1001, 6131 "Lucien Hubert," 427–441.

members participated in the Algeciras Conference in 1906, where Franz von Arenberg and Auguste d'Arenberg particularly pushed for an agreement on Morocco. The Arenbergs descended from the same aristocratic family based in Belgium but belonged to the German and the French branch respectively. Franz was vice-president of the German Colonial Society in Berlin, and Auguste was the president of the French Committee of French Africa in Paris. Moreover, they were members of parliament in their countries.[96] If ever colonial differences emerged between France and Germany, the Arenbergs urged the French and German parliaments to reach an agreement.[97]

In the view of republican observers in France, the aristocrats undermined the nineteenth-century project of democratic nationalism and tried to reestablish their power on (trans-)colonial territory. As early as 1893, when Chailley founded the ICI and scoured the French political elite for a flagship to represent the young institution, he was met with almost unanimous rejection. The upper ranks of the Third Republic advanced the nationalist argument that they were "Republicans and not internationalists" and denied their support for the ICI.

Chailley complained bitterly about those who still thought that internationalism ran counter to democracy:

> It is a lamentable phenomenon that democracies show a certain indifference, perhaps a certain uneasiness in the face of international associations. They are naturally suspicious and withdraw into themselves; they show an exclusive and grudging patriotism and think that they like their country less if they like another country; they do not respect those cosmopolitan families who maintain friendships and alliances that transcend the *patrie* ... families that are like bridges over the borders to connect the peoples and to allow them to mingle with each other, to appreciate each other, to associate, to help each other.[98]

Chailley exposed this reluctance of democratic nation-states to support international associations during the ICI's meeting of 1898, while some of the "cosmopolitan families," such as the Arenbergs, were present and displayed their consent.

While aristocrats were overrepresented in the colonial administrations and the ICI, the denunciation had deeper roots in republican notions of how a nation should colonize. Republicans in France usually favored the Algerian model, that is, the legal integration of the colony into the territory of the

---

[96] Andurain, "Réseaux d'Affaires," 85–102.
[97] F. von Arenberg "Opinions Européennes Avant la Conférence" *L'Europe Coloniale* (December 27, 1906); "La Question du Maroc" *L'Écho de Paris* 22, no. 7612 (April 30, 1905); Archives Arenberg, Carton Franz von Arenberg, Questions Politiques, Article "Franz von Arenberg," no name and date; ICI, *Compte Rendu 1907*, 66.
[98] ICI, *Compte Rendu 1897*, 50.

motherland. As Algeria was legally a part of France, it stood for the republican ideal of assimilative colonialism.[99] The ICI's ideal of colonial autonomy and its inclination to favor transcolonial cooperation over the strong influence by the state contradicted the republican project of assimilation. Consequently, the aristocracy in the ICI came under suspicion of betraying the Republican ideal of democratic nationalism.

Although the ICI was not a bastion of aristocratic atavism, noble networks helped its members to weave their own political web across the colonial world. ICI members naturally courted noble families who loomed large in the higher ranks of administrations, both in the metropole and in the colonies. What is more, they showed sincere respect for noble lifestyles that allowed for colonial commitment and for holding up transnational worldviews. The Dutch expert of Islam Christiaan Snouck Hurgronje, an academic beyond suspicion of aristocratic propensity, reported from the 1909 meeting of the ICI that "I hold this meeting in high esteem because it gave me the possibility to meet Lord Reay, Dernburg (the latter rude as the former noble), Chailley (whom I know already because of his Javanese journey), Anton from Jena etc. etc. Prince Hendrik presided over the session. He is intellectually more gifted than his brother Johann Albrecht who eagerly took part in our works."[100] Snouck Hurgronje's sympathy was undoubtedly with the nobles in the ICI (Lord Reay, Prince Hendrik, Duke Johann Albrecht). Unlike the German parvenu Dernburg, Lord Reay represented the time-honored nobility with extensive colonial experience. He was no exception: in the period before 1914, ten out of the seventeen British members were Lords and Earls. Together with the Dutch prince Henry of Mecklenburg and the president of the German Colonial Society, Duke Johann Albrecht of Mecklenburg, they represented the ongoing influence of peers in the civil service of democracies and in allegedly liberal colonial policies. They did not make the ICI an aristocratic institution but certainly provided networks to secure political and transcolonial connections.

The strong solidarity European ICI members developed over the Moroccan compromise and the aristocratic networks they used raise the question why the ICI labeled its transnational project international and not European. A closer look at the concept of Europe among ICI members illustrates that Europe represented a deficient and asymmetric transnationalism. Seen from the ICI's perspective, a European Colonial Institute would have differed from an International Colonial Institute in essence. The reasons lay in the Congo.

Pouvourville's "European ideal" cited above was clearly directed against British hegemony in colonial matters. As we have seen, between 1900 and

---

[99] Bancel et al., *La République coloniale*.
[100] Snouck Hurgronje to Nöldeke, June 29, 1909, in Koningsveld, *Orientalism and Islam*, 150–151; ULCSH, G. 27 Institut Colonial International Brussels.

1914, an anti-British attitude was latent in the ICI as French- and German-speakers dominated its meetings. Anti-British particularism took on a dramatic scale after the turn of the century. In that period, several ICI members contributed to the French journal *L'Europe Coloniale* – with its full and revealing title *Organe Hebdomadaire des Intérêts Coloniaux de l'Europe Continentale: Allemagne – Autriche – Belgique – Danemark – Espagne – France – Hollande – Italie – Portugal – Russie*. *L'Europe Coloniale* was the most aggressive continental press organ to attack British colonial policy. It openly fought against the "anglo-yankee-australian" expansion and took the Spanish-American War as the starting point to launch "a European action against the Anglo-Saxon crusade." The journal, whose editors were close to Chailley's French Colonial Union, suspected the Anglo-Saxons of wanting to expand their influence over the whole globe. In India, in the Spanish Antilles, in Africa, in Belgian Congo, and in Transvaal, the Anglo-Saxons allegedly tried to "bleed Europe to death ... any humiliation of our continent is a national satisfaction for them."[101] This British aggressive expansionism, *L'Europe Coloniale* concluded, was the "manifestation of a menacing imperialism that aims at Continental Europe," and cooperating with London in colonial matters would be like "kissing Judas." To counterbalance its influence, *L'Europe Coloniale* cherished a "European Union" against the British – and without them.[102] The anti-British stance of Belgian, French, and German colonial activists along with the Spanish aversion to the United States, seemed to give rise to an alliance among continental colonialists and consolidated their desire for a continental and colonial Europe.

What seemed to be an asymmetric transnational design of a continental Europe, however, had also individualistic origins. The anti-British attitude of *L'Europe Coloniale* was responsive to the British campaign against forced rubber collection in Léopold's Congo Free State. British and American journalists led the field of those who accused Léopold of killing millions of Congolese to satisfy his greed for rubber. Léopold, who often bribed his way out of any difficulty, used *L'Europe Coloniale* to attack Britain and the United States and bring the continental powers on his side. Although the paper denied all accusations, Léopold funded it.[103] He bribed *L'Europe Coloniale* to divert the attention from the rubber scandal and tried to conspire against the British and American sources that shamed his quasi-genocide in the Congo.

---

[101] BNF, Arsenal Fol-JO-2431, "L'Europe Coloniale: Son programme, sa raison d'être, son objectif," *L'Europe Coloniale* 1, no. 1 (October 9, 1904).
[102] Ibid.; and "L'Union Européenne," *L'Europe Coloniale* 1, no. 1 (October 9, 1904).
[103] BNF, Arsenal Fol-JO-2431, "L'Europe Coloniale: Son programme, sa raison d'être, son objectif," *L'Europe Coloniale* 1, no. 1 (October 9, 1904); "L'Union Européenne," *L'Europe Coloniale* 1, no. 1 (October 9, 1904).

Léopold lost this press war and had to resign as head of the Congo Free State in 1908. With him, *L'Europe Coloniale et Continentale* disappeared, both as a journal and as a transnational concept. Subsequently, the ICI established itself as the only transnational colonial institution and continued to portray itself as internationalist rather than European. In so doing, it appealed to both the British and the Americans to participate in its inclusive internationalism. The initial reluctance of British colonialists to join the ICI has to be seen against this background. Yet, when Léopold stepped back as the head of the Congo Free State in 1908, more delegates from the United Kingdom joined the ICI and British institutions such as the Royal Colonial Institute became interested in shared colonial knowledge. Within the ICI, they would soon play an important role.

Curiously, while the Congo Free State disappeared, the ideal of a "colonizing state" without motherland prevailed. When the Belgian King Léopold and his International African Association founded the Congo Free State in 1885, lawyers described it as an independent "civilizing state" (*État civilisateur*). By "civilization," they meant the integration into the world market and not so much the assimilation of people and laws.[104] In 1903, an international lawyer in the ICI, Édouard Descamps, felt the need to reemphasize the original international character of the Congo Free State and published a book entitled *L'État Civilisateur*. The book was responsive to the crisis of the CFS, during which Léopold came under attack for having betrayed the internationalist ideal – and his internationally monitored civilizing mission to replace slavery in the Congo with free labor and capitalism. In the midst of the Congo scandals, Descamps thus praised and idealized the original *État civilisateur*, which he viewed as being established "in the name of science and humanity" and dedicated to fighting slavery and "liberating the black race." Descamps was a devoted Christian and a confident internationalist who organized the Hague Peace Conference (1899), set up the Permanent Court of Arbitration (1899), and would be named special delegate of the League of Nations to establish the Permanent Court of International Justice (1922).[105] The CFS, Descamps explained, was exemplary because its legitimacy was not rooted in ethnic homogeneity or underpinned by a contract with the people, like in a nation-state. Instead, it was a "colony without metropole" and therefore a "colonizing state" and a "civilizing state."[106] Its "existence as an autonomous colonizing state," Descamps argued, allowed it to be concerned with colonization first, as "opposed to states that colonize secondarily and additionally only. The latter pursue nationalist purposes as their principal goal."[107] This state, he

---

[104] Wauters, *Histoire Politique*, 11.
[105] "Descamps, Édouard," *Biographie Coloniale Belge*, vol. 4, 219–230.
[106] Descamps, *L'Afrique Nouvelle: Essai sur l'état civilisateur*, 36.
[107] Ibid., 35.

concluded, was not a nation-state, but "finds its fundamental legitimacy in the right to assist human beings, who are – like us – made for progress."[108] According to Descamps, its legitimacy as a state originated in its program to civilize central Africa and its inhabitants. For him, the Congo Free State was therefore not a national power but a moral power.[109] More importantly, it gave autonomy to the colonial experts of the ICI.

Since the civilizing state was an autonomous and "un-national" state by definition, it gave all international experts the opportunity to make a career. The ICI seemed interested in turning all colonies into such entities governed by science and not by nationalism. It was therefore the transnational scientific community that would shape the colonial future. Indeed, colonial scientists, much more than any other group, dominated the ICI. Cherishing the ideal of a universal colonial science in theory, the ICI gave scholars the opportunity to meet in person at the annual assemblies. While they had long exchanged ideas and experiences via the circulation of publications, the ICI meetings gave them the possibility to meet and develop long-lasting friendships. In the beginning, those friendships were grounded in the individualistic agenda of winning the favor of luminaries and of capitalizing on higher-quality work of other scholars. Chailley, for instance, courted the Dutch Arabist Christiaan Snouck Hurgronje, the most famous specialist on the Muslim world around 1900. Chailley used Snouck Hurgronje's detailed knowledge about the Dutch Indies and his connections with Dutch administrators and Indonesian notables to write his handbook about colonial policies in Java. Only later did they meet frequently in a more convivial atmosphere to discuss their colonial experience over extended dinners.[110] The German Arabist Carl Heinrich Becker equally took advantage of the ICI meetings in the Netherlands to spend several days in Snouck Hurgronje's house. Later, Becker returned whenever possible, attracted by Snouck Hurgronje's sister.[111] Such friendships among ICI members emerged from individualist careerism but also developed into truly "transnational" friendships.

Neither the Morocco question nor World War I meant the parting of ways for ICI members. While German ICI member Becker succumbed to nationalist fervor at the outbreak of the war, he wrote to his Dutch friend Snouck Hurgronje:

---

[108] Ibid., 37.
[109] Ibid., 27.
[110] ULCSH, Or8952, A224: Chailley (UCF) to Snouck Hurgronje, June 20, 1897; and A 225: Chailley to Snouck Hurgronje, January 26, 1913.
[111] ULCSH, Or8952 A141, Becker to Snouck Hurgronje, May 20, 1909; Or 8952 A142 Becker to Snouck Hurgronje, May 24, 1909; Or 8952 A142 Becker to Snouck Hurgronje, June 8, 1909.

> Our fatherland fights for its existence ... those are glory days for us. But eminent values of our civilization [Kulturwerte] will also be irretrievably lost. The learned men, and our international science of Islam [Orientalistik] in particular, will suffer considerably. If Germany wins the war, the Orientalistik will thrive ... but it will be a national science. If we lose, it will be superseded. Both prospects make me succumb to grief. It was above all internationality that stimulated science.[112]

Although Becker's lamentation did not reduce his nationalist attitude, he continued to use the ICI networks during the war. Via Snouck Hurgronje, he interrogated Chailley – the head of the ICI who was promoted to a high-ranking position in the French Ministry of War – about friends and relatives who had died on the French battlefields.[113] He also made inquiries about his friend and fellow ICI member Louis Massignon, who was one of the few scholars who actually fought in the war and went missing. Such were the moments when Becker regretted the "total defeat of Internationalism" and a war that had been "a surrender of ideas to reality."[114] He was not aware that the ICI's transnational agenda was already a reality and would not only survive the war but even grow stronger out of it.

We can conclude that there were five reasons to establish the ICI – or to join it in its early days. First, embracing the ICI's internationalism served nationalist aims and helped governments to build and legitimize their empires. By joining the ICI, representatives from the Netherlands, Belgium, and the United States profited from international colonial experience to make their empires fit for competition with other empires. By 1900, most colonial ministries had learned to capitalize on the ICI's production of colonial knowledge and, as Belgian and German officials remarked, to use its "reservoir of information to which the founders of overseas colonies added all their accumulated experience."[115] In their imagination, the ICI was a colonial archive that provided them with best practices of colonial government. They would soon support the ICI logistically, ideologically, and financially. Moreover, Spanish delegates used their membership to rehabilitate Spain's colonial empire and its reputation. Second, an international colonial organization enabled small nations such as Belgium and the Netherlands to increase their agency within Europe. They could use the ICI to invert power relations and to outdo representatives of more potent nations. Dwarfs in Europe, they were indeed giants in the field of colonialism.[116] Members of small nations were thus easier

---

[112] ULCSH, Or8952, A149, Becker to Snouck Hurgronje, November 17, 1917.
[113] ULCSH, Or8952, A150, Becker to Snouck Hurgronje, November 21, 1914.
[114] ULCSH, Or8952, A152, Becker to Snouck Hurgronje, June 25, 1915 and July 24, 1915.
[115] BArch, R1001/6186, 5: German Ambassador in Brussels to Caprivi January 9, 1894, Article "L'Institut Colonial International," Indépendance Belge (January 9, 1894).
[116] Wesseling, "The Giant," 58–70.

to recruit. Third, the ICI initially embraced all types of colonialism. Apart from the above-mentioned nationalities, Russians and Latin Americans became members of the ICI. They had no overseas colonies but were engaged in internal colonial settlement of their countries. While they were quite active in the early days of the ICI, Russians and Latin Americans began to consider their concepts of internal settler colonialism to be in contradiction with the ICI's focus on replacing European settlers with indigenous collaborators. The United States, instead, capitalized on the ICI's experience to shift its paradigm from internal frontier colonialism to a policy that took the indigenous population in the new overseas colonies into account. Fourth, personal and ideological rivalry within nations pushed individuals to participate in the ICI. Rivalry emerged between assimilationists and associationists in France, between Pan-Germans and self-declared liberal colonialists in Germany, and between protectionists and free traders in Belgium. Fifth, rivalries within nations also led an emerging caste of colonial experts to build an individual career in colonial internationalism. By joining the ICI, they increased the probability of receiving information, improving their reputation, and securing funding. Individuals such as Joseph Chailley, and not colonial governments, were the driving force behind the foundation of the ICI. For these individuals, transnational cooperation became more important than loyalty to their own imperial nation.

Since the ICI was mainly a project of individuals and not of nations, they could create a transnational sphere in which colonialism had more credit than nationalism. The main dividing line did not run between French, British, and German colonialisms. Instead, a gap opened between colonial nationalists and colonial internationalists in each country, such as between Pan-Germans and German ICI members and between assimilationists and associationists in France. The main reason for this rupture was the dissociation of ICI members from the nationalist groups and authorities in the metropole. On the one hand, ICI members wanted to avoid an imperial conflict among European powers that threatened their colonial project as a whole. On the other hand, colonial experts in the ICI developed a strong sense of autonomy from their nation-states. As we will see, ICI members became professionals around 1900 and their professionalism and esprit de corps as colonial experts outpaced their nationalism. Even more so, the transnational colonial job market provided possibilities for them to build a career – regardless of nationalist restraints. For obvious reasons, they acquired professional skills through their transnational careers and knowledge transfers rather than by sticking to a nationalist ideology. The ICI gave them the opportunity to engage in networking and to acquire a set of colonial skills. It is thus for utilitarian reasons that they cherished the autonomy of colonial science and technology in the ICI.

1.3 The Constitution of an Institution: Promoting and Financing Colonial Internationalism

Once the founding father had laid the foundation of the ICI, its members turned it into a transnational colonial institution and had it funded but not controlled by national governments. They used three strategies to transnationalize the ICI. First, they declared it a learned society with a scientific purpose that was beyond national interests. Second, they acquired funding from governments that was not earmarked and that enabled them to act independently of donor nations. Third, they established a recruitment system that favored colonial expertise over national belonging. Taken together, these strategies ensured the transnational character of the ICI and its autonomy.

Between 1894 and 1914, 136 members from 11 countries turned the ICI into a virtual laboratory of colonialism. At fifteen week-long plenary meetings, these experts explored new techniques of colonial rule and development. To meet its objective of making science more colonial and colonization more scientific, the ICI published extensive reports that constituted a veritable *Bibliothèque Coloniale Internationale*, a name that editors chose for the series of ICI publications. More than fifty volumes of the *Bibliothèque Coloniale Internationale* appeared between 1893 and 1914 alone. Thirty-one of these volumes were comparative studies on colonial science, technology, and development. They covered the recruitment of administrators and the labor force, railway construction, irrigation, and mining as well as the establishment of protectorates, land tenure, and colonial law. Another sixteen volumes contained detailed minutes of the ICI's fifteen plenary meetings held between 1894 and 1913. In addition to the conference proceedings, the ICI published expert reports on alcohol and opium trade as well as on big-game hunting in the colonies. Taken together with thousands of individual publications by ICI members, those studies left hardly any stone in the colonies unturned. In its publications, the ICI claimed to avoid over-generalizing colonial theories and doctrines in favor of more detailed progress reports by colonial practitioners.[117] They did not want to gain their knowledge from theoretical science but from empirical experience. To achieve this goal, the ICI predominantly bundled reports from different colonies in a comparative and particularistic way, adding general comments during the plenary meetings. This gradual process aimed at synthesizing colonial knowledge, without theorizing too much.

Even though the volumes of the *Bibliothèque Coloniale Internationale* did not always live up to their empirical aspirations, colonial governments held them in high esteem and they circulated globally.[118] ICI publications could be

---

[117] ICI, *Compte Rendu 1900*, 123, 195, 208.
[118] Subscribing to the ICI's publications: Argentina, Australia, Canada, Greece, Guatemala, India, Japan, Siam South Africa, Switzerland, and Uruguay. See ICI, *Compte Rendu 1929*, 61.

1.3 THE CONSTITUTION OF AN INSTITUTION

found in colonial offices, in public libraries, and even in the sparse book collections of colonial administrations overseas like in German Cameroon, in Portuguese Mozambique, and in Dutch Sumatra.[119] Colonial officers cherished the particularistic arrangement that gave them the opportunity to compare different techniques of governing in other colonies. Frequently, colonial administrations – for example, in German East Africa – urged colonial ministries in the metropole to purchase and forward the ICI's publications, while complaining bitterly if the authorities back home failed to send them immediately upon publication.[120] Inspired by the ICI's *Bibliothèque Coloniale Internationale*, colonial administrators put reliable strategies and techniques of colonial rule and development to the test in their own colonies. The ICI's colonial science was thus applied science.

While developing a transnational colonial science, the ICI cooperated closely with other international learned societies within Europe such as the Institute of International Law (1876) and the International Institute of Statistics (1885) on which the ICI was modeled.[121] Some members literally accumulated memberships in nongovernmental institutions. The first president of the ICI, the economist Léon Say, appeared in the registers of twenty different associations, many of them international.[122] Due to overlapping memberships, the ICI launched joint projects, for example, with the Institute of International Law to draft an international convention for the recruitment of workers in the colonies.[123] Yet, while the Institute of International Law openly intervened in political affairs, the ICI pursued a seemingly quietist strategy.[124]

For the ICI, participation in projects with the label "international" was a means to make its colonialist ends sound moral and scientific. Apart from using the moral language of internationalism, the ICI's dedication to internationalist movements was not ideological but practical and therefore transnational rather than international. For practical reasons, the ICI members were involved in many, if not all internationalist initiatives around 1900. Since colonial science covered a wide field, ICI members sat in most international learned societies and attended almost all international scientific congresses. But they were also involved in more radical internationalist movements.

---

[119] The *Reichskommissariat* in Duala owned several ICI volumes. On Sumatra, see "Institut Colonial International," *De Sumatra Post* (July 23, 1910).
[120] BArch, R1001, 6188, Nr. 71: Governor German East Africa to Kolonialbtheilung, February 25, 1897; Nr. 107: Governor German East Africa to Koloniabtheilung, September 9, 1898.
[121] ICI, *Compte Rendu 1897*, 63; Schnee, *Deutsches Koloniallexikon*, 99–100.
[122] ICI, *Compte Rendu 1897*, 52–53.
[123] ICI, *Compte Rendu 1899*, 53–54; ICI, *La Main d'Oeuvre aux Colonies*, 3 vols. See also Daviron, "Mobilizing Labour."
[124] Koskenniemi, *Gentle Civilizer*.

One ICI member, the Belgian Émile Vandervelde, was among the leaders of socialist internationalism. Even an international women's rights activist network around the famous Indonesian feminist Raden Adjeng Kartini had strong supporters in the ICI, whose members were also in touch with Pan-African internationalists such as W. E. B. Du Bois.[125] ICI members strategically socialized in international diplomatic and international law circles, for example, those who would initiate the League of Nations. The ICI was also a corporative member of the World Congress of International Associations, launched by the Union of International Associations in 1910, the only organization for which internationalism was an end in itself.[126] Yet, for the ICI, internationalism was a means and not an end in itself. Most of its memberships, then, served to develop the ICI's colonial and not its international cause. Thus, the ICI used these internationalist movements without declaring internationalism its ultimate goal.

In its early days, the ICI cultivated an image of absolute neutrality and styled itself as a scientific and apolitical institution, heralding that "at the International Colonial Institute, we never want to give advice and we have always refused to impose doctrines."[127] The statutes banned "political debates" from the institute's meetings and recommended to avoid "any questions which might be likely to cause national ill-feeling."[128] Apart from providing a comfort zone against quick-tempered nationalists, the ICI's anti-political impetus was conducive to a portrayal of colonialism as a transnational science – thereby obliterating its bad reputation as a nationalist ideology. By acting like a "disinterested" learned society, its members tried to counter their image as a colonial lobby group.[129] In line with its scientific aspiration, its official purpose was to develop best practice techniques of colonization through comparison of colonial methods and the transfer of governmental technologies.

ICI members skillfully escaped supervision by European governments, while using them for their own transnational projects. As we have seen, the ICI soon won influence among government officials in the metropole and overseas, although it officially kept a low profile in colonial politics. To get access to the upper ranks of political decision-makers in the metropole, the founding fathers used colonial lobby groups that were not overly nationalistic,

---

[125] Kartini, *Letters*, xiii.
[126] Laqua et al., *International Organizations*; ULCSH, F.6 Congrès Mondial des Associations Internationales 1913.
[127] ICI, *Compte Rendu 1900*, 123, 195, 208.
[128] "Article 12 of the Statutes," in ICI, *Compte Rendu 1909*, 30; *Notice Institut Colonial International*, 24.
[129] Ageron, *France Coloniale ou Parti Colonial?*; Grupp, *Deutschland, Frankreich und die Kolonien*; Andrew and Kanya-Forstner, "The French Colonial Party," 99–128; Viaene, "King Leopold's Imperialism," 741–790.

1.3 THE CONSTITUTION OF AN INSTITUTION

such as the French Colonial Union, the Royal Asiatic Society, and the German Colonial Society.[130] The German Colonial Society, for example, persuaded the colonial division within the German foreign ministry that the ICI was an "opportunity to profit from the rich experiences of other colonial powers."[131] With the assistance of such lobby groups, the ICI then recruited its members among the political elite of each state and gained indirect influence among decision-makers.

Soon, ICI members roamed the floors of colonial ministries in the Netherlands, Belgium, Germany, and France. Its agents in the colonial offices provided the ICI with insider knowledge and documents about railway building, colonial law, tropical hygiene, and the recruitment of a labor force, which the ICI used for comparative studies.[132] Frequently, colonial ministries went as far as carrying out the ICI's instructions to launch surveys among overseas administrators on tropical hygiene and indigenous law. German, French, Dutch, and particularly Belgian colonial ministries and embassies distributed ICI surveys around the tropical world.[133] Administrators, settlers, missionaries, and colonial subjects alike responded to these requests by delivering the most recent news from the colonial perspective. Some even accepted the ICI as a more authoritative institution than their nation's colonial authorities. For example, the Portuguese expat newspaper *The Beira Post* in Mozambique looked in admiration to "the Pleiades of politicians and scholars of global reputation" who ran the ICI and were better informed than the Portuguese colonial authorities.[134] By the turn of the century, the ICI certainly knew more about everyday colonial life than the armchair administrators in the colonial offices of the metropoles.

Once the ICI had recruited eminent members, these notables talked their national governments into funding its transnational project. Governmental subsidies made up the most important part of the ICI's budget. Before World War I, the ICI received financial aid from the Belgian, Dutch, and French colonial ministries each subsidizing it with 1,500 to 2,000 francs annually. In the first years of its existence, Russia and Chile donated smaller amounts but backed out of the project toward the turn of the century, when they realized

---

[130] For example, the German Colonial Society. See HZA La 140 Bü 246, Reay to Hohenlohe-Langenburg, January 1893.

[131] BArch, R 1001, 6186: Akten Institut Colonial International, Nr. 1-4: Deutsche Gesandtschaft in Belgien to Caprivi, January 9, 1894; Nr. 15: Hohenlohe to Kolonialabtheilung, June 1, 1894.

[132] BArch, R 1001, 6186: Akten Institut Colonial International, Nr. 1-4: Deutsche Gesandtschaft in Belgien to Caprivi, January 9, 1894; Nr. 15: Abschrift Janssen to Hohenlohe June 15, 1894.

[133] BArch, R 1001 6187 ICI, Nr 3 Vohsen to Dernburg, March 4, 1907; Nr. 34: Dernburg to Vohsen, January 2, 1909.

[134] "Instituto Colonial Internacional," *The Beira Post* (Mozambique, May 27, 1913).

that the ICI dismissed the internal settler colonialism that had shaped those countries.[135] German colonial administrations in Cameroon, German East Africa, and Jiaozhou each assigned 250 marks to the ICI from their already low budget. These small contributions from overseas were above all symbolic – but revealed that administrators held the ICI's work in high esteem.[136] Only after 1900, the colonial authorities in Berlin siphoned off up to 2,500 francs annually for the ICI from a special Africa-Fund. These sums were far from being enough to run the ICI, but they contributed to remunerate its only permanent employee, Secretary General Camille Janssen. Another 10,000 francs derived from membership fees (50 francs annually for effective members and 15 francs for associated members) and from the sale of the ICI's publications.[137]

Despite government funding, the ICI struggled continually not to be in the red. The income from selling publications was negligible, although sending the ICI's periodicals to governments often aroused their interest in funding the whole institute. In 1912, the ICI earned only 3,797 francs from selling its conference proceedings and special reports – though this represented the highest profit from publications the ICI had seen since its founding. In the same year, the ICI had to spend 8,000 francs to balance the costs of the *Recueil International de Législation Coloniale*, a comparative report on colonial law. The *Recueil* had 218 subscribers but earned the ICI no more than 2,800 francs.[138] What kept the ICI alive in its early days were one-off payments and donations.[139] The biggest donation prior to the World War I came from the Belgian entrepreneur Albert Thys, who was responsible for the construction of the Matadí–Léopoldville railway in the Congo and who owned several mining companies in the Katanga region. In 1900, Thys funded the ICI with a subsidy of 6,000 francs, taken from the budget of his railway company. This sum enabled the institute to publish an encyclopedic three-volume series on railway construction in the colonies.[140] These rare injections of capital enabled the ICI to hold frequent meetings and refund the travel costs for a couple of its members.

The financial situation changed for the better as soon as colonial governments embraced the development policy that the ICI designed and promoted. The financial takeoff started before World War I with a surplus of 8,000 francs in 1912 but took full effect in the interwar period. By the 1930s, for example,

---

[135] See AMAEB, D 4782 INCIDI, Report on "Session Extraordinaire du 6 Juin 1896."
[136] ICI, *Compte Rendu 1913*, 84.
[137] ICI, *Compte Rendu 1897*, 58.
[138] ICI, *Compte Rendu 1913*, 83–84.
[139] ICI, *Compte Rendu 1913*, 34.
[140] ICI, *Compte Rendu 1900*, 255. Albert Thys had already funded the Institute in 1894 with 2,500 francs, taken from the budget of the Compagnie du Congo pour le Commerce et l'Industrie: ABAE, D 4782 Manuscript of the procès verbaux, January 8, 1894.

all French colonies granted opulent subsidies to the ICI. Indochina led the field with 20,000 francs.[141] More importantly, the British government – which had exercised restraint before the war – joined the donor countries with 50,000 francs annually.[142] By that time, the circulation of the ICI publications increased, because they interested not only colonial officials but also experts of the League of Nations, the International Labor Organization, and other international institutions.

Increasing membership spoke to the growing importance of the ICI, which explicitly recruited individuals as colonial experts and not as representatives of a nation. The number of members was restricted to 60 by 1894 and then was gradually raised to 200 by 1913. A strong notion of exclusivity led the founding fathers to accept members by invitation only. In practice, only 136 joined, because the leaders valued quality over quantity. ICI members proposed candidates from their own country who were then elected by all ICI members during the annual "extraordinary sessions."[143] Older members approached potential candidates in person and chose them according to their colonial expertise and their social status. The ICI categorized members into effective, associated, and corresponding members. Effective members were supposed to be "among those who distinguished themselves in colonial policies, be it in the colonial service of each nation or in the fields of colonial law, political economy or the administration of colonies." The associated members were "persons with special knowledge" who might live in the metropole whereas corresponding members generally resided in the colonies and were a source of first-hand information.[144] It was thus the main concern of the ICI to enroll experts only and to choose them from among politicians, colonial administrators, scholars, and technicians. Overall, the recruitment scheme valued expertise over nationality. Nevertheless, the ICI used national networks for recruitment. Many of the German members, for example, were recruited from the semi-official Colonial Council, which advised the German government on colonial matters.[145] The same goes for the influential Belgian Colonial Council (1908) whose members were equally in the ICI. In France, powerful lobby groups like Chailley's Colonial Union became the national branch of the ICI.

At times, critics reproached the ICI for simply assembling has-beens and wannabes in equal shares. While it is true that many members had already

---

[141] ANOM, FP 100APOM/222–223, ICI, Correspondance Louwers avec Section Française, Louwers to Olivier, December 29, 1938.
[142] NAK, CO 323/1043/1 Request ICI for financial support from British Government, 1929; ICI, *Compte Rendu 1931*, 71.
[143] AMAEB, D 4782 (D 89) INCIDI, Rapports Sessions Extraordinaires.
[144] As corresponding members rarely participated in the ICI's activities, the general assembly decided in 1897 to open the group of "associated members" to those who had not lived in the colonies. ICI, *Compte Rendu 1899*, 19–21.
[145] Pogge-von Strandmann, *Imperialismus vom Grünen Tisch*.

retired from colonial service and some had not yet been to the colonies, the experience of colonial practice was greater in the ICI than in the average state institution. By 1900, the bulk of the ICI's members were legal experts, both in colonial and international law, like the British Lord Reay and the Belgian Édouard Descamps. The second most important group comprised the *anciens*, former governors and administrators, whose authority, however, no one dared to challenge. They sided with colonial engineers and agronomists who vouched for the practical relevance of the ICI. Those "technicians of colonization" were emblematic for the ICI's self-conception as a virtual laboratory for colonial techniques. In a similar way, specialists in tropical medicine contributed to its status as an expert institution. In addition, a smaller number of colonial entrepreneurs joined. Executives such as Albert Thys and the German bank director and millionaire Karl von der Heydt compensated for their low numbers by restless activity. They connected the ICI with capitalists in Europe and the Americas. In accordance with the ICI's inclination to scientific colonization, missionaries and military members were underrepresented. Before World War I, only two missionaries and two navy officers were among the 136 members. The striking absence of those who represented conquest and evangelization was no coincidence. It expressed the ICI's desire to delete all traces of colonial methods it considered as outdated.

While some called the expertise in the ICI in doubt, it did not strike observers that Africans and Asians were lacking on the membership lists. No one questioned the fact that all ICI members were white, male, and pursued a lifestyle that can be qualified as bourgeois. Their financial resources allowed them to commit themselves to politics, high society life, and the study of the possessions overseas. Moreover, many of the ICI's members had a seat in national parliaments or were part of the upper ranks of bureaucracy. Most of them taught at universities. Almost all of them were members of colonial interest groups or learned societies, which operated on a national basis.

According to the statutes, the system of national representation in the ICI was proportional, but the quota system had little importance in practice. In theory, each country was assigned a number of seats that was in accordance with its supposed colonial "importance." In 1894, the ICI reserved eleven places for British delegates, seven for French, six for Dutch, five for Germans, three for Belgians, three for Spanish, three for Italians, three for Portuguese, two for Danish, and one for an Austrian (accepted by Oscar Lenz who was in fact German-born and employed by German colonial societies). The frontier colonizers also participated: Russians received five seats and Americans and Latin Americans had three seats each.[146] The quota system, however, concealed

---

[146] See ICI, *Compte Rendu 1894*.

the fact that the "French intellectual element dominated the sessions," as the German government laconically observed.[147] This "French element" comprised all members who could speak French, among them Belgians, Dutch, Spanish, Italians, Portuguese, and even Germans themselves.

Thus, prior to World War I, the ICI's official language was French, a fact that caused astonishingly few protests and even fewer communication problems. With French being the diplomatic and transnational language of the Belle Époque, most of the well-educated ICI members spoke it fluently. When the French geographer Henri Froidevaux participated for the first time in an ICI meeting in Germany, he was surprised to hear all the members "speak in excellent French," not only during the sessions but also in the animated debates "*hors séances.*"[148] Writing from The Hague in September 1895, the British Alfred Lyall described one of the ICI meetings to his brother: "We meet in a large official room, where speeches are made and papers discussed on colonial questions; the official language being French, I have not yet made any oratorical display. But my French enables me to understand very well what is said, and to me the debates are interesting, especially when the French members take part in it."[149] Such modesty by a British imperialist was hitherto unheard of and gave proof of Lyall's desire to support the ICI's transnational project. English was officially the ICI's second language, but the majority of the members preferred French. Chailley himself was unable to write simple letters in English.[150] Before World War I, the ICI printed its publications in French only, mainly because it was unable to pay translators. It was not until after the Great War that the ICI sporadically commissioned university students to translate its proceedings. Hence, British colonial experts who did not speak French became increasingly interested in the bilingual publications and therefore in the ICI (see Figure 1.1).

While the founding fathers had been at pains to encourage like-minded colonial enthusiasts from the big powers to join the ICI in 1893, all prominent colonial experts signed up for a membership after 1900. Among them were Frederick Lugard, Hubert Lyautey, Bernhard Dernburg, and Dirk Fock – leaders who consequently remodeled the colonial policy of Great Britain, France, Germany, and the Netherlands respectively.[151] All of them admitted the ICI's great influence on their reformist colonial policy, which originated in

---

[147] BArch, R 1001, 6186: Akten betreffend das ICI Nr. 1–4: Dt. Gesandtschaft in Belgien to Caprivi, January 9, 1894.

[148] BArch, R 1001, 6186: Akten betreffend das ICI, Nr. 89: Questions Diplomatiques et Coloniales July 1, 1904: Froideveaux: La Session de Wiesbaden de l'ICI, 11–25.

[149] Durand, *Alfred Comyn Lyall*, 364.

[150] ANOM, FP 100 APOM/93-98, 1: Union Coloniale, Chailley, Projet de Mission aux Indes Anglaises et en Indochine, Chailley to Constable, publisher at the India Office, December 9, 1896.

[151] BArch, R 1001 6187 ICI, Nr. 9: Dernburg to Vohsen, March 23, 1907.

Figure 1.1 Meeting of the INCIDI (former ICI) at Lisbon in 1957
© INCIDI (ed.), *Pluralisme Ethnique Et Culturel Dans Les Sociétés Intertropicales, Compte Rendu De La 30ème Session À Lisbonne 1957* (Brussels: INCIDI, 1957)

the 1890s and reached its heyday between 1908 (when Dernburg reformed the German colonial administration) and 1922 (when Lugard published his famous dual mandate theory that reiterated indirect rule). At the same time, ICI members helped newcomers such as the United States and Italy to organize their new empires. When meetings became more frequent after 1900 and were held annually instead of biennially, the ICI strengthened its transnational esprit de corps.

Around 1900, the ICI's internationalism was more and less than the sum of its nationalist parts. More because it became transnational, less because individualist ambitions were the driving force. Individuals such as Joseph Chailley, Camille Janssen, and Albert Thys had egoistic reasons to spend much time and money on the ICI. Chailley wanted to oust his nationalist rivals in France, Janssen got himself a paid job as secretary-general of the ICI, and Thys used it to acquire international expertise and capital for his railway constructing company in the Congo. Without the enthusiasm of these three individuals, the ICI would have had a short life.

After 1900, transnationalism became a priority in the ICI, though not a ubiquity. Nationalism lingered on, but it was something members tended to promote back home and not within the ICI. The exclusion of fervent nationalists such as the German Carl Peters spoke to that agenda. Individuals who joined the ICI might have been nationalist on one occasion and transnational on another. Yet the ICI itself largely was a transnational space in which nations became unimportant for the colonial purpose it pursued. Obviously, transnationalism was not a word people used in the 1890s but this was often what they meant when they spoke about internationalism. The ICI's internationalism was scientific and not one of international relations. The priority of the ICI members was neither their nation nor the relationship between or "inter-" nations. Their priority lay beyond the nation and constituted an autonomous colonial sphere. Thus, the ICI could have easily gone by the name of Transnational Colonial Institute. As they lacked the word, they labeled it "international." Tellingly, the ICI members equally avoided the words "empire" and "imperial." The term empire seemed to evoke an amalgamated space that comprised one nation and its colonies. These nation-empires had caused much trouble and brought back the period of conquest and extinction. It was more promising to turn colonialism into a progressive and transnational science. Around 1900, empires had no potential for becoming such a progressive transnational tool. Since ICI members avoided the term empire, they never described their project as "inter-imperial" cooperation. Instead, they frequently used the expression "inter-colonial" assuming that there was an autonomous colonial space.[152] Chapter 2 is about that transcolonial space.

[152] Sohier, "Pour une Collaboration Juridique Intercoloniale," 27–28.

2

A Transcolonial Governmentality Sui Generis

The Invention of Emulative Development

The shift from nationalist to transnational colonialism in Europe triggered a move from colonial government toward transcolonial governmentality overseas. Instead of ruling through a bureaucracy centered in a metropole, ICI member Lord Reay explained in 1903 that administrators needed a "colonial instinct, which is an instinct *sui generis*."[1] Many ICI members contended to have acquired their expert instinct by personal experience rather than deducing it from theories developed in the motherland. The ICI provided them with a transcolonial "reservoir of information to which the founders of overseas colonies added all their accumulated experience."[2] This chapter demonstrates that the ICI processed these transcolonial experiences and turned them into governmental techniques of colonial development.

The members of the ICI thought of their transcolonial development schemes as governmental in the Foucauldian sense of the word, meaning that a state institution was unnecessary to impose a certain agenda on a society and cause it to participate in its own transformation. This approach could be more adequately described as functional governance, a doctrine prevalent in the UN and among international development agencies after 1945 (Chapter 9). ICI members knew about the lack of an efficient centralized power in the colonies. They offered a decentralized transformation of colonial societies with the help of techniques developed through transcolonial comparison and transfer. What is more, their governmental program was to incite a "colonial instinct" equally among the colonized population. ICI members wanted them to participate in and contribute to the colonial order. The main purpose of this order was economic development, to which the colonized population should contribute at their own pace and in harmony with their own nature.

As early as the 1890s, the ICI invented a transcolonial version of economic development, which differed from the typical state-led development schemes of the 1930s in that it was not necessarily centrally planned and administered. Instead of seeking financial aid directly from the European governments, the

---

[1] ICI, *Compte Rendu 1903*, 46–48.
[2] BArch, R1001/6186, 5: German Ambassador in Brussels to Caprivi, January 9, 1894, Article "L'Institut Colonial International," *Indépendance Belge* (January 9, 1894).

ICI developers attracted capital from the international market. The ICI's transcolonial development scheme was collaborative, emulative, and governmental. To design cheap and governmental tools of development, ICI members emulated technologies of development successfully field-tested in other colonies. This emulative development scheme led to the idea of "slow development" that claimed to take local conditions and customs into account. Guided by their "colonial instinct *sui generis*," they designed a transcolonial development scheme through which they felt closer to other colonial experts than to their compatriots in the metropole. Solidarity among colonial experts was thus the precondition of transcolonial development schemes.

What distinguished the ICI's notion of development from unvarnished exploitation was its combination with rudimentary welfare schemes and ethical discourses. Members of the ICI promoted a holistic development that left the lives of the colonized workers and their environment intact. Searching for a third way between the preservation of an allegedly authentic indigenous society and a great leap forward, they advocated a temperate and gradual transformation toward a capitalist society. ICI members increasingly appealed to an applied colonial science that they developed from their own thorough knowledge of colonial societies.

For different reasons, five transnational subgroups – tropical hygienists, utilitarian free traders, Christian paternalists, humanitarian theorists, and advocates of social and transcolonial legislation – in the ICI held that the indigenous workers should be at the origin of development. Tropical hygienists ironically advanced racial theories to endorse the indigenization of development efforts. Utilitarian free traders expected development on the cheap from the employment of the colonized. Ethical and humanitarian attitudes drove Christian paternalists and advocates of social legislation to promote the protection of indigenous workers from predatory capitalism. Embracing cultural relativism, colonial lawyers codified customary law and ultimately implemented a transcolonial "indigenous" law, which should guide the colonized toward a more productive life. Cooperating across colonial and disciplinary boundaries, these five groups wanted to bring about a slow and sustained transformation toward a capitalist society. The notion of sustained and holistic development was not intuitive but was the result of a long and nonlinear process. In theory, that process led ICI members to adopt governmental schemes that highlighted the productive role of the colonized population. In practice, transcolonial and sustained development schemes often failed, while nevertheless securing funding and new employment possibilities for the ICI members.

2.1 A Transcolonial Science of Comparison and Experience

The most important transcolonial initiative of the ICI members was to promote an applied science of transcolonial development. In 1900, around half of the ICI's members were scholars at universities, but equally important were experts who developed their knowledge from practical experience. Lord Reay underlined that "we refer only to practical problems, which our members develop from their personal experience that they acquired as colonial administrators. That is why the exchange of views is very fertile, even if it discourages the theorists. To be sure, a Colonial Institute does not give itself away to doctrines."[3]

In theory, the ICI's version of colonial science was empirical. Its proclaimed aim was to substitute theoretical approaches developed in the motherland with the method of colonial comparison and transfers between different colonies. Madagascar's governor-general Gallieni, for example, traced Chailley's journey to Java because he expected to "be inspired by the practice on the ground instead of following mere theories. The latter might exist in their own right at congresses of geographical societies, but they become inapplicable if we want to use them on the ground in our overseas possessions."[4] To develop applicable techniques was the greatest concern of the ICI and comparison was the way to do so. Consequently, the first paragraph of its statutes stipulated that the ICI had the purpose of "facilitating and spreading the comparative study" to determine the most efficient way of administration, legislation, and exploitation of economic resources.[5]

For profit-seeking ICI members, transcolonial science was functionalist and not idealistic. Arguing that they needed transcolonial experience for successful development projects allowed the colonial experts to receive more funding. Chailley's functionalist approach in the ICI's governmentality project was innovative and to some extent prefigured functional governance, which became popular in the UN and international development agencies after 1945 (Chapter 9). When Chailley asked the French Ministry for the Colonies and the Department for Public Instruction to finance his research trip to British India in 1896, he argued that it was the only way to gain real experience. While he had already bought 1,000 books to study the religions and castes of India, along with the British colonial legislation and education, he insisted that he needed to travel personally to the crown colony because it was "what a laboratory is to the chemist or the physicist."[6] ICI members frequently evoked the idea of the transcolonial laboratory and partly realized

---

[3] ICI, *Compte Rendu 1903*, 46–52.
[4] ANOM 100 APOM 93, Union Coloniale, Correspondance Gallieni, Gallieni to Depincé, January 12, 1901.
[5] BArch, R1001/6186, 7: German Ambassador Brussels to Caprivi, January 9, 1894, "L'Institut Colonial International," *Indépendance Belge* (January 9, 1894).
[6] ANOM FP 100 APOM/93-98 Union Coloniale: Chailley Mission aux Indes Anglaises 1900-1901, Chailley to Ministère de l'Instruction Publique, July 29, 1900.

it with regard to colonial agriculture and medicine.[7] Conveying the impression of establishing a neutral colonial science based on experience even increased the possibility of ICI members receiving funding.

In the 1890s, the ICI turned into a travel agency for scientists that made comparative and transcolonial experience possible. Most importantly, the ICI provided transcolonial networks and recommendation letters. These letters enabled them to travel without restraints in foreign colonies. Chailley, for example, approached the governor-general of the Dutch Indies via his Dutch colleagues in the ICI. When Chailley traveled to Dutch Java in 1900, the governor ordered his administrators to provide him with food, accommodation, official documents, and collegial company. Owing to the governor's support, Chailley obtained access to administrative archives, military bases, and state hospitals in Dutch Java.[8] Having received carte blanche, he scrutinized every aspect of Dutch colonization in Java and collected data, which he then processed in his voluminous book on Dutch colonial administration.[9]

Even colonial ministries made use of the ICI's transcolonial networks, especially if their missions needed to be kept secret from a nationalist lobby at home. As late as 1909, the German colonial minister and ICI member Bernhard Dernburg confidentially approached American colonial internationalists who gave him reference letters to travel in the cotton-producing states of the United States. Visiting the exploitative cotton plantations in the semi-colonial Deep South, he engaged in a sort of industrial espionage and studied how plantation owners prepared and "educated" Afro-Americans for "manual work."[10] Another member of the German colonial ministry, Alfred Zimmermann, who had been an ICI member since 1897, visited the Dutch East Indies, British possessions, and French Tunisia with the help of reference letters from ICI members. He made wide use of their knowledge and advice to publish a five-volume series on *The European Colonies*.[11] Like-minded internationalists from Great Britain translated his oeuvre into English, while Zimmermann proofread scientific articles written by his Belgian colleagues about German colonialism and vice-versa.[12]

---

[7] ARGB, Zaire 68: Rapport d'Emil Zimmermann, Coopération Belgo-Allemande, December 20, 1910.
[8] ANOM 100APOM 93, Union Coloniale, Chailley-Bert, Voyage aux Indes Néerlandaises, Mai-Juillet 1897, Article "De Heer Chailley-Bert."
[9] Chailley, *Java et ses Habitants*.
[10] BArch, R 1001, 6631, 6: Dernburg to Warburg August 26, 1909. On Dernburg's journey, see Zimmerman, *Alabama in Africa*, 195.
[11] BArch, N2345/53, 1: Letter of recommendation by Leroy Beaulieu, March 11, 1894; Zimmermann, *Die Europäischen Kolonien*.
[12] BArch, N2345/48, 3: Thozée to Zimmermann, January 22, 1894; BArch N 2345/47, 8: Strachey to Zimmermann and Danckelmann, December 12, 1902.

For those colonial internationalists who were not able to acquire this comparative experience personally, the ICI documented and condensed colonial experience. A learned society, it enabled specialists to keep up with the latest developments in the interdisciplinary field of colonial science. While specialists attended international congresses in their own field, they profited from the interdisciplinary exchange in the ICI and the possibility to apply their knowledge to colonial contexts. The German Arabist Becker wrote in 1912 that he "just came back from the meeting of the International Colonial Institute in Brussels ... it was very interesting. We got to know each other very well. The topics were accurate, the presentations good and the debates sometimes nuanced. Questions concerning currency, forced labor, and acclimatization were problems I was able to learn from."[13] The ICI and the interdisciplinary exchange among its members played a crucial role in "colonizing" different scientific disciplines by making them available to the transcolonial community of experts.

2.2 From Tropical Hygiene to Racist Anthropology: The ICI and the Acclimatization Dilemma

When members of the ICI met for the first time in 1894, they chose to discuss the one topic that was least likely to cause nationalist clashes among its members: the unhealthy climate in the colonies.[14] The ICI invited Georges Treille, professor of naval hygiene and exotic pathology and inspector general of the French Service de Santé des Colonies.[15] Treille made a plea for transnational cooperation and evoked the European sense of community with regard to climatic menaces overseas:

> In these diverse [colonial] climes, a *rapprochement* of interests is prepared which is like an international fusion, and the regrettable divisions of the old Europe disappear. The new colonies open themselves liberally to every European, with disregard to his nationality .... This solidarity of European interests – in an attempt to civilize the barbarian and unexploited countries – places huge duties on international science.[16]

Treille's scientific understanding of transnational solidarity fit the program of the ICI very well, since it portrayed itself as the alma mater of the colonial sciences. This is why the subject figured high on the agenda of sessions held in

---

[13] ULCSH, Or. 8952 A145, Becker to Snouck Hurgonje, July 6, 1912.
[14] See Curtin, *Disease and Empire*; Osborne, *Emergence of Tropical Medicine*; Arnold, *Warm Climates*; MacLeod and Lewis, *Disease, Medicine, and Empire*. For global contexts, see Anderson, *Colonial Pathologies*.
[15] Treille, *Organisation Sanitaire*, 60.
[16] Treille, *De l'Acclimatation*, 6.

1894, 1895, 1900, 1908, 1909, 1911, 1912, and 1913, with the deliberations continuing after World War I. In the 1890s, mortality rates among European administrators were the ICI's main concern, since they stood in the way of efficient administration and development. Its long-term member Gustave Dryepondt, the head of the Congo Free State's medical service who worked with an international team of researchers at the medical laboratory in Léopoldville, revealed in a comparative study that in French Dahomey, more than a quarter of the administrative staff had succumbed to tropical diseases.[17] On average, 16 percent of the French administrators in the African colonies died between 1887 and 1912.[18] A German ICI member added that out of 164 administrators and soldiers who served in German Cameroon between 1885 and 1896, only one-third completed their service, while two-thirds either died or became invalid due to blackwater fever, malaria, or dysentery.[19] Such high numbers of casualties not only disabled the colonial administration but also reflected very badly on them back in Europe, as members of the ICI emphasized when meeting in The Hague in 1895:

> Isn't it the idea of the insalubrious climate that wards off men and capitals from tropical Africa? It is useless to search for other reasons! ... A double benefit derives from taking care of the administrators' life to allow them to endure in the colonies: the state can introduce an element of stability to the colonial administration and inspire confidence among the masses in the colonial project. Are not these the two ingredients that guarantee the success of the whole enterprise?[20]

Since the reputation of the entire colonial project – and its funding – was dependent on the good health of the Europeans, the ICI urged for immediate and professional solutions to avoid high mortality rates.[21]

In the 1890s, more than fifteen tropical hygienists and heads of colonial sanitary services joined the ICI, which pioneered globalizing tropical medicine. While the first international congress of tropical medicine was held as late as 1913, the ICI offered a platform to specialists in the field as early as 1894. Most of these experts pursued transnational careers and were no strangers to foreign colonies. Before the German Empire acquired its own colonies, German doctors had often practiced in the Dutch East Indies, where their skills had been in high demand.[22] Albert Plehn, a member of the ICI and vice-president

---

[17] Dryepondt and Van Canpenhout, *Rapport Sur les Travaux*; Société Royale de Médicine, *Rapports*, 433.
[18] Cohen, *Rulers*, 23.
[19] Plehn, *Beiträge zur Kenntnis*, 24.
[20] ICI, *Compte-Rendu 1895*, 97.
[21] On the debate about mortality, see Curtin, *Death by Migration*.
[22] Snouck Hurgonje to Nöldeke, January 4, 1919, in Koningsveld, *Orientalism and Islam*, 270.

of the International Society for Tropical Hygiene, had started his career in the Dutch East Indies, where he systematized the use of quinine prophylaxis against malaria.[23] Later, he organized the containment of malaria, blackwater fever, dysentery, and beri beri in German Cameroon.[24] Another German member of the ICI, Hans Ziemann, had visited several foreign colonies before he began to direct the hospital in Douala. He was a member of the British Society for Tropical Medicine and Hygiene and the Société de Pathologie Exotique in Paris.[25] In Paris, he met Raphaël Blanchard, a French entomologist who had obtained his degree in Germany and Austria.[26] The British malaria expert and Nobel Prize winner Ronald Ross held Blanchard in high esteem and applied his methods in India.[27]

To promote tropical medicine, ICI members established new research institutes in their home countries. In 1902, Blanchard joined forces with the founder of the ICI, Joseph Chailley, to set up the French Institut de Médicine Coloniale, which they modeled after the London School of Tropical Medicine and the Liverpool Tropical School of Diseases by adapting their curriculums.[28] Specializing in tropical pathology, hygiene, and parasitology, Blanchard's Institut de Médicine Coloniale evolved into an international training school for tropical doctors: in the first year of its existence, thirteen French, one Belgian, three Columbian, one Haitian, and two Russian students graduated from the school.[29] In Germany, Robert Koch and ICI member Franz von Arenberg initiated the creation of the Institute for Maritime and Tropical Diseases (1900) in Hamburg and modeled it after similar Dutch and British institutes in Weltevreden and Simla, with the objective of preparing German doctors for their service in the colonies.[30]

Transnational networks emerged predominantly in the new field of parasitology, which used microbiological approaches to prove that parasites caused diseases that had traditionally been ascribed to bad air or foul soil.[31] Instead of developing their own national traditions of parasitological research,

---

[23] *Archiv für Schiffs- und Tropen-Hygiene* 35 (1931), 205; Plehn, *Beiträge*, 18.
[24] Rumberger, "Plehn, Friedrich," 524.
[25] "Hans Ziemann," in *Deutsches Koloniallexikon*, vol. 3, 748.
[26] Blanchard, "L'Entomologie"; Opinel, "The Emergence of French Medical Entomology," 387–405.
[27] Bynum and Overy, *The Beast in the Mosquito*, 486.
[28] Opinel, "The Emergence," 391; Blanchard, *L'Insitut de Médicine Coloniale*, 7.
[29] Blanchard, *L'Insitut de Médicine Coloniale*, 19.
[30] ICI, *Compte Rendu 1907*, 65; and "Errichtung eines Instituts für Tropenhygiene," *Deutsche Kolonialzeitung* 13 (March 13, 1899), 106.
[31] We cannot confirm Osborne's claim that tropical medicine can only be explained within its national context. See Osborne, *The Emergence of Tropical Medicine*, 2. For a nuanced interpretation, see Neill, *Networks*; Digby et al., *Crossing Colonial Historiographies*; Mertens and Lachenal, "The History of 'Belgian' Tropical Medicine," 1249–1272; McVety, *The Rinderpest Campaigns*, 25–35.

many experts looked to Italy as an example. There, malaria caused the deaths of an estimated ten to twenty thousand individuals per year. Parasitological research flourished in malaria-ridden Italy and its experienced physicians were in high demand in all the colonies. In Léopold's Congo, for example, almost half of the doctors employed by the Free Congo State were Italians.[32] The French colonial ministry frequently sent colonial doctors to study in Italy before they established themselves in the French empire.[33] The renowned German bacteriologist Robert Koch had also visited Italy frequently, as well as Dutch Java, before he investigated the origins of sleeping sickness in German East Africa.[34]

After World War I, ICI members pursued careers in international organizations. Émile Brumpt joined the League of Nations' Health Committee, which supported his epidemiological studies in the "warm countries," funded by the Rockefeller Foundation.[35] Gustavo Pittaluga, an Italian ICI member specializing in malaria studies, became vice-president of the League of Nations' hygiene commission. Before the war, he had headed the General Spanish Health Directory and advanced the Spanish colonial health service in Equatorial Guinea.[36] Both Brumpt and Pittaluga were also members of the League's malaria commission.[37] Hence, ICI members were pioneers of international parasitological research. Its leaders made use of their networks of *tropical* medicine to answer a most pertinent *colonial* question: Was economic development through the colonial settlement of Europeans in the "warm" regions medically possible?

Thinking of tropical medicine as an applied science, the ICI tried to find out whether medical experts would be able to immunize European settlers against the harmful tropical climate and its specific diseases. The purpose was to know whether white settlers would be productive enough to bring about economic development. Members of the ICI contemplated three different medical approaches to tackle the problem: traditional tropical hygiene, the new science of bacteriology, and racial theories. Traditional hygienists found the causes of tropical diseases in "external" environmental factors such as high

---

[32] An ICI member employed in the CFS. See Baccari, *Il Congo*, 70; Vellut, "European Medicine," 67–87.
[33] ANOM FM Mis/99, Dossier Médecin principal Jean Legendre.
[34] "Ergebnisse der wissenschaftlichen Expedition des Geheimen Medizinalrats Professor Dr. Koch nach Italien zur Erforschung der Malaria," *Deutsche Medizinische Wochenschrift* 5 (1899), 344–347; BArch R 6619/75.
[35] Brumpt, *Titres et Travaux*, cited in Opinel and Gachelin, "Emile Brumpt's Contribution," 299–308. For the continuity between colonial and international health organizations, see Borowy, *Coming to Terms*, 15 and 198; Farley, *To Cast out Disease*, vii.
[36] Baganet Cobas, "Dr. Gustavo Pittaluga," 11–19. See also Pittaluga, *Elementos de Parasitologia*; Webb, *Humanity's Burden*, 134.
[37] Société des Nations, *Publications Hygiene*, 4.

temperatures, humidity, and the emanation of the soil (miasma).[38] Bacteriologists, instead, used microbiology to search for the "internal" causative agents of tropical diseases: they had identified mosquitoes as the vectors, and germs as the agents, of endemo-epidemic diseases.[39] A third group started from the idea that different "races" reacted differently to tropical diseases and used statistical data to prove the inability of the white race to settle in the tropics, which they thought led to racial degeneration.

A long debate led ICI members to conclude that traditional hygienists were unable to immunize white settlers against the hostile tropical climate. Traditional instructions hardly improved upon naval handbooks of the early nineteenth century, which claimed that sweating and anemia damaged the organism of the Europeans who sojourned in the tropics. To avoid deficient sweating, they prescribed frequent showers, baths, and ventilation, as well as appropriate clothes and awnings to keep the sun away.[40] As a cure against anemia, naval doctors recommended a self-reliant prophylaxis that prescribed fresh vegetables and invigorating sleep. Traditionalists also highlighted the therapeutic effects of hill stations, which allegedly relieved European bodies from the pressures of the hot lowland climate.[41] Although ICI members established such sanatoria in the highlands of the Dutch Indies, British India, German East Africa, and the Congo Free State in the 1890s, they agreed that hill stations alone could hardly guarantee a fully healthy and productive life in the colonies.[42] After all, frequent visits to hill stations prevented farmers and workers from pushing ahead with production and development. To be sure, traditional doctors also suggested the taking of prophylactic quinine and arsenic against endemic diseases such as malaria.[43] But in the 1890s, many ICI members considered prescriptions for quinine and arsenic attributes of trial-and-error medicine rather than deriving from professional and purposeful medication. As a result, most members of the ICI dismissed traditional tropical hygiene as deficient.

More surprisingly, ICI members equally rejected the bacteriologists' undertaking to combine microbiological knowledge with sanitation measures to control infectious diseases such as malaria and sleeping sickness. In the 1890s, the skepticism toward bacteriologists was unexpected given that they promised new methods to immunize Europeans against these diseases.[44] After

---

[38] On miasma theories, see McNeill, *Mosquito Empires*, 30 and 80.
[39] Neill, *Networks*, 13. The role of mosquitoes had been known for a long time. See McNeill, *Mosquito Empires*, 196.
[40] ICI, *Compte Rendu 1894*, 57.
[41] ICI, *Compte Rendu 1900*, 141.
[42] ICI, *Compte Rendu 1911*, 105, 141, and 192.
[43] ICI, *Compte Rendu 1894*, 50–51.
[44] For an overview, see Arnold, *Warm Climates and Western Medicine*; Lyons, *The Colonial Disease*.

all, Treille had initially hoped that bacteriologists might provide remedies and finally enable white settlers to acclimatize in the tropics:

> For some localities in the intertropical zone, the history of colonization is effectively no more than a long chronology of lamentable disasters. Thousands and thousands of men have succumbed again and again to its climate. They are sad victims of the ignorance of the hygienic prescriptions and of the wrong choice of a place to settle. But the ruin of the first enterprises, the horror of the murderous epidemics, the following misery and abandonment, all of this will now pass slowly into oblivion and disappear from the memory of men.[45]

Despite this hope to erase the memory of vulnerable and costly settler projects, bacteriologists were still a long way off from fulfilling their promise of immunization. Although transcolonial efforts to combat sleeping sickness and other diseases were under way, there was no prophylaxis. Eradicating the mosquitoes that transmitted malaria and sleeping sickness proved costly and complicated.[46] At the same time, ICI members felt uneasy about the bacteriological revolution and its consequences. Drawing on his own experience in the Congo, Dryepondt cautioned his colleagues against the pitfalls of bacteriologist arguments: if it was not the climate in general – represented by the traditional "miasma" school of thinking – but identifiable microbes that were at the origin of tropical maladies, then Europeans would be able to do physical work in the tropics: "The climate can be dangerous to those who work, it is true, but the miasmas are not the problem. The White who labors manually is *not* more exposed to the bites of the anopheles, stegomyia or tsetse flies ... than the White who works in his office."[47] Dryepondt knew very well that "pathetic and lazy colonizers, who want the blacks, the domestics, and the boys to do all the work" frequently found excuses to avoid physical work.[48] Bacteriologists held these excuses up to ridicule. Without admitting it, ICI members were certainly among those "lazy colonizers" who thought that whites should not work in the tropics. More importantly, ICI leaders categorically dismissed mass settlements, even in territories with few endemic diseases such as Algeria. His utilitarian attitude led Chailley to believe that economic development was less costly and risky if Europeans employed indigenous farmers and workers. Hence, ultimately, most ICI members turned against bacteriologists who promised economic development through white settler-farmers. The latter seemed to be a burden for the development effort.

---

[45] Treille, *De l'Acclimatation*, 8.
[46] Lyons, *The Colonial Disease*, 229.
[47] ICI, *Compte Rendu 1911*, 112.
[48] Ibid., 114

In the 1890s, doctors in the ICI increasingly adopted theories of racial degeneration. They started from the idea that racial acclimatization was the main operation to enable colonization: "By white colonization, we understand exclusively the acclimatization of the race, i.e. the adaption to the climate of a whole population, not only during the lifetime of the first arrivals, but also their progeny, conserving from generation to generation the distinctive qualities of their ascendants, without any mixture with the indigenous."[49] Unlike bacteriologists, however, they defined the settlers' acclimatization as a pathological process: if transplanted to a foreign environment, European organisms allegedly suffered severely.[50] The consequence was not only weakness and temporary disease but also collective degeneration, racial decline, and even extinction of the "white race."[51] Endorsing this racialized medical science resulted in an "acclimatization dilemma," according to which the entire white race would degenerate and become sterile once its members tried to acclimatize themselves to a tropical environment.[52]

The pathologization of the acclimatization process was partly inspired by Arthur de Gobineau's *Essay on the Inequality of Human Races*. In the essay, he argued that a "civilized" race might lose its purity if it conquered a weaker race. When they entered in contact, hybridization would inevitably lead to the degeneration of the superior race.[53] At the 1889 International Colonial Congress, some of the ICI's founding fathers had attended a lecture by Gobineau's disciple Gustave Le Bon, who explicitly situated racial encounter and decline within a colonial setting.[54] By combining Darwinist ideas of racial evolution and the rise-and-fall model of empires, Le Bon showed himself to be critical toward colonial settler societies. He identified a recurrent pattern in world history according to which the more numerous races – no matter what their "character" was like – absorbed the less numerous ethnicities. He cited the example of white families living in the midst of a black population, who "will disappear in a few generations without leaving any trace. This has been the fate of all conquerors who were strong in weaponry, but weak in number." And more dramatically: "All great empires that unite dissimilar peoples can only be created by force and are condemned to perish by violence."[55] Being French, he naturally directed his criticism toward French policy in Algeria where the French gave the land to European settlers.[56] ICI founder Joseph

---

[49] ICI, *Rapport Preliminaire*, 10.
[50] On degeneration, see Anderson, *Colonial Pathologies*, 2.
[51] For the American context, see Anderson, "Immunities of Empire," 94–118.
[52] Acclimatization means the process during which an organism adjusts itself to a new environment and is modified. See Jennings, *Curing the Colonizers*, 8–39.
[53] Geulen, *Geschichte*, 71.
[54] *Congrès Colonial International de Paris*, 29.
[55] Le Bon, "The Influence of Race in History," 7 and 11.
[56] Le Bon, "Algeria and the Ideas Prevailing in France," 4–5.

Chailley, among others, had attended Le Bon's lecture. Since Chailley had long claimed that the French settler policy in Algeria had been a fatal error and a financial disaster, Le Bon provided him with a racial justification against settler colonialism. This combination would also shape the program of the ICI

While influenced by racial theory, the ICI superficially claimed to do justice to its empirical approach. In 1909, the ICI convened a committee on the "Acclimatization of the Population of the White Race in Tropical Countries." Among the members of the committee were outstanding tropical hygienists who explored the practice of settling Europeans in the colonies. To put their evolutionary theory about racial degeneration to a test, they sent a questionnaire to Europeans living in tropical regions who had given birth to children there.[57] European settlers who answered the survey naturally denied any signs of racial degeneration among themselves or their children. In its final verdict, however, the ICI's committee argued that it would be irresponsible to send white women to the colonies, whom they feared would produce *dégénerés*. Such a colonial policy would equal, as one member put it, "a crime against the parents and a crime against *la Patrie*."[58]

To be sure, not all ICI members believed in racial degeneration, but all of them used racial theories to explain their empirical realities and to rationalize their pragmatic interests. Representatives of the "old colonies" with larger settler communities, for example, were in favor of "indigenization" of Europeans, arguing that some of them had long undergone processes of "mestization."[59] Charles Grall, the head of the Native Health Service in French Indochina, among others, stated that acclimatization was an "unrealizable task," unless Europeans managed to "indigenize ... in other words: the body achieves a mixed temperament, half way between that of the European and the native. That is the creole temperament, the only one compatible with tropical regions."[60] Despite the 1905 ban on miscegenation in South West Africa, German ICI members also considered race mixing as a process that could keep the colonial project alive.[61] The most radical proposition came from the Dutch physician Emanuel Moresco, the first secretary of the government of the Dutch Indies. In a report *On the Conditions of the Métis and the Attitude of the Governments with Regard to Them*, which Moresco prepared for the 1911 meeting of the ICI, he proposed an "exchange of qualities" between the Europeans and non-Europeans by intermarriage. In that way,

---

[57] ICI, *Compte Rendu 1911*, vol. 1, 139.
[58] ICI, *Compte Rendu 1911*, 109.
[59] Speech by "mestizo" Isaac at *Congrès Colonial International*, 84–85.
[60] ICI, *Compte Rendu 1912*, 87. Cited after Jennings, *Curing*, 16. On the French case, see Saada and Noiriel, *Les Enfants de la Colonie*.
[61] Kundrus, *Moderne Imperialisten*, 219–280; Lindner, *Koloniale Begegnungen*, 317–361; Hartmann, "Die Mischrassen," 907–908.

he argued, the intelligence of white men could be joined with the indigenous' immunity to tropical diseases.[62] Moresco's argument was racist and pragmatic alike, since he believed that colonial societies would "benefit in the most profitable way from their [the mestizo's] aptitudes."[63] He held important posts in the Dutch colonial administration and would later become the Dutch delegate for colonial policy at the League of Nations and a member of the International Labor Organization.[64] Echoing Moresco, the Spanish ICI member Antonio Maria Fabié even sent a delegation to the Spanish Philippines that investigated the possibilities to "blend the races" (*fundir las razas*) of the colonizers and the colonized in order to make the Filipinos progress and the Spanish apt to live in the tropical climate.[65] As Creole settlers argued in the ICI's meetings, a certain degree of indigenization was necessary for making settler colonies productive. Their pragmatic approach differed from the "pure" armchair racism of the metropole but was no less racist in essence.

If even Creole settler activists deemed indigenization appropriate, it was unclear to the majority of the ICI's members why the costly process of settlement and indigenization was necessary at all. Endorsing Chailley's utilitarian arguments against expensive settler societies, they identified the indigenous population alone as being the productive factor of colonial economies. For that reason, the ICI's attention slowly shifted from immunizing the whites to saving the indigenous from demographic decline. Around 1900, ICI members launched the earliest campaigns against indigenous "depopulation." Hans Ziemann, the German colonial physician in the ICI, was among the first to introduce a rudimentary pronatalist policy in German colonies. Apart from introducing healthier diets, he fought against abortions and prided himself on having equipped 50 percent of the Cameroon's native huts with windowpanes and awnings to protect the younger inhabitants from heat and mosquitoes.[66] The ICI particularly highlighted the work of hygienists in German East Africa who were the first to inoculate Africans against the sleeping sickness and to deliver quinine against malaria, with the colonial police enforcing the hygienist measures and escorting reluctant patients to the hospital.[67]

Comparison finally led ICI members to conclude that a successful development policy needed not only immunized indigenous workers but also

---

[62] Moresco, *De la Condition*, 6. On mestization, see Bosma and Raben, *Being Dutch*, 114–115.
[63] Moresco, *De la Condition*, 12. However, Moresco excluded the black "race" from the mixing with Europeans.
[64] Stuart Cohen, "Emanuel Moresco," 132–141.
[65] Fabié, *Mi Gestion Ministerial*, 648.
[66] Ziemann, *Über das Bevölkerungs- und Rassenproblem*, 8–10.
[67] ICI, *Compte Rendu 1913*, 154.

indigenous medical staff. ICI member and physician Albert Jullien, who was responsible for thousands of African workers perishing during the construction of the Congo-Matadí railway in the 1890s, looked for examples abroad to clear his own name and improve the Congolese medical service. He turned to the highly successful sanitation policy during the construction of the Panama and Suez Canals. Jullien ascribed the Congolese fiasco of the 1890s to a lack of resources and the poor number of sixteen official European physicians in the Congo (in 1911), with only four being specialized in combating the rapid spread of sleeping sickness and malaria. Hence, taking the successful containment of malaria during the construction of the Panama Canal as an example, Jullien increased the number of indigenous doctors, and created the nursing schools in Boma and Léopoldville. The graduates of these schools informed the workers about the use of clean water, the danger of the mosquitoes, and the nourishment of children. After Jullien had started campaigns to vaccinate African construction workers, plantation owners equally asked him to immunize their Congolese employees. Jullien explained to the ICI that Congolese doctors and their auxiliaries executed these vaccination campaigns successfully because the population was more likely to accept them as trustworthy.[68] Similar campaigns of combating indigenous depopulation became a priority of the ICI and its development schemes.[69]

Giving priority to indigenous workers at the turn of the century, most ICI colonial experts discouraged European settlers from going to the colonies. Indeed, the emigration to French possessions was in steady decline by the end of the nineteenth century even though it had been quite important before.[70] The Belgians refrained almost completely from settler colonialism, following Léopold II who had famously stated that "the Belgians do not emigrate."[71] German colonial experts actively prevented potential settlers from emigrating to their African colonies while encouraging them to go to the Americas.[72] In order to so, the German Colonial Society created a Central Information Bureau for Emigrants, which advised Germans against emigrating to German colonies "due to the bad climate."[73]

Le Bon's racial theories substantiated the utilitarian and pragmatic idea among ICI members that a colonial economy was more productive if based on an indigenous workforce rather than a costly settler society that was rarely

---

[68] Ibid., 121, 123, 132, and 134..
[69] Frequently cited in the ICI. See Strauss, *Depopulation*.
[70] Poiré, *L'Émigration*, 13.
[71] Stengers, "Leopold II," 46–71.
[72] For the low number of Germans in the colonies (no more than 25,000), see Conrad, *Globalisation and the Nation*, 81–82.
[73] BARch, R 8023, 109, fol. 4, Leitfaden für die Auskunftserteilung an Auswanderer., BArch R 8023, 109, fol. 131.

able to look after itself. The absence of settlers, however, did not make Europeans irrelevant. ICI members were selfish enough to favor their own "expert rule" over the establishment of vulnerable settler societies. Under the guidance of well-trained European experts, they assumed, the "native races" would finally develop their own potential and the resources of their land. Taken together, racist, utilitarian, and selfish reasons led to the same conclusion: colonial rule needed a firm basis in the indigenous societies. Thus, ICI members publicly heralded the "triumph of the natives" and with it the triumph of ICI experts who guided them.[74]

As ICI members capitalized on non-European contributions to the economy, they publicly showed their will to start a dialogue with the colonized "races," for example, when more than fifteen ICI members participated in the First Universal Races Congress held in London in 1911. The purpose of the Universal Races Congress was "to discuss in the light of science and the modern conscience the general relations subsisting between the peoples of the West and those of the East, between the so-called white and the so-called colored peoples, with a view to encouraging between them a fuller understanding, the most friendly feelings, and a heartier co-operation."[75] Although this congress was hardly anti-colonialist in the sense that few spokesmen of the colonized peoples were present, its members witnessed the participation of W. E. B. Du Bois and Indian delegates. Du Bois would later play a key role in the Pan-African movement and participants from India would become supporters of the Indian National Congress and therefore the Indian independence movement. Hence, ICI members chose to be in touch with nationalists from the colonized world, even if they did not share their agenda of emancipation. Instead, Dutch ICI member Jacques H. Abendanon declared in a rather vague way that "colour should form no part at all of our estimate of the worth of human beings."[76] Indeed, it was the "worth" of the colonized that made ICI members align racial theories with their utilitarian interests.

2.3 Utilitarians in the ICI and the Governmentality of Free Trade

An important group of free traders in the ICI gave a fresh impetus to utilitarian schemes of transcolonial development. Entrepreneurs and free trade activists who lost ground in protectionist Europe made themselves at ease in the transcolonial space.[77] Joseph Chailley was probably the ICI's most eminent advocate of free trade and economic liberalism. As early as 1886, he had addressed the British anti-protectionist Cobden-Club, translated Anglo-

---

[74] Treille, *De l'Acclimatation*, 4.
[75] Spiller, *Papers on Inter-Racial Problems*, v (preface).
[76] First Universal Races Congress, *Record of the Proceedings*, 52.
[77] Pitts, *Turn to Empire*; Fitzpatrick, *Liberal Imperialism*.

Saxon free trade literature into French, and called Adam Smith one of his intellectual ancestors.[78] This made him an outspoken adversary of the protectionist economic system through which the French state had monopolized colonial trade during the ancien régime, and which was on the rise again in the 1890s.[79] When Chailley edited the *New Dictionary of Political Economy* together with the first ICI president Léon Say, they described their liberalism in the following way: "We are of the liberal school ... the school of progress ... liberty, freedom of commerce, liberty of the individual, free trade, and free initiative ... are our doctrines." Their doctrines owed much to Léon Say's grandfather, the liberal economist Jean-Baptiste Say, who had promoted security of property, free trade, and a noninterventionist state in the early nineteenth century.

What made free traders of the ICI special was that they partly extended elements of their economic liberalism to the colonies. Arguing along utilitarian (and, as always, racial) lines, they hoped that free trade would motivate the colonized to be more productive and participate in the colonial economy. Therefore, they intended to apply Say's "use-value" credo to the colonies. This credo purported that the value of a product is predominantly in its immediate utility. The colonies should be turned into such "useful" elements that created value through colonial exploitation and development. Say and Chailley subsequently played an important part in coining the utilitarian concept of *mise en valeur*, which they defined as economic development rather than exploitation of the colonies.[80] To develop the colonies, they wanted to mobilize the productive power of all individuals, including foreigners and the colonized population.[81] Chailley particularly highlighted the role of indigenous workers, entrepreneurs, and merchants for the *mise en valeur* and recommended to emulate the economic success of Ghanaian cocoa planters in British Gold Coast. Anticipating development theories of the 1950s, he proposed to "turn [the indigenous population] into happy people" by including them in the capitalist world: "Every other civilization has created needs among people: creating needs leads to wage labor; wage labor creates wealth," and wealth results in "what we call civilization."[82] For Chailley and Say, internationalizing and liberalizing the colonial economy was not an ideology but a necessary precondition of development.

While the founding fathers of the ICI were mostly free traders, new members converted from economic nationalism to free trade. The conversion of German entrepreneur Julius Scharlach from a nationalist Pan-Germanism

---

[78] "The Cobden Club Dinner," *The Times* (London, 33993, July 3, 1893), 7.
[79] Chailley, *Les Compagnies*.
[80] Persell, *The French Colonial Lobby*, 97–114; Conklin, *A Mission to Civilize*, 39.
[81] Say and Chailley, *Nouveau Dictionnaire*, viii–ix.
[82] Préface Chailley in Fauchère, *La Mise en Valeur*, VII and IX.

to colonial internationalism and ICI membership illustrates the attractive power of free trade. Scharlach, whom insiders called the "most influential man in the [German] Colonial Department," initially mobilized both national and international resources to his own benefit.[83] He was the co-founder of Pan-German associations and had the support of fervent jingoists. At the same time, he headed the multinational South West Africa Company Limited. While his company received a land- and mining concession from the German government, it registered at the London stock market to raise capital. As German investors hesitated to put money into the exploitation of copper mines in German South-West Africa, the majority of shareholders turned out to be British nationals. Although such a takeover was common, Scharlach earned harsh criticism from the Pan-German lobby that wanted ethnic purity also in capitalist projects. Scharlach, however, ignored the Pan-German protests and even sold parts of his concessions to Cecil Rhodes' De Beers Consolidated Mines Ltd., who paid £5,000 to subsequently exploit the diamond deposits on the companies' territory.[84] ICI members such as Scharlach and the Belgian railway entrepreneur Albert Thys openly used the ICI's meetings to win over investors.

The ICI was not alone in attracting international capital to the colonies. Colonial governments not only accepted but also actively encouraged such a policy of internationalization and transcolonial cooperation. When British companies took over at least seven rubber plantations in German East Africa between 1900 and 1909, the German governor welcomed them for investing money and taking the risk of cultivating new unproven rubber plants.[85] The same is true for the French and the Belgian Congo, where the Dutch Nieuwe Afrikaansche Handels-Vennootschap had over fifty factories to produce and process cotton, palm oil, palm kernel, and plantation rubber. By 1918, it operated seven steamers and thirty-nine lighters on the Congo River.[86] Belgian capitalists, in turn, ran more than ten rubber estates in British Malaya and transferred cultivation methods for the high-yielding Hevea trees from Congo to Malaya.[87] Dutch planters were particularly active in German East Africa and brought capital and experience in sisal planting from the Dutch East Indies with them.[88] The ICI was an important platform for entrepreneurs to initiate their deals. Among the directors of the Belgian-

---

[83] Koponen, *Development for Exploitation*, 145.
[84] "South West Africa Company Limited," *Deutsches Koloniallexikon*, vol. 2, 277.
[85] BArch R 8024 167 "East African Rubber Plantation Company," *Frankfurter Zeitung* (December 19, 1909); "Die Umgründung Deutscher Unternehmungen in Englische Limited-Gesellschaften."
[86] Van der Laan, "Trading in the Congo," 245.
[87] *Bulletin Agricole du Congo Belge* 1, no. 1 (1910), 141.
[88] BArch R 8024/128: Deutsche Agaven GmbH.

German Gesellschaft Südkamerun, for example, were the ICI members Scharlach, Thys, Woermann, and Delcommune.[89]

ICI meetings and more specialized congresses in which ICI members participated provided not only an opportunity to strike deals but also to establish networks of mutual trust, as the director of the most important British experimental station for colonial agriculture in Trinidad explained:

> We have this advantage, that we are able to obtain personal knowledge of each other at the Congresses .... Let me assume, for example, that I want to import sugar cane into Trinidad. If I sent to my friend [and Dutch ICI member], Dr. van Hall, for these sugar canes, and he sent me a certificate that there was no disease in the district from which these canes were taken ... I should not have the slightest hesitation in admitting these to our colony .... But if the Director of Agriculture in some little-known part of the world were to do the same, and sent me a certificate similar to the one supplied by Dr. van Hall, I should want to know first of all whether he was competent to give a certificate, or whether any preventive measures taken at the place of origin were efficient.[90]

Van Hall seemed to be a trustworthy trade partner because of his ICI membership and the expertise and familiarity that came along with it.

Thinking along lines of profitability for their individual enterprises, entrepreneurs in the ICI acted independently of any political prerogatives but pressed every button if political statements served their purpose. In this regard, their part-time nationalism was little more than a means to moneymaking. Among those part-time nationalists in the ICI were the directors of the European shipping lines servicing the colonies, Adolph Woermann (Woermann-Linie, Hamburg), Jules Charles-Roux (Compagnie Générale Transatlantique, Marseille), and Félicien Cattier (Compagnie Maritime Belge, Antwerp).[91] They became fervent nationalists when they wanted subsidies from their national governments. But more frequently, they styled themselves as internationalists. Woermann, for example, traded with all colonies in West Africa and depended on a multinational clientele of passengers and the cargo of foreign companies.[92] A similar ideological flexibility characterized bankers, such as Karl von der Heydt (German Disconto-Gesellschaft) and Albert Thys (Belgian Banque d'Outre-Mer). They used international capital for their colonial projects, which equally profited from national subsidies and political "protection" from their respective governments.[93]

---

[89] *Der Tropenpflanzer* 4 (1900), 558; Eckert, *Grundbesitz*, 73.
[90] *Proceedings of the Third International Congress of Tropical Agriculture*, 110.
[91] Aillaud, *Jules Charles-Roux*.
[92] The Woermann-Linie received subsidies in the 1880s, on demand of the German Colonial Society. See Müller, *Politische Geschichte*, vol. 19, 20–28.
[93] International banking networks: AGRB, Banque d'Outre-Mer, 16: Correspondance (F. Cattier), 25–26.

Although the free traders were ideologically inconsistent in praxis, they flocked to the ICI in high numbers, because it was the last institution to support their temporary inclination to free trade. While most colonizing countries turned to protectionism in the 1890s, the ICI commemorated free trade ideals or even tried to reintroduce them into the transcolonial field. This was particularly true for a new economic strategy that the ICI invented and disseminated: the idea of transcolonial and emulative development.

2.4 The Invention of Emulative Development: The Congo Railway

The ICI shaped and disseminated an internationalist version of colonial development policies that predated the nationalist development plans of the 1930s and built upon the method of colonial comparison.[94] Habitually, historians see the British Colonial Secretary Joseph Chamberlain at the origin of the idea that colonies were underdeveloped estates that had to be made self-sufficient through controlled and pertinent investment from the motherland.[95] Yet, long before Chamberlain became colonial secretary in 1895 and popularized the term "development," ICI members had promoted the concept. Together with Chailley, the French ICI member Ernest Roume established the basis for the *mise en valeur* of French West Africa and their British colleague Alfred Lyall had been among the first to use the word "development" in English.[96] Another colonial internationalist from Britain, George Baden-Powell, claimed that he had "for years past used the analogy of the estate that needed development by means of good management, good roads, and the investment of capital. This analogy has become suddenly popularized because of its assertion by the new Secretary for the Colonies [Chamberlain], whose businesslike vigor on behalf of a proper and adequate development of Colonial resources we all greet with such confidence." Speaking at the Royal Colonial Institute in London in 1896, Baden-Powell argued along the lines of the ICI that the development of colonial Africa "cannot be handled in completeness unless we also carry in mind what our good neighbors in Africa are doing and intend to do. The question is essentially international as well as national." He advocated a "friendly co-operation of all Powers for the development of Africa" and traveled to the French colonies to study their efforts of *mise en valeur*.[97] For him, development was a joint effort and required transcolonial comparison and cooperation.

---

[94] On British development policy, see Davis and Huttenback, *Mammon*; Havinden and Meredith, *Colonialism and Development*; R. M. Kesner, *Economic Control*.
[95] Carland, *The Colonial Office*, 101. In general, see Arndt, *Economic Development*.
[96] Hodge, *Triumph of the Expert*, 34.
[97] The brother of ICI member Baden Henry Baden-Powell. See Baden-Powell, "Development of Tropical Africa," 219–220, 229, and 234.

2.4 THE INVENTION OF EMULATIVE DEVELOPMENT 83

The ICI's concept of development differed from Chamberlain's definition in the sense that it relied on international capital instead of national investments. More importantly, ICI promoted transcolonial cooperation and knowledge transfers to reduce the costs of development projects, a strategy that can be called emulative development. Instead of making the motherland invest large sums, which were useless if deployed in an inefficient way, the ICI wanted to exchange knowledge about efficient techniques between colonial experts. Thus, the main method to reduce costs was to compare developmental techniques tested in other colonies to ultimately emulate the most efficient ones. This transcolonial method resulted in comparative or emulative development. A rudimentary theory of emulative development appeared first in Paul Leroy-Beaulieu's book *On Colonization among Modern Peoples* (1874), which became a classic. Leroy-Beaulieu, who was the first-ever member of the ICI, had compared colonization efforts in a diachronic and synchronic perspective to identify "principles" that were most "useful" to the prosperity of colonies.[98] Putting his project into practice, the ICI compared different development efforts, chose the most efficient attempt, and adopted it in other colonies. Chailley, a disciple of Leroy-Beaulieu in economic matters, concluded that "progress is brought about by the cooperation of all."[99]

The most spectacular case of transcolonial and emulative development was the construction of the railway line from Matadí to Léopoldville in the Congo Free State in the 1890s. It became the ICI's showcase project because it successfully combined international investment and comparative development. The Belgian ICI member Albert Thys started building the railway line that connected the Congo's interior to the Atlantic in 1890 and finished it in record time, only eight years later. Before building the railway, Thys studied efforts to construct colonial railways in a comparative way. While his comparative studies led him to recruit thirty-two experienced African artisans who had built the railway in Dakar in French West Africa and spoke French, he equally concluded that French state-led railway construction had been inefficient and protracted.[100] He unfavorably compared the time-consuming bureaucratic process and the allocation of funds by the French parliament to the immediate availability of international capital. Unlike the French state-enterprises, Thys' Compagnie du Chemin de fer du Congo was a private joint-stock company, whose capital amounted to

---

[98] Leroy-Beaulieu, *De la Colonisation*, v.
[99] Say and Chailley, *Nouveau Dictionnaire*, ix.
[100] Cornet, *La Bataille*, 181. In later comparative surveys, Thys' project is exemplary. See ANOM 50COL78, Mission d'études des chemins de fer d'Eugène Salesses (1904/1906); AMAEB, AE 204 Correspondance France, 1/88 EIC CONGO Governor Lieutenant to Sécrétaire d'État Bruxelles, July 26, 1905: Voyage Mr. Salesses; Salesses, *Les Chemins de Fer*, 32.

twenty-five million Francs and came from Belgium, Great Britain, and Germany. Thys used the ICI's networks to win shareholders. Three members of the Congo Railway's Directory Board were equally members of the ICI, along with the chief engineer and the main doctor of the construction site.[101] To give immediate satisfaction to shareholders in Europe, Thys built the track as fast as possible. Unlike the French, he admitted that the velocity of railway building was more important than any attempt at "perfection."[102] To proceed quickly, Thys emulated employment strategies developed by the Dutch in the East Indies. He employed subcontractors who were responsible for a restricted group of workers and introduced a system of bonuses that awarded each subcontractor if the works advanced faster than scheduled.[103] In addition, to increase the efficiency and velocity of the construction site, Thys internationalized his workforce.

The Congo railway showed that transcolonial development projects rarely improved on outright exploitation. Around 10,000 "colonial subjects" from around the globe worked on the Congo railway, and the ICI played an important part in facilitating their recruitment. The internationalization of the work force was necessary because the pace of construction proved deadly for employees. Between November 1891 and June 1892 alone, 900 African workers died due to work accidents, diseases, and exhaustion. Construction was particularly difficult, given the rugged mountains, the lack of labor force, and the epidemic-ridden environment, which did not allow for pack animals to transport the material. Hence, death rates amounted to 17 percent or even more, both among Africans and Europeans.[104] Given the high mortality, the local Congolese refused to sign up for jobs, and Thys had to recruit workers from other colonies. Apart from an international group of engineers and workers, comprising Italian, Danish, German, Swiss, Dutch, Greek, and Luxembourger citizens, recruitment agents enrolled African blue-collar workers from as far as Zanzibar, British Nigeria, French Senegal, German Togo, and Portuguese Angola.[105] As the multitude of languages spoken at the construction site reminded observers of the "legendary construction site of the Babel tower," it became the symbol of transcolonial development.[106] Thys also employed 3,000 Asian and Antillean workers, until many of them died in the

---

[101] Compagnie du Congo, *The Congo-Railway*, 4; "Georges de Laveleye," *Biographie Coloniale Belge*, vol. 4, 497.
[102] Cornet, *La Bataille*, 26.
[103] Thys, "Les Chemins de Fer," 19.
[104] Thomas, *Violence and Colonial Order*, 310; Cornet, *La Bataille*, 209; ICI, *Compte Rendu 1897*, 95.
[105] AGRB Louwers 2 (29) Lettres et Notes and manuscript; Départ pour le Tanganika, February 24, 1902; Cornet, *La Bataille*, 219.
[106] "Chemin de fer du Congo. Personnel Ouvrier," *Le Congo Illustré* 1 (1892), 52.

insalubrious climate or became victims of the "deficient organization of work," as officials euphemistically admitted.[107]

The transcolonial scheme almost failed because of the "protectionist" policies of colonial states. After the French and British administrations, in particular, learned about the mortal conditions in the Congo, they banned Thys' recruitment agents (around 400 of them) from their territories and introduced travel bans for their subjects. In 1894, for example, France denied West Africans departure from the French colonial territory unless they received official permission.[108] Recruitment agents had to buy a recruitment franchise from the French administration, which also restricted the number of workers that were allowed to leave the colony. For every African who left the colony, 500 francs had to be paid to the government. The administration only reimbursed this sum if the person returned to the colony within one year.[109] As early as 1891, British Sierra Leone had asked Thys for a deposit of £30,000 as a warrant so that 600 subjects who left for the Congo would be treated according to the contract and returned in sound condition.[110]

The ICI intervened against these isolationist tendencies that threatened the project of transcolonial development. In its sessions in 1895, 1897, 1899, and in 1912, it responded to the overall need of workers by drafting agreements on mutual labor recruitments in the colonies, a task that kept lawyers in the ICI busy well into the interwar period.[111] The most important feature of a future convention of cross-colonial recruitment was that the workers signed the contract voluntarily and in full awareness of its content. Thus, ICI members joined forces with the Institute of International Law to draft exemplary recruitment contracts that would protect the workers against exploitation in foreign colonies. The model contracts stipulated that the employment could not exceed a period of five years, reduced the working time to ten hours a day, and fixed the salary from the beginning. The model contracts also sought to ensure medical assistance and prescribed that the transport between colony of origin and employment country had to be free. Families should not be separated.[112]

Although it is unclear whether colonial administrations used the ICI's templates, they seemed to be confident that the situation would improve. In the mid-1890s, British Colonial Secretary Chamberlain had a note sent to Thys

---

[107] ICI, *Compte Rendu 1897*, 95.
[108] All of them needed a passport to leave. See AMAEB AE 204 Correspondance France 6/53 Emigrations des Naturels du Loango, August 28, 1885.
[109] Solus, "Le Régime er l'Organisation du Travail"; A preliminary regulation from 1888: AMAEB AE 204 Correspondance France 6/51: EIC Affaires Étrangères to Noitoua, Résident, February 3, 1886.
[110] Cornet, *La Bataille*, 220.
[111] On the interwar period, see Fall, *Le Travail au Sénégal*.
[112] ICI, *Compte Rendu 1899*, 58–62.

that explicitly allowed for the recruitment of workers in Sierra Leone, Nigeria, and Gold Coast.[113] Adjacent colonies, such as German Cameroon, French Congo, Portuguese Angola, and the Congo Free State equally agreed that workers could freely circulate between their territories. An official ordinance from 1895, for example, allowed the free circulation of Africans from the French Congo to the Congo Free State.[114]

Thys' railway project was officially transcolonial and emulative, but the reasons for its efficiency were less pleasant. The rapid construction of the railway was mainly due to the waste of African lives and not to the emulation of railway building techniques. Also, the narrative of internationalization was only partly true. First, the capital supporting the railway company was far from being international; it was predominantly Belgian. Namely, the Belgian government held 40 percent of the shares and Belgian private investors another 31 percent. British and German capitalists held only 20 percent and 8 percent respectively.[115] Second, the company's success was hardly due to the transcolonial cooperation but grounded in Léopold's newly introduced protectionist policy. In 1890, when Thys' railway company started operating, the head of the Congo Free State ended the open-door policy and monopolized the lucrative rubber extraction in the whole colony. Investors were aware of this neo-mercantilist policy that nevertheless enabled Thys' railway company to become rich by transporting rubber to the coast. In this way, the company benefited from Léopold's greed for rubber, as investors were abundant and shares, initially offered for 500 francs, soared to a height of 16,000 francs overnight. The chief engineer of the railroad went into raptures over the development: "People were going literally crazy. It was enough to put the word caoutchouc on a brochure and the capital arrived in great quantities."[116]

Despite the high mortality on the Congo railway, Thys also succeeded in using the ICI to establish his development efforts as a transcolonial model of paternalistic governmentality. Speaking to the ICI members, he claimed to have constantly improved the working conditions on the construction site. After initial problems, workers were allegedly adequately lodged, provided with food (officially a daily ration of 500 g rice, 250 g biscuits or beans, and 250 g dried meat or fish), and had access to medical care. All of them, he argued, personally received a regular salary and cash in hand from the company's accountants. As soon as Thys improved the hygienic standards and regularized the work schedule, he reported, Congolese job seekers even approached him to ask for employment. Thys felt vindicated that his "humane" way of organizing the building site – which was rather paternalistic,

---

[113] Cornet, *La Bataille*, 320.
[114] AMAEB, AE 204 Correspondance France, 2/114.
[115] Thys, *Au Congo et au Kassaï*; Cornet, *La Bataille*, 163.
[116] ICI, *Compte Rendu 1904*, 243.

2.4 THE INVENTION OF EMULATIVE DEVELOPMENT 87

with guaranteed salaries, accommodation, food, and a rudimentary show business to entertain the workers – appealed to the Congolese.[117] In his view, this paternalistic development policy was the first step to introduce capitalism to Africa.

What is more, Thys declared Africans fully compatible with the capitalist system. As early as 1889, he predicted that the natural inclination of the Congolese to commerce would open the way to African development. He particularly emphasized that "the African is born a merchant" and that the commercial spirit had saved Africans from sharing the fate of the Indians in America, that is to say, extermination.[118] Being a stout utilitarian, Thys believed that people were worthy to live because they were economically useful. At the same time, he explained to the ICI members that a capitalist open-door policy would have saved the Congolese from Léopold's cruel suppression, which was only possible because the king monopolized trade and controlled the access to the territory. The liberalization of commerce, instead, would allow the Congolese to capitalize on their own work.[119]

Thys' learning process that resulted in an ideology of paternalistic guidance toward capitalism struck a chord among other ICI members who styled themselves as liberal reformers and facilitators of emulative development. French administrators excelled in emulative development, mainly at the initiative of French ICI member Ernest Roume who was at the origin of the French *mise en valeur*, a comprehensive program combining economic development, infrastructure measures, medical care, professional education, and a rising standard of living for colonial subjects.[120] After being an active member in the ICI, Roume became governor-general of French West Africa in 1902. Upon his inauguration, he immediately dispatched French informants to Holland and Belgium to analyze their use of the indigenous labor force for developing their colonies. Apart from observing Dutch and Belgian colonies, he sent commissions to British territories to study the efficient organization of commercial ports and he reorganized the port of Dakar accordingly.[121] The *mise en valeur* thus started long before it became an official ideology in the interwar period, and it inspired both the German colonial minister Dernburg and the British reformer Frederick Lugard.[122]

---

[117] Thys, "Les Chemins de Fer," 19.
[118] Compagnie du Congo, *Le Chemin de fer du Congo*, 119.
[119] ICI, *Compte Rendu 1908*, 207–209.
[120] Conklin, *A Mission to Civilize*, 39; Aldrich, "Imperial Mise En Valeur," 917–936; Constantine, *The Making*, 14.
[121] Lugard, *Dual Mandate*, 499.
[122] Sarraut, *La Mise en Valeur*; Lugard, *Dual Mandate*, 499.

Apart from the ICI, transimperial initiatives from the Global South pushed Roume to frame his *mise en valeur*. When he became governor in 1902, more than 400 "Syro-Lebanese" immigrants lived in French West Africa. They had left the Ottoman Empire in search of new opportunities but still held strong ties with Lebanon and its global diaspora, especially the one in Marseille. They started as precarious traveling merchants but soon penetrated the West African interior and started buying rubber from Africans, which they sold at a profit to German companies. Unlike the French trading firms, the Lebanese paid Africans in cash. In so doing, they forced French firms to do the same.[123] While French merchants lobbied the administration to expel Lebanese merchants, Roume was more reluctant to do so, declaring that they had the right to participate in free trade due to "their status as Europeans" guaranteed "by international conventions" between France and the Ottoman Empire.[124] Roume intended to control and tax the Lebanese, without suppressing their commercial and financial activities. Thus, during Roume's tenure, their official number rose to over 1,300, with many more unregistered. Governors who followed him would apply much more restrictive measures. By then, however, the Lebanese played an important role in commerce, construction, railway building, and banking. This enabled them to provide the African population with loans, which was in line with the ICI's plans to promote economic incentives among the African population. ICI members continued to speak generously of the transimperial Lebanese diaspora throughout its existence.[125]

In 1907, the French ICI member and deputy in the French parliament Lucien Hubert popularized Roume's policy in Germany. He gave several lectures, wrote a dozen newspaper articles, and met with German ICI members Lindequist and Dernburg, who headed the new German Colonial Office. Dernburg, a liberal banker who became colonial minister in 1908 to reorganize the German colonial economy in a rational way, had traveled to the US and Dutch colonies. He set out to reform German colonialism along utilitarian lines and made a plea for development policy with the help of private capital.[126] Most importantly, he emulated the French *mise en valeur* by translating it into German (*Inwertsetzung*), claiming that it would also lead to the "improvement of the living situation of blacks and whites."[127] Although his approach was less transcolonial, he advocated a development policy that was grounded in emulation and went beyond mere exploitation.

---

[123] Desbordes, *L'immigration*, 21, 46–68.
[124] Ibid., 56.
[125] INCIDI, *Compte Rendu 1957*, 162.
[126] Froment, *Le Devoir*, 12.
[127] Dernburg, *Zielpunkte*, 5; Schubert, *Der Schwarze Fremde*, 299; *La Verité sur le Congo* (March 15, 1906), 112.

2.5 A Humanitarianism of Free Trade: Redefining Exploitation as Development

Unlike Chamberlain, whose notion of development followed a purely capitalist logic of investment and return, ICI members gradually embraced a social logic of forging structures that would be conducive to long-term growth and included "welfare" elements. One of them was the governor of French West Africa, Ernest Roume, who understood colonial development also as a liberal and humanitarian act that should protect the indigenous population from exploitation. Trained in the ICI, his comparative studies led him to abolish the remainders of nominal slavery in African cotton and grain production in the Sahel zone of French West Africa. In 1905, he issued a decree that aimed at "putting an end to practices leading to the alienation of a person's liberty." The decree allowed thousands of slave-like workers to leave their masters or to renegotiate the conditions of their employment with them. Roume also introduced a multilevel court system that gave slaves or servants the possibility to claim their rights to property, grain, and livestock.[128] His anti-slavery campaign earned Roume much fame.

More generally, the ICI's agenda resembled the humanitarian efforts of abolitionists to extinct slavery. Several ICI members had indeed played an important role at the Anti-Slavery Congress in Brussels and even signed the Anti-Slavery Act of 1890 for their countries. The Act coordinated the efforts to abolish the trade with slaves, arms, and alcohol in the colonies. While the Act only suppressed slave raiding and -trading, but not slavery as such, ICI members such as Roume actually banned slavery.[129] Going beyond the Brussels Act, they claimed that this fight against slavery was a "general humanitarian duty that required the cooperation of all powers, also of those who did not have colonies in Africa."[130] While the ICI thought of Africans as born merchants who actively contributed to commerce, it equally used the abolitionist argument to legitimize colonization in the first place.

It seemed that the ICI member's definition of human rights for the colonized equaled the right of the colonized to participate in a liberal economy and to possess private property. They declared participation in the market a human right.[131] In 1907, the French ICI member Lucien Hubert used German newspapers to call for a "European duty in Africa." Hubert proposed an international declaration "to respect native law as well as native property

---

[128] Roberts, "The End of Slavery," 684–713.
[129] Miers and Roberts, *The End of Slavery*, 17 and 282–309; Ribi Forclaz, *Humanitarian Imperialism*, 31–34.
[130] BArch, R 1001, 6131 Internationales Ethnographisches Büro, Nr. 59: Memorandum "Internationale Zusammenarbeit zur Einschränkung des Waffenverkehrs und Rolle von 1890."
[131] ICI, *Compte Rendu 1899*, 545.

rights, and family constitution. Life opportunities of the colonized have to be protected and they should be granted free work and salaries. Like the French Revolution has proclaimed human rights for the grown-up and civilized peoples, the civilized world of today must claim the human rights" for all the colonized peoples. His plea for economic liberalization received public support from Belgian, British, Dutch, German, and Portuguese colonial officials.[132] Going beyond simple abolitionist arguments, an eminent ICI member equally proclaimed at the International Congress of Colonial Sociology in 1900 that the age of extermination and expropriation of the indigenous peoples was over. Instead, the "humanitarian ideas" of the late nineteenth century "have put an end to slave trade and extermination ... from now on, the colonizing peoples are forced to respect native property rights on the soil of their territory."[133] The resolutions of the congress contained "humanitarian" principles that the League of Nations is generally said to have introduced in the interwar period. Since "only free and salaried labor has serious results," its members demanded to abolish any kind of coerced labor (including for public works).[134] Finally, the congress issued a resolution in the name of "good government" that "the congress recommends the free exercise of the right to petition."[135] This right to send petitions and complaints to the colonial authorities would be reinvented twenty years later, when the League of Nations introduced colonial mandates and the right to send petitions to the League.

The Dutch case shows that ICI members were more likely to push for the "humanitarian" liberalization of colonial economies than other colonial experts. Around 1830, the Dutch had introduced a system of forced cultivation in the Indies to produce cheap cash crops. Between the 1830s and the 1860s, Indonesian peasants had to grow cash crops and Dutch trading companies earned a fortune by selling the cheaply produced crops on the European market. In 1860, the forced cultivation scheme in the Dutch Indies provoked the first humanitarian campaign against forced labor. The campaign's leader was a Dutch administrator and bestselling author called Multatuli, who pleaded for fair trade with the colony and later became a model for humanitarians and fair trade activists. But it was a future ICI member who took political and legal action. In the 1860s, the Dutch Minister of Colonial Affairs

---

[132] BArch R 1001, 6131 Internationales Ethnographisches Büro, Nr. 58: "Internationale Konferenz für Eingeborenenschutz: Ein Vorschlag von Lucien Hubert," *Die Woche* 9, no. 9 (March 2, 1907); See also Nr. 48–55: "Lucien Hubert, Le Rapprochement Franco-Allemand," *La Grande Revue* 11, no. 10 (July 10, 1907), 427–441.

[133] BArch, N2345/54 Aufsätze, 5: "Respect de la Propriété Indigène," *Congrès International de Sociologie Coloniale* (Paris, 1900).

[134] *Congrès International de Sociologie Coloniale* [*Procès-Verbaux Sommaires*], 36.

[135] Ibid., 32.

Fransen van de Putte, who would be a founding member of the ICI, indeed launched an initiative to abolish the forced cultivation system and to liberalize the economy of the Dutch Indies.[136] Other Dutch ICI members were largely responsible for introducing this shift, which partly enabled peasants in the colonies to produce for a capitalist system and to their own benefit. While in reality coerced labor did not completely disappear, the Dutch ICI members had earned themselves a reputation of being liberal and humanitarian reformers.[137]

By 1900, many ICI members indeed believed in the governmental force of the free market to make the colonized peoples participate in the project of colonial development. Thys had been first to verbalize this idea after he had realized that "fair wages" induced Congolese men to ask for work at the railway construction site. Chailley endorsed this governmental idea. State-led schooling and legal measures, Chailley explained, could not adequately teach the benefits of capitalism to the indigenous population: they had to experience the benefits of capitalism themselves. In this way, they had to be educated to work for progress, "not by apologies and theories," but "by acts."[138]

2.6 Toward Paternalistic Development Schemes of Christian Reformers

Around 1900, a more interventionist group of paternalistic development theorists gained ground within the ICI: Christian philanthropists. They were a potpourri consisting of British abolitionists, Dutch moralists, and socially minded Catholics from Belgium and France. Christians were naturally in line with Albert Thys' paternalistic approach, in which he used governmental techniques to turn his workers into capitalists, including moral education, saving banks, and rudimentary welfare schemes. Hence, the Christians' paternalistic agenda did not necessarily contradict that of the free traders. Both Christian abolitionists and free traders claimed to liberate slaves and to turn them into potential workers for the colonial economy.[139] In the Dutch case, the combination of economic liberalism and Protestant paternalism was well established.

Dutch colonial experts engaged in Christian and paternalistic development schemes because and not despite of their economic liberalism. The Protestant nation had a long tradition of liberal trade. Yet, in the nineteenth century, some Dutch ICI members seemed to be ashamed of not extending this

---

[136] "Max Havelaarfonds," *Het Nieuws van den Dag voor Nederlandsch-Indië* (January 9, 1911). See also Deventer, "Havelaar-Voorspel," 199–215.
[137] Locher-Scholten in Fitzpatrick, *Liberal Imperialism*, 27–28.
[138] Say and Chailley, *Nouveau Dictionnaire*, xviii.
[139] Ribi Forclaz, *Humanitarian Imperialism*; Barnett, *Empire of Humanity*.

tradition to Dutch colonies. As we have seen, they had used their ill-famed system of forced cultivation to exploit Java between 1830 and the 1860s. Referring to the Dutch colonial guilt of forcing the Javanese to grow cash crops for Europeans, the Dutch ICI member Conrad Theodor van Deventer proposed in 1899 in a groundbreaking article that the inhabitants of the Dutch Indies, who had particularly suffered from the forced cultivation system, should receive an indemnity from the Dutch government.[140] Two years later, the Dutch government took action.

In 1901, the Dutch government inaugurated the first state-led development scheme for a colony, in the framework of a more extensive and religiously inspired so-called ethical policy. After Christian parties had won the Dutch elections in 1901, they put Deventer's idea of indemnities into practice and introduced the so-called ethical policy in the Dutch Indies. According to official sources, the Dutch government invested more than 200 million guilders and designed a ten-year development plan that anticipated the characteristic elements of modern development policies: increasing the area of irrigated rice fields, constructing roads, granting Indonesian peasants access to credit banks, inducing migration to less populated areas, and teaching the Indonesians how to scientifically grow staple foods. The Dutch also started campaigns to bring about prosperity, a higher standard of living, and welfare (*welvaart*) for the indigenous population.[141] The ethical period, starting in 1901, seemed to be the first state-led development scheme ever.

The Dutch ethical policy was more transcolonial than generally assumed. For example, hundreds of agronomists from around the world worked at the agricultural research institute at Buitenzorg on Dutch Java. Together, they increased the yield of cash crops and developed governmental schemes that encouraged Javanese farmers to grow scientifically improved plants. Several ICI members were among the researchers at Buitenzorg, whose director, Melchior Treub, became an honorary member of the ICI (see Chapter 4). What is more, the research stations were partly funded by European and American planters who were about to acquire huge plantation estates on the Indonesian island of Sumatra. International capital invested in this European-owned plantation belt in Sumatra played an important part in bringing money to the colony.[142] Those plantations ran on the exploitation of imported workers from China, among others.

---

[140] Deventer and Fransen van de Putte, "Ter Gedachtenis," 128–137.
[141] For example, 187 million guilders went into irrigation projects. Although the development plan failed, there seemed to have been lasting effects. See Cribb, "Development Policy," 232; Locher-Scholten, *Ethiek in Fragmenten*, 11–54 and 176–208. See Boomgaard, "The Welfare Services in Indonesia," 65–67, on agricultural schools, and 75–77 on credit banks.
[142] Stoler, *Capitalism and Confrontation*.

2.6 TOWARD PATERNALISTIC DEVELOPMENT SCHEMES

All in all, it seems that the Dutch metropole spent less money on the development of the Indies than it wanted to acknowledge and the scheme often worked to the benefit of Europeans only. Ninety percent of the invested money went into irrigation schemes, which predominantly supplied European plantations. What is more, the Dutch had raised the money for this scheme by increasing the tax on land (*land rent*), which was an additional burden for the Indonesians.[143]

Raden Adjeng Kartini, the Javanese "Princess" widely read by ICI members, confirmed in one of her letters that Dutch investments had little effect:

> The Government has spent tons of gold to give water to the land in the dry season, and also in building heavy barriers against floods in the wet season, but so far without result. Splendid canals have been dug, which have provided work for thousands, it is true, but they appear to be of little practical value. During the East Winds the land perishes with thirst, and during the West Winds everything floats upon the water.[144]

She added that the Javanese were unlikely to participate in development projects because they were "burdened by heavy taxes, under the load of which they can move but slowly."[145] Since ICI members edited her letters, she might have inspired them to reject large-scale and cost-intensive development projects, an idea the ICI adhered to until the 1960s.

Tellingly, while ICI members paid their respects to the Dutch ethical policy, they cited it less frequently as a model than the cultivation system, which had enforced crop improvement but co-opted peasants and villages. Combining ethical arguments with the model of small-scale development, paternalistic Christians in the ICI emphasized the need to protect their subjects from the excesses of colonial conquest and the dangers that came with capitalism. While fostering gradual economic development, they claimed to prevent the indigenous population from overhastily jumping into modernity. Catholics, in particular, assumed a protective stance, both against exploitative capitalists and impatient administrators who used force and violence to impose their schemes of "development." ICI member Franz von Arenberg, a leader of the Catholic Center Party in Germany, for example, frequently unveiled colonial scandals in German Togo. He received firsthand information about mistreatment from missionaries in Togo and sent an entire list of undesirable colonial administrators to the colonial authorities in Berlin.[146]

---

[143] Post, *Rapport sur l'Irrigation*, 330.
[144] Kartini, *Letters*, 33.
[145] Ibid.
[146] Archives Arenberg, Franz von Arenberg, "Aus den Geheimnissen der Zentrumskamarilla," *Die Post* 575 (December 8, 1906).

To be sure, the Christians in the ICI were no missionaries in the traditional sense but instead adopted the position of social reformers. Within Europe, they had long advocated a rudimentary welfare policy to counter the progress of Socialist movements in the industrialized centers. In the early twentieth century, they wanted to take this paternalistic welfare policy to the colonies, particularly to the Belgian Congo. There, the discovery and exploitation of copper deposits and other resources led to a quick industrialization, symbolized by the foundation of the mining town Elisabethville in 1910. Octave Louwers, a Belgian lawyer who would succeed Janssen as secretary-general of the ICI in the 1920s, stood for an important group of social-minded Christians who gained a foothold in colonial policies between 1900 and 1930.[147]

Louwers arrived in the Congo in 1901, only a few weeks after he had graduated in European law. He became a judge in the Mayumbe region and a prosecutor in the Congo's first capital Boma – yet without any additional training and without understanding the language of the Congolese litigants. He was surprised about the sudden power he had over the Congolese who "very seriously and without laughing ... call me 'Monsieur le Juge' all the time."[148] Unfamiliar with local customs and colonial legislation alike, Louwers referred to the law of God and grandiloquently claimed that he "used the Judgement of Solomon" as a model for his own verdicts. Instead of arguing along the lines of either customary or colonial law, Louwers used every verdict to "deliver a homily to the litigants," which would improve their general morale in everyday life.[149]

Adding to Louwers' Solomonic paternalism was the desire to protect Congolese workers against European companies. The case of a Congolese railway worker, whom the sources call Sanassi, illustrates his social paternalism. An employee at the Mayumbe railway construction site, Sanassi used Louwers to claim his rights after he had lost his left hand due to an explosion at the site. The railway building company asserted that Sanassi had carelessly handled the explosives and that the worker alone was to blame for the accident. Fighting for an invalidity indemnity, Sanassi managed to bring the case before Louwers. The latter invoked articles 258–260 and 647 of the Civil Code of the Congo Free State, which were exact copies of article 1382–1384 of the Belgian Civil Code. It was an innovation that Louwers declared this law universally applicable, which included the Congolese employees. The Belgian judge argued that "the employers and captains of industries and companies are responsible for the harms and damages done to their employees who work for

---

[147] See Daughton, *An Empire Divided*.
[148] AGRB, Louwers Papers 2: Départ au Congo, February 2, 1901.
[149] It is not clear but possible that Cane was Catholic. See AGRB Louwers Papers: Souvenirs de son Passage à Boma: Cane to Louwers, January 13, 1902.

them, given that the employer always has a miniscule part in the accident." Giving proof of his paternalism, he reasoned that employers had to protect the workers against their own carelessness by frequent controls and surveillance, especially if the employees were unexperienced. This interpretation led the court to conclude that Sanassi was to blame only partially and he received an indemnity that was modest but more than one might expect in a colonial context.[150]

In his memoirs, Louwers prided himself on being a just judge and famous among the Congolese, who traveled long distances to see him:

> If you were in Boma, you would see, every day, the arrival of long [processions] of natives coming from the interior and walking towards the house of the "palaver judge" – this is my house. Sometimes whole villages come to me, queuing in long lines .... The reason for this is that all of them are in some sort of palaver and want to make the best of it. A conflict arose between them and the sorcerer or head of their village has passed a judgement on them that failed to satisfy them. This is why they come to the white authorities.[151]

Louwers heard and judged five to six of these appeal cases every day. They contributed to forming his paternalistic self-image but also caused far-reaching structural changes.

Louwers was not alone in attempting to reconcile economic development with the education of African workers. A year before Louwers left for the Congo, several ICI members were among the 400 participants of the International Congress of Colonial Sociology. In 1900, the congress recommended a governmental strategy to make the colonized participate in the capitalist economy. They wanted to "develop among the colonized a sense of providence and for saving up money."[152] The initiative to introduce saving banks came from Belgian Catholic reformers such as Louwers who urged the colonized population to plan ahead, a skill the ICI members believed most indigenous peoples lacked.[153] Catholic Belgian reformers indeed designed a so-called social assistance for the Congolese and introduced saving banks in the colony before World War I.[154]

After Louwers returned to Europe, he styled himself the most prolific expert in Congolese colonial law and became a frequent contributor to the ICI's

---

[150] However, they reduced the indemnity considerably: AGRB Louwers Papers 4 Souvenirs de son Passage: Louwers, January 16, 1902.
[151] AGRB, Louwers Papers 2: Départ au Congo, February 2, 1901.
[152] Ibid., 22.
[153] Ibid., 27.
[154] AGRB, Louwers Papers 247 (274) Assistance Sociale au Congo 1940: Rapport sur l'Assistance Sociale à Coquilhatville 1939, 4–5. On Congolese reactions, see Hunt, *A Nervous State*, 101–130.

comparative collections of colonial legislation. He published the first edition of the Codes and Laws of Belgian Congo in 1914 and ensured the seven subsequent editions.[155] While in his early days as a judge and prosecutor, he referred to Catholicism and welfare paternalism, his later approach was in line with the ICI's overall initiative to codify customary and colonial law on a transcolonial level.

2.7 Legal Governmentality and the Invention of Transcolonial Law

In the early twentieth century, ICI members turned colonial legislation into a tool for economic development, which comprised elements of exploitation of resources, protection of workers, and the preservation of indigenous cultures. Dissociating themselves from King Léopold's fatal exploitation of the Congolese people, ICI members promoted a moderate development that combined cultural relativism with the gradual introduction of capitalism. To preserve local customs while enabling the penetration of capitalism, they intended to reconcile "preservationist" customary law with "capitalist" European law. Chailley famously argued that indigenous societies had to "develop within their own milieu" to preserve their own culture on the way to economic progress. This process required the preservation of customary law, which they defined as the unwritten habits and traditions that were legally binding for members of a specific kinship group. What is more, Chailley and the most eminent colonial lawyers in the ICI, the French Arthur Girault and the Belgian Félicien Cattier, agreed that many of the colonized societies had a time-honored "civilization" of their own, such as India, Indonesia, and Islamic regions in Africa.[156] These civilizations looked back on a long legal tradition and Girault and Cattier advised the colonial administrations to refrain from outright legal Europeanization if they wanted to bring about prosperity and development for all.[157]

Customary law certainly got into conflict with the desire to introduce capitalism through European law, but this legal rivalry did not jeopardize the ICI's ultimate goal of making the colonial society more productive by combining both. In the 1890s, the ICI made property legislation in both customary and European law an essential element of its "development efforts." These efforts often resembled outright expropriation. Rather naturally, ICI

---

[155] Louwers, *Codes et Lois*.
[156] ANOM 100APOM 93, Union Coloniale, Chailley-Bert, Voyage aux Indes: "Chailley-Bert Over Java," *Nieuwe Rotterdaamsche Courant* (August 27, 1897).
[157] Only labor contracts should be modeled on European examples to guarantee the development of capitalism. See Girault, "Condition des Indigènes," 49–59 and 62–63. See also Cattier, *Droit et Administration*; Girault, *Principes de Colonisation*; El Mechat, "Sur les Principes," 119–144.

members endorsed the view that the colonial state had the right to take possession of resources that were of public interest, such as forests and mines.[158] ICI members had extensive experience in legitimizing the exploitation of these resources by evoking customary law. As early as 1878, ICI member Baden Henry Baden-Powell had pushed through a law in British India based on the assumption that "all forest rights had traditionally been the formal prerogative of the territorial sovereign." By making this reference to customary law, he gave moral support to the administration's decision "that local communities therefore had no rights [to collect wood in the forest, etc.] that were not officially and explicitly granted." India's 1878 forest law became a model for the rest of the British Empire and similar regulations were in place in Dutch Java.[159] It is well known that Léopold advanced similar arguments to exploit the rubber forests in the Congo Free State.

Around 1900, however, liberal members in the ICI such as the Dutch Fransen van der Putte pleaded for the introduction of individual property for the indigenous population, arguing that only private ownership would motivate indigenous landowners to develop their lands and participate in the capitalist market.[160] At the 1903 meeting of the ICI, he made it clear that "we need a class of big indigenous landowners."[161] More precisely, free traders in the ICI recommended the European-style registration of property according to the Torrens Act that enabled owners to register their land in a central register. Once they did so, the land eternally belonged to them individually. In theory, both the colonized and colonizers could register their land. In practice, the complicated registration process and the neglect of collective rights to indigenous lands gave Europeans an advantage in the Torrens system.[162]

More paternalistic voices in the ICI warned that the liberal Torrens Act might ruin indigenous landowners, especially in colonies where European settlers had interest in land.[163] The Torrens Act had indeed had devastating effects for the indigenous population in Australia. Girault reported that French Algeria had equally introduced the Torrens Act in 1873. As a result, indigenous landowners sold their lands to European speculators and poor settlers, often under dubious conditions. The European buyers lacked the will or the capital to cultivate and develop it.[164] Thus, Algeria abolished the system in 1897. Up to 1900, a similar system of individual property was in place in the

---

[158] ICI, *Compte Rendu 1904*, 169–170; ICI, *Le régime minier*; ICI, *Le régime forestier*.
[159] Ross, *Ecology and Power*, 284–286. It did not remain uncontested, though. See ICI, *Compte Rendu 1900*, 95.
[160] ICI, *Compte Rendu 1903*, 64, 90.
[161] ICI, *Compte Rendu 1903*, 151.
[162] ICI, *Compte Rendu 1899*, 521.
[163] ICI, *Compte Rendu 1903*, 84.
[164] Ibid., 121.

Punjab in India. Although there were few European settlers there, high land taxes had pushed Indian landowners into the debt trap.[165] According to Girault, taxation and debts finished Indians off and they lost their private property in the end to usurious moneylenders.[166] Given these reports, the ICI's paternalists assumed that the colonized populations were unable to survive in a neoliberal system governed by the Torrens Act.

The debates over the legal conditions of development led ICI members to compare laws in different colonies and to find the "best way to legislate in the colonies." Lawyers in the ICI published three volumes on comparative legislation in 1906 and issued the periodical *Recueil International de Législation Coloniale* from 1910 to the interwar period.[167] More importantly, ICI members were responsible for introducing courts in several Asian and African colonies, notably Camille Janssen in the Congo Free State from 1885 onwards, Ernest Roume in French West Africa from 1903 onwards, and Cornelis van Vollenhoven in the Dutch Indies from 1901 onwards. Influenced by the ICI's cultural relativism, they wanted the colonial court system to be dualistic, reserving European courts and laws for Europeans and indigenous courts and laws for the colonized.[168] While they established indigenous courts in most districts of the three colonies, it remained unclear what legal code the judges should apply in areas with unwritten customary law. Given their unfamiliarity with local customs, ICI members pushed for their codification, both to apprehend and to control them. In 1900, some of them issued a statement at the International Congress for Colonial Sociology that urged colonial administrations to collect indigenous customs and codify them. They added that "these codes have to compile indigenous customs without altering them."[169] The contrary was true.

Not falling short of their own expectations, ICI members had participated in launching the first transcolonial survey on customary laws by establishing the Internationale Vereinigung für Vergleichende Rechtswissenschaft und Volkswirtschaftslehre (IVVR) in 1895.[170] An international association based in Germany and devoted to the comparison of law, the IVVR initiated the comparative compilation of customary law of African and Oceanian

---

[165] ICI, *Compte Rendu 1900*, 102; ICI, *Compte Rendu*, 129.
[166] Girault, "Condition des Indigènes," 53–54.
[167] It had severe financial difficulties. See BArch R 1001/5530 Renkin to Janssen, December 6, 1912; Vohsen to RKA, November 26, 1912; ICI, *La meilleure manière de légiférer pour les colonies* (Bruxelles, 1905).
[168] Conklin, *A Mission to Civilize*, 39; Plasman, "Un État de Non-droit?," 27–49.
[169] *Congrès International de Sociologie Coloniale. Procès-Verbaux Sommaires*, 31–34.
[170] Codification projects before 1895 were fragmentary and had little impact. See Renucci, "Les Magistrats Dans les Colonies," 687–697.

2.7 LEGAL GOVERNMENTALITY & TRANSCOLONIAL LAW

peoples.[171] An international group of donors, including the German Colonial Department, the German Colonial Society, and Chailley's French Colonial Union, funded the project, while a Dutch sociologist published the results.[172] Via the ICI's networks, the IVVR sent questionnaires to district officers, missionaries, anthropologists, and overseas merchants and also consulted indigenous informants.[173] When the first questionnaire of the IVVR arrived in French Sudan, its governor was enthusiastic about the project. He addressed a circular to all regions, districts, and the remotest military post. In the circular, he explained that the French colonial administration attached "great importance to this project – *not only* from a scientific point of view and because it is our duty to contribute to the project of the Internationaler Verein by sending them comprehensive and thoroughly researched documents – *but also* because this study is of highest value for those who come to serve in Sudan after us or who are interested in this colony."[174] The IVVR's model prompted several other surveys and a hunt for customary laws in Africa and beyond.[175]

One of the most pertinent questions for the ICI was how administrators could use customary property law, succession law, and trade law to facilitate development projects. To answer this question, the IVVR used a uniform questionnaire drafted by the German lawyer Albert Hermann Post, who coined the term "ethnological jurisprudence" and shaped the idea of legal anthropology that influenced British legal anthropology as much as it fascinated officials in the Dutch, Belgian, Italian, and French Empires.[176] The questionnaire asked for details in the field of family and gender relations, birth, childhood, marriage, old age, illness, succession, political organization, slavery, legal procedure, punishment, vengeance, land tenure, property, and trade relations. Post believed that customs were similar in most parts of the world and the IVVR collected them on a transcolonial level. ICI members were not only the first to collect customary law on a trans*colonial* level, they also

---

[171] The main instigator was ICI member Felix Meyer. See Van der Lith, "Rechtsverhältnisse," 1–21.
[172] Steinmetz, *Rechtsverhältnisse von Eingeborenen Völkern*, iii. See also Schröder, *Prügelstrafe*, 23.
[173] ICI, *Compte Rendu 1895*, 21; BArch R 1001/5530 IVVR (Meyer) to Kolonialabtheilung, March 3, 1896; IVVR (Meyer) to Kolonialabtheilung, [March?] 7, 1896; ICI, *Compte Rendu 1912*, 203.
[174] "Note-Circulaire du Lieutenant-Gouverneur du Soudan du 13.01.1897," in Ortoli and Aubert, *Coutumiers Juridiques*, 1–2.
[175] Clozel and Villamur, *Les Coutumes Indigènes*.
[176] Post and Sugden, "Ethnological Jurisprudence," 31–40; Adam, "Modern Ethnological Jurisprudence," 216–229; Lyall, "Early German Legal Anthropology," 114–138; Post, *Afrikanische Jurisprudenz*, iv. It integrated elements of the famous Garson and Royal Anthropological Institute, *Notes and Queries*.

launched a project of trans*ethnic* codification, such as the codification of *adat* customary law in the Dutch Indies (Chapter 5).[177]

Compiling a "transethnic" law code, in particular, gave colonizers the opportunity to manipulate and reinvent customary law and to make it compatible with commercial and political interests. Roume thus recommended to administrators that "to achieve this goal, you compare differing habits, which, although details seem to differ at first sight, nevertheless present to the keen observer common points that help to determine a general character."[178] While bringing customary law in line with European commercial interests, the IVVR could still claim that it was more "authentic" than European or European-made "indigenous" law. Indeed, the IVVR relied on African contributors such as Faama Mademba Si from Senegal, who wrote an extensive report on the customary law of the Sansanding region on the Niger River, which seemed to be the most "authentic" contribution to the IVVR's collection of customary law. However, Mademba Si was more than a simple informant, and in his transethnic description of customary law in West Africa, he manipulated the facts for his own benefit and that of French "development" of the region.

Mademba Si's story is well known, as is his contribution to the French penetration and "development" of West Africa's interior.[179] Of noble origin, Mademba Si entered the French colonial service as early as 1869. Trained in France, he assumed the difficult task of constructing telegraph lines across Senegal's hinterland. As he proved a reliable collaborator to the French, they naturalized him and entrusted him with several military campaigns to conquer parts of West Africa's interior. Ultimately, the French governor named him king of a loosely defined region around Sansanding in the Segu district that was linguistically and religiously diverse. Pretending to develop the region, Mademba Si made extensive use of corvée, raised taxes that did not exist, and enriched himself. In 1899, when complaints about Mademba Si's abuse of the local population, including rapes and murders, reached the French head of the Segu district, he had no other choice than to revoke him from his post and imprison him. A few months later, however, the French reinstalled him as a king of Sansanding, which he remained until his death in 1918. His kingship was an invention that had never existed in local customs.

Throughout his rule, Mademba Si eagerly published to legitimize his kingdom and his behavior by evoking the customary law of the Sansanding area. The IVVR gave Mademba Si the opportunity to portray himself as the rightful ruler to an international audience. Skillfully, he combined elements of different customs and added invented traditions to substantiate his rule. His

---

[177] Lev, "Colonial Law," 57–74; Mamdani, *Define and Rule*, 34–42; Van Vollenhoven et al. *Van Vollenhoven on Indonesian Adat Law*, xxix–lxvii.
[178] Clozel, "Circulaire,"18–20; Ginio, "Negotiating Legal Authority," 115–135.
[179] Roberts, "The Case of Faama Mademba Sy," 185–204.

invention of a single customary law of the region was absurd, given that the Bambara, Fulbe, Maraka, and Bozo groups who lived there differed widely in language, customs, and their degree of Islamization. Observers remarked that "regrettably, the author does not distinguish between the four different groups but lumps them together. His contribution thus partly diminishes in value. The differences in the social organization are thus less pronounced."[180] Mademba Si's report was a typical example of a transethnic design of customary law.

Combining real and invented customs into a new transethnic customary law, Mademba Si defended his rule as a king, as well as the economic exploitation of the region. Most importantly, he explained that within customary law, the king remained uncontested and was "sacrosanct and chosen by God as his representative on earth." He reiterated the strategy of the French colonizers claiming that the land always belonged to the conqueror and that "any unoccupied land belongs to the king and is his domain." The king then might distribute land among individual concessionaires.[181] Mademba Si explained further his right to levy taxes by the fact that there is generally "no tax on land but the *diaka* paid to the king." He made himself the supreme judge and evoked customary law to prove that "the king is the supreme authority and when he issued a judgement, there is no appeal."[182] The French must have approved of his invention of customary law, which allowed them to maintain their loyal collaborator in power and use him to control and "develop" the region. In 1903, the IVVR published Mademba Si's manipulated and transethnic compilation of customary law in German and made it known to an international audience.[183]

Transethnic and transcolonial codification projects became even more pertinent in industrializing mining zones of central Africa. In the Belgian Congo, the codification mission gained a transethnic and transcolonial dimension around 1910, when labor migration resulted in the mixing of different customary law groups.[184] To assess the consequences of legal mixing, ICI members specifically observed the development of Elisabethville, a mining town that emerged in the vicinity of Katanga's new copper mines and became an official city in 1910.[185] In the same year, several mining companies from Elisabethville, headed by the Union Minière du Haut Katanga, launched the transcolonial recruitment agency Bourse du Travail du Katanga: this recruitment agency enlisted workers from different regions in Belgian Congo and the

---

[180] Mademba Si, "Bambara, Sarakolesen," 62.
[181] Ibid., 85–86.
[182] Ibid., 87 and 65–66.
[183] Belmessous, *Native Claims*, 15–16.
[184] Dibwe dia Mwembu, *Histoire des Conditions*; Larmer, "Permanent precarity," 173–175.
[185] Fetter, *The Creation of Elisabethville*.

British colony of Northern Rhodesia.[186] From 1908 onwards, railway lines connected Katanga to South Africa and Portuguese Mozambique and facilitated the transcolonial recruitment of workers. Elisabethville grew by a rate of 2,000 African newcomers per year.[187] It soon became clear that Elisabethville was unique because most workers did not return to their region of origin but settled near the plants. They thus lived permanently outside their customary environment, a situation that Europeans feared would lead to alienation and legal confusion and expose Africans to subversive ideologies. For more than a decade, ICI members Girault and Cattier had pondered how to deal with those "detribalized" Africans who could not develop within their "own milieu."[188]

Fearing that multiethnicity and legal plurality might be a threat to economic stability, colonial lawyers made Elisabethville the most important research center on customary law in central Africa and a testing ground for the mixing of customary laws.[189] The main instigator of the research was Antoine Sohier, a Belgian jurist and head of the appeal court in Elisabethville who arrived in Katanga in 1910 and would later join and influence the ICI.[190] As the steering committee of the Union Minière du Haut Katanga also became a corporative member of the ICI, colonial internationalists closely accompanied the economic and legislative development of Elisabethville. Sohier, in particular, spoke to the needs of the Union Minière when he identified the "legislative incoherence" as a major obstacle to economic progress in the Katanga region, assuming that legal pluralism brought ethnic rivalry to the fore and instilled unrest among the workers.[191]

Applying customary law also enabled ICI members to fabricate a shift from outright exploitation to softer development. The new Belgian government, which took over the Congo from Léopold in 1908, publicly declared their intention to preserve customary law and assume responsibility for the protection of indigenous rights through legal codes. Before 1908, Léopold II had given indigenous land as concessions to rubber-collecting companies. After 1908, Belgian administrators first seemed to continue this policy by granting concession to the new mining companies. Pressure came from the international media that accused the Belgians of repeating history and giving concessions to ruthless companies such as the Union Minière du Haut Katanga. Faced with these accusations, the new government wanted to show good will. The constitution-like Charte Coloniale of 1908, which marked the

---

[186] Higginson, *A Working Class*, 26.
[187] Mainly in the 1920s. See ibid., 74.
[188] Girault, "Condition des Indigènes," 52–53.
[189] The main thinkers were Sohier, *Traité Élémentaire*; Possoz, *Élements du droit*.
[190] Landmeters and Tousignant, "Civiliser les Indigènes par le Droit"; AGRB, Louwers Papers, 164 Correspondance Hardy: Louwers to Hardy, May 4, 1935.
[191] Sohier, *Memoires and Souvenirs*, 123.

2.7 LEGAL GOVERNMENTALITY & TRANSCOLONIAL LAW 103

takeover of Léopold's exploitative Congo Free State by the Belgian parliament, indeed sought to establish legal security and stipulated that all Africans in the Congo were subject to customary law.[192]

By declaring the African quarters of Elisabethville a *centre extra-coutumier*, the Belgians transferred the idea of upholding indirect rule and the customary law to urban environments.[193] Colonial lawyers such as Antoine Sohier accompanied the emergence of the self-governed *centres* and saw in them "the departing point for working on the reconstruction of the indigenous society and the restoration of a traditional policy that guides the evolution of our subjects within the framework of their customs."[194] While paying lip service to the coexistence of various customary laws, Sohier provided the basis for a single customary law in the Congo. Throughout his life, he stuck to the idea that "in the same that our [European] jurisdictions have to refer to the general principles of European law, the customary jurisdictions need first of all refer to the general principles of customary law."[195] He and his collaborators even took an overarching "Bantu law" and "negro law" that bundled up essential habits of all Bantu-speaking peoples for granted.[196] Well into the interwar period, lawyers in Elisabethville reiterated that a transethnic code should be the purpose of codification projects. "Unlike the ethnographers who describe predominantly varieties" of customs, one of them insisted, they wanted to draft "the elementary law ... of all negro legal groups."[197] ICI members endorsed this view and made a case for an "average customary law" that combined the most important rules of the different customary traditions. They imagined that such a transethnic customary law might solve the problems caused by detribalization.[198]

In practice, Sohier soon abandoned the idea of an "average customary law" and brought his legislative activity in line with the needs of the European economic interests. In the *centres*, it was not customary but indigenous law that ruled, a law entirely made by Europeans, similar to the French *Indigénat*. The French had developed the *Indigénat* in Algeria to punish crimes only Africans could commit, such as not greeting a European.[199]. In Belgian Congo, Europeans drafted a similar penal law for the Africans of the *centres*.[200] This

---

[192] Stengers, *Belgique et Congo*.
[193] Young, *Politics in Congo*, 70.
[194] Sohier, *Traité Élémentaire*, 3.
[195] Ibid., 31.
[196] Ibid., 8; Possoz, "Polygamie," 49; Tempels, *La Philosophie Bantoue*.
[197] Possoz, "Principes de Droit Nègre," 104.
[198] AGRB, Louwers Papers 236 (263) Session ICI 1936: Rapport Charles sur Centres Extra-coutumiers 1936, 46.
[199] Mann, "What Was the Indigénat?," 331–353; Brunet la Ruche and Manière, "De l'exception," 117–142.
[200] Sohier, *Pratique des Juridictions*, 26.

penal law was neither customary nor European but exclusively made for the mine workers. Since their working conditions in the mines were poor and dangerous, and the hygienic situation in the *centres* appalling (they lacked water supply), the workers deserted. Belgians made the law to persecute African workers who fled to Northern Rhodesia or other neighboring colonies.[201] As late as the 1920s, Belgian administrators would issue special indigenous regulations in the infamous Masters and Servants Acts, which enabled European employers to declare allegedly disloyal workers criminals and to chastise them personally if they "deserted" their contracts.[202] As they fled to foreign colonies, indigenous penal law was transcolonial.

Several ICI members condemned the harsh measures against "deserters" and drafted labor contracts that gave more rights to African labor migrants. Having discussed recruitment strategies already during Thys' construction of the Congo-Matadí railway in the 1890s, the ICI designed a *transcolonial* indigenous law that stipulated both the protection and the punishment of African workers. A leader of the Catholic Party in Belgium and member of the Institute of International Law, Édouard Descamps, explained that only the security of the contracts and a resulting mutual trust would make the *mise en valeur* with the help of the indigenous workers possible.[203] Descamps received support from leading ICI members, such as Secretary-General Janssen, whose opinion was authoritative when he addressed the issue in the 1912 session of the ICI. Janssen wanted to avoid any kind of forced recruitment and insisted that the contract be signed directly at the place of recruitment. He even intended to accord African workers the right to break a contract, provided that they had good reasons and assumed the costs of repatriation to their country of origin. Janssen turned against any form of corporal punishment inflicted by the employer on those who did not obey or did not fulfill their contract. Finally, he categorically rejected forced labor, even the "compulsory labor" ordered by colonial administrations and governments. As Benoit Daviron has concluded, Janssen's position was "resolutely progressive." Far from being unique, Albert Thys and the Dutch liberals in the ICI endorsed Janssen's position.[204] Before World War I, however, the ICI did not manage to stipulate an international convention. Instead, ICI members introduced bilateral transcolonial agreements that contained fragments of the model contracts they had designed. Around 1910, the Belgians negotiated new agreements to facilitate cross-border recruitment of workers for the emerging mining

---

[201] Sohier, "Pour une Collaboration Juridique Intercoloniale," 27–28.
[202] Lannoy "Le Régime et l'Organisation," 38–40, 90.
[203] ICI, *Compte Rendu 1899*, 53–54; ICI, *La Main d'Oeuvre*.
[204] ICI, *Compte Rendu 1912*, 247–248; Daviron, "Mobilizing Labor," 488.

industry.[205] Similar agreements between, say, Portuguese Mozambique and South African mining areas, became the norm.[206]

In practice, transcolonial laws often served to control African labor migrants rather than protecting them. In Belgian Congo, transcolonial law became the rule during the interwar period. Every time the Belgian administration decreed new laws concerning the African population, it added explicitly that these laws also applied to "the natives of the Congo and the adjacent colonies." In other versions, they used the formula "neighboring" colonies.[207] Consequently, laws stipulated in the Belgian Congo were also valid for African labor migrants from British Tanganyika, Northern Rhodesia, French Congo, and Portuguese Angola. Sohier declared this "intercolonial cooperation" necessary, especially to unify penal law across the colonies and to facilitate the persecution of African workers who had disobeyed their employers, no matter whether they came from Congo or abroad.[208]

Thus, Congolese indigenous penal law became transcolonial to persecute African workers who fled to Northern Rhodesia or other neighboring colonies. Quite the opposite, the transcolonial penal law did not apply to Europeans. ICI members tended to criticize that. Sohier publicized a case that began before World War I but extended well into the interwar period. As Sohier styled himself the protector of the African population, he tried to prosecute the Scottish recruitment agent Mac Ivor (a pseudonym), who forcibly recruited workers in Congo and Northern Rhodesia to work in the mines of Katanga. When Sohier summoned Mac Ivor for the first time, the latter threatened to use his contacts to upper-rank administrators and entrepreneurs in the Congo to have Sohier laid off. But Sohier, who had a strong sense of the independence of judges, kept on observing Mac Ivor, whom he called a "trafficker." The lawyer refused to "ignore the separation of powers" and to "abolish implicitly the articles of the Penal Code" by letting Mac Ivor go. When the Scotsman raided an entire village a few months later and killed one man who refused to be recruited, Sohier took action. He personally went to visit the village and publicly accused Mac Ivor of forced recruitment, which the Charte Coloniale had banned. Mac Ivor, however, fled to Northern Rhodesia to escape the sentence.[209] He was never convicted, due to the lack of a transcolonial agreement to

---

[205] AMAEB AE 202 Correspondance puissances étrangères; AE 204 Correspondance France 5/300 EIC Dept. Intérieur to Dept. Extérieur, August 28, 1905: Étude de recrutement d'artisans noirs originaires des possessions portugaises; AE 204 Correspondance France 6/3: EIC Gouverneur to Sécrétaire d'État, May 9, 1898; AE 204 Correspondance France 6/10 and 6/11.

[206] Harries, *Work, Culture, and Identity*. Generally, see Seibert, "More Continuity than Change?," 369–386.

[207] Sohier, "Le Décret du 24 Julliet 1918," 23.

[208] Sohier, "Pour une Collaboration Juridique Intercoloniale," 27–28.

[209] Sohier, "Un Début de Carrière Judiciaire."

prosecute European criminals. Sohier's attempt to condemn Mac Ivor, however, was not only an act of equity. Protecting African workers from criminal recruiters was also a way to gain them for the cause of colonial development.

Adding transcolonial and transethnic methods to their repertoire provided lawyers in the ICI with four options for designing new codes for the colonies: first, maintaining a fragmented variety of local ethnic laws according to the doctrine of cultural relativism; second, drafting a new transethnic code based on the idea that different customary traditions had similar basic rules; third, imposing European law on the indigenous population; fourth, introducing an invented indigenous law that was not customary law but a specific legal code that ascribed an inferior status to the indigenous peoples and legally segregated them from Europeans.[210] To be sure, ICI members combined these four procedures to secure "governmental" rule and development efforts. While Europeans kept up appearances of maintaining and codifying customary law, it is understood that they interpreted, manipulated, and redefined it in the process of codification.[211] Property and inheritance law, in particular, was rigged. In the field of commercial law, they often imposed European law. In addition, colonial administrations invented an "indigenous" penal code, such as the famous French "indigénat" to ensure legal segregation and the legal privileges of the colonizers. However, although the ICI claimed it, there was never a strict dualism between European and customary law but rather a subsidiary hierarchy between them.[212]

In sum, the ICI promoted a specific colonial law for legislative development that went beyond the distinction between customary, indigenous, and European law. Colonial law became a tool for what they imagined as being sustained development. ICI members never fully abandoned the codification of customary law and frequently used customary arguments to legitimize their political and economic interests. But transethnic codification projects failed to materialize, apart from regions with a longer Islamic tradition. While in the Dutch Indies, transethnic *adat* law (a mix of Islamic and customary law, see Chapter 5) became generally accepted and even provided the constitutional basis for a unified and stable law of the independent Indonesian nation after 1945, there was no such uniform transethnic code in sub-Saharan African colonies.[213] There, customary law remained highly fragmented, although the colonized needed a reliable transethnic system of norms to escape the caprices of the colonial state. Thus, sub-Saharan African colonies lacked a (customary) legal basis once they became independent. In most colonies, laws for

---

[210] Braillon, "Nouvelles Perspectives," 143–163; Mann, "What Was the Indigénat," 331–353.
[211] Roberts, *Litigants and Households*, 35–70; Chanock, *Law, Custom, and Social Order*; Mamdani, *Define and Rule*, 42.
[212] Saada, "Penser le Fait Colonial"; Benton, *Law and Colonial Cultures*, 1–2.
[213] Lev, "Colonial Law," 70.

non-Europeans resembled European-made indigenous law rather than customary code. The ICI's *Recueil International de Législation Coloniale*, stands for this legal amalgam and the general shift to a "mixed" and therefore arbitrary colonial law. In the *Recueil*, customary law was strikingly absent. Instead, it contained a mix of superficial ethnographic material and specific colonial laws concerning property, taxes, and commerce. Throughout its existence, the ICI collected firsthand information from administrations in the *Recueil* and in special editions to find a best practice of legislative development.[214]

ICI members assigned law in the colonies a new functional priority: they believed that colonial law must facilitate economic development, or at least not stand in its way. They had reinvented colonial law as a method to bring about social and economic change. In theory, they believed in education through law. In practice, the reverse was true and their program resembled an early version of functionalism: the subordination of colonial law under social change, induced by colonial domination and development schemes. Anticipating progressive anthropological theories of the 1930s, ICI members also applied functionalism to customary law and argued that "customs change over time and other observers among other groups of the same people will come to different conclusions."[215] Well into the interwar period, ICI members emphasized that it "would indeed be wrong to imagine the indigenous societies in Africa as clichés in a given system and resistant to any kind of innovation. The custom, particularly because it is conservative and because it serves to protect a society, adapts itself to new conditions of existence."[216] Developmental colonialism was this new condition of existence.

2.8 The Global Career of Transcolonial Development Schemes

Transcolonial development schemes quickly raised interest among colonizers and colonized alike. As we have seen, Gandhi's journal *Indian Opinion* followed ICI leader Chailley in arguing that the British had not invested enough money in India, where many lived in "great poverty and where commerce and trade are entirely local and therefore without real importance."[217] Gandhi seemed to be interested in an Indian economy with more local participation and the support of international capital, which approximated him to the ICI's approach.

---

[214] BArch R 1001/6187, 82, "Auf den Erlass vom 3. März 1909 Nr. KA VI 2094/11584, Nr. 132 betreffend das Internationale Koloniale Institut in Brüssel"; R1001/6187, 74: "Kaiserliches Gouvernement Togo 18.Juni 1909: Anfrage des Internationalen Kolonial-Instituts."
[215] Steinmetz, *Rechtsverhältnisse*, iv.
[216] AGRB, Louwers Papers 236 (263) Session ICI 1936: Rapport Charles sur Centres extracoutumiers 1936.
[217] *Indian Opinion* (October 6, 1905), 15.

Among West African entrepreneurs, who had already been part of a global trade network, the ICI's plans for a transcolonial railway network raised entrepreneurial hopes. The African entrepreneurs of Gold Coast and Nigeria wondered if they could profit from Chailley's proposal to create a common zone of trade and a transcolonial railway network at the Anglo-French economic conference on West Africa in 1919. They also became interested in his proposition to coordinate the activities of shipping lines, standardize bills of lading, and align customs regulations.[218] Although the ICI rarely put its transcolonial plans into practice, they seemed to appeal to the colonized entrepreneurs.

More important was the ICI's transcolonial development scheme for colonial newcomers such as the United States. Immediately after the United States took possession of the Philippines, Puerto Rico, and Cuba in 1898, the US government sent several research missions to other colonies and consulted ICI members on how to "govern a tropical colony."[219] In his official report, the American ICI member Oscar Phelps Austin used the publications of ICI members and followed Albert Thys when claiming that fair wages would make colonial subjects contribute to the development of the colony. Only by introducing capitalism, roads, railways, and irrigation systems, Austin continued, would the United States render its colonies self-sufficient. At the same time, Austin warned that "guidance in development" was necessary. Restricted state intervention should bring about the diversification of agriculture, support smallholders, and encourage the colonized to grow cash crops. While he saw in individual property a tool of encouragement, he also considered soft coercion a possible way to make the colonized participate in a liberal economy. The precondition of such an economy was a stable currency, chartered companies, and labor immigration. He was equally in favor of preserving indigenous culture and hoped that a liberal policy toward the indigenous populations might win their loyalty.[220] Like the ICI, Austin encouraged the US government to take steps to improve the "material, mental, and moral condition of the people of the colony."[221]

Development projects inspired by the ICI not only became a model for newcomers but also for well-established colonial powers such as Great Britain. When the most eminent colonial reformer Frederick Lugard wrote his allegedly path-breaking developmental manifesto *The Dual Mandate in British Tropical Africa* in 1922, he had two main sources. First, he referred to the British experience and the introduction of indirect rule and other reforms after the 1856 Sepoy rebellion in India, which had caused the British to model their policy on the more peaceful Dutch Java. His second

---

[218] *The Gold Coast Nation* (July 6, 1919), 3; *The Nigerian Pioneer* (June 3, 1921), 6.
[219] Ireland, *Tropical Colonization*, vii.
[220] US Dept. of the Treasury, *Colonial Administration*, 2822
[221] Ibid., 2638.

source was the ICI and the writings of its members. His idea of the dual mandate had much in common with the ICI's program of emulative development, cultural relativism, and indirect rule. In his landmark plea for a new "native policy," Lugard explicitly referred to Ernest Roume's development program and hailed him for the comparative study of British, American, Dutch, Belgian, and French colonial trade, which became the basis of his own developmental policy. Moreover, Lugard admired the German Kolonialwirtschaftliches Komittee (Committee for Colonial Economy), a semi-private society that was close to the ICI and responsible for sending out "botanical and agricultural expeditions to German and other colonies to report on economic possibilities and the ways scientific methods could improve and boost native industries."[222] Thus, Lugard, probably the most famous colonial reformer of his time, took the development schemes of ICI members as an example.

In terms of long-lasting effects, the League of Nations would be inspired by the ICI's soft development program. In 1920, the soon-to-be secretary general of the ICI, Octave Louwers, brought the ICI's developmentalist attitude into the League of Nations' Permanent Mandates Commission (PMC). Together with eight other ICI members who joined the PMC in the course of the 1920s, they had an important impact on its agenda. Louwers reiterated the ICI's idea that "liberty of work, respect of the property of native territories, and commercial freedom" were the new and old priorities of colonial policy.[223]

Only occasionally did transcolonial and governmental projects of "soft" development live up to the expectations they raised. Transcolonial agreements on labor recruitment succeeded partly – attempts to turn Africans into a capitalist and money-saving middle class less so. Nevertheless, transcolonial and governmental schemes of development became well established. The reason for success was that they helped to increase the autonomy of self-styled experts and provided a legitimization for colonial rule. Moreover, the ICI also designed them to hide away the wars they waged on the colonized populations. In the nine conference proceedings the ICI published between 1904 and 1913, for example, they never mentioned a single word about the devastating onslaughts of German troops on the Herero and Nama in German South West Africa and rarely referred to Léopold's fatal exploitation of the Congolese people. Instead, ICI members spilled much ink on the allegedly progressive role of colonialism. Apart from transcolonial transfers, intercolonial comparison became a tool for them to prove their progressive attitude and conceal colonial violence.

---

[222] Lugard, *Dual Mandate*, 498–499.
[223] ANOM 100APOM223, Louwers to Neveu, April 25, 1929; Louwers, "Camille Janssen," 437–440.

3

Politics of Comparison

The Dutch Model and the Reform of Colonial Training Schools

Beginning in the mid-nineteenth century, colonial experts all over the world propagated the Dutch East Indies – much more than British India – as an example of successful native policy and of professional colonial administration.[1] To unravel the secrets behind the Dutch administrative achievements, the French Ministry of the Navy and the Colonies dispatched Joseph Chailley in 1893 on an official mission to "study the recruitment of colonial administrators in Holland."[2] His journey was the founding act of methodological colonial comparison and resulted in the establishment of the ICI. Based on comparison and transfers, Chailley and the ICI inaugurated an era of colonial reform, which indeed transformed the training of colonial administrators in Western Europe and the United States. At the origin of this transformation was a call for professionalization that supposedly marked the shift from military to civil administration and from the rule over territory to the rule over people.[3] The purpose was to replace settler colonization with a small group of professionals who ruled through indigenous collaborators, as it seemed to be the case in the Dutch Indies.

Taking off around 1908, the reform of training schools for colonial staff in the metropoles owed a lot to the transnational comparisons and transfers among ICI members.[4] To be sure, the state-run colonial training schools that emerged at that time in most metropoles seem to belong to a nationalistic history, as do comparisons that contrast specific national styles of colonial

---

[1] On the British model, see Crowder, "Indirect Rule," 197–204; Dimier, *Le Discours Idéologique*, 11. On the Dutch model, see Wesseling, "The Giant"; Wesseling, *Imperialism and Colonialism*; Gouda; "Mimicry and Projection." See also Kuitenbrouwer, *Nederland*. Problematizing the Dutch "rational" model, see Stoler, *Along the Archival Grain*.
[2] Chailley, *La Hollande et les Fonctionnaires*, 9 and preface.
[3] For a general overview, see Gann and Duignan, *African Proconsuls*. On France and Britain, see Thomas, *The French Colonial Mind*; Prior, *Exporting Empire*; Kirk-Greene, *Britain's Imperial Administrators*; Metcalf, *Ideologies*; Whitehead, *Colonial Educators*; Dewey, *Anglo-Indian Attitudes*; Stockwell, *The British End*; Pietsch, *Empire of Scholars*. On Africans, see Keese, *Living with Ambiguity*.
[4] Haupt and Kocka, *Comparative and Transnational History*.

administration. While it is true that each nation-state ultimately institutionalized its own recruitment, selection, training, remuneration, and old-age provisions, this chapter unveils how the ICI members used transnational networks and comparison to dictate exactly these terms of employment. What is more, the training of technocratic staff was widely transnational and prefigured what historians have called "technocratic internationalism."[5] The latter ultimately resulted in the League of Nations' "international public administration," which many ICI members joined. As historians have shown with regard to the League of Nations' staff, international staff appeared as "brokers" in a transnational field, using both national and transnational infrastructure and symbolic capital.[6] ICI members, by using comparison and transfers to find the ideal training for colonial officials, preformed this transnational field and introduced early forms of functional governance. This process was rather transnational than transcolonial because it entailed an exclusion of non-Europeans in the colonies from the colonial career.

The idealization of the Dutch colonial policy, however, was no more than a function of colonial comparisons, which aimed at increasing the agency of colonial experts. This chapter distinguishes between three functions of the comparative method. First, comparisons were political, because colonizers used them intentionally in a contrasting way to produce stereotypes for the idealization and stigmatization of other empires.[7] The stigmatization of other empires was common in the age of high imperialism, and the Spanish attracted most criticism. ICI members, however, rather used stereotypes to idealize the "other" empires. Colonial experts of the ICI were particularly inclined to use idealizing stereotype-comparisons, because they hoped that an exemplary "other" would coax their own governments to pay more attention and money to the colonial cause. Second, comparisons aimed at identifying similarities between colonial approaches of different countries to unveil shared ideas and universal ideals to which all colonizers subscribed. One ICI member made it clear that "before comparing, we need to know what exactly we compare. We collect meticulously diverse documents from all latitudes; with their help, we do not necessarily develop a unified colonial system, but we become aware of a certain state of the mind we share."[8] The awareness of similarities helped to identify the archetype of empire. The Roman Empire was the most likely candidate to be such an archetype, but it soon gave way to the archetype of a governmental empire that allegedly ensured economic and human progress through science, efficient administration, and a certain degree of self-government. Tellingly, ICI members did not find this archetype in the past but in the idealized future.

---

[5] Kaiser and Schot, *Writing the Rules*, 21–73.
[6] Gram-Skjoldager and Ikonomou, "Making Sense of the League," 420–444.
[7] Gibson, *The Black Legend*.
[8] ICI, *Compte Rendu 1907*, 99.

Third, and most importantly, colonial comparisons were dialectical, in the sense that they enabled experts to develop successful techniques of colonization and to dismiss unrewarding methods. After identifying successful micro-techniques of colonial governmentality, ICI members combined them to improve colonial administration as a whole. The object of dialectical comparisons were prototypes, that is, successfully tested techniques developed elsewhere that were worth imitation. These micro-techniques potentially existed all over the colonial world, also in otherwise stigmatized empires such as the Spanish empire. As we will see, it is the combination of prototype-, stereotype-, and archetype-comparisons that led colonial internationalists to introduce new training schools for administrators. In this process, the ICI members borrowed techniques from all empires, not only from the Dutch.

By 1900, prototype-, stereotype-, and archetype-comparisons prompted the professionalization of colonial administration in all empires, yet only for European officials. The number of European colonial experts overseas increased, and their selection, training, and payment improved significantly. Much to the taste of the ICI, "colonial expert" became a job title and a salaried profession. Around 1910, entering the colonial service as a European came along with health insurance and old-age pensions. Although small numbers of non-Europeans continued to be lower-ranked administrators, they had no access to those benefits. Health insurance and old-age pensions, in particular, remained a privilege of the Europeans. Taken by their own financial interests, the ICI members forgot their initial project to govern through the local populations. In some cases, Europeans replaced non-Europeans in the administration.

Two cases from German East Africa show how different the governments treated European and non-European experts in the colonial service. After graduating from an agricultural school in Munich in 1909, the German agronomic expert Adolf Gresser took up a position in Togo. Only a year later, Gresser "returned to Germany because his physical condition was not fit for the tropical climate." He lived on paid convalescent leave for a year, before the German Colonial Office employed him for another two months. Although the German Colonial Service Law (1910) required his removal from the Colonial Service because of his *Tropendienstuntauglichkeit* (unfitness for service in the tropics), the Colonial Office gave him a new post at a small agricultural research station in German East Africa. Once again, he quit this position after a month, claiming to be unfit for the tropical climate. Thereupon, the governor sent him to the healthier Biological-Agricultural Institute at Amani in the Usambara Mountains. Yet, in the meantime, the agricultural advisor of the East African government had filed a lawsuit against Gresser for the "physical abuse of natives." Gresser admitted to have indeed "kicked a native lightly in the bottom because he had not greeted him." On another occasion, he had "dealt one or more severe blows with the fist and the rifle butt" to an East

African worker whom he considered to have "behaved clumsily." Gresser invoked the "right to use corporal punishment" valid in the German colonies as an excuse. He had no excuse, though, for his aggression against his denouncer, whom he attacked in August 1913 "on a hotel terrace in Dar es Salaam with a riding whip."[9] As the Colonial Office seemed to have been slow at initiating a dishonorable discharge, Gresser demanded to keep his honorary titles and receive an old-age pension. Although he had served only one and a half years and forfeited his membership in the Colonial Service, the German minister of justice determined after World War I that he should receive an old-age pension as a member of the German Civil Service.[10]

German authorities reacted the opposite way when the Javanese botanist Raden Soleman made a similar, though more modest request. Soleman was a botanist and draftsman from the Netherlands' Indies, headhunted by German ICI members and agronomists who brought him to East Africa in 1902. In the German Protectorate, Soleman helped to launch the famous Biological-Agricultural Institute of Amani. As agricultural expert, he received a salary of 140 rupees.[11] His employers at Amani spoke highly of him, claiming that his work was of the "highest importance" for the institute and that he was "very useful." During the fourteen years of his service, he had only been ill twice and always rapidly returned to service. When the British troops conquered German East Africa in World War I and most Germans had left, Soleman remained in Amani. Speaking and writing German fluently, he was suspect to the British. Soleman petitioned Berlin to send him money for his repatriation to Java. According to his contract, the German Colonial Service was responsible for providing him a third-class ticket for his return. Only after persistent pressure from Soleman's mentors did the German authorities promise to help him. However, neither the ticket, nor his pending salary was ever paid. Desperately, he wrote: "Until today, my hope was in vain, and I have not received a penny. I ask the German Colonial Office to send me the money as soon as possible, because I continue to have a hard time here and I would like to return home."[12] It is unknown what happened to Soleman. All his German colleagues officially retired and received an old-age pension after the war.[13]

Soleman had come to East Africa in 1902 because German agronomists admired the Dutch agricultural policy in the Indies. Their admiration derived from an idealization of Dutch rationality and professional government. Java, in particular, was considered exceptional for its rational administration,

---

[9] BArch R2/43/I/946: Gutachten des Reichsministeriums des Inneren.
[10] BArch R2/43/I/946: Gutachten des Reichsministers der Justiz.
[11] BArch R1001/8651/203: Direktor Amani to RKA, December 14, 1914.
[12] BArch R 1001/8651/218: Raden Soleman to RKA, July 9, 1921.
[13] BArch R2/43/I/946: Schreiben Reichsminister für Wiederaufbau, November 29, 1919.

profitability, and alleged liberality toward the Javanese. While such stereotypes often stimulated a general interest in the Dutch policy, the emulation of its colonial methods and "prototypes" was selective and purposeful.[14] Since they knew that Javanese practitioners such as Soleman had concrete experience in applied colonial techniques, Germans in East Africa – who happened to be ICI members – employed him. Along with him, they recruited European planters, as well as Javanese and Chinese tobacco planters, who had worked on Sumatra and Java. The governor of German East Africa explained that "we can only be successful if we use the help of Chinese and Javanese tobacco planters. I therefore asked the imperial consulate in Singapore to recruit twenty Chinese workers, one overseer, ten Javanese, and two Chinese gardeners and asked him to send them here together with their habitual supply and tools."[15] Why did Dutch Java have a comparatively good reputation?

3.1 Colonial Comparison and the Role of the Dutch Stereotype

The myth of Dutch exceptionalism had deep roots in the nineteenth century, because Java became the only profitable colony. British publicists first popularized Java as the pearl of all islands that even outshined the British crown colony. They praised Java's dual administration (native and European) and admired its system of economic exploitation through the cultivation system. As we have seen, the Dutch administration used the cultivation system to force Javanese village communities to dedicate one-third of their fields to cash crop production – mainly sugar, coffee, and indigo. It was mandatory for the peasants to sell the yields of this compulsory cultivation to an official Dutch trading society that sold them in Europe.[16] Between 1840 and 1873, this *Cultuurstelsel* earned the Dutch state a fortune that colonial experts estimated at 1.5 billion francs.[17] In Java, the system induced the native rural communities to abandon subsistence agriculture and produce for the European market.

The cultivation system rose to global prominence after James William Money, a British administrator and lawyer from Calcutta, immortalized it in his bestseller *Java or How to Manage a Colony: Showing a Practical Solution of the Questions now Affecting British India* (1861). Money's book – written as a response to the post-1857 crisis of the British Empire – was a

---

[14] Chailley, *Java et ses Habitants*, vii.
[15] BArch R 1001/8647: Governor Wissmann to Reichskanzler Hohenlohe, February 11, 1896.
[16] Wesseling, "Le Modèle Colonial," 231. On the cultivation system in general, see Fasseur, *The Politics*; Elson, *Village Java*; O'Malley, "Plantations 1830–1940"; Klaveren, *The Dutch Colonial System*, 120–121.
[17] *Congrès Colonial International*, 160.

whole-hearted appeal to model British colonial policy on the more successful Dutch rule in Java:

> A new system was inaugurated in 1832, which, in twenty-five years, quadrupled the revenue, paid off the debt, changed the yearly deficit to a large yearly surplus, trebled the trade, improved the administration, diminished crime and litigation, gave peace, security and affluence to the people, combined the interests of Europeans and Native, and, more wonderful still, nearly doubled an Oriental population[18]

Money argued that emulating such as system was a way to reconcile the British with the Indians, because it tutored them on how to capitalize on the colonial economy without forcing them into cultural assimilation. The Dutch model thus stood out by successfully replacing cultural assimilation with economic assimilation.[19]

Even more importantly, the *Cultuurstelsel* had inspired Europeans to build new empires. King Léopold II of Belgium, who had devoured Money's book, studied Java in detail, modeling his Congo Free State on it. "Apart from Holland," Léopold claimed, "there are no governments who know how to make colonies productive."[20] He applied a modified version of the cultivation system in the Congo Free State: he pressed the Congolese village communities to supply his agents with a quota of wild rubber from Congolese woods.[21]

To be sure, Multatuli's documentary novel *Max Havelaar: Or the Coffee Auctions of the Dutch Trading Company* (1860) abated the zeal of admirers substantially – by proving Money wrong. Multatuli blamed the cultivation system for having caused flight, poverty, and famines among the Javanese. Several journalistic accounts confirmed that up to half of the population fled from populous regions to escape forced cultivation of cash crops. Those who remained often starved, as they reduced self-sufficient rice production.[22] As outlined in Chapter 2, the success of Max Havelaar and a subsequent campaign against inhumane colonial policies led the liberal Dutch government of the 1860s to gradually abolish the lucrative – but repressive– cultivation system. From this time, the cultivation system fell into disrepute in Holland (but not colonialism per se, which Multatuli had never criticized). Liberal

---

[18] Money, *Java*, ix.
[19] Ibid.
[20] AMAEB, Beyens Papers, Léopold to Beyens, July 20, 1878.
[21] "Kultursystem," in *Deutsches Koloniallexikon*, 388. On Léopold's fascination with Java, see Le Febve de Vivy, *Documents d'Histoire*, 20 and 31; Stengers, "Modèle Colonial," 69.
[22] Unlike many interpretations claim, Multatuli's novel was not "anti-imperialist" and did not question colonialism in general. See Multatuli, *Max Havelaar*; Van Laak, *Literatur*. For more on flight, violence, and punishment, see Soest, *Geschiedenis*, 197–204; US Dept. of the Treasury, *Colonial Administration*, 2227; Stuchtey, *Die Europäische Expansion*, 26.

politicians abolished the trade monopoly and introduced what they called a free market economy.²³

Dutch ICI members, in particular, had been quick at condemning the cultivation system and turned its abolition into a symbol of their own liberality and "ethical" attitude. As we have seen, ICI leader Fransen van de Putte had been the driving force behind the abolition of the *Cultuurstelsel* in the 1860s. In the 1890s, ICI member Conrad T. van Deventer introduced the idea of an ethical policy, claiming that the Netherlands had a moral duty to reimburse the Javanese people for their suffering during the period of the cultivation system.²⁴ Driven by an apologetic civilizing mission, the "ethicals" launched the first ever state-led development program in 1901 and promised the Indonesians material progress and participation in the colonial administration. To the international community, this "ethical policy" (1901–1942) seemed to confirm once more that the Dutch colonial policy was always ahead of its time. For the other ICI members, Java came to epitomize a modern colony with a supposedly cooperative native policy and a rational drive to economic development.²⁵

3.2 "Applying Compulsion in Some Modernized and Improved Form": Paradoxes of the Ethical Policy

The transition from forced cultivation to the "ethical policy" itself was based on a stereotype that did not correspond to the realities on the ground. The Dutch had never abolished the cultivation system completely but only its unprofitable branches. Until the 1890s, they maintained the forced production of coffee. As late as 1898, more than 250,000 families in 14 out of the 20 Javanese residencies still had to produce two-thirds of Java's coffee, until the Dutch colonial government lost interest in coffee cultivation because of the decay of the coffee prices on the world market.²⁶ At the same time, Dutch liberals accepted forced labor to develop the former Sultanate of Deli on Sumatra's East Coast into one of the most profitable plantation complexes in the colonial world, which accounted for one-third of the exported cash crops from the Dutch Indies. J. T. Cremer, another ICI member, who headed the planter society Deli Maatschappij and was Dutch colonial minister between 1897 and 1901, had initiated the so-called Koelie-ordonnatie (Coolie-Ordinance, 1880), which allowed the planters to control and punish their

---

[23] On the contemporary discussion, see Pierson, *Java*.
[24] Deventer, "Een Eereschuld," 205–257; Bertrand, "Politique Éthique," 2–41.
[25] Schmutzer, *Dutch Colonial Policy*.
[26] US Dept. of the Treasury, *Colonial Administration*; Worsfold, *A Visit to Java*, 158–159 and 164.

workers as desired.[27] As a result, indentured "coolies" from China and Java worked "in slave-like conditions" to produce evermore yields, with plantations rather resembling prison complexes than capitalist enterprises.[28] Given their success, the new slave plantations became a prototype for other colonial powers, though they hardly advertised it as a stereotype.

The ensuing ethical era was ethical only by the stereotyped standards of the colonizers. While the foreign workers suffered on the Deli plantations in Sumatra, the "free" peasants in Java had to finance the highly praised development projects of the ethical policy, such as the famous state-run and allegedly free irrigation system. Paid for by native land tax, the irrigation system moreover tended to benefit the European planters of water-intensive sugar cane plantations to the detriment of indigenous staple food cultivated in the rice fields.[29] Compromising their ethical principle, the Dutch led a devastating war against the insurgent Sultanate of Aceh in Northern Sumatra between 1873 and 1914, with millions of casualties and thousands fleeing the area and the costs of war amounting to over 250 million Florins.[30] The ICI was aware of the war, as its Dutch member Christiaan Snouck Hurgronje served as an advisor during the campaign and replaced former scorched earth tactics by "divide and rule" strategies to win the war. They celebrated this strategy as progressive.[31]

All colonial internationalists paid lip service to the allegedly exemplary "ethical policy," while the fascination for the *Cultuurstelsel*'s payout remained. The prototype ousted the stereotype. At the ICI's meeting of 1897, for example, secretary-general Chailley spoke generously about the cultivation system: the efficiency of the system, he suggested, was as important as liberty, because it brought demographic growth and prosperity to all.[32] However, Chailley was well aware of its moral condemnation. When he noticed the stenographer in the ICI's meeting room, he added hastily: "But now that there are stenographers attached to the International Colonial Institute, I do not want that, when in twenty years the students will read in the proceedings of this session that I defended a system, which I reject."[33] The Belgian debate was more impulsive. When the Belgian ICI member Albert Thys warned King Léopold in the 1890s that the stigmatized system had become a source of shame for the Dutch colonizers, Léopold replied cynically: "So what! I will also

---

[27] Kooreman, *De Koelie Ordonnantie*; Breman, *Koelies*; "Sumatra's Oostkust. Landbouw," *Staatsblad van Nederlandsch-Indië* 133 (n.d.); Stoler, *Capitalism and Confrontation*.
[28] Ross, *Ecology and Power*, 112–113.
[29] On continued forced labor recruitment, tax paying, and conflicts about water, see Klaveren, *The Dutch*, 68–69.
[30] Worsfold, *A Visit to Java*, 161; Kreike, "Genocide in the Kampongs?," 297–316.
[31] The ICI also recommended literature on the Aceh wars. See Petit, *La Conquête*.
[32] ICI, *Compte Rendu 1897*, 126–127.
[33] Ibid., 132.

show regret once I will be old."[34] He thought forced cultivation a necessary tool to "civilize and moralize the indolent and corrupted" natives and a precondition for the liberalization of the colonial economy.[35]

American colonizers equally rehabilitated the cultivation system by suggesting that it compared favorably with slavery in the United States. Assuming that the *Cultuurstelsel* was to the East Indies what slavery was to the Americas, ICI member Austin considered both "so far as results can be measured in dollars and cents, a success." The cultivation system, however, was "softer." Thus, Austin informed the US government about the advantages of the *Cultuurstelsel* in 1903. Although he pretended to be generally opposed to forced cultivation, he thought it necessary to educate "idle natives": "it has become fashionable to emphasize the good sides of that institution and to hint at the possibility of applying compulsion in some modernized and improved form as a remedy for the ingrained inactivity or inefficiency of free natives." He added that the "wish that such a system might be adapted to other countries" was frequent among the colonial administrators by the turn of the century.[36] Unlike slavery, the cultivation system was not yet dead.

While taking the emulation of the *Cultuurstelsel* prototype into consideration, ICI members cultivated the stereotype of a liberal and participative Dutch policy. The dualist administration in Java undoubtedly set the standards for such a policy. Indeed, as early as 1836, the Regulations on the Policy of the Government of the Netherlands Indies, Chapter IV, Article 77 stipulated that "as far as circumstances permit, the indigenous people are left under the immediate leadership of their own heads of government, be they appointed or recognized. They are subject to higher supervision as it is determined by general and special regulations by the Governor General."[37] In the 1890s, Dutch ICI members contributed to the development of the native administration (*Inlands Bestuur*) in Java, giving it more weight in the face of the European administration and supervision (*Binnenlands Bestuur*). In this dualist system, there were thirty-six residencies, headed by Dutch residents who named Indonesian regents at the head of the *Inlands Bestuur* and supervised their work. The Dutch chose regents from loyal notable families. Regents had a few secretaries to control the elected village head of the residency. In many ways, the Dutch use of indigenous collaborators resembled the administrative approach of British India. However, the latter had fallen into disrepute after the so-called Sepoy rebellion of 1857, whose outbreak Money and others had blamed on the repressive British administration.

[34] Thys, "Devons-nous Coloniser au Congo," 15.
[35] Letter to Duke of Brabant (Léopold II) July 26, 1863, in Le Febve de Vivy, *Documents d'Histoire Précoloniale*, 19.
[36] US Dept. of the Treasury, *Colonial Administration*, 2775.
[37] Snouck Hurgronje, "De Inlandsche Bestuursambtenaren," 212.

3.2 PARADOXES OF THE ETHICAL POLICY

In the 1890s, Dutch ICI members became patrons of the *Inlands Bestuur*. Indonesian administrators particularly praised the support of ICI member Snouck Hurgronje who was an advisor to the Dutch colonial government in native affairs.[38] Snouck Hurgronje patronized several promising Javanese adolescents, with whom he regularly met over lunch to plan their career in the administration of Java. Achmad Djajadiningrat, a young man from a noble family in the Bantam Residency in Java was one of them. Snouck Hurgonje was a mentor for him and his siblings and helped all of them become high-ranking civil servants in the *Inlands Bestuur*. Djajadiningrat thought of Snouck Hurgonje as "a man to whom my whole family owes much and who had had the biggest influence on my intellectual life and aspirations until the end of my career."[39] Snouck Hurgonje paid for Djajadiningrat's education and talked the Dutch higher burgher school Koning Willem III into accepting him, although this famous *Gymnasium* established in 1864 had almost exclusively been for Europeans and Creoles. Thanks to Snouck Hurgonje, Djajadiningrat made a career in the *Inlands Bestuur* and became regent of Serang in Western Java.

Another Dutch ICI member, the international lawyer Emanuel Moresco, went even further and lobbied for participation of Indonesian administrators in the legislation of the colony. In 1911, he pushed for the creation of a People's Council (Volksraad) in the Dutch Indies, which would hold its first session in 1918. This consultative council was composed of both Europeans and Indonesians and theoretically laid the ground for a future self-government of the colony.[40] While the Dutch administration always had the last word, the Volksraad gave Indonesians the opportunity to publicly comment on lawmaking in the colonies.

The ICI used Snouck Hurgonje's paternalistic empowerment of Indonesian administrators and Moresco's Volksraad as an opportunity to portray the Dutch Indies as an archetype of liberality and the ICI as a promoter of indigenous participation. The reality was certainly quite different. Although Djajadiningrat came from a privileged family and had the unconditional support of Snouck Hurgonje, he still suffered from the discriminating treatment by European superiors. Like many other Indonesian administrators, he constantly felt the "hostile attitude of most European administrative officials," who thought that he would never reach the "intellectual level of the Europeans."[41] Those Europeans could always overrule Indonesian decisions, be it in matters of administration or legislation.

---

[38] Snouck Hurgronje, *The Achehnese*.
[39] Djajadiningrat, *Herinneringen*, 62–87.
[40] Moresco had studied councils in British India for the Dutch colonial ministry. See Moresco, *De Wetgevende Raden*. When the Volksraad was finally established in 1918, only two-fifths of the seats were for Indonesians. See Moresco, *Les Indes*, 30–31.
[41] Djajadiningrat, *Herinerinngen*, 62–87.

Perpetuating the myth of efficient administration, however, enabled ICI members to idealize the Dutch model to obtain more funding from their own governments. In 1901, the Dutch "ethical" government was indeed the first colonial power to make significant investments that allegedly led to economic development and demographic growth in Java. By way of comparison, the French ICI member Chailley tried to push Paris to imitate the Dutch and invest more in the colonies: "Java, the pearl of the Dutch Indies, has 30 million inhabitants and a budget of 300 million francs, which has made the Dutch Treasury swell, enriched thousands of colonists and caused an incredible increase of the indigenous population."[42] Chailley exaggerated the success of the "rational" Dutch administration only to belittle the Algerian antimodel. In his talks and publications, he forwarded the figure of fifty billion francs, which the conquest, pacification, and settlement of Algeria had cost the French taxpayer.[43] According to him, the expenses for Algeria had soared because of an inflated settler administration, whereas efficient technocrats governed the Dutch Indies and made the native population productive. The German ICI member Zimmermann equally urged the Colonial Office in Berlin to increase the funding of the agronomic research institute of Amani in German East Africa, arguing that "the small country of Holland, on the contrary raises the money necessary to finance its *Plantentuin.*" The Plantentuin was the Dutch agronomic research institute in Java that would play an important role in increasing the Indies' agricultural productivity (see Figure 3.1).[44]

3.3 The Method of Prototype Comparison: "Why Invent If Inventions Already Exist?"

In the colonies, persuasive stereotype-comparisons gave way to the ICI's practical interest in prototype-comparisons, which supposedly served "to lead the colonies rapidly and safely to prosperity."[45] Prototypes are generally early samples or releases that serve to test inventions and register their positive and negative properties. Based on the outcome of the test, future replications can thus be remediated and enhanced. This method was particularly time-saving and efficient, as Chailley claimed: "Why invent, if inventions already

---

[42] Chailley, *Java* (1914b), xxix.
[43] "Le Maroc et l'Opinion Publique," *Bulletin du Comité de l'Afrique Française* (January 1908), 10.
[44] BArch R 1001/8651, 86–87: Rheinische Handel- Plantagen Gesellschaft to Kolonialamt, September 1, 1908.
    ICI, *Compte-Rendu 1895*, 188.
[45] Chailley, "Les Anglais," 842.

3.3 THE METHOD OF PROTOTYPE COMPARISON

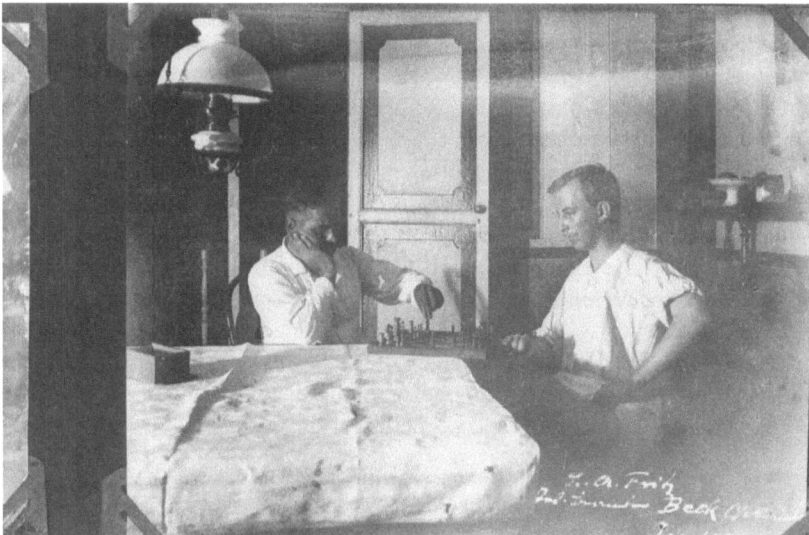

Figure 3.1 German colonial officer and Dutch telegraph operator playing chess in Yap (Caroline Islands)
© Bildbestand Der Deutschen Kolonialgesellschaft, Universitätsbibliothek Frankfurt/Main, Image 066-4200 016

exist? ... It is more effective to look around us."[46] If prototype colonial techniques had proven successful in one colony, administrators applied them to other colonies, especially the "new possessions" in Africa. Hence, the ICI engaged in a diffusionist policy of imitation and adaptation, with prototype comparison and transfers being the most cherished "method" of "colonial science."[47] Unlike the intentionally politicized stereotypes, prototype comparisons allowed ICI members to have a more differentiated view on empires. Prototypes differed from stereotypes in that they made selective comparisons and transfers of knowledge possible. Karl Rathgen, the ICI member and head of the Colonial Institute in Hamburg, which trained colonial administrators since 1908, stressed that "there can be no question of imitating standardized models."[48]

Prototype comparisons aimed at the adaptation of successfully tested colonial techniques, but ICI members also engaged in a detailed error analysis to identify failures and shortcomings. Colonial specialists in the ICI were well

[46] Chailley, *Java*, ix.
[47] Haupt and Kocka, *Comparative and Transnational History*.
[48] Rathgen, *Beamtentum*, 83.

aware that other colonies were complex realms of experience that provided examples in certain fields only. ICI members agreed that, as one German scientist put it, "an expert is a man who has made all the mistakes which can be made, in a narrow field."[49] The ICI's philosophy was to let others make the mistakes and then to learn from their experience. A British agronomist, for example, envied the younger colonizers such as Germany and Italy as they "have the advantage of our experience as well as our mistakes to guide them."[50] Chailley thought along similar lines. Although he claimed that Algeria had been a total failure, and that also "the British have, in the course of their history, committed horrifying errors," he considered certain elements of French policy in Algeria or British colonial rule as exemplary.[51] Instead of advocating indiscriminate plagiarism, Chailley deliberately used the term "adaptation" to describe transfers of techniques between colonies as processes of methodological selection and adaptation.[52]

3.4 Using Comparisons: The Identification of Administrative Deficits

In the 1890s, ICI members identified the recruitment and training of colonial administrators to be the most deficient colonial technique. As Paul Leroy Beaulieu, Europe's most eminent theorist of colonization and the ICI's intellectual ancestor, wrote as early as 1874:

> More than any other country, France has committed capital errors in the recruitment of its colonial administrators. There are no rules except hazard and favoritism ... it is time for France to imitate the British and the Dutch and to create a corps of administrators who are specially chosen and instructed.[53]

Some fifteen years later, the European colonial reformers proceeded to action and professionalized the recruitment of specialized colonial administrators. Most initiatives came from ICI members. In 1893, Chailley established the ICI mainly to learn more about the recruitment of administrators in other countries. Between 1894 and 1900, the ICI published several shelf-filling volumes that analyzed the *Recruitment of Colonial Functionaries* in a comparative way. Those publications inspired other ICI members and led to a substantial reform of the training systems of all colonizing countries.[54] The reforms were

---

[49] Mackay, *A Dictionary*, 35.
[50] Barnes, "Agricultural Education," 71.
[51] Chailley, "Les Anglais," 842.
[52] Chailley, *Java* (1900), ix.
[53] Leroy-Beaulieu, *De la Colonisation*, 695. Cited in Singaravélou, *Professer l'Empire*, 46.
[54] It is interesting to see how the comparative knowledge on administration produced by the ICI, *Les Fonctionnaires* was reproduced in Cohen, *Rulers of Empire*, who also wrote an article on administration in the INCIDI's journal *Civilisations* in 1970. I used both the ICI

embedded in a European-wide project to professionalize colonial administration and thus protect it against criticism.[55] Reformers thought colonial "good governance" by professional and specialized administrators was crucial to mobilizing human and natural resources in the colonies.

The ICI tended to take the "best" from each system to mold the ideal European administrator. Such exemplary colonial administrators were supposed to combine three essential qualities. Against the background of the acclimatization debate, they needed physical and psychological preparation for extended sojourns in the tropics. Second, the new strategy to encourage the colonized population to participate in the administration required the knowledge of indigenous languages and culture. Third, the reformers wanted colonial officials to govern independently of the "unprofessional" and "ignorant" bureaucracy in Europe: they intended to relocate sovereignty and transfer from the metropole to the colony. There, expert administrators should be free to accumulate sovereignty or to redistribute it among their indigenous assistants. These three paradigms resulted in the three priorities assigned to the newly established colonial training schools: resilience (both moral and physical), anthropological knowledge, and autonomy.

In the early 1890s, hardly any colonizing country operated centralized and specialized schools to train civil servants for the colonies. Actually, neither France nor Germany had an autonomous colonial ministry. They treated colonial matters in the Naval and Foreign Ministry respectively. In 1889, the French established the École Coloniale as a training school for colonial administrators, but prior to World War I, the institution supplied only 15 percent of French colonial administrators.[56] In Germany, candidates provisionally attended seminars at the Commercial School and the Seminar for Oriental Languages in Berlin (1887), which taught mostly Asiatic languages to German diplomats.[57] The Seminar was far from being the colonial academy it often claimed to be. The only African language taught there was Swahili, the mother tongue in German East Africa. As late as 1912, only 2 percent of the 317 graduates had chosen Swahili, while the majority had learned Turkish or Eastern Asian languages.[58] Great Britain had kept the colonial administration decentralized, divided among the India Office, the Colonial Office, and the Sudan Political Service. The India Office was most developed but awaited restructuring and professionalization, while the Colonial Office did not take

---

and Cohen for the chapter on administration in my dissertation dating from 2016. Referring to the ICI and Cohen in 2018, Kwaschik, *Griff nach dem Weltwissen*, came to strikingly similar conclusions.

[55] Rathgen, *Beamtentum*, 46; Gann and Duignan, *The Rulers*, 57.
[56] Cohen, *Rulers of Empire*, 30. In general, see Delavignette, *Freedom*.
[57] BArch R2/42741, 45: Kolonialabtheilung, September [1908].
[58] Mangold, *Eine "Weltbürgerliche Wissenschaft,"* 234.

charge of important colonies, such as Northern and Southern Nigeria, until 1900.[59] According to historian John Darwin, it was not the official India or Colonial Offices but "the chaotic pluralism of private and sub-imperial interests" that was running the British Empire.[60] As there was no unified colonial service, there was no professional selection process. The Colonial Service chose its governors in secret sessions, and the selection of colonial administrators was a matter of patronage rather than competition.[61] The India Office, while establishing a competitive examination, recruited its employees among the graduates from public schools and Oxbridge and chose explicitly from among the "sons of fathers" who had already served in the Civil Service at home or in the colonies. After their graduation, the selected candidates went through a one-year phase of preparation, but the India Office did not maintain any special schools for administrators for the Crown Colony.[62] The Sudan Political Service – responsible for the government of the recently conquered Sudan regions – referred to a system of "athletocracy" by recruiting among the best sportsmen of public schools.[63] After Joseph Chamberlain had become the head of the Colonial Office in 1895, he could not but conclude that the service is "lamentably weak, both at home and abroad."[64] The weakness continued well into the twentieth century and was partly due to the liberal skepticism toward state centralization and the self-assertion of Oxbridge graduates who dominated the Colonial Service.[65]

Not even the highly prestigious British Colonial Service lived up to its own expectations, In the reform period between 1900 and 1914, more British delegates joined the ICI. Their presence showed that countries with a "prestigious" colonial service, such as Britain and the Netherlands, also saw the ICI as an instrument to (re)establish the reputation of colonial administrations.

3.5 Early Reforms between the Dutch Archetype and the Plurality of Prototypes

Unlike stereotypes about a regressive Spanish empire would make believe, the first initiative to reform corrupted colonial services came from the long-

---

[59] Kaminsky, *The India Office*, 16–17; Carland, *The Colonial Office*, 10.
[60] Darwin, "Imperialism and the Victorians," 641. His verdict is based on Robinson et al., *Africa and the Victorians*.
[61] For a controversial view on the topic, wee Porter, *The Absent-Minded Imperialists*. More concretely, see Gann and Duignan, *Rulers of British Africa*, 46 and 170; Kirk-Greene, *Britain's Imperial Administrators*, 179. There was, however, a competitive examination for the India Office.
[62] Kirk-Greene, *Britain's Imperial Administrators*, 15.
[63] Ibid., 168.
[64] Ibid., 52–53.
[65] Stockwell, *The British End*, 5–6.

standing Spanish Overseas Ministry in 1890. This was no coincidence. Administrative reforms were more likely to happen in colonies where an established Creole society contested the administrative interference by the metropole, such as in the Dutch East Indies in 1848 and in Cuba in 1890.[66] The crisis-ridden Spanish empire took the lead in reforming the careers of its colonial administrators as a direct response to the threat of imperial disintegration in Cuba.[67] The ongoing conflict between Cuban separatists and administrators who were loyal to Spain divided the colony. When the future ICI member Antonio Fabié became the head of the Overseas Ministry in 1890, he intended to grant autonomy rights to the separatist *criollos* (Spaniards born in Cuba), who had turned against the *peninsulares* (Spanish mainlanders), who monopolized the administration in Cuba. Fabié's reforms aimed at reconciliation with the Cuban *criollos* to stop the series of separatist wars and to reestablish the islands' economic productivity.[68] Autonomy rights should appease the independence movements and avoid outright independence at the same time.

Fabié tried to appease the radicalizing Cuban separatist movement by loosening the grip of the *peninsulares* on the administration and internal Cuban affairs.[69] Fabié blamed the "immoral" and corrupted *peninsulares* for using their administrative posts to accumulate wealth. In an unofficial report, the Overseas Ministry held them responsible for the loss of forty-four million pesos that went missing between 1880 and 1890.[70] Fabié set out to "purify" the administration and launched substantial reforms to make the administration "more efficient" and to reestablish "the rule of justice."[71] In particular, Fabié issued a law that made judges and fiscal officers in Cuba irremovable to guarantee their integrity.[72] To avoid nepotism, he introduced age restrictions for certain administrative positions. He prohibited the falsifications of accounts and receipts, a common practice of deception among corrupt colonial administrators.[73] Other administrative measures were supposed to trigger

---

[66] The ICI did not mention the Dutch case of 1848, however. See Bosma and Raben, *Being "Dutch,"* 188–206.
[67] On Cuba, see Pérez, *Cuba*.
[68] Balfour, *The End of the Spanish Empire*, 10; Schmidt-Nowara, *The Conquest of History*; McCoy et al., *Endless Empire*; Schmidt-Nowara and Nieto-Phillips, *Interpreting Spanish Colonialism*.
[69] Curiously, Fabié is ignored in Huetz de Lemps, *L'Archipel* and in Balfour, *Spanish Empire*, 9–10.
[70] Quiroz, "Corrupción, Burocracia Colonial," 105. The corruption caused outrage. See Cabrera, *Cuba y sus Jueces*; Schmidt-Nowara, "Imperio y Crisis Colonial," 31–90.
[71] Fabié, *Mi Gestion Ministerial*, 26–27.
[72] Ibid., 28.
[73] Resolución Adoptada por el Ministerio de Ultramar el 23. Septiembre 1890, cited in ibid., 50.

the development (*fomento* or *desarollo*) of the colonies, brought about by real experts who took the place of corrupt administrative elites.[74]

In the Philippines, his reform project of the 1890s comprised the formation of a "corps of specialized *funcionarios*," who spoke the "local languages and dialects."[75] Instead of assimilating colonial legislation to the metropolitan model, Fabié respected the *derecho indiano* (indigenous law), which he viewed as better adapted to local specificities. The model for his reforms in the Philippines was Dutch Java, a colony with a huge creole population that he admired for having combined political autonomy with a tariff system that increased the revenues of the metropole. While Fabié favored the colonies' restricted autonomy, he ruled out the possibility of full independence: the "Spanish family is one and indivisible," he claimed (by excluding the native *indios*). Instead, he pursued a straightforward protectionist economic policy.[76]

The *peninsulares*, who called themselves *Españoles incondicionales*, accused Fabié of introducing "self-government" to the Spanish colonies.[77] At their instigation, he had to resign as a colonial minister. His successors withdrew essential regulations of his legislation and his adversaries seized power.[78] The international community in general and the ICI in particular had regarded Fabié's reforms with interest. But the relapse into the vices of the old Empire – monopoly exploitation and genocidal warfare against Cuban separatists in the 1890s– earned the Spanish harsh criticism.[79] The ICI, in particular, deplored the failure of Fabié's progressive reforms of administrative autonomy.[80] According to ICI members, its failure anticipated the end of the Spanish empire, which took effect as the United States defeated Spain in 1898.[81]

Seen from the point of view of comparative colonialists, the French did a better job, especially because Chailley and Paul Leroy-Beaulieu, colonial reformer and the first member of the ICI, propagated the Dutch archetype as a model, while combining it with prototype-transfers from German and British recruitment for colonial service.[82] Three years after Fabié's reforms in Spain, Chailley received 500 francs from the French colonial authorities, on condition of preparing a detailed report for Paris of how to model colonial

---

[74] Fabié, *Mi Gestion Ministerial*, 53.
[75] Ibid., 646.
[76] Ibid., 10 and 21.
[77] Ibid., 44 and 647.
[78] ICI, *Les Fonctionnaires*, viii, 16–36.
[79] Lewis, *On the Government*, lix, 148–149; Fabié, *Mi Gestion Ministerial*, 579.
[80] ICI, *Les Fonctionnaires*, viii, 16–36.
[81] Hopkins, *American Empire*, 337–440.
[82] Cohen, *Rulers*, 18 and 38.

training on the Dutch example.[83] Chailley's mission was part of a program to restructure French colonial administration, launched in the late 1880s by undersecretary of state in the Ministry of the Navy and the Colonies, Eugène Étienne. In 1889, Étienne had established the École Coloniale in Paris as a professional school for administrators but had dashed Chailley's expectations to become its first director.[84] Nevertheless, he conceded and ultimately allowed Chailley to travel to Holland.[85] After Étienne resigned from his post in 1893, Chailley denounced Étienne's École Coloniale as a laudable project, which had nevertheless epically failed to produce professional administrators. Jumping on the bandwagon of colonial reform, Chailley visited the Dutch Colonial Ministry interviewed officials in charge, studied the relevant literature, and participated in the dinner that led to the foundation of the ICI.

French colonizers had closely followed the Dutch passage from the *kontors* of the East Indies Company to the establishment of professional colonial schools in Delft (1842–1900) and Leiden (1864–1891).[86] While the training school in Delft had operated since 1842, the colonial reformer and co-founder of the ICI Fransen van de Putte had reorganized the education of Dutch colonial administrators in the 1860s. He had created the Leiden colonial school in 1864 and introduced a mandatory and central exam for colonial administrators (*groot-ambtenaarsexamen*).[87] Long-serving colonial administrators designed and oversaw this centralized and standardized exam, which Dutch citizens could pass either in the metropole or in Batavia. The competitive examination in the *groot-ambtenaarsexamen* became a prototype of successful expert selection and training. Chailley valued it higher than the competitive examination of the India Office (which was the only competitive recruitment examination in Europe apart from the Dutch great exam).[88] In his report to the French colonial authorities, Chailley lauded the Dutch system for giving priority to specialization, autonomy, and anthropological knowledge – characteristics that the British India Office allegedly lacked.

What was so exceptional about the Dutch training of colonial officials? Most importantly, it was mandatory for candidates to take the great exam to familiarize Dutch candidates with the indigenous culture and use it as a tool

---

[83] ANOM FM MIS//63/bis, Folder 1, "Chailley Bert, Mission aux Pays-Bas en vue d'étudier le mode de recrutement des fonctionnaires coloniaux": Jamais to Chailley, October 5, 1892.

[84] It had served as a seminary for Indochinese students before and had a "native section" throughout its existence. See Cohen, *Rulers of Empire*, 37. On the context, see Kwaschik, *Der Griff nach dem Weltwissen*, 52–63.

[85] ANOM FM MIS//63/bis, Folder 1, "Chailley Bert, Mission aux Pays-Bas," Letter Etienne to Chailley, January 20, 1892.

[86] Chailley, *La Hollande*, 18.

[87] "Koninklijk Beslut van 10 September 1864," *Ned. Staatsblad*, 93.

[88] For a detailed description of the Indian Civil Service, see Gilmour, *The Ruling Caste*.

for indirect rule. The curriculum comprised history, geography, and ethnography of the Dutch East Indies, as well as Muslim law, local customs, and indigenous administration. Future administrators had to speak at least one vernacular, either Malay or Javanese.[89] The ICI highlighted that they "learn and perfectly speak the indigenous languages."[90] The exam took place annually and was open to "Dutch citizens, indigenous subjects of Holland and children born to parents of European civilization dwelling in the East Indies." While the Dutch colonial ministry recruited two-thirds of the administrators in the metropole, Chailley concluded that it chose the rest among the Creole candidates in the Dutch Indies (this perception was probably wrong, as there were Creoles who took the exam in Europe and then returned to Indonesia).[91] To be adequately prepared, the Dutch gave administrators their training in Europe before they sent them to the colonies for an apprenticeship.[92]

Dutch administrators enjoyed a comparably ample amount of autonomy from the metropole. Once the Colonial Ministry had assigned the graduates a post in the Indies, the governor-general in Batavia was free to employ them – without interference by The Hague. This regulation strengthened the autonomy of the authorities overseas and allowed the governor-general to react quickly to temporary needs. Colonial experts all over Europe praised this autonomy as a guarantee for effective administration. Chailley contrasted it to the authoritarian French approach. For fear of autonomy and the accumulation of power, Paris controlled district officers more closely and forced them to swap posts every two years.[93] This so-called *rouage* led to a high turnover among the "kings of the bush" – as wary observers in the metropole called the officials in the colonies – and kept them from engaging themselves in local languages and customs.[94]

Adding to autonomy in the Dutch empire was flexibility. While regular administrators of the Dutch East Indies had to pass the great exam, Batavia recruited legal specialists and technical experts straight from universities and technical schools. Lawyers, botanists, and foresters went directly to occupy technical posts in the Dutch Indies. For want of specialized schools in botany and forestry, the Dutch even sent their trainees to high-tech schools in

---

[89] "Koninklijk Beslut van 20 Juli 1893," *Ned. Staatsblad* 117, cited in ICI, *Les Fonctionnaires*, vol. 2, 50.
[90] ICI, *Compte Rendu 1895*, 375.
[91] Chailley, *La Hollande*, 43; Bosma and Raben, *Being "Dutch,"* 186 and 192.
[92] Few "creole" children entered the *Binnenlands Bestuur*. See ibid., 132.
[93] Studies on the French colonial service remain largely biographical and autobiographical. See Colombani, *Mémoires Coloniales*; Simonis, *Le Commandant en Tournée*; Clauzel, *La France*. Going beyond biographies: Dimier, "Formation des administrateurs."
[94] Girault, "Rapport sur la Surveillance à Éxcercer," in ICI, *Compte Rendu 1908*, 290; See also Bouche, *Histoire de la Colonisation*, 135.

3.5 EARLY REFORMS

Germany, before they embarked for the Indies.[95] For the Dutch authorities, the expertise of colonial administrators was often more important than national belonging, which shows their inclination to the autonomy of colonial experts.

Chailley was aware that the Dutch recruitment system was not without errors and considered it only the "least imperfect of all," together with the British system.[96] His main criticism was the age of Dutch candidates and the lack of a physical test. Unlike the British Service that accepted candidates between nineteen and twenty-two only, there was no age restriction for the Dutch Colonial Service Chailley assumed that many Dutch recruits might be "too young to reassert themselves in the colonies or too old and lacking suppleness."[97] Without any age restriction that guaranteed resistance to the demoralizing milieu in the tropics, they would become a risk for the administration. Moreover, Chailley noted, the Dutch had failed to test the candidates' physical or moral aptitudes. Here again, the British cut a better figure by introducing moral tests for their civil servants (or guaranteed "morality" by recruiting the elite from universities). Chailley deemed it unlikely that such tested administrators were abusive toward the colonial subjects or ridiculed "the good reputation of the metropole" through misbehavior.[98]

In terms of physical tests, both the German and the British model stood out. They came closest to the ICI's recommendation by extending the physical entrance tests formerly ensured by the army to the civil administrators as well, in an effort to assure the candidates' resistance to changing environmental conditions.[99] German authorities, in particular, attached great importance to the medical test and even forged a new term to describe it: all candidates had to present themselves to the colonial authorities in Berlin to have their *Tropendiensttauglichkeit* – the suitability for longer sojourns in the tropics – certified by a single official physician, Dr. Steudel.[100] The negative counterpart was the *Tropendienstuntauglichkeit*, a legal term describing a medical status of life-threatening incompatibility with the tropical environment. Before sending candidates to the colonies, the doctor and his team vetted the candidates on the viability of heart, lungs, nervous systems, and visual and auditory organs. He also tested their tolerance of quinine. Steudel rejected candidates both for racist and for moral reasons. Arguing along racist lines, he tended to veto blond Europeans because they seemed to be more vulnerable in the tropics than Southern Europeans. Dismissing candidates who drank alcohol or

---

[95] Chailley, *La Hollande*, 81.
[96] Ibid., 86.
[97] Ibid., 21–22.
[98] Ibid., 25.
[99] ICI, *Compte Rendu 1895*, 292.
[100] Tesch, *Laufbahn*, 23; Haarhaus, *Das Recht*, 18.

smoked, the only vice accepted was the corpulence of "moderately adipose persons suitable for colonial service."[101]

Unlike the Germans, who established clear criteria for fitness, British authorities adhered to a holistic concept of general education and cultivated equestrian sports and cricket as an integral preparation for colonial service. Sports games were part of the public schools' ideology to form British students' character during their university career. Experts argued that it had the side-effect of strengthening the physique before they left for the colonies and helped them to maintain it on the spot. The British colonial administration became famous for explicitly recruiting administrators among those who had succeeded in rugby, rowing, cricket, athletics, or hockey competitions between Oxford and Cambridge.[102]

Not all colonial experts subscribed to the certified health. Bacteriologists at tropical institutes were naturally skeptical regarding the British obsession with holism. They promised to immunize Europeans through exogenous medication by drugs and vaccination, rather than by autogenous training of body strength. In their laboratories, they had identified the exogenous parasites to be the reason for tropical diseases – consequently they had to be contained with "exogenous" counteragents. Their findings made the prediction of *Tropendiensttauglichkeit* through health certificates unlikely. Indeed, much to the chagrin of the colonial authorities, the *Tropendienstuntauglichkeit* often developed only in the colonies, although doctors in Europe had pronounced administrators healthy in Europe. Thys, who had been at pains to recruit engineers and workers for the construction of the Congo railway, complained about this impossibility of testing the Europeans' *Tropendiensttauglichkeit*: "It is a bit like buying a razor blade: you can only tell if it is good after having used it."[103]

Despite this insecurity, all colonial powers introduced medical tests after 1900. The French and Dutch colonial reformers, inspired by the British enthusiasm for sports, incorporated sports in general and equestrian sports in particular in the candidates' curricula.[104] In many ways, this policy contradicted their proclaimed agenda of relying on indigenous cooperators.

3.6 The Era of Reform Around 1908

Back in France, Chailley's 1893 report on the Dutch system caused a great stir. Given that the French colonial administration was a branch of the Naval

---

[101] Tesch, *Laufbahn*, 24.
[102] Gayffier-Bonneville, "La Formation des Administrateurs," 36; Gann and Duignan, *Rulers of British Africa*, 200.
[103] ICI, *Compte Rendu 1897*, 103.
[104] Rathgen, *Beamtentum*, 72.

Ministry, reformers warned that they lagged behind the Dutch, the British, and even the Spanish: "The subordination of colonial matter to the views of the marine and war strategies is, in reality, one of the principal reasons for the stagnation of our colonial possessions."[105]

The French government reacted. In 1894, one year after Chailley had submitted his report, France established an autonomous colonial ministry.[106] In 1896, the École Coloniale introduced entrance examinations to guarantee the quality of its students, and the candidates had to compete for colonial posts in a *concours*, provided that they held a certificate of moral and physical suitability.[107] To prepare colonial administrators, Chailley personally gave classes on comparative colonialism at the École Libre des Sciences Politiques, a university that soon rivaled the École Coloniale as an institution to train colonial administrators. There, Chailley offered courses on anthropology and overseas legislation. His comparative approach inspired Lyautey to establish a system of "associationist" indirect rule in Morocco after 1912. Chailley had recommended that the "natives" should fill the lower ranks of administration to avoid the import of a "European proletariat" of underpaid functionaries. Yet Chailley also made clear that privileges of the administrative profession applied to Europeans only. They should be paid sufficiently and receive an old-age pension.[108]

Unlike Chailley's classes, the École Coloniale failed to teach indigenous languages, customs, and ethnography. The first director, Paul Dislère, preferred teaching European law instead of indigenous laws and withdrew ethnography from the curriculum.[109] Although Dislère was an expert in Dutch colonial policy and corresponded with Dutch plantation companies on new methods in the production of indigo, tobacco, and quinine in Java, he did not embrace the idealized Dutch system of a participative colonial state.[110] Anthropological elements such as language courses in the native idioms were rare and remained a significant lacuna in the preparatory classes. Only later did teachers like the famous anthropologist Maurice Delafosse bring the École Coloniale's curriculum in line with the Dutch model.[111] Delafosse, a future member of the ICI and famous *indigènologue*, had proven Africa's old-age civilization by translating Arabic sources on the region, notably the famous *Tarikh al-Fettach*, which familiarized Europeans with the history of the

---

[105] Leroy-Beaulieu, *De la Colonisation*, 740.
[106] Chailley, *La Hollande*, 10.
[107] Enders, "L'École Nationale," 272.
[108] ANOM, FP 100APOM/321: Lettres Chailley à Lyautey, Folder: Maroc Situation Politique 1917–1918: "Notes Cours 1917–1918: Le Maroc et ... l'Administration d'un Peuple Protégé."
[109] Cohen, *Rulers of Empire*, 37–48.
[110] ANOM, Min. des Colonies, École Coloniale, Fonds Paul Dislère FR ANOM 122COL13.
[111] Cohen, *Rulers of Empire*, 48.

Songhai Empire.[112] Under his auspices, the École Coloniale introduced courses in West African Manding languages in 1910.[113] By 1912, the École Coloniale – soon to be endearingly called "Colo" – finally established a precarious monopoly over the training of French colonial administrators.

While Chailley's journey to the Netherlands prompted colonial reforms in France, his reports also inspired the Dutch to remodel their own colonial training.[114] They abandoned the time-honored Delft school to the profit of a reformed colonial school, affiliated with the university in Leiden. Candidates were now able to take courses offered at the university and benefited from the diversity of language courses and the anthropological disciplines that had found their way into Dutch academia. To standardize the training and centralize it in Europe, they closed down all training schools for higher civil servants in the East Indies.[115] Moreover, they followed Chailley's advice to imitate the British system by introducing an age limit, as well as physical and moral tests for the candidates.[116] Finally, they launched a debate about how to make indirect rule more efficient, inspired by Chailley's recommendation to make use of the established but restricted class of an indigenous aristocracy, instead of relying on representatives of *"de kleine man"* (the common people).[117] He made similar recommendations to the British.

Chailley and the ICI also led the British to reform the recruitment of their colonial administrators. They realized that recruiting colonial officials among the educated elite in Oxford or Cambridge would result in the formation of "scholars rather than administrators."[118] Indeed, by 1908, three-fourths of the British colonial servants had graduated from Oxford or Cambridge.[119] The earliest training school for colonial administrators, the Haileybury College (1806–1855) had modeled its curriculum on the liberal arts education at Cambridge University.[120] Even Thomas Babington Macaulay's reorganization of British colonial training in the 1850s had hardly touched upon the ideal of holistic elite formation, promoting a classic Oxbridge education that privileged Greek and Latin over Arabic and Hindi.[121] Convinced that modern science and rationality can only be expressed through European languages, Macaulay

---

[112] Delafosse *Haut-Sénégal-Niger*; Amselle and Sibeud, *Maurice Delafosse*.
[113] Cohen, *Rulers of Empire*, 48.
[114] Deventer, "Drie Boeken over Indië," 145–146; Hasselmann, "De Practische Resultaten," 155–166.
[115] Bosma and Raben, *Being "Dutch,"* 300.
[116] Chailley, *La Hollande*, 25–26; ICI, *Les Fonctionnaires*, vol. 3, 14.
[117] Deventer, "Drie Boeken over Indië," 149.
[118] ICI, *Compte Rendu 1895*, 331–332.
[119] Rathgen, *Beamtentum*, 65. Ninety-three percent had attended public schools. See Kirk-Greene, *Britain's Imperial Administrators*, 17.
[120] Lowell, *Colonial Civil Service*, 12.
[121] ICI, *Compte Rendu 1895*, 326; Rathgen, *Beamtentum*, 57–61.

3.6 THE ERA OF REFORM AROUND 1908

had dismissed indigenous languages as negligible. According to Chailley, the British "Macaulayism" lingered on in the 1890s.[122] Indeed, the US Taft report confirmed in 1903 that the competitive examinations to enter the Civil Service in India gave more credit to those who excelled in Greek or Latin (750 marks each) than to those who learned Sanskrit or Arabic (500 marks each), with the former being compulsory and the latter optional.[123] Instructors at the Colonial Institute in Hamburg even ridiculed the British for producing "Renaissance men" and "human encyclopedias." Modern administrators, they claimed, should be "less humanistic and more realistic."[124]

These charges against the British did not go unnoticed across the channel, especially because an internal reform movement thought the same way. Chamberlain had already initiated a review committee. Referring to its result, he introduced pre-posting training for British administrators. Knowing that it was hard to find staff for service in unhealthy colonies, however, no one wanted to introduce a difficult exam that deterred young British gentlemen from making a colonial career.[125] Thus, under Chamberlain, patronage prevailed and exams were pro forma. Between 1908 and 1925, pre-posting training was centered in the Imperial Institute in South Kensington, London.[126] Not an official training school, the Imperial Institute offered no more than rudimentary courses in hygiene, penal law, civil law, accounting, and tropical agriculture.[127]

More importantly, the ICI's *spiritus rector* Joseph Chailley became the initiator of reforms in British India. After extended travels in 1900/1 and 1904/5, he published an in-depth study about the British crown colony, under the title *L'Inde Britannique* (1910). He wrote the account in close cooperation with both British and Indian officials he had met on his journey and registered their grievances and complaints. In this 500-page volume, he regarded British India with sympathy but lamented the deep social cleft between the British officials and the Indian society. He urged the British to accept more Indians into the administration. In 1910, the secretary of state for India, Lord Morley, had Chailley's report translated into English, under the more discriminating title *Administrative Problems of British India*. Chailley's close friend and informant, the secretary of the Financial Department in India and ICI member Sir William Meyer, translated the book into English. Meyer's English version

---

[122] Gann and Duignan remarked that administrators were "adaptable." See Gann and Duignan, *Rulers of British Africa*, 51.
[123] "Examination for the Civil Service in India," cited in US Dept. of the Treasury, *Colonial Administration*, 1268–1271.
[124] Zache, *Die Ausbildung*, 8–9.
[125] Jeffries, *Colonial Empire*, 12.
[126] Kirk-Greene, *Britain's Imperial Administrators*, 133; Golant, *Image of Empire*.
[127] Rathgen, *Beamtentum*, 73; ICI, *Compte Rendu 1895*, 334 and 340.

resembled occasionally a reinterpretation rather than a translation and inflated Chailley's latent criticism of the British system. Given Meyer's influence on the writing and translation of the book, it included a good deal of British auto-criticism. The publication became a standard reference for British rule in India and cemented his reputation as a contributor to a "solid and self-supporting dominion in the East."[128]

With regard to the "native policy," it condemned the British assimilative policy of educating mostly Hindus at Anglo-Indian universities. Instead of creating "men fit for subordinate official posts," the author(s) complained, the British assimilation policy had produced fervent adversaries to British rule and politicized "intellectuals" who tried to beat the British at their own game.[129] Instead of assimilating the literate Hindus and teaching them European-style general "intelligence," *Administrative Problems of British India* recommended making use of the traditional Muslim nobility, who supposedly had ruled the subcontinent for ages. They had a historically acquired "character" to rule as intermediaries and could be used for executive tasks – instead of producing assimilated, but potentially subversive, Hindus. Indeed, by 1900, Indian Muslims had only made up 5 percent of the higher administrative positions held by Indians. Chailley advised the British to increase their number and to use them as executive forces, who "accepted" British supremacy, just as Snouck Hurgonje had done it in the Dutch possessions.[130] British administrators gladly embraced these ideas. Henry Boy Scotts of the Bengal Civil Service, for example, wrote after visiting Java: "Unquestionably a study of Java and of its government is one of the first duties of an Indian governor, and if that is fairly undertaken it will lead, I think, inevitably to this conclusion, that in many matters it is a mistake to insist that our Oriental subjects should conform to our Western ideas."[131]

The ICI loomed even larger in the reform of German colonial training. Germany did not operate any central educational institution. Since 1893, candidates for the colonial service had to go through the three-month fast-track course at the Seminar for Oriental Languages in Berlin.[132] Physicians were prepared at the Hamburg Institute for Naval and Tropical Diseases, and botanists received some practical learning at the botanical gardens in Berlin.[133]

---

[128] Strachey, *India*, ix–x.
[129] Chailley, *Administrative Problems*, 562.
[130] Ibid., 203, 561–566. For the view of a British ICI member on the impact, see Lyall, "Islam in India," in Lyall, *Asiatic Studies*, translated into French as *Etudes Sur les Moeurs Religieuses et Sociales de l'Extrême-Orient* (Paris, 1907–1908); Eckert, *Herrschen und Verwalten*, 37.
[131] Boys, *Some Notes on Java*, iii–iv.
[132] Tesch, *Laufbahn*, 25; Haarhaus, *Das Recht*, 42.
[133] Zache, *Die Ausbildung*, 5; Haarhaus, *Das Recht*, 41–42; Tesch, *Laufbahn*, 26.

3.6 THE ERA OF REFORM AROUND 1908

On the initiative of German ICI members, the city of Hamburg established the Colonial Institute as a university for colonial studies in 1908.[134] Launched by the German Colonial Society, and partly funded by the new Colonial Office (1907), the ICI member Karl Rathgen became its first director and turned it into the most eminent colonial training center in Germany.[135] Rathgen based the Colonial Institute's organization on the comparative studies published by the ICI and consulted its members on how to organize a training school that was at the same time a research institution.[136]

In his opening address at the Colonial Institute, he echoed Chailley's stereotypes by blaming the British system for producing "gentlemen" and "universitymen," who lacked specialized knowledge. If the British even privileged sports over indigenous languages, Rathgen moaned, it did not stand up as a model of modern schooling.[137] He cited his British colleagues in the ICI, Sir Hubert Jerningham and Alfred Lyall, to testify as witnesses that in Britain "until today, a colonial education does not exist and has never existed."[138] Only the detailed knowledge of indigenous languages, their customs and laws, and their religion and superstitions, Rathgen continued, allowed the Europeans to rule, while the "ignoramus" administrator was doomed to fail. In his view, colonial administrators faced new, demanding responsibilities, such as tax-raising, infrastructure measures, and the protection of indigenous labor, all subsumed under the overall goal of the development (*Nutzbarmachung*) of the colonies.[139] By copying successful strategies of other colonial powers and avoiding their errors, Rathgen hoped to realize a colonial university that accorded with the ICI's priorities.

Despite his fierce criticism of the British training, Rathgen borrowed from the recently reformed institutions in Britain and the Netherlands. He studied the courses offered by the British Imperial Institute on hygiene, law, and accounting. Another model was a colonial school created by Dutch colonial minister Fock, a member of the ICI, in 1908. Fock's school offered postgraduate training for a small administrative elite of advanced officers who had already served between six and ten years in the colonies. In the spirit of professional development, they studied comparative colonial administration, economy, finance, statistics, and law, with the purpose of making exploitation and administration more efficient. While Rathgen considered the Dutch

---

[134] Ruppenthal, *Kolonialismus*.
[135] Rathgen, *Beamtentum*, 39.
[136] Ibid., 88.
[137] Ibid., 65.
[138] Ibid., 39 and 88. Jerningham's and Lyall's quotes can be found in ICI, *Compte Rendu 1905*, 283 and 278.
[139] Ibid., 43.

in-service training exemplary, he was more skeptical toward the French École Coloniale.[140] Although he respected its graduates, he dismissed its inflexible and strict curriculum prior to the anthropological reforms instigated by Maurice Delafosse.[141] Rather than taking the École Coloniale as a model for the Colonial Institute, Rathgen praised the colonial institutes that local chambers of commerce had established in Marseille, Lyon, Bordeaux, Nantes, Havre, and Nancy.[142] However, Hamburg's inclination to commerce did not lower the desire to turn its Colonial Institute into a training school for administrators and an academic research institute.

When the Colonial Institute in Hamburg began to function in 1908, its eclectic character reflected these experiences made in other colonizing countries. Thirty-two lecturers taught history, law, economy, languages, geography (*Landeskunde*), ethnography (*Völkerkunde*), and hygiene. Its inclination to colonial research and its academic ambitions are evident in the fact that it developed into the official Hamburg University. This derived from Rathgen's double purpose of conveying technical knowledge and engaging in scientific research alike:[143] Arthur Girault, a French member of the ICI, had advised Rathgen on offering colonial doctorates, because the introduction of colonial dissertations in France had also vitalized colonial science as a whole.[144] Like in France and in the Netherlands, the promotion of an explicitly colonial science at European universities and the formation of specialized colonial administrators went hand in hand.

The prerogatives of the Colonial Institute represented the reformist zeal that the ICI had kicked off in Europe. The professional education of colonial administrators, Europeans now agreed, consisted of a solid preparation in European universities, aiming at the "knowledge" of the indigenous cultures and the *mise en valeur* of colonial territories. While mastering indigenous languages was indispensable, accounting, statistics, administrative law, and economic management outranked Maucaulayist and Humboldtian ideals of classic education. A flexible curriculum – composed by the candidates according to their chosen position and destiny – was crucial to allow for individual specialization and ultimately efficient administration.

---

[140] Ibid., 73.
[141] Ibid., 79.
[142] Regional institutes, especially the Institut Colonial in Marseille, held close ties with the ICI because they were internal rivals of the colonial elite in Paris. See Heckel and Cyprien, *L'Enseignement Colonial*, introduction; and Klein, "La Création de l'École Coloniale de Lyon," 158.
[143] Haarhaus, *Das Recht*, 44–45.
[144] Rathgen, *Beamtentum*, 51.

3.7 Ousting Indigenous Administrators

Curiously, when ICI members initiated the reform of colonial administrations in the mid-1890s, their focus on *European* candidates led them to neglect and even repress indigenous administrators.[145] The Dutch reforms, in particular, worked to the detriment of the Indonesians. The number of Europeans who arrived in the Dutch Indies doubled around 1900. Mostly well-educated, they occupied higher administrative positions and the new jobs created by the ethical policy inaugurated in 1901. The military academy and training schools in Batavia and Semarang closed down and deprived Creoles and indigenous Indonesians of the opportunity to sneak into an administrative career. The government also blighted the initiative of Djajadiningrat and others to establish a university that was open to Indonesians (only in 1920 did it allow the formation of the Technical University in Bandung).[146] Chailley observed that the Dutch law from 1867 regarding indigenous participation had remained *lettre morte*. Between 1864 and 1893, the Dutch administration had admitted only one Indonesian – a noble vizir's grandson of the Yogyakarta sultanate – to the higher division.[147]

Europeans who occupied the upper ranks never fully handed over the reins to Indonesians. As Snouck Hurgronje, who had helped Indonesians to hold higher posts in the colonial administration complained in 1908:

> The number of European civil servants has been steadily increasing, and their involvement has spread to more and more aspects of administrative duties. The Inland chiefs have become more civil servants than before, but their role in administrative duties has increased honor in subordination rather than independence; in the administrative family they form, so to speak, the category of children and servants.[148]

Although the Dutch administration was said to rely heavily on Indonesian subalterns, the training for the *groot-ambtenaarsexamen* ousted Indonesian intermediaries. Chailley pointed out that the teaching of Malay and Javanese languages, as well as Indonesian culture and law, enabled Europeans to understand and control Indonesian subaltern officers. Hence, Dutch candidates who excelled in Javanese or Malay were among the first to be chosen for the colonial service, regardless of the grades they received in the other disciplines.[149] Thanks to their language skills, Chailley argued, the Dutch did not have to rely on unreliable interpreters whose power was a steady concern in

---

[145] Stoler, *Race and the Education*, 44.
[146] Bosma and Raben, *Being "Dutch,"* 300 and 314–320.
[147] Chailley, *La Hollande*, 20.
[148] Snouck Hurgronje, "De Inlandsche Bestuursambtenaren," 215.
[149] "Koninklijk Beslut van 20 Juli 1893, e" *Ned. Staatsblad* 117, cited in ICI, *Les Fonctionnaires*, vol. 2, 50.

most empires.[150] Paradoxically, the Dutch reform relegated the Indonesians to second rank and deprived them of agency.

Indonesian officials who remained in their positions were underpaid, as Raden Adjeng Kartini reported in one of her letters:

> Many native officials are so ill-paid that it is a wonder how they can get along at all on their meagre salaries, A district registrar who all day long writes his back crooked, earns at the end of the month, the incredibly large sum of 25 florins. On that he and his family must live, and pay house rent; he must dress himself neatly, and also keep up his prestige over the lesser officials.[151]

Those in rural areas, Kartini added, "must keep a little carriage and a horse ... for journeys into the country" and were responsible for the "entertainment of the Comptroller, the Regents, and sometimes also the Assistant-Resident when they come on tours of inspection."[152] Given the lack of an adequate salary and old-age pensions, she understood well why corruption gained ground among them.

In France, the École Coloniale equally contributed to exclude non-Europeans from becoming professional administrators. From 1886 onwards, the École Cambodgienne in Paris had trained thirteen upper-class Cambodians to become administrators. When the École Coloniale replaced the École Cambodgienne in 1893, it focused on the training of young French candidates rather than educating non-European collaborators. While the École Coloniale maintained an indigenous section and a quota for Cambodian students, the quality of their classes deteriorated and their education became insignificant.[153] In British West Africa, this policy turned into numbers. In 1883, "the Gold Coast Africans held nine of the 43 highest posts in Government," whereas "in 1908, only five of the colony's 274 officers were Africans."[154]

One reason for this policy was that reformers established training schools in Europe only. Despite all reforms, Indians had to take the entrance exam for the British Indian Civil Service in Europe, and in the 1890s, no more than four to five Indians succeeded every year.[155] Despite the plea for a practical, professional, and native-oriented education, the ICI members advised against transferring training schools to the colonies. The German Rathgen, for example, valued preparatory classes in Europe over training schools in the

---

[150] For example, see Trotha, *Koloniale Herrschaft*, 186.
[151] Kartini, *Letters*, 33.
[152] Ibid., 34.
[153] Edwards, *Cambodge*, 74–75.
[154] In contrast, a quarter of the Indian Civil Service consisted of non-Europeans by 1937. See Anderson and Cohen, *The Government*, xix.
[155] Lowell, *Colonial*, 42.

colonies.[156] Only after a comprehensive training in Europe should candidates complete an "internship" in the colonies.[157] Also in German colonies, like in Cameroon, the number of civil servants from the metropole tripled between 1905 and 1914.[158] The same goes for British colonies. In 1901, "the administrative staffs of Northern and Southern Nigeria together amounted to about fifty officers. By 1905, they had increased to over 150, and by 1909 to over 250."[159] Around that time, the colonial ministries sent hundreds of European "experts" to the colonies to prove their will to professionalization. Belgium sent hundreds of medical officers after it took over the Congo from Léopold's private predatory system, showing its will to implement a "positive" colonialism. In British West Africa, the Medical Service established in 1902 excluded Africans, while European medical staff soared to 120 in 1905 and steadily rose to 170 in 1909. At the same time, the British claimed that the death rate among European administrators in West Africa decreased: "it was 20.6 per thousand in 1903, fell to 12.8 per thousand in 1924." The news made more and more British men join the colonial service.[160]

The focus on training within Europe originated in the imagined fear of immoralized and separatist societies overseas. Following the ICI's traditional anti-settlerism, its members apprehended the influence of immoral settlers who might infiltrate the administration, also to the detriment of the indigenous population. Only a preparation in Europe, one member of the ICI claimed, ensured the administrators' morality and respect toward the indigenous majority. They needed to acquire a "spirit of absolute impartiality" in Europe, to prevent them from favoring European settler interests over native needs, as it had happened in the self-governing British settler colonies.[161] This remark unveiled the ICI's concerns with separatist settler movements that had emerged in the British dominions. It exposed that the ICI's program of colonial autonomy was not meant to be a settler project but a rule of independent experts.

A second explanation for the Europeanization of colonial training is the rise of colonial and anthropological research at European universities around 1900. While the training within Europe provided for a solid general education, it increasingly provided the possibility for anthropological and linguistic specialization. Newly founded departments at European universities offered specialized classes in colonial science, languages, and anthropology. Following Chailley's report on Dutch colonial training, for example, the Delft colonial

---

[156] Rathgen, *Beamtentum*, 52.
[157] Ibid.
[158] Hausen, *Deutsche Kolonialherrschaft*, 120.
[159] Jeffries, *Colonial Empire*, 18.
[160] Ibid., xix and 17. See also Perham, *Native Administration*.
[161] ICI, *Comtpe Rendu 1895*, 402.

school in the Netherlands closed down (in 1900), to the benefit of a more diverse program at Leiden University.[162] At Leiden and Hamburg, future administrators could learn most indigenous languages spoken in the colonies, together with their law. The French also diversified their anthropological and linguistic program, for example, at the École française d'Éxtreme Orient.[163] Candidates for the Sudan Service in Britain received anthropological training from 1908 onwards.[164] This integration of colonial careers into a diversified metropolitan academia rooted training in Europe.

Thirdly, the ICI favored internationalization over indigenization. The Colonial Institute in Hamburg accepted visiting students from Britain, Belgium, and the Netherlands but no inhabitants of their own colonies.[165] In all countries, the reformed curricula stipulated that candidates for colonial service had to speak English, more than any other language, before they left for the colonies.[166] At international colonial congresses, ICI members presented plans for a École Coloniale et Mondiale situated either at the International Agricultural Institute in Rome or at colonial museums in Tervuren, Washington, and Berlin.[167] Belgian administrators came closest to establishing an international training school in Brussels.[168] Cyrill van Overbergh, an internationalist and future editor of the *Mouvement sociologique international*, designed an "École Mondiale" in Tervuren, funded by the revenues from the Congo Free State. He wanted it to be a comprehensive international university that dedicated one out of three departments to instructing specialists destined for the Congo. Van Overbergh foresaw a general training in sports, morality, languages, and administration, as well as specialized careers for colonial cooks and experts in railway metaling. It should be open to all Europeans, who were supposed to study there between two months and three years.[169] Léopold II was about to inaugurate the school when he had to abdicate as the head of the Congo Free State in 1908. With his abdication, Belgium put the project aside and only partly realized it in 1920, when the Union of International Associations revived the project and established a School for International Affairs.[170] By then, the

---

[162] ICI, *Les Fonctionnaires Coloniaux*, 27; Rathgen, *Beamtentum*, 70.
[163] ICI, *Comtpe Rendu 1895*, 419; Singaravélou, "L'Enseignement Supérieur Colonial," 71–92.
[164] Cohen, *Government and Administration*.
[165] StaHa 364-366 Kolonialinstitut, 203 Besichtigung des Instituts durch Fremde, 5–6.
[166] For Germany, see BArch R2/42741: Bedingungen zur Auswahl von Bewerbern der Kolonial-Beamten-Laufbahn 1905. For Belgium, see Heckel and Cyprien, *L'Enseignement Colonial*, 180.
[167] Wildeman "Ce qui devait être un Insitut Colonial et Mondial," 1–5.
[168] Clerck, "L'Administration Coloniale Belge," 189.
[169] Overbergh, *École Mondiale*.
[170] Rathgen, *Beamtentum*, 89; CO 830 323, Foreign Office, 386: Union des Associations Internationales, March 12, 1920.

League of Nations was searching for experienced staff, without having its own training schools. No wonder they also recruited ICI members for sections concerning the colonized territories, abolition, and tropical hygiene.

3.8 Lobbying for Higher Salaries and Old-Age Pensions

During the professionalization process, it turned out that the main purpose of ICI experts was to secure a decent living for themselves, during and after their service. Even the three priorities that they advanced in the training of administrators – physical and moral health, anthropological knowledge, and autonomy – were often no more than an excuse to request higher wages and old-age pensions. One of the most important arguments in favor of higher wages was to guarantee the "moral health" of the administrators.

No institution other than the ICI, staffed with former administrators and ambitious reformers, was more credible when it stated that colonial administrators were "human and not all heroes, or examples of disinterest."[171] ICI experts emphasized that colonies lacked legal institutions, state bureaucracy, and a civil society that might control the colonial "kings of the bush." In such a legal and political vacuum, they argued, administrators were seduced by immorality.[172] The reform should make sure that administrators resisted the unsound temptations of an allegedly irrational environment. What is more, any legal regulation seemed to be in vain if "honest administrators" did not watch over the application of the rules. Jacques Spanjaard, the director of the Delft school, saw in the formation of "honest men" the only way to ensure the practical application of theoretical laws.[173] Those honest men had to accumulate responsibilities and could not rely on external help. They had to be "integral men," as one French administrator put it.[174] Given the lack of democratic or institutional control, ICI members regarded moral integrity as the only warrant to avoid corruption and abuse.

The argument that preparatory classes guaranteed moral integrity was also a way to increase the administrators' much cherished autonomy. ICI members suggested that a scrupulous selection and preparation of administrators could obviate the need for the metropole's control of "moral" and financial integrity among colonial officials. ICI members particularly turned against the unpopular colonial inspectorate. First introduced in the French empire in 1815, the inspectorate stood for the interference by incompetent bureaucrats from the

---

[171] ICI, *Compte Rendu 1895*, 274.
[172] Girault, "Rapport sur la surveillance," 291–292; US Dept. of the Treasury, *Colonial Administration*, 2624; Deschamps, *Roi de la Brousse*.
[173] ICI, *Compte Rendu 1895*, 402–408.
[174] Deschamps, *Roi de la Brousse*.

motherland.[175] Every two or three years, the French *Direction de Control* sent inspectors to the colonies to "unveil irregularities" in the colonial administration "without making noise in the world" and before scandals caused a stir in the motherland.[176] An inspectorate also existed in the Congo Free State, where *inspecteurs d'état* paid spontaneous and unannounced visits to the administrators.[177] Unlike other countries, the French inspectors not only controlled the financial situation but also the moral behavior of their governors. ICI member Girault delegitimized the inspectorate as a legacy of the Old Regime.[178] The German Hans Haarhaus contrasted the French with the Dutch system, whose administrators were completely independent of bureaucracy in the metropole.[179] By evoking the recruitment reform, they promised to avoid corruption and immorality a priori without any ex post inspectorate.

What is more, ICI reformers used several strategies to increase their salaries and social benefits, for example, by arguing in favor of "moralizing" family reunion. They promised to domesticate the administrators' impulsive masculinity by sending white women to the colonies, whose presence, they argued, would render them honest and integral.[180] ICI members advanced the Dutch as an example, who brought the administrators' families to the Indies, suggesting that the wives created a moralizing milieu in an uncivilized environment. Indeed, almost half of the 240,000 Europeans in the Dutch East Indies were women.[181] By contrast, the British and German Colonial Offices discouraged officers from marrying when they were young and left for the colonies.[182] While family members joined the administrators in British India, they were often absent and traveled to Europe frequently.[183]

In the Dutch Indies, the salary of the officials was three up to times higher than in the administration of the metropole. ICI members argued that this large income allowed the Dutch administrators to marry in the first place. They also gave them the ability to frequently "evacuate" women and children

---

[175] Garner, *Watchdogs of Empire*.
[176] Girault, "Rapport sur la Surveillance," 291, 300.
[177] Gann and Duignan, *The Rulers of Belgian Africa*, 91.
[178] Girault, "Rapport sur la Surveillance," 291, 300.
[179] Haarhaus, *Das Recht*, 136.
[180] The gender aspects of colonial administration cannot be treated here in detail. See Hall, *Cultures of Empire*; Burton, *Gender, Sexuality*; Kundrus, "Weiblicher Kulturimperialismus," 213–235; Ha, *French Women*; Kirk-Greene, "Forging a Relationship," 62–82.
[181] Locher-Scholten, *Women and the Colonial State*, 17. For an Overview, see Clancy-Smith and Gouda, *Domesticating the Empire*.
[182] Gann and Duignan, *Rulers of British Africa*, 203; Tesch, *Die Laufbahn*, 17; Wolff, *Die Landmesser*, 83.
[183] Gilmour, *The Ruling Caste*; Buettner, *Empire Families*.

3.8 LOBBYING FOR HIGHER SALARIES & PENSIONS

during the hot periods.[184] So did the British, who had to offer the Oxbridge elites adequate salaries, which "served to attract the best class of men England could give." As a rule, British governors earned twice the salary of their French or German colleagues.[185] Keen to follow the Dutch and British example, Chailley's French Colonial Union lobbied to pay higher wages to French *fonctionnaires*, who were mostly unmarried. Chailley himself organized recruitment events to find potential wives for the administrators.[186] Modeled on the British Women's Emigration Association, the French Colonial Union finally set up a Société française d'émigration des femmes in 1897, which sent a few women to the colonies but not without testing their morality and physical ability beforehand.[187] The French colonial minister supported these initiatives: according to him, the presence of the family in general, and women in particular, was conducive to increasing the administrator's morals and avoiding colonial scandals.[188] In Germany, the wife of hygienist and ICI member Hans Ziemann, Grete, held the families in the Dutch East Indies up as an example of successful acclimatization – of men, women, and children alike.[189] Thus, the German Colonial Society founded a women's section in 1908 and chose 107 women to go to the colonies in 1912. However, only twenty-nine of them were married there, while the others worked as dressmakers or returned to Germany.[190] In 1910, the Belgians announced plans to pay an additional 1,000 francs to married officials, who often earned no more than 1,800 francs. Yet, as a one-way trip for women cost around 2,000 francs, the subvention had little effect.[191] It was not until the 1920s that a substantial number of women emigrated to the colonies in Africa and Asia.[192]

Whatever ensured the morality of administrators, be it careful selection or the presence of a family, the ICI argued that higher salaries were the basis for it.[193] The German colonial lobby, for example, advanced the higher costs of living for families and especially the high prices for "milk, meat, and black

---

[184] ICI, *Compte Rendu 1895*, 274; Leclercq, *Un Séjour dans l'Île de Java*, 262. On the high costs of marriage, see Bosma and Raben, *Being "Dutch,"* 113.
[185] Gann and Duignan, *Rulers of British Africa*, 159. Concerning the Dutch case, see Bosma and Raben, *Being "Dutch,"* xix.
[186] "Allocution de M. Comte de Haussonville," in D'Haussonville and Chailley, *L'Emigration des Femmes*, 6.
[187] For example, see Ha, *French Women*.
[188] Heckel and Cyprien, *L'Enseignement Colonial*, 47.
[189] Wildenthal, *German Women for Empire*, 6.
[190] *Deutsches Koloniallexikon*, vol. 1, 662.
[191] Sohier, *Mémoires et Souvenirs*, 130; Clerck, "L'Administration Coloniale," 189.
[192] Locher-Scholten, *Women and the Colonial State*; Wildenthal, *German Women for Empire*, 265.
[193] See, for the German example, BArch R2/42741: Bedingungen zur Auswahl von Bewerbern der Kolonial-Beamten-Laufbahn 1905.

bread" overseas.[194] Newcomers such as the US government also recommended high wages to "secure a wide field of selection amongst a class of men who are constitutionally high-minded and honest."[195] It is understood that higher salaries were not only a means to counteract abuse and corruption but also served the self-interest of the colonial administrators. To make the colonies a home for families, the ICI also demanded long-term contracts and old-age pensions for colonial officials.

The Dutch administrators served a comparably long term of twenty years.[196] Their extended tenure compared favorably to the German and French case, where the average tenure of governors between 1884 and 1914 was four and a half and three years respectively.[197] As a German administrator from East Africa enviously observed, most of his colleagues in the Dutch East Indies "are permanently appointed and can consider their employment an employment for life, whereas the civil servants here ... can be dismissed with a notice period of half a year, even if they have already served for six years."[198] If born in the Indies, Dutch administrators brought their families with them and dwelled in the same region. Many of them even stayed in the colonies after their retirement – at the fixed age of forty-five – and received a pension that made up a quarter of their salary. Although these old-age provisions had long been a privilege of those administrators who held a diploma from the Delft training school (around 10 percent), experts of colonial administration such as the German Hans Haarhaus declared them a precondition of the professionalization of colonial careers.[199]

However, ICI members considered a boost in wages useless if it was not combined with the benefits of social security and old-age pensions. Given that *Tropendienstuntauglichkeit* remained a high risk and the main reason for administrators to abandon their service, the ICI was concerned about their lives after the service.[200] The ICI wanted to present administrators with the prospect of a stable career and retirement planning. As it was strictly forbidden for colonial administrators in all empires to make money on the side (amongst the restrictions of side jobs were bans on purchasing land, starting a

---

[194] BArch R2/42741: Schreiben AA Kolonialabtheilung [?] 1905.
[195] Ireland, *Tropical Colonization*, 60.
[196] See, for example, the regulations of the families traveling to the East Indies, "Koninklijk Beslut van 19 Februari 1872 houdende vaststelling van het overtochtsreglement," *Indisch Staatsblad* 125, cited in ICI, *Les Fonctionnaires*, 163–164.
[197] Gann and Duignan, *The Rulers of German Africa*, 68.
[198] BArch R 1001/8651: Die Versuchsstation in Ost-Usambara Amani, 79: Abschrift Erlass Direktor Amani, May 4, 1908.
[199] Haarhaus, *Das Recht*, 77; Bosma and Raben, *Being "Dutch*,*"* 202.
[200] ICI, *Compte Rendu 1895*, 296. In the French Colonial Service, 16 percent of the administrators employed between 1887 and 1912 died and only a few completed their tenure. See Cohen, *Rulers of Empire*, 23.

3.8 LOBBYING FOR HIGHER SALARIES & PENSIONS 145

business, "exploring minable deposits," and publishing without permission), they had to rely on their official income and social benefits.[201]

Around 1900, only the Dutch paid adequate old-age pensions, while shorter tenure in the other empires prevented them from doing the same.[202] Kartini described aptly how privileged the Dutch administrators were:

> In India too one is entitled to a pension after twenty years' service, and the clergy after only ten years. India is an El Dorado for the officials, and yet many Hollanders speak of it as a "horrible Ape-land." I get so infernally mad when I hear them speak of "Horrible India." They forget all too often that this "horrible Ape-land" fills many empty pockets with gold.[203]

Granting pension payments was difficult in France, where the law foresaw a maximum term of service of only twelve years. It was a serious problem in Germany, where the colonial administration hired administrators for three years in German Southwest Africa, two years in German East Africa, and only one and a half years in insalubrious Togo and Cameroon.[204] In Belgium, a decree from 1888 foresaw a tenure of three years and Léopold gave a retirement allowance only to a few administrators who had "distinguished themselves in accomplishing their task."[205] Only the twenty years of service in the Dutch Indies enabled the Dutch state to pay appropriate old-age pensions.[206]

This changed in 1910, when the Belgians, the Germans, and the British introduced professional administration and new laws for the colonial bureaucracy. The Belgian ICI member Jules Renkin augmented the tenure in the Congo to at least ten years (increased to eighteen in 1921 and twenty-three in 1934), after which officials had the right to a pension for the rest of their life. European administrators received civil servant status, old-age pensions, and subsidies if they brought their wives.[207] Their family and near relatives equally received a pension if the administrator deceased.[208]

The Germans had hitherto recruited colonial administrators among the regular *Beamtenschaft* (the German Civil Service in the metropole) and reintegrated them into the metropole's civil service after they had served in the

---

[201] BArch, R2 42695, Auszug Protokoll des Kolonialraths October 26, 1898; BArch, R2 42695, Hohenlohe, Anmerkung October 19, 1898; Haarhaus, *Das Recht*, 56.
[202] For the debate in German parliament about old-age pensions, see "Reichstag, 80. Sitzung, May 5, 1910," *Verhandlungen des Reichstags* (Berlin 1910), 2944.
[203] Kartini, *Letters*, 19–20.
[204] Tesch, *Die Laufbahn*, 17; ICI, *Compte Rendu 1895*, 300. In the CFS, the administrators signed contracts for three years. ICI, *Les Fonctionnaires*, vol. 2, 241.
[205] Clerck, "L'Administration Coloniale," 189.
[206] "Koninklijk Beslut van 10 April 1881 op het verleenen can pensionen," *Indisch Staatsblad* 142, in ICI, *Les Fonctionnaires*, vol. 2, 208.
[207] Clerck, "L'Administration Coloniale," 128–200.
[208] *Bulletin Agricole du Congo Belge* 1, no. 1 (1910), 4.

colonies.[209] This swap of the so-called *Altbeamte* (senior civil servants) guaranteed administrators a pension based on the lengthy service in both colonial and metropolitan bureaucracy. It allowed the German state to pay the lowest wages to their colonial administrators, even less than the Belgian or Portuguese officials received.[210] According to the ICI, the German system ran counter to the Dutch ideal and was hardly acceptable for those colonial experts who promoted a separate and autonomous career for colonial professionals.

This is why, in 1910, the ICI member and German colonial minister Bernhard Dernburg instigated a new *Reichskolonialbeamtengesetz* (Imperial Law on Colonial Civil Servants), which guaranteed elevated wages and adjusted the pension system.[211] The number of permanent and pensionable posts increased and colonial officers had the right to a disproportionally high old-age pension after six years of service. Their salaries were tax-free and they had the right to six months of vacation after eighteen months of service.[212] Dernburg's reorganization of the Colonial Civil Service "regularized the positions of colonial officials, unified conditions of service, laid down explicit conditions of tenure, survivor's benefits and the like. Pay scales improved and became at least comparable to those attaining at home, if not better."[213]

Britain made similar reforms. ICI member Robert Herbert had initiated a Government Pensions Act as early as 1865, but the regulations he introduced did not take full effect. It was only after the ICI revived the topic that Britain established a systematic pension system in 1911 and became "the precedence of colonial governorships in terms of salary and the various grading of governorships into classes."[214] British administrators were divided into different income classes and received a fixed salary with corresponding retirement allowances – provided that they had pursued their profession for at least ten years.[215] Between 1900 and 1910, the British Colonial Office doubled its correspondence, improved its management, built railways, and founded the London School of Tropical Medicine.[216] In 1904, the Indian Office and, in

---

[209] Tesch, *Die Laufbahn*, 15–16; BArch R2/42689: Letter Reichsfinanzministerium, November 19, 1908. See, in general, Zurstrassen, *Ein Stück deutscher Erde*.

[210] In 1913, the governor of German East Africa earned £1,893 a year, while the governor-general of Nigeria earned £7,500, the governor-general of Angola £2,200, and the governor-general of Belgian Congo £2,058. The head of French West Africa received £2,469. See Gann and Duignan, *Rulers of British Africa*, 159.

[211] Spidel, *The German Colonial Service*. Preliminary reforms dated back to 1900. See Hausen, *Deutsche Kolonialherrschaft*, 77.

[212] Hausen, *Deutsche Kolonialherrschaft*, 110–114.

[213] Gann and Duignan, *Rulers of German Africa*, 54.

[214] Lowell, *Colonial Civil Service*, 5.

[215] Kirk-Greene, "The Progress of Pro-Consuls," 181–183; Blakeley, "Pensions and Professionalism," 138–153.

[216] Gann and Duignan, *Rulers of British Africa*, 57–62.

1907, the Colonial Office were thoroughly reorganized, separating the white settler colonies (Dominion Department) from the Tropical Colonies (Crown Colonies and General).[217] They created a "General Department" with tasks as varied as personnel management, audit, and old-age pensions.[218] Since each British colony had its own pensions rules, transfers of officials between different colonies became a paralyzing problem for the British Empire. A mixed pensions system dating from 1869 had collapsed immediately, and it was not until 1907–1908 that an Inter-Departmental Committee proposed new solutions for "mixed pensions." However, the process was delayed, also because British officials refused to draw inspiration from more centralized systems in Dutch, French, Belgian, and German empires. Only shortly before World War I, when they embraced comparative methods and transcolonial exchange, did they move forward. In 1914, British colonies in West Africa introduced a scheme for widows' and orphans' pensions and drafted a similar one for East Africa. More significant reforms occurred only in the 1920s, before the Warren Fisher Commission centralized colonial services in 1930.[219] The US government, instead, introduced new regulations after the American Historical Society had thoroughly studied the British, French, and Dutch colonial service and concluded that administrators "must be tempted into [the service] by large pay, security of tenure and liberal pensions."[220] German ICI members established a colonial ministry in 1907 and the number of specialist advisors increased from five to nine.[221] The Dutch also reformed the training of its officials.

The year 1910 marked the watershed for most European colonial administrators because they received the status of civil servants and all the privileges that came with it. From then on, the state partly funded their training, paid them higher salaries, provided them with a health insurance, entitled them to paid vacation, took care of their families, and secured their old-age pensions. Becoming an administrator became more attractive. The ICI was not behind all those reforms but worked hard to make them happen. Ironically, the focus on Europeans led the reformers to ignore the colonized population, which never enjoyed similar privileges. While the Europeans transferred their welfare state to the colony, they excluded the colonized from its benefits. Djajadiningrat complained that the Indonesians "too must have the prospect of advancing through eagerness and seniority, just as someone of similar abilities in the Binnenlandsch Bestuur."[222]

---

[217] Ibid., 64.
[218] Ibid., 62.
[219] Jeffries, *Colonial Empire*, 22–24.
[220] Lowell, *Colonial Civil Service*, 5.
[221] Gann and Duignan, *Rulers of German Africa*, 51.
[222] Djajadiningrat, *Herinneringen*, 265.

The ICI thus served as a lobby for European administrators and was responsible for inaugurating a reform era between 1893 and 1910. Chailley's 1893 study trip to the Netherlands set off an avalanche of reform in all European empires. It originated in the ICI's method and politics of comparison: ICI members used comparative stereotyping but also provided the basis for transfers of ideas and "intercolonial learning" through prototype comparisons. The Dutch provided the new archetype of efficient governmentality but played an ambiguous role with regard to various prototype transfers. As such, Dutch colonialism became a model for both native cooperation and compulsion, for small-scale agriculture and large plantation economies, and for Indonesian participation and exclusion. This ambiguity manifested itself especially in prototype transfers in colonial agronomy.

4

Cultivating the Myth of Transcolonial Progress

The ICI and the Global Career of Buitenzorg's Agronomic Laboratory

In 1902, the Javanese botanist Raden Soleman disembarked in Dar es Salaam, the capital of German East Africa. A native of the Dutch East Indies, he had worked for the Dutch at the Buitenzorg botanical garden on the island of Java before he set sail for East Africa. From Dar es Salaam, he continued traveling inland until he arrived at the hill station of Amani. At Amani, German colonial agronomists and ICI members were about to launch a biological-agricultural institute, modeled on the famous agronomic research station that had operated for decades in Buitenzorg. To do so, ICI members Franz Stuhlmann and Albrecht Zimmermann had studied the Javanese example thoroughly and recruited Raden Soleman as an expert for the Amani project.[1] He remained at Amani for fourteen years and contributed to establishing the biggest agronomic research institute in Africa.[2]

Raden Soleman's story is truly transcolonial, as is the story of agronomic knowledge transfers. Soleman's transfer to East Africa was the outcome of the ICI's initiative to use expertise from foreign colonies and emulate field-tested techniques of economic development. From Buitenzorg, ICI members transferred agronomic expertise, improved plants, and initiated new planting techniques and governmental schemes of agricultural work in other parts of the colonial world.[3] In around the year 1900, the botanical garden at Buitenzorg received much attention, as it had become the most important and up-to-date research institute for tropical agriculture in the world. Combining transcolonial knowledge production and the genetic engineering of plants, its managers turned botanical science into an applied science of colonial farming.[4] By encouraging Javanese farmers to grow scientifically improved cash crops, Buitenzorg introduced a new governmental model of agricultural development that spread across all empires. Historians concluded

---

[1] BArch R1001/8651/ 203: Direktor Amani to RKA, December 14, 1914.
[2] R 1001/8651/218: Raden Soleman to RKA, July 9, 1921.
[3] Goss, *The Floracrats*, 33–58 and 85.
[4] Wille, *Mannen Van De Microscoop*; Cittadino, *Nature as the Laboratory*, 134–143; Drayton, *Nature's Government*, 247. It is absent, however in Hodge, *Triumph of the Expert*, 90–143.

that Buitenzorg's "improvement efforts in the East Indies stood out not only for their botanical sophistication (the product of Javanese farming skills as much as the scientific standing of Buitenzorg gardens) but also for their unusual socio-ecological attentiveness."[5] Observers thus tied Buitenzorg's project of agronomic governmentality to the Dutch ethical policy of the early twentieth century, which promised to develop the Indies in the framework of a more moral colonialism.[6]

Although colonial experts exaggerated Buitenzorg's achievements, its reputation was at the origin of a new era of transcolonial transfers that relied on the allegedly more progressive "Eastern model" of colonial cash crop production.[7] Buitenzorg's "Eastern" model seemed to oust the "Western" model of suppressive American plantation economies. Up to 1900, "colonial" plants and planting techniques often came from the American South and Latin America. Most prominent were transfers of cotton growing techniques from the Deep South in the United States to the new colonies in Africa.[8] It seemed that those traditionally slave-based American plantation systems primarily influenced colonial agriculture of the early twentieth century.[9] The Western American template of exploitative plantation work seemed to be most suitable for the new colonies in Africa. Yet Buitenzorg's fame suggests another story. For colonial governments in Africa and elsewhere, Buitenzorg's Eastern model became the symbol for an economy of free indigenous peasants who used scientifically improved crops for independent smallholder cultivation. This Eastern model of free indigenous smallholder production steadily gained ground among colonizers around the world. The Eastern model earned itself a global reputation as a more "humane" type of colonial economy, because it encouraged the colonized to participate in agricultural production instead of coercing them, as in the Western American model.[10] The myth of Buitenzorg's liberality predated and anticipated the interwar idea of an allegedly humanitarian colonialism.[11] It remained, however, a myth.[12]

---

[5] Ross, *Ecology and Power*, 419. See also 126, 328–335. On Java in general, see 293–294.
[6] Maat, *Science Cultivating Practice*; Moon, *Technology and Ethical Idealism*.
[7] On Buitenzorg's reputation, see Raby, *American Tropics*; Zangger, *Koloniale Schweiz*; Schär, *Tropenliebe*, 189–190.
[8] Zimmerman, *Alabama in Africa*, 16; Beckert, "From Tuskegee to Togo," 498–526.
[9] It seemed that West Africa adopted the American model, East Africa the Asian model. See Zimmerman, "Ruling Africa," 93–108.
[10] Wesseling, "The Netherlands," 38–60. On "humane" colonialism in the interwar-period, see Pedersen, *The Guardians*, 1–16.
[11] Unlike Goss, I argue that it became an ideal before World War I. See Goss, "Decent Colonialism?," 187–214.
[12] Bosma, *The Sugar Plantation*, 4.

4.1 The Birth of the Buitenzorg Myth

Between the 1880s and the 1930s, several hundred international botanists stayed at Buitenzorg as research fellows, among them were many ICI members. The up-to-date laboratories provided an exceptional opportunity to study tropical plants and their use for the colonial economy. Among the fellows was the German botanist Georg Volkens, who gave a detailed description of the gardens to the members of the German Colonial Congress in 1902:

> It was comprised of an enclosure of fifty-eight hectares, with approximately 10,000 different species of tropical plants, an agricultural *jardin d'essai*, a "virgin forest," trial fields, and a mountain garden. Eight laboratories conducted research in fields as varied as agricultural chemistry, pharmacology, agricultural zoology, phytopathology, physiology, and forestry. The laboratories contained the most modern equipment available, including microscopes, gas lighting, water supply systems, and darkrooms.[13]

ICI member Chailley, who had made a pilgrimage to Buitenzorg in 1900, added that all over the Dutch East Indies, there were experimental stations affiliated with Buitenzorg that specialized in the improvement of coffee, tobacco, indigo, rice, and sugar cultivation. Moreover, the stations housed a herbarium with 200,000 specimens, a 6,000-volume strong library, a museum, and a reading room with 200 scientific periodicals, which were available to researchers. Treub turned the botanical gardens into a veritable research institute that published the multilingual *Annales du Jardin Botanique de Buitenzorg* in which the fellows presented their research output.[14] Buitenzorg undoubtedly represented a modernity that European academia had long claimed for itself.

Botanists representing the Western model, such as the young American botanist David Fairchild, also stayed at Buitenzorg to study colonial agronomy. In his autobiography, with the rather pretentious title *The World Was My Garden*, he explained how Buitenzorg had helped him to make a career in the United States. Fairchild had visited Buitenzorg in 1895 on the invitation of its reputed Dutch director Melchior Treub, who was responsible for transforming the earlier botanical garden into an extensive scientific research institute. He stayed for eight months to do research in the so-called foreigners' laboratory that was equipped with microscopes and the most modern lab apparatus. With the help of the Javanese employees of the garden, Fairchild familiarized himself with tropical plant taxonomy and went on collecting trips around the Indonesian islands. After his return to the United States, he

---

[13] Volkens, "Der Botanische Garten zu Buitenzorg," 182–183, 189.
[14] Chailley, *Java*, xlii–xliii.

became the head of the Office of Seed and Plant Introduction and imported more than 30,000 new tropical plants to the United States, including soy beans, pistachios, mangos, and nectarines. He established his own botanical garden in Florida, named "The Kampong" after the term for traditional Javanese agricultural villages frequently used by the Dutch colonial administration. In the 1930s, he would become the most famous botanist in the United States.[15] Walking down memory lane in 1934, Fairchild recalled: "If there has ever been any one period of our lives more than another that had impressed our whole outlook on science it was the period of our first stay in the Botanic Gardens of Buitenzorg ... it was then and remains to this day one of the most remarkable scientific institutions in the world."[16] Unsurprisingly, colonial authorities in the United States took Buitenzorg as a model for establishing their own agronomic research institutions in the Philippines.[17]

ICI members took the lead in promoting Buitenzorg as a transcolonial model for a scientific colonial agriculture. Most of them traveled to Buitenzorg. Their own experience gained at Buitenzorg added significantly to their fame. When Buitenzorg was mentioned, colonial experts suddenly put imperial rivalries on hold and were full of admiration.[18] For administrators in the Belgian Congo, the botanical garden was "the most important in the world."[19] In 1915, even the future director of the Kew Botanic Gardens in London, Arthur W. Hill, had to admit that Buitenzorg was "probably the most complete and extensive botanical establishment in the world."[20] ICI member Auguste Chevalier, who later became the head of the Permanent Mission of Agriculture at the French colonial ministry, called it "the largest establishment in the world for the perfecting of tropical agriculture."[21] At the German Colonial Congress of 1902, Georg Volkens celebrated Buitenzorg for radiating "pure science."[22]

Other than those specialized experts, many colonial administrators stopped over at Buitenzorg on their way to the colonies and during their frequent holidays. Soon, it also became a tourist destination for Europeans who took the grand tour of Asia. "Every globetrotter knows the botanical gardens of Buitenzorg," concluded the *German Colonial Encyclopaedia* in 1914.[23] Indeed, Buitenzorg figured prominently in the famous *Baedeker* travel guide for India,

---

[15] Fairchild, *The World*, 61–81.
[16] Fairchild and Barbour, "The Crisis at Buitenzorg," 33–34.
[17] Merrill, *Report on Investigations*, 75; Chailley, *Java* (1914), xlv.
[18] On the pre-history, see Weber, "Collecting Colonial Nature," 72–95.
[19] "Le Dr. Treub," *Bulletin Agricole du Congo Belge* 1 (1910), 320.
[20] Hill, "The History and Functions," 210–211; Zangger, *Koloniale Schweiz*, 384–385.
[21] Letter A. Chevalier to G. Angoulvant, June 24, 1922, in Angoulvant, *Les Indes Néerlandaises*, 748.
[22] Volkens, "Der Botanische Garten," 182–193.
[23] "Buitenzorg," *Deutsches Koloniallexikon*, vol. 1, 250–251.

4.1 THE BIRTH OF THE BUITENZORG MYTH   153

suggesting to travelers that it was worth taking a detour to the Indonesian island of Java, just to admire the famous botanical garden. Japanese travel guides provided detailed maps for exploring the extensive gardens.[24] As Buitenzorg gave visitors access to its photo laboratory and its darkrooms, most of them brought pictures home with them, which they used in their numerous publications and talks about the Javanese research laboratory.

To explain why Buitenzorg became an institution of international significance, it is necessary to consider both its commensurable scientific achievements and its symbolic function in global discursive structures. Not only did its directors succeed in improving Javanese agriculture, they also excelled in advertising and exaggerating their achievements. Colonialists around the world admired and imitated Buitenzorg because of the garden's quantifiable success in local agriculture but also because it served to portray colonialism as a progressive force in world history. Thus, it is necessary to give equal attention to Buitenzorg's real impact and its symbolic meaning for the colonial project as a whole.

Buitenzorg became a global success because colonial propagandists and ICI members, in particular, turned it into a symbol of progressivism by mythologizing it in three ways: they magnified its productivity, inflated its emancipative effects on the "natives," and overstated its internationalist nature. Their admiration for Buitenzorg actually became an effort toward mythologization, rather than simply celebrating the botanical garden – in that there was a distinctive effort toward partial obscuration and selective perception. The Javanese population spoke out loudly against this mythologization. The focus on processes of mythologization does not imply that Buitenzorg's productivity, its emancipative effort, and its internationalism were mere fiction. Most mythologization processes spring from a truth but manipulate and misrepresent the facts in a way that serves a more far-reaching purpose.[25]

The outcome of the mythologization process was a Buitenzorg cult rather than a Buitenzorg myth, but proponents did indeed use the narrative structures of classical myths to describe its origins. A much-cited foundational myth suggested that Buitenzorg's botanist Justus Hasskarl was at the origin of the garden's global reputation because of his theft of cinchona seeds from Peru and illegal importation of them to Java in 1852, where biologists improved the plant's yield and developed the largest quinine production facility in the world.[26] Various versions of Hasskarls' heroic act circulated in the literature, portrayed mostly as a foundational journey and an act of "botanical

---

[24] See map of "Buitenzorg," in Baedeker, *Indien*; Imperial Japanese, *An Official Guide to Eastern Asia*.
[25] A well-known case of obscuring indigenous knowledge at Buitenzorg was the medication for beri-beri. See Pols, "European Physicians and Botanists," 173–208.
[26] King, *A Manual of Cinchona*, 7.

espionage."[27] Buitenzorg also had a founding father, Melchior Treub, who allegedly turned the botanical garden into the world's most international and most modern agronomic research laboratory in the 1890s, although the garden had a much longer history of indigenous participation and scientific innovation.[28] Nevertheless, Treub became honorary member of the ICI. He stood for the idea that colonialism was not destructive but would lead underdeveloped natives into a prosperous future, without the use of force. Buitenzorg became the symbol for this myth of the good empire and played therefore an essential part in the framing of a new colonialist worldview.

We can identify seven different fields through which colonial propagandists mythologized Buitenzorg: improvement of economic plants, agricultural education and famine prevention, internationalism, the smallholder scheme, the shift from the Western to the "modern" Eastern model, global plant transfers, and the emulation of Buitenzorg in other colonies.

4.2 The Improvement Project between Plant Engineering and Social Engineering

It is remarkable that Americans like Fairchild and Germans like Volkens felt the need to go to Buitenzorg to perfect their knowledge in genetic engineering and chemical agriculture, despite coming from countries with a solid scientific infrastructure. Seen against this background, Buitenzorg turned European worldviews upside down. Scientific progress was not located in Europe but in the tropics, especially with regard to plant improvement.

In the 1890s, Melchior Treub had indeed shifted Buitenzorg's passive botany, which consisted mainly of cataloging and categorizing tropical plants in the *herbarium*, to an applied science that increased the output of agriculture in the Dutch Indies. The focus was narrowed to the improvement of cash crops, because they were also marketable in Europe. To achieve a higher yield, the laboratories adopted a Darwinist plant biology and engaged in genetic engineering, the development of new planting techniques, the production of more efficient fertilizers, and research on how to combat plant diseases.

In the early twentieth century, the improvement of marketable plants seemed to be a total success. For example, the sugar output per cultivated hectare was the highest in the world and had relegated Hawaii to second place by 1900.[29] Responding to the rubber boom of the early twentieth century, Otto de Vries, the director of the central rubber station at Buitenzorg, worked together with ten scientific researchers to establish experimental

---

[27] Bosma, "Franz Junghuhn's," 175–206.
[28] Zeijlstra, *Melchior Treub*; Weber and Wille, "Laborious Transformations."
[29] Bosma, *The Sugar Plantation*, 88–140; Klaveren, *The Dutch Colonial System*, 182.

rubber plantations and make their output more efficient.[30] After some years of experimentation, his laboratories were able to increase the Hevea rubber tree's resistance to diseases and the wind by shield budding and plant breeding.[31] After developing the Hevea seeds into highly productive and disease-resistant plants, Buitenzorg exported them around the world. In addition, Buitenzorg's chemical laboratories enhanced fertilizers and pesticides to protect plantations from insects and plant disease. This attempt was backed by methods of mixed gardening, such as "intercalary planting," which helped Javanese planters to avoid expensive fertilizers.[32] The innovative research made Java a leader in modern colonial agriculture and anticipated the development policies of the twentieth century. By 1900, tropical regions around the world requested improved plants from Buitenzorg.

While the scientific improvement of plants was successful, it is unclear whether applicable improvement happened in Buitenzorg's laboratories or outside in the fields of European and Javanese planters. Most success stories about increased crop yields derived from Buitenzorg's publications and Treub's propaganda campaign in its favor. The Javanese themselves must have contributed in a significant way to the improvement project. After all, this is why German colonial agronomists had recruited Raden Soleman. By the same token, European planters, who were about to establish large plantations on the Indonesian island of Sumatra, experimented independently of Buitenzorg, and denied its usefulness for practical agriculture. Thus, the association of sugar planters refused to leave experimentation to Buitenzorg alone and tried to control the improvement of its sugar production themselves.[33]

4.3 Realities and Myths of Internationalization: The Silencing of Indigenous Knowledge

Today it is well known that Buitenzorg attracted specialists from all over the world who contributed to plant improvement. Since the 1880s, Treub made the internationalization of Buitenzorg's scientific staff part of the overall Dutch strategy to take advantage of foreign experts.[34] First, European experts visited Buitenzorg upon the invitation of the Dutch colonial governor in Java. He paid researchers a stipend while also providing transportation, accommodation, and a working space for four to five months.[35] Among foreigners, this "most

---

[30] Vries, *Estate Rubber*; Dean, *Brazil and the Struggle for Rubber*, 63.
[31] Coster, "The Work of the West Java Research Institute," 56–69.
[32] Chailley, *Java* (1914), xliv.
[33] Ibid., 66 and 87.
[34] Treub, *Der Botanische Garten*.
[35] BArch, R 1001/8604, Nr. 44/45: Generalkonsulat Niederländisch-Indien to Kolonialabtheilung, April 29, 1898.

liberal way" of granting access to the laboratory became so popular that Buitenzorg quickly ran out of stipends.[36]

When applications by far exceeded the available stipends, researchers came to Buitenzorg at their own expense and stayed for up to two years. For instance, German botanists – in tandem with colonial interest groups and academies of science – lobbied the German government to establish its own Buitenzorg scholarship. In 1898, Berlin agreed to fund such a scholarship, on the condition that it was "pursuing not only scientific but also practical purposes and letting the colonial undersecretary designate one fellow at least every fourth year."[37] In total, some fifty Germans became official visiting fellows at Buitenzorg – on both Dutch and German grants – between the 1880s and 1914. They not only contributed to agronomic research in Java but also sent plants, seeds, and technological know-how back to Germany "for the colonial mission of the German *Reich*."[38] In 1904, the Swiss government launched a similar scholarship, which enabled around twenty Swiss scientists to visit Buitenzorg.[39] While German-speaking researchers were always the majority among the foreigners at Buitenzorg, there were also Russian, American, Austrian, British, French, and Belgian fellows.[40] Most of them published the results of their research in the famous *Annales du Jardin Botanique de Buitenzorg*.

To satisfy their demands, Dutch authorities equipped one of the workshops for visiting researchers, offered them lodgings, occasionally a small remuneration, and free classes in the pidgin versions of Javanese and Malay.[41] Visitors benefited from their rudimentary language skills to gain knowledge about the local fauna. Thus, the American Fairchild, who exchanged ideas with British, German, and Belgian researchers at Buitenzorg, also learned from the local population: "As I learned a little Malay, I was astonished when chatting with the Javanese, Sundanese and Madurese working in the garden to realize their knowledge of the plants." Mantri Oedam was one of those, who particularly impressed Fairchild: "Oedam was a really remarkable botanist in many ways, familiar with every plant in the garden and knew not only its native name but its botanical name as well. He had that rare faculty of form memory."[42]

---

[36] BArch, R 1001/8604, Akademie der Wissenschaften to Foreign Ministry, August 24, 1897; Abschrift December 13, 1895, Engler and Schwendener to Minister für Geistliches, Unterricht und Medizinal-Angelegenheiten.

[37] BArch, R 1001/8604, Nr. 45/56: Minister des Inneren und Reichsschatzamt, May 31, 1898.

[38] BArch, R 1001/8604, Nr. 78-80: Verzeichnis der aus Java mitgebrachten Nutzpflanzen and Nr. 78-85: Letter Giesenhagen to Hohenlohe (Foreign Ministry), April 27, 1900.

[39] Zangger, *Koloniale Schweiz*, 384-385.

[40] Dammermann, "The Quinquagenary of the Foreigners," 1-54.

[41] Chailley, *Java*, xlix.

[42] Fairchild, *The World*, 64.

By 1900, there were as many as 300 of those non-European experts. Treub, in particular, downplayed their role, claiming that "the native personnel is composed of about a hundred individuals, among whom are [only] three employees who have special botanical knowledge."[43] This could hardly be true given the transcolonial interest in their faculties. Treub, who styled himself the founding father of the internationalist research institute, also failed to mention that the garden was built on existing traditions and had made use of indigenous knowledge from its earliest days. In 1845, the German botanist Justus Karl Hasskarl had openly stated that his knowledge about the local plants and their comparative categorization came from the "natives." His project was to know "what the natives had to say about the value and usefulness of plants that grow in their regions and make the results known in order to give others guidelines to further analyze them and later to make the knowledge known to general benefit."[44]

While Western researchers at Buitenzorg learned from the Javanese and Sundanese experts, they never credited them in their publications, nor did they reward them in any other way. Fairchild gave proof of his colonial mentality as he described them as mere servants during his inaugurating tour of the gardens with Melchior Treub in 1895:

> Everybody had a "boy," so Treub turned his own boy, Mario, over to me. I had never had a servant of my own and felt myself a prince. Incidentally, I never had a servant since who cared for me as Mario did. From mounting microtome sections on microscopic slides to managing a caravan across the mountains, he took care of everything. Each morning I rose early, as one does in the tropics, and Mario would serve me with coffee.[45]

Although those "servants" and "employees" played an important role in enabling, inspiring, and conducting research, official reports omitted them and instead laid emphasis on cooperation among *Western* scholars only, whose synergies and cross-fertilizations were allegedly the only source of scientific progress. Apart from Fairchild, no employee or visitor of the gardens mentioned the Javanese. Because of this silence, it is difficult to estimate how extensive biopiracy – the appropriation of "native" knowledge – was. It is certain, however, that the focus on Buitenzorg's internationalism concealed the contribution of Indonesian experts even more. While Buitenzorg's internationalization was a fact, it was part of the mythologization effort to focus on this dimension only. The role of Javanese experts who also became internationalists, such as Raden Soleman who went to German East Africa, is literally unknown. German botanists deliberately concealed their contribution:

---

[43] Headrick, *Tentacles of Progress*, 221.
[44] Hasskarl, *Aanteekeningen Over het Nut*, vi.
[45] Ibid., 64; Gross, *The Floracrats*, 72.

Soleman's German superior at Amani used the Javanese's plant paintings for his own publications, without giving credit to him.[46]

4.4 Javanese Perspectives on the Failure of Agricultural Education and Famine Prevention

Treub's innovative idea was to combine plant engineering with social engineering.[47] He claimed to give equal weight to the spreading of improved plants among the Javanese peasants and teaching them more efficient planting methods. To make supposedly rational farming methods popular, he reinvigorated the agricultural school that had existed since 1876. The school accepted a very limited number of sons of Indonesian elites, who would study and spread European agronomic knowledge across the colony.[48] It became a symbol of colonial governmentality and social engineering.

ICI member Chailley went to see Treub's scheme of agronomic governmentality for himself and popularized it in public lectures and publications. However, he tended to describe the theory instead of the reality: according to him, the Dutch colonial government had reserved a budget of 109,000 florins to fund these agricultural classes, which were held in vernacular languages. Around 1900, Treub professionalized the school. He trained Javanese agricultural assistants called *mantris*, hoping that these mobile teachers would spread agronomic knowledge and scientifically selected seeds. Their "education" started with a three-year course, in which indigenous and *metis* students not only learned how to grow cash crops but also received training in accounting and were instructed to use credit offered by the colonial banks. Javanese farmers were supposed to learn predominantly on test fields, where agricultural teachers demonstrated how they could benefit from scientific cultivation methods. Once the graduates had returned to their fields, Buitenzorg inspectors supervised their cultivation of tea, coffee, or rice and evaluated the results. A much talked about novelty, for example, was a dry rice version that required less irrigation and water supply.[49] Chailley deemed this system the most modern approach to colonialism.

Officially, the purpose of involving indigenous farmers in cash crop production was to increase both the output of the colonial economy and the living standard of the colonized populations. In so doing, Buitenzorg was supposed to bring about progress in both European and indigenous societies and thus the progress of humanity in general. At the same time, the selective perception of the scientific achievements by the founding father Melchior Treub

---

[46] R 1001/8651/203: Direktor Amani to RKA, December 14, 1919.
[47] Goss, *The Floracrats*, 79.
[48] Maat, *Science Cultivating Practice*, 41.
[49] Chailley, *Java*, xliv.

obfuscated earlier scientific approaches that explicitly made use of indigenous knowledge and methods.

Yet, while plant improvement may have been successful, the transformation of indigenous cultivation techniques by agricultural education was eventually derailed, if it was ever fully attempted. While Treub's new agricultural school opened in 1903 with ten indigenous students, only seven of them graduated in 1907 to become agricultural advisors. The next cohort was more numerous, yet seventeen advisors were hardly enough to transform the indigenous agriculture in even a minor part of Java.[50] In the rare cases that Europeans imposed new planting methods on the Javanese population, their intervention did not necessarily lead to an increased yield. For example, when Javanese sugar planters suffered from low sugar prices and high competition between 1900 and 1914, they tried to apply new methods as recommended by European agronomic experts. They planted sugar earlier in the year and cultivated rice after the sugar harvest to use the fields more efficiently. The result was sobering: "as cropping cycles became more crowded, the problem of overlap between the crops intensified; if cane were harvested late, it prevented peasants from putting in a dry season second crop before putting their land to rice in the wet season. When rice was scheduled to be followed by cane, peasants often employed the quicker-maturing but lower-yielding *padi dengahan*." Thus, the techniques intended for improvement often led to a deterioration.[51]

More importantly, periods of food insecurity and famines were frequent and relativized Buitenzorg's ascent. While Buitenzorg was not the cause of the famines, it nevertheless failed to provide the remedies its founder had promised. One significant famine occurred between 1900 and 1904 in Java.[52] It was so far-reaching that the Dutch government had to provide significant funds for relief work, amounting to four million florins.[53] After the famine, it set up a welfare committee to prevent food shortages in the future. One of its members was the regent of Serang in Western Java, Achmad Djajadiningrat. He would publicly unveil the shortcomings of the Buitenzorg system.

Unlike Treub and Chailley, Djajadiningrat judged Buitenzorg not by its plans but by its impact, and it seemed to have had very little. The regent of Serang harshly criticized the government for its failure to improve agriculture for the benefit of the larger population. He remarked that there were few agricultural advisors, and even fewer Javanese among them, who were familiar

---

[50] Goss, *The Floracrats*, 89-91.
[51] Elson, *Javanese Peasants*, 170-171.
[52] Hugenholtz, "Famine and Food Supply in Java," 155-188; Boomgaard, "From Subsistence," 35-50.
[53] Tetteroo, *How They Survived*, 47.

with local conditions. He proposed giving the Javanese a more significant position in an expanded agricultural school at Buitenzorg. In his own regency of Serang, he explained, there were many well-educated candidates. But he could send only two of them to higher agricultural schools "because there were no more places available."[54] He concluded that "despite the increasing zeal and knowledge, with which the European and the native officials take the case, despite the costs that are spent, native agriculture generally remains as it used to be ... some improvements, which are observed here and there, are never of perpetual nature, but usually stand and fall with a few persons."[55]

Chailley's review of the agricultural school differed significantly from Djajaniningrat's assessment. Chailley neither mentioned the poor impact of the school, nor did he address the failure of Buitenzorg methods. Oftentimes, Buitenzorg methods had not been tested in a "normal environment" and did not work in the fields. Thus, farmers who had to produce cash crops often refused to apply Buitenzorg methods. As the farmers' resistance continued, the government responded by enforcing cultivation, euphemistically called *perintah alus*, or "soft persuasion." This was particularly ironic with regard to the new era of "ethical policy" toward the Indonesians that the Dutch had proclaimed in 1901.[56] Despite these shortcomings, Chailley promoted Javanese colonial agriculture as a model of a successful smallholder system.

The Dutch colonial government recalled Treub from his post in 1909, as soon as it realized that he had failed to bring about the transition. Observers agreed that his scientific achievements remained unmatched, while his social and economic policy had failed. His successor, H. J. Lovink, promised to pay more attention to traditions of indigenous farming and "to increase together with the Javanese farmer his rice yields economically, taking into account his development, workforce and his capital."[57] Lovink became the head of the newly established Agricultural Department in the Netherlands East Indies, which also seized control of Buitenzorg. Despite his efforts, food shortages continued far into the interwar period. The crucial problem remained, along with the debate surrounding it. When Clifford Geertz developed his theory of "agricultural involution" from a Javanese case study in 1963, he concluded that the colonial development policy had brought about change but not progress for the Javanese population.[58]

---

[54] Djajadiningrat, *Herinneringen*, 264–265.
[55] Ibid.
[56] Moon, *Technology*, 31–39.
[57] Cited in Goss, *The Floracrats*, 92.
[58] Geertz, *Agricultural Involution*.

4.5 The Ideal of a Smallholder Agriculture and the Role of European Planters

When Lovink replaced Treub, he made a renewed effort to promote small-scale farming and particularly urged village communities and small farmers to improve rice production. His reforms seemed to benefit the Javanese to the detriment of the colonial export economy. He increased the number of agricultural schools to eight and trained twenty-six official Javanese "extension agents," who "educated" local farmers and oversaw their efforts to improve their yield. Javanese farmers could learn how to boost their rice yields, improve cultivation techniques, use fertilizers, and receive seeds and plants from new seed gardens and nurseries. They received a theoretical education in botany, plant physiology, irrigation, and dry farming. In addition, the administration kept them informed about newly introduced cash crops such as peanuts and cassava. The Javanese agronomic teacher M. Oemarsanoesi, for example, edited instructive pamphlets, gave talks, accompanied experiments in the fields, and advised farmers on the use of fertilizers and selected rice varieties.

Hence, some farmers turned their own fields into trial fields. Using this opportunity, the Department of Agriculture distributed new rice varieties such as *padi baok* to 109 villages in 1914. By 1917, six districts out of eight carried out experiments with rice varieties. Local rulers supported these efforts, such as the sultan of Yogyakarta and the susuhunan of Surakarta, who each financed an agricultural school. The schools trained mostly sons of farmers whom they expected to return to their fields. In so doing, they hoped to popularize the disease-resistant *Skrivimankotti* rice variety that had proven to be highly productive in Dutch Surinam.[59]

Yet, once again, the results of these efforts rarely lived up to the expectations. The value of "improved" varieties was often unclear to the farmers for whom their cultivation was a losing bargain. In the case of *Skrivimankotti* rice, the peasants realized that it was productive but not profitable. They preferred local rice of better quality that outsold *Skrivimankotti*. Moreover, the Dutch administration had not taken local modes of production into account. It banned women, who played a vital role in Javanese agriculture, from the agricultural schools. Their Eurocentric attitude led them to assume that agriculture was naturally male-dominated. The promotion of "improved" small-scale farming – if it was an improvement at all – was omnipresent and sophisticated only in the manifold publications of the promoters. The farmers' reality on the ground often differed widely from the plans of the administration.[60]

---

[59] Ibid., 56–66.
[60] Ibid., 57–58.

Why did the "smallholder scheme" fail again? The answer to that question might lie in another version of the Buitenzorg story that its admirers rarely told. Buitenzorg's priorities were never the smallholder farmers in Java but rather the European planters in Java and Sumatra's famous "plantation belt." Buitenzorg developed improved economic plants for them, because they funded the research institutes. To turn Buitenzorg into a veritable research institute and to increase his financial freedom for agronomic science there, Melchior Treub had organized a system of private funding between 1880 and 1909. In exchange for seeds and scientific advice, European plantation owners financed the research at the laboratories. This was also a way the tea planters of the Dutch Indies remunerated the head of Buitenzorg's microbiological division who directed research on tea plants. Similarly, the General Syndicate for Sugar Production funded the commission for the cultivation of sugar. Tobacco and coffee stations had similar funding systems and Buitenzorg's success depended on their favors.[61]

The plantation system was diametrically opposed to the smallholder system and recalled the "Western" model of coercive plantation economies in the Americas. As Ann-Laura Stoler has shown, many Javanese would soon go to work on the plantations in East Sumatra, instead of launching their own farms in Java. The working conditions there resembled those of Chinese workers who had few rights and worked partly under conditions akin to slavery. They were indentured laborers and received severe punishments if they did not follow the rules of the plantations. In the interwar period, these workers rose against their oppressors and made the violent atmosphere visible that finally gave the plantations the bad reputation they deserved.[62] Her analysis of the anti-smallholder model ties into Clifford Geertz findings about the sugar farmers in Java:

> Until the latter half of the 19th century, the sugar mills in Java bought or commandeered a large percentage of their cane from independent peasant cultivators. But as scientific methods made possible increasing yields per acre, the Dutch introduced the system of land renting and direct supervision of the cultivation of the primary crop already described .... The undeniably improved efficiency of this sort of vertical integration (at least in narrowly technical terms) was gained at the cost of a tendency to reduce the landowning peasant's role to that of a passive renter living mindlessly off the proceeds of his sugar rents: "in place of the peasant ingeniousness came the coolie submissiveness."[63]

---

[61] Van Klaveren, *The Dutch*, 182.
[62] Stoler, *Capitalism and Confrontation*.
[63] Geertz, *The Social History*, 49.

While Buitenzorg represented both Java's smallholder system and Sumatra's plantation system, most international observers highlighted the smallholder schemes. This selective perception must be understood in the light of a broader development in colonial theory of the early twentieth century. Buitenzorg's reputation for alleged progressiveness spread throughout the world, building upon the transatlantic exchanges of agronomic knowledge. As we will see, this mythologization was central to European imperialists' attempts to transfer the Western plantation model from the Americas to new commodity frontiers in Africa during the late nineteenth century.

4.6 Mythologizing the Shift from Latin America to Africa: Transatlantic Agronomic Transfers

The early modern period had seen a fruitful economy built on global plant exchange. The imperialists of the nineteenth century claimed to incorporate the hitherto neglected tropical regions into this system in a more strategic way. While the global redistribution of plants dated back to the post-Columbian period of colonial expansion, it indeed reached an unprecedented scale in the late nineteenth century. The scramble for Africa gave a new impetus for the transfer of commercial agricultural products. Assuming that the African continent was uncivilized and its inhabitants incapable of exploiting their own resources, European colonizers set out to make its agriculture more efficient and profitable. To achieve this aim, they sought out models from other tropical regions. In the late nineteenth century, before the Buitenzorg model's rise to prominence among imperialists, colonial administrators in Africa particularly admired South America, which was famous for its productive plantations and appeared to have a similar labor market, with a predominantly black body of workers. Yet they were aware that this system had its roots in slavery and brutal exploitation. Claiming that they would turn away from this "Western model" of a post-slavery plantation economy to embrace the "Eastern model" of Javanese smallholder production became one of the major colonialist narratives of the twentieth century. This narrative was only plausible if the Javanese example and Buitenzorg were mythologized to the extent that they epitomized an anti-slavery model.

While colonial botanists borrowed heavily from Latin America, its reputation was in steady decline by 1900. Its diminution was only partly due to the continued system of slavery, which Brazil abolished only in 1888, but also stemmed from raised concerns among Europeans about a "white slavery" that would use European immigrants to replace the former slaves on the plantations.[64] Indeed, throughout the nineteenth century, abolitionists had

---

[64] Degler, *Neither Black Nor White*.

promoted the relocation of cash crop production such as sugar from the West Indies to East India, insisting that "we only need to substitute East India, for West India sugar – and the British atmosphere would be purified at once, from the poisonous infection of slavery."[65]

By 1900, colonial propagandists around the globe took up that idea and added that Latin America had lagged behind in establishing a modern cash crop economy built on the improvement of economic plants. To Euro-American imperialists, the Eastern tropics seemed to be more advanced in grounding their cash crop production in the improvement of plants through genetic engineering. Buitenzorg, in particular, became a symbol of this forward-looking and "scientific" colonial agronomy.

It has to be clear that this "shift" from the Western model to the Eastern model happened on a discursive level, in the sense that colonial propagandists invoked it to legitimize their rule, predominantly in Africa. While they turned to the East, they continued to import economic plants, and with them planting models, from North and South America. One of those plants was the *Hevea Brasiliensis* rubber tree grown in the Pará region of Northern Brazil. Additionally, coffee, tea, cocoa, and sugar plants attracted the attention of European colonial botanists.

Thus, most colonial administrations sent missions to Latin America. In 1899, ten German plantation companies, several chocolate factories, the private German Committee for Colonial Economy, and the German Foreign Ministry, funded an expedition to Central and South America to analyze and imitate the planting techniques for cocoa, coffee, caoutchouc and vanilla in order to launch a profitable plantation economy in German Africa.[66] The expedition sent back thousands of seeds and seedlings to experimental stations and plantations in the German colonies, among them Criollo cocoa, coffee plants, and Hevea rubber trees. The most important German colonial botanist and ICI member, Franz Stuhlmann, obtained almost 120 of these for acclimatization in East Africa. Other than that, private plantations also received seeds.[67]

Between 1896 and 1914, the French colonial ministry alone dispatched thirteen commissions to Latin America. One of the most favored destinations was the rubber producing Pará region. Famed for producing the best quality rubber, the Pará region witnessed frequent visits from European caoutchouc commissions. All the colonizing countries wanted to profit from the rubber boom at the onset of the century, which had led to steadily increasing prices

---

[65] Bosma, *The Sugar Plantation*, 44–45 and 57–61, quote on page 61.
[66] BArch 1001, 7841 Plantagen und Eingeborenen-Kulturen in Mittel- und Südamerika. Reise Dr. Preuss; Karsten, "Paul Preuß," 222–227.
[67] Preuss, *Expedition*, 424–425.

that reached their highest peak in 1903.⁶⁸ In 1898 and 1901, the French colonial ministry sent Eugène Poisson to Pará, who returned with 100,000 seeds of the profitable *Hevea brasiliensis* rubber trees and 350,000 grains of the less qualitative, but easily conservable, *Manihot glazivoii*.⁶⁹ These samples provided the basis for rubber plantations in the French colonies in Africa and Indochina, where they triumphed over the less profitable autochthonous varieties.⁷⁰ Participating in the harvest of Hevea plants in Brazil, Eugène Poisson had also observed the processing of the rubber. Poisson made his Brazilian Hevea seeds available to French botanical gardens and the French colonies. In addition, the Boma agricultural research station in the Congo Free State also received seeds from the Poisson mission.⁷¹ Having similar intentions, the Belgian King Léopold had already imported *Hevea brasiliensis* plants himself, as well as several Brazilian workers. He wanted them to develop an intensive rubber production on professionally organized plantations to substitute the extensive gatherer economy, which had earned the king a fortune in the 1890s but had exhausted the wild rubber trees and caused the death of thousands of Congolese workers.⁷²

The American model was thus still important in providing "new" colonies with plants and methods. The history of transferring cotton farming from the South of the United States to West Africa is only one example to illustrate this. But in their publications, colonial agronomists, whether in Africa or elsewhere, often preferred to highlight the role of Buitenzorg. And indeed, based on its mythologization, colonizers around the world built little Buitenzorgs as symbols of their own progressive attitude and as a means to attract funding.

4.7 Turning to the East: Transfers of Improved Plants and Their Failure

Those who "turned to the East" were mostly colonial careerists who hoped to gain a good reputation by emulating the Buitenzorg model. Germans were the first to transfer Buitenzorg's staff, improved seeds, and plants from Java and Sumatra to their colony in East Africa. ICI members Franz Stuhlmann, Walter Busse, and Albrecht Zimmermann, were central to this transfer. Stuhlmann and Busse had researched at Buitenzorg at the turn of the century, while Albrecht Zimmermann was the head of the Javanese coffee experimental

---

[68] Tully, *The Devil's Milk*.
[69] ANOM FM AFFPOL MIS 76bis, Mission d'études des arbres à caoutchouc au Brésil d'Eugène Poisson (1898/1901).
[70] Poisson, *Rapport sur une mission*, 14; Chevalier, "La Situation des Plantations," 309–310.
[71] Padirac, "L'Importance Économique," xvii.
[72] Tully: *The Devil's Milk*, 101–122.

station between 1896 and 1901.[73] In 1902, those Buitenzorg veterans closed down an abortive experimental station for colonial agriculture in German East Africa and replaced it with a professional Biological-Agricultural Institute in Amani.[74] Because of his Buitenzorg experience, Stuhlmann was appointed the first director of the institute in Amani and later designated Albrecht Zimmermann as his successor. Walter Busse stayed in Java and organized the transfer of cash crop seeds and laboratory material from Buitenzorg to Amani. What is more, they modeled the new Biological-Agricultural Research Institute in Amani on the Buitenzorg "prototype": it was part of a hill station complex in the Eastern Usambara Mountains that combined agronomic trial fields and several laboratories with the features of a spa town. Its priority was to import cultivable plants that were vital to colonial life.[75]

As early as 1896, Franz Stuhlmann and Walter Busse had started to introduce cinchona trees from Dutch Java. The bark on the cinchona trees contained quinine – the most important palliative against malaria and other tropical maladies – in great quantities. Early on, the global circulation of cinchona trees was subjected to a process of mythologization. As we have seen, Hasskarl allegedly had brought the trees from the West to the East, from Peru to Java, in 1852. By that time, cinchona was so rare that it was said to be "balanced with gold." Yet, grown on large plantations in Java, cinchona trees seemed to be a great success. Chemists and botanists in Buitenzorg supposedly increased the quantity of quinine in the tree's bark from 0.4 percent to 18 percent. At the same time, the free distribution of seedlings to Javanese peasants boosted the Javanese production of quinine. Increased production reportedly reduced the price of this precious remedy by 80 percent.[76] In terms of turnover, quinine became the most important medication in the world, with Java providing for 97 percent of global quinine production by 1930. Stuhlmann and Busse copied these methods in German East Africa, bought ever more refined species from Java, and employed Indian specialists to guarantee their prosperity. In 1907, they had planted 25,355 trees in Amani and 66,700 trees on private plantations, which represented the success of the project in German East Africa.[77] Nevertheless, cinchona failed to bring in a profit. Historian Andrew Goss showed that "by 1895, even the Javanese cinchona plantations were not profitable anymore" and only government subsidies in the Netherlands East Indies kept the cinchona economy alive.

---

[73] Zimmermann, *Der Botanische Garten*.
[74] Paasche, *Deutsch-Ostafrika*, 246.
[75] BArch, R 1001/8604, Direktor der botanischen Zentralstelle für die Kolonien zu Berlin, Engler, to AA Kolonialabteilung, November 30, 1906.
[76] Webb, *Humanity's Burden*, 106; Porter, *The Greatest Benefit to Mankind*, 465–466.
[77] Stuhlmann, *Beiträge zur Kulturgeschichte*, 434–440. On the Dutch case, see Sambuc, "Le Developement Économique," 288–289.

4.7 TURNING TO THE EAST

While the cinchona economy in Java had no commercial future, the mythologization of Dutch rationality and will to improve led the Germans to establish huge plantations in East Africa. After all, quinine seemed to ensure the supply of manpower and stabilize colonial rule.[78]

At around the same time, Albrecht Zimmermann introduced rubber cultures to Amani. Botanists in Java had imported Hevea rubber trees from Brazil and had increased their productivity. In order to introduce systematic rubber production to Africa, Zimmermann then imported the improved seeds from Buitenzorg to Amani.[79] He hoped that professional Hevea plantations would soon replace the traditional *Raubbau* (robber economy) in Africa, the harvest of caoutchouc from wild rubber trees. Dismissing the forced rubber collection in Léopold's Congo, he saw the future of caoutchouc production on intensive rubber plantations as taking place in Brazil or Dutch Java. The French specialist for rubber cultivation, Camille Spire, shared his high regard for Hevea rubber from Java. In 1901, the French colonial minister had sent Spire on an official mission to Buitenzorg. Spire shipped plants and seeds from Buitenzorg to Paris, where agronomists analyzed them and forwarded them to French colonies in Africa. In so doing, Spire continued a long tradition of French agricultural missions to Java, which had already led to the establishment of rubber plantations in Indo-China. Following the Dutch example, Spire wanted to encourage the cultivation of rubber trees by distributing the seeds among colonists, administrators, and indigenous farmers.[80] The success of "improved" Hevea rubber from the Dutch Indies was short-lived, however, as the synthetic production of rubber limited conventional production in the interwar period.[81] In Africa, rubber from Java did not gain traction in any case.

Zimmermann, who had been Buitenzorg's expert for coffee planting for seven years and had done extensive research on parasite infestation of coffee, styled himself the savior of East African plantation economy. There, early and random efforts to plant 10,000 hectares of *Coffea arabica* and *Coffea liberica* had proven disastrous. In 1901, Zimmermann arrived from Buitenzorg determined to combat a coffee disease that had hitherto been unknown in Africa. He identified it as *blorok*, a disease he got to know in Buitenzorg. Zimmermann also used grafting methods developed in Buitenzorg to replace vulnerable plants with the more resilient *Coffea canephora*, and he imported

---

[78] Goss, *The Floracrats*, 56.
[79] Zimmermann, *Der Manihot-Kautschuk*, 311.
[80] FR ANOM 50COL 14: Mission à Java de Camille Spire, pour l'étude du jardin botanique et du laboratoire de Buitenzorg (1901). See also Spire and Spire, *Le Caoutchouc*, 200–209, 225 and 233–234.
[81] Tully, *The Devil's Milk*, 48.

seeds of improved *Coffea arabica* from Java.[82] Few of these attempts succeeded, but Zimmermann claimed that his attempts contributed to mastering the coffee crises of the early twentieth century, when the world market price of coffee collapsed.[83] Zimmermann's advice was highly regarded in France, and as late as 1914, Chailley's French Colonial Union dispatched the agricultural inspector of Madagascar, Fauchère, to Java, to study the cultivation of coffee at Buitenzorg and apply it to French Africa.[84]

The transfer of raw materials for the colonial plantation economy went hand in hand with the employment of Javanese and Indian staff in German East Africa, who were more experienced with methods and technologies of cash crop cultivation.[85] As we have seen, Buitenzorg agronomists trained Javanese peasants to grow the improved crops, a process that was only nominally free of coercion. This allegedly more liberal Eastern model equally found its way into German East Africa, where Amani's agricultural instructors seemed to encourage an African smallholder agriculture. However, as in the Dutch Indies, the government resorted to forced cultivation if African farmers refused to grow new crops, especially cotton. Enforced cultivation caused the so-called Maji-Maji rebellion against German colonial rule in 1905–1907.[86] It is unclear if people were compelled to grow crops from Buitenzorg, but it is certain that its emulation did not liberalize colonial rule at all.

4.8 The Consequences of Mythologization: Emulating Buitenzorg throughout Africa and Beyond

The immaculate reputation of Buitenzorg led colonial governments to finance enormous projects to emulate it. German colonial internationalists, for example, used the Buitenzorg myth to make Berlin fund similar stations not only in Amani but also in West- and Central Africa. In German Cameroon, which traditionally borrowed extensively from the Western model to establish cocoa plantations in the 1890s, the botanist Otto Warburg was the driving force behind a laboratory modeled on the Eastern example. Warburg came from a Jewish merchant family in Hamburg and spent several years in Buitenzorg during the 1880s. He founded the German Committee for Colonial Economy in 1896, which claimed to make the German colonies more

---

[82] Zimmermann, "Erster Jahresbericht," 441.
[83] Clarence-Smith: "The Coffee Crisis," 100–119.
[84] FR ANOM 50COL68, Mission d'études sur la culture du café aux Indes néerlandaises par Fauchère, inspecteur d'agriculture à Madagascar, à l'initiative de l'Union coloniale française (1914); Fauchère, *Culture Pratique*, 168–169; Koningsberger and Zimmermann, *De dierlijke vijanden der koffiecultur*; Zimmermann, *Kaffee*.
[85] Zimmermann, "Erster Jahresbericht," 435.
[86] Iliffe, *A Modern History*, 168–178.

profitable. In 1899, the Committee urged the German government to create a "laboratory in connection with a botanical garden" in Victoria at the foot of Mount Cameroon. Warburg designed a multifunctional laboratory that provided for all the needs of the colony: agricultural engineers would improve the fertilization of the soil, phytopathologists would combat the pests infecting tropical crops, zoologists would improve stockbreeding, pharmacologists would test new drugs, hygienists would analyze contagious epidemics, and, finally, chemists would examine new elements unknown in Europe. Moreover, in Warburg's opinion, such a laboratory would boost the production of cash crops, and he proposed that the directors of the surrounding coffee, tobacco, and cinchona plantations should bear the costs.[87] Although smaller than Amani, Warburg's laboratory in Victoria became a miniature Buitenzorg, with its own chemical and botanical laboratories, trial fields, an experimental station for the clearing and reforestation of the "virgin" woods, and a training school to teach practical agriculture to the colonized peasants.[88]

At the same time, the Belgian colonial administration used the Buitenzorg model to whitewash the ill-reputed cash crop production in their Congo colony. In an attempt to make the international community forget the rubber scandals under Léopold II, the Belgian colonial government sent its "personnel technique agricole" to Java and to the British Indies.[89] Even before Brussels revoked Léopold as the king of the Congo in 1908, a horticulturist trained at Buitenzorg became responsible for establishing a botanical garden in Eala not far from the Congo River.[90] Belgian botanist-administrators claimed to be turning Eala into a "Congolese Buitenzorg."[91] Among other plants, they imported coconut palms, coffee, cocoa, and bamboo directly from Buitenzorg.[92]

The British botanist William Thiselton-Dyer, who was director of the Royal Botanic Gardens in Kew between 1885 and 1905, was the main instigator of the emulation of the Buitenzorg model in the British Empire.[93] The research station in Aburi (Gold Coast), in particular, followed this model and sent traveling instructors to the Ghanaian cocoa planters. Although they had used plants from São Tomé and were oriented toward America, Buitenzorg became important to them in times of crisis. When the São Tomé plants fell prey to fungal infestation during the World War I and deficient planting techniques

---

[87] Warburg, "Warum ist die Errichtung," 294–295.
[88] Thillard, "La Culture du Tabac."
[89] "Rapport présenté aux Chambres par le Ministre des Colonies," *Bulletin Agricole du Congo Belge* 1 (1910), 15–16.
[90] Pynaert, "Le Jardin d'Eala," 211.
[91] Wildeman, *Mission Emile Laurent*, cxliv.
[92] *Bulletin Agricole du Congo Belge et du Ruanda-Urundi* 1 (1910), 14 and 16.
[93] "Early History of Buitenzorg Botanic Gardens," *Bulletin of Miscellaneous Information (Royal Gardens, Kew)* 79 (1893), 248 and 253.

led to the decline of cocoa plantations in British West Africa, Buitenzorg experts were on hand with help and advice.[94] The director of the Institute for Plant Disease, C. J. J. van Hall, had closely observed and studied the cocoa smallholders in Ghana. He advised them on how to combat diseases and use budding methods developed at Buitenzorg. Also, in Southern Nigeria, officials published, recommended, and spread Hall's tutorials in English.[95]

In French Africa, the colonial administration established similar agronomic institutes and training schools for the African populations. After Chailley had promoted Buitenzorg, Auguste Chevalier, who was the *spiritus rector* of French colonial agronomy and edited the most important journal of colonial agriculture in France, was given the task of reorganizing the colonial agronomy of French Africa. Chevalier favored the participation of indigenous peasants in developing a stable colonial economy. To teach them efficient and modern planting techniques, Chevalier set out to establish specialized research stations for the cultivation of cotton, cocoa, coffee, and oleaginous plants. In search of a model for these stations, Chevalier traveled to the British and the Dutch Indies. On Chevaliers' initiative, the French colonial administration emulated Buitenzorg's laboratories and copied its scientific journals on tropical agriculture to spread a new version of agriculture.[96] Chevalier established research institutes for tea, Hevea rubber, and coffee in Indochina. In Senegal, he created a research station for groundnut production, a cash crop grown by Senegalese farmers that provided for half of the exports of French West Africa.[97] Chevalier's initiative was the prelude to the reform of the French colonial agronomy in West Africa (see Figure 4.1).

Ultimately, Buitenzorg became a model for much of the world affected by the intertwined processes of imperialism and global capitalist development in the late nineteenth and early twentieth centuries. Illustrative of the widening scope and transnational nature of its influence, the German Jew Otto Warburg used his botanical initiation at Buitenzorg to support Zionist colonization in Palestine. In 1903, while still directing several colonial cash crop companies in German Togo and Cameroon, he became the head of the Zionist Commission for the Exploration of Palestine. Warburg figured prominently in the Palestine Land Development Company (1908), which acquired territory in Palestine and trained Jewish settlers in farming and agronomy.[98]

---

[94] Chevalier, "Alerte aux Plantations."
[95] The links between British West Africa and Buitenzorg need further research. These hints on Buitenzorg's role are taken from Hall, *Cocoa*, vi, 146, and 382–392.
[96] Chevalier, "Le Fonctionnement du Laboratoire," 3–11; Chevalier, "Historique de la Revue de Botanique," 1.
[97] Bonneuil, "Auguste Chevalier," 20.
[98] Warburg, "Warum ist die Errichtung," 296; Warburg, "Über Wissenschaftliche Institute," 202.

4.8 THE CONSEQUENCES OF MYTHOLOGIZATION

Figure 4.1 French Governor-General of Indochina Pierre Pasquier visits Java, dinner in the garden, around 1929
© University Of Leiden, Digital Archives, Southeast Asian & Caribbean Images, Kitlv 118338: http://Hdl.Handle.Net/1887.1/Item:887261

Confirming the importance of the "Eastern model," West African botanists such as the "repatriated" Afro-Brazilian Michel Ahyi, who was active in Togo and Ghana, imported trees and plants from East Asia in the 1920s and 1930s. That was surprising, given that Afro-Americans who returned to West Africa after the end of slavery, maintained good relations with American producers and their extensive range of economic plants. Ahyi, however, traveled from Togo to Formosa to introduce quite important economic plants to West Africa: "I had to identify the name of the plant myself, after I returned from Formosa, China, because I learned there that the Chinese multiplied it extensively and used it to produce building timber and roof timbering ... I also introduced Pithécolobium sama, called the 'rain-tree' that provided a lot of shadow."

The trees soon adorned the streets of Lomé.[99] The transcolonial transfers were thus far from being an exclusively European affair, who nevertheless were responsible for spreading the Buitenzorg myth.

4.9 Cultivating the Buitenzorg Myth

Buitenzorg was undoubtedly the most frequently cited model for an efficient colonial agronomy and its emulation became fashionable among colonial administrations of the early twentieth century. However, its mythologization resulted in the fact that the "new" Buitenzorgs rarely mirrored the original's success and never lived up to expectations. It became clear to colonial agronomists that "improved" crops from Buitenzorg often failed when transferred to a different setting, such as coffee and pesticides from Java when planted in German East Africa. Furthermore, indigenous peasants often refused to plant the foreign crops or even rebelled against them, when colonial administrations made use of forced cultivation.[100]

Why did the Buitenzorg myth become so important and live on, despite its shortcomings? First of all, the international scientists at Buitenzorg needed positive news because their funding came mostly from private investors. The institute thus depended on its self-display of efficiency, rationality, and humanity. Second, foreign researchers who had been at Buitenzorg perpetuated the myth, given that a fellowship at the most modern agronomic institute could boost their careers. Third, Buitenzorg seemed to confirm colonial narratives about helpless native populations that needed agricultural education so as not to starve. To give substance to this idea, Europeans obscured the contribution of Javanese experts such as Raden Soleman and the poor impact on the improvement of the situation of the Javanese population. Fourth, and most importantly, it helped to portray colonialism as a progressive project. Hundreds of colonial administrators, publicists, and self-styled colonial experts referred to Buitenzorg when searching for a successful model of profitable but humane colonialism. Before the World War I, there were few examples of a colonial policy that lived up to the expectations of moral and material progress that colonial propagandists had raised. Not even Buitenzorg seemed to come close to such an ideal of a supposedly efficient and humanitarian colonial future. To use it as a symbol of colonial governmentality, Buitenzorg needed to be mythologized, and its negative sides hidden from the global public. From the perspective of European imperialists, therefore, turning it into the prototype of a "good colonialism" helped to legitimize colonization all over the world. So did the manipulation of native and Islamic law, which ICI members used to encourage development.

[99] Interview Robert Ahyi: Si Lomé m'était contée, 74.
[100] See the absence of Buitenzorg in Beckert, *Empire of Cotton*.

5

The Adatization of Islamic Law and Muslim Codes of Development

ICI members deemed transcolonial cooperation necessary to respond to the agitated "world of Islam" that transcended the internal borders of the colonial world from Indonesia to Senegal and from Mozambique to Algeria.[1] Although fearing a collective Pan-Islamist uprising against colonial rule, ICI members soon realized that the globality of Islam was defined by its diversity. Referring to strategies of colonial governmentality, ICI experts could claim that Islamic law was actually a customary law grounded in local conditions rather than in a single law imposed by the Qur'an. This redefinition of Islamic law as *adat* (customary) resulted in a significant transcolonial project of "adatization" of Islamic law. The diversity gave ICI members the opportunity to invent, redefine, and manipulate Islamic law by mixing different local traditions or Islamic schools of jurisprudence.[2] This invention and manipulation of Islamic law by the colonizers also provided the basis for subtler strategies of domination, repression or dispossession. In particular, they could use Islamic law to get access to profitable *ḥabūs* - landed property that was in the way of colonization. The debate about the *ḥabūs* became so pertinent in the Islamic world that anti-colonialists sent a petition to the American president Woodrow Wilson in 1919 and asked him to stop the expropriation of *ḥabūs*. Yet, in the 1920s and 1930s, colonial internationalists continued using Islam in general and the globality of Islam in particular to sustain and enhance colonial rule. Referring to Islamic law, ICI members promoted the revival of Islamic craft guilds as a tool to develop the colonial world in a sustained way. They saw in craft guilds the basic element of a "Muslim labor code" that might lead to a corporate reorganization of colonial societies as a third way between capitalism and socialism.

---

[1] For a general overview, see Motadel, *Islam*; Clancy-Smith, *Rebel and Saint*; Robinson, *Muslim Societies*; Hiskett, *The Course of Islam*; Levtzion and Pouwels, *The History of Islam in Africa*; Christelow, *Muslim Law Courts*.
[2] For Islamic law, see Hallaq, *A History of Islamic Legal Theories*.

5.1 Theory Meets Praxis: The ICI as a Hub for Exchange about Colonial Islam

ICI members assisted colonial governments that ruled the Muslim world from Rabat to Batavia and from Algiers to Dar es Salaam. Three of them stood out. Christiaan Snouck Hurgronje directed the Office for Native Affairs in the Dutch Indies for seventeen years. Marcel Morand dominated the policy of the French Service for Indigenous Affairs in Algeria from the turn of the century well into the inter-war period.[3] The German expert of Islam Carl Heinrich Becker prepared colonial administrators for service in Muslim Africa, while he served as the main advisor to the governor in German East Africa.[4] Together with ICI members such as Hubert Lyautey, Henri de Castries, and Louis Massignon, Becker dominated Islamic policy in most colonies between 1890 and the 1920s.[5]

An essential contribution to their reputation as experts was their close contact with Muslim scholars and intellectuals. They were well aware that theological debates within the Muslim community had been globalized throughout the nineteenth century. The global debates raised questions about the nature and the future of Islam under colonial rule. In the Najd region on the Arabian Peninsula, the Wahhabi movement set out to purge Islam of unorthodox and idolatry practices like the worship of saints. Even though politically opposed, the Dutch Arabist Snouck Hurgronje and the Wahhabi leaders would agree that local traditions had corrupted and weakened Islam and dissolved the unity of Islamic law. According to them, Islamic law resembled a customary rather than a divine law. Different Salafist movements argued in a similar way. Other Muslim thinkers agreed but reacted in the opposite way: Sayyid Jamāl ad-Dīn al-Afghānī or Muḥammad ʿAbduh saw in the modernization and rationalization of Islam and its laws the only way to shake off colonial rule.[6] As we will see, the ICI experts tried to use both this new global consciousness and the resulting realignment of Islam to redefine the religion for their own purposes. Those purposes were openly colonial.

The Dutch ICI member and Arabist Christiaan Snouck Hurgronje was the *spiritus rector* of Islamic studies and in high demand as a specialist on Muslim policy in colonial contexts. He had risen to fame during the 1890s, when he had assisted the Dutch colonial government in defeating the insurgent Aceh sultanate in Northern Sumatra (1873–1904).[7] Although the Dutch won the war by using excessive violence, Snouck Hurgronje made the world believe

---

[3] Arabi, "Orienting the Gaze," 43–72.
[4] Pesek, "Sulayman b. Nasir al-Lamki," 225–229.
[5] Burke, *The Ethnographic State*.
[6] Snouck Hurgronje, *Oeuvres Choisies*, 58–59; Aydin, *The Idea*, 8–9.
[7] Snouck Hurgronje, *The Achehnese*; Kuitenbrouwer and Poeze, *Dutch Scholarship*, 70.

that his detailed knowledge of Acehnese Islam and its notion of a holy war was the decisive factor.[8] Starting in the 1890s, colonial experts lined up to ask for Snouck Hurgronje's advice. The French leader of the ICI, Joseph Chailley, met him in Batavia in 1897 and haunted him whenever he was in Europe.[9] The head of the Algerian Service of Indigenous Affairs, Edmond Doutté, studied Dutch in order to read Snouck Hurgronje's report on the Acehnese. He convinced Snouck Hurgronje to become an unofficial advisor to the Indigenous Affairs Department in Algiers.[10] Shortly thereafter, Snouck Hurgronje became an official advisor to the French government in Morocco.[11] British colonial authorities translated Snouck Hurgronje's works on the Acehnese, commissioned him to study the relations of Indian Muslims with Mecca, and circulated his publications among the administrators in the empire.[12] German ICI member Becker sought advice from Snouck Hurgronje on German policies in East Africa and relied on him when establishing Islamic studies at the Colonial Institute in Hamburg. In 1909, he wrote to Snouck Hurgronje that he was "happy to create something which is completely new for Germany and modelled on your courses" in Leiden.[13] The exchange on colonial policies between Hamburg and Leiden ultimately resulted in the exchange of students between the two colonial universities.[14]

So why was Snouck Hurgronje so popular among the colonizers? Apart from his expertise, the answer was his reassuring way of persuading colonial administrators that the transcolonial solidarity between Muslims – falsely demonized as an aggressive Pan-Islamism – was not a threat but a chance for colonial governments. The latter were constantly concerned about "radicalized" Muslims who returned from the pilgrimage to Mecca. The Indian Civil Service, for example, commissioned Snouck Hurgronje to study the pilgrimage from British India to Mecca and its consequences for Indian Islam.[15] The German administration, in particular, feared that Muslims might accept the Ottoman caliphate in Istanbul as the "Supreme Lord of all Muhammedans" and rebel in his name.[16] ICI members Snouck Hurgronje and Becker ridiculed

---

[8] Snouck Hurgronje to Nöldeke April 25, 1891; Koningsveld, *Orientalism and Islam*, 27.
[9] ULCSH, Or8952, A225: Chailley to Snouck Hurgronje, February 1, 1913; ULCSH, Or8952, A224: Chailley (UCF) to Snouck Hurgronje, June 20, 1897 and A225: Chailley to Snouck Hurgronje, January 26, 1913.
[10] ULCSH, Or. 8952 A273: Doutté to Snouck Hurgronje, February 24, 1901.
[11] ULCSH, Or. 8952 A183: Postcard Lucien Bouvat to Snouck Hurgronje, July 26, 1916.
[12] ULCSH, Or. 8952 A233: Constable to Snouck Hurgronje, May 27, 1891.
[13] ULCSH, Or8952, A140: Becker to Snouck Hurgronje [? First letter 140]; Or. 8952 A141: Becker to Snouck Hurgronje, January 1, 1909.
[14] ULCSH, Or 8952, A145: Becker to Snouck Hurgronje, June 4, 1912.
[15] ULCSH, Or. 8952 A233: Constable to Snouck Hurgronje, May 27, 1891; Slight, *The British Empire*, 62–123.
[16] Snouck Hurgronje, "The Holy War," 249–284.

these concerns about Pan-Islamic insurrections as amateurish.[17] Snouck Hurgronje informed them that Muslims had long accepted government by the strongest power and not by the most holy one. He argued that in the twentieth century, 90 percent of Muslims lived under non-Muslim rulers.[18]

Nevertheless, radical versions of Islam continued to raise concerns. After all, Islamic messianism had engendered violent Mahdiist revolts in Egyptian Sudan (1881), British India (1889), and German Cameroon (1907).[19] The Mahdiist eschatology was said to create emotions that were hard to control.[20] Against the background of the Aceh jihad, Snouck Hurgronje recommended that colonial governments should immediately "fight these fanatic movements with violence."[21] But he also added reassuringly that they were local phenomena. Both the geographic distance and religious factionalism prevented local Mahdi rebellions from spreading in the Islamic world. Indeed, confessionalism seemed to be a natural barrier to a Pan-Islamist union.

This was slightly different with Sufi brotherhoods (khouans). Colonial administrators warned against the rebellious character of the "panislamist Khouanism," particularly the Sanūsīya order that resisted German, French, British, and Italian colonizers in Northern and Central Africa.[22] Their conspiratorial meetings in which they convulsed in hysteria, their allegedly socialist community spirit, and their military "fanaticism" led the colonial powers to see in them the veritable "Islamic peril."[23] Algerian Sufi brothers, the governor-general in Algeria calculated, paid annual taxes amounting to 702,180 francs to brethren outside Algeria. Their monasteries served as places of sanctuary, and the colonial governments suspected them of hiding not only illegal foreigners but also criminals. To make things worse, the Sufi brotherhoods possessed extensive territories qualified as waqf or ḥabūs, holy community lands that were inalienable according to Muslim law. Therefore, the government characterized them both as a "state within a state" that levied taxes from ca. 300,000 Algerian Sufi brothers and as "the very soul of Panislamism" that did not respect colonial borders.[24]

Snouck Hurgronje generally agreed regarding the potential dangers of Muslim mysticism and its particular inclination to refute authority. Yet he also informed the colonizers that it did not matter much if external laws imposed on the Sufis were Muslim or Christian or secular.[25] Sufis allegedly

---

[17] Becker, L'Islam, 10.
[18] Snouck Hurgronje, Oeuvres Choisies, 108 and 47–50.
[19] Becker, L'Islam, 9.
[20] Snouck Hurgronje, Politique Musulmane, 101–102.
[21] Ibid., 76.
[22] On Senegal, see Diouf, Tolerance, 9.
[23] Billiard, "Étude sur la Condition Politique," 18; Triaud, La Légende noire de la Sanûsiyya.
[24] Depont and Coppolani, Les Confréries, 252–253.
[25] Snouck Hurgronje, Politique Musulmane, 71.

contested authority and not ideology. After all, Snouck Hurgronje explained, they were an elite phenomenon and not a fanaticized mob. Quite frequently, they had indeed been open to accepting Western authority. While Snouck Hurgronje thought it impossible to reform or dismantle them because of their eminent political and social role, he pleaded for cooperation.[26]

Inspired by Snouck Hurgronje and Muslim lawyers close to the ICI, the Algerian government indeed realized that Sufi brotherhoods were "devoted to governments who knew how to approach them."[27] A Muslim professor at the madrassa of Algiers and clerk in the French administration, Mohand Said Ibnou Zekri from Kabylia, had pushed for such a reinterpretation of brotherhoods in his reformist book *Risāla*, dating from 1903. He provided the French with firsthand knowledge about the Sufi lodges (*zāwiyah*), especially in "Berber" Kabylia, where customary law and Islamic law blurred. These *zāwiyahs* had had a bad reputation among French colonizers because of their participation in the "insurrection" of 1871. An early modernizer of Islam, Ibnou Zekri suggested instead that the French administration could easily turn the declining *zāwiyahs* into strongholds of the colonial state and even make them "Republican *zāwiyahs*."[28] Ibnou Zekri always remained close to ICI members and his son would become the first Algerian to join the Institute in the 1950s.

Against the background of such initiatives, an official report reinterpreted the history of the French conquest in Algeria and found instances of successful French cooperation with the *Tijāniyyah* brotherhood, which had "always regarded us as the rightful occupant of Algerian territory by the will of God." Both the French and the *Tijāniyyah* had profited from mutual military support, and the former conquered Algeria with the help of the latter. Against the background of international models and the rereading of Algeria's own history, governor-general Jules Cambon launched a policy of alliance with the most important brotherhoods in Algeria. Cambon frequently arranged his colonial policies with his brother Paul, an ICI member and the instigator of French indirect rule over the protectorate in Tunisia.[29] Increasingly, most ICI members considered Islam and partially also Sufi brotherhoods a useful tool for colonization, ascribed civilizational power to them, and declared Islam a co-colonizer to Europeans. When the German Becker, a follower of Snouck Hurgronje, spoke before Chailley's French

---

[26] Ibid., 72–73.
[27] Depont and Coppolani, *Les Confréries Religieuses Musulmanes*, 263.
[28] Pouillon, *Dictionnaire*, 654–655; Kamel, *L'Islam kabyle*, 46–97.
[29] Depont and Coppolani, *Les* Confréries, 265, 271; Cambon, *Paul Cambon* vol. 1, for example, 201; Trumbull, *An Empire of Facts*, 118.

Colonial Union in 1910, he summed up that for most of the colonial powers, Islam was not a rival but an ally.[30]

Based on the idea of Islam as a co-colonizer, administrators actively engaged with Muslim religious authorities. A well-known way to do so was to receive fatwas that allowed Muslims to live under European colonial rule.[31] Islamic jurists, the muftis, issued fatwas in Mecca or Medina, which were then globally accepted by believers as guidelines for lawful behavior. As early as the 1850s, the British rulers in India had asked muftis from Mecca to issue a fatwa that authorized Indian Muslims to live under the rule of the infidel colonizers.[32] Snouck Hurgronje was familiar with this use of fatwas to stabilize colonial rule and presented the Dutch government with the strategy.[33] At his instigation, the Dutch paid the ulema Sayyid Uthman, a descendant of the Prophet who had become mufti in Batavia, 100 guilders a month to publicly preach loyalty to the Dutch government. When the Dutch queen was enthroned in 1898, Uthman not only recognized her as a sovereign but also praised her as the protector of Indonesian Muslims.[34] In Algeria, governor-general Jules Cambon traveled to Mecca in 1893 and received a fatwa from the muftis that reproduced the British and Dutch ones almost verbatim. The Meccan fatwa authorized Algerian Muslims to live under French rule, provided that they were free to practice their religion and that Muslim jurisdiction was applied to them.[35] Cambon took advantage of his journey to Mecca to secure another fatwa. This fatwa excommunicated the leaders of the *Sanūsīya* brotherhood, who were supposedly about to establish a sovereign state in central Africa and had opposed French troops north of Lake Chad.[36]

The ICI recommended the fatwa policy as one strategy for the successful realization of native policy.[37] It was soon applied in all colonies with Muslim populations.[38] Yet, using institutions of Islamic law was not enough for the colonizers. In the Dutch Indies, Snouck Hurgronje had suggested to his collaborator Sayyed Uthman to go beyond the fatwa policy in order to influence and control the life of Indonesian Muslims. Commissioned by Snouck Hurgronje, Uthman actively interfered with the jurisdiction of Muslim *qāḍīs*.

---

[30] Becker, *L'Islam*, 19.
[31] Fatwas are generally defined as "nonbinding legal opinions issued by a qualified Islamic scholar in response to a question posed by an individual, judge, or government." *The Princeton Encyclopedia*, 173.
[32] Hunter, *The Indian Musalmans*, 217–219.
[33] Snouck Hurgronje to Directeur van Onderwijs, April 5, 1891, in Snouck Hurgronje, *Ambtelijke Adviezen*, vol. 2, 1512.
[34] Snouck Hurgronje, "Islam und Phonograph," 426.
[35] Depont and Coppolani, *Les Confréries*, 35 and 37.
[36] Ibid., viii.
[37] Morand in ICI, *Compte Rendu 1909*, 441, note 2.
[38] Umar, *Islam and Colonialism*, 30.

To guide – or manipulate – their decisions, he edited a handbook for jurists. The handbook claimed to synthesize Islamic law and was enforced on the Muslim judges as a mandatory book of reference for decisions taken in Muslim courts. Those guidelines had not been an official codification of law, but they anticipated future developments in Muslim policy: the manipulation and reinvention of Islamic Law under colonial rule.[39]

5.2 From Divine Law to Customary Law: The Adatization of Islam

International experts of Islam joined Snouck Hurgronje in deconstructing Islamic law only to reinvent and reconstruct it for their own benefit. The most important strategy in deconstructing Islamic law was to identify the weak points of its system. There were two options for pursuing this goal. The first was to reveal the internal contradictions of Islamic law. The second option was to expose the external influences that had corrupted the legal system of Islam. ICI members from the Netherlands excelled in both approaches. They were at the center of reinventing Islam as a "soft" and dynamic law that enabled them to use it for colonial purposes.

The soft character of Islamic law was inherent to the legal system of Islam. Snouck Hurgronje argued that Islamic law had been a dynamic and evolving corpus during the first three centuries of its existence. At that time, it absorbed influences from the civilizations that Muslims conquered and was a highly syncretistic religion. It was obvious that passages in the Qur'an had been taken from Christianity, Judaism, and also Roman law, revealing that Muhammed not only interpreted divine revelations but also completed them.[40] Snouck Hurgronje emphasized that the Qur'an itself was put into writing relatively late and that at the moment it had become inalterable, it also became insufficient. Therefore, the Sunna was added as a legal source, consisting of six authoritative collections of the Prophet's words and deeds. When these failed to do justice to the complexity of reality, the consensus of the (early) Muslim community (*Ijmā'*) was attributed the authority to decide on cases that were neither covered by the Qur'an nor by the Sunna. Islamic scholars then invented ever more refined legal instruments to decide on complicated issues: *Qiyās* were conclusions of analogy, *ra'ī* were the personal and rational judgments of a judge, while *'adāt* and *'urf* were the local customs that had to be taken into account. The repertoire of legal sources thus comprised Qur'an, Sunna, analogy, logic, and customs – and not even in that order, because it was possible to counter a Qur'anic verse with arguments taken from the Sunna.[41]

---

[39] Snouck Hurgronje, *Politique Musulmane*, 70.
[40] Snouck Hurgronje, *Oeuvres Choisies*, 51.
[41] Ibid., 217–273.

As a result, the varying historical and political contexts determined the evolution of Islamic laws and produced a wide range of contradictory regulations. "So many sects, parties and tendencies," Snouck Hurgronje resumed, "so many collections of rules that apply to a small group only."[42] Moreover, the lack of a stable clergy and an imperious caliphate allowed every Muslim to follow their own versions of Islam.[43] Starting in the tenth century, Snouck Hurgronje added, Islam had stopped modernizing its legal corpus. This outdated law did not live up to the necessities of the modern world in the nineteenth century. According to him, aphorisms, which Arabs loved to insert into their conversations, illustrated the alleged mismatch between Islamic law and modern everyday life: the phrases "necessity ignores all laws" or "necessity follows its own laws" (al-ḍarūra lahā aḥkam) could be overheard from Casablanca to Batavia. In many fatwas, Snouck Hurgronje found the expression "because of necessity or constraint" (li-ajl al-ḍarūra) that served to give authority to a claim not covered by the Qur'an or the Sunna.[44]

According to Snouck Hurgronje, the use of "necessity" (ḍarūra) as a legal argument had two antithetical consequences. On the one hand, ḍarūra was a means for Islamic law to declare itself irrelevant. It offered a legal possibility to suspend the law and declare a state of exception, especially in times of colonial invasion. But even earlier, Islamic law had surrendered to local customs, owing to its own inflexible rigidity. On the other hand, the legal argument of "necessity" provided a means to safeguard the authority of Islamic law. According to ḍarūra, it was actually lawful to respond to the "necessities" of modernity and to bring about the modernization of Islamic law. Indeed, modernization was under way, Snouck Hurgronje argued by making reference to reforms in the Ottoman Empire and Egypt that combined Islamic and European civil law.[45] Taking those countries as an example, Snouck Hurgronje concluded that Islamic law had to be modernized in order to survive. He did so by using arguments he found in the Islamic legal repertoire, such as the ḍarūra. If Islamic law had always adapted to local customs, it could also adapt to the necessities of global modernity.

The legal flexibility of Islamic law and its "customary" character was also due to influences from outside the system. The long history of Islamic expansion revealed its capacity to incorporate elements of foreign customs. The practice of Islam in the Dutch East Indies, British India, German East Africa, and French North Africa was a case in point. Snouck Hurgronje had spent several years of his intellectual life proving that Islam had reached Indonesia not directly from the Arabian Peninsula but via India. On the way, he argued,

---

[42] Ibid., 223.
[43] Snouck Hurgronje, "Politique Musulmane de la Hollande," 27.
[44] Snouck Hurgronje, *Oeuvres Choisies*, 247–248.
[45] Ibid., 247–251.

5.2 FROM DIVINE LAW TO CUSTOMARY LAW

it had absorbed Hindu and Buddhist elements before carrying them to Indonesia.⁴⁶ There, again, it had blended with local customary law. ICI member Becker agreed and was even believed to have singled out elements of India's syncretistic "popular Islam" as far as East Africa, where Swahili-speaking ulema used religious texts from Bombay and the Malabar Coast.⁴⁷ These texts were shot through with rites from Indian traditions, including the use of holy water or the art of oneiromancy.⁴⁸ According to Becker, no region equaled British India in its variety of Islamic sects. He assumed that this was due to the adaption of Islam to the caste system.⁴⁹

With regard to diversity, Becker claimed, African Islam was in no way inferior to the varieties of Asian Islam. Becker evoked the works of Edmond Doutté, who had analyzed the magical practices of Islam in the Maghreb. The mysticism of North African Islam ascribed *barakah* (more or less "benediction") to saints but also to things and situations of personal contemplative ecstasy. This "animist" tradition was backed by the omnipresence of beliefs in curses or the harmful effects of the "evil eye." Doutté had concluded that Islam "absorbed the old beliefs in magic" more easily than any other religion. Customary law was deeply rooted in indigenous societies and nowhere replaced by Islam: "While the beliefs change, the rites persist."⁵⁰ This was an attitude shared by both Arabists and anthropologists working in West Africa.⁵¹

Moreover, Becker remarked that, unlike Christianity, Islam did not spread through missionary activity. Instead, economic expansion and military conquest carried Islam to Asia and Africa.⁵² This implied that it was not dogmatically trained missionaries who spread Islam but merchants, soldiers, and administrators.⁵³ These laymen were dogmatically undisciplined and often misinterpreted Islamic rules. While some recited prayers without understanding their content, others did not even maintain the outward appearance of the rituals. In Java, for example, Islamic law had never gained a foothold. Snouck Hurgronje observed that in Aceh, people did not pray five times a day, and in other regions in Java, Muslims ignored the fasting period.⁵⁴ These accounts led some ICI members to believe that Islamic law officially in force in the Dutch Indies had actually nothing to do with Islam.

---

⁴⁶ ULCSH, Or. 8952 A140: Becker to Snouck Hurgronje, January 31, 1907; Snouck Hurgronje, *Politique Musulmane*, 72.
⁴⁷ Becker, "Materialien," 30.
⁴⁸ Ibid., 33.
⁴⁹ Ibid., 5.
⁵⁰ Doutté, *Magie et Religion*, 602; Becker, "Materialien," 31.
⁵¹ Le Chatelier, *Les Confréries Musulmanes*.
⁵² ULCSH, Or. 8952 A: 144 Becker to Snouck Hurgronje, May 19, 1911.
⁵³ Snouck Hurgronje, "Politique Musulmane de la Hollande," 29–30.
⁵⁴ Ibid., 28 and 50.

It was exactly the idea that Islamic law in the Dutch Indies had nothing to do with Islam that inspired Dutch ICI member Cornelis van Vollenhoven to launch the biggest codification project of customary Islamic law in the history of colonialism. Around 1900, Van Vollenhoven became obsessed with the idea that behind the Islamic label, the customary *adat* law ruled in the Dutch Indies. In his view, customary *adat* law had not only infiltrated but completely taken over Islamic law. ICI members encouraged Van Vollenhoven to collect indigenous *adat law* in the Dutch Indies.[55] By indigenizing Islamic law through adatization, it became easier to manipulate it. Van Vollenhoven chose the term *adat*, the Arabic word for custom, which designated the customary traditions in Indonesia. Paradoxically, Van Vollenhoven chose an Arabic term to prove that *adats* had little to do with Islam. Instead, he argued that these customs had become authoritative, and to neglect them resulted in punishment. Therefore, Van Vollenhoven insisted on using the expression *adat* law: "They are *adat* on account of their uncodified state and *law* because they carry sanctions."[56] Starting in 1900, Van Vollenhoven's collaborators collected *adats* to ultimately systematize them in forty-five volumes of so-called *Adatsrechtbundel*.[57] To promote its use, Van Vollenhoven published extensively on the theory and practice of *adat* law. He spread his theory via the ICI, where he earned himself the honorific nickname "Homer of adat law."[58]

To uncover superficially Islamicized *adat* law, Van Vollenhoven instructed his collaborators, who collected elements of customary law in extensive fieldwork in the Dutch Indies, to distrust any report on the legal force of Islamic or Hindu law. He even prohibited his assistants to consult written texts or interrogate the Indonesians about their legal mentalities. He wanted them to rely on the close observation of everyday practice only.[59] Even if Indonesians knew about Islamic legal concepts, – like *melk* (right of ownership) or *sarakat* (common property) – he cautioned that their existence in a code did not prove they were applied in practice.[60] Therefore, he believed that only anthropological methods – and participant observations, in particular – allowed him to identify and understand *adat* law.

Van Vollenhoven's survey followed recurring patterns of ethno-juridical research by searching for fragmentation and the plurality of customs. With utmost care, his collaborators analyzed native collectivities and their

---

[55] Van Vollenhoven, "The Study of Adat Law," 27 and 31. Van Vollenhoven, "La Politique Coloniale," 409; Snouck Hurgronje to Nöldeke May 1, 1921, in Koningsveld, *Orientalism and Islam*, 288.
[56] Van Vollenhoven, "The Elements of Adat Law."
[57] Van Vollenhoven, *Adatrechtbundels*, 45 vols., published 1911–1955.
[58] ICI, *Compte Rendu 1920*, 143.
[59] Van Vollenhoven, "Adat Guide (1910)," 262–265.
[60] Van Vollenhoven, "The Elements of Adat," 12.

territorially or genealogically determined solidarity. This approach helped to "naturally" compartmentalize the territory under investigation into "law areas" that were inhabited by "jural communities" (*rechtsgemeenschappen*). Aceh, for example, constituted such an autonomous legal community.[61] The fragmentation of *adat* law provided the colonial administration with the possibility of using both "divide and rule" and "define and rule" strategies to impose its will. In the fifty volumes of collected *adat* law, Van Vollenhoven indeed defined and partially invented *adat*. In the Dutch Indies, *adat* law would become the ruling law and even provided the basis for the new constitutional law after Indonesia's independence in 1945.

To make colonial authorities familiar with his insights and further develop *adat* law, Van Vollenhoven entered the ICI in 1913. Up to that date, he had published predominantly in Dutch, a language that few colonial officials understood. While the Dutch terminology of his *adat*-theory was hard to translate, he nevertheless hoped to spread its principles. Speaking before the ICI in 1921, Van Vollenhoven extended his diagnosis beyond the borders of the Dutch Indies. He had always regarded the Malay Archipelago (including the Philippines), Indochina, and Madagascar as one cultural unit, in which Indonesian *adat* law prevailed. Later, he added British India to the map of *adat* law countries.[62] In all of those territories, he complained, colonial administrators had mistakenly assumed that religious laws – Islamic or Hindu – governed the population. According to him, this ignorance of *adat* law had led to severe misunderstandings and conflicts. In Bengal in British India, for example, administrators had committed the original sin of declaring the religious codes (Muslim, Buddhist, and Hindu) as a basis and source of native law. The same error had been repeated over and over again, the last time in Burma in 1898.[63] Even worse for him was the imposing of English law. These Anglo-Indian Codes fostered assimilation, which Van Vollenhoven considered to be even more detrimental to colonial policy, as assimilation was diametrically opposed to the nature of *adat*. It was indeed only in 1915 that the British contemplated a serious codification of customary law that might have existed under the guise of Islamic, Hindu, or English law.[64] The logic behind adatization soon spread to all colonies with a Muslim population and particularly shaped native policy in North Africa, where administrators admired the Dutch example.

The members of the ICI loomed large in launching adatization processes across all colonies, mainly because it emphasized Islam's plurality. This plurality had indeed always been inherent to the various forms of Islam around the

---

[61] Ibid., 57–60.
[62] Holleman (ed.), *Van Vollenhoven on Indonesian Adat Law*, xxx.
[63] Van Vollenhoven, "La Politique Coloniale," 374.
[64] Ibid., 375.

world but became more visible through the comparative and transcolonial approach at the end of the nineteenth and in the early twentieth century. The ICI members were pioneers in comparing Islam in different colonies. In a similar way, Pan-Islamic dialogue across empires made differences visible. Muslim intellectuals saw in this plurality a harbinger of decline. In a way, emergent Pan-Islamic revivalist and preservationist movements, such as the Salafiya and the Wahabiya, responded to the adatization project by preaching a return to the original and uniform Islamic code of the Qur'an. Another branch of Pan-Islamists reacted the opposite way. It claimed that Islam would erode from within in a paradoxical tension between orthodox aspiration and heterodox reality. Thus, it turned to reform and wanted to overcome its customary character by modernizing Islam and Islamic law, as the Ottoman Empire and Egypt had done it in the 1870s. We will see that ICI members also tried to use this modernized Islamic law to rule their own colonies.

The adatization project was also much to the taste of most ICI members, as it confirmed their belief in cultural relativism. The primary result of adatization was the primacy of customary law. As the fragmentation of customary law had long served to legitimize colonial pacification and domination, it helped to justify colonial rule. Also, Islam's supposed plurality and flexibility deprived independence movements of a unifying emancipative ideology. Adatization was also a way of containing Islamic independence movements. Thus, it is hardly surprising that ICI members endorsed the idea that Muslim law was neither Muslim nor a law. Again, it was Snouck Hurgronje who put it bluntly: "Muslim law is not a law."[65]

The interpretation of Islam as plural and vulnerable, which Muslim intellectuals and the ICI's experts on Islam shared for different reasons, attracted the attention of colonial administrations all over the world. The territory they administered was congruent with those regions that had seen the convergence of local customs and Islamic culture. The adatization project taught them that Islam might be an opportunity for colonial rulers rather than a threat to colonial rule. As it was potentially open to further modification, they started programs to modify it according to their own interests. Manipulative codification and transformative modernization were two means to the ends of imposing colonial rule. This initiative fell on fertile ground in Algeria, where ICI member and head of the Service of Indigenous Affairs, Marcel Morand, started a project to codify Islamic law. Morand was a declared follower of Snouck Hurgronje, although Snouck Hurgronje theoretically discredited the codification of Muslim law to preserve its dynamic character.[66]

---

[65] Snouck Hurgronje, *Oeuvres Choisies*, 261.
[66] Contacts beyond the common membership in the ICI seem only to have started in 1923. See ULCSH, Or. 8952 D103: Morand to Snouck Hurgronje, September 27, 1927; ULCSH, Or. 8952 A144: Becker to Snouck Hurgronje, May 19, 1911.

5.3 The Codification of Islamic Law in Algeria

Algeria's governor-general Jonnart started the most reckless attempt to use Islam's globality, diversity, and dynamics for colonial purposes.[67] In 1905, he commissioned Marcel Morand, the director of the Algiers School of Law, who specialized in Muslim law and native customs, to produce a codification of Algeria's Muslim law. Along with the head of Algeria's indigenous affairs at that time, Jean-Dominique Luciani, he put together an expert commission that comprised both Europeans and Algerian ulama.[68] It took them eleven years to publish the code. The process was particularly time consuming: While Morand set the agenda and drafted the Code's preliminary version, the individual paragraphs were sent to Muslim and European judges, as well as to European court presidents in Algeria's bigger cities. All of them could comment on the draft, with the commission discussing their objections and occasionally changing the Code in response. Although the Code never came into force, tribunals in the colonies constantly referred to it and colonial administrators appreciated Morand's Code and grounded their juridical argumentation on it.[69]

Morand also responded to the appeal of ICI members at the International Congress of Colonial Sociology in 1900 to reevaluate not only indigenous jurisprudence but also their legal codes.[70] The ICI, with its comprehensive publications on colonial law, was his main source of information and stimulation. A member of the ICI since 1907, Morand had always consulted its members for potential models of codification in other countries.[71] Snouck Hurgronje and Becker, in particular, inspired his general idea of Islamic law.[72] He saw in the use of law a tool for control, knowing that Snouck Hurgronje had used *adat* law to refine measures of counterinsurgency in Aceh. Moreover, he had observed British attempts in India to transcribe the law of the *Khodja* sect to stamp out its unclear status between Shiism and Sunnism that caused them to rebel against colonial authorities.[73]

From studying codification projects in other parts of the world, Morand had also learned about the variety of Islamic law. He agreed with Snouck Hurgronje that history had proven the inconsistency of the two main sources

---

[67] The first French administrator to collect elements of Islamic Law in Algeria was Louis Rinn. See Rinn, *Marabouts*; and Trumbull, *An Empire of Facts*, 20–25 and 64–71.
[68] Pouillon, *Dictionnaire des orientalistes*, 252.
[69] Ibid.; "Marcel Morand," 747.
[70] Morand saw the congress and the ICI at the origin of native legislation. See Morand, *Introduction à l'Étude*, 19, note 2.
[71] Morand, *Avant-projet de Code*, 9.
[72] In 1923, Algeria's government sent a copy to Snouck Hurgronje: ULCSH Or. 8952 A277: Letter Doutté to Snouck Hurgronje, September 8, 1923, and September 20, 1923.
[73] Morand, *Avant-projet de Code*, 9.

of law – the Qur'an and the collection of traditions in the Sunna – and therefore their openness to interpretation. He was familiar with the Dutch strategies of adatization of Islamic law. In addition, Morand informed himself about the four orthodox Islamic schools of law (*madhahib*) that dominated in different parts of the world. In British India, two rudimentary handbooks were in use to inform administrators about the predominating Ḥanafī school but that were not necessarily applicable to other colonies with Mālikī or Ḥanbalī or Šāfi'ī rites. This is why Anglo-Indian authors started translating Mālikī legal texts valid in West Africa.[74] The existence of different schools of law in Sunni Islam would become one of the most important tools for the French to manipulate Islamic law.

Complicating matters was the specific situation in Algeria, where the colonial authorities applied French law to French settlers and Islamic law to Algerian Muslims. This duality, Morand remarked, was, however, not absolute. According to a decree from April 17, 1889, "necessity" divested land tenure law from Muslim jurisdiction. "The Muslims residing in Algeria," Morand observed, "are governed by Muslim law only in the fields of personal status, succession, some of their buildings and the use of testimonies for evidence." French law, however, would soon rule over matters of land tenure and real estate because it guaranteed "the security of transactions, the development of colonization, and the very interest of the natives whose land tenure system risks to bring down the price of the land. These necessities command that in the future, there will be only one land tenure system in Algeria, which is French law."[75] The French administrators thus aimed at controlling the most important economic resource in colonial Algeria – land. Morand would teach them how to use Islamic law for that purpose.

Morand's codification of Algerian Muslim law covered four domains: civil status (*statut personnel*), inheritance law (*loi de succession*), certain regulations concerning real estate (*immobilier*), and testimony (*prevue des obligations*). The commission was particularly curious about Muslim notions on the possession of land.[76] This was particularly true for the ḥabūs lands, which were inalienable real estate according to Islamic laws. As the founder of a ḥabūs immobilized the land mostly by will – while assuring the *usufruct* rights to his heirs – the French Supreme Court treated the ḥabūs as subject to inheritance law. As a consequence, they escaped French property law, which did not have any legal equivalent to the ḥabūs.[77]

Morand's codification was a farce. He himself drafted the first version in French, which was then translated into Arabic and sent to Muslim judges.

---

[74] Russel and Suhrawardy, *First Steps in Muslim Jurisprudence*, xiv.
[75] Morand, *Avant-projet de Code*, 12–13.
[76] Ibid.
[77] Ibid., 17.

5.3 THE CODIFICATION OF ISLAMIC LAW IN ALGERIA

Although Muslims, most of the qāḍīs seem to have accepted the codification project. Overall, they only asked for insignificant changes. Morand turned most of these cautious requests down, arguing that "this request contradicts Muslim law and cannot be changed." It was Morand who defined the nature of Muslim law.[78] The other members of the codification commission, which consisted of nine Europeans and three Muslims, who were moreover loyal to the French government, abided by Morand's decisions.

A few qāḍīs could use the International Congress of Colonial Sociology to contest the French policy of manipulating Islamic law. Remaining anonymous, one of them lamented that "the cadis used to be omnipotent and were competent in all fields of law: civil, penal, and criminal. They even could impose the death penalty ... what remains today of that power? What do we have left of our multiple skills? Very few, if not to say nothing." As early as 1866, the French state had started to oust Algerian qāḍīs, who challenged French competence: "It is extremely difficult ... for strangers to assimilate Arabic morals, to get to the bottom of their usages and customs."[79] Generally, however, many qāḍīs participated in the codification project and tried to bring in their own as well as colonial interests: "Law has to speak to the multiple interests that seem to be in jeopardy and has to safeguard the property of the natives, the rights of the buyer, and the necessities of colonization. This is the main point."[80] The "necessities of colonization" was a code that the French administration used to justify expropriations and in some cases forced labor. Nevertheless, a subtle protest was possible.

Morand managed to silence their protests by arguing that his version of Islamic law was authoritative because eminent Muslim scholars from Egypt and the Ottoman Empire endorsed it. He explicitly referred to the "Europeanized" *Mecelle* codes of the Ottoman Empire (1877) and the Egyptian civil code (1876).[81] This strategy he had adopted from ICI leader Joseph Chailley, who had promoted the use of Europeanized law from Egypt and the Ottoman Empire in the colonies with a Muslim majority.

In the 1890s, Joseph Chailley had proudly trumpeted his friendship with the Ottoman minister and legislator Sawas Pasha. An Ottoman minister of foreign affairs, Sawas Pasha had contributed to the codification of Ottoman Muslim law in the 1870s. The result of this reorganization of Ottoman law was the so-called *Mecelle* code that combined Islamic Ḥanafī law with elements of European law and stood for Europe's semi-colonial influence in the Ottoman Empire. Chailley admired Sawas Pasha for his ability to express

---

[78] Gouvernement Général de l'Algérie, *Projet de Codification*, 57.
[79] "Mémoire présenté par un cadi Algerien," *Congrès international de sociologie coloniale*, vol. 2, 131.
[80] Ibid., 138.
[81] Morand, *Avant-Projet de Code*, 7.

European prerogatives in terms of Islamic law: "Sawas Pasha tells us that every occidental truth can be in the long term understood and accepted by Muslims, provided that it had been islamisized."[82] Sawas Pasha – who was a Christian and had become a French national by choice – was a member of Chailley's French Colonial Union and a proponent of the French civilizing mission.

Sawas Pasha's concept of Muslim law derived from the Ottoman debates on the modernization of the law and its combination with European, mainly French, law. He emphasized its compatibility with European law and its ability to develop and to adapt to changing situations. According to him, the history of Islam had proven this flexibility during its expansion, when it changed significantly while being applied to new circumstances and the necessities of their population. But Islam's flexibility to adapt to local specificities went hand in hand with its capacity to adjust to change over time. To substantiate his claim, Sawas Pasha cited the "legislating prophet" Muhammad, claiming that "the laws cannot be changed but by the necessities of the time [*exigences du temps*]."[83] Like European specialists, he claimed that Islam was a dynamic religion that reacted to necessities of global change. Its modernization was not only possible but also necessary. Colonial administrators were more than happy to share this attitude and acted on Sawas Pasha's authority as an Ottoman legislator. He gave lectures at Chailley's Colonial Union as early as 1893, in which he proposed the framing of modern European law in Islamic terms and its application all over the colonized world.[84] For the European colonizers, Sawas Pasha's Christianity was of secondary importance, a view not necessarily shared by Muslims. While Arabists such as Becker or Snouck Hurgronje harshly criticized him for his crude manipulation of Ottoman law, colonial administrators in Algeria and Tunisia tried to emulate his approach and adopt the Europeanized Ottoman law.

Morand, in particular, left no doubt that his version of Islamic law was the correct one, arguing that it originated in the reformed *sharia* codes that governed Turkey and Egypt. Egypt had also "modernized" its legal codes under the guidance of Europeans and integrated elements of the French civil code.[85] Morand claimed that Muslim governments of those countries had made those codes. According to him, they represented the most modern version of Islamic law, with which Algerian judges had to be familiarized. Most importantly, he ascribed the highest authority to verdicts of the Egyptian mixed courts, which had been imposed on Egypt by its European creditors in the 1870s and staffed with European judges.[86] When Morand completed the

---

[82] ICI, *Compte Rendu 1904*, 74.
[83] Sawas, *Le Droit Musulman Expliqué*, 22.
[84] Ibid., 1.
[85] See the Ottoman Mecelle Code (1877) and the Egyptian Civil Code (1876).
[86] Skovgaard-Petersen, *Defining Islam*, 60.

final version of the code, he did his best to Europeanize Algerian Muslim law, by portraying the modifications as a reform that came from within Islam. For example, the legal category of slavery disappeared from the code, although some Muslim judges pointed to the traditionally tolerated existence of slaves in the Southern regions.[87]

The full extent of the code's manipulative potential unfolds in Morand's substitution of the local *Mālikī* rite with the foreign *Ḥanafī* rite. The *Ḥanafī* rite dominated the Ottoman and Egyptian codes and used all legal sources available, including analogy (*qiyas*), the rational decision of the judge (*ihstisan*), or local customs (*adat, urf*). As a consequence, the *Ḥanafī* rite gave more room for interpretation than the *Mālikī* version that traditionally applied to Algeria. It also provided married women with more rights concerning personal property and the possibility to divorce their husbands. Introducing the *Ḥanafī* rite to Algeria helped Morand to portray Algerian *Mālikī* rites as lagging behind the advances of Islamic reformism. He did not hide his intentions in this regard: "The dispositions of the *Ḥanafī* rite are often more human, more open [*large*], more tolerant than those of the *Mālikī* rite. We should, without hesitation, and even though the majority of Algerians are *Mālikī*, rule out the *Mālikī* code and prefer the *Ḥanafī* to it."[88] But whenever convenience required it, Morand reserved for himself the right to mix different rites. The global diversity of Islam provided Morand with the means to combine its elements to create his own "Islamic law."

Morand repudiated traditions that he considered "anachronistic" or "incoherent." The "anachronistic" judgments included the notion that a non-Muslim could not legally marry a Muslim or that a Muslim man could repudiate his wife anytime without reason.[89] Among these "incoherent" *qāḍī* judgments was the right to turn mobile property into *ḥabūs*. Morand also overruled the judgment that an expropriation of a *ḥabūs* did not change its character as a *ḥabūs*. Finally, he declared the impossibility to mortgage a *ḥabūs* unlawful, as many Muslims protected their property from seizure by the state by declaring it a *ḥabūs*.[90] Obviously, Morand's intervention with regard to the *ḥabūs* aimed at reducing their number, because they stood in the way of European acquisition of Algerian land.

Several other elements of the code aimed at reducing collective property (mostly *arch* land). Under the guise of simplifying inheritance law, the codification commission reduced the potential heirs to the nuclear family. By the same token, Morand's Muslim law prohibited adoptions. Both regulations aimed at increasing the possibility that there would be no heir to a possession,

---

[87] Gouvernement Général de l'Algérie, *Projet de Codification*, 11–12.
[88] Morand, *Avant-projet de Code*, 13.
[89] Ibid., 3.
[90] Ibid., 2–3.

which then – according to the Egyptian *Ḥanafī* law – fell into the hands of the *beit-al-mal*, a quasi-state-owned administrative institution. In Algeria, however, there was no *beit-al-mal* or institution that administered ownerless land. It was therefore bestowed on the colonial state. Several *qāḍī*s protested against this regulation when they commented on the original draft. A local judge from Arzew complained that the *Mālikī* code conveyed land without an heir to a pious Muslim institution. But if the *Ḥanafī* rite should be applied, he proposed to "say openly that it is the state who inherits, as the appellation 'beit-el-mal' does not mean anything to us."[91] Added to these regulations was a stipulation that facilitated the liquidation of collective land: if only one of the owners wanted to liquidate his parcel of land, the others had to agree, buy the land from him, or dissolve the entirety of collective land.[92]

To draft his code, Morand had chosen to mix different schools of law and to take advantage of two "Europeanized" legislative sources, the *Mecelle* code of the Ottoman Empire and the Egyptian civil code.[93] While Muslim sovereigns had officially written these codes, they produced them in semi-colonial spaces that enabled the penetration of European law into the new codes of these countries. It goes without saying that this invented law was conducive to the substantiation of the colonial state in Algeria because it simulated indirect rule. Doutté concluded that the Algerian code actually "not only codifies but also modifies Muslim law."[94] ICI members who had inspired Morand's codification project now took it as an example. French administrators who were responsible for the codification and its application in Algeria gave lectures on their Islamic policy back in Europe.[95] Indeed, Morand's code inspired similar projects as far away as Russia, which was the first semi-colonial power to codify *sharīʿah* law for its entire colony in Turkestan. In 1908 and 1909, the so-called Pahlen Commission codified predominantly family law, civil status, and succession law. Pahlen's commission explicitly referred to the developments in Algeria.[96] While certain Islamic experts in the ICI criticized the Algerian efforts of open Europeanization of Islamic law, colonial administrators in North Africa proved that they were able to express the necessities of colonization in terms of Islamic law, especially with regard to the expropriation of *ḥabūs*.

---

[91] Gouvernement Général de l'Algérie, *Projet de Codification*, 43–49 and 26.
[92] Ibid., 60.
[93] Ibid., 7.
[94] ULCSH Or. 8952 A278: Doutté to Snouck Hurgronje, October 11, 1923.
[95] ULCSH, Or. 8952 A277: Doutté to Snouck Hurgronje, September 8, 1923, and October 9, 1923.
[96] Morand, *Avant-Projet de Code*, 9–10. On the Pahlen Commission, see Morrison, "Creating a Colonial Shariʿa," 127–149.

5.4 The "Modernization" of Muslim Law in the Tunisian Protectorate

Algeria was a settler colony and it gave priority to European settlers. Tunisia, by contrast, seemed to be different. In Tunisia, the ICI member Paul Cambon had established a system of indirect rule that claimed to respect local laws and institutions. Declared a protectorate in 1883, Tunisia represented an anti-Algeria, based on a more modern and respectful form of colonization. French policy in Tunisia, however, did not differ in a significant way from the colonial policy in Algeria.

When the French established their protectorate over Tunisia in the 1880s, they had compelled the Tunisian bey to reform the country's legal system according to the Ottoman and Egyptian models. They employed two specialists for this task. One of them was Sawas Pasha, the Christian Ottoman who held close ties with the French colonial lobby. Sawas Pasha was seconded by a much younger Tunisian-Italian Arabist from Florence, David Santillana, who would complete the draft of the new Tunisian code for the French government.[97] Theoretically, Santillana's expertise was in Tunisian *Mālikī* law. Yet his methods did not differ significantly from Sawas Pasha's approach. For both, the Ottoman *Mecelle* and the precedential decisions of the Egyptian mixed courts served as models, as it did during Morand's codification of Muslim law in Algeria. The Ottoman and Egyptian experiences provided practical insights into the fusion of French civil law with Muslim regulations (*Mecelle* in the Ottoman Empire) and the application of British common law within a Muslim environment (the mixed courts in Egypt).

Sawas Pasha cooperated with Santillana and the French resident general to elaborate the new code. All of them invoked the Islamic concept of "necessity" as a source of legitimacy for the modernization of Muslim law. In his introduction to the *Avant-projet de Code Civil et Commercial Tunisien* (1899), Santillana claimed that the predominant *Mālikī* rite in Tunisia stipulated that laws should be made according to their social utility. The *Mālikī* doctors of law Al-Tasouli and Ibn Farhoun endorsed this view by explaining that custom and tradition can be converted into law, while Ibn Nadjim admitted that "necessity made us accept many things that are normally prohibited according too rigid principles." Santillana also invoked the *Ḥanafī* inclination to analogy as a legal instrument, which allegedly confirmed that "the law does not follow absolute rules, like grammar or logic ... rather it incessantly adopts to the circumstances that engendered it." Mollah Tcheragh Abi concluded in the introduction that the Muslim *shariah* law – if it can be called a law at all, because it is not an organic law – is in no way immobile or unmodifiable"[98] According to

---

[97] Santillana, *Code Civil*; Santillana, *Istituzioni di Diritto Musulmano*.
[98] Santillana, *Code civil*, v; Morand, *Avant-Projet de Code*, 14.

him, all Muslims, no matter which school of law they adhered to, agreed on the importance of "necessity," which determined the law.

Like Morand's codification project, Santillana's code also combined different schools of law for the benefit of the Europeans. Both Morand and Santillana cited the Ottoman *Mecelle* that claimed that "it is wrong to stick to one single school of law ... we have to pick the best from every imam." A judge from the mixed courts in Egypt agreed that a sovereign might choose among a great variety of interpretations and therefore "has the choice to apply whatever religious rule he wants to apply." Finally, the famous mufti of Cairo, Muhammad Abduh, told the Algerian and Tunisian legislators that he was of *Šāfi'ī* origin but often used the *Ḥanafī* rite for his verdicts. Tunisian lawmakers would happily embrace the same strategy. Ultimately, both the Ottoman and the Egyptian courts mixed rites in their decision, a practice that would become common in Tunisia as well.[99]

Sawas Pasha, who had conducted a preliminary study about the codification of Tunisian law, had picked up on the "mixed rites" codification, stating that both the *Mālikī* and the *Ḥanafī* rites were in force in Tunisia. Before the arrival of the Europeans, the *sharī'a* courts had two sections, one for each rite. Litigants could choose the judge who was specialized in their orientation. In addition to this duality, there was also an independent court for local usages and non-religious administrative law.[100] Thus, even Tunisia provided the colonial guardians with plenty of possibilities to mix different rites. Santillana's team of legislators used all these sources to establish the new code, along with the vast corpus of fatwas circulating in the Muslim world.[101]

Unlike the Algerian code, the Tunisian code openly integrated elements of European law, even though the legislators tried to couch them in Muslim concepts. Already, Sawas Pasha had recommended to add European legislation in commercial and civil law and to win Muslim scholars over for the use of "scientific" and "rational" methods. The commission was officially charged with "codifying civil, commercial and penal legislation based on the model of the French Code."[102] When it published the Tunisian Code, many regulations were derived from the French *Code Civil*, as well as German, Swiss, and Italian commercial law. Santillana's code made no secret of those sources. It allowed for the tracing of the origins of every single law by adding its sources to the paragraphs that contained them. At least the possibility to verify the regulations was taken from the Muslim *isnād*

---

[99] Ibid., 14–15.
[100] Estournelles, *La Politique Française en Tunisie*, 366–368.
[101] Van Vollenhoven, "Notice Complementaire," 413–416.
[102] Santillana, *Code Civil*, I.

tradition, which held verifiability in high esteem. The code was formally Muslim but partly of European content.

The commission involved Muslim laws only if they were consistent with the European legislation. Thus, Santillana assumed the task to "search ... in Muslim jurisprudence, and in the older Tunisian legislation, all those rules that could be useful with regard to the principles of modern law or the current conditions of the native society."[103] Unlike other members of the commission, Santillana did not dismiss Muslim law as immobile and dogmatic and therefore irreconcilable with European law. According to Santillana, an Aristotelian spirit guided Islamic legislation, which regarded all humans as political and social beings and took their needs into account. Both materialism and utilitarianism determined Muslim laws: "The purpose of the law is social utility."[104] In his view, the principles inherent to all law were also present in Islam: procedural sincerity (*bona fide*), equality before the law, and the ultimate purpose to abolish all unjust damage (*dharar*). Arguing in this functionalist tradition enabled Santillana to justify the modernization (and Europeanization) of Islamic law – allegedly out of its own impetus. There was only one component that Islamic jurisprudence lacked, the Italian Arabist claimed: the "synthesizing spirit."[105] This lacuna should be filled by the codification of Tunisian law.

Drafted in the late 1880s and early 1890s, the codification was brought to a successful end in 1899. But only the commercial code came into force in 1906 under the title *Code des Obligations et Contracts*.[106] Its main purpose was to secure the observance of contracts by two individuals or juristic persons and to guarantee their mutual obligations. While contract law was a universal necessity in all societies, it was also a typically "colonial" concern. According to the mastermind of French colonial law and ICI member, Arthur Girault, the "natives" often broke employment agreements with Europeans because of their moral dishonesty.[107]

The code was mainly focused on contract law but touched upon various issues concerning everyday life. Therefore, an important passage was dedicated to the *ḥabūs*, which were omnipresent in Tunisian daily life. The foundation of such a *ḥabūs* required a contract and it was by analyzing the Muslim traditions of contract law that Santillana found an instrument in Muslim law to turn the inalienable *ḥabūs* into private property.

---

[103] Ibid., I.
[104] Ibid., IV.
[105] Ibid., XI.
[106] Ibid.
[107] Girault, *Principes de Colonisation*, 537.

5.5 "Tunisian Law Provides Us with a Means": Dispossession between Settler Colonialism and Protectorates

European law often governed real estate regulations in the French colonies – and in the protectorates. Depriving native law of control over real estate was one essential purpose of colonial law's dual paradigm, as formulated by Chailley in the ICI: "the emancipation of the individual and the emancipation of property."[108] Two instruments were available to achieve this dual goal, namely, a personal status (yet not a civil status, which was for citizens only) for each individual and individual land titles. The colonial state had to provide for a system that enabled the systematic registration of individuals and their property. Registering individuals and their property was an onerous task, as the ICI expert for land tenure in the colonies Günther Anton explained. In the 1890s, the high court of Algiers, for example, had counted fifty thousand Algerians with the name Muhammed ben Ahmed. This made it almost impossible for courts to distinguish among individuals, to identify criminals, or to register landowners. Collectively owned land and "family communism" were further obstacles to constitute private property.[109]

Colonizers from all countries agreed that there was only one remedy to these problems: the "Torrens Title." Theoretically, the Torrens system was a central register for individual land titles, which was public, transparent, and accessible. Once a title was registered, it became the indisputable property of the person who had submitted it for inclusion on the register. In practice, the Torrens system manifested itself in a variety of slightly differing forms of centralized land registers, inspired by Australian colonization law, the German *Grundbuch*, and notions of French civil law. The Torrens system originated in Australia and had played a vital role in providing the white settlers in South Australia with colonial land. It was therefore the legacy of nineteenth-century settler colonies. Tellingly, even ICI members who claimed to prefer schemes of indirect rule promoted the Torrens Act. Chailley's father-in-law Paul Bert was the first to apply it in French Indochina in 1885.[110] All the French colonies adopted the system, ranging from the Algerian settler colony to the Tunisian protectorate and the West-African possessions, where concessionaires received extended territories from the colonial governments.[111] In 1897, Gallieni introduced it to Madagascar.[112] The Belgian Hubert von Neuss, who joined the ICI later, copied the Torrens Title from Tunisia when reorganizing

---

[108] ICI, *Compte Rendu 1904*, 77.
[109] Anton, *Französische Agrarpolitik*, 102–103.
[110] Chailley-Bert, *Dix Années*, 9; Girault, *Principes de Colonisation*, 594.
[111] ICI, *Compte Rendu 1900*, 691; ANOM, FM MIS Carton 76, Folder Noel Pardon, Pardon to Colonial Minister, May 25, 1906: Application de L'Acte Torrens, Demande de Mission Gratuite.
[112] Gallieni, *Madagascar*, 524; ICI, *Compte Rendu 1900*, 695.

the real property law of the Congo Free State in the 1890s.[113] It spread further to the Italian and German colonies and was in force in the mandates of Syria, Lebanon, and Palestine from the 1920s onwards.[114]

The ICI members celebrated the Torrens system for its efficacy and claimed that its superiority derived from its unambiguity, its verifiability, and its publicity. According to the ICI specialist of land law Günther Anton, who had traveled to several European colonies to study their regulation of property, the advantages of the Torrens system were evident. An individual who intended to buy a territory could consult the central register about the land's legitimate owner, about potential rights on the land claimed by a third party, or about its possible encumbrance such as an outstanding mortgage or unpaid property taxes. While the claims of a third party suspended a transfer of the land, an encumbrance lessened its value. If the registered land title did not contain any endorsements of this kind, the purchase contract was concluded and the buyer received the land, "purified" of any hidden charges. But it only entered in his full possession after the buyer's title appeared in the central register.[115]

Applied to the colonies, the Torrens system worked in favor of the Europeans, although it left it to the colonized to choose if they wanted to register their lands.[116] Few of them did, as the procedure was unfamiliar, costly, and included traveling to the administrative centers. ICI specialists in colonial law such as Anton had to admit that the introduction of the Torrens Act would be "disastrous" for indigenous farmers.[117] Conflicts were frequent, when either side registered land that used to be collective land. Anton reported that European colonists and investors had constantly complained about the contestations of their titles long after they had purchased territory from the colonized. Sometimes the lands had been used as temporary pastures by nomads or the local residents. In other cases, the lands had been considered sacred. More frequently, the land was collectively owned and one of the owners had sold parts of it without the consent of his co-proprietors. In similar cases, groups had the right of usufruct or the right to hunt or collect firewood on the territory. By introducing a central land register that guaranteed that a territory was free of these burdens, the colonial powers hoped to assure the full rights to a purchased territory and facilitate its transfer – mostly to Europeans.[118]

---

[113] Comeliau, "Hubert van Neuss," 653–656; Stengel, *Der Kongostaat*, 27, based on Descamps' publications.
[114] Soulmagnon, *La Loi Tunisienne*; Gavish, *The Survey of Palestine*, 129–134.
[115] ICI, *Compte Rendu 1900*, 674.
[116] Ibid., 674.
[117] Ibid., 680.
[118] Ibid., 670 and 674.

A case from West Africa, reported by the Togolese Etsè Amedon, illustrates the disputes that emerged through the clash of collective land ownership and the new land title system, which the German administration introduced in Togo as early as 1906. Amedon was a member of the Bè community on the Togolese coast that had, he explained, "alliances (not only alliances but kinship relations) with the people of Togoville." This relationship was unstable, but "at a certain moment in history, [Togoville] had legal preeminence over the population of Bè" and rights to its collective land. So far so good, but "this story caused problems when the Germans arrived," Amedon explained, "who declared the land that they wanted to plant coconut trees public utility." To avoid expropriation, the territory was sold to the Germans: "the chefs of Togoville came to Bè to sell its land, because they thought it belongs to them." Yet, if the land belonged to them at all, it never belonged to them alone. In the decades to follow, the Togolese fiercely debated this land sale, which left a mark in Togolese collective memory as the "epoch of the famous land title 255."[119] Léonidas Quashie, a Togolese lawyer from Lomé, reported that "we have always had a lot of law suits concerning land, land titles, etc.," since Germans had introduced land titles as early as 1906 and claimed that it caused more trouble than the "attribution of land by the state" in parts of French West African colonies.[120]

The ICI saw in the Torrens title and individual property one "governmental" way to make the colonized more productive. Quashie's report suggested that this plan proved to be successful because "in Togo, since the time of the Germans, individuals are the owners of land," including the Togolese themselves who used their possession to become successful plantation owners.[121] However, no one mentioned that these plantation owners in Togo were predominantly Afro-Brazilians who had returned to West Africa after the end of slavery in Brazil, brought capital and networks with them, and rose to prominence as businessmen and politicians. Referring to Tunisia, the ICI tried to prove statistically that the Torrens Title might also benefit the indigenous population. Between 1886 and 1892, there were only 251 registrations in Tunisia, 130 by French, 73 by Italians, and 34 by Tunisians. The reluctance of the Tunisians, ICI members explained, was mainly due to the high registration fees. When the administration reduced the fees in 1892, the demand rose slightly and reached the overall number of 2,089 until 1897. Finally, in 1898, there were 236 Tunisians, 224 French, and 123 Italians who had registered their lands.[122] Although the ICI saw progress at work, the interest in registration remained generally low and Tunisians who registered might have acted as

---

[119] Interview Etsè Amedon, in Marguerat and Pelei, *Si Lomé*, vol. 2, 14.
[120] Interview Quashie, in Marguerat and Pelei, *Si Lomé*, vol. 2, 110.
[121] Ibid., 110.
[122] ICI, *Compte Rendu 1900*, 680.

5.5 "TUNISIAN LAW PROVIDES US WITH A MEANS" 197

straw men for Europeans. They contributed to the invalidation of indigenous land rights. For example, the Torrens system enabled a single owner of collective land to demand the inscription of his property. If he asked for registration, the other owners were not allowed to refuse this. They could either buy his part or divide the territory. The ICI argued that both decisions were legal in Muslim law. The result, however, was the liquidation or dismemberment of the Tunisian's real estate.[123] Only in certain regions did this system bring about the intended transition to private property and capitalism.

While the ICI continued to emphasize the merits of the Torrens Title, governors often ignored the Torrens system and continued to make use of outright expropriation, declaring the dispossession as necessary for "public utility."[124] At the outset of the twentieth century, the priority of colonial governments was to appropriate the most fertile land for cash crop production.[125] While land grabbing for colonial agriculture lingered on, the discovery of extensive subterranean resources renewed the interest in land tenure regimes and access regulations. In 1904, the ICI undertook a vast study on the legal access to resources for mining companies (*régime minier*), which was closely intertwined with the debates on the legal access to land (*régime foncier*). The ICI debated whether subterranean resources belonged to the owner of the surface plot (*accession*), to the state (*domanialité*), to the discoverer (*occupation*), to the state because it has to be defined as res nullius (*souveraineté*), or to those concessionary companies who are most apt to exploit them (*adjudication*).[126] The ICI members tended to prefer professional concessionary companies who guaranteed the most effective exploitation. While the colonial state was also supposed to profit from the resources, the colonial government should invite tenders on an international scale, in order to ensure competent exploitation.[127]

Whenever ICI members were involved in codifying collective property law, such as during the IVVR's codification of customary law in West Africa, they emphasized the "customary" right of the conqueror to use public domain (forests, fishing grounds, pastures, etc.) and identified potential crown land owned by a sovereign but used by the people.[128] Indigenous lawyers, such as the Senegalese Mademba Si appeared as the key witnesses for the legal appropriation of collectively owned land. Contributing to the IVVR's codification project in 1903, Mademba Si mixed customary and Islamic law in West

---

[123] Ibid., 687.
[124] Expropriations started in 1838. See Massignon, *Écrits Mémorables*, vol. 1, 664.
[125] Girault, *Principes de Colonisation* vol. 2, 33–34.
[126] ICI, *Compte Rendu 1904*, 169–170.
[127] Ibid., 172.
[128] Steinmetz, *Rechtsverhältnisse*, 1–13. On the collectivity problem, see Rolin, "Du Respect des Coutumes," in ICI, *Compte Rendu 1921*, 271.

Africa law to explain that "the conquering race does not pay any kind of compensation for the use of the land to the conquered, because through the conquest, all land rightfully belongs to the former."[129] Arthur Girault picked up on this idea: once the colonial power had defeated the sovereign by conquest, he argued, it assumed the sovereign's role. In India, for example, the British crown had asserted itself as the legal successor to the Muslim sovereigns since 1854. In his courses on colonial legislation, Girault explained to future administrators that most of the land in Muslim countries belonged to the sovereigns and was only bestowed upon those who cultivated it. The commoners had the right to *usufruct* only. According to him, most colonial governments naturally decreed that "all the mobiles and immobiles of the royal domain are now domains of the state."[130]

In those colonies that lacked a recognizable sovereign, the colonizers invoked the labor theory of property, which they portrayed as universally accepted. The German Anton, specialist on the comparison of colonial land tenure, informed the ICI members of a paragraph in the Qur'an that assigned the right to occupy a territory to those who cultivated it. It was therefore unnecessary to refer to Locke's famous labor theory of property if the holy book of the Muslims said the very same thing. Colonial administrators were able to use Islamic law as an argument in favor of occupation and dispossession.[131] Nevertheless, expropriation persisted.

Land grabbing was most obvious in settler colonies. Although the Algerian colonial government abolished the Torrens system in 1897, it continued to seize the land of Algerians. In 1906, for instance, the French government created a new colonization center in the mixed commune of Berrouaghia. To acquire land in that area, it expropriated extensive territories inhabited by the Beni-bou-Yagoub. Among the dispossessed lands was a ḥabūs of one thousand hectares, which was inalienable according to Islamic law. The Beni-Bou-Ygoub resisted bitterly and sent frequent petitions to the French parliament protesting against the violation of the inalienability of the ḥabūs. The French General Assembly urged Algiers to stop the expropriation but failed to take appropriate measures.[132]

The debate about inalienable ḥabūs, however, made ICI members pause and rethink policies of expropriation. After all, the expropriation of ḥabūs seemed to be more likely to provoke anti-colonial revolts across Muslim countries. This is particularly true for the ḥabūs endowments in Tunisia, which were generally not seized, to keep up with the appearance of indirect rule and

---

[129] Mademba Si, "Bambara, Sarakolesen," 86.
[130] Girault, *Principes de Colonisation*, vol. 2, 39–40.
[131] Anton, *Französische Agrarpolitik*, 60.
[132] "Notice sur les travaux parlementaires de l'année 1906," *Revue Algérienne, Tunisienne et Marocaine de Législation et de Jurisprudence* 23 (1907), 1.

respect for a time-honored institution in Islamic law. "The pious foundation of the *ḥabūs*" Snouck Hurgronje warned "belong naturally to the realm of the holy law"[133] However, while Islamic law considered the *ḥabūs* as immobile, inalienable, and "elevated to the other world," they were dedicated to quite worldly purposes: making money. According to the colonizers, they did not make enough money, and they sought ways to dilute their inalienable and "holy" status.[134] The intensive study of Islamic laws at the beginning of the twentieth century indeed provided the colonizers with more subtle possibilities to acquire land.

The private *ḥabūs* (also called *waqf*) was a profit-yielding property that its owner declared inalienable by turning it into a pious endowment.[135] In doing so, the land could not be sold or given away. In exchange, parts of its profits – deriving from the production of crops on its soil, for example – were endowed to mosques or madrasas. Several reasons might lead landowners to declare their land estate a *ḥabūs*. One of them was to secure a families' continued possession of the land, which expressed the owner's social status. Another reason was to protect the land from confiscation by the state. A supervisory board administered the *ḥabūs* and watched over its mortmain character. While the *ḥabūs* supervisory board now legally possessed the land or real estate (*dominium eminens*), the former owner kept the right to use it and make profits from it (usufruct or *dominium utile*). He and his heirs retained the usufruct eternally, as long as they did not abuse their rights and neglect its exploitation.

Alongside the private *ḥabūs*, which was perpetually used by the family that had turned it into an inalienable property, there were public *ḥabūs* such as mosques and public gardens. Traditionally, Muslims turned a private *ḥabūs* without legal heirs into a public *ḥabūs*, which was then both possessed and exploited by a pious foundation. A supervisory board watched over all these modifications of the status but did not necessarily register them. According to the *Mālikī* handbooks, *ḥabūs* could be created by oral agreement only, without the obligation to put the contract into writing. This made it difficult for the colonial powers to distinguish *ḥabūs* from alienable land.[136]

It is understood that the *ḥabūs* were an obstacle to European colonization. In Ottoman Tunisia, experts reckoned, one-third of all territory had been qualified *ḥabūs* – and was theoretically inalienable. By 1898, the gains of the Tunisian *ḥabūs* amounted to 1,268,886 francs.[137] Cyrenaica was entirely covered with *ḥabūs* owned by the *Sanūsīya* brotherhood, much to the chagrin

---

[133] Snouck Hurgronje, "Politique Musulmane de la Hollande," 67.
[134] Ibid., 56.
[135] On the endowments in North Africa, see Hoexter, *Endowments, Rulers and Community*.
[136] Baldinetti, *David Santillana*, 23.
[137] ICI, *Compte Rendu 1900*, 658.

of the Italians who were eager to colonize it. They sent Santillana there to find out how they could be removed from the *Sanūsīs* by using arguments from Muslim law.[138] While codifying Tunisian law for the French and searching for solutions to alienate *ḥabūs*, he had found a contractual procedure called *Inzāl* that allowed both Muslims and Europeans to "purchase" *ḥabūs*.

Referring to Santillana, the ICI encouraged making use of the *Inzāl* (frenchified into *enzel*), which actually allowed for the alienation of *ḥabūs* by giving leaseholders the perpetual right to use it. Muslim jurists had introduced the *Inzāl* to help out *ḥabūs djemaas* (supervising boards) that were unable to administer and exploit the totality of their *ḥabūs* and that failed to convert some of them into capital. The advisory boards needed capital to exploit the other *ḥabūs* in its custody. The *Inzāl* was even more important, as uncultivated and unexploited *ḥabūs* risked losing their status of inalienability, according to the *Mālikī* rite.

Mālikī jurists therefore stipulated that only the *dominium eminens*, but not the *dominium utile*, was inalienable. Thus, instead of buying *ḥabūs* land – which was unlawful – persons could lease the *usufruct* for an extensive period of ninety-nine years or more. Instead of a onetime purchase, they committed to pay an eternal and immutable rent. Receiving such a *dominium utile* often resulted in open possession-taking. Moreover, the tenant could provide the administrative council of *ḥabūs* with a piece of land of equal value. If the administrative council accepted, he received full property rights over the *ḥabūs*.[139]

Since the establishment of the protectorate in Tunisia, the French had adapted a "soft" version of the *Inzāl*. They urged the bey to enable long-term leases, while formerly a lease on *ḥabūs* land was possible for three years only. A new decree facilitated the lease for ten years, renewable twice. The tenant had to pay rent to the supervising board and use an equal amount of money to increase the yield and make it more profitable. This increase in profit was then to be paid back to the usufructuary when the bail ended. However, at any time, this restricted bail could be turned into to a hereditary bail. The ICI popularized this "colonial" version of the *Inzāl* among European administrators.[140]

These provisory rules were soon replaced by Santillana's 1906 code, which declared the *Inzāl* a legal contract according to Tunisian law.[141] The *Code des Obligations et Contrats* reveals Santillana's strategy to couch European interests in Islamic terms and therefore make it a more "legitimate" law. The concept of *Inzāl*, he claimed, could also be found in Roman law, where it

---

[138] Baldinetti, *David Santillana*.
[139] ICI, *Compte Rendu 1900*, 660–663; Santillana, *Istituzioni di diritto*, vol. 1, 4.
[140] ICI, *Compte Rendu 1900*, 664.
[141] Santillana, *Code Civil*, 400–413.

was called the "emphytheotic lease," a contract by which the owner of an uncultivated piece of land granted it to another either in perpetuity or for a long time – on the condition that he cultivated the land, enhanced its yield, and paid an annual rent.[142] This system also resembled the so-called *precaria* law of the European Middle Ages. The equivalence between European and Islamic traditions, Santillana claimed, was possible because of a more general similarity between legal concepts. Like the Europeans, who occasionally distinguished between rights of possession and use, the Muslim scholar Ibn Nadjim (or Nujaym) distinguished between the two elements of property, the right to possess something (*droit sur la chose, rakba, corpus rei*) and the right to use something (*droit qui a pour objet l'utilité ou la jouissance, antifaa, utilitas*).

Ibn Nadjim's definition was taken from the Ottoman *Mecelle*, which had made wide use of his interpretation of Qur'anic law.[143] While the general concepts of possession and use of land property were taken from the "modernized" *Mecelle* code, Santillana found the details of the contract in local rites. He cited the *Mālikī* and *Ḥanafī* definitions of *Inzāl*, which shared this interpretation. The definition of the main North African theorist of *Inzāl*, Bairam, came closest to the Roman definition of the emphytheotic lease and stipulated that the "*Inzāl* is a contract by which the administrator of a *ḥabūs* gives a virgin territory to another person who cultivates it – with the plantations belonging to the person who established them – and who pays an annual rent to the pious foundation ... this is, without any doubt, a lease of the territory, unlimited in time."[144] After defining the *Inzāl*, Santillana explained its different varieties that existed all over North Africa, thereby emphasizing its universal validity.

The rest of the paragraph on the *Inzāl* stipulated that it had to be a written contract to be valid and that the leaseholder received "full property rights" once the contract had been concluded. The leaseholder could sell his rights on the land to others, even without previous notification of the original owner (the *ḥabūs* administration).[145] All these rules helped to make the "acquisition" of the *ḥabūs* easier for potential purchasers. The colonial state in Tunisia made use of this legal possibility when it gave legal force to Santillana's code.

This *Inzāl* system played into the hands of newly arrived European colonists. If leasing a *ḥabūs*, they did not need a huge amount of capital to buy land immediately upon arrival. Instead, they leased a *ḥabūs* and paid an annual rent until the day they could afford to offer the *djemaa* a new territory in exchange. By 1897, the system was well established. The government put the *ḥabūs* up to

---

[142] "Emphytheosis," in: Bouvier, *A Law Dictionary*, 525.
[143] Mallat, *Introduction to Middle Eastern Law*, 246.
[144] Santillana, *Code Civil*, 402.
[145] Ibid., 403–413.

auction. Among 11,823 alienated ḥabūs, 8,322 were acquired by European colonists.[146] Santillana, who entered the service of the Italian state after he had drafted the code for the French, continued to work on issues related to ḥabūs after the World War I. He headed the Commission for the Study of Islamic Questions Relating to Colonial Interests, which the Italian colonial ministry sent to Cyrenaica to verify the Sanūsīya's right to own the ḥabūs that dominated the region. Arguing on the authority of Kahlil, the authoritative scholar of the Mālikī rite he had translated into Italian, Santillana claimed that the Sanūsīya had to deliver the proof of their possession by presenting testimonies of the oral contracts. Although Santillana's mission was not very successful, his investigations resulted in doubts on 23,000 hectares of ḥabūs land, on which the Sanūsīya had no testable right.[147] In the meantime, his *Code des Obligations et Contrats*, and with it the Inzāl contract, was applied in Morocco, Syria, Somalia, and Lebanon. In Algeria, however, it was not applied, given that the government continued to expropriate the land without pretending that this happened in accordance with their own laws.[148]

Much more than in Algeria, the French argued along the lines of Muslim law in the Tunisian protectorate. However, the purpose remained the same. A number of ḥabūs had to be pushed back and its territories had to be opened for colonization. "Tunisian law provides us with a means to do so," the ICI expert on land tenure in the colonies, Günther Anton, informed the members of the ICI in its 1900 meeting. He made reference to Santillana's code and spread the word about a new argument of "Islamic law" in favor of colonial dispossession. The ḥabūs policy became a significant cause for disagreement in international politics of the twentieth century. In 1919, the nationalist Emir Khaled from Algeria sent a petition to the US President Wilson and portrayed the expropriation as one of the worst French colonial crimes. He argued that "today, despite the law that separates the Churches and the State, the few ḥabūs that still exist are administered by the French government, under the guise of a tutelage."[149] As late as 1938, the Italian governor of Libya, Italo Balbo, complained at the predominantly fascist International Congress on Africa that the North African ḥabūs did not serve religious and public purposes anymore. Instead, they had allegedly become strongholds "for personal interests and – like in the case of the Senussia [Sanūsīya] – to aliment the rebellion." He asked the fascist state to intervene, though by respecting

---

[146] ICI, *Compte Rendu 1900*, 660–663; Santillana, *Istituzioni di Diritto*, vol. 1, 4.
[147] Baldinetti, *David Santillana*.
[148] Concerning Morocco, see "Dahir du 6. Septembre 1913," *Bulletin Officiel* 47 (September 19, 1913), cited in 100APOM/321 Lettres Chailley à Lyautey, Folder Maroc: Production Agricole et leur Communication 1912–1915.
[149] Petition printed in Ageron, *Genèse de l'Algerie*, 172.

Islamic laws.[150] At the same congress in 1938, a French ICI member reported that the Sultan of Morocco had centralized the control over 16,000 ḥabūs properties in the protectorate. They thus came under the indirect control of the French colonial power.[151]

5.6 Islamic Craft Guilds and the Muslim Code of Labor in the 1920s

The initial concern that Islam in general and Pan-Islam in particular might pose a threat to colonial rule proved unfounded. Colonial internationalists developed and exchanged strategies to use Islamic law for colonial purposes. Most of those strategies originated in the East Indies before colonial administrators imported them to Africa. In particular, the fatwa policy was a product of transnational communication among colonial experts. It included Muslim collaborators, who "sold" their own expertise and issued authoritative fatwas in favor of the colonial power. But specialists on Islam went even further and aimed to manipulate the details of Islamic law, which was said to penetrate deep into the everyday life of colonial subjects.

One strategy to modify Islamic law was to *adatize* Islamic law by declaring it a customary law that could be modified according to local and temporary circumstances. The lack of a Muslim clergy and the fragmentation in different *madhāhib* (schools of jurisprudence) substantiated their claim that no Muslim could ever know what Islamic law is. Only European internationalists with their bird's-eye view on transcolonial Islam would be able to grasp the true nature of global Islam. Consequently, colonial internationalists of the ICI claimed to be able to have a better understanding of Islam than the regionally bound Muslim theologians. The invention and codification of *adat* law and its strategic use to drive a wedge between Muslim rebels and the local population in Dutch Sumatra is the most prominent outcome of creative mixing of legal traditions. At the same time, colonial scientists confirmed that Islamic law provided the means to adapt itself to changing circumstances. Not only did the Qur'an, the Sunna, or the fatwas prove that Islamic law was open to individual interpretation; the use of concepts such as "necessity" also pointed to the flexibility of Islamic law. Even non-Muslims could use the non-religious concept of necessity to argue against Qur'anic prescriptions.

Given the diversity of Islam, colonial administrations combined different legal traditions of Islamic law to create new codes. They applied traditions that resembled Western legal concepts. Apart from spreading the more "European" Ḥanafī *madhab* all over the colonial world, experts also borrowed elements from the Ottoman *Mecelle* code, which had been modeled on the European

---

[150] Balbo, "La Politica Sociale Fascista," RAI, CSMSA, vol. 1, 740.
[151] Lyautey, "La Politique du Protectorat en Afrique Marocaine," in RAI, CSMSA, 987

civil law earlier in the nineteenth century. Such amendments taken from the semi-colonial Ottoman Empire were added to "autochthonous" rules that had been chosen for their compatibility with the prerogatives of colonial rule. The *Inzāl* contract, which enabled both Europeans and Muslims to acquire theoretically inalienable *ḥabūs* property is a case in point. The contract had long been used in Islamic law and came close to European notions of usufruct rights on land. Colonizers then applied it to contexts where the system had been unknown before.

By the 1920s, members of the ICI refined their strategy and used customary Islamic law to bring about "soft" economic development toward a corporative colonial society. They promoted Islamic craft guilds as a governmental tool to reorganize the colonial society and economy. Craft guilds loomed large in the *Mālikī* version of Islamic law and had particularly gained momentum under the Fatimids' expansion in North Africa during the tenth century.[152] In 1923, French ICI members Lyautey and Massignon, who headed the French Service of Indigenous Affairs in Morocco, intended to revive the craft guilds and commissioned a Survey on Muslim Corporations of Artisans and Merchants in Morocco. Moroccan experts such as Idrīs al-Moqri informed them about Islamic corporative law: each craft guild had an *amīn* at its head who served as a syndic and representative. Islamic *'urf* (customs) and *'adab* (honorable conduct of life and social intercourse) seemed to govern them. Craft guilds existed in every city and were most visible at the local *sūq* (market) but also had a strong rooting among the Berbers in the mountainous inland of Morocco. Each corporation seemed to have the monopoly on the production of a certain good and held the exclusive right of selling it in the *sūq*.[153] In Fez alone, there were 164 guilds with 9,000 members, among them shoemakers, tanners, dyers, silk dealers, blacksmiths, carpenters, plumbers for water supply, road sweepers, oil merchants, clock makers, olive pressers, engineers, couscous producers, librarians, artists who ornamented plaster walls, and tourist guides.[154]

Craft guilds seemed to provide the basis for a corporatist society. Lyautey and Massignon saw in them basic entities of artisanal production, market control, social cohesion, mutual aid, and even political representation. Each craft guild had a representative assembly that acted as a court with the *amīn* as a judge. Customs and bylaws of these corporations proposed consecutive steps of conflict resolution. Rural corporations organized themselves in case of natural disasters, for example, by collectively fighting locust infestations.[155] Administrators hoped to avoid democratic reforms by ruling via the craft

---

[152] Massignon, *Écrits Mémorables*, 166.
[153] *Enquête sur les Corporations*, v–vi.
[154] Ibid., 13.
[155] Ibid., 62–63 and 68.

guild's *amīns*, who controlled guild members. Massignon equally believed that craft guilds were mutual aid societies that assisted their members in case of work accidents and unemployment. In so doing, Massignon hoped, they would be able to ward off communist and syndicalist ways of organizing worker collectivities. In Tunisia, for example, "the tribunal of the *'orf* or customary law, where the cheiikh el medina from Tunis solves conflicts among corporatives, has resisted with pain the infiltration of the communist propaganda upon the new professions (dockers, railway workers, tram workers) for two years."[156] Thus, in the view of most ICI members, corporations provided a third way between capitalism and socialism. They could prevent the colonized from joining European-style trade unions and picking up socialist ideas. Since both the total individualization of capitalism and the collectivization of socialism were suspected to destroy the stability of indigenous societies, ICI members relied on craft guilds to avoid the transformative shock the colonized allegedly hardly survived.

Curiously, some of the publicly owned *ḥabūs* also fell into the category of corporations because the Muslim community employed professional officials (the *nazir al ḥabūs*) to administer them in accordance with corporative and Islamic law. Apart from managing the public *sūq* and other market places, the *ḥabūs* corporations looked after the lighting of a city, its sewage system, and its water supply, which was highly important for the mosques, fountains, and public gardens.[157] The *ḥabūs* corporations were literally at the heart of North African cities and, in this case, should remain in the hands of the colonized.

To the delight of ICI members, corporations seemed to have a long tradition from India to Madagascar and from Morocco to Senegal. What is more, colonial administrations around the world emulated the French revival of craft guilds in North Africa. In 1924, the governor of Tripolitania, Giuseppe Volpi, employed French experts of the Service of Indigenous Arts in Morocco to create a similar preservationist department in the Italian colony.[158] On the occasion of the 1919 World Fair, administrators from British India inquired about the French program to revive the North African rug industry, which allegedly preserved the traditional family businesses and craft guilds.[159] The British administrators had discovered the existence of similar craft guild traditions in India, which already appeared in the Vedas and the Laws of Manu. They set out to organize their revival.[160] Indian economists indeed looked back on a long corporative tradition. In an important study on Indian

---

[156] However, this strategy was not always successful. See *Enquête sur les Corporations*, 117–118.
[157] Ibid., 78–79.
[158] Ricard, "Les Arts Tripolitains," 203–235.
[159] Pommereau, "The Invention of the Moroccan Carpet," 228.
[160] Hough, *The Co-operative Movement*, 51.

cooperative economy, the economist Hiralal Lallubhai Kaji explained that castes in India had originally been no more than occupational units and professional corporations. Unlike the ill-reputed castes of the twentieth century, he argued, the original castes had been voluntary economic associations rather than hereditary social classes. Thus, the primordial castes were much more flexible and less exclusive. Bemoaning that in the new castes, "membership by choice has gone and membership by birth has come," Indian experts such as Kaji recommended reviving these original professional castes.[161] He received support from a certain Mahatma Gandhi, who made the revival of the artisanate a precondition of regaining Indian dignity and the ability to achieve self-sufficiency and ultimately self-government.[162] Massingon would declare Gandhi's approach exemplary and admired him throughout his life.[163] Apart from the romantization of Gandhi, the alignment of corporations and castes reveals the will to engage in a transcolonial dialogue and find overarching solutions for responding to the penetration of colonial capitalism.

The transcolonial reinvigoration of corporations and cooperatives received its own panel at the International and Intercolonial Congress of the Indigenous Societies held at Paris in 1931. Before an international audience, ICI member Massignon cautioned against the disappearance of craft guilds under colonial rule. He claimed that only around 25,000 corporative artisans were left in North Africa, whose products, moreover, were driven out of the markets by cheap European commodity. He presented concrete evidence for the decline of craft guilds across the Islamic world: Turkey abolished them in 1924. In Syria, where Massignon had studied craft guilds in 1927 and 1928, "syndicalism substituted corporatism." The same development was about to hit Tunisia and Jordan.[164] He then outlined his preservationist program, which had stopped the decline in Morocco.

News reached the International Labor Office in 1930 that Massignon intended to use corporations to stabilize the colonial economy.[165] The ILO's directors made this approach their own, not least because it had "a certain relation with our own enquiry on the *artisanat*," which had so far been, however, rudimentary. The ILO's directory sent its attaché Roger Plissard on a ten-day study trip to Tunisia to learn whether the corporations were "really efficient" or if their decline was irreversible. In Tunis, he analyzed "the working conditions of Northern Africa" that could provide the basis for a future policy in the "larger domain of the working conditions in a Muslim

---

[161] Kaji, *Co-operation in India*, 14.
[162] He also promoted cooperative schemes. See Karve, *Co-operatives*, 4.
[163] Massignon, "L'Artisanat Indigène," 177.
[164] Massignon, *Écrits Mémorables*, vol. 2, 623.
[165] ILO Archives, N206/1/01/8, Muslim Labour, Plissard: Report de Mission à Paris, 1931, 1–2.

society." Plissard's object of study included the famous Tunisian *chouachis* corporation of artisans, which produced *šāšiyyas* (typical Maghrebi cylindrical cap) for the entire Islamic world, and the weavers of Kairouan. The ILO made the craft guilds a priority of its strategy in the Muslim world, and its director Albert Thomas personally pursued the issue during a journey to Egypt.[166]

The ILO's directors showed interest in corporations because they seemed to be an instrument to secure social peace in Muslim countries and were said to prevent a proletarian revolution. Generally, the ILO favored corporatist conflict solutions that were consensual and brought together employers, workers, and states.[167] Like Massignon, ILO experts thought of corporations as predominantly Muslim institutions that had the virtue of establishing "social unity." This "Muslim solidarity," the ILO concluded, was an additional bond that united master and apprentice and "tempered" the opposition between them. Since the ILO concluded that "the Koran governs work," Muslim corporations seemed to establish social peace beyond their immediate religious or economic purpose.[168] This idea shaped the ILO's approach to "Muslim Labor," which was mainly labor in the colonies.

In the 1930s, corporatism became the central strategy of the ILO in its development of a "Muslim code of labor" that could be applied to the entire Muslim world, a field that was completely new to the ILO. Plissard saw a chance that 240 million Muslims who inhabited the colonial world from Morocco to the Dutch Indies would turn away from communist ideas and revive their time-honored corporative systems: "They constitute a special proletariat because they are artisans trained like our ancient corporations of the old regime by a long practice to the pleasure and the purposefulness of work."[169]

As it happened, the ICI equally promoted the revival of this artisanate in the Dutch Indies and in sub-Saharan Africa. According to ICI members, corporations did justice to any kind of segmented and tribal society: they were big enough to guarantee social peace but small enough not to turn into syndicalist and nationalist organizations such as the Sarekat Islam in Java. The segmentary result of corporative policy, ICI member Henri Labouret argued, made them also compatible with tribal societies in West Africa, and corporatives should be extended to these regions.[170] Step by step, colonial administrations around the world discovered the multifunctional nature of corporatism.

As the ICI members increased their efforts to rule through "Muslim" craft guilds, they got closer to the fascist state corporatism that emerged in the

---

[166] Ibid., 7.
[167] This changed in 1944. See Seekings, "The ILO and Welfare Reform," 155.
[168] ILO Archives: N/206/1/01/8: Muslim Labour: Plissard: Rapport de Mission à Paris.
[169] Ibid.
[170] Labouret, "Le Paysannat Indigène en AOF," 20 and 28.

1930s. Predominantly, though not exclusively, fascists promoted it as a means to transform society into a fascist planned economy. Italy was leading the field since Mussolini had proclaimed the "Corporate State" and established the Ministry of Corporations in July 1926. For a start, Italy introduced meta-corporations of Industry, Agriculture, Trade, Transport, Banking, Professionals and Artists, and Seamen and Airmen. These corporations not only united employers and employees in a single professional body but were also the basic organ of political representation. Italian fascists exported the ideal of the corporative state to Libya and Ethiopia (as well as to Spain and axis Europe in general).[171] Both German and Italian fascists would try to use Islamic infrastructure to impose their colonial policy, as we will see in Chapter 7.

The manipulation of Muslim law has to be seen within the broader context of a colonial "native policy." Mixing customary and Muslim law allowed ICI experts to use it and to manipulate it for colonial purposes. The use of Islamic "traditions" continued in the interwar-period, when new institutions of colonial internationalism portrayed themselves as the defender of the indigenous peoples and heralded a new era of colonialism. More importantly, the manipulation of Islamic institutions fully unfolded in the 1930s, when the ICI lent itself to the emerging project of fascist colonialism.

[171] Bosworth, *Mussolini*, 224.

6

Creating an "Anti-Geneva Bloc" and the Question of Representivity

> Reference was made to the impression which had been received by various British members who had taken part in the proceedings of the [International Colonial] Institute that the active interest in the Institute which is displayed by various Continental Colonial powers is due to their desire to use the Institute for the purpose of creating an anti-Geneva Colonial "bloc." It was agreed that if in fact this tendency exists, it would be a great mistake (apart from any other considerations) for the Government of this country to take any active part even to the extent of lending their support to the private British members.[1]

As if no one learned a lesson from World War I, the interwar period took polarization to the extreme. Not immune to the politics of polarization, it seemed natural to the British colonial authorities to see in the ICI a conservative antidote to the supposedly more emancipative Permanent Mandates Commission (PMC) of the League of Nations, established in Geneva in 1921 under British auspices to guide fourteen-mandate territories to independence. The ICI had resumed its activity in 1920. Its first meeting in postwar Brussels was a déjà-vu. It featured the founding fathers from 1894: the bustling secretary Janssen who would bring the members back together; the mastermind Chailley who won over the liberals with his seemingly progressive native policy; the lord Reay who secured the support of the numerous aristocratic colonial governors; and the philanthropist Arenberg whose presence anticipated the role Catholic do-gooders would play in legitimizing colonialism.

The ICI's old guard aroused suspicion of mobilizing to defend the prewar colonies against liberalization in the new mandates. The PMC, which declared the former German and Ottoman colonies international mandates in 1919, indeed propagated the "well-being" of the colonized populations in the mandates and allowed them to send petitions to Geneva if this well-being came

---

[1] CO 323 1114/10: ICI, Group of British members, Note of a meeting held on November 28, 1931.

under threat.² British colonial officials claimed that the League's mandate system was a way to spread their allegedly liberal Anglo-Saxon colonialism. To emphasize its own liberality, the British Colonial Office accused the ICI of putting together a continental "anti-Geneva Colonial bloc," which defended classic continental colonialism against the PMC's reforms. While London would refuse to fund the ICI throughout the 1920s for that reason, we will see that British colonial policy nevertheless came pretty close to the ICI's agenda. London's reluctance to fund the ICI's "continental" colonialism was certainly painful for the ICI, as one of its main donors, the Belgian railway colonizer Albert Thys, had perished in 1913.³ Yet, by considering the financially precarious ICI a potential threat to the state-backed PMC, the Colonial Office affirmed the ICI's importance.

Despite the PMC's financial and legitimating head start, the ICI rose to prominence in the interwar period and would finally outlive the PMC. Indeed, the ICI represented the colonial lobby much more than the PMC. Although the PMC got more publicity, the ICI was closer to the colonial practice. It also had a more extensive network across the colonial world. At the five ICI congresses held throughout the 1920s, one could bump into the most illustrious colonial experts of the time, including members of the PMC and "liberal" colonizers such as the British Frederick Lugard and the French Hubert Lyautey. Organizations with a progressive reputation, among them the League of Nations, the International Labor Organization (ILO), and the International Institute of African Languages and Cultures (IIALC), sent delegates to attend the ICI's sessions and sought its expertise by recruiting their staff among its members. During most of the 1920s, both the ICI and the PMC considered themselves as progressive.

The public expected a storm of international conflict brewing between the French-speaking ICI and the British-influenced PMC but ultimately, they would cooperate.⁴ In colonial matters, the ICI chose an anthropological approach of cultural relativism, which was opposed to the PMC's mission to civilize and assimilate the mandates under its rule. Curiously, both organizations settled the potential conflict by cooperating closely in practical transnational and transcolonial matters, instead of engaging in idealistic international conflicts.

Whether the ICI or the PMC was more progressive depends very much on the definition of the term. The PMC was progressive to the extent that it promised the inhabitants of the mandates gradual emancipation, proportional to their degree of civilization. It understood civilization as a process of assimilation to (imagined) European habits. The ten members of the PMC,

---

² Pedersen, *The Guardians*, 83–88.
³ ICI, *Compte Rendu 1920*, 67–69.
⁴ On the "national" infrastructure of these international organizations, see Gram-Skjoldager and Ikonomou, "Making Sense of the League," 420–444.

who had the power of determining a group's degree of civilization, were supposed to be neutral experts. They met in Geneva and received knowledge about the mandates only through indigenous petitions and delegates of the mandatory powers who tried to disprove the petitions. The almost 200 colonial enthusiasts who joined the ICI were experts of a different kind. They held the view that they were more progressive because they knew the real nature of the colonized. Unlike PMC members, they encountered them on a daily basis and relied on anthropological studies that used informants among the local population. Accordingly, ICI members claimed to have a structural knowledge of the colonized societies, whereas the PMC members had only punctual insights in specific political conflicts and isolated scandals treated in the petitions. The way the ICI saw it, anthropological knowledge was indispensable to adequately understand and slowly transform indigenous societies instead of assimilating them to European lifestyles in an abrupt way. The PMC's lack of anthropological knowledge and colonial experience, along with the rule that banned PMC members from traveling to the mandate territories, allowed ICI members to accuse it of Eurocentrism. ICI members preferred cultural relativism, which seemed to be more progressive. Today, we would use a different category when comparing the ICI and the PMC: the ICI was not more progressive but certainly more representative than the PMC.

The question of who adequately represented the colonies and its inhabitants dominated the interwar period. The PMC officially declared itself the advocate of the colonized but actually represented the interests of the colonizers. It read the petitions sent by representatives of the populations in the mandates but ultimately gave credit to the colonial powers who defended their cause personally at the PMC's sessions in Geneva. Overall, the PMC took the petitions into account but rarely treated them with seriousness.[5] Unlike the PMC, the ICI saw itself as representative for colonies that wanted increased autonomy from the metropoles. Within these autonomous colonies, it also saw room for indigenous representation and tried to determine who legitimately qualified to speak for the colonized population. ICI members participated actively in introducing representative bodies in the colonies and even sent indigenous delegates to represent their colony in international organizations. While they considered indigenous technocrats and taxpayers as potential delegates who could speak for the indigenous population, they ousted radical anti-colonial nationalists.

Non-Europeans participated actively in these debates about who might be representative. Achmad Djajadiningrat from Indonesia and Joseph Ephraim Casely Hayford from Ghana were among those who joined representative councils. Although educated in the Western style, these delegates tried to extend their power to the benefit of the colonized. Their understanding of

---

[5] For a view from Africa, see Callahan *Mandates and Empire*.

representation was one that assumed that they were on equal terms with the Europeans without emulating them. They launched a wide debate about whether they were representatives or delegates or the like and to what extent they might have a mandate to speak for a bigger group. The ICI even assessed their representativeness by measuring the contribution of African and Asian taxpayers to the colonial economy. In so doing, they put the question of whether the masses deserved representation in times of increased taxation on the table.

This chapter shows that the debates about the status of colonies in the interwar period were not so much about sovereignty as about representation. To be sure, when Wilson declared the right to self-determination in 1917, this formula provoked claims for national sovereignty in many parts of the world. But Wilson's declaration only partially led colonized populations to claim a right to national sovereignty and, as a consequence, independence. Rather, they actively engaged in the debate about self-determination in the sense of representation and not sovereignty. In the 1920s, the number of candidates who could potentially speak for the colonized or represent a colony soared: international organizations, colonial governments, technocrats, philanthropist organizations, indigenous chiefs, elected colonial councils, trade union federations, entrepreneurs, parties, and leaders of anti-colonial movements were among them. The ICI loomed large in defining those who were allowed to speak for the colonized.

I argue here that Europeans, be they members of the PMC or the ICI, be they liberals or conservatives, launched and used the debate about representivity to delegitimize any delegate who spoke for the colonized population. They developed a doctrine of unrepresenatation. Curiously, this doctrine would ultimately lead the colonized population to the conclusion that the only way to real representation was via an independent democratic nation state and mass participation. Ironically and unconsciously, the ICI pushed the inhabitants of the colonies to embrace nationalism and representation through the masses.

In the 1920s, the ICI was certainly no anti-Geneva bloc if judged by its personnel. The same advocates of colonial domination sat in the ICI and the PMC. In the 1930s, when colonial internationalists adopted explicitly anti-liberal positions, the ICI increasingly denounced Geneva as unrepresentative. As we will see, the late ICI's anti-liberalism was the beginning of its turn to fascism. Its fascistization was gradual. After Chailley's death in 1926, the old guard in the ICI slowly gave way to young radicals. In 1929, the ICI voted against the ILO's project to ban forced labor from the colonies, in the early 1930s it embraced a fascist economic Eurafrica, and by 1938 Italian fascists accomplished the take-over of the ICI. Curiously, it was during the ICI's turn to fascism in the 1930s that the British Colonial Office started funding it, revealing that fascism and liberalism had joined forces to perpetuate colonialism.

6.1 ICI Networks and the Postwar Redistribution of Mandates

At the Peace Conferences in Paris, ICI members realized that the diplomats of 1919 cared little for the colonies and knew literally nothing about them. When the Belgian delegate Pierre Orts, an ICI member since 1909 and future PMC member, presented Belgian colonial demands to European heads of state at the Council of the Ten on January 30, 1919, he expected something like the spirit of 1884/5, when Europeans assembled in Berlin to partition Africa. This spirit he found to be completely absent in Paris. When Orts and the other Belgian delegates entered the conference room to expose their plans for Africa to the Council of the Ten, there were no chairs for them. Squeezed into a corner and "knee to knee with Clemenceau," Orts began his one-hour presentation, only to be interrupted regularly to have his speech translated. The translation stole half of his speaking time. More disappointingly, the Council of the Ten obviously lacked the geographical knowledge about Africa to follow Orts, who lamented that "I have never again spoken to an audience so openly indifferent and so careless in hiding its ennui. Finally, I turned away from the principal table to the experts of the various delegations."[6] While the experts at least pretended to listen to him, they seemed to be much more concerned with postwar Europe and made unlikely candidates to represent colonial interests.

In the eyes of ICI member Orts, the Peace Conference of 1919 was unlikely to adopt the spirit of colonial internationalism that had reigned during the partition of Africa in 1884/5. It seemed that European diplomacy and colonial diplomacy had grown apart. A new imperial rivalry about the redistribution of former German and Ottoman colonies seemed to oust colonial internationalism. Against all odds, the Belgian Colonial Ministry invoked its long involvement in colonial internationalism to demand a "legitimate reparation for the damages caused by three years of a war that Germans had inflicted on us."[7] During this devastating war, the Belgian colonial army had conquered Ruanda-Urundi and fertile lands in Tanzania from the Germans. In 1919, Belgium warned against the aggressive imperial diplomacy that had led to World War I and referred to the more harmonious colonial diplomacy among colonial internationalists. The ICI stood for the autonomous colonial internationalism that allegedly ran counter to imperial gunboat diplomacy in Paris.

Since the European diplomats showed little interest in the details of colonial bargaining, Belgians launched unofficial talks by using the ICI's networks. Orts, in particular, tried to gain acceptance for a barter trade with Portugal, which controlled navigable parts of the Congo River on Angolan territory that

---

[6] AGRB, Papiers Orts, Carton 389: Orts, *Souvenirs de Ma Carrière*, 152–153.
[7] Ibid.; Note in Annex, "La Conférence de la Paix," 2.

gave access to the Belgian Congo. As Belgium made the Congo River a priority, it was willing to give the territories its colonial army had conquered in German East Africa to Portuguese Mozambique as a recompense. Orts had already received positive signals from the former Portuguese governor of Mozambique, Alfredo Augusto Freire d'Andrade, who was close to the ICI and his future colleague in the PMC.[8] However, a potential agreement with Lisbon also needed the consent of Portugal's longtime protector, Great Britain. Thus, Belgians pushed for an unofficial meeting between Orts and the British secretary of state for the colonies, Alfred Milner. They met in the Parisian Hotel Crillon on March 20, 1919.

The meeting between Orts and Milner was extraordinary because, officially, the British government had so far belittled and even questioned the contribution of the Belgian colonial troops during the conquest of German territory in East Africa. Milner, in particular, had held the view that Belgian troops had completely depended on British supply and support. When he met Orts in March 1919, he seemed to have changed his mind. Milner welcomed the Belgian delegate with the remark that they should "not let the Conference decide for us, but find an agreement between ourselves." He understood very well that a tête-à-tête with a single Belgian diplomat was more expedient than a multilateral squabbling. Orts appreciated that the British secretary of state for the colonies had finally agreed to hear the Belgian demands, indeed for the first time after its colonial troops had conquered important parts of German East Africa. Milner was "convinced that the Conference will ratify our agreement."[9]

The ensuing debate, however, showed that Milner was no member of the ICI and stood for the imperial diplomacy that lacked any sense for solidarity among colonizers. He made clear from the beginning that "we [the British government] shall fight to the last to have you out of this country," not specifying if "this country" meant Ruanda-Urundi, German East Africa, or the Congo. Orts pretended not to be impressed at all but later admitted that Milner "had the British Empire behind him" and personified all its power: "Upright, he was taller by more than a head and such a majestic height often incites those who have the physical advantage to abuse of the advantage he has."[10] Milner naturally aligned with the official attitude of the Peace Conference that a barter trade was out of question. More than that, he wanted to secure Ruanda for Britain to realize the British railway connection from Cape to Cairo. Orts feared that he would come away empty-handed.

[8] Ibid., 148–150.
[9] AGRB Louwers Papers, 170 (197) Conference de la Paix à Paris 1919: Report Louwers on Conversation Orts-Milner, March 20, 1919.
[10] AGRB, Papiers Orts 389: *Souvenirs de ma Carrière*, 154.

Despite Orts' fears, Milner did not go as far as escalating unofficial negotiations and they reached an agreement. Orts was able to secure Ruanda and Urundi as a mandate for Belgium. He conceded Tanzania to Milner, securing a free port zone in Kigoma for the Belgians from which it could transport anything in a sealed train across Tanzania to Congo. The Rwandan Kagera region in the West of Lake Victoria remained British, because Milner wanted a corridor for building a railway to Uganda. The Peace Conference rubberstamped these so-called Orts-Milner agreements.[11] Ultimately, the arcane diplomacy seemed to have worked out for both sides, although Belgium did not lay hands on the Portuguese territory in the end. The Orts-Milner agreement provided the way for the Signatory Powers' new mandate system, which internationalized the former German colonies in Africa and gave them as mandates to Belgium, Britain, and France.

What did ICI members make of the new mandate system once it was on its way? ICI members, who were said to defend the colonies against the politically "liberal" mandates in their "anti-Geneva bloc," actually endorsed the mandates system, mainly because it bore the mark of classic colonial internationalism and because it would increase the autonomy of colonial administrators with respect to the metropole. Orts observed that many higher-ranking colonial officials preferred to govern a mandate over a proper colony, because this gave them the ability to "react against the routine of metropolitan administrations and to resist the influence of financial forces whose requirements were impossible to reconcile with the material and moral development of the indigenous populations"[12]

They also pushed for applying the logic of the Congo Act of 1884/5 to all the colonial possessions (both mandates and colonies). After all, the Congo Free State had been a sovereign state, at the mercy of the international community but independent of the metropole, and ICI members hoped for a similar sovereign status of all the colonies in 1919 to increase the autonomy of colonial administrations.[13] Second, like in 1884/5, they set their hope in the internationalization of the territories to attract more capital and investment.[14] The new Peace Treaty of 1919 seemed to confirm ICI members in their agenda of making colonial territory self-sufficient and financially autonomous.

The ICI members, who represented colonial administrators more than any other institution, welcomed the mandates that helped its members to escape the tight grip of the bureaucracy in the metropole and allowed them to raise taxes and levy customs tariffs. They thought of mandates as the first step to dominion status and an independent state governed by colonial experts. ICI

---

[11] Ibid., 156.
[12] AGRB, Papiers Orts 389: *Souvenirs de Ma Carrière*, 187.
[13] ICI, *Compte Rendu 1920*, 96.
[14] Ibid., 85–100.

members Pierre Orts and Leopoldo Palacios, who were among the most prominent theorists of the mandate system, particularly emphasized its dominion status. Both traced the idea of the mandate back to the South African apartheid schemer Jan Smuts. Smuts represented the South African dominion, a (as we will see controversial) model for colonial autonomy from the metropole.[15]

6.2 The Reestablishment of the ICI and the Question of Self-Determination

Sixteen people met in 1920 in Brussels to reestablish the ICI. Thirteen among them had been members of the ICI since the turn of the century. In 1920, Camille Janssen had secured modest subsidies from the Belgian Foreign Ministry, the Belgian Colonial Ministry, the Belgian Ministry of Science and Arts, the Dutch Colonial Ministry, and the Italian government.[16] Janssen had an obvious interest in reviving the ICI, as he was its only salaried employee, receiving 20,000 francs per year.[17] He took the initiative to reestablish it. In 1920, Joseph Chailley became both its new and old president. A new impetus came from the Belgians Pierre Orts and Octave Louwers, as well as Dutch vice-president Dirk Fock, who would soon become governor-general of the Dutch Indies. Five British members joined as well, despite London's fear of the "anti-Geneva bloc."

Milner, who was familiar with the potential power of unofficial networks among colonial internationalists, was behind the British refusal to fund the ICI, when he was secretary of state for the colonies between 1919 and 1921. In March 1920, Lord Reay, a founding member of the ICI, sent a private note to Milner, informing him that the old guard of the ICI had "resuscitated" the Institute. He lobbied Milner for official funding from the Colonial Office. Reay's strategy was typical of the ICI's prewar use of "political" comparisons. In his request to Milner, he compared Britain unfavorably to Belgium, France, the Netherlands, and Portugal, who all contributed to the ICI's budget and warned Milner that Great Britain must keep pace with them. He also evoked the traditional ties between the ICI and the Colonial Office.[18]

Reay inexpertly mistimed his request. Milner and the British government were busy establishing their pet child, the League of Nations. Moreover, the

---

[15] AGRB, Papiers Orts, 433: Revendications Belges en Afrique, Annexe, 69.
[16] ICI, *Compte Rendu 1920*, 80–81.
[17] AGRB, Louwers Papers 51 (78): Correspondance Vandervelde 1928, letter Louwers to Vandervelde, November 1927; AGRB, Louwers Papers 234 (261) ICI 1926, Karnbeek to Louwers October 1, 1926.
[18] CO 830 323 ICI, 373: Reay to Milner, March 31, 1920; and 376: Beckett (Colonial Office) to Campbell, March 20, 1920.

younger staff of the Colonial Office had never heard about the ICI. They had to consult the better-informed Foreign Office on the ICI's activities but finally made their own judgment and denied its value for Britain: "It must be observed that until we obtained the information [about the ICI] furnished us by Mr. Tafton from the Foreign Office, we were really hardly aware of the existence of the International Colonial Institute, which seems to indicate that its functions are not specially, or primarily, of use to this Department and the Colonies and Protectorates."[19] With the staff of the Colonial Office being skeptical or ignorant regarding the ICI, the Colonial Office rejected the ICI's first request for support out of hand. In his official rejection letter to Reay, Milner explained that the Royal Colonial Institute in Britain did a good job although it had never requested subsidies. He predicted that the colonial administrations overseas would complain about the subsidies to a non-British institution whose output was hardly accessible to English speakers.[20] Given these harsh words, there was absolutely no hope to be set on Great Britain.

Milner was not quite right, however. British colonial internationalists continued to hold important positions in the British Empire and urged bureaucratic staff back home to value the ICI's international cooperation. One of them was the committed ICI member and Indian High Commissioner William Meyer. When he heard about the reestablishment of the ICI in 1921, he traveled immediately to Europe to join its second session, "as the principal representative of the Empire." He even prepared a paper on the question of how to train "Colonial Magistracies" in the new postwar context of more autonomous colonial administrations.[21] Meyer was not the only prominent British member of the ICI. The omnipresent Frederick Lugard worked hard to recruit new members for the ICI, the undersecretary of the colonies, William Ormsby-Gore, became one of the ICI's most active members, as did the editor of the Cambridge History of the British Empire, Arthur Percival Newton, and later on the governor of Punjab and compiler of the official *Survey on Africa*, Malcom Hailey. They stand for the ICI's growing influence in British colonial circles.

The ICI members who met in 1920 had big plans: it announced their intention to make the colonies self-supportable and self-governing. They interpreted Wilson's proclamation of self-determination from 1917 as a chance for colonial administrators to turn their colonies into more autonomous entities. Economic self-determination was the first step toward achieving this goal. Based on the assumption that Europe should not dictate the economic policy of a colony, ICI members outlined their plan to cut the colonies

---

[19] CO 830 323 ICI, 377–378: Draft Memorandum.
[20] CO 830 323 ICI, Milner to [?]; 379: Milner to Reay, April 17, 1920.
[21] *The Uganda Herald* (May 6, 1921); *East African Chronicle* (May 14, 1921), 12.

off from the metropoles and instead cooperate more closely among themselves. In their debate on commercial autonomy at the meeting in 1920, they took up the idea of equality between European citizens in Africa and proposed to turn sub-Saharan Africa into a common customs union. They also wanted to harmonize its trade laws: "It is the shared interest of the colonizing nations to agree on a uniform customs regime ... that allows commercial flows to go their natural way."[22] However, they rejected all attempts of the metropoles to impose a more global free trade system on the colonies and mandates as "anti-economic and anti-colonial."[23] Throughout the 1920s, they would plead for replacing the metropole-colony relation with "inter-imperial trade" and "co-operation between all the great colonizing nations."[24]

Economic self-determination naturally presupposed political self-government and the ICI proclaimed that the time of self-government had come "not only for the European population but also for the indigenous population." To be sure, self-government was still a matter of "degree" and not of complete independence, but the ICI was convinced that it should be "accompanied by the possibility for the population to make its opinions and desires heard." More precisely, they aimed at the introduction of representative bodies such as the newly founded People's Council (Volksraad) in the Dutch Indies, which they presented as exemplary at the ICI's session in 1920.[25] Its indigenous members were partly nominated and partly elected. What is more, colonial governments in India and British Gold Coast for the first time in colonial history introduced constitutions such as the Government of India Act in 1919 to provide a solid legal basis for questions of representation.[26] The League of Nations also established clear rules for the mandate territories and the "communities" who lived there. Article 22 of the League's Covenant confirmed that "the wishes of these communities must be a principal consideration in the selection of the Mandatory," and the PMC theoretically granted them the "constitutional" right to send petitions to Geneva.[27] The constitutionalism appeared to be part of progressive postwar reforms.

While the ICI equally pushed for autonomy and self-determination, the question arose of who exactly might be the subjects of self-determination. Who was able to represent the indigenous population of the colony? According to the ICI members, the main body of representation in Europe, the democratic nation-state, was nonexistent. Who had the legitimacy to speak for the indigenous population? If no nation-state existed, could they be

---

[22] ICI, *Compte Rendu 1920*, 49.
[23] Ibid., 94–95.
[24] ICI, *Compte Rendu 1931*, 14–15.
[25] ICI, *Compte Rendu 1920*, 158.
[26] Legg, "Dyarchy," 44–56.
[27] Pedersen, "Samoa," 235.

delegates in international organizations? Was the Europeanized elite legitimized to speak for the masses? Should the colonial government be a technocratic government? What was the role of the diaspora who embraced nationalist ideas but was abroad?

In the years following World War I, the question of representation became the crucial question in the debate about self-determination. The ensuing debate proved to be regressive, however, because colonial governments used the "question" of representation as an excuse not to grant self-determination to the colonized population. Both PMC and ICI members argued that radicals who spoke for the colonized population were not authorized to do so, because they were not representative. For example, when delegates of the Duala from Cameroon, who had concluded several contracts with the German colonizers before World War I, sent a petition to the Peace Conference in August 1919 asking to have a say in the decision about the redistribution of their territory, the conference ignored them.[28] Only the governor of French Equatorial Africa met with the four most important Duala chiefs to win their support for a French mandate in Cameroon. Yet the Duala chiefs told him that "we await the coming of all allies" and made clear that they might prefer the British, which led Paris to claim that the Duala did not represent the Cameroonians. They accused the Duala of "turning the entire territory of the Cameroons into a second Liberia, whose government they would assume themselves."[29] The 1920s were thus the period of denied representivity. Denied representivity resulted in denied self-government. Those who gained autonomy were the colonial administrations overseas, not the colonized populations.

6.3 Representation and the "Exosmosis" between Colonies and Mandates

Like the British Colonial Office, many Europeans believed that the PMC represented the new mandates and the ICI spoke for the prewar colonies. Reality was more complex. Be it out of mutual respect or of mutual suspicion, the ICI and the PMC exchanged members and tried to recruit experts from each other. By 1926, half of the PMC's members were equally in the ICI. In the whole period of the PMC's existence between 1921 and 1937, more than one-third of PMC delegates (ten out of twenty-eight) were active members in the ICI: Pierre Orts, Frederick Lugard, Malcolm Hailey, William Ormsby-Gore, Daniel François Willem Van Rees, Frederick Van Asbeck, José Frazão Count of Penha Garcia, Kunio Yanagita, Leopoldo Palacios, and Ernest Roume. Their activity in both institutions was compatible and mostly reconcilable rather

---

[28] Eckert, *Grundbesitz*; Austen und Derrick, *Middlemen*, 145.
[29] Joseph, "Un Prétendant Royal," 340–341.

than contradicting: In less than a week during 1936, the international hero of colonial reformism Frederick Lugard jetted from the session of the Mandates PMC in Genova to the ICI's meeting in London (and finally to the meeting of the International African Institute in Paris).[30] The ICI, the PMC, and the ILO often coordinated their schedule, making sure that the PMC sessions and ICI meetings did not coincide.[31]

While memberships overlapped, the intellectual origins of the PMC's and the ICI's agendas seemed irreconcilable. On paper, the PMC wanted to Europeanize the mandates' inhabitants and guide them to higher stages of civilization and self-government, while the ICI wanted to preserve their culture as the basis for a soft and governmental development. When Pierre Orts became a member of the PMC he became aware that he "presided from now on over the social, political, economic evolution of over 21 million human beings, ranging in the racial hierarchy from the most primitive forms of humanity to the peoples of high antique civilization – like the Syrians of Damascus – our likes in some fields of activity but politically minor and, consequently, unable until further notice of governing themselves."[32] The intellectual origins of the PMC's civilizing mission, Mark Mazower has shown, came from British settler lobbyists Alfred Milner and Jan Smuts. Milner intended to use the League to "prolong the life of an empire of white rule through international cooperation."[33] The South African Smuts had designed the PMC's mandate system, which hierarchized colonized peoples according to their civilizational status and the ability to govern themselves. They were assigned a status between advanced (A-mandate), semi-advanced (B-Mandate) and backwards (C-Mandates). This status described their proximity to potential self-government. To legitimize this hierarchy, Smuts appropriated the civilizing mission (hitherto not very strong in British colonial theory) and gave it an "unmistakably racial coloration." Indeed, the PMC's civilizational standard relegated mandates in Africa to the lowest stage, as those who had lost all hope for potential "civilization." While Milner interpreted internationalism as a union of white settlers "from Cape Town to the Zambezi," Smuts' South Africa capitalized on the mandates system by taking over the former German South West African settler colony in 1920.[34] Although they considered themselves as Kantians and Hegelians, the "intellectual" background seemed to be rather practical. Nevertheless, the PMC's

---

[30] CO 3232 1400/II: Lugard to Chancellor, June 18, 1936.
[31] LoN Archives, R2295, 6A/10036/486 Extrait letter ICI to Catastini, February 1, 1929 and Extrait letter Catastini to Louwers, February 2, 1929.
[32] AGRB Orts Papers 439 Ouvrages: *Le Système des Mandats*, 3.
[33] Mazower, *No Entchanted Palace*, 30.
[34] Mazower, *No Entchanted Palace*, 32.

civilizing mission seemed to be at odds with the ICI's anti-settlerist approach and thus unrepresentative for interwar colonial reformism.

Given the PMC's origin in settler ideology, a group of ICI experts inclined to area studies harshly criticized the League and the PMC, claiming that they were unrepresentative, racist, and not worth the name League of Nations. The Arabist Snouck Hurgronje evoked the wrongdoings of segregationist settler societies, most importantly South Africa and the southern part of the United States, and their color bar. He then dismissed the League for being equally racist and for excluding Islamic countries, in particular. Instead, he advocated a "League of Races," to "assure peace and tranquility for the entire humanity." Every human group would send delegates there.[35] Although most ICI members agreed with Snouck Hurgronje on the League's Eurocentrism and lack of anthropological knowledge, Snouck Hurgronje could not find a majority among them to promote a "League of Races" before he died in 1936 and fascists from Italy took over the ICI.

Members of the PMC hardly reacted to such allegations, also because they were quite pragmatic and far from being consistent in applying the civilizational hierarchy. In his reflections on *Le système des mandats de la Société des Nations* (1927), the senior member of both the ICI and the PMC, Pierre Orts, revealed that there had never actually been an intellectual origin of the mandates system, but only a pragmatic one: "A solution that gave satisfaction to the traditional aspirations of British and French politics."[36] Like the ICI, the League was not a merely utopian project by "starry-eyed idealists" but tended to understand itself as utilitarian, pragmatic, and functionalist, which made it easier for ICI members to join its commissions and committees.[37] One of the League's intellectual fathers, David Mitrany, a trained colonial internationalist close to the ICI who propagated a functionalist cooperation between international companies, organizations, and NGOs to solve global problems, stood for this "ideology of pragmatism." So did the Swiss head of the PMC, William E. Rappard, who was close to neoliberal circles and seemed to get along quite well with the utilitarians in the ICI.[38]

Thus, hidden by the much-cited rhetorics of civilization, functional and practical approaches shaped the PMC's mandates rules. The PMC buried, in the fine print, practical requirements for the mandatory powers that had little to do with civilizing and developing people. In Syria and Lebanon, France was supposed to manage and pacify the different ethno-religious groups, while

---

[35] Snouck Hurgronje, "L'Islam," 419–421, 426, and 428.
[36] AGRB Orts Papers 439 Ouvrages: *Le Système des Mandats*, 6.
[37] Kaiga, *Britain and the Intellectual Origins*, 2–3.
[38] Pedersen, *The Guardians*, 9; Slobodian, *Globalists*, 94–95.

protecting the cultural autonomy of (Christian) minorities in particular.[39] Australia was to ensure the exploitation of phosphates in its mandate in Nauru.[40] And, in Palestine the mandate should support the Zionist settlement. The PMC implemented elements of the civilizing mission and rarely granted the right to self-determination in a consistent way. Moreover, practically all colonial officials whom the mandatory powers sent to Geneva for the annual hearings of the PMC's reports about the mandates were long-standing ICI members: The French Robert de Caix and Albert Duchêne, the Belgians Halewyck de Heusch and Pierrre Ryckmans, as well as the British Ormsby-Gore (who was in the PMC only between 1921 and 1922 and then became undersecretary and secretary of the colonies)[41] It would be too simplistic to assume that the ideological dividing line ran between the PMC and the ICI. Both bodies were split up into internal factions that make it impossible to draw a sharp line between a conservative and a progressive raison d'être. The PMC, but also other bodies of the League of Nations, recruited ICI members. Louwers, C. Neytzell De Wilde, and José D'Almada, for example, were in the Slavery Commission of the League.[42]

As with the PMC and the ICI themselves, spheres of mandates and colonies blurred in the 1920s. PMC members were confident that mandates had a knock-on effect on regular colonies. Daniel François Willem van Rees, a member of both the ICI and the PMC, predicted an "inevitable exosmosis" through which the colonies would be forced to align their policy with the more "liberal" mandates: "Its influence will not be limited to walls and frontiers: the reforms which will be accomplished in one country, as also the dominating spirit which inspired such reforms, will inevitably be propagated elsewhere."[43]

Van Rees, however, was wrong in assuming that the mandate system would bring about a change in the colonies. The contrary was the case, since mandatory powers administered mandates like colonies. All mandatory powers were primarily colonial powers who had always administered colonies and then took over the mandates. When they received a mandate in 1919, they aligned their administration and legislation to the adjacent colonies, under the guise of making administration more efficient. The British, for example, made the colonies of Kenya and Uganda a customs union in 1917, soon to be joined by the Tanganyika mandate. In 1920, they legally assimilated the mandate to

---

[39] "Mandate for Syria and Lebanon," Art. 8, in: C P M 466/C. 529 M. 314 1922 VI/C. 667 M. 396. 1922 VI.
[40] Société des Nations, *Procès-Verbal de la Onzième Session*, 20.
[41] Pedersen, *The Guardians*, 69; LoN Archives, R 4109, 6A/2639/1612, Report of the Mission to the Session (Twenty-Third) of the ICI held in London 1936.
[42] LoN Archives, R 4109, 6A/2639/1612, Report of the Mission to the Session (Twenty-Third) of the ICI held in London 1936.
[43] ICI, *Compte Rendu 1927*, 39.

the colonies. The British governor in Accra made the laws for both the Gold Coast colony and the mandate of British Togoland. Administrators from French West Africa merged the administration from Dahomey and French Togoland, although the latter kept budgetary autonomy.[44] Thus, colonial rule and mandate rule converged. Increasingly, the assumption that the ICI might represent the colonies and the PMC the mandates proved mistaken.

In the mid-1920s, the PMC struggled to respond to widespread criticism that in practice the powers governed the mandates like colonies and that the practice in the mandate did not live up to the theory. Since the ICI had the reputation of being a body that represented the colonial administrations, the PMC wanted it to make a public statement against the inversed "exosmosis." Since the PMC could not prevent Britain, France, and Belgium from integrating mandates into the legal and administrative system of adjacent colonies, it turned to the ICI as a representative umbrella organization of all colonial administrations. The PMC wanted the ICI to pay lip service to the PMC's theory of the mandates' liberality, which allegedly distinguished it from the old "despotic" colonies. In 1924, the PMC urged the ICI to put the mandates on the agenda of its next meeting. It was also a test to determine definitively whether the ICI was indeed an anti-Geneva project or supported the PMC's cause.[45] It was, however, not until 1927 that Van Rees personally reified the mandate theory at the ICI meeting. By that time, international lawyers had addressed errors and inconsistencies between theory and practice.[46] Moreover, Germans had joined the PMC in 1927 and used their readmission to voice loud criticism that the mandatory powers France, Belgium, and Britain ruled the mandates like colonies and that Germany would be a much more reliable mandatory power in putting the theory into practice. Responding to both international lawyers and German revisionists, Van Rees wanted to "eliminate completely all divergence of views," about the nature of the mandates.[47]

In the ICI, Van Rees explained that mandates and colonies differed in essence. Mandates had a more autonomous status and their inhabitants benefited from a specific form of legal representation. Unlike colonial powers, he claimed, mandatory powers had no "right to sovereignty" in the mandates, which lay in the hands of the League. Consequently, he evoked the "principle of non-annexation," proclaimed at the Peace Conference in Paris, which prohibited the mandatory powers to integrate the mandates into the legal and administrative system of the motherland.[48] With the option of annexation

---

[44] Hailey, *An African Survey*, 171–190.
[45] LoN Archives, R 60, 1/338117x/2709, Catastini to Secretary General, May 17, 1924; ICI, *Compte Rendu 1927*, 11 and 21.
[46] Wheatley, "Mandatory Interpretation," 207.
[47] ICI, *Compte Rendu 1927*, 39.
[48] Ibid., 21.

dropped, the option for the indigenous inhabitants to become citizens of the metropole and equals before European law was also gone. Claiming that the inhabitants of mandates had distinct "national statutes" and that "they are neither citizens nor subjects and that they cannot be, by any general measure, assimilated to [the motherland's] own nationals."[49]

While the principle of non-annexation seemed to make European citizenship for the non-Europeans in the mandates impossible, Van Rees emphasized that Article 22 conceded instead "the legal recognition of the peoples inhabiting the territories, who thus enjoy an independent juridical personality."[50] This legal recognition of the "natives" as a potential subject of international law was "the most innovative" part of the mandate rules, as Van Rees had announced proudly. Being such a "juridical personality" was the precondition to send petitions to the PMC and consequently to be treated as a litigant party before international law.

Van Rees' words were well chosen. He did not go as far as considering the mandates' inhabitants a proto-state but only admitted their independent status as a legal entity. Thus, they seemed to have the chance to open a legal case and act as a plaintiff. What is more, being an "independent juridical personality" implied some kind of representative body, as a spokesman had to represent the interests of a larger group. However, as the PMC and the ICI regarded few inhabitants of the mandates able to govern themselves, a nation-state was out of question as a representative body. Also with regard to representation, they came close to the status of a nongovernmental organization, such as an association, an incorporate organization, or a corporation. The ICI very much endorsed this view, as it was about to redefine the colonial state as a corporative state.

There is no doubt that Van Rees pushed his theory about the "legal person" of the mandates too far. In practice, petitions sent by inhabitants of the mandates mattered little. In 90 percent of the cases, the PMC refused to consider their petitions by declaring them prima facie unfounded, imprecise, and partially unlawful.[51] More frequently, the PMC rejected the inhabitants' complaints on the grounds that they were not representative. For example, when a group of Togolese sent four petitions in 1927 to protest against the abuses of French mandatory rule, the PMC ruled that the petitions were not "precise" enough to serve as legal documents. More importantly, it argued that the petitions did not concern the interests of the Togolese population as a whole, because German agents had allegedly provoked the politically motivated petitions.[52] Once the PMC rejected a petition, no appeals were possible.

---

[49] Ibid., 25.
[50] Ibid., 17.
[51] Pedersen, *The Guardians*, 91.
[52] ICI, *Compte Rendu 1927*, 42.

As Susan Pedersen has shown, the petitions were not legal documents. In the rare cases that the PMC rebuked mandatory powers, it was up to them alone to implement the PMC's recommendations, which were not legally binding. But the PMC rarely took action to improve the sort of the mandatized peoples.[53]

The unresolved question of who could send petitions and adequately represent the mandates' population gave the PMC the opportunity to refuse all complaints, even if they came from professional lawyers. One of them was the above-mentioned Ghanaian lawyer Casely Hayford, one of the few Africans to follow the development of the ICI from its foundation. Long before World War I, Casely Hayford had referred to international law and Locke's labor theory of property to tax the European colonizers with being inefficient, irrational, and unable to develop the land they had conquered.[54] Given this failure of the great powers, Casely Hayford concluded that Europeans had no legitimacy to possess colonies and speak on behalf of their inhabitants. After World War I, he was among the first to write petitions to Geneva, even though he lived in a colony and not in a mandate.

Writing from the British Gold Coast colony, Casely Hayford sent three petitions on behalf of the Adjigo family from neighboring Togo (a French mandate) between 1924 and 1927. The Adjigo were an Anglophone and Germanophone merchant family who were unsatisfied with the French rule over their territory. For some thirty years, the Adjigo had rivaled with the Lawson family for the control of the Togolese city of Anécho. Before the war, the German colonial administration had chosen to use the Lawson family for their purposes and had deported the Adjigo family. After 1919, when the French mandate was established, the Adjigo hoped for their reinstatement. But the French governor did not rehabilitate the Adjigo family and equally sent its leaders to "obligatory residence" in Northern Togo.[55] After the Adjigos' own appeals to return from exile had failed, Casely Hayford advocated for them and sent three consecutive petitions on their behalf to the PMC.

Although the French mandatory power had unnecessarily curtailed the rights of the Adjigo, the PMC rejected Casely Hayford's petitions.[56] More than that, Pierre Orts claimed in the PMC's fourteenth session in 1929 that the representation of a single family by a "foreign" lawyer was "an abuse of the right of petition," also adding that Casely Hayford had "falsely" claimed that the French administration had failed to forward one of his petitions to the PMC.[57] The PMC's refusal to accept Casely Hayford's petition was particularly

---

[53] Pedersen, "Samoa," 235.
[54] Casely Hayford, *Gold Coast*, 5.
[55] Antonelli, "Le droit de petition."
[56] C. 564.1927.VI. LoN, PMC, *Report on the Work of the Twelfth Session 1927*, 8.
[57] Antonelli, "Le Droit de Petition."

absurd because a French general inspector of the colonies, M. Picanon, who traveled to the French colonies to control the work of the officials, accused the governor of Togo, Paul Auguste Francois Bonnecarrère, of having wrongly deported the Adjigo and thus continuing the German policy of divide and rule. Casely Hayford, who was certainly the best informed African of his time, got to know about Picanon's critique. He also knew that Picanon recommended replacing Bonnecarrère with a new governor who was willing to cooperate with the Adjigo. Pierre Orts, who was less well informed, accused Casely Hayford, who had evoked Picanon to make his case in his petition, of having forged this story. However, it was true that Paris finally called Bonnecarrère to order and almost deposed him. In the end, he had to accept the return of the Adjigo family from exile.[58] Thus, while the PMC had refused the Adjigo and their representative Casely Hayford basic rights, the French colonial government finally solved the problem through its own inspectorate.

6.4 Refusing Representation and "Abusive Petitions"

Because the petitioners had no nation-state, no representative body, and no accredited advocate, the PMC could refuse all petitions as sectarian and irrelevant. It accepted neither the Adjigos' demand for justice nor petitions coming from other "minorities" such as the Kurds and the Assyrians in Iraq.[59] The PMC's refusal to accept Casely Hayford as a lawyer of the Adjigo, and Orts' attempt to discredit him, caused a long debate about representation. Orts called nonrepresentative petitions "abusive petitions," and this expression found its way in European and African media. "Abusive" were those petitions that seemed to spam the PMC's letterbox in Geneva and were allegedly off-topic. Casely Hayford himself addressed the topic in the *Gold Coast Leader*. In France, colonial journals such as *L'Afrique Française* and *Les Annales Coloniales* brought up the issue of allegedly abusive petitions. Following their campaign, the governments of France and Belgium asked the PMC to introduce a safety filter to avoid the "abuse of the right to petitions." Orts proposed that the Casely Hayford case should become a precedent for this procedure and a deterrence for abusers. He recommended an end to discussing any topic related to the Adjigo case and to ban Casely Hayford from the right to address any petition to the PMC.[60]

The question of representation received a new stimulus by the public debate over outsiders who spoke on behalf of the native population, especially if Europeans spoke for Africans. This was the case in May 1928, when the International Office for the Protection of Native Races, an association of

---

[58] Gayibor, *Histoire des Togolais*, 233–234.
[59] Pedersen, *The Guardians*, 281.
[60] Antonelli, "Le Droit de Petition."

European philanthropists who were close to the PMC and the ICI, sent a petition to the PMC that was no less than a sweeping blow to the mandate system. The Office referred to a study by Harvard professor and soon-to-be ICI member Raymond Leslie Buell, who had traveled Africa for several months and collected his observations in a book titled *The Native Problems of Africa*. In his book, Buell harshly criticized British rule in Tanganyika, Belgian rule in Ruanda-Urundi, and French rule in Togo and Cameroon. These allegations became the nucleus of the petition. It was ICI and PMC member Van Rees who processed the petition. Buell had spared none of the mandatory powers and accused them of having violated the rules they had made themselves: The Belgian officials forcibly recruited inhabitants of Ruanda-Urundi for the private mining company Union Minière du Haut-Katanga in Southern Congo. French officials in Cameroon had given former German tobacco plantations to a French company although they should have sold them at auction. In French Togo and Cameroon, the administration obliged the inhabitants to contribute to public works, without paying them any salary. The same happened in Tanganyika, where the British officials also pushed back African coffee planters to leave the fertile lands to Europeans.[61]

The PMC considered none of Buell's allegations as legitimate, although their weight increased through the support of the International Office for the Protection of Native Races. Geneva concluded that Buell's reproaches were "either without foundation or are not of a nature to occasion any intervention."[62] Instead, the colonialist press denounced Buell as being an outsider, who had only traveled in Africa for a short period of three months, too short to be actually able to understand the situation. Endorsed by PMC members, colonialist journals such as *L'Afrique Française* accused Buell of retrieving his information from the "meaningless muckraking newspapers" because his sources were African journalists who wrote for the *Negro World*, the *Gold Coast Independent*, and Casely Hayford's *Gold Coast Leader*. Ironically, the *Afrique Française* blamed Buell of a "racist bias" that made him an unreflecting defender of the African cause.[63] Dismissed as the advocate of the Africans, the American Buell turned away from the PMC. He would join the ICI instead.

6.5 Looming Independence? The ICI and Representative Councils in the Colonies

Unlike the PMC, ICI members sought ways to organize indigenous representation within the colonies and even advocated the introduction of a

---

[61] LoN Archives, 6A/4479/758, *Petition of the Bureau International pour la Défense des Indigènes*, May 24, 1929, 78.
[62] LoN Archives 6A/4479/758, Confidential Draft Conclusion of the PMC, July 11, 1929.
[63] LoN Archives 6A/4479/758, *Afrique Française* (June 1928), 148.

constitution and elections. At the ICI's 1927 meeting, its members agreed on the importance of "representative councils." Cautiously, they added that no colonial expert would "completely reject the idea of equipping the colonies with an organism capable to inform the government about the feelings and the needs of the population, apart from official sources, and such an organism has always a representative character." The innovative element of the ICI's representative scheme was to break with individual chiefs who had habitually represented the population without having its support.[64]

The progressive Dutch members of the ICI particularly pushed for representative councils, after they had designed and introduced the Volksraad in Indonesia. The Dutch lawyer Emmanuel Moresco and father of the Volksraad, in particular, felt the need to put an end to the policy of paramount chiefs, because their monopoly on representation allowed "neither criticism nor a public and controversial debate" among wider circles of the population.[65] As a liberal, Moresco assumed that a "controversial debate" was a necessary process on the way to secure adequate representation. He received support from Belgian and French colonial administrators who argued that only elections enabled a critical debate and, as a result, the adequate representation of the entire population. Some of the French delegates in the ICI had pushed for a Central Indochinese Assembly that was, however, far from being realized, also for lack of a precedence.[66] The ICI wanted to fill this gap by studying forms of indigenous representation in a comparative way. As they assumed that the Asian colonies were on the brink of self-government, they focused on the American Philippines, in British India, in Dutch Indonesia, and in French Indochina.

A few minutes into the debate at the 1927 meeting, it became clear that many ICI members subscribed to nationalist evolutionism. For them, the emergence of nationalist movements in the colonized world was inevitable. Moresco cautioned his colleagues that "peoples are not made to be eternally dominated by other people ... there comes the day when they have to be their own leaders. At least, natural evolution shows this tendency. The consequence is that, in principle, each colony is a nation in the making. It is evident that we do not have the right to oppose ourselves to thus evolution."[67] Moresco's prediction resembled the PMC's philosophy of gradual emancipation, although he believed that the driving force behind emancipation were nationalists from overseas and not civilizers from Europe. Notwithstanding, his belief in an evolutionist path-dependency led him to assume that a model for colonial emancipation could be found in the "European constitutional

---

[64] We can see this already in the 1920 meeting. See ICI, *Compte Rendu 1920*, 157, 164.
[65] ICI, *Compte Rendu 1927*, 74–75.
[66] Ibid., 71–111.
[67] Ibid., 108.

history." He indeed pleaded to start by turning colonies into constitutional states that clearly regulated the relationship between "those who govern and those who are governed."[68] To draft a constitution, the composition of the representative organs, as well as the reach of their powers, required an exact definition.

In the 1920s, representative bodies that deserved this name were few in the colonized world. Those who existed had a young history and were predominantly located in Asia. Around 1900, the US Taft Commission (influenced by the early ICI) had recommended and actually introduced a bicameral system in the Philippines and even organized elections (with a very restricted franchise) in 1907.[69] In British India, the Morley-Minto reforms of 1909 increased the number of Indians in the representative Councils of the Provinces. In 1919, the Government of India Act introduced a bicameral system with a Council of State and the partly elected Indian Legislative Assembly. The latest, and probably most widely known representative organ, was the Volksraad (People's Council) in Dutch Java. Designed by Moresco and launched in 1918 as a consultative organ, it obtained legislative power in 1925. In the same year, the British Gold Coast colony introduced a constitution and increased the number of Africans in the Legislative Council to nine out of thirty.

All these representative organs should have theoretically shifted gradually from a consultative and administrative role to legislative functions. Even if this transition into a law-making body succeeded, as in the Netherlands Indies, the colonial governor could veto all decisions and laws the respective body had made. In all cases, the members of representative councils were partly nominated and partly elected, though through a census suffrage and via provincial councils that made sure that only profiteers, notables, and chiefs could vote. Through this system, the colonial governments made sure to have a majority of loyal members. The councils met irregularly. The Gold Coast Legislative Council, for example, met between two and five times a year.[70] The Volksraad exemplified this controlled and therefore selective representation.

Like no other representative body in the colonies, the Volksraad in the Dutch Indies raised hopes of participation among the Indonesians just to disappoint them. While it remains unclear whether the Dutch introduced the Volksraad as a reward for the Indonesian war contribution or if it was a concession toward participatory demands from the proto-nationalist groups Sarekat Islam (1910) and Budi Utomo (1908), it is certain that Dutch ICI members particularly pushed for an Indonesian representative body already before the war. ICI member and prewar director of education in the Netherlands Indies, Jacques H. Abendanon, wanted all Indonesians to have

---

[68] Ibid., 74–75.
[69] Brownlee, *Authoritarianism*, 73–74; Hutchcroft, "Colonial Masters," 277–306.
[70] Wight, *The Gold Coast*, 56.

"the right to vote" to educate them for an independent democracy in the future.[71] Moresco designed it, J. P. van Limburg Stirum launched it while being governor-general in 1918, and his successor, the ICI's vice president Dirk Fock, expanded its legal powers in 1925. At its inauguration in 1918, the Volksraad had thirty-eight members. The colonial government appointed half of them, while the municipal and local councils (which existed since 1903 and were elected) dispatched the other half. Over the years, Indonesians never made up more than 45 percent of the Volksraad's delegates. At least a quarter of the appointed Indonesians were chosen for their loyalty to the Dutch colonizers. Among the Indonesians whom the local councils elected, eleven out of nineteen were former government officials (*priyayi*) who received a Dutch pension and depended on the state. Up to 1925, the Volksraad had no legislative powers but the governor-general had to consult it on matters of budget and military conscription, among others.[72] After Fock had accredited the Volksraad with extended legislative – and not only consultative – power in 1925, it engaged only reluctantly in claiming the right to make laws. Between 1927 and 1941, the Volksraad only made a few amendments to government ordinances and the governor withdrew a handful of decrees because of the Volksraad's criticism. However, the Volksraad made use of the initiative to propose laws only six times. The Europeans rejected three of these drafts out of hand.[73] Given this self-restriction of the Volksraad and the governor's veto power, the Dutch colonial government was overconfident and even accepted moderate Indonesian nationalists as members in the Volksraad. Tjipto Mangoenkoesoemo was among them. The Dutch had exiled him before World War I because he had co-founded the protonationalist Budi Utomo society. In the Volksraad, however, he kept a low profile and carried no weight.

Discussing the Volksraad at the 1927 meeting led ICI members to the remarkable conclusion that voters in a mass democracy might be easier to control than the elite who had embraced European-style nationalism. The former Belgian colonial minister Louis Franck truly believed that "the political system has to be responsive to the soul of the masses and translate their aspirations and needs." Others even declared that they were ready to risk "decolonization" as long as colonial experts, and not the indigenous nationalists, were in control of this process. To undermine the revolutionary fervor of "semi-European" nationalist leaders, the ICI considered democratic elections and the participation of the "masses," even if such a grassroots democracy marked the end of official colonial rule.[74]

---

[71] ICI, *Compte Rendu 1920*, 48
[72] Wedema, *'Ethiek' und Macht*, 125–130.
[73] McTurnan Kahin, *Nationalism and Revolution*, 40.
[74] ICI, *Compte Rendu 1927*, 104.

Less well-meaning members of the ICI endorsed this view, claiming that the masses in the colonies were easier to manipulate than fully-fledged nationalist and communist leaders. The Dutch Schuman added that "the masses ... don't know exactly how a parliamentary system works. But I guess this is the same in Western Europe."[75] His remark aroused scornful laughs among the bourgeois members of the ICI. Seen against this background, it was a strategic move of the ICI to declare the "masses" who lived in the colonies the true sovereign. Those masses were allegedly more representative than the "semi-European" agitators who had gathered in European cities such as Paris, London, Hamburg, and Brussels. While colonial experts took great pains to portray these exiled nationalist leaders as "alienated," "detribalized," and communist, they argued that the authentic population in the colony should speak for itself.

The history of representative bodies in India and Indonesia left ICI members with the impression that emancipative movements in the colonies might easily be mitigated by reforms and restrictive participation. The British Newton and the Dutch Moresco referred to the Swaraj movement in British India to confirm the strategy of co-opting nationalists. The Swaraj party had emerged in 1923 to reinstate Gandhi's strategy of civil disobedience. A year earlier, Gandhi had suspended his struggle to avoid an escalation following a deadly clash between protesters of Gandhi's Non-Cooperation Movement and the colonial police. The Swaraj was the section of the Indian National Congress party that wanted to continue with the protests. But unlike Gandhi's Non-Cooperation Movement, Swaraj leaders chose to join and use the provincial and central legislative councils established by the British. They intended to use the British infrastructure to sabotage its imperial rule and make it fall. One of them, Vithalbhai Patel, was even elected to become the president of the Central Legislative Assembly, introduced in 1919 as the lower house of a bicameral system in British India. However, the Central Legislative Assembly had tellingly few opportunities to actually make or change laws. As most representative organs in the colonies, the Central Legislative Assembly in British India was a farce. Patel's successes as its president were often more rhetorical than substantial. He pushed through a law to extend primary education in India but only in certain regions. Finally, he gradually adapted to the unpolitical administrative life of the council. This, at least, is the interpretation of the ICI members.

At the 1927 meeting, Moresco narrated the short history of the Swaraj in the Central Legislative Assembly as a history of surrender:

> In the first phase, the Swaraj movement had a completely negative attitude [toward British representative councils] ... in the second phase,

[75] Ibid., 100.

they abandoned their attitude of complete abstention; they participated in the elections and entered the councils in huge number with the intention of obstructing its work and bringing about a "deadlock"; this plan failed. Finally, in the third phase, they actively participated in the works.

Thus, Moresco concluded in a triumphalist way: "the non-cooperation movement was weakened and will ultimately vanish." More importantly, he made a general rule out of this de-radicalization through pseudo-democratization: "If there is one thing to learn from this story, it is that ... we do not have to fear an obstructive and reactionary movement in its early stage."[76] The ICI members were so arrogant that they did not even take anti-colonial movements seriously.

While progressive members of the ICI endorsed democratization in principle, they spilled much ink to explain how the lack of a national identity and solidarity stood in the way of full and immediate democratization. The segmentary character ascribed to indigenous societies became the most powerful argument against democratization. French members explained that Indochina was ethnically divided into "Annamites, Cambodians, Laotians, Chinese" who were allegedly unable to be in a parliament together.[77] In India, British officials declared Muslims and Hindus irreconcilable, an attitude that delivered the excuse to refuse independence for another decade, before the partition of British India made decolonization possible. This fear of potential fragmentation through democratization was indeed an excuse, even more because models for proportional representation existed and worked to the benefit of the colonial power. There were proportional systems of representation with the minor error that the proportions were wrong. Councils in Ceylon and Chochinchina, but above all the Volksraad in Java were based on proportional representation that took into account the existence of different ethnic groups (Europeans, Javanese, Chinese, Arabs).[78] The quota for so-called "foreign Orientals" (Chinese and Arab) in the Volksraad was a means to maintain colonial rule: the Dutch knew that Chinese and Arab minorities always supported the cause of the Dutch colonial government. This "political segregation" served as a divide-and-rule practice in most colonies.[79] Nevertheless, the ICI invented the causality between democratization and sectarian conflict because it could use it to argue against full democratization. This pseudo-causality and the imagined dilemma that democratization would result in sectarian chaos became the main argument to maintain imperial rule after World War II.

---

[76] Ibid., 106.
[77] Ibid., 97.
[78] Ibid., 80–81.
[79] Hailey, *African Survey*, 170.

6.5 LOOMING INDEPENDENCE?   233

The second most important argument against democratization was the allegedly natural inequality of indigenous societies. Indochina, one ICI member argued, had already a hierarchically ordered society with kings (of Cambodia) and emperors (of Annam) whose authority the French needed to maintain in order to not destabilize the system.[80] The most concrete and partly convincing example ICI members advanced was the process of (pseudo-)democratization in the Philippines, where the United States had established an upper house (the Philippine Commission) and a lower house (the elected Philippine Assembly) in the early twentieth century. Elections to the Assembly took place in 1907, but the US administration used strategies of restriction, misinformation, and discouragement to keep the turnout down to 1.4 percent of the Filipino population.[81] It is no wonder that the elections benefited mostly the elite that had traditionally cooperated with the colonial administration. ICI members closely observed the success of the corrupt upper classes and used it as a proof that the Filipinos were not yet ready for a democratic election. After all, they argued, the "caziques" (a small group of well-off notables) had had a comeback in the elections and aggravated political division and class differences in the Philippines.[82]

Democratization, the ICI wanted to make believe, privileged those who were already privileged. Despite considering the sovereignty of the masses, the ICI kept to its paternalistic attitude and claimed that only a just colonial ruler could protect the weak, empower the lower classes, and guarantee minority rights. This brought ICI members closer to the position of the PMC members who refused to accept anyone as the legitimate representative of the mandates' population. Ironically, the underlying logic was, as Van Rees remarked at the ICI meeting, that the population of the mandates and colonies were unrepresentable if they did not develop a national spirit of solidarity. Looking at European history, he assumed that a representative system required first a proto-nationalist sentiment. Dutch members, in particular, saw few alternatives to a nationalist evolutionism in the sense of a "natural and inevitable evolution of indigenous societies to an advanced degree of independence and political liberty."[83]

A debate concerning the Gold Coast Legislative Council shows that the issue with representation was not exclusively European. Ghanaians, for example, engaged in a fierce debate about the nature of representation. In Gold Coast, the Aborigines Rights Protection Society, established in 1897 by Ghana's progressive coastal elite, did not accept the Legislative Council as an adequate representative body, because it privileged the chiefs who cooperated with the

---

[80] ICI, *Compte Rendu 1927*, 94 and 97.
[81] Brownlee, *Authoritarianism*, 73, cited after Paredes, *Pilippine Colonial Democracy*, 44.
[82] ICI, *Compte Rendu 1927*, 80–81.
[83] Ibid., 76.

British government. The Aborigines Rights Protection Society even sent a petition to the British government claiming that the Ashanti chiefs whom the British invited to join the Legislative Council broke with the custom of taking decisions together with the elders. According to the Aborigines Rights Protection Society, Ashanti chiefs such as Ofori Atta were not legislators but only executed decisions made by a collective Ashanti "state council." The petition stated that "it was therefore an act of high courage in Sir Ofori Atta to accept membership and risk the consequences of breach of custom." Thus, they concluded "it is against native law and custom for a chief to sit in a legislative assembly."[84]

The ensuing debate focused on the question of whether Ashanti chiefs were delegates or representatives. Delegates, according to Ashanti legal philosophy, had a "mandate of their constituency" and could take decisions on their own, if on its behalf. Representatives, instead, always had to consult the collective "sovereign" before voting on any single law in the Legislative Council. Chief Nana Ayirebi Acquah, for example, had a seat in the Legislative Council and represented the Central Province. He voiced his concern about the inability to vote spontaneously in the Legislative Council:

> Our people will not understand us and they will likely say that the farmers are not having good price for their cacao, but that when we as their representatives go down to Accra to guide their interests we simply sit down tight without saying anything in their favor with the result that now the import duty on cotton goods is increased to their detriment.[85]

But overall, Nana Ayirebi Acquah found the debate absurd and alluded to the fact that the British government used the debate to question the chiefs' legitimacy and representiveness:

> Last week we were told in this House [of the Legislative Council] on a particularly simple question of amendment that we had no mandate; but in my opinion it is the practice in all civilized countries that once a person is elected by his constituency, he automatically receives their mandate and then can represent their interest in any matter of vital importance whether charged or not.[86]

While the ICI had the merit of pushing for a broader basis of representation to overcome the cooperation with individual chiefs and privileged ethnic groups, it backtracked with regard to immediate democratization. Ironically, the final outcome of the representation debate was that democracy was only possible in the colonies if there was a national electorate and therefore a

---

[84] Wight, *Legislative Council*, 96–97.
[85] Ibid., 96–97.
[86] Ibid. 99.

nation. A keen observer of the Gold Coast Legislative Council would cite Edmund Burke to illustrate this point: "Parliament is not a congress of ambassadors from different and hostile interests; which interests each must maintain, as an agent or advocate, against other agents or advocates; but parliament is a deliberative assembly of one nation, with one interest, that of the whole."[87] The ICI used this idea to deny the colonized populations democratic representation. By implication, however, their message was that the colonized had to be a nation first before becoming a democracy. Unintendedly, this played into the hands of the nationalists, as the nationalist option seemed without any alternative.

6.6 The Failure of Representation through International Organizations and the Birth of Nationalism

Focusing on the colonies, the ICI members considered the diasporic groups that gathered in Paris, London, Hamburg, and Brussels as nonrepresentative, especially because of their allegedly alienated and detribalized status as semi-Westerners. ICI members ignored Europeanized non-Europeans explicitly, which became clear during the Panafrican Congress held in Paris in 1919. The Panafrican Congress was far from being anti-colonial and simply aimed at improving the situation of Africans within the colonial context. But the leaders of the ICI refused to accept their claims as representative. When the Congress was about to start in 1919, the ICI's rising star and future secretary-general Octave Louwers wrote to Pierre Orts that they should not send official representatives to the event, not to "officialize the Congress" and to keep it a "private" initiative.[88] Because Colonial Ministries from France and Great Britain even prevented African leaders from participating in the Panafrican Congress and sent government representatives instead, it became no more than a meeting of predominantly European philanthropists.[89]

Well into the 1920s, the ICI underestimated the anti-imperial nature of new international movements and therefore did not consider them a serious threat to the colonial system. Its arrogant belief in the indisputable legitimacy of colonialism manifested itself in 1928, when the PMC compiled a list of "international associations that are concerned with colonial questions" and asked the ICI's secretary-general, Octave Louwers, to contribute to the list. Louwers indicated that the PMC had failed to list the Universal Negro Improvement Association and African Communities League and the League Against Imperialism. Garvey's Universal Negro Improvement Association had

---

[87] Ibid., 99.
[88] AGRB Louwers Papers, Dossier O. Louwers 170 (197) Conference de la Paix à Paris 1919 Notes et documents, Louwers to Orts, February 19, 1919.
[89] W. E. B. Du Bois, "Winds of Time," *Chicago Defender* (May 26, 1926).

started to promote the emancipation of all Africans as early as 1913. The League Against Imperialism had met in 1927 for the first time and was influenced by Communist ideas. Louwers seemed to see them as philanthropist organizations but not serious anti-imperial movements.[90] Instead, the ICI confided in its own governmental skills to persuade Africans about the benefits of empire. In 1931, it invited the "assimilated" Senegalese Blaise Diagne, who became the first non-Westerner to speak at an ICI meeting. Diagne had been naturalized French, was elected to the parliament in Paris, and became an employee of the Colonial Ministry in Paris, which he represented at the ICI's meeting. He confirmed the ICI's belief that colonization was a beneficial project and he warned supporters of independence movement: "once it has been undertaken, no retreat can be thought of."[91]

While ignoring the anti-imperialist initiatives of the diaspora in Europe and the United States, the ICI was much more concerned with those groups who might turn to anti-colonial nationalism inside the colonies. ICI members came up with the idea of sending them as delegates to international organizations to give them the feeling of representing their people. For example, to mitigate the nationalist fervor of Indonesian Volksraad members, Dutch colonial internationalists invited them to join international organizations as representatives of the Dutch Indies.[92] Indonesians happily accepted this "third way" of representation because the imperial constitution denied them real participation through the Volksraad and offered no chance to join the parliament of the metropole.

Achmad Djajadiningrat, the former Indonesian regent of Serang and protégé of Dutch ICI member Snouck Hurgronje, was one among those Volksraad members who represented the Dutch Indies at international congresses. After Snouck Hurgronje had made it possible for Djajadiningrat to begin a career within the administration of the Dutch Indies, the offspring of an Indonesian *priyayi* family attended two meetings of the League of Nations and participated in the debates on forced labor at the International Labor Congress in 1929. Djajadiningrat had long admired Geneva as the center of internationalism and had learned French to speak the language of diplomats. He felt proud to be part of the Dutch delegation, particularly because its leading diplomat, Mgr. Nolens, who treated him as a Dutch national and always "called me 'mon patriote'" when he presented him to foreign delegations in Geneva. Djajadiningrat recalled: "Although I am, as the reader knows, a convinced advocate of the politics of association, I do not need to say how pleased I was to hear a great Netherlander such as Mgr. Nolens calling me 'compatriote.'"[93]

---

[90] LoN Archives, R 2325, 6A/5167/758 Friis to Louwers, July 21, 1928.
[91] ICI, *Compte Rendu 1931*, 20.
[92] Bertrand, *État Colonial*, 443–509.
[93] Djajadiningrat, *Herinneringen*, 349–351.

6.6 FAILURE OF REPRESENTATION

When Djajadiningrat attended the International Labor Congress in Geneva, he admired the fierce but fruitful negotiations between employers and trade unions about the global working conditions.[94] For him, the ILO delivered the proof that two strictly opposed parties were able to reach agreements that occasionally even did justice to the necessities of the powerless. It was remarkable in his eyes that the ILO thought of class relations also in terms of race relations, especially when it discussed the labor conflicts in the Indies and in South Africa.[95] At the International Labor Congress, Djajadiningrat met Indonesian human rights activist and proto-nationalist Hadji Agoes Salim, who had been a member of the Volksraad for Sarekat Islam, then joined the Dutch Trade Union Federation and held close ties with the International Transport Worker's Federation.[96] Mohammed Hatta, soon-to-be independence leader, was equally at the ILO.[97] Given the inclusion of more of these radical forces such as Salim, Djajadiningrat found the negotiation about labor rights in the ILO much more stimulating than the bureaucratic procedures of the League.

While he admired the ILO, Djajadiningrat considered the League of Nations no more than a big palaver and a "complaints department" ("klachtenbureau") where delegates did not take far-reaching decisions but enmeshed themselves in rhetorically brilliant self-pitying.[98] Given the presence of high-ranking diplomats, Djajadiningrat was afraid to participate in the debates that revolved around opium trade, disarmament, and intellectual cooperation: "But I have nevertheless given a speech in French in the name of the governmental delegation." Yet, it soon "occurred to me that my task was predominantly to provide information about the situation in Indonesia for our delegation, so that I did not need really deep-going knowledge about the different topics." The diplomats' superficial knowledge about Indonesia and their paternalistic attitude struck him.[99] Indonesia was only a minor topic on the League's agenda and instead of tackling colonial problems, diplomats accused Djajadiningrat's country of being hub for the trafficking of women. Faced with this reproach, and given that he had already introduced protective measures for Indonesian women through the Volksraad in 1925, Djajadiningrat left the League disappointed.[100] Apparently, the Dutch delegation had brought him to have native support to disprove these allegations. Moreover, he became aware of the Dutch strategy to bring only loyal

---

[94] On the ILO, see Maul, *Human Rights*.
[95] Djajadiningrat, *Herinneringen*, 349–351.
[96] Mrázek, *Sjahrir*, 69.
[97] ILO Archive, N206/1/01/3: J. Goudal to Phelan September 3, 1927.
[98] Djajadiningrat, *Herinneringen*, 358–363.
[99] Ibid., 349–351 and 358–363.
[100] Locher-Scholten, *Women and the Colonial State*, 50.

Indonesians to the League, especially when he met his colleague from the Volksraad, Pangeran Adipati Soejono, who was in favor of Dutch colonial rule.[101]

Both the League and the ILO saw in the Indonesians "technical advisors" rather than political representatives. Neither the loyalist Djajadiningrat nor the socialist Salim, who participated in the meetings of the Dutch Federation of Trade Unions, were taken seriously. Djajadiningrat immediately realized that he "was only a technical advisor, and could not say anything on my own initiative."[102] Consequently, both could use their presence in Europe to get involved in subversive activism. In Amsterdam, Salim co-organized Perhimpoenan Indonesia, the association that represented the Indonesian nationalists in the Netherlands. Djajadiningrat met with nationalist students in the Netherlands who provided him with an invitation to the meeting of the League Against Imperialism in Frankfurt in July 1929. He tricked the Dutch colonial ministry into allowing him to go to Germany by claiming to study German society and its "middle classes." He added: "I did not find this difficult because I had anyways decided to make a journey in Europe to study its middle classes ... further I told the Dutch embassy in Berlin that the Colonial Ministry had approved my participation in the anti-imperial world congress in Frankfurt."[103] At the congress, which lasted one week and was under the influence of the Communist International, Djajadiningrat met for the first time with revolutionary leaders such as the Chinese Sun-Yat-Sen, Chivapragupta of the Indian National Congress, representatives of Iraq's National Party, the Afro-American civil rights activist William Pickens, and the leader of the Latin American anti-imperialists, Manuel Ugarte. For Djajadiningrat, this was "the most international congress" because it brought together (male and female) delegates from colonized countries.[104]

In the end, however, Djajadiningrat, Salim, and Casely Hayford relied on representative councils in the colonies, which promised to bring about gradual change instead of banking on international organizations. Neither the League of Nations, nor the ILO, nor Communist Internationalism seemed to speak to their needs. The internationalism of these organizations was more or less Eurocentric and had little to offer to the colonized middle class.[105] Djajadiningrat, who was interested in Marxism but despised Sovietism, found good and bad in this communist agenda. While he endorsed the anti-imperialists' fight for the right of trade unions to form coalitions and umbrella

---

[101] Colenbrander, "Bij het Aftreden," 380.
[102] Djajadiningrat, *Herinneringen*, 350.
[103] Ibid., 353.
[104] Ibid., 354.
[105] On the particularities of a non-European middle class, see Dejung et al., *The Global Bourgeoisie*, 1–40; Melber, *The Rise of Africa's Middle Class*, 1–16.

organizations in the colonies, he was skeptical toward the dominant Soviet-Chinese agenda to use rebel movements in Asia to realize their geopolitical goals and engage in an "anti-imperial imperialism" in this region.[106] By renouncing communism and radical anti-colonialism, he avoided persecution that hit others: in the very same moment, Sukarno was arrested in Java for his leadership in the Partai Nasional Indonesia he had founded in 1927. Although Sukarno shared a socialist and nationalist agenda with Djajadiningrat, the more radical Sukarno never became a member of the Volksraad. Like Djajadiningrat, Casely Hayford chose a more moderate approach. He turned away from the League's internationalism and back to the Legislative Council in Gold Coast to push for reforms and independence. This was very much what the ICI wanted them to do. It was only after Indonesia's independence in 1949 that an offspring of the Djajadiningrat family joined the ICI and became its first permanent non-European member, a year before Indonesia joined the UN. Before World War II, however, the ICI's focus was on representation in the colonies, especially when indigenous taxpayers asked for it.

6.7 The ICI's Campaign for Financial and Political Autonomy in the Colonies

In the 1920s, the majority of the colonized became taxpayers and expected representation for their contribution. As the metropoles struggled with rebuilding a war-torn Europe, they refrained from bigger investments in the colonies and partly abandoned early development programs such as the Dutch ethical policy.[107] Consequently, the burden to finance the colonies was on the local taxpayers. ICI members were enthusiastic about taxation, as it seemed to increase both economic autarky and political autonomy. World War I had shown that autarky was possible, since most colonies seemed to have been self-sufficient and even bailed out sectors of the European war industry. During and after the war, metropoles used resources from their empires to contribute to the rebuilding of Europe. ICI members welcomed this new creditworthiness of the colonial economy. Yet they wanted the colonial economy to be more than a complementary economy. They hoped that the colonies would soon be able to pay for their own economic development and finance a rudimentary welfare state. To achieve this goal of self-sufficiency and self-development, colonial internationalists tried to cut financial and political ties with the motherland. Autonomy of the colonial administration and taxation of the local population seemed to be two sides of the same coin on which the ICI engraved the principles of autarky and autonomy.

---

[106] Djajadiningrat, *Herinneringen*, 355–357.
[107] Booth, "Colonial Revenue," 44 and 52.

The principle of financial autonomy became the pater noster of the ICI, whose members repeatedly reiterated the idea that mandates were models for colonies in that they were "entities quite distinct from the Powers who are called to govern them. It follows that the powers are obliged to respect rigorously the integrity and the political statute of these territories, that any unoccupied and unclaimed land in those territories form part and parcel thereof, and that any revenues belong to their own public treasury."[108] The mandate constitution of 1919 disallowed the mandatory power to exploit its trust and stipulated that all revenues from land and labor had to feed back into the territory and its inhabitants.[109] Financial autonomy of colonial possessions was not a new idea. The French law on budgetary autonomy of the overseas possessions, for example, came into force as early as 1900. Thenceforth, French colonies were supposed to be self-sufficient, which led to the introduction of the poll tax.[110]

World War I, in particular, was the testing ground for colonial internationalists to see how far they could push autonomy. Renowned colonial internationalists refused to levy troops and taxes to support the metropole.[111] Colonial disobedience particularly came from the ICI's milieu. ICI members such as Ernest Roume celebrated the refusal of the Dutch-born governor of French West Africa, Joost van Voellenhoven, to levy indigenous troops for Paris and the war in Europe.[112] Arguing that France had to act resolutely along colonial lines, Van Voellenhoven told the "diplomats" in Paris that he needed manpower in French West Africa to keep the colonial economy going and could not waste their lives on European battlefields.[113] "French West Africa has to shape its own destiny," he claimed, lamenting the labor shortage caused by the war.[114] After refusing to recruit soldiers in French West Africa, Paris accused Van Voellenhoven of unpatriotic behavior and released him from his duties as governor.[115] Van Voellenhoven, who had been born to Dutch parents in Algeria and was on good terms with colonial experts in Germany

---

[108] ICI, *Compte Rendu 1927*, 25.
[109] Ibid., 27.
[110] Coquery-Vidrovitch, *Le Congo*, 116.
[111] Colonial governors in British East Africa, German East Africa, British Gold Coast, and Togo even refused to participate in the war at all, evoking the neutrality of their colony. See Nasson, "British Imperial Africa," 133.
[112] Mainly via Chailley's *Union Coloniale*: IdF, Fonds Terrier MS 5925, vol. 2, fol. 365–375, Gouverneur AOF Vollenhoven to Ministre des Colonies, November 10, 1917, "Situation Politique de la Colonie."
[113] Comité d'Initiative, *Une Âme de Chef*, 38–56.
[114] Ibid., 169.
[115] IdF, Fonds Terrier, MS 5925, vol. 1, fol. 255–277: Van Vollenhoven to Ministre des colonies, September 22, 1917: "Reorganisation de l'Ouest-Africain;" Comité d'Initiative, *Une Âme de Chef*, 57–70.

6.7 ICI'S CAMPAIGN FOR AUTONOMY IN COLONIES

and the Netherlands, subsequently faced a xenophobic campaign that questioned his loyalty to France. Nevertheless, he continued to call for colonial autonomy from France and advocated a "Franco-British federation in West Africa" that should result in an exclusively colonial "League of Nations" in which the metropoles played a minor role.[116]

A more ambiguous case was the disobedience of British ICI member William Meyer during World War I in India. Before the war, Meyer had become a devoted internationalist who translated Chailley's *Administrative Problems of British India* (1910) into English. During the war, he was a member of the Viceroy's Council in British India and responsible for financing the recruitment of Indian soldiers, also for territories outside the crown colony. The "Finance Minister of India," as Chamberlain called him, seemed to have denied financial support to recruit Indian railway workers and soldiers for service outside the Indian sphere of influence. In particular, he refused to levy taxes in India for the British military campaign in Iraq – on the grounds that the Mesopotamia campaign "strained the Indian financial and monetary systems to the limit."[117] Accused of disloyalty, a parliamentary committee investigated Meyer's case. Although the committee found him innocent of all charges, he was "held up to public odium and contempt" in the British media. The press advanced his German name and internationalist activities in the ICI to call his Britishness into question.[118]

In many cases, however, the war had proven autonomists such as Van Voellenhoven and Meyer right, because the colonies were economically stable even though the war cut them off from the motherland. During the war, economic self-sufficiency had become a fact. After the war, metropolitan governments had to accept the fact that both financial and administrative autonomy was the only way to bring about an organic and self-sufficient organization of a colony. Thus, colonial internationalists such as Meyer took over posts to remodel the relation between metropole and motherland in the postwar era.[119]

Meyer, who was the ICI's vice-president and became the first high commissioner for India according to the new Government of India Act in 1920, was responsible for giving India an autonomous status comparable to the dominion status of Britain's former white settler colonies.[120] He had already been a part of India's decentralization committee before the war. During the war,

---

[116] Ibid., 169.
[117] Tomlinson, "Meyer, Sir William Stevenson." The 1918 Montagu-Chelmsford Report committed Britain to postwar reforms to promote gradual Indian self-government. See Garton, "The Dominions, Ireland and India," 162.
[118] House of Commons, *Parliamentary Debates 1917*, 2230–2232; 2251; 2198–2199; 1584.
[119] Tomlinson, "Meyer."
[120] On the context, see Gorman, *The Emergence*, 113–114.

Meyer de-linked the rupee from its fixed exchange rate with the sterling and made Indian finances autonomous from the metropole. After the war, the Indian government succeeded in removing the defense of the Middle East from the list of its strategic obligations in future imperial defense planning.[121] Meyer owed a lot to the ICI's schemes of autonomy and therefore attended all its meetings between 1920 and 1922. At the meetings, he lobbied for a more independent "colonial magistracy." He also headed the Indian delegations at the first and second assemblies of the League of Nations (1920–1921).[122]

In a similar way, the second ICI vice-president in 1920, the Dutch Dirk Fock, became responsible for the decentralization of the Dutch colonies. As the postwar governor-general in the Dutch Indies, he set himself the task of strengthening municipal self-government (which the Dutch had introduced to the Indies as early as 1903). In 1907, long before Meyer in British India, Fock had drafted two bills that rendered the finances of Dutch India independent of the metropole. One of them, the *Indische Comptabliteitswet*, granted Dutch India a legal personality and allowed it to take out a loan without the consent of The Hague.[123] Fock's policy benefited the autarky of the Dutch Indies. In the interwar period, when imports from Europe to the Dutch East Indies fell from 61 percent to 42 percent, the economic autonomy increased.[124]

As the colonies cut themselves off from the metropoles, unofficial talks within the ICI brought about bilateral agreements between the colonies to support each other. Franco-Belgian cooperation in the two Congos, for instance, became exemplary. Their agreements stipulated remissions of customs duty and the mutual right to persecute "delinquents, smugglers, and criminals" on the others' territory.[125]

6.8 No Taxation without Representation?

The key to financial independence was the taxation of the colonized population, which increased significantly in the 1920s.[126] As the ICI revealed in a comparative survey on taxation, reforms in the 1920s and 1930s made taxation more comprehensive and complex but not necessarily fairer. In Belgian Congo, for example, the number of taxpayers rose from 648,832 in 1915 to

---

[121] Tomlinson, "Meyer."
[122] *The Uganda Herald* (May 6, 1921); *East African Chronicle* (May 14, 1921), 12.
[123] Wedema, *"Ethiek" und Macht*, 125–130.
[124] *Annuaire de Documentation Coloniale Comparée* 1 (1927), 176.
[125] Fontaine, "L'Alliance Franco-Belge," 148–149.
[126] Traditional accounts about financing and taxing empire were hardly interested in the contributions of indigenous taxpayers. See Davis and Huttenback, *Mammon*; Marseille, *Empire Colonial et Capitalisme Français*. For a more comprehensive view, see Havik, Keese, and Santos, *Administration and Taxation*.

6.8 NO TAXATION WITHOUT REPRESENTATION? 243

2,637,552 in 1936.[127] In terms of complexity, the Dutch blazed the trail by introducing the first system of gradual taxation in 1920 and even had exemptions for low-income earners.[128] Shortly after, the Belgian Congo reformed its tax system, carefully avoiding connotations with the longer history of Léopold's enforced "rubber tax" and the wide use of forced cultivation during the World War I. Aware of its bad reputation, Brussels introduced a progressive tax system. This system was gradual not with regard to individual salaries but in proportion to the development of the region in which the taxpayer lived. Thus, residents of the highly developed capital Léopoldville paid seventy-five francs annually, while the inhabitants of the poorer inland districts paid only ten Francs.[129] In Senegal, similar regulations stipulated that inhabitants of the groundnut producing areas would pay ten francs, the less well-off regions only seven.[130] In 1933, all of French West Africa introduced a progressive income tax. The British in Eastern Africa usually preferred the traditional poll and hut tax, as they lacked tax registers and the bureaucratic infrastructure to collect the taxes. They would follow the path of gradual taxation in the 1930s.

The ICI was particularly interested in the amount the indigenous population contributed to the overall income of the colony and found out that indigenous taxpayers contributed up to 50 percent of the overall budget of a colony.[131] The ICI's study revealed that in Swaziland and Basutoland, where few Europeans lived and whose African inhabitants made their money in the South African mining industry, indigenous taxes were around 50 percent of the colonies' budget. In Uganda, it was 30 percent. In colonies that relied both on European and non-European producers, such as in British Kenya and Belgian Congo, their contribution was around 20 percent. In classical settler colonies, the revenues from the native tax were low, such as in Northern Rhodesia were it was only 10 percent. In the coastal colonies of Western Africa, the amount was also relatively low because tariff revenues were much more important than direct taxes on individuals. Nigerians contributed only 13 percent, whereas customs revenues in the British colony accounted for 72 percent. And British Gold Coast refrained from levying income taxes at all because the colonial government relied on import duties and export duties for cocoa, which were cheaper to collect and more profitable.[132] In 1933, the direct

---

[127] ICI, *Compte Rendu 1939, Reports*, 44.
[128] Ibid., 94.
[129] Ibid., 22.
[130] Tandjigora, "Fiscalité Coloniale," 213–226.
[131] The ICI published its comparative study on tax contributions in 1939, but most of the data was from the 1920s and early 1930s.
[132] Based on reports in ICI, *Compte Rendu 1939*. See also Gardner, *Taxing Colonial Africa*, 5 and 44. For Belgian Congo, see Booth, "Varieties of Exploitation," 70.

taxes provided still for only £860, which rose slowly to £40,000 in 1937, which, however, seemed negligible in face of an overall income of £3,774,000.[133] Despite these exceptions, the 1920s and 1930s saw the rise of tax burden in all colonies.[134]

It seems that the ICI's study, which had the merit of unveiling the importance of native taxes for the colonial budget, still underestimated the indigenous contribution by far: in French West Africa, for example, it reached up to 98 percent.[135] This was particularly true in the 1920s, when subventions from Paris were rare and French West Africa paid back basically all loans and subsidies it had received from Paris within one year. Hence, West Africans were not only contributing to the colonial budget but funded it completely. By and large, British colonies also financed themselves entirely out of local revenues by 1914.[136] Most colonies used their local resources to pay back loans: well into the 1930s, Kenya spent 30 percent, Nigeria 31 percent, and Nyasaland 44 percent of their respective budget on the liquidation of debts.[137] The financial independence of the Belgian Congo advanced more slowly and at the cost of indebtedness. In 1926, Brussels stopped its annual advances to the colony.[138] In the late 1920s, the Congo still spent 17 percent of its expenditure to pay off debts.[139]

Apart from regular taxes, compulsory labor contributed to the self-sufficiency of the colonies. In French West Africa, one important reason for self-sufficiency was the so-called *prestations*, compulsory labor for all kinds of public works. The ICI's report had explicitly emphasized that all colonies used compulsory labor, even after the ILO banned forced labor in 1930. Even the British colonies and the Netherlands' Indies (whose government only partially abolished forced labor in 1927) made use of the "labor tax." No matter if they lived in Niger or in Tanzania, colonial law obliged each male adult to work between twenty and twenty-five days per year for the colonizers to build streets, railways, and schools. Once the railways were ready to operate, revenues from the service were an important source of income, especially in Nigeria (most important), Gold Coast (second most important), and Kenya (third most important source).[140]

The diversification of taxes led to overtaxation, while the revenues also served to fund colonial institutions in Europe. Colonial administrations

---

[133] ICI, *Compte Rendu 1939*, 78.
[134] Frankema, "Raising Revenue," 460.
[135] Huillery, "The Black Man's Burden," 1–38.
[136] Gardner, *Taxing Colonial Africa*, 66.
[137] Gardner, "Fiscal Policies," 145.
[138] Jonghe, *La Politique Financière du Congo*, 9.
[139] Gardner, "Fiscal Policies," 145.
[140] Gardner, *Taxing Colonial Africa*, 7–8.

6.8 NO TAXATION WITHOUT REPRESENTATION?   245

combined the income tax with various other taxes: import and export duties, property and land tax, a dog tax, and court fees. On top of that, they invented taxes that did not necessarily exist in Europe, such as a tax on polygamy, a bicycle tax, a cattle tax, the passport fee for labor migrants, and, in case people were not able to pay their taxes, more compulsory labor. The ICI listed all these taxes and concluded that many Africans were overtaxed.[141] In Belgian Congo, for example, 20–60 percent of cash available to the Congolese fed into the tax systems.[142] While Africans were relatively overtaxed, the European administrators were relatively overpaid. Taxpayers of French West Africa, for example, covered the salaries of all French colonial staff, among them 8 governors and 120 rank and file administrators.[143] They alone devoured 13 percent of French West Africa's budget.[144] Africans also paid for colonial institutions in the metropole. The ICI revealed that the Congolese of Belgian Africa contributed to the budget of the Belgian Colonial Office and paid for the Congo Museum in Tervuren.[145]

The important contribution of African taxpayers put the question of representation on the table. In 1928, Casely Hayford explained, in his role as a member of the Gold Coast Legislative Council, that the Ghanaian delegates represented the interests of the taxpayers and therefore needed more influence on the colonial budget.[146] As early as 1917, he had mounted a no taxation without representation campaign. Tax revolts became more frequent.[147] They expressed the will of the masses and gave them a certain amount of agency. Adding to these rather new developments was the question of who could legitimately collect taxes. Paramount chiefs mostly supported the tax policy of the colonial administration because they capitalized on it. Increasingly, anti-colonial nationalists criticized the chiefs for cooperating with the government. In Gold Coast, for example, the Aborigines' Rights Protection Society, which mainly consisted of the coastal economic and intellectual elite, argued that "chiefs who cooperated with the British would become servants of the government and would no longer be representative of their people."[148]

Chiefs continued to play a role in collecting taxes for the European administration but their legitimacy eroded in face of a more self-conscious civil society and anti-colonial leaders of a new kind. As tax revolts became more frequent in the 1920s and 1930s, chiefs indeed gradually gave way to a "neutral"

---

[141] ICI, *Compte Rendu 1939, Reports*, 72,
[142] Peemans, "Capital Accumulation," 165–212.
[143] Coquery-Vidrovitch, "Le Financement de la Mise en Valeur," 239.
[144] Huillery, "The Black Man's Burden," 6.
[145] ICI, *Compte Rendu 1939, Reports*, 16.
[146] "Debates Legislative Council" (October 26, 1928), cited in Priestley, "The Gold Coast Select Committee," 548.
[147] Booth, "Colonial Revenue," 44.
[148] Shaloff, "The Income Tax," 360.

bureaucracy of tax collectors. In the Dutch Indies, for example, colonial administrators set out to dismantle tax farming, a system that the VOC had introduced and perfected in the nineteenth century. It had allowed Chinese immigrants to collect taxes from the Indonesian population, to the benefit of the Dutch state.[149] This transition was not always smooth, and where taxation of individuals was impossible, highly inhuman forms of collective collection persisted. In Java and Nigeria, the village remained the most important tax unit, formed the basis of assessment, and was collectively held responsible for the payment. The ICI considered this method of collective responsibility exemplary.[150] As we will see, villages would have a revival as tax units in corporate schemes of colonial economy.

Unfair taxation on a racist basis existed in all colonies. What would be taken to the extreme in South Africa, namely, that the Africans in the segregated reserves received little money from tax revenues, was also the norm elsewhere. The dualist colonial state foresaw a fiscal segregation along racial lines, mainly between European and non-European taxpayers, who were each subject to different tax laws. Theoretically, European taxes benefited the Europeans and so-called native taxes the indigenous population. Colonial administrations pretended to uphold a dual state in matters of taxation, following a separate but equal logic. Financial commissioners in Kenya, for example, analyzed "the contribution made to taxation both direct and indirect by the different racial communities" and measured "the amount of money expended in the interest of each community, in particular on natives and non-natives." The different communities were "European, native, Indian, Goan, Arab," which formed different tax groups.[151] The ICI was aware that fiscal segregation mostly served to guarantee privileges for European settlers, especially with regard to land taxes.[152] In the French colonies, Europeans often received concessions with exemptions from taxes.[153] In British colonies, direct taxes on land for Europeans were kept at a minimum to attract settlers.[154] Overall, between 1912 and 1918, direct taxes paid by European settlers in Kenya were negligible and were below 1 percent of the colony's overall budget.[155]

In all colonial tax systems, be they old or new, the colonized population paid way more than it got in return. During the Great Depression, colonial administrations pushed tax exploitation to an extreme. In the Gold Coast colony, the government planned to introduce an income tax in 1931 and return only

---

[149] Wahid, "In the Shadow of Opium," 110.
[150] ICI, *Compte Rendu 1939, Reports*, 82.
[151] Ibid., 67.
[152] Ibid., 96.
[153] Coquery-Vidrovitch, *Le Congo*.
[154] Frankema, "Colonial Taxation and Government," 139.
[155] Gardner, *Taxing Colonial Africa*, 52.

6.8 NO TAXATION WITHOUT REPRESENTATION? 247

50 percent of it to the Ghanaians, which led to fierce protests because they outnumbered Europeans by far.[156] At the same time, the governor refused to redistribute the cocoa taxes among the Ghanaians who had paid them. Questioned by the ICI on the nature of tax redistribution in Gold Coast in the 1930s, British delegates stated in a cynical way:

> However satisfactory the system of taxation in the Colony or Southern territories of the Gold Coast may be from the point of view of raising revenue for the purpose of the central government, the fact that over most of the territory there has no means of raising a steady income from direct taxes for the financing of native treasuries has serious disadvantages. Thus the 'stools' or native administrations finance themselves by raising occasional levies ... the only other means of financing the native administrations are by the proceeds of court fines, market fees and the rent and sales of land.[157]

To finance "native" self-government and their welfare state, Ghanaians were supposed to pay extra taxes and sell their land! Absurdities were even taken further. In British Swaziland, which was segregated into European territories and non-European reserves, the amount received from the dog tax equaled the expenditures on agricultural development and education for the Africans. In Swaziland's budget of the 1930s, the revenues from the dog tax amounted to £2,600 and the expenses for education and agricultural development in the African reserve to £2,650. What made this statistic even more absurd was that the dog tax mostly came from African dog owners.[158]

Also in the mixed zones around industrial agglomerations, the colonized tended to pay for infrastructure and measures of hygiene, whereas Europeans hardly paid any taxes at all.[159] While European and indigenous workers shared a common space to work in, fiscal and legal segregation separated them in those mixed zones. The Congolese population, for example, paid for local streets in the "mixed sections" that both Europeans and Congolese used.[160] Although the ICI was aware of this problem, it endorsed fiscal segregation, arguing that it allowed the indigenous population to benefit from their own taxes. As we have seen, this rarely happened.

If the colonized showed themselves loyal to the colonizers, they were occasionally promoted into the European tax group. If colonial subjects worked for the Europeans, they could switch sides and be exempted from taxes, such as the soldiers of the standing colonial armies. Members of the Belgian Force Publique and the British King's African Rifles, for example, did

---

[156] Shaloff, "The Income Tax," 359–375.
[157] ICI, *Compte Rendu 1939, Reports*, 78.
[158] Ibid., 50.
[159] Ibid., 11.
[160] Ibid., 15.

not pay taxes. Their exemption led to a significant loss in revenues, because they were among the few Africans who indeed received a salary. Around 300,000 Force Publique members were active during the war. After the war, Force Publique and police in the Congo numbered 12,000.[161]

On the flip side, the most important indigenous taxpayers often received the right to vote for the legislative councils. If they paid a higher amount of taxes, the Europeans considered them more "representative." All elections were based on a census suffrage. Occasionally, Europeans even integrated commercial associations with nationalist tendencies into this system. The most famous case was the Sarekat Islam in the Dutch Indies, originally a corporation of batik producers from Java who tried to protect their profession and trade. Sarekat Islam combined Islamic mysticism, local traditions, and commercial interests. ICI member Snouck Hurgronje considered them as a reasonable movement that was capable to organize self-government and two of its members received a seat in the Volksraad.[162] Only later, when Sarekat Islam showed clearly nationalist and communist tendencies, did some of its members enter into conflict with the Dutch authorities.

The European members of the representative councils were also entrepreneurs and corporations, a fact that anticipated the colonizers' strategy to favor economic over democratic representation. The ICI partly subscribed to this scheme that gained currency when the ideal of a corporate state gathered steam during the Great Depression and with the rise of fascist movements in Europe. Actually, the existing representative organs in the colonies had long built on corporate representation, especially in the Asian colonies. Indonesian critics such as the Sarekat Islam had long held the view that the "Volksraad is capitalist."[163] At the 1927 meeting of the ICI, Portuguese members emphasized the economic character of their representative system. In Portuguese India, the council consisted of "eleven members elected among economic associations or among the indigenous population." In Timor, there were four members in the council: "one representing the municipal council, one the Portuguese merchants, one the Chinese and Arab merchants, and one for the farmers."[164] The only representative council in Indochina that advised the governor-general (Chef de la Colonie), the Conseil du Gouvernement, was composed of eighteen heads of the civil service division (chefs de service) and twelve "representatives of economic interests," along with five natives.[165]

---

[161] AGRB, Louwers Papers 243 (270), Assistance Sociale au Congo, Oeuvre de M. Tibbaut 1913–1914: Étude sur la creation de l'Epargne au Congo Belge, November 2, 1913.
[162] Netherlands Indies Government, *Overzicht van de gestie der Centraal Sarikat-Islam in het Jaar 1921*, 18.
[163] Netherlands Indies Government, *Sarekat Islam Congres 1916–1918*, vol. 3, 7.
[164] ICI, *Compte Rendu 1927*, 84.
[165] Ibid., 96.

In Kenya, the Convention of Associations, consisting of white farmers and planters became the "Unofficial Parliament" in 1911, which the governor consulted frequently.[166] In Nigeria, the "four Chambers of Commerce and the banking and shipping interests" played an important role in the council, as well as one African representative of the Niger traders.[167] In the Gold Coast Legislative Council, three Europeans represented banks, commerce, and shipping interests, and two were delegates of the Chamber of Commerce and Chamber of Mines. They also had representatives in the Provincial Countries. Among the official members were the director of public works, the director of agriculture, the general manager of the railway, the comptroller of customs, and the chief inspector of labor.[168] All of the provincial (consultative) councils and the Chambers of Commerce and of Agriculture sent their leaders as delegates to the council.

In 1927, economic representation seemed to be a solution to organize a potentially independent colony-state, at least in the "more advanced" Asian colonies. It is important to note that the will to autonomy went as far as desiring independence. Independence, to be sure, had different degrees. Its advocates often evoked a dominion-status but, increasingly, their schemes took the shape of a fully sovereign nation-state. The ICI members were convinced that the difference in civilizational status would automatically require their tutelage, regardless of an official status as a colony. Moresco also dismissed the idea of economic disadvantages in case of independence: "During the United States' war for independence they posed this about the British: We will lose the American market and what will than happen to our commerce? Well, we know now that the trade between America and Great Britain has not suffered at all. On the contrary, it has miraculously increased." The same, he argued, was true for the colonies in Asia in 1927: "Even from the material point of view, we do not have to be scared of the evolution that leads the peoples of Asia to free themselves from European domination." For Moresco, independence was inevitable, and only a matter of "degree."[169]

6.9 Representing the New "Generation of the War" in the ICI

From 1927 onwards, however, a new generation gained influence in the ICI whose will to equip the colonies with representative bodies fell behind their forefathers' schemes of gradual emancipation. The Belgian Pierre Orts, who had joined the ICI in 1909, observed a shift from the "generation of the

---
[166] Hailey, *African Survey*, 166–167.
[167] Ibid., 172.
[168] Wight, *The Gold Coast*, 43 and 63.
[169] ICI, *Compte Rendu 1927*, 108–109.

Congo" to the "generation of the war."[170] By evoking the "generation of the Congo," he alluded to the project of the ICI's founding fathers of 1894 to replace Léopold's failed pseudo-internationalism with a new and constructive colonial internationalism. The forerunners of 1894 continued to be the pacesetters in the 1920s. After 1927, however, the generation of Congo reformers gradually gave way to a generation whose internationalist fervor had been attenuated by World War I. The retirement of the Secretary-General Camille Janssen in 1926 and the death of the ideologue Joseph Chailley in 1928 were the harbingers of radicalization. Janssen was replaced with the bellicose Belgian lawyer Octave Louwers.[171] Chailley's influence ebbed away more gradually and ceded only with the death of his disciples Lyautey, Lugard, and Snouck Hurgronje between 1934 and 1936. By then, the influence of Italian fascists on colonial schemes grew.

Institutional and ideological changes accompanied the shift in the ICI's personnel. In the mid-1920s, Louwers created national branches of the ICI in the member states. The French Colonial Union, for example, became the ICI's official branch in France. This shift from individual membership to corporate membership of national branches certainly contributed to the ICI's renationalization. The corporative remodeling of the ICI continued with the corporative membership of Belgian mining companies. To no small degree, the reorganization resulted in a professionalization of the ICI. The French Colonial Union met regularly to prepare its contributions to the ICI's general assembly. Louwers also abolished the category of loosely "associated members" and only accepted full members who could be obliged to participate more actively in the ICI's work.[172] Taken together, these measures brought about a professionalization as well as a renationalization that led to a more stable operational basis.

A genuinely new and weighty decision of Louwers' ICI was to abandon its neutrality, by deciding that the debates in the general assembly "can end in a vote."[173] The decision to take decisions was prominently put to a test in 1929. In that year, the ILO officially asked the ICI to comment on its ambitious scheme to ban forced labor from the globe, which also included the colonies. The ILO saw in the ICI the representative body of "autonomous" colonial administrations and addressed its members as the "most authoritative specialists in colonial matters."[174] The ICI's independent valuation of the role of forced labor in the colonies seemed to be more reliable than the official

---

[170] AGRB, Papiers Orts, 389: Orts, *Souvenirs de Ma Carrière*, 22.
[171] AGRB, Louwers Papers 234 (261) ICI 1926, Séance du Bureau Renforcé, October 2, 1926.
[172] Ibid., October 1, 1926.
[173] Ibid.
[174] ILO Archives, N206/1/01/5 ILO to Louwers, November 11, 1929.

assessment from European governments. For that reason, the ILO wrote to Louwers in 1929 that "it would be extremely interesting for the proceeding of our work to be acquainted with the ideas of the International Colonial Institute about questions of forced labor."[175] The request was not among the wisest of the ILO's initiatives.

With only two abstentions – the Nigerian governor-general Palmer and the liberal Dutch Moresco – the ICI voted against an international convention that banned forced labor from colonial territories.[176] In the preceding debate, two groups justified their negative vote with two different strains of argument. The ICI's more authoritarian members made clear that their expertise was above international law. They considered themselves as men of action rather than men of law.[177] They justified their vote by pretending that underdeveloped and culturally different societies required special action, which included compulsory labor. Supposedly, no "universal law" condemning forced labor could ever apply to the colonies. The Portuguese delegates, who had so far kept a low profile in the ICI, felt a particular need to act "according to experience and not to theory."[178]

ICI members who upheld humanitarian appearances equally found a reason to vote down the ban on forced labor. They invoked article 421 of the Versailles Treaty that stipulated that international conventions did not apply to colonies "where owing to the local conditions the convention is inapplicable."[179] Advancing a humanitarian approach, they argued that compulsory labor was necessary to protect the health and life of the native race, to combat disease, and to implement hygiene policies.[180] Their most powerful, if also the most cynical, allegation was that the ILO was Eurocentric and had never consulted the representatives of the workers in the colonies: "Please allow me to ask," the Portuguese Penha Garcia exclaimed, "how many indigenous workers and patrons have you seen in Genova?" The ICI members reacted with "laughter and signs of approval" to his allegations against the ILO's Eurocentrism. Indeed, the ILO had little knowledge of the working conditions in the colonies.[181]

---

[175] ILO Archives, N206/1/01/5 ILO to Louwers, [? 1929].
[176] ICI, *Compte Rendu 1929*, 131–132.
[177] Ibid., 72.
[178] Ibid., 55–56.
[179] *Les Cahiers Coloniaux de L'Institut Colonial de Marseille*, 551–552 (August 19/26, 1929), 310, in AGRB Louwers Papers 235 (263): XXeme session de l'ICI: "La législation du travail indigène et les méthodes de mise en valeur des colonies 1929 Intervention de M. O. Louwers."
[180] ICI, *Compte Rendu 1929*, 74.
[181] Ibid., 114.

The ICI's official statement against the abolition of forced labor sounds like a collection of pretexts:

> In the colonies, more than in Europe, where a better organization of labor, the press and parliaments provide an effective control which serves to prevent many abuses, a particularly attentive and active supervision by the governments concerned of all matters affecting labor is essential to ensure the effectual and practical application of the laws on the subject ... the evolution of labor legislation must proceed at a pace corresponding with the rate of development of the native populations. A uniform labor legislation for all colonies is therefore impossible, the rate of progress varying from colony to colony .... All questions referring to health and to the protection of the workers must have the precedence over all others .... In the present state of affairs, there is room for international agreements only in a limited measure and between colonial powers only.[182]

The last point is important. ICI members complained that there were only six or seven colonizing countries represented at the ILO, against thirty-six non-colonial powers.[183] The ICI members claimed that the ICI was the only international institution that represented exclusively colonizing states. To explain their vote in favor of forced labor, Louwers rushed to Geneva. He warned the ILO not to "leave colonial questions to those countries who do not have to find solutions for colonial questions." Going back to an age-old interest of the ICI, Louwers proposed instead to draft an international convention that standardized labor contracts between employers and employees in the colonies. "Colonizing countries," he resumed, were perfectly able to "exercise the mutual control" with regard to the protection of workers' rights.[184]

Despite its total failure, the ILO's request had officialized the ICI's status as the representative organ of colonial administrators and regarded it as more trustworthy than the governments in the motherlands. For that reason, the ILO felt the need to remain on good terms with the increasingly influential ICI.[185] Its leaders thought that "political motives" had led the ICI members to vote against the forced labor convention.[186] Those "political motives" could be found among the new Portuguese and Italian lobby in the ICI, who had introduced the aggressive and cynical language of fascism to its meetings. To push back this fascist faction, the ILO tried to strengthen the moderate party in the ICI and set their hopes on Octave Louwers. The conservative secretary-general became the ILO's go-to guy in colonial matters, as its leaders agreed in

---

[182] Ibid., 131–132.
[183] Ibid., 58.
[184] ILO Archives, N206/1/01/5 Letter Weaver to Thomas, September 12, 1929.
[185] ILO, *International Labour Conference 1930*, 277.
[186] ILO Archives, N206/1/01/5 [?] to Phelan, September 6, 1929.

their secret correspondence: "We have to keep on the right side of him. We will ultimately see if we can offer him a more official participation in our activities."[187] Through Louwers, the ILO would create "a small group of influential members in the Institute who would regard the Office as worth rather more serious and sympathetic consideration."[188] Ironically, the ILO would realize this scheme by headhunting ICI members to join its Committee of Experts on Native Labor. This Committee had been established in 1927 to draft the Convention against forced labor and to protect "native labor" in the future. Liberal ICI members Van Rees and Albrecht Gohr, as well as Louwers joined the ILO's Committee.[189] Thus, even after the ICI's vote in favor of forced labor, moderate colonial internationalists and the ILO were on exceptionally good terms.[190]

Despite the ILO's proselytism, the regressive party in the ICI grew stronger. In the early 1930s, the group's confidence grew and it started to ridicule humanitarian justifications of colonialism. This development was in line with a general shift in colonial paradigms. In 1931, France celebrated the centenary of Algeria's conquest and turned the festivities in Paris into the biggest international colonial exhibition the world had seen so far. Many ICI members took part in the innumerable workshops organized during the festivities. Slowly, they embraced the brutal rhetoric of settler colonialism that the ICI had actively fought against since the 1890s. Neo-settlerists from Portugal and Italy in the ICI celebrated the comeback of an anti-humanitarian settler language. Others openly celebrated South Africa's apartheid policies and the cruel repression that came with it. At the ICI meeting in 1931, ICI delegates from France, enthused by the internationalist celebration of Algeria's conquest, claimed openly that they were proud of their imperialist conquest (even though the ICI had avoided the term imperialism for its aggressive connotations and despotic reputation). Aggressively, the French delegates exclaimed at the ICI meeting that if socialists called the French colonial policy imperialist, they would simply and proudly agree. For the first time in the ICI's history, members became emotional and chanted the slogan "Long live imperialism" at the ICI meeting in 1931.[191] It is hardly surprising that Italy's violent conquest of Ethiopia in 1935 did not meet with much criticism within the ICI.

6.10 Representing Fascism and Liberalism

The ICI reached its highest degree of representation in the 1930s, when Britain started funding it. Curiously, Britain started officially supporting the ICI at the

---

[187] ILO Archives, N206/1/01/5 Weaver to Thomas, September 12, 1929.
[188] ILO Archives, N206/1/01/5 Summary report Goudal to Phelan, September 6, 1929.
[189] Zimmermann, "Special Circumstances in Geneva," 234–237.
[190] ILO Archives, N206/1/01/5 ILO to Franck, [1929].
[191] ICI, Comtpe Rendu 1931, 51.

very moment it turned into a veritable "anti-Geneva bloc," ousted the PMC, and swung to fascist positions. Up to 1931, the British had refused to accept the ICI as representative. After Louwers became secretary-general of the ICI in 1927, he mounted a campaign to get subsidies from the British government. He found support in the conservatives via the under-secretary of state for the colonies, William Ormsby-Gore, who was also a member of the ICI (since 1924) and the PMC. To gain Britain's goodwill, the ICI published the conference proceedings in English and Louwers traveled to England to "give the British group a representation that was proportional to the colonial power of the Empire" and to make a member of the royal family participate.[192] His campaign was successful to the extent that the British group in the ICI grew significantly. In 1929, the Colonial Office informed the India Office, the Dominion Office, the Foreign Ministry, and the colonial governments overseas about the ICI and its request to subscribe to its publications and to fund it.[193]

While British conservatives wanted to fund the ICI, the Labour-led government (1929-1931) and the Colonial Office remained skeptical.[194] The rank-and-file of the Colonial Office had long rejected the cooperation with the ICI because it caused additional work for an already understaffed administration.[195] In 1929, a spokesman of the Colonial Office denied the ICI's international character because, "it is not 'official' and I have not been able to find any justification for its assumption of the title 'international' beyond the fact that its members are chosen from the countries which have colonies."[196] The Colonial Office also blamed the ICI for its defense of forced labor: "The Powers behind the Institute, France, Belgium, Portugal and to a lesser extent Holland, are committed to forms of forced labor to which Great Britain is opposed (see 'prestation' and 'in lieu of military service')." They had little doubt that "demands will be made to make use of the Institute to obstruct any progress at Geneva next year over the drafting and acceptance of a Forced Labor Convention."[197] The anti-Geneva ghost haunted the British, and it was quite real by 1930.

Against the advice of the Labour Party and the Colonial Office, the conservatives expedited British funding of the ICI, supported by administrators in India and the Foreign Office, which traditionally held close ties with the ICI.[198] The Foreign Secretary of the conservative government, Austen Chamberlain,

---

[192] CO 323 984/7: Louwers to Ormsby-Gore, August 25, 1927.
[193] CO 323 1043/1: Note November 26, 1928.
[194] CO 323 1043/1: Foreign Office to Colonial Office, April 10, 1929; and IOR/L/E/7/1540/2971: Colonial Office to Treasury, April 10, 1929.
[195] CO 323 984 7: Colonial Office to Foreign Office, 1929.
[196] Ibid.
[197] CO 323 1043/1: Circular R.V. Vernon, no date.
[198] CO 323 1043/1: Foreign Office to Vernon (Colonial Office), July 19, 1929.

6.10 REPRESENTING FASCISM AND LIBERALISM

had declared a British funding of the ICI an "eminent desire" on the grounds that "closer co-operation and the exchange of useful information between foreign governments in colonial matters is likely not only to be of immediate benefit to the various colonies concerned but also to lead to the sources of friction and so to improve relations generally between the countries."[199] British India equally pushed for funding, and it spent already 4,500 Belgian francs annually on ICI publications.[200] The British members of the ICI, who now met regularly in the rooms of the British Empire Society equally worked hard to get the funding. Among them were the editor of the *Cambridge History of the British Empire*, A. P. Newton, the Swiss-born but naturalized explorer Hanns Vischer, and Ormsby-Gore.[201] Lugard initially turned against official funding, arguing that neither did the International Institute of African Languages and Cultures in London receive financial support from the state and that both institutions should maintain their neutrality. But he would change his mind. Finally, business interests seemed to play a role and had a spokesman in the British ambassador in Belgium, George Grahame, who added that "We have a good deal to do with M. Louwers in the way of official business."[202] They all obtained satisfaction when the conservatives got back to power in 1931.

Starting in 1931, the British government allocated an annual sum of 50,000 Belgian francs or £300 for a time span of three years. The Colonial Office had finally agreed that it considered it inappropriate for "the greatest colonial power ... to be held aloof from the Institute"[203] The British paid less than the French (£343), but its subvention was higher than the Belgian (£228), Dutch (£286), Italian (£155) and Spanish (only £18) contributions.[204] At least £120 came from colonial governors overseas.[205] While the British seemed to have suspended the payment prematurely in 1932, the enthusiasm for the ICI grew. In 1936, the ICI held its session in London.[206] The Colonial Office co-organized the event, which was a full success. Both Colonial Office staff and the duke of Kent participated in the meeting.[207] The Colonial Office's higher-ranking staff enthusiastically helped to prepare the panels on education of Africans through broadcasting, cinema, and press. Mass media seemed to be

---

[199] CO 323 1043/1: Foreign Office to Colonial Office, April 10, 1929; and IOR/L/E/7/1540/2971: Colonial Office to Treasury, April 10, 1929.
[200] CO 323 1043/1: Note November 26, 1928.
[201] BLA, IOR/L/E/7/1540/2971: Grindle to Undersecretary of State, April 21, 1928.
[202] IOR/L/E/7/1540/2971: Grahame to Ormsby-Gore, November 19, 1928.
[203] CO 323 1043/1: Reply to Skevington, May 15, 1929.
[204] CO 323 1043/1: Note February 25, 1929.
[205] CO 323 1400/II: Howell (CO) to Lugard, January 30, 1936.
[206] Ibid.
[207] CO 323 1400/II: Maffey to Lugard, September 22, 1936.

the future of colonial governmentality and a means to "uplift natives." The London congress was the last ICI meeting before the fascists took over.

While anti-colonial movements emerged in 1919 across the world and demanded sovereignty, both the PMC and the ICI questioned their representativeness. Their governmental strategy consisted of accepting loyal groups as representative and dismissing critical voices as unrepresentative. Both the PMC and the ICI delegitimized anti-colonialists who organized themselves in Paris, Amsterdam, and Frankfurt, arguing that these alienated Westernized milieus had abandoned the authentic lifestyles of their kinsmen in the colonies. The ICI, in particular, highlighted the representative councils in the colonies and claimed that they responded to the authentic situation in the colony. By styling itself the representative of colonial authenticity, the ICI arrogated the right to define and redefine who might speak for the colonized. Among the candidates were chiefs, assimilated elites, taxpayers, entrepreneurs, the masses, etc. The PMC and the ICI strategically kept the debate going and it never ended. It served to increase the power and autonomy of the colonial administrations and to perpetuate their colonial rule. By the mid-1930s, the new fascist regimes in Europe increasingly saw the ICI as more representative in colonial matters than the PMC. Under pressure of the fascists, the PMC ceased to exist.

7

Inventing Fascist Eurafrica at the Volta Congress

Fascist colonial internationalism culminated in the international Volta Congress on Africa, held in Rome in 1938. The Volta Congress was the biggest colonial congress of the interwar period, and the Italian organizers invited colonial experts of all stripes. A curious mix of republicans liberals, conservatives, monarchists, fascists, philanthropists, paternalists, social reformers, progressive anthropologists, experimental economists, Christians, and Islamophiles attended the Congress. Since the new fascist colonialism propagated in Rome was syncretistic, most of them found their interests represented and banked on the fascists to realize their agenda.[1] ICI members, in particular, joined forces with the fascists, and even reformers of the PMC teamed up with them. Their suggestion to create a transcolonial Eurafrican empire as a basis for a transnational fascism in Europe seemed absurd. But many participants of the Volta Congress took it seriously.

This chapter shows how fascists picked up the ICI's version of "reformed colonialism" and even subscribed to very progressive approaches in anthropology. Syncretizing preexisting ideologies, their approach differed in kind from the PMC's program but not in its colonial essence. Under the influence of racist theories, the Volta Congress substituted the PMC's civilizing mission (which wanted to Europeanize the colonized populations before granting them independence) with the rule of cultural relativism (which suggested that the colonized populations had to live according to their own rules and culture as the basis of restricted self-government).[2] To achieve this goal, the Volta Congress emulated and perpetuated the ICI's anthropology, which had relied on cultural relativism and indirect rule since 1894. Yet it slightly diluted cultural relativism through a typically fascist program of social engineering that it applied to indigenous societies. The desire to combine cultural relativism and social engineering led them to embrace the social anthropology of Bronislaw Malinowksi, who had redefined his discipline and seemed to be an unlikely supporter of the fascist cause. Thus, in its outreach, the Volta

---

[1] For an overview, see Alcalde, "Transnational Consensus," 243–252; Passmore, "Writing the History," 287–304.
[2] On cultural relativism in the interwar period, see Cooper, "Reconstructing Empire," 198.

Congress aligned with the anthropological turn of the 1920s, represented by Bronislaw Malinowski and the ICI, instead of going with the somewhat antiquated civilizing mission of the PMC.

The concrete framework for this fascist reform of colonialism was what participants called a "Eurafrican" empire. They thus reanimated the idea of Eurafrica, which Pan-European liberals and internationalist socialists had delineated in the 1920, before French and German colonial internationalists appropriated the concept to "reconcile Europe via Africa."[3] In the late 1920s, the idea of Eurafrica indeed became a vehicle for German and Italian colonial propagandists to reconcile their fascist colonial projects with the allegedly well-meaning French and British ones.[4] At the Volta Congress, they combined pan-European and neo-imperial worldviews. They designed fascist Eurafrica as a "good" empire that relied on a corporate economy and restricted self-government for the conquered peoples. Both principles found acceptance among the ICI members and even admiration among "liberal" colonizers. This compatibility was one important reason why allegedly liberal colonial reformers and progressive scientists enthusiastically supported the Volta Congress. It also shows that there was hardly something like a "liberal" colonialism.

The history of the ICI and its involvement in fascism represents the interwar colonialisms in a much more adequate way than a one-sided focus on the PMC does.[5] What is more, the continuities of the fascist period can also explain the imperial concepts of the post-1945 period, most importantly the legacy of the planned economy and its corporative and cooperative character. It was the legacy of the ICI and not the one of the PMC that shaped post-WWII colonial policies. The most influential, yet often neglected, legacy was the creation of corporate and cooperative empires.

7.1 The Volta Congress and Fascist Colonial Internationalism

In October 1938, when fascist governments were about to plunge the world into ruin, colonial internationalists flocked into Rome to attend the weeklong Volta Congress on Africa. Officially, the Italian Royal Academy and the Volta Endowment organized the congress as a follow up to the Volta Congress on Europe held in 1932. Behind the scenes, it was the trailblazers of Italian

---

[3] Ageron, "L'Idée d'Eurafrique," 463.
[4] Hansen and Jonsson, Eurafrica; Montarsolo, L'Eurafrique; Linne, Deutschland, 82.
[5] On fascist internationalism, see Hedinger and Hofmann, "Editorial: Axis empires," 161–165; Herren, "Fascist Internationalism," 191–212; Alcalde, "Transnational Consensus," 243–252; Passmore, "Writing the History," 287–304; Reichardt and Nolzen, Faschismus; Kott and Patel, Nazism across Borders; Framke, Delhi – Rom – Berlin; Motadel, "The Global Authoritarian Moment," 843–877.

fascism who staged the Congress: the monarcho-fascist philosopher Francesco Orestano, the co-organizer of the March on Rome and governor of Libya Italo Balbo, seconded by Mussolini's former interior minister and ICI member Luigi Federzoni.[6] Reassembling 126 colonial experts from 15 countries for 7 days, the Convegno Volta was the biggest congress on colonial Africa the world had seen so far. Delegates came from Italy (62) France (16), Britain (16), Germany (15), Belgium (5), Poland (2), Spain (2), Bulgaria, Yugoslavia, Norway, Holland, Portugal, the Vatican, Sweden, and Switzerland (1 each). They gave 180 talks in 15 different languages on the latest development in colonial policy and science. As we will see, the Volta Congress became a milestone in the history of colonial internationalism.

At the Volta Congress, fascists, national socialists, racists, conservatives, Catholics, Protestants, liberals, and socially minded philanthropists sat down at the same table. They shared a similar colonial purpose. Hence, no one objected when the fascist organizers invited their fellow Nazi ideologists and thus readmitted Germans to the ranks of colonial internationalism. Even British participants of the Volta Congress agreed that the "new Germany" should receive full equality in African affairs. Thus, the Congress members officially decided to "grant the Equality of the Privilege and Responsibility which Germany asks." Most of them considered the German delegation at the Congress as highly competent in African culture, languages, anthropology, and politics.[7] The German delegation included SS-Oberführer Karl Jung, the head of the NSDAP's colonial economy section Kurt Weigelt, the *lebensraum* sloganeers Karl Haushofer and Richard Thurnwald, the organicist Franz Heske, and the chairman of the colonial physicians in the NSDAP, Peter Mühlens, who would later perform human experiments in concentration camps. While the Germans had had no colonies for twenty years, they took advantage of the Volta Congress to show that the Third Reich had kept its colonial toolbox available and in good condition. The Volta Congress raised hopes among them to return to Africa. Karl Haushofer, in particular, had cast an eye on the idea of Eurafrica, made famous by the Italian Africanist Paolo d'Agostino Orsini, as a potential opportunity for Germany to return to Africa via the backdoor of fascist solidarity.[8]

The fascist agenda did not deter liberals affiliated to the League of Nations, nor did it repel ICI members who considered themselves philanthropists and progressives. At least six former or current employees of the League of Nations attended the congress: Julius Ruppel of the PMC, as well as Eduardo Piola Caselli, Charles-Auguste Le Neveu, Eugène Pittard, Alberto Pirelli, and Luca

---

[6] On Italy, see Ben-Ghiat and Fuller, *Italian Colonialism*; Camilleri, *Staatsangehörigkeit*; Bernhard, "Borrowing from Mussolini," 617–643.
[7] Tracy Philipps, "The Volta Meeting in Rome," 20–21 and 24–25.
[8] D'Agostino Orsini, *Eurafrica* was part of Haushofer's personal library.

Pietromarchi. Future UN officials such as Pierre Ryckmans also traveled to Rome. Apart from the fascist co-organizer Federzoni, the ICI participants were Angiolo Mori, Carlo Rossetti, Octave Louwers, Pierre Ryckmans, Georges Hardy, Henri Labouret, Charles-Auguste Le Neveu, Louis Massignon, Marcel Olivier, François Sorel, U. Fritz Herbert Ruxton, Hanns Vischer, Antonio Vicente Perreire, Pierrre Lyautey, and James Erasmus Tracy Philipps (the last two would only join the ICI shortly after the Volta Congress).[9] Those who thought of themselves as progressive colonizers did not bother debating with outspoken Nazis about colonial policies.

Most participants hoped for careers in the emerging fascist empires. ICI members such as Louwers saw in the international congress a job market, where they could advertise their colonial expertise. After all, Italy had opened a new field of colonization by conquering Ethiopia, and it needed experts.[10] Since Italians explicitly declared the technical administration of the new territories a common European project, they made colonial experts sit up around the world. Louwers, for example, used the Congress to promote the ICI and its ability to develop "reliable and rational colonial doctrines."[11] He then quoted several publications of ICI members to advertise their work and expertise. Without doubt, Louwers also hoped to get more financial support for the ICI.

Opportunism, however, was only a secondary reason for liberals to attend the Volta Congress, the first being the convergence of liberal and fascist colonialism. The topics treated at the Volta Congress were diverse but tended to emphasize the merits of native policy, which the fascists defined as "social policy towards the indigenous population."[12] Most of the topics resembled the ICI's program of scientific colonialism: the governmental role of Africanists in colonization, the question of the acclimatization of white settlers, the reaction of Africans to European penetration, the preservation of native cultures and religions, the "association" of the native population, and cooperation between European colonial powers.

The organizers invited anthropologists, sociologists, and economists to share their scientific approaches of how to transform the colonized societies without destroying them. The ICI's secretary-general Louwers, who gave his talk prominently right after the inauguration, put this approach in a nutshell: "We have to preserve the indigenous population in their traditional

---

[9] The most liberal ICI members, predominantly from the Netherlands, absented themselves from the Congress.
[10] Already in the late 1920s, Louwers had traveled to Italy to recruit more members for the ICI: AGRB Louwers Papers, Correspondence avec Zoli 1933 168 (195), Louwers to Zoli, June 14, 1933
[11] Louwers, "Orientation Actuelle des Études sur l'Afrique," in RAI, *CSMSA*, vol. 1, 61.
[12] Ibid., 22.

environment and grant them a maximum of independence and administrative autonomy."[13] Most importantly, participants subscribed to the innovative discipline of social anthropology, which gave the colonized a rational function in society and did not only see them as culturally or biologically determined beings.

Given its liberal agenda, the Volta Congress was certainly an attempt to reconcile the world with Italy's brutal conquest of Libya and Ethiopia, without losing the fascist face. The fascist organizers portrayed the conquest as a necessary phase that provided the basis for a constructive and cooperative native policy. During 7 days and 126 talks, the Italian gas attacks and bombings during the conquest of Libya and Ethiopia were completely absent. Instead, the Italians established a narrative of the revival of the tolerant Roman Empire that embraced all the peoples it had conquered. Thus, they announced plans to "give them universal values in the Roman style" without forcing them into "our historical civilization that does not appear to be transmittable" and concluded: "this is our law and not that of violence."[14] This narrative also appealed to the self-styled progressive colonizers in the ICI.

The Volta Congress has been widely overlooked and therefore underestimated by historians, certainly because the surrounding events diminished its importance. Four days before the inauguration of the Congress, on September 30, 1938, Britain, France, and Italy confirmed Hitler's annexation of portions of Czechoslovakia in Munich. Although the conference participants saw in the Munich Agreement a confirmation of European solidarity, their own amity conference got little attention.[15] The conference proceedings appeared only in late 1939, when the war hit the headlines. In the words of ICI member Octave Louwers, the congress was "overtaken by the events."[16]

Yet, while the memory of the event almost got lost in the shuffle of the war, Volta's structural legacy lingered on. Eminent ICI members perpetuated the Congress' memory after World War II[17] The French ICI member Louis Massignon announced in 1951 that the Volta Congress was at the origin of "Eurafrica" in the sense of a cultural, economic, and political symbiosis of Europeans and Africans.[18] The ICI's secretary-general Octave Louwers published a condensed remake of its proceedings in 1949. To make Volta a landmark, he summarized the most important contributions and complained that the Congress had "not had the impact it deserved," referring to the lack of

---

[13] Louwers, "Orientation Actuelle," 61.
[14] De Vecchi, "Politica Sociale Verso gli Indigeni," in RAI, *CSMSA* vol. 1, 719.
[15] RAI, *CSMSA*, vol. 1, 1581.
[16] Louwers, *Le Congrès Volta*.
[17] AGRB Louwers papers 237 264 INCIDI anciennement ICI, Démission de M. O. Louwers 1950: Begminot to Louwers, October 2, 1950.
[18] Massignon, *Écrits Mémorables*, vol 1, 665.

attention to a Congress that would secretly shape postwar colonial policy.[19] The former British district commissioner in Uganda and ICI member James Erasmus Tracy Philipps had already published an extensive summary in the *Journal of the Royal African Society* in 1939. Like Louwers, Tracy Philipps celebrated the fascists' will to establish a "practice of European solidarity" in Africa to fight diseases and under-population on the continent and organize the mass education of Africans.[20] After World War II, Louwers and Tracy Philipps continued to glorify the Congress and neither of them showed any sense of guilt. As we will see, fascist influence on colonialism survived the war with little damage and partly laid the basis for postwar colonial policy.

The British Tracy Philipps and the Belgian Louwers stand for the progressive and philanthropist colonialists who fell for fascism, partly because it promised to realize colonial projects that the ICI had long hoped to implement. Tracy Philipps was a humanitarian activist who had organized schemes of refugee resettlement after World War I. In the 1930s, he became district officer in Uganda and tried to reform the British system of indirect rule. He disempowered the chiefs whom the British administration traditionally used to govern Uganda and directly consulted the population about their griefs and desires. The governor of Uganda regarded his initiative as disobedience and removed him from his post for having single-handedly "democratized" colonial rule. Once he was fired, Tracy Philipps went to fascist Italy and promoted Mussolini's colonial schemes as a model. He claimed that fascist imperialism might "make a greater appeal to the African" because British colonial rule was too pitiful. As African legal concepts highlighted retaliation, he argued, "dictators such as the earlier Caesars and Mussolini, are more sympathetically intelligible to average Africans."[21] Like many ICI members, Tracy Philipps saw in fascism a way to improve and apply his own ideas. While parts of the British media accused him of being an agent of the fascists, he was quickly acquitted, mainly because his colonial ideals did not differ in essence from imperialist and racist positions in Britain. Immersed in racist thinking, Tracy Philipps did not see any fascist "propaganda fide" emanating from the fascist Congress organizers, whom he described as friendly and "natural." Nor did the participation of German Nazis to the Congress change his mind.[22]

The Christian internationalist Octave Louwers, who wanted to introduce a paternalistic welfare policy to the colonies, equally considered the Volta Congress unproblematic because it propagated a common European effort to develop Africa that would be more successful than the League of Nations.

---

[19] Louwers, *Le Congrès Volta*, 3.
[20] Tracy Philipps, "The Volta Meeting in Rome," 19–32.
[21] Tracy Philipps, "Editorial letter," 140–142.
[22] Tracy Philipps, "The Volta Meeting in Rome," 20–21 and 24–25.

Louwers believed that "it is through this effort of coordination and cooperation that Africa becomes a module of Europe's unity."[23] It was indeed the most important message of the Volta meeting that only a united Europe was able to lift Africa to a higher level of development. In his opening remarks, the futurist and fascist journalist Francesco Orestano proclaimed the need to defend the "European political and civil Empire" against "any antagonism and subversion." By creating the united "Europe of tomorrow," he explained, Africa would develop faster. The mutual effort in the colonies would automatically bring about a "pan-African" space of economic cooperation, which would become an integral part of the European economy. Several speakers at the Congress quoted the duce's mot that "Africa is the complementary continent of Europe."[24] The Congress participants even went beyond this merger and envisaged a Eurafrican empire.

In 1951, the French ICI member Louis Massignon claimed that he had "seen the birth of Eurafrica at the Volta Congress of 1938, in Mussolini's Rome"[25] Massignon was an Arabist and Islamophile who saw in the fusion of Catholic and Islamic cultures the basis for a reinforced unity between Europe and (North) Africa. He shared this desire of a Eurafrica with the fascists. Conference organizer and governor of Libya, Italo Balbo, proudly reported on Mussolini's visit to Tripoli in 1937, during which the duce "unsheathed the 'Sword of Islam,' promising that Fascism would defend its Moslem subjects and help them to greatness."[26] Balbo then outlined his achievements in Libya, where he had allegedly established mosques, Koranic schools, Islamic tribunals, and supported the sacred sites of the marabouts. He promoted an empire with "the maximal respect for the Muslim religion."[27] French participants of the Congress, who generally kept a low profile, vociferously agreed with this policy. ICI member Le Neveu added that French colonizers such as Lyautey had never considered Islam "an inferior but a different civilization"[28] In the theory of the Volta Congress, the Islamic civilization was the basis for a Eurafrican cooperation among equals. In reality, the co-optation of Islam was, as Italo Balbo put it in a more honest moment at the Volta Congress, the "ultimate *instrumentum regni*" for Europeans in Africa.[29]

---

[23] Louwers, *Congrès Volta*, 128.
[24] RAI, *CSMSA*, vol. 1, 23–24.
[25] Massignon, *Écrits Mémorables*, vol 1, 665.
[26] Bosworth, *Mussolini*, 319.
[27] Balbo "La Politica Sociale Fascista," 739.
[28] Ibid., 601.
[29] Ibid., 746.

7.2 Neo-Roman Ideologies and the Fascist Eurafrican Empire

Eurafrica, a concept that is generally said to have emerged only after 1945 to reconcile the imperial hangover with the process of Europeanization, was much more than an Islamo-Catholic spiritual community. The fascist Eurafrica promoted at Rome was first of all one of a common economic area in Africa, whose resources supplied and strengthened a united Europe. Orestano thought of it as economic cooperation based on a "pan-african" transport network with railroads, roads, and air connections. Like ICI members, he promoted "emulative acts" to transfer field-tested strategies of colonial exploitation to lesser developed regions.[30] Inspired by the fascist corporate state, Tracy Philipps designed a "Higher Council of Economic Development, sub-divided into Economic Regional councils, composed of the European Powers of colonial experience in Africa."[31] These schemes coincided with Mussolini's dictum that Africa was the "complementary continent of Europe" and the plans of the head of the NSDAP's colonial department Kurt Weigelt, who also happened to be a CEO at the Deutsche Bank and at Lufthansa. At the Volta Congress, Weigelt saw his project of a complementary economic *Ergänzungsraum* in Africa confirmed. He owned plantations in Cameroon and sought solutions to supply the Germans with invigorating fat supply. To close the "fat gap" in German Europe, he intended importing groundnuts and palm oil from Africa.[32] The economic Eurafrica of all those men mostly worked to the economic detriment of Africa.

What should the political organization of Eurafrica look like? Unsurprisingly, the Italian organizers of the Volta Congress resurrected the Roman Empire as the ideal political frame for Eurafrica.[33] Federzoni emphasized that Italy had already "resumed the oeuvre of Rome" and had "become imperial again."[34] Geographically, the Roman and the Eurafrican empires were congruent. What is more, the ideal of the Roman Empire appealed to all colonizers, be they fascist or not. British liberals naturally subscribed to it, as did French republicans and German Nazis of the Third Reich. The Roman Empire reconciled all antagonisms. It stood for settler colonialism and indirect rule, authority and participation, conquest and civilization, tribes and citizens, unity and diversity, religious syncretism and cultural pluralism, Europe and Africa. All these antagonisms had coexisted in the Roman Empire, in which the participants saw both strength and tolerance.

---

[30] Ibid., 24
[31] Tracy Philipps, "The Volta Meeting," 25–26.
[32] RAI, *CSMSA*, vol. 1, 23; and vol. 2, 1486.
[33] For Mussolini's Eurafrican plans, see Podestà, Eurafrica; Corban, forthcoming.
[34] RAI, *CSMSA*, vol. 1, 35–36.

Figure 7.1 Italian fascists visiting the Nazi-Reichskolonialbund around 1938
(© Bildbestand Der Deutschen Kolonialgesellschaft, Universitätsbibliothek Frankfurt/Main, Image 059-8064-08)

The Eurafrican empire of the Volta Congress was designed to be unique but not unprecedented. The revival of an international empire of the Roman kind had intrigued the ICI for almost a decade. At the international celebrations for the centenary of Algeria's conquest in 1930 and 1931, ICI members such as the Belgian Louwers had noted the comeback of a Eurafrican empire.[35] The French used the occasion to celebrate their Algerian settler colony but also displayed their will to align their new empire with the British and Dutch (and,

---

[35] See AGRB Louwers Papers 241 (268) Congrès centenaire de l'Algérie, Alger May 1930 Rapport sur le Congrès.

as it happened the Roman) model of indirect rule and cultural relativism. While French republicans had long avoided the term "empire" for its despotic connotations, they now revived it. At the ICI's session of 1931, which explicitly took place during the centenary celebrations in Paris, a French delegate put the new imperial spirit straight: "Some say that France is an imperialist nation and sometimes they attach a pejorative meaning to this term. I exposed our doctrine to you. If this is being imperialist, all right! Then long live imperialism!"[36] At the Volta Congress, the French Louis Bertrand equally declared the conquest of Algeria and the recent Italian conquest of Libya and Ethiopia the rebirth of a common Latin Africa.[37] Obviously, Latin Africa was to perpetuate the Roman Empire. This new imperialist spirit reflected both a more aggressive colonialist language and a reconceptualization of the empire as a more inclusive Roman-style political entity.

At the Volta Congress of 1938, Italians equally redefined empire, by dismissing the meaning that the PMC and Socialists had given it. Cesare Maria De Vecchi, one of the fascist *quadrumviri* whom Mussolini had made governor of Somalia, elaborated on the fascist empire whose origins he saw in the universality of the Roman model. According to him, it was "cynical" to justify imperial expansion as either "democratic" (as settler colonialists claimed because it was the colonialism of everyman) or "humanitarian" (as the PMC and advocates of the civilizing mission claimed) because it obviously involved violent conquest.[38] This ridicule of humanitarian colonialism was certainly directed against the PMC, which had claimed to make empires a space of opportunity and material improvement for its indigenous inhabitants. De Vecchi unsurprisingly also dismissed Lenin's definition of imperialism as the inevitable outcome of the expansive forces inherent in capitalism. Colonial expansion, De Vecchi cautioned, was not a consequence of "historical materialism" or "economic determinism."[39] Instead, it derived from a "spiritual unity of will and action."[40] To democratic and humanitarian justifications of colonialism, he opposed the time-honored legitimacy and "universalist character" of the Roman Empire: "the fascist doctrine of the State returns to the imperial forms that have their roots in the Roman and Christian" tradition. In face of the imperium, all other justifications appeared to be "inhumane."[41]

By evoking the alleged inclusiveness and universality of the Roman Empire's rule, De Vecchi reconciled the fascist neo-imperialism with the self-government promoted by progressive colonial experts of the 1920s. He

---

[36] ICI, *Compte Rendu 1931*, 51.
[37] Bertrand, "L'Afrique Latine," 208.
[38] Vecchi di Val Cismon "Politica Sociale," 708 and 713.
[39] Ibid., 709.
[40] Ibid., 712.
[41] Ibid., 709–10.

claimed that the Eurafrican empire was the "cohesive cement of all races and all customs." It was understood that in this empire, colonies should rather be called "provinces" and that the indigenous upper and middle classes should govern these provinces.⁴² In Rome, he argued, provincial autonomy followed the model of the Greek polis and entailed legal and cultural autonomy. De Vecchi defined the Roman province as a "territory to which the metropolitan law could not be transplanted, but where the existing customs and laws inherited from the predecessor can easily be applied." He wanted the conquered people who lived in the provinces to accept the imperial state and "become one with it and see it as an expression of their own personality," following the Roman doctrine "patriam unam diversis gentibus" within a setting of the imperial *pax romana*.⁴³ Louwers represented the progressive participants of the Congress who endorsed legal autonomy in the provinces. Based on the ICI's studies, he vouched for the fact that African populations were not primitive at all but had sophisticated legal systems that were rational and efficient: "Their legal life was intense and varied .... Native law was guided by a spirit of practice that equaled in many regards the law of the highly developed nations."⁴⁴ Self-government in the provinces based on local laws was therefore unproblematic. Like the Roman Empire, Corrado Zoli added, every language group (Amharic, Tigrinya, Galla, Arabic speakers) would receive its own province in Italian Ethiopia "to protect their ethnic individuality."⁴⁵ Such designs of a federal organization of empire would become prominent after World War II and even in the independent states after decolonization.

As the fascists pressed ahead with the retribalization of European society, they learned to cherish the supposedly tribal spirit of the Africans. The neotribalism theoretically worked to the benefit of the colonial population. His fascination with fascist colonialism, for example, led Tracy Philipps to celebrate the African "totemic clan" as a more organic unity of mutual solidarity and insurance. The Volta Congress seemed to support his claim that the African tradition of a spiritual *Volksgemeinschaft* compared favorably with the moribund European civilization. The ethnic groups in Africa reminded Tracy Philipps of the "semi-ancestral Animism akin in substance to the Animism of Greece and Rome in the Prime of their Civilisation."⁴⁶ Tracy Philipps' obsession with tribalism was in no way inferior to the Italian fascists. Since 1922, the organizer of the congress, Italo Balbo, had claimed the title of *ras* for himself. *Ras* was an Ethiopian word for a tribal chieftain and became a

---

⁴² Ibid.
⁴³ Ibid., 725–727.
⁴⁴ Louwers, "Orientation Actuelle," 69.
⁴⁵ Ibid., 84.
⁴⁶ Tracy Philipps, "The Volta Meeting in Rome," 25–26.

title in the fascist political hierarchy. The neo-tribalism, which rested on a complete misinterpretation of African societies, spread among the participants of the Volta Congress.

What role did race play in the Eurafrican empire? Within a unified Eurafrican empire, race became the only marker of otherness, albeit with surprising results. Among the racists was Luca Pietromarchi, who had been vice-commissioner of Eritrea between 1916 and 1918 and Italian representative at the League of Nations from 1923 to 1930. After turning to fascism, Pietromarchi evoked the racist Hamite hypothesis to promote a potential solidarity between Europeans and Africans of Hamite blood. Pietromarchi categorized the Hamites as an elite race who lived predominantly in North Africa but had spread their genes as far as sub-Saharan territories. While Hamites would never accept inferiority with regard to Europeans, he argued, they were superior to "Negroid Africans" because they were a "race endowed with precious qualities, among them their extreme tendency to spirituality" and their "religious fervor."

Pietromarchi believed that the intense spirituality and religious fervor made the Hamites congenial to fascists. Because of the spirituality inherent to their race, Hamites had once easily converted to Christianity, as symbolized by the North African Christian leaders Athanasius and Saint Augustine. They maintained their extreme spirituality in times of Islamization. Since religious extremism was in their blood and not only a cultural phenomenon, Pietromarchi argued, Hamites transformed Islam when it came to Africa rather than being changed by Islam. The Islam of Berbers and Tuaregs, Pietromarchi concluded, became "aggressive, intransigent and fanatic." That made them ideal partners for the fascists who claimed the same characteristics for themselves.[47] After all, some Libyans had proven their combative spirit when fighting alongside the Italians in the war against Ethiopia in 1935, as Italo Balbo proudly related.[48]

In the 1930s, the ambitious Libyan governor Italo Balbo had already taken measures to implement the fascist-Hamite fusion, even by offering Italian citizenship to Libyans. He had incorporated some of them in the fascist militarized state by creating the Gioventù Araba del Littorio in 1935. A paramilitary group that would become a branch of the Gioventù Italiana del Littorio, the Gioventù Araba del Littorio gave military and "spiritual," that is, ideological training to Libyan children and youngsters. Balbo made being a member in the Gioventù Araba del Littorio a prerequisite for attaining Italian

---

[47] Andalusia served him as a precedent that proved that the Aryan race could successfully merge with the Hamite race. See Pietromarchi, "Comportamento delle Strippi Camitiche," in RAI, CSMSA, vol. 1, 610–620, partly quoted in Louwers, *Le Congrès Volta*, 46–50.

[48] Balbo, "La Politica Sociale Fascista," 747.

citizenship, an idea he promoted during the Volta Congress and implemented one year later, in 1939. In a similar way, he believed Ethiopia should be organized along fascist lines: "In Addis Ababa ... the local fascio has assembled over a thousand native children in its schools, where they are given free lunch and are clothed in the uniform of the 'Gioventù Etiopica del Littorio.' This institution already has important ramifications in most of the large centers of the Empire."[49] This reeducation, however, had poor results and was no more than fascist propaganda. As only 8 percent of young Libyans had been schooled by 1936 (and schooling included the Gioventù Araba del Littoral), this institution seems to have been less of a success than Balbo claimed. Only around 10,300 Libyans would be granted Italian citizenship until the end of the war.[50] In reality, most Libyans and Ethiopians were kept segregated from the Italians and denied political rights.[51] The real purpose was to rule through them and not with them. Balbo nevertheless kept on promoting the symbiosis of Christians and Muslims.

7.3 The Anti-Geneva Consensus

Apart from creating an economic, political, and cultural unity with Africa, the Eurafrican empire was meant to revive European solidarity and substitute for the League of Nations. Most of the participants paid homage to Mussolini, who had left the League in 1933, in their talks. Like German Nazis, Italian fascists blamed the makers of the Versailles treaty and the League's PMC for their refusal to give them colonial territories in 1919 (see Figure 7.1). Only a new fascist League, Italo Balbo believed, could give Italy the opportunity to have its possessions confirmed by a new Eurafrican community.[52] Italians and Germans naturally despised the League of Nations; but a Polish participant also assessed that the "League in Geneva has failed in bringing the peoples of the world nearer to each other" and instead "quarreled before the colored population, and exposed its weakness before them."[53] Neither liberal participants of the Volta Congress nor those affiliated the League of Nations protested against the plan to dissolve the League. Their opportunism was a triumph of fascist colonial internationalism over the allegedly liberal colonial internationalism of the League. The Volta Congress in Rome left no doubt that it was indeed an anti-Geneva bloc.

As quixotic as the Volta Congress' plans of a Eurafrican empire seemed to be, they curiously coincided with ideas of the most progressive anthropologist

---

[49] Zoli, "The Organization," 85–86.
[50] Baldinetti, *The Origins of the Libyan Nation*, 48–53.
[51] Kotschnig, "Review of the School," 168.
[52] Balbo, "La Politica Sociale Fascista," 733.
[53] Sapieha, "Gründe für die Europäsiche Solidarität," in RAI, *CSMSA*, vol 2, 1507.

of the time, Bronislaw Malinowski. It was a great success of the organizers to win Malinowski's favor and support. Although Malinowski was absent from the Congress, he agreed to send two papers and warm greetings to Rome. His absence allowed a creative misreading of his writings, but the links of his theory with the fascist project were so striking that no manipulation was needed. Like the participants of the Volta Congress, Malinowski argued in favor of a world government in form of an empire of indirect rule, which he called alternately "a federation of mankind, a super state, a [reformed] League of Nations, or commonwealth of peoples." Malinowski's new League of Nations took the form of a good empire. It should curtail the sovereignty of nation-states but allow cultural diversity, mainly to avoid aggressive nationalist wars. For the "preliterate people" he foresaw more "tribal or national" autonomy under the control of "a special colonial committee composed primarily of anthropologists." In this colonial super state, "the treatment of colored labor would have to change fundamentally, since one of the requirements of this plan is equality as well as freedom in the future of living."[54] His model for such a peace-bringing colonization seems to have been the Hapsburg Empire. Malinowski had experienced Hapsburg as a relatively tolerant empire when he grew up in Poland. He romanticized his youth in the "good" empire, which had allowed for cultural diversity by hedging exaggerated nationalisms.[55] Thus, Hapsburg and Rome seemed to him empires of indirect rule, just like the British liberal empire to which he lent his anthropological expertise.

7.4 Bronislaw Malinowski's Colonial Anthropology and Fascist Functionalism

Malinowski's scientific approach of functionalist anthropology was indeed compatible with fascist needs. In his first paper at the Volta Congress, "The Scientific Basis of Applied Anthropology," he roughly outlined this approach, which theoretically justified a Christian-Islamic Eurafrica.[56] Generally speaking, Malinowski's anthropology stated that the social behavior of "savages" and "civilized" people were not so different. Even if the "savage" tribal societies seemed to spawn irrational and inefficient customs, Malinowski presumed that they had a function for the society as a whole and were indeed rational within this system. The parts worked together to create a more balanced and

---

[54] Malinowski, *Freedom and Civilization*, 334–336.
[55] Gellner, *Language and Solitude*, 143–144. Malinowski's support for Lugard's indirect rule is widely known but his involvement in fascist colonialism less so. See Foks, "Bronislaw Malinowski," 35–57.
[56] Malinowski, "The Scientific Basis," in RAI, *CSMSA*, vol. 1, 5–24; Yale University Library Manuscripts and Archives, MS 19 Malinowski papers, b.16 f.134.

efficient economy, culture, and political stability. In his view, culture was a complex, holistic thing and the anthropologist observer could only understand it if he saw it as a unity and an interconnected whole. All members of society participated in this interconnected whole and their behavior had a function in the system.[57] As he presupposed that both "savage" and "civilized" societies had their own rationality, both could be analyzed with the same methods. For the participants of the Volta Congress, Malinowski's functionalism sounded very much like the fascist ideal of a state.

Italian fascists saw in Malinowski's functionalist society the equivalent of the organic society they intended to create in Italy and beyond. "From the standpoint of ethnology," the specialist of "primitive religions" Raffaele Pettazzoni commented on Malinowski, "even a primitive civilization such as those we find among African populations, is always an organism, a unique structure consisting of several elements. You cannot touch one of its elements without provoking trouble in the balance of its totality [ensemble]."[58] In Malinowski's functionalist society, all customs and behaviors of groups functioned as integral parts to support a bigger rational whole. Even if the parts seemed to be irrational, such as customary dances and feasts, they made sense if analyzed with regard to their function for the groups' balanced economy, cultural coherence, and political stability. Malinowski explained that culture was a concrete reality and an integral unit whose elements were interdependent and whose parts existed only as means to a common goal. This holism sounded very much like the imagined fascist state. In the ideal fascist society, individuals and collectivities subordinated themselves to an overarching whole, a body of which they were the organs. The state's organs were the family and corporations who had to function properly and subordinate them to keep the state alive. Both organic and functionalist societies allowed dynamic activism (if it did not threaten the hierarchy) and spirituality (as a means of cultural cohesion). Although Malinowski's two papers were read out in absentia, they became the most referenced contributions at the Conference.

Obviously, the fascists were not aware that Malinowski's functionalism was heuristic and a tool to understand social life, as well as a method to reestablish the rationality of allegedly savage tribes. Nevertheless, some of them claimed the idea for themselves, as it helped them to conceptualize the fascist state they wanted to bring about. While Malinowski's functionalism was a way to analyze societies, the fascists' functionalism was one of action and their aim was to create a functionalist society. They wanted to bring about an organic society in which each member had its place. Almost logically, this entailed that those who did not have a function in the fascist society had to be excluded or

---

[57] Gellner, *Language and Solitude*, 134.
[58] RAI, *CSMSA*, vol. 1, 754. The ICI equally wanted to preserve "native" institutions and culture.

eliminated. Obviously, fascists also tended to rewrite history as a function of the fascist present. To them, Malinowski's functionalism seemed highly compatible with fascist socio-political programs. Thus, while Nazis would ban Malinowski's works in Germany, the Volta Congress celebrated his approach. That Malinowski himself did not attend the Congress was proof of a rather unilateral declaration of sympathy. But Malinowski was not completely innocent.

While Malinowski was hardly a fascist, ICI members looked up to him as a theorist of colonial administration. In his second paper, entitled "Modern Anthropology and European Rule in Africa," he urged his anthropologist colleagues to do "useful" research for the benefit of the colonial administration.[59] Malinowski had popularized this "practical anthropology" since 1929 with the support of the International Institute of African Languages and Cultures.[60] Louwers added in his talk at the Volta Congress that the ICI had made practical anthropology a tool for colonial administration as early as the 1890s. Unlike the International African Institute in London, the ICI never wanted to uncouple anthropology from colonial studies. Indeed, the ICI had always wanted to know what happened to social functions when indigenous peoples got in touch with European colonizers.[61] Malinowski's triumph at the Volta Congress was thus based on the fact that ICI members thought his way anyways.

Malinowski had more practical advice for the colonial administrators that was very much in line with the ICI's approach. While anthropologists had to study "Africans in transition," it was the task of colonial administrators to accompany and control this change. Referring to functionalist theory, Malinowski claimed that African cultures were so complex and intertwined that they could not be changed "by a stroke of pen" but only "slowly and gradually."[62] Fearing a culture shock, his advice for administrators was to watch over the graduality of change, for the capitalists not to invest too much capital, for the industrialists not to industrialize too quickly, and for all of them to thoroughly study the culture of the people they colonized. This had been the ICI's program from the 1890s onwards. Malinowski's plea for a soft way into capitalism, in particular, coincided with the ICI's guidelines issued at its 1933 meeting: "The capital in our colonies should be similar to enthusiasm; it should never lack but it also should not overflow either."[63] Malinowski gave a prominent place to anthropologists in the colonial machine and wanted them to govern the new Eurafrican empire.[64]

---

[59] Yale University Library Manuscripts and Archives, MS 19 Malinowski papers, b.16 f.135.
[60] Malinowski, "Practical Anthropology," 22–38.
[61] Louwers, "Orientation Actuelle," 60–63.
[62] Ibid., 880–881.
[63] ICI, *Comtpe rendu 1933*, 42, cited in Louwers, *Congrès Volta de 1938*, 101.
[64] Valentin Mudimbe, *The Invention of Africa*, 33.

Italian fascists adopted the Volta version of Malinowski's functionalist approach, claiming that colonial domination had made functionalist ethnology automatically "the ethnology of cultural encounters."[65] Raffaele, for example, endorsed a "historicized functionalism" and promoted the comparative study of colonial societies in which two cultures met and induced the modification of functionalist elements. He combined elements of functionalism with the *Kulturkreistheorie* (theory of cultural areas, or civilizations) that dominated German and Austrian anthropology in the 1930s and was linked to racist approaches.[66] Unlike the functionalists, the *Kulturkreistheorie* laid emphasis on the historical development and determination of different cultures or civilizations. Each allegedly had its own racial ethnohistory. The different cultural areas thus followed multiple and different logics.[67] From that emerged the question of what happened when two cultural areas got in touch through expansion of one of them. In the 1920s, anthropologists increasingly asked that question: Would it lead to a diffusion of one culture, to the end of the inferior culture, or to a mix of cultures? Would this be an encounter of civilizations or a clash of civilizations? The closer German-speaking *Kulturkreis* ethnologists were to the 1930s, the more they tended to believe in the end of allegedly inferior culture areas or civilizations.[68]

With particular reference to Ankermann, Pettazzoni blamed German ethnologists for having long been concerned with the physical "bastardization of two races" in colonial situations. Unlike them, Pettazzoni refused to frame colonial encounters in terms of the physical mixture of races. Rather, he claimed to be interested in the functionalist transformations that emerged from the contact of two civilizations, assuming that these were of a higher and lower degree of organization. He thus pleaded for the comparative study of the contact between "differing civilizations." In the 1930s, this could only be a contact between colonizers and colonized. His program was a new form of ethnological colonialism that differed from the old one in its rationale if not in its purpose of maintaining colonial rule. After 1945, the ICI would pick up the idea of an encounter of civilizations.[69]

---

[65] Pettazzoni, "Orientamenti atuali," in: RAI, *CSMSA*, 57.
[66] Ibid.; Penny, "Traditions in the German Language," 79–95; Penny and Bunzl, *Worldly Provincialism*.
[67] This distinguished the *Kulturkreis* approach from Darwinist evolutionism, which was unilinear.
[68] Zimmerman, *Anthropology and Antihumanism*.
[69] Pettazoni "Orientamenti Atuali," 58–59.

7.5 Liberalism, Fascism, and the Encounter of "Differing Civilizations"

Unwittingly, Malinowski and Pettazoni became the harbingers of the ICI's strategic renaming after 1945, as they framed the colonial encounter as one of "differing civilizations" instead of racial distinctiveness. Louwers, who would reestablish the ICI in 1949 under the name International Institute of Differing Civilizations, reiterated Malinowski's contribution and Pettazoni's interpretation at the Volta Congress in his conference report published in 1949: "This is one of the most authentic and penetrating studies about the colonial process and the phenomenon of the mutual penetration of differing civilizations that I have ever read."[70]

The main legacy of the Volta Congress was the invention of Eurafrica as a framework for the encounter of differing civilizations. After 1945, this idea persisted, but it was unclear if a Eurafrican *empire* was an adequate frame for the encounter of differing civilizations or if Eurafrica allowed for nominal *independence*. Malinowski's idea of a technocratic "rule of the anthropologists" made both a "good empire" and nominal independence thinkable. Indeed, for Malinowski, there was a short step from "British indirect rule" to "independent" rule and he even used both interchangeably.[71] In this regard, he was in line with the ICI members who had a similar ambiguous attitude and were ready to accept independence if they could maintain their influence. A Eurafrica based on expert governmentality without nominal government became a possibility.

In a similar way, the Volta Congress had brought colonizers from liberal and fascist countries closer to each other, in a sinister analogy to the Munich Conference that took place almost at the same time, some thousand kilometers north. Participants from Great Britain, such as the former governor-general of Sudan, Sir John Maffey, claimed that the two events of 1938 testified to a new European spirit. He admitted that he had had no expectations when he received the invitation to come to Rome: "I looked at the document and asked myself for what they wanted me in Italy ... I did not regard the invitation with a great deal of pleasure, neither with much anticipation of enjoyment." But during the conference, he took a liking to solidarity with the fascist colonizers: "Nothing had separated us here ... it has brought us closer together in this Rome, so old and yet today so young, fulfilling her mission."[72] Not only Maffey, but also the French participants like Eugène Pittard returned home with this new mission to give the project of "Eurafrica, as we call it now," more substance.[73]

---

[70] Louwers, *Congrès Volta 1938*, 71.
[71] Malinowski, *Freedom and Civilization*, 335.
[72] RAI, *CSMSA*, vol. 2, 1581.
[73] RAI, *CSMSA*, vol. 2, 1582.

7.6 The Corporatist Economy of Eurafrica

The syncretistic nature of the Volta Congress manifested itself in the idea of a corporatist Eurafrican economy, which combined a centralized corporatist state organization with grassroots agricultural cooperatives. In his inaugural speech at the Volta Congress, the Italian minister of education proclaimed that Mussolini's Italy was an "Italy of the Fasci and of the Corporations (and this means the political, social, and economic unity)."[74] Italian fascist corporatism had emerged in the interwar period as a counter project to the capitalist economy of individualistic and liberal democracies.[75] Its advocates proposed that economic and political interests should be represented by a limited number of monopolistic and noncompetitive corporations that were functionally differentiated and licensed or even created by the state authority.[76] Italy established twenty-two corporations in 1934 that were "organs of the state" and represented the industry and agriculture. They advised the government how to bring about economic development through a planned economy. To do so, they also established and controlled small-scale cooperative initiatives from below.[77] Apart from controlling the national economy, corporations should undermine socialist tendencies by uniting employers and employees of a certain branch under one umbrella corporation. By dismantling class solidarity among the workers, this system prevented class struggles. Employers and employees were supposed to settle conflicts within the corporative frame. The welfare state was replaced by paternalistic support of the employer for an employee of a corporation. Italian fascists almost naturally assumed that the corporative state should be extended to their colonies.

Bruno Biagi, who was about to transform Italy into a corporatist state, urged the colonial internationalists at the Volta Congress to extend "institutions of consortia and corporations to the fields of supplies and sales" in Africa.[78] According to Biagi, the colonies were already Eurafrican, because European settlers and African workers lived in its territory. For him, Africans were a "productive factor, a machine that has to be kept most efficient." To get the most out of them, he deemed a corporative economy most suitable. He chose the Europeans to be heads of the corporations, to guide the African workers and also to represent them politically. What is more, white settlers who employed Africans should "assist" them in case of disease, unemployment, inability to pay taxes, etc. Through this corporative system of European "assistance" for the African workers, Biagi argued, a welfare state became

---

[74] Ibid., vol. 1, 37.
[75] Podestà, *Il mito dell'impero*, 261–288.
[76] Costa Pinto, *Corporatism and Fascism*, 5.
[77] ILO, *International Labour Conference Twentieth Session 1936*, 50–54.
[78] Biagi, "Politica Sociale Verso gli Indigeni," in RAI, *CSMSA*, vol. 2, 859.

unnecessary and it was less likely that trade unions would gain ground in the colonies. Because he thought a welfare state was too expensive for the colonies anyways, and he rejected democratic schemes of representation promoted by trade unions, the corporative colony seemed to be the best form of economic organization. In Biagi's paternalistic system, which saw welfare emerging from an individual pact between white employer and black employee rather than from a legally binding social contract between classes, Africans were supposed to "collaborate" with the higher ranked settlers. Biagi used corporative language to describe his Eurafrican settler-indigenous unit and called it a "legal-economic institution."[79] While most of his ideas were common sense among the colonial experts, his superficial views on Africa were particularly uninformed, contradictory, and carelessly presented. The participants of the Volta Congress gave more credit to experienced administrators who ascribed a more active role to the colonized population.

The governor of Libya, Italo Balbo, claimed for himself to have established a rudimentary corporative economy in North Africa. Historians of fascist Italy often like to emphasize that, had Balbo not made a career in the fascist state, he would probably have gone down in history as a liberal. Indeed, in mainland Italy, he criticized the corporate state, because its representatives had not been democratically elected but named from above.[80] His policy in Libya, instead, was typically corporatist. He wanted to make the Libyans participate in public and economic life, however without "exposing them to democratic ideology and ballot rigging."[81] Thus, he delighted himself that the "*homo oeconomicus* of the liberal economy ... gave way to the 'organized' one, made by the fascist regime." He concluded that "it would be absurd if the Fascist State – who honorably developed the regime of the controlled economy based on the corporative organization – paid no attention to the Arabs of the Libyan province."[82]

As a governor, Balbo supported corporatist and cooperative schemes such as the consortium for the dates of Fezzan and the cooperative of the fishermen in Pisida. To implement a controlled economy, Balbo had prescribed fixed salaries for workers and regulated the costs for manpower (in the same breath, he indicated that a controlled economy required occasionally forced labor). To come into the limelight, Balbo subsumed all temporary state-led economic measures under the corporatist label. He had allegedly initiated the planting of 1.5 million palm trees, the nursing of 800,000 olive trees, and the breeding of a million livestock. Although a systematic corporative policy was lacking in Libya, he claimed that the central government controlled the economy

[79] Ibid., 856 and 858–859.
[80] Bosworth, *Mussolini*, 324.
[81] Balbo, "La Politica Sociale Fascista," 743.
[82] Ibid., 735–736.

through corporatist structures. According to him, corporative and cooperative policies were responsible for the drilling of artesian wells, the fight against desertification, the free redistribution of domain land (to less than a hundred Libyans) in 1937, the introduction of small loans from savings bank, and the evacuation of 300,000 cattle from Western to Eastern Libya when a drought threatened them in 1936.[83] Balbo labeled all this as corporative.

Corporatism was not the monopoly of the Italian fascists, and a much more sophisticated plan for a corporate colony came from the above-mentioned Arabist Louis Massignon.[84] He had revived the corporative traditions of North Africa in the 1920s and deemed the smaller entities of craft guilds an adequate way of stabilizing colonial society and establishing an organic unit with the motherland. Massignon was a prominent member of the ICI and actively participated in the Volta Congress. Echoing Malinowski, he was interested in the "functioning of the *ensemble*" and, echoing the fascists, he presupposed an "organic structure of societies."[85] He found the organic structure in the old North African elite of manufacturing artisans, organized in craft guilds, which he wanted to be the new corporative elite that participated in colonial production and administration. The colonial state, he urged, should lay both economy and political representation in the hands of the craft guilds, which artisans had formed beginning in the fifteenth century in total harmony with North Africa's Islamic law, culture, and society. He turned Morocco into his testing ground, where the French ICI member Hubert Lyautey had established a prototype of indirect rule.

In the 1920s, the Direction of Indigenous Affairs in Morocco employed Massignon to save the corporative economy of North Africa. He spent his life fighting "de-incorporated" societies in the colonies that he considered the equivalent of an uprooted or unnatural society. In his view, de-incorporation was the inevitable outcome of industrialization and proletarization, which seemed to be a consequence of European colonial penetration. The penetration of industrial capitalism in North Africa potentially led de-incorporated indigenous populations to embrace socialist ideologies As Massignon had a strong aversion against the "unrestrained syndicalism," he intended to slow down industrialization. For him, this "industrialization had ruined the artisanate after the First World War" and needed to be restricted.[86] His nostalgia for corporatism concerned both the European and the colonial world, which he thought of in a single frame. Thus, he stood up against what he called a "clash of cultures" in the colonies between a capitalist and a corporatist economy by reviving the craft guilds as the nucleus of colonial societies.

---

[83] Ibid., 735–737.
[84] Pasetti, "Corporatist Connections," 65–94.
[85] Massignon, Écrits Mémorables, vol. 1, 596.
[86] Ibid., 605.

At the Volta Congress, Massignon sensed for the first time that his corporate project was not purely preservationist but indeed coincided with the futurist project of a spiritually organized "Eurafrican" empire. Massignon's Eurafrica had two dimensions. The first, North-South dimension, blurred the sharp distinction between motherland and colony, seeing it as a single, potentially corporate empire. Inspired by neo-Roman visions of empire among Italian fascists, the Eurafrican corporate empire also spoke to Massignon's very personal inclination to a mystical worldview. Massignon was a type of Eurafricanist formerly unheard of: since the early 1920s, he was on his way to become a Catholic Muslim, a category he earned the merit to have invented and partially lived. His syncretistic approach linked Islam, Catholicism, and partly Judaism and led him to search for universal elements in all Abrahamic religions. As these had fruitfully coexisted in medieval Al-Andalus, he believed in Islamic Spain as an archetype of an Abrahamic Eurafrica. Most importantly, Al-Andalus had also seen the heyday of craft guilds. Its Muslim governors had even reshaped Islamic law to include regulations for a corporative life. Massignon found similarities both in mysticism and in craft guilds that rested on the spiritual solidarity among its members. For him, Muslim, Jewish, and Christian craft guilds formed the nucleus of a particularly moral economy that might enable a coexistence of Muslims, Christians, and Jews in colonial North Africa. The second, South-South dimension in Massignon's scheme was then the "social cooperation in North Africa." He personally helped to revive craft guilds in the whole of North Africa, where France and Italy joined forces to align their native "social" policy and geared it towards a corporative policy that pushed back an allegedly "segmented society."[87]

French political leaders shared Massignon's Eurafrican corporatism, though in a laicist version. While Lyautey embraced Eurafricanism in the 1920s, the liberal propagator of French development policies and ICI-sympathizer Albert Sarraut suggested in 1937 that a joint *mise en valeur* through "a Eurafrican corporation" might be the way for France to peacefully coexist with the Third Reich and avoid war.[88] His overall goal was to push back communism, and a Eurafrican corporation with the Nazis seemed to be the best way to achieve this goal. One year later, at the Volta Congress, corporatist activists such as Balbo and Massignon combined the centralized corporative organization of the state with the promotion of grassroots corporations and cooperatives. As we will see in Chapter 8 in more detail, the ICI propagated corporations and cooperatives in all colonies. Colonial corporatism would have a long legacy in Eurafrica well beyond World War II and even in times of independence.

[87] Ibid., 665.
[88] Montarsolo, *L'Eurafrique*, 23–34.

7.7 The ICI's Fascist Turn

Overall, the Volta Congress was a great success for the ICI and not only because it pushed the cause of colonial internationalism. A broader audience took interest in the work of the ICI and it gained in popularity. It could also improve its financial situation by selling its publications to new clients. Polish scientific institutions, for example, bought the complete works of the *Bibliothèque Coloniale Internationale* after Polish scientists had attended the Congress in Rome.[89] It also recruited new members at the Volta Congress.

The ICI members were so taken by the Volta Congress that they held the subsequent session in 1939 in Rome, where Italian fascists dominated the session. Tracy Philipps noted the growing gap between the "democratic" and the "totalitarian countries" and observed that the absence of French delegates "weakened" the democrats.[90] Yet, representatives of both sides still attended the 1939 meeting, which reiterated the compatibility of liberal and fascist colonialism. Together, the participants of the Rome meeting even visited sites of interior colonization in Italy and the settler colonies in Libya.

At the Rome session of 1939, it became clear that the ICI had adopted the amalgam of humanitarian aid, settler colonialism, the Volta ideology, and its plan to revive the Roman Empire. Tracy Philipps' exalting report on the ICI's excursion to fascist settler colonies in Italy and Libya testified to this amalgam of allegedly unrelated ideologies:

> Most interesting and impressive visits were made by the Members of the Institut to the clean and fertile farms of a friendly and frugal peasantry who flourish upon soil solidified and reclaimed, by the Government's enterprise and energy, from the vast and malarial Pontine Marshes which had defied the efforts of previous ages. Horace and Cicero have recorded picturesquely how they shivered and became sick of an ague after passing through this pestilent waste. The technique of the reclamation and refertilisation, the repopulation and reproductivity of the Pontine Swamps and of the parts of Libya about Cyrene are models for this kind of settlement or recolonisation of land. For Colonial Powers, here are examples of what can be achieved by a not wealthy country of great tradition, tradition which included within its colonial administration such divergent elements as Palestine and the *ultimos in orbe Britannos*. These modern achievements, witnessed by so many Members of the Institut, arise from a combination of constructive imagination with a *risorgimento* of dynamic energy. This combination is what, in Europe's overseas colonies, was also felt and manifested in our time by two great Europeans, Gallieni and Lyautey, as the power of poetry in action. The Members of the Institut

---

[89] ICI, *Compte Rendu* 1939, 40. On Polish colonialism, see Ureña Valerio, *Colonial Fantasies*.

[90] Tracy Philipps, "The XXIVth Biennial Session of the ICI," 17–21.

have lived to see the Pontine Marshes thick with corn. Love for the peasant people of Italy has been felt by every Englishman who has lived among them. Whatever our political views, few will wish to deny that the maker of modern Italy has also been animated and energized.[91]

Renouncing their decade-old doctrine of anti-settlerism, members of the ICI visited fascist settler colonies in Italy and in Italo Balbo'sLibya [92] They evoked the colonial spirit of the Roman Empire that the fascist government had perfected. But they also linked it to progressive native policies of indirect rule, as represented by Lyautey and his policy in the French protectorate over Morocco. In the same way, Tracy Philipps' admiration for both fascist settler colonialism and schemes of French indirect rule revealed that Europeans generally agreed on their overall colonial ideology. Colonialism remained Europe's lowest common denominator despite the continent tearing itself apart in World War I.

Analyzing the ICI enables us to tell the whole story of interwar colonial internationalism from 1920, when the "liberal" PMC set the tone, to the late 1930s, when fascism became prevalent. After World War I, European media declared the allegedly liberal and humanitarian PMC a novelty. Its activity in Geneva received much attention from friends and foes alike, and historians continued to highlight its progressive role for the interwar period.[93] The ICI and the Volta Congress, instead, have received little attention, although their fascist colonial internationalism soon supplanted the supposedly humanitarian approach of the League's PMC. Going beyond such dichotomies, the development of the ICI in the 1930s shows that the allegedly "liberal" and the fascist colonialism were partly compatible. The fascist version of colonial internationalism fell on fertile ground among "progressive" ICI members. Thus, seen across the two decades, the ICI represents the full range of colonial internationalisms, especially the often-forgotten fascist version of a Eurafrican empire, which continued to shape Europe's policies after 1945.

[91] Ibid., 20.
[92] Ballinger, "Colonial Twilight," 819–826.
[93] Pedersen, *The Guardians*, 24–25.

8

False Authenticity

The Fokon'olona and the Cooperative World Commonwealth

In the early 1930s, Freppel Cotta from Goa in India traveled to Italy to study agricultural cooperatives. Cotta was one of the most important Indian experts on farmer cooperatives. Since Italy had started colonizing itself by extending internal colonization under Mussolini, we can label Cotta's journey transcolonial and aiming at transfers of cooperative technologies. For him, ideal cooperative societies were economically self-sufficient mutual aid societies, whose members shared tools, knowledge, funds, seeds, and marketing strategies. Once the farmers who joined paid sufficient membership fees, cooperatives ideally served as credit banks that issued low-interest loans to its members. In India, colonial administrators and Indian economists alike saw in these collective credit banks a way to fight usurers who gave high-interest loans to native farmers and often ruined them.[1] Mixing philanthropic arguments and colonialist interests, ICI members endorsed Coppa's view that cooperatives "will eventually break through the iron ring of usury [and] will compel the payment of fair prices" through joint marketing.[2] This model, inspired by the European cooperative movement, spread in the colonial world of the 1920s.[3] Cotta initially adhered to the liberal British Rochdale model, which was about a century old and had become the core ideology of the International Cooperative Alliance (1895). The Rochdale principles presupposed that membership in agricultural cooperatives was voluntary and that members should democratically elect their own management board, which acted autonomously of the state.[4] His study trip to fascist Italy, however, suggests that the colonial cooperative system was less liberal.

It was only on paper, however, that fascist Italy adhered to the Rochdale principles. To keep up appearances of a cooperative grassroots movement, Italian fascists had defined cooperatives as voluntary associations of farmers. As in liberal countries, their official purpose was to provide loans to the

---

[1] Cotta, *Agricultural Co-operation*.
[2] Kat Angelino, *Colonial Policy*, vol. 1, 401, cited in Strickland, *Co-operation for Africa*, 41.
[3] For an overview, see Eckert, "Useful Instruments of Participation," 97–118; Nyanchonga, "Mutualism and Cooperative Work," 585–616.
[4] Cotta, *Agricultural Co-operation*, 7.

members "for productive purposes and at low interest," to buy seeds and tools, to organize the collective marketing of the products, to construct buildings for common and individual use, and to improve the moral and the material conditions of the farmers. Each member had to pay an entrance fee and buy a share of at least 100 lire. In theory, the members elected a general assembly that named a president and manager.[5] According to fascist ideologies, they had to be self-supporting, without financial help from the state or outside banks. But government subsidies were possible, especially for wine producing cooperatives.[6]

In reality, the fascist cooperative policy was hardly liberal and autonomous. When Mussolini came to power, he dissolved preexisting autonomous cooperatives (which had been predominantly Socialist and Christian) and aligned them with fascist forms of collective agriculture. At the meeting of the Grand Council in 1925, Mussolini laid down the two main principles of the fascist cooperative movement: the unity of the movement and the supremacy of the state to coordinate it. To put it plainly, unity meant political loyalty to fascism and the supremacy of the state implied the total control by fascist bureaucrats.[7] In 1931, Mussolini created the Ente Nazionale Fascista Della Cooperazione, a state agency that controlled and coordinated all cooperative activity according to the fascist "planned economy."[8] This institution could dissolve cooperatives at any time or replace the elected presidents with fascist loyalists.[9] Agricultural cooperatives turned into tools to spread the fascist doctrine among the rural population.[10] Moreover, it dictated the "joint effort to reclaim new land," guided by an ideology of small-scale settler colonization both within Italy and beyond.[11]

Why did Freppel Cotta, who studied cooperatives worldwide in a comparative way, and who cherished the liberal British and Scandinavian versions, highlight the fascist cooperative scheme? In his widely read publication on Italian cooperatives, he defended his praise of the fascist policy: "As we are treating of Co-operation and not of political systems, any praise or blame attached to the Fascist and any other regime will relate solely to the facts which form the subject of our study."[12] In his view, fascist cooperatives aligned with a general trend of state intervention in planned economies, such as the Soviet kolkhoz and the German "blood and soil" policy. More importantly, state

---

[5] Ibid., 32.
[6] Ibid., 10.
[7] Ibid., 7.
[8] Ibid., 136–137.
[9] Hobson, "Review of Freppel Cotta," 605–607.
[10] Cotta, *Agricultural Co-operation*, 129.
[11] For example, the reclamation of Ostia. See ibid., 39.
[12] Ibid., 7.

control also loomed large in colonial cooperativism. As early as 1912, British India had introduced a Registrar of Cooperative Societies who had all power to deny certain groups from forming cooperatives and could dissolve them at any time.[13]

In this regard, the fascist cooperative policy did not differ much from cooperative policies in the Republican and liberal empires. Like the Eurafrican ideologists of the Volta Congress, Cotta saw corporative and cooperative designs as an opportunity to link the economy of Europe with the colonial economies overseas. For him, transfers between the systems to improve the whole were highly important. That is why he promoted a "Co-operative World Commonwealth" that linked all initiatives around the world.[14] This Commonwealth seemed to speak to liberal, socialist, fascist, and colonialist initiatives alike.

In the 1930s, agricultural cooperatives were indeed on everyone's lips. Colonizers evoked cooperatives to stabilize colonial rule. Frederick Lugard, the main promoter of indirect rule and an active ICI member made cooperatives a pillar of colonial governmentality. In the late 1920s, he redefined his colonial doctrine of indirect rule as cooperative rule: "The fundamental principle of the [cooperative] system is identical with that of 'Indirect Rule' – which could better be named Co-operative Rule – the essential purpose of both being to teach personal responsibility and initiative. Nowhere more than in Africa can the principle of deliberate and organized co-operation towards a definite and recognized objective be of greater value."[15] Lugard's plan to induce personal responsibility and initiative among the colonized became the main purpose of cooperative governmentality, which also guided indigenous experts. In 1929, the Indian economist Sumant Khanderao Muranjan of the All-India Co-operative Committee explained how cooperatives would substitute castes and "bring fresh strength and hope to the small producer without impairing in any way his initiative and ... to rid society of the overgrowth of middlemen which has thrust itself between the producer and the consumer."[16] Many regarded cooperatives a means to prepare peasants for the colonial economy and equally leave peasant poverty and indebtedness behind.[17] In sum, cooperatives served to make the average peasant participate in the colonial economy.

In the 1930s, ICI members wrote official guidelines for administrators for how to implement cooperatives in collaboration with the indigenous population. The 1,837-pages-strong African Survey edited by ICI member Malcolm

---

[13] Rhodes, *Empire and Co-operation*, 129.
[14] Cotta, *Agricultural Co-operation*, 139.
[15] Strickland, *Co-operation for Africa*, vi–vii; Rhodes, *Empire and Co-operation*, 207–208.
[16] Muranjan, "Prolegomena," in Kaji, *Co-operation in India*, 1.
[17] For India, see Ali, *A Local History of Global Capital*, 94–107.

Hailey for the Royal Institute of International Affairs concluded that "the success of the movement in Asia and elsewhere has naturally suggested that in Africa also co-operation might solve some of the problems created by the impact of new forces on native life."[18] ICI member Raymond Leslie Buell, who compiled an equally comprehensive survey of 1,011 pages for the Harvard Bureau of International Research, particularly adored the contribution of the French cooperative Indigenous Provident Societies to the "improvement of native life" in West Africa.[19] Apart from being ICI members, these authors shared the opinion that only native self-government and self-production would strengthen the colonial economy and bring about sustainable development. Some of them even promised that cooperatives would pave the way to independence. Writing a guidebook of 1,293 pages for the Dutch colonial administration, ICI member Arnold De Kat Angelino saw cooperatives at the "core" of a "rejuvenating" economic development that would lead to autonomy and ultimately independence.[20]

Anti-colonial nationalists indeed saw in cooperatives a basis for the emancipation of the masses. As early as 1920, the National Congress of British West Africa had created the West African Co-operative Association. Its vice president, Casely Hayford, proudly announced that "cooperation" had become "the greatest word of the century." Cooperatives loomed large in a broader Pan-African movement of self-improvement and self-government and cooperation was not only a way to economic autonomy, but also to political empowerment.[21] Muranjan's colleague in India, Hiralal Lallubahi Kaji, had calculated that, by 1929, around 10 percent of the Indian rural population was enrolled in cooperatives. He concluded that "none can deny that the Co-operative Movement, having thus a larger membership than any other single movement, is the most important national movement in India to-day and will increase in importance in the future."[22] According to Cotta, this nationalist dimension was inherent to the Rochdale principles, which stipulated that "co-operation is above class and party."[23] On the flip side, the colonial and the fascist states abused this principle to ban any kind of opposition and multi-party systems. Both evoked the "liberal" Rochdale principle to admit only loyal cooperatives and dissolve the rest.[24]

---

[18] Hailey, *African Survey*, 1466.
[19] Buell, *The Native Problem*, 351.
[20] Kat Angelino, *Colonial Policy*, vol. 1, 378 and 452; and Strickland, *Co-operation for Africa*, 38–39.
[21] *Gold Coast Leader* (July 24–31, 1920), 5–6. See also Hopkins, "Economic Aspects," 135–136.
[22] Kaji, *Co-operation in India*, 12.
[23] Cotta, *Agricultural Co-operation*, 139.
[24] Ibid., 129.

Which role did cooperatives play in the history of colonialism between the 1920s and the 1950s? I argue in this chapter that self-styled progressive colonizers promoted corporatist and cooperative schemes as the most liberal and participative way to development. They tended to make use of precolonial indigenous cooperative schemes such as the *fokon'olona* in Madagascar to show how much they respected authentic institutions. In theory, cooperatives allowed the indigenous populations to realize self-government, higher income, a self-supportive welfare system, and democratic representation. However, propagating the "soft power" of cooperatives concealed the coercive force behind them. Looking at concrete cases unveils that even indigenous cooperatives such as the *fokon'olona* became an instrument of oppression and coercion. Unlike Rita Rhodes' seminal study, which maintained that British colonizers in India used the cooperatives to "transfer Western enlightenment and British liberalism to India," I argue that they used them to impose Western rule.[25] Toward the end of colonial rule, colonizers used cooperatives to perpetuate a governmental system of oppression and self-repression. Even after independence, international organizations and the elites of the independent nation-states used them to maintain a system of (post)colonial governmentality.

8.1 The Decline of Settler Cooperatives

In the overseas colonies of the nineteenth century, cooperative thought had been a constitutive element of white settler societies who understood themselves as self-reliant developers of unexplored rural territories who relied on mutual help rather than government backing. They intended to transfer autonomous cooperative schemes, which Raiffeisen, Schultze-Delitzsch, and the Rochdale Society had developed in mid-nineteenth century Europe, to Africa. For this reason, European-style cooperatives emerged earliest in settler colonies such as South Africa, Southern Rhodesia, and Kenya. Those settler societies considered themselves an inherently cooperative society. The spokesman of British settlers in Kenya, Major Legett, proclaimed in 1906: "The cultivation of the co-operative spirit, the interchange of ideas, advice, etc, could not be too strongly insisted upon as tending to the mutual good of all."[26] Cooperatives were a means for white farmers to secure a stable prize for their produce. Maize farmers in South Africa, for example, formed an important cooperative production and marketing society and mounted the pressure on those who were not members of cooperatives to hold back their high quality maize to keep the prize high. The South African Maize Breeders',

---

[25] Rhodes, *Empire and Co-operation*, 127.
[26] *Times of East Africa* (July 7, 1906), 3.

Growers', and Judges' Association warned that "it is essential that the farmer should receive a fair prize for his product .... All maize growers still having stocks of maize, either white or yellow, provided they are good, should hold on as long as possible. Really good grain must be getting scarce."[27]

Unlike the way settler narratives portrayed it, they hardly launched a cooperative movement from below but relied on a cooperative policy from above. It was the colonial governments who triggered the settler cooperative movement by establishing rural credit banks. The Union of South Africa took the lead with a Land Bank in 1912, followed by a Registrar of Co-operative Societies and an inspection team that secured good administration and the solvency of the borrowers. Southern Rhodesia started registering cooperatives in 1909 and set up a Land Bank in 1924. Kenya centralized the granting of credit to cooperatives by a new Land Bank in 1931. While settler cooperatives had existed before these governmentalist initiatives, the take-off came in the interwar period. The Kenya Farmers Association, for example, established a wheat pool and a maize pool and tried to monopolize the marketing of these products. Overall, settler colonies used these cooperatives for the benefit of the white farmers.[28]

ICI members indirectly contributed to the settler cooperative movement. Karl von der Heydt, who used the ICI to promote his monetarization projects of the colonies, was the head of credit banks in Tanga and Dar-es-Salam in German East Africa. Reserved predominantly for European planters and their associations, these banks had three million marks in capital. Before World War I, similar institutions emerged in German South West Africa. In 1911, the ICI recommended them as a model for other colonies and encouraged the establishment of cooperative credit institutions that might serve for creating a middle class in the colonies.[29]

Much to the taste of the ICI, settlers shared their experience on a transcolonial level and tried to spread successful models of cooperation. E. W. Evans, for example, the director of the Farmers' Co-operative Meat Industries and of the Agricultural Union in Australia and New Zealand traveled the whole of Africa to talk about the cooperative experience on the other side of the globe. In addition to British settlers, he also informed Portuguese settlers in Mozambique about the latest developments in Australia, New Zealand, and Canada, the success of creameries in Natal, and the prospects for a federation of cooperatives in Southern Africa. He ended up proposing a Federation of Producers of the Empire, and apparently the Portuguese settlers hoped to get access to that supra-cooperative to sell their produce overseas.[30]

---

[27] *Rhodesia Herald* (December 16, 1921), 4.
[28] Hailey, *African Survey*, 1469.
[29] ICI, *L'Organisation du Crédit*, 39–40.
[30] "Federação da Associação Cooperativa dos Farmeiros da União," *O Africano* 731 (April 19, 1919).

When the economic crisis and low commodity prices hit the European exporters in the 1930s, colonial administrations started to rethink their policy. Apart from the sales crisis among European exporters, Africans who worked on white farms and plantations, such as in Kenya and Rhodesia, could not pay their taxes anymore. The crisis entailed significant losses for the budget of the colonial state and the administration slowly turned away from settlers to highlight the benefits of African farming for the cash crop economy. One expression of this shift was the will to use cooperative institutions to control the marketing of African products, such as in Kenya, where the governor introduced the Marketing of Native Crops Ordinance in 1935.[31]

8.2 The Shift to "Indigenous" Cooperative Schemes and the Birth of Compulsory Provident Societies

The ICI had promoted cooperative schemes for the indigenous population long before World War I, because they seemed to be self-organized cells of economic development and self-financed welfare associations. In 1911, the Dutch ICI member Jacques H. Abendanon made a plea to introduce cooperative credit institutions for the small indigenous "industry and commerce" that did not have access to loans provided by European banks. The way to raise capital for these organizations was nebulous but resembled a sort of crowd funding: "This organization has to rely on the principles of mutuality, of cooperation and of self-help, with the financial and moral support of the state." Cooperative credit unions should operate on a local and regional level, while Abendanon's schemes of mutuality should extend to the entire colonial economy: "Apart from the credit associations we need cooperatives for the purchase of primary materials and tools for the joint production and marketing." Abendanon appealed to the colonial state to provide training and education for the use of machines and to help the indigenous producers to get access to markets.[32] More than that, British ICI member Claude Francis Strickland added later that cooperatives were a "soft" way to develop the colonies and civilize their inhabitants: "I want to use Cooperation and to some extent it is already being used as a means of educating people for self-government and modern life in every way, not only in agriculture and small crafts, but also in their private lives, in health and personal life."[33] The ICI's cooperative schemes went significantly beyond the original purpose of colonial cooperatives to fight famine and make indigenous peasants more independent from private moneylenders and brokers.[34]

---

[31] Anderson and Throup, "Africans and Agricultural Production," 329.
[32] ICI, L'Organisation du Crédit, 138–139.
[33] Strickland, "The Cooperative Movement in the East," 815.
[34] For an overview, see Mann and Guyer, "Imposing a Guide on the Indigène," 124–151.

Colonial cooperatives, as ICI members imagined them, differed from the European cooperative movement of the nineteenth century in their degree of voluntary participation. ICI experts officially respected the standards set by the International Cooperative Alliance (1895), claiming that membership in cooperatives was voluntary by definition.[35] Yet they hoped that tribal, religious, and small-town solidarity in the colonies would be a cohesive, if not coercive, factor to make the indigenous population participate in cooperative schemes. According to them, tribal and religious solidarity created an atmosphere of mutual obligation. A sense of mutual obligation was necessary for cooperatives to be successful in lending money, tools, and expertise to its members. As we will see, this idea led to the acceptance of compulsory membership under colonial rule.

As ICI members saw it, cooperatives thrived predominantly in Muslim and animist societies with a high degree of mutual obligation. While Islam in urban North Africa provided the basis for corporative solidarity, it seemed to be equally important for the rural and agricultural cooperatives in both North and sub-Saharan Africa. The so-called Provident Societies (Sociétés de Prévoyance) that France had introduced in Algeria seemed to prove that point. By 1889, there were already 68 Provident Societies with 159,000 members.[36] In Tunisia, the French successfully introduced Provident Societies to monitor local cooperatives such as the weavers of Djerid, the Horticultural Cooperative Association of Gabès, and the Gardeners of Soliman.[37] In Morocco, cooperatives became equally successful, amounting to 52 Provident Societies with 835,000 members by 1935. In Indochina, however, the attempt to introduce Provident Societies in 1907 failed.[38] International colonial experts explained the varying success with the natural inclination of tribal communities who built on religious solidarity to form mutual aid societies. They claimed that "Islam contributed with its collectivist glue" to establish an economic cooperative tradition.[39] In the 1920s, the ILO took up these ideas of "Muslim solidarity," suggesting that it led to a "certain social stability."[40] ICI member Henri Labouret particularly emphasized the cooperative character of Muslim brotherhoods and other "liturgical communities" that had a common lineage and morale, as well as a shared social, legal, and economic system. Going beyond Muslim solidarity, the French theorist of Provident Societies Marcel Boyer added animist societies to the

---

[35] Rhodes, *Empire and Co-operation*, 28, 199–200.
[36] Boyer, *Les Sociétés de Prévoyance*, 21.
[37] Ibid., 23.
[38] Ibid., 11.
[39] Ibid., 132.
[40] ILO Archives, N206/1/01/8 Rapport de Mission à Paris, October 1931.

intrinsically cooperativist groups. Secret societies in West Africa, for example, were a "manifestation of mutuality" for him.[41]

Around 1900, ICI member Louis Milliot proclaimed the cooperative nature of Islamic law, although the cooperative schemes he advanced to make his point resembled sharecropping and even serfdom and were moreover highly controversial among Islamic jurists. Milliot popularized the *muzāra'a*, which was a contract in Islamic law that established a society of joint sowing and cultivation. Indeed, Islamic jurists such as Ibn Salamoun and Ahmad ad-Dardir had called the *muzāra'a* the "society for sowing" and "the society for labor."[42] Its legal origins could be found in the Sunna: Shortly after the conquest of Medina, Muhammad had allegedly concluded a *muzāra'a* contract with a group of Jews, who then sowed and cultivated the Muslim oasis of Khaïbar, for which they received half of the harvest. Despite this episode in the holy Sunna, the representative of another legal school, Abou Hanifa, claimed that the importance of the *muzāra'a* was highly exaggerated. In his eyes, it was not a contract at all but a "favor" the Jews did to Muhammad. More importantly, any *muzāra'a* should be based on a voluntary contract between equals who shared both risks and profits, for example, by pooling seeds and labor and receiving equal shares of the harvest. However, the most frequent version of the *muzāra'a* in North Africa of the nineteenth century were the so-called *khammes*: an oral "contract" between landlord and agricultural laborers, stipulating that the laborers cultivated land and received only one-fifth of the harvest.[43] The *khammes* resembled a classic scheme of sharecropping and often turned into outright serfdom. Milliot insisted that the modern version of the *muzāra'a* was a form of cooperation among equals and the proof that the "the idea of mutual aid shapes the Muslim religion."[44] In the 1930s, French economists incited the ILO to use the *khammes* for the economic development of Muslim colonies. The ILO also widely ignored their coercive character.[45]

Generally, the introduction of Provident Societies in Algeria was indeed more violent than the French made believe. Most typically, they destroyed local cooperative institutions before rebuilding them under the name of Provident Societies. In the mid-nineteenth century, the French army in Algeria had destroyed granaries and silos, claiming that they supplied the rebels who resisted French penetration. Only when the French had conquered and controlled a territory did they revive the silos, for the first time in 1864 in the Milianah subdivision.[46] But it was not until 1894 that an organic law in

---

[41] Boyer, *Les Sociétés de Prévoyance*, 31 and 33.
[42] Milliot, *L'Association Agricole*, 19.
[43] Ibid., 19–20.
[44] Ibid., 83 and 66.
[45] ILO Archives, N206/1/01/8, Report de Mission à Paris, 1931, 3.
[46] Boyer, *Les Sociétés de Prévoyance*, 18.

Algeria imposed a comprehensive network of Provident Societies that theoretically covered each commune, tribe, and *douar* (tent village). In 1908, there were 190 societies with around 520,000 members and a capital of 18,000,000 francs.[47] This amount sounded impressive, but it also placed an additional financial burden on the farmers. Apart from paying membership fees, each member had to pay two to four francs for each plow possessed and two cents for each sheep raised. The Provident Societies' capital was insufficient to provide for droughts. When a famine hit North Africa in 1909, Provident Societies hardly lived up to expectations of providing the population with food.[48]

As a response to this disaster, membership became compulsory in 1909. Consequently, the autonomy of the Provident Societies was nominal at best. They were theoretically self-organized but actually state-controlled. The members elected an administrative council, but the French administration appointed its president and its treasurer. In theory, the council watched over the building up of reserves and decided whether members in need received loans or not. In practice, the French administrators took these decisions.[49] The control became even tighter when the French extended the Provident Societies to sub-Saharan Africa.[50]

In 1910, the ICI member Ernest Roume, who had become governor of French West Africa (AOF) in 1902, introduced Provident Societies to Senegal. He had studied indigenous mutual aid societies among the Bambara and in Guinea, learned about colonial finances in the ICI, and provisionally copied the new Provident Societies' legislation from Algeria.[51] His original purpose was to constitute seed storages against famines and teach the indigenous population "providence." This plan was highly cynical, given that West Africans had long operated their own grain reserves. Among the Serer in precolonial Senegal, for example, it was common to set aside seventy to eighty kilos of seeds per family to provide for difficult times. In Lower Casamance (Senegal), individuals stored rice to survive until the next harvest. Also in the Sahel zone, their proximity to the desert had taught the inhabitants to build up reserves. The Serer even organized the joint marketing of their crops, a strategy that the French destroyed and only reintroduced in the early 1930s. What is more, the colonized population had to finance their own cooperative life. In AOF, both members and observers complained that the membership fees were an "additional tax." From 1915 onwards, the AOF collected

---

[47] Ibid., 21.
[48] Milliot, *L'Association Agricole*, 266.
[49] Ibid., 264 and 274.
[50] Boyer, *Les Sociétés de Prévoyance*, 9.
[51] Ibid., 41–42.

membership fees together with the general taxes. The governor, instead, refused to fund the Provident Societies on a regular basis.[52]

Another colonial internationalist, Joost van Voellenhoven, took over from Roume during World War I and established a more comprehensive network of Provident Societies that slowly extended to the whole of French West Africa. But it was only in the 1930s that Provident Societies reached a critical mass to become a factor in the colonial economy. Across French West Africa, there were several hundred Provident Societies with around five million members. In 1934, they had an overall capital of thirty-seven million francs. This led the French to conclude that "we indeed observe the birth of an 'African cooperatism.'"[53] However, many of those Provident Societies existed only on paper.

As a rule, the Provident Societies created after the cooperative turn of the 1930s were much more diverse than the earlier versions: their tasks included distribution of seeds, development of cash crop production in the colonies near the coast, the improvement of plants, and the introduction of new agro-industrial methods. Gradually, they developed into mutual aid societies for credit, joint production, and common marketing. Concurrently, the funding of the societies became more professional. The governor introduced agricultural banks, and the Mutual Agricultural Credit Banks completely took over the credit business from Provident Societies in 1933. In so doing, the French broke with the idea of cooperative self-sufficiency. Muslims did not pay an interest rate, as did all the others, but an administrative fee that equaled the interest. Also new in 1933 was that Provident Societies could theoretically insure their members against cattle and plant diseases as well as natural disasters.[54] It was not before 1933 that Provident Societies officially turned into marketing boards and thus became fully-fledged cooperatives as the French government imagined them.[55] Joint marketing worked to the benefit of both farmers and the French colonial state. Arranged marketing policies, such as holding back groundnuts in Senegal, helped to determine the price for the produce on the world market. As Senegal provided 10 percent of the world's groundnut production, they could at least impose the selling price in West Africa by withholding their harvest or by flooding the market.[56]

Showing tendencies toward a corporatist organization of its empire, the French administration was able to use those Provident Societies to control production and to implement the long-term planning of the economic development of the colony.[57] In terms of development, the French used the

---

[52] Ibid., 37, 54, and 103.
[53] Ibid., 41–42, 130, and 133.
[54] Ibid., 71–72, and 85.
[55] Ibid., 9.
[56] Ibid., 89.
[57] FR ANOM 93COL17 on the 1929 loan, Boyer, *Les Sociétés de Prévoyance*, 88.

cooperative storage of various seeds from a certain region to single out the best seeds and improve them in the local environment that suited them best. The "perfecting of the local variants" marked the beginning of systematic and localized crop improvement within the cooperatives that added to the improvement efforts in research stations such as Bambey in Senegal for groundnuts.[58] By "localizing" crop improvement, it solved the long-standing problem of incompatibility of scientifically improved plants with varying local conditions. This policy, however, led to conflicts with the local population. For fear of Africans delivering their spoiled produce only to the granaries, the French administration forced them to deliver their best. Although the law had little effect, it provoked the opposition of entrepreneurs such as the Serer in Senegal, who were reluctant to send their best seeds to the granaries of the Provident Societies because they wanted to use them for their own sophisticated systems of crop improvement and storage.[59]

Colonial experts celebrated the Provident Societies as inherently "indigenous" but in fact used them to establish a coercive economy. As we have seen, membership was mostly compulsory and involved the payment of a significant membership fee. The French justified this compulsory fee by claiming that it was an indigenous tradition. In Labé in the Fouta-Djalon (Guinea), for example, administrators traced the "success" of their Provident Societies back to the preexisting Farilha system, in which the religious leader traditionally received 10 percent of the farmers' harvest. The French district officers used Muslim leaders to do the same for the Provident Societies. Yet the farmers heavily disliked the system of those "indigenized" Provident Societies, as they had already done in times of the Farilha. What is more, those Provident Societies had the right to expropriate land and real estate and were used to justify obligatory labor for "public works." The only relief for the farmers was that the Provident Societies hardly worked in the way they should: only twenty out of ninety-five Provident Societies in the region were active.[60]

8.3 Franco-Belgian Exmosis and Christian Paternalism in the Congo

For a short period before World War I, the French Providence System inspired Belgian ICI members to introduce their own mutual credit societies in the Congo.[61] They studied the providence system in French West Africa before launching their own program. In 1912, ten Belgian ICI members joined forces

---

[58] Ibid., 97–98.
[59] Ibid., 39.
[60] Ibid., 42 and 63–64.
[61] AGRB Louwers Papers 243 (270): Assistance Sociale au Congo, Oeuvre de M. Tibbaut 1913-1914: "Les Accidents du Travail au Congo," *Journal du Congo* (1914); Boyer, *Les Sociétés de Prévoyance*, 11.

with the famous Solvay Institute in Brussels, which specialized in social engineering, to establish the Society of Social Assistance in the Congo. The aim of this Society was to "change the mentality of the natives" toward providence in general and saving money in particular.[62] They calculated that 52,000 Congolese indeed received a salary, be it as workers for Belgian railway and mining companies or as members of the colonial army.[63] This optimistic estimate led Belgian ICI members to work toward a Congo-wide network of mutual saving banks. Fascinated with the idea of teaching the Congolese providence, the Social Assistance intended to treat salaried workers like soldiers of the Congolese colonial army by forcing them to save money. Congolese soldiers in the Force Publique paid parts of their salaries into a "reserve of salaries." Only when they officially finished their service did they receive the amount they had been forced to save over the years. What was a means to prevent soldiers from deserting the army should also be applied to regular workers.[64] To verify the identity of the depositors, the Social Assistance used dactyloscopy. It tried to register the fingerprints of all Congolese to use them for identification as depositors, including in the illiterate countryside. The United States served as a model for the "digital imprint" for general identification, because it had successfully introduced such a system in the Philippines.[65] The immediate result of this initiative was rather meager. By 1914, there were five indigenous savings banks in Congo with only 133,000 Belgian Francs deposited.[66] Like in French West Africa, these banks were state-run rather than cooperatively organized.

In the 1920s, Belgian and French experts jointly developed new ideas of how to organize a cooperative society in Africa. The French district officer and economic advisor of the AOF's governor, Robert Delavignette, corresponded frequently with the Belgian founder of the Social Assistance, Octave Louwers. Both were prominent ICI members and as such met almost annually. To no small degree, Delavignette shaped the economic policy of the AOF, as he advised the governor Jules Brévié. Delavignette also became Brévié's man in the ICI, which allowed the governor to keep himself informed about international developments. For example, Louwers sent Belgian publications on economy and finances in the Congo to Delavignette, who wrapped them up and forwarded them to Brévié.[67]

---

[62] AGRB, Louwers Papers 243 (270): Draft for survey sent to administrators, missionaries, merchants, and planters.
[63] Ibid., Étude sur la creation de l'Epargne au Congo Belge, November 2, 1913.
[64] Ibid.
[65] Ibid., Projet: Base d'une institution d'épargne à développer dans la colonie.
[66] AGRB, Louwers Papers 244 (271): Assistance Sociale au Congo 1914: Banque du Congo Belge to Œuvre d'Assistance Sociale au Congo, May 19, 1914.
[67] AGRB, Louwers Papers, Correspondance Delavignette 1933–1957 158 (185): Delavignette to Louwers, March 3, 1933.

Louwers and Delavignette shared a romantic vision of African peasantry as the basis of a stable colonial economy.[68] They discovered their common admiration for Belgian ethnologist Lucien Lévy-Bruhl, who claimed that "primitive people" were not inferior but only worked from a different mindset. Instead of using rationality and logics, Lévy-Bruhl argued, their existence was shaped by their belief in a mythical solidarity between individuals, the initiated kin-group, the animist environment, and the ancestors in the otherworld. This unconditional solidarity, which Lévy-Bruhl also called "mystical participation," seemed to provide the basis for a mutualist and cooperative society. Based on this assumption, the French district officer Delavignette and the Belgian jurist Louwers discussed how to implement the cooperative policy and identified similarities between the agrarian customs in the AOF and Belgian Congo.[69]

Based on this correspondence, the governor of AOF, Jules Brévié, concluded that cooperatives were the right way to win back the hearts of the West Africans. After World War I, he observed, the "superstitious belief in European superiority" among "our administrees" was about to fade and conflicts were likely to occur. Through Provident Societies, however, he assumed "the masses will be with us."[70] He facilitated the creation of the state-controlled Provident Societies but also looked to British West Africa, where a cooperative movement emerged independently of the state.[71] Combining approaches of direct and indirect rule, he saw the Provident Societies as an autonomous way of "real indigenous self-administration" and at the same time as an instrument to control the population.[72]

While Delavignette and Louwers agreed on the general "indigenist" approach to African cooperativism, the actual policy of the Belgians in the Congo was highly paternalistic and came from Christian milieus. Their Christian paternalism stands for the strong influence of Christian social reformers in European colonial policy of the 1920s. The Belgian Social Assistance, as it became known in the 1920s, intended to use thrift societies to transform Congolese habits according to Christian social policy. They promoted the "cooperative" unit of the family as the basis of society and the most common entity of mutualism. Again, saving money should help the Congolese men to pay the bride price, get married, and have numerous children. At the same time, the ideal of saving money would lead Congolese men to renounce polygamy. Moreover, they saw providence as a way to

---

[68] On Delavignette, see Dimier, Le gouvernement, 92–93.
[69] AGRB, Louwers Papers 158 (185): Correspondance Delavignette: Letter Delavignette to Louwers, December 1, 1932
[70] Gouvernement Général, Circulaires de M. le Gouverneur, 20–23.
[71] Boyer, Les Sociétés de Prévoyance, 11.
[72] Gouvernement Général, Circulaires de M. le Gouverneur, 54.

abolish the alleged custom of destroying the property of a dead person on the occasion of his or her funeral. Saved capital would also help to acquire real estate, build brick houses, and equip households with hygienic items that lived up to modern sanitation standards and enabled children to grow up safely with all modern conveniences such as lighting, furniture, and different clothes for every day of the week. It would help the Congolese to start a business or get seeds and machines for agriculture. They subsumed all these points under social and economic "development" of the Congolese and labeled it a "humanitarian" initiative.[73]

The Belgians, however, failed to fund this initiative. In 1925, four-fifths of metropolitan loans in the budget for the Congo was for maintaining order, peace, security, and for the administration. "Consequently," a report concluded, "there is not much left to spend on the social and economic organization .... The insufficiency of credits for financing the social policy is particularly striking."[74] What the Belgians spent on improving the "social order" went to hygiene, education, missionary activity, and programs to increase birthrates.[75] As a result, in the late 1920s, the Belgian Social Assistance degenerated into a missionary effort to teach Congolese women how to become good housewives and stop spending the money their husbands supposedly earned. It was "her role to make the best out of the few Francs that her husband earned, for the benefit of the whole family." For that purpose, the Social Assistance opened no more than a handful of saving banks and consumer cooperatives called "Economat" in the major Congolese cities.[76]

8.4 The Search for Authentic Cooperatives and the Hypocrisy of British Indirect Rule

Although ICI members introduced Provident Societies to French and Belgian Africa, other ICI members were less enthusiastic about them. Upholding appearances of their liberalism, the British ICI members criticized the paternalistic cooperatives in France and Belgium for their lack of liberality and self-organization.[77] They openly denied their cooperative character on the grounds that membership was compulsory. Given the strict control by the colonial state, many ICI were reluctant to promote Provident Societies as a cooperative

---

[73] AGRB, Louwers Papers 249 (170): Assistance Sociale au Congo, Œuvre de M. Tibbaut 1913-1914, Draft Survey

[74] Jonghe, *La Politique Financière*, 16.

[75] Gardner, "Fiscal Policies,"145.

[76] AGRB, Louwers Papers 247 (274): Assistance Sociale au Congo 1940: Rapport sur l'Activité de l'Assistance Sociale à Coquilhatville 1939, 4-5. On Congolese reactions, see Hunt, *A Nervous State*, 101-130.

[77] On the British approach, see Windel, "Cooperatives and the Technocrats."

ideal. They seemed to be a means of direct rather than indirect rule, which was the ICI's doctrine. Upholding its image of endorsing a soft colonial governmentality, the ICI demanded more authentic indigenous cooperative schemes that operated independently of the government.

The British ICI member Strickland became the main promoter of these liberal and authentic schemes. International media called him the undisputed "apostle of cooperation in Africa." After being registrar of cooperative societies in the Punjab in British India, he had indeed introduced cooperative policies to Tanganyika, Zanzibar, Nigeria, and even Palestine. Colonial administrations around the world sought his expertise, also because he seemed to have "really entered the minds of the natives," as the official Gazette of French West Africa remarked.[78] Admiration for his expertise extended from the ICI members to the highest colonial administrators such as the French governor of French West Africa, Jules Brévié.[79] Strickland made Brévié rethink French cooperative schemes. The French government took the sophisticated cooperative legislation in British East Africa and in India as a model and called it a "new power for colonization."[80]

Strickland used the ICI to portray himself as the most important expert of independent and self-organized cooperatives.[81] In the company of colonial internationalists, he tended to emphasize that the colonial state had to keep completely aloof from giving loans to the population or aiding it in cooperation-building because farmers would be insouciant in paying it back if it was not their own money. No state-funded central banks and district banks, he argued, could replace the educational character of mutual credit societies. While his approach was neoliberal, it was not individualistic, as individualism generally contradicted cooperative schemes. Hence, curiously, he also advocated the family as the smallest unit of a cooperative society. In so doing, he came closer to the Belgian model than he intended to.[82] He would also abandon his liberal ideal as an advisor to the British colonial administration in India, Kenya, and Zanzibar.[83]

Kenyan farmers provided the most famous example for an independent cooperative scheme as Strickland imagined it. The most famous was the Kilimanjaro Natives' Planter Association (KNPA), an entirely African cooperative formed by the Chagga coffee growers in the Kilimanjaro region

---

[78] Gouvernement général, *Bulletin Hebdomadaire*, 16–19.
[79] AGRB, Louwers Papers 158 (185): Correspondance Delavignette: Delavignette to Louwers December 1, 1932; Boyer, *Les Sociétés de Prévoyance*, 107.
[80] Gouvernement général, *Bulletin Hebdomadaire*, 16–19.
[81] Rhodes, *Empire and Co-operation* focuses mainly on white cooperatives. India plays a minor role, Africa is absent.
[82] Strickland, *Co-operation for Africa*, 427–428.
[83] On his role in India, see Rhodes, *Empire and Co-operation*, 183.

in the mid-1920s.⁸⁴ By 1925, there were 4,500 farmers who cultivated about 1,500 acres and produced 80 tons of Arabica coffee. As European planters spread rumors about their plantations being a source of pests and diseases, the Chagga felt the need to organize. The interpreter and clerk Joseph Merinyo set up the KNPA in 1925. The managing committee, together with its staff and clerks, was responsible for the marketing of the produce, which included regular market reports about prices and their development. The Cooperative provided common facilities for the purchase of seeds and tools as well as organizing transport, storage, and the fight against pests and diseases. Most importantly, the cooperative gave loans to its members and encouraged "the spirit and practice of thrift, mutual help and self-help." In every society, a professional secretary took care of the bookkeeping and money transactions. Habitually, each village elected its own representative to the committee, which was named the all-African managing committee. The funds derived from a one cent of a shilling per pound weight of parchment for the coffee that was sold. By 1929, it had 27,000 members, but the collapse of coffee prices brought it into financial difficulties.⁸⁵ Nevertheless, the KNPA stood on its own feet and did not receive outside help or funding, with the colonial government temporarily even withdrawing administrative support.

In the late 1920s, however, Strickland became an advisor to the Kenyan government and tried to seize control of the KNPA. He used the KNPA's financial weakness to bring the KNPA in line with British coffee legislation and to influence its price policy.⁸⁶ Staging an intrigue, the colonial government coaxed the KNPA's vice chairman to stand up against the founding father and first president of the cooperative, Joseph Merinyo. Adding insult to injury, it accused Merinyo's supporters of having stolen £4,500 from the association funds. The leaders were imprisoned and substituted. The government in Nairobi remodeled the cooperative according to its own rules and imposed a European manager. In 1932, all cooperatives got officially registered under the new Co-operative Societies Ordinance. They were decentralized and it became mandatory for all Chagga to sell their coffee through the new state-controlled cooperative.⁸⁷ Strickland's alleged liberalism was a farce.

Strickland delivered the ultimate proof of his hypocrisy during his attempt to transform Zanzibar's clove industry into a state-controlled cooperative economy. In 1931, he "was invited by the Zanzibar Government, through the Colonial Office, to visit the Protectorate and advise on the reorganization

---

⁸⁴ It has been analyzed on various occasions. See Iliffe, *A Modern History* 274–280; Erdmann, *Jenseits des Mythos*; Eckert, *Herrschen und Verwalten*, 56–61.
⁸⁵ "A short account of the Kilimanjaro Native Co-operative Union Ltd.," *The East African Agricutlural Journal* 12, no. 1 (1946), 45–48; quote: 46.
⁸⁶ Rogers, "The Kilimanjaro Native Planters Association," 105.
⁸⁷ "A Short Account of the Kilimanjaro Native Co-operative," 47.

of the clove industry, particularly from the cooperative point of view."[88] Such a transformation was implausible, however, given that the inhomogeneous group of Arab plantation owners, Indian financiers, and Swahili labor migrants from the mainland who worked on the plantations would certainly not turn to a production based on mutual help and solidarity. As if to prove his amateurish approach, Strickland had to admit that he had little knowledge about clove production and its social organization: "An element of uncertainty has thus been introduced in my inquiries."[89] Yet his inclination to self-display was back as soon as he had to present the results of his survey. Disregarding his own ignorance, Strickland drafted a Cooperative Societies Decree, designed a Clove Grower's Association for Zanzibar, and laid down its bylaws in great detail.[90]

In his confidential report to the colonial governor, Strickland recommended to force the clove planters to adopt his rather strange plans, such as the "compulsory planting of areca-palms and other conspicuous trees at each corner of a plantation," to fix the boundaries of each compound.[91] Other recommendations sounded more cooperative but were no less problematic. The purpose was to "reduce the high rates paid in recent years for the picking of cloves and at the same time to ensure that uniform rates were paid."[92] By reducing the salaries, Arabs should then pay back their debts to the Indian financiers. As Strickland proposed: "The agricultural classes are indebted to non-agriculturalists and are unable, through lack of organization, of character, and of alternative sources of credit, to free themselves."[93] This plea for a cooperative liberation from debts was in reality a way to reduce the debts of Arab plantation owners through wage dumping. Knowing about the shallowness of his recommendations, Strickland insisted that his report remained confidential: "Premature disclosure will to some extent defeat their purpose."[94]

Strickland's scheming met with disapproval among quite successful African and Asian cooperative initiatives in the British Empire. In 1934, the Nigerian nationalist Louis Mbanefo publicly disapproved of Strickland's interventionist cooperativism that gave the colonial state full control over the societies. Mbanefo argued that only an alignment with tribal structures would lead to a sustained existence of the cooperative and its success.[95] In Nigeria and Gold Coast, native cooperatives were on the rise, along with an awareness that West

---

[88] Strickland, *Confidential Report 1931*, 2
[89] Ibid., 2
[90] Ibid., cover letter.
[91] Ibid., 4.
[92] *Zanzibar Protectorate Blue Book for the Year 1935* [Nairobi? 1936?], 181.
[93] Strickland, *Confidential Report 1931*, 11.
[94] Ibid., cover letter.
[95] Windel, "Mass Education," 100–101.

8.4 AUTHENTIC COOPERATIVES & HYPOCRISY

Africans can use them to control their own resources and economy. To do so, the highest organ of native representation in West Africa promoted cooperation on the biggest scale. When the National Congress of British West Africa met for the first time in 1920, the deputies were "strongly convinced that the time has come for the co-operation of peoples of the British West African Dependencies in promoting their economical development." They recommended "the formation of a Corporation, to be known as the British West African Co-operative Association ... to found Banks, promote shipping facilities, establish Co-operative Stores, and produce buying centers." The vice president of the National Congress, Casely Hayford, proudly announced that "cooperation" had become "the greatest word of the century." For the National Congress, cooperation was not only a way to economic autonomy but also to political empowerment.[96]

When the West African National Congress proclaimed the cooperative age in 1920, several farmers' associations had long existed among the cocoa farmers of Gold Coast and Nigeria. In 1925, the bustling West African businessman Winifried Tete-Ansa founded the famous West African Co-operative Producers Ltd. to give them a powerful and representative umbrella organization. It assembled most cocoa farmers' associations, important merchants, and selected politicians. The majority of traditional farmer's associations in Western Africa joined the West African Co-operative Producers Ltd., which ultimately controlled 60 percent of the West African cocoa production. To supply the farmers with capital, Tete-Ansa set up a bank that issued loans. Moreover, he established links with Afro-Americans in the United States, which he saw as the main market for West Africans products. Tete-Ansa argued that the farmers should be able to directly sell their produce to the United States, bypassing the European colonizers. Consequently, Tete-Ansa's cooperative scheme was truly Pan-African and was designed to bring about economic self-determination for the West Africans.[97]

A similar Pan-African cooperative project was launched by Davidson Don Tengo Jabavu in South Africa, in tandem with Afro-American attempts to improve the agricultural output of former slaves in the United States.[98] Before World War I, Jabavu had observed that the white famers in South Africa "have about fifty agricultural associations all united by a Congress, meeting annually. We, who are four times as numerous, have practically no such organization nor one so perfect in machinery." Thus, he got involved in starting a "new Native Farmers' Association" in 1918, "with such success that it has produced no small revival in agriculture amongst us and we still hope for great things

---

[96] *Gold Coast Leader* (July 24–31, 1920), 5–6; Hopkins, "Economic Aspects," 135–136.
[97] Ibid.
[98] *Umteteli wa Bantu* (Johannesburg, December 18, 1920), 2.

therefrom."[99] Jabavu became among the most eminent experts on cooperation and sought inspiration from the Tuskegee Institute in Alabama, where black educators tried to improve the lives and agricultural production of former slaves. To some extent, Jabavu was in line with the ICI's approach to use cooperatives for a slow transition to a capitalist mode of production. In the United States, he argued, "the slaves were all unleashed into liberty with a suddenness that has proved harmful both to the owners and the freed."[100] In 1919, he set up the Native Farmers' Association with the help of an "American Negro Farm demonstrator" from Tuskegee, who was a specialist in dry farming. Like in the United States, he used cooperative schemes to train and "educate" African farmers.[101]

Like most Europeans, the ICI members rarely mentioned Jabavu's and Tete-Ansa's Pan-African cooperative schemes, certainly because they were too independent and at the same time not "indigenous" enough. The West African Co-operative Producers Ltd., for example, was too nationalist and too capitalist for the ICI. On the one hand, its approach contradicted the ICI's ideal of small-scale cooperatives whose members knew each other personally. On the other hand, ICI members feared that indigenous mega-cooperatives were able to oust European companies and become an instrument of liberation from the colonizers. Although the West African Co-operative Producers Ltd. collapsed a few years after its foundation, it established a solidarity among West Africans that engendered more weighty cooperative projects in the future. This solidarity proved efficient during the famous cocoa hold-ups that Ghanaian farmers' associations organized collectively in the 1930s to enforce higher prices on European buyers such as the United African Company. The biggest cocoa hold up of 1937–1938 was "national" in the sense that most farmers held back their produce. It spoke to an economic nationalism that indeed could threaten colonial rule.[102]

8.5 Cooperatives and the End of the "Asian Model" in India and Indonesia

In its search for a more "authentic" indigenous cooperative model, the ICI turned to India, where cooperative schemes had a long history. The *nidhis*, for example, received international attention. These mutual loan associations had emerged in mid-nineteenth century Madras and were thus as old as the European Raiffeisen and Rochdale schemes. A French cooperativist observed that *nidhi* members met "annually to depose a little sum." The accumulated

---

[99] Jabavu, *The Black Problem*, 83.
[100] Ibid., 55.
[101] Ibid., 110.
[102] Austin, "Capitalists and Chiefs," 63–95.

capital enabled the *nidhis* to provide members with short-term and long-term loans. What was special about the *nidhis* was the security agreement, which stipulated that members received the whole amount of their deposits after seven years. This bylaw ensured that members who received loans in the first seven years of their membership paid them back, in order not to lose the total amount of their deposits after their seven years' membership.[103] In so doing, the *nidhis* avoided a collapse of the credit system, which happened frequently if borrowers did not repay their credit. In the early twentieth century, the *nidhi* spread to the United Provinces, the Punjab, and Bengal. In 1901, there were over 200 *nidhis* with some 36,000 members in India. However, Indian experts considered the *nidhis* a purely urban institution that was "confined to middle-class town-dwellers and had not reached the agriculturalists."[104]

ICI members celebrated the British colonial government taking up another Indian cooperative tradition, the so-called *takavi*-loans. The *takavi*-loan dated back to the Mughal period and helped victims of natural disasters with government loans that had a comparably low interest rate of 5 to 6 percent. *Takavi*-loans constantly increased in significance and amounted to two million pounds by 1903. By then, however, British cooperative lawyers had laid hands on them: only the state-controlled Cooperative Unions were allowed to receive such loans and could then forward them to smaller cooperatives.[105] Indeed, *takavi*-loans became inefficient in the British era, given that "they were only granted at the end of much official procedure and delay."[106]

According to some ICI members, the British were grievously mistaken when they neglected the *nidhis* and the *takavi*-loans to the benefit of a state-controlled and interventionist cooperative policy. In 1904, the British administration indeed introduced the Co-operative Credit Societies Act to create a network of officially registered and tightly controlled cooperatives. Nominally, any ten people in a village could register as a cooperative. The cooperatives were partly exempted from taxes to relieve them of multiple levies.[107] Yet central cooperative unions supervised them. By 1908, there were 15 of those unions that watched over 1,766 rural and 227 urban cooperatives with 184,889 members. A general registrar controlled their accounts. While a majority of them seem to have been self-supporting, many seized the opportunity to borrow from the state banks and thus increased their dependency on the administration.[108]

---

[103] Philip, "La Coopération aux Indes," 183.
[104] Qureshi, *The Future*, 4.
[105] ICI, *L'Organisation du Crédit*, 120–123.
[106] Qureshi, *The Future*, 5.
[107] Ibid., 6–7.
[108] ICI, *L'Organisation du Crédit*, 120–123.

For the Indians, cooperatives played an ambiguous role, especially because the British government used official cooperatives to impose obligatory labor and held their members collectively responsible for reimbursement of the loans. Bylaws forced the members to participate in joint work "for consolidation of holdings, for schemes of co-operative fencing, for lift irrigation projects and for similar programs." In some cooperatives, there was a "compulsory abjuration of intoxicating drinks or attendance at school of children of members of co-operative societies." Government officials declared that these measures were "enforced not out of doctrinaire considerations, but having regard to the social requirements."[109]

Most importantly, the bylaws made members collectively responsible for the amortization of loans originally given to individual members. The rural cooperatives, in particular, had an unlimited liability and were thus collectively responsible to pay back the money.[110] What was a way for the British to ensure the reimbursement of loans and security for the credit banks was also highly unfair for the members, especially because there were also fake cooperatives that fooled them out of their money.[111]

Despite its stabilizing intent, the system of unlimited liability was an important reason why the British cooperative system finally failed. The Indian cooperative system collapsed in 1929. While some observers related the collapse to the global economic crisis of 1929, colonial administrations said that the fault was almost exclusively with corrupt and irresponsible Indian management boards (*Panchayats*).[112] Their favoritism allegedly led to the common practice of granting loans to untrustworthy borrowers. The ICI had already warned in 1911 that borrowers rarely had to state the purpose for which they intended to use the loans. Many seemed to use the cooperative loans to pay off older debts, with a higher interest rate.[113] British authorities confirmed that cooperatives had failed in its original purpose to replace usurious moneylenders.[114] The MacLagan Committee, which examined the decline of the Indian cooperatives during World War I, denounced the use of loans for speculative purposes, the absence of a background check for borrowers, as well as the fact that capital came from external banks and not from the members themselves, which would have guaranteed a more responsible use of the funds.[115] A survey revealed that only 10 percent of

---

[109] Mehta, *Co-operative Farming*, 5.
[110] ICI, *L'Organisation du Crédit*, 120–123.
[111] Niyogi, *The Co-operative Movement*, 10.
[112] Hailey, *African Survey*, 1466.
[113] ICI, *L'Organisation du Crédit*, 120–123.
[114] Niyogi, *The Co-operative Movement*, 4.
[115] Qureshi, *The Future*, 8–9; IOR/V/26/340/2 1915 Co-operation in India (Maclagan) Committee 1914–15: Report, Simla, 1915.

8.5 COOPERATIVES & END OF "ASIAN MODEL"   303

the officially registered cooperatives were efficient in 1917, a number that dropped to 2 percent in 1935.[116]

The failure of the Indian cooperative system became a matter of global debate and the ILO and the League of Nations even hired Indian experts to explain its collapse. In 1939, Anwar Iqbal Qureshi, an Indian economist who specialized in cooperative credit systems and Islamic concepts of interest rates, became a temporary member of the Financial and Economic Section of the League of Nations.

Anwar Iqbal Qureshi came up with a very different explanation for the collapse of the cooperative system in India: instead of accusing the Indian management boards of being corrupt, he detected a fault with the British introducing unlimited liability for agricultural cooperatives in the Co-operative Credit Societies Act of 1904. Qureshi was aware that the typical colonial strategy of shuffling off all financial responsibility and risk to the Indians ultimately led to the failure of the system. He observed that a collective of guarantors did not stabilize the cooperatives but disabled them from the start.[117] According to Qureshi, well-off farmers, who had much to lose in case of unlimited liability, did not join the societies in the first place: "Seeing that they risk the whole of their property by becoming members," the rich farmers refused to join. Consequently, the cooperatives "may often degenerate into an organization of poor and inefficient farmers of the locality, dependent in its activity only from outside (State) resources."[118]

At the League of Nations and in his publications, Qureshi also made a proposition for how to improve the system. The only way to avoid such a failure, he argued, was to diversify the functions of the cooperatives and to turn them into multipurpose societies: "By multiple society I mean a society which caters for all the needs of the farmers and not only for credit requirements. A mistake has been made in most countries for laying too much stress on co-operative credit," for the farmers would take the loans and then forget about the common purpose. It was therefore necessary to combine it with marketing, common transport and machinery, insurance for the peasants, and mutual aid institutions. Only these elements, Qureshi concluded, constituted a cooperative spirit and a sense of responsibility. He urged the British government to secure "efficient and paid management," instead of letting the Indians take all the costs.[119] But the system remained deficient and seemed problematic to the ICI members who kept up the illusion of a strictly indirect rule and colonial governmentality.

---

[116] Niyogi, *The Co-operative Movement*, 4.
[117] *Times of East Africa* (September 8, 1906), 6.
[118] Qureshi, *The Future*, 22–23.
[119] Ibid. He received support from Niyogi, *The Co-operative Movement*, 5.

Even before the failure of the Indian system, Dutch Indonesia had suffered a similar fate, and ultimately the ICI dismissed both as a model for a successful cooperative economy.[120] Before World War I, the Dutch cooperative system was the ICI's exemplary student. ICI member and former minister of education and industry for Dutch India Johannes Hendrik Carpentier-Alting was involved in monitoring the Dutch cooperative policy and the ICI got access to his confidential reports. At the ICI's meeting of 1911, its members celebrated the Dutch Indies for their sophisticated "cooperative" credit institutions. In the frame of its "ethical policy," the Dutch Department of Popular Credit provided loans to the villages through village and division banks. Unlike the British, the Dutch government paid for the administration, among them were 212 Indonesian bank clerks. Village commissions also administered significant amounts of money. Between 1909 and 1912, village banks increased from 369 to 585 and division banks increased from 66 to 75. Over 90 percent of the banks were in Java, and the Javanese increasingly deposited money in the banks. In 1911, Javanese villagers had cash deposits of about 889,066 florins, of which they deposited 700,769 in the division banks, while 188,297 florins were administered by the village commissions. At the same time, the banks gave loans to the villages to buy machines and iron tools.[121]

In the late 1920s, however, the well-developed cooperative economy of Java lost its appeal among colonial internationalists. The Javanese system broke down in the 1920s, because few of the villagers were able to pay back their loans. Before World War I, the "ethical" Dutch government had equipped the banks with a capital of 1,830,000 florins, of which 1,643,500 were used for loans. The borrowers repaid only 93,000 florins, while 1,550,500 remained unsettled.[122] Critics such as Strickland blamed the absence of self-organized cooperative banks for this failure. The colonized, he repeated, would only pay back loans if they had received them from their own "cooperative" peer group. Contributing to the failure was apparently also the unusually high interest rates that reached up to 40 percent. At the end of the day, Strickland concluded, the Dutch had failed to "educate" the people to be economical. Even Dutch colonizers agreed with him. In 1927, the Dutch government issued a new law that favored the creation of seemingly authentic grassroots cooperatives. By 1930, the new law had led to the registration of 81 new societies that added to 519 cooperatives that the Javanese had formed without a specific law.[123]

For the first time in the history of the ICI, the Eastern model belied its expectations. Apart from the fact that cooperative policy in India, Indonesia,

---

[120] On the failures, see Hailey, *African Survey*, 1466.
[121] ICI, *L'Organisation du Crédit*, 110.
[122] Ibid.
[123] Strickland, *Co-operation for Africa*, 427–428.

and Indochina had failed, the state-controlled cooperatives in Asia hardly lived up to the ideal of grassroots economic development and successful indigenous self-government. To uphold its ideal of indigenization and rule through autochthonous institutions, the ICI had to find a better example.

8.6 The Authentic Way of Cooperative Compulsion: The *Fokon'olona* in Madagascar

Ideal cooperatives should give Africans and Asians the possibility to stay themselves, while slowly transforming them individually and collectively into more productive subjects. ICI members, in particular, started from the premise that the overhasty contact with modernity would distort their natural self and forms of collectivism. Only a careful moral and material uplifting that was inherent to their own societies was said to be successful. Only cooperative traditions inherent to native societies, ICI members argued, could be used to achieve this goal. After dismissing British and Dutch top-down cooperatives, the ICI found an allegedly truly indigenous cooperative model in Madagascar, in the so-called *fokon'olona* system.

Yet, while the ICI promoted the *fokon'olona* of Madagascar as truly indigenous cooperative institutions, the French administration actually used them to impose a repressive system of forced labor and collective punishment. Tellingly, under the guise of the "most" indigenous *fokon'olona*, the colonial government of Madagascar pursued a policy of economic development and indirect disciplining that was violent at its core. Partly, this policy was a response to the ILO's initiative to ban forced labor in 1930. Fascists and ICI members openly rejected the ILO's proposition, declaring at the International and Intercolonial Congress of Indigenous Societies (Paris, 1931) that the combination of "forced labor and the salariat are the only possibilities" to transform "pastoral societies" in the colonies and make them more productive.[124] In the ensuing debate, during which the both the ICI and the French government voted against the ban on forced labor, France had to show good will. After all, it did not want to go down in history as an illiberal power. Hence, although France did not sign the convention banning forced labor in the colonies, it pretended to stop all kinds of forced labor unless it was part of indigenous traditions. Ironically, the ILO, who banned forced labor from the colonies, would promote the *fokon'olona* later on as an adequate means of development in the Global South. Well into the postcolonial era, international organizations would recommend the use of *fokon'olona* for sustained development, ignoring the repressive role they had played under colonial rule.

---

[124] Gorini, "Le Salariat et le Paysannat," 120.

Literally, *fokon'olona* meant an "association of human beings" who shared a common goal and followed common rules: the verb *mifoko* implied that people formed collectives to achieve a common purpose.[125] At the beginning of the twentieth century, the *fokon'olona* were known as mutual aid societies, predominantly in rice production. They coordinated their irrigation efforts and tried to improve rice production with regard to yield and quality. In case of food shortages, they advanced rice to their members, who had to pay those seed loans back with an interest of 25 percent of the harvest. The *fokon'olona* took care of the purchase and the improvement of both paddy and white rice and also sold it in a communal way.[126]

Originally, the term *fokon'olona* seemed to have designated mere kinship groups that built on traditional clan and lineage structures of the Merina people in central Madagascar. The Merina king Andrianampoinimerina had made them official in 1787 to give his rule a more firm basis among communes and individuals. Over the nineteenth century, the *fokon'olona* developed into more extensive interest groups whose corporate spirit went beyond the genealogical self-conception, yet without overcoming it completely. The main purpose became the joint organization of rice cultivation and irrigation. What was specific about the *fokon'olona* community was that each individual member was accountable for economic and public life to thrive.[127] The French colonial administration, keen on transforming the Malagasy society to its own benefit, sensed that it might use the *fokon'olona* system for its own purposes.

First, Europeans declared these communal self-help groups exemplary because they seemed to be fully compatible with preexisting clan and lineage-structures.[128] This ethnicization and biologization was a very Eurocentric interpretation of the *fokon'olona*. Sometimes they were indeed congruent with families, villages, tribes, clans, lineages, and even castes, but mostly their networks transgressed these kinship segments. After all, *fokon'olona* built upon economic ties between villages rather than a fixed territorial unity and ethnic purity. Nevertheless, as an official report of the French colonial government concluded, their members claimed a common ancestry. Hence, the *fokon'olona* were "really adapted to the indigenous mentality."[129] Based on these assumptions, the French administration hoped that these ethnoeconomic entities would make modernization without detribalization possible.

---

[125] Foreword by G. Julien, in Delteil, *Le Fokon'olona*, v.
[126] ICI, *L'Organisation du Crédit*, 95.
[127] Cahuzac, *Essai sur les Institutions*, 75.
[128] For definitions by the French ethnographic state, see Condominas, *Fokon'olona*, 22. He was occasionally mistaken. See Serre-Ratsimandisa, "Théorie et Pratique du Fokonolona," 41.
[129] Delteil, *Le Fokon'olona*, 93.

8.6 AUTHENTIC WAY OF COOPERATIVE COMPULSION

Colonial officials were even more intrigued about the *fokon'olona* being almost congruent with their own ideas of cooperative life. They were responsible for mutual aid in cultivation; shared tools; collective credit; joint house building; organization of a welfare state to take care of the poor, the ill, and the elders; storage of overproduction in silos (such as rice); and even the settlement of conflicts on a local scale. All these measures seemed to be destined to improve the lives of the Malagasy population and to help develop the colonial economy. According to the *fokon'olona* expert Pierre Delteil, it was the "role of the Civilizing State to oversee this evolution and to direct it."[130]

In the eyes of the French, their most important activity was the irrigation of rice fields and the production of rice. The rice fields were communal property of the *fokon'olona*, whereas each individual was responsible for the cultivation of a certain division called *hetra*. The individuals had the right to bequeath the *hetra* to their children or even sell it, if the buyer was a member of his community. A complete stranger could only buy the land if the *fokon'olona* accepted him as one of their own.[131] Overall, the *fokon'olona* seemed to resemble the cooperative ideal of a shared economy with bylaws that regulated community life and sanctioned any wrongdoing that threatened this life. This is why it had both communal and judiciary functions.

More critical observers warned that *fokon'olonas* were highly conservative institutions that established solidarity without eliminating hierarchies. Solidarity rested upon the belief in a common ancestor and a couple of saints. Behind this illusion of solidarity was a hierarchical system that helped to impose the rule of the Merina kings.[132] When the Merina king Andrianampoinimerina had officially introduced the *fokon'olona* in 1787, he had done so to maintain the privileges of the upper *Andriana* caste. The *Andriana* could claim the collaboration of two lower castes, the nominally free but actually dependent *Hova* and the slaves called *Andevo*. Through the *fokon'olona*, the upper caste obliged the lower castes to work for the common purpose, either by appealing to the solidarity of the group to engage in works necessary for the survival of the community or by short-term obligation to work called *valin-tanana*. Apart from cultivating their own fields, the slaves, in particular, contributed disproportionally to the well-being of the other castes. They seemed to do so voluntarily, but in reality, they followed a well-established customary system that benefited the upper classes. Hence, the *fokon'olona* were not cooperative associations among equals and enabled various forms of enforced labor.[133]

---

[130] Ibid., 94.
[131] Condominas, *Fokon'olona et Collectivités Rurales*, 30.
[132] Ibid., 24.
[133] Serre-Ratsimandisa, "Théorie et Pratique du Fokonolona," 41.

While allegedly securing economic "solidarity," the *fokon'olona* were a political institution that indirectly served to put the government's policy into practice. Members (who could also be called *fokon'olona*) appointed a chairman who was then responsible for establishing order and implementing royal decrees. Kings used them to collect taxes, although the royalty returned a certain amount to them to organize communal life. As we have seen, they played the role of courts. More than that, *fokon'olonas* started imposing a moral code for individual behavior in 1869. In that year, the Merina kings adopted Protestantism and banned exogamy and alcohol from the *fokon'olona* in their realm. The *fokon'olona* also watched over the observance of the Sunday rest. They became a governmental tool for the Merina kings to control the individual lives of their subjects.[134]

After France had conquered Madagascar in 1896, it made use of the *fokon'olona* to establish a pseudo-indigenous and repressive regime of "indirect rule." In 1902, a French decree on the administrative organization of the Imerina codified and redefined the *fokon'olona*. They became official indigenous administrative units called *fokon-tany*. The decree forced all inhabitants of those districts to become member of a *fokon'olona*: "It is obligatory for every *indigène* to become a member in the fokon'olona of the locality where he or she habitually resides." Members were then allowed to elect three nominees, among whom the colonial governor chose one to represent them – or imposed his own candidate if he saw public order threatened. Merina taxpayers had to provide the salary and staff of this representative, traditionally called *mpiadidy*. The *mpiadidy* headed the administration of the *fokon'olona*. According to the French decree, he and the other members of the *fokon'olona* had to organize the communities' jurisdiction, maintain streets and telegraph lines, establish irrigation systems and canals, fight endemic diseases, and take measures of public hygiene. They also had to take care of elders, widows, and orphans.[135]

Referring to colonialist strategies of collective punishment, the French decree of 1902 stipulated that members of a *fokon'olona* were jointly responsible before the governor for not naming and delivering criminals to the colonial government. In these and other cases, the French governor had the right to impose a fine of five francs on each individual member of the *fokon'olona* and was allowed to take the aggregate from the *fokon'olona's* common treasury.[136] The French *fokon'olona* decree therefore legitimized collective responsibility and collective punishment by claiming that it was an

---

[134] Bloch, "Decision-Making in Councils," 29–62.
[135] "Organisation de l'Administration Indigène de l'Imerina, Décret du 9 mars 1902," *Journal Offciel de Madagascar* (April 30, 1902), 7391.
[136] Ibid.

8.6 AUTHENTIC WAY OF COOPERATIVE COMPULSION 309

old Merina tradition. Article 14 of the decree held the members of the *fokon'olona* collectively responsible if one patch of land remained uncultivated.[137]

The *fokon'olona* appealed so much to the French that the French governor Gallieni extended them to the whole island. In the days of the Merina kings, this system existed only in their domain and was the basis of their domination. Gallieni imposed them on the rest of the island, explicitly to "fight against the inertia of the populations who, neglecting their agricultural labor, risk becoming victims of famines."[138] Those "inert" non-Merina societies, who had organized their communal life in a completely different way, fought the *fokon'olonas'* enforced cultivation tooth and nail.[139]

The French publicized their *fokon'olona* policy in the 1920s and the 1930s to convince the international community of its respect for indigenous population. In that period, France was struggling to legitimize its refusal to subscribe to the ILO's ban on forced labor in the colonies. In 1926, the governor of Madagascar had indeed issued a decree that allowed requisitioning labor for public works. But he had to withdraw it in 1929, mainly due to international pressure and France signing the League of Nations' Slavery Convention that stipulated in Article 5 to "progressively and as soon as possible ... put an end to the practice of" forced and compulsory labor.[140] Nevertheless, the French colonial ministry argued that obligatory labor was necessary to build up an infrastructure and bring about economic development. It pretended that obligatory labor benefited both the colonizers and colonized and their common interest. Faced with international criticism, the French governors used the *fokon'olona* label to conceal the perdurability of forced labor.[141]

It was convenient that in that very moment anthropologists and colonial lawyers discovered the *fokon'olona*, as a preexisting "indigenous" institutions that allowed obligatory communal labor of "public interest." Anthropologists vouched for the authenticity of obligatory labor in the *fokon'olona*: In an important study published in 1931, Gustave Julien and the legal anthropologist Pierre Delteil portrayed the *fokon'olona* as a progressive and cooperative institution, while emphasizing its legitimate use of obligatory labor. Delteil demonstrated that *fokon'olona* were egalitarian systems, meaning that each individual, no matter if they were men, women, children, or elders, participated in the work for the common purpose. He added that the commitment to

---

[137] Delteil, *Le Fokon'olona*, 79–80.
[138] Ibid., 79.
[139] Serre-Ratsimandisa, "Théorie et Pratique du Fokonolona," 37–58: 42–43. See also Paillard, "Domination Coloniale," 73–104.
[140] ILO, *International Labour Conference. Fourteenth Session 1930*, 272; ILO, *International Labour Conference Session Geneva 1928*, 287.
[141] See his preface in Delteil, *Le Fokon'olona*, x.

the common cause was obligatory according to the *lalana velona*, the customary law of the Merina and that any wrongdoing justified the exclusion and the "civil death" of a member. The main purpose was building and maintaining the irrigation systems, which the Merina king had always assured by a "corvée d'État." Even if an individual member refused to cultivate his land, Delteil explained, the king who officially owned all land had the right to enslave him. He cited the Merina king, who was about to punish a member of the *fokon'olona* who simply wanted to exchange his infertile piece of land against a more fertile one:

> Andrianampoinimerina had said: "Bring me the lazy guy, I will take care of him ... bring him to me and I will have him sold as a slave. All the fields of my kingdom have to be brought into cultivation [se valent] ... it is not only the chiefs who are responsible, it is also the fokon'olona. The neighbor has to denounce the neighbor."[142]

Instead of condemning the king's leaning toward slavery, Delteil admired him for being a just "conqueror, legislator, engineer and also a very wise administrator." After all, he added, the king had done all that to fight famines.[143] The quote also proved that the *fokon'olona* were far from being a democratic and egalitarian institution. It was the king who made the final decisions. From 1896 onwards, the French colonial administration replaced the king as the institution that had the last word. The self-styled *fokon'olona* experts received indirect support from the famous French anthropologist Marcel Mauss who identified systems of "mutual obligations" in all indigenous societies in his widely read essay *The Gift* (1924).[144] In French West Africa, a much-cited example were the so-called *flanton* or *kari* societies among the Bambara in Mali. The *kari* were mixed gender age groups that had received their initiation – circumcision or excision – in the same year and thus entered community life at the same moment. These groups had common rites, feasts, and leaders. By the 1930s, French anthropologists laid stronger emphasis on *kari* being "not only societies of mutual aid but also working cooperatives, especially for agricultural work." To prove their cooperative character, French anthropologists argued that the *kari* group often helped an individual member who was about to marry to cultivate the fields of his future father-in-law. In so doing, they collectively paid off the member's dowry. This form of solidarity among young people was certainly far from being a cooperative in the European sense. Nevertheless, the French interpreted it as such. What they wanted to achieve with this reinterpretation became clearer when it came to communal work: "The Kari interferes, for example, to clear the land to open it

---

[142] Ibid., xiv–xv and 3.
[143] Ibid., 3–4.
[144] Mauss, "Essai Sur le Don," 30–186.

up for cultivation, to build roads and tracks, and to accomplish the *corvées municipales*."[145] French administrators always found a way to define forced labor as a natural indigenous institution. When the French administrators started promoting cooperatives on a bigger scale in 1930, they used all these anthropological ideas of mutual obligations to justify their system of obligatory labor.[146]

The *fokon'olona* saw a revival during the cooperative turn of 1930, when they became a symbol for sustained development. When a French decree officially introduced "agricultural credit, mutual insurance, and cooperation in Madagascar and Dependencies" in April 1930, the *fokon'olona* became once again the core of the cooperative reorganization of the colony. The decree declared that the *fokon'olona* "may act as local credit funds and carry out work such as the clearing of woods, recovery of marsh-land, irrigation, etc." When Pierre Delteil reedited the former *fokon'olona* conventions in 1931, he explained that the obligation to work was an integral part of *fokon'olona* regulations: "In almost all conventions, similar dispositions concern the common tasks. We have seen the measures taken to ascertain the *mise en valeur* of the land. The *obligation au travail* can be found almost everywhere; any individual who does not contribute with any labor is suspect, the means securing his livelihood can be disputed."[147] Delteil was positive about all of these oppressive rules.

The ICI's fascination with colonial governmentality shone out in Delteil's résumé about the traditional function of the *fokon'olona*: "Thus, the fokon'olona conventions assured the maximum of tranquility in the country, without the government seeing itself obliged to being concerned with it. After the conquest, the French administration could not help but wishing and favoring their re-establishment."[148] Because they "favor concord, cohesion, and mutual aid," Delteil recommended them in 1931 to "hasten the progress of indigenous peoples on the path to civilization."[149] Yet, in Madagascar, putting the *fokon'olona* system in place progressed more slowly than steadily. It did not seem that the cooperative organization of society was as universal and universally accepted as the French administration wanted to make the world believe. By 1938, there were 339 indigenous cooperatives in Madagascar with 10,148 members that were based on the *fokon'olona*, 32 "indigenous" credit funds with 5,636 members, and 4 other cooperatives with another 679 members.[150] While the practical implementation was a disappointment, the French

---

[145] Boyer, *Les Sociétés de Prévoyance*, 35–36.
[146] Anonymous, "Co-operative Societies among Natives," 358.
[147] Delteil, *Le Fokon'olona*, 70.
[148] Ibid., 72.
[149] Ibid., 89.
[150] Shaffer, *Historical Dictionary*, 297–298.

emulated the *fokon'olona* scheme in other colonies of its empire. As early as 1926 and 1927, the French themselves had introduced a similar system of using local communities as credit societies in Indochina.[151] Madagascar also inspired French West Africa to introduce camouflaged coerced labor and to extend the cooperative system.[152]

In the 1930s, other colonial powers who subscribed to the cooperative turn became interested in the *fokon'olona*. Indeed, the revival of *fokon'olona* in the French cooperative legislation of the 1930s received much more international attention than the original societies of the 1880s, although the topic of obligatory labor was absent.[153] Public interest was fostered by the rumors that the *fokon'olona* had originally been "Indonesian" and that this advanced socioeconomic concept had migrated to Madagascar. It thus seemed applicable to both Asian and African contexts. Referring to the French decree of 1930, administrations of other colonies in Africa set out to emulate the *fokon'olona* system. In Belgian Congo, for example, rural planners took the *fokon'olona* as the underlying "principle of collective and solidary responsibility."[154] The system entered international colonial mindsets during the International Colonial Exposition in Paris in 1931 and became famous among ICI members. Finally, the ILO requested information from the Malagasy government and gave the *fokon'olona* a prominent place in its recommendations of how to organize "native cooperation."[155]

The *fokon'olona* had long-lasting effects. In Madagascar, the French governor reinvigorated the *fokon'olona* system in the 1950s under the name of "autochthonous rural collectivities" with an elected council and further developed it into "modern autochthonous rural communities." After independence, the Malagasy government used the *fokon'olona* as a basis of its constitution. In the late 1970s, the German development agency GTZ declared them authentic and a model for participatory development policies, which originated in pre-colonial societies.[156] In the 1980s, the World Bank celebrated them in the same way the international community did in the 1930s.[157] As late as 2001, an ILO-report on the elimination of forced labor exempted the *fokon'olona* from the definition of forced labor, stating that

---

[151] Gelders, "Le Paysannat Indigène," 98.

[152] Related to the so-called deuxieme portion. See ILO, *International Labour Conference Fourteenth Session*.

[153] "Co-operative Societies Among Natives," *Annals of Public and Cooperative Economics*, 11, no. 3 (1935), 358.

[154] Gelders, "Le Paysannat Indigène," 98.

[155] "Co-operative Societies among Natives," 358.

[156] Gallon, "Mythos oder Methode," 181–197.

[157] World Bank. *Report No. 2898*.

8.6 AUTHENTIC WAY OF COOPERATIVE COMPULSION 313

this definition does not apply to ... labor in the collective interest made compulsory and carried out under the application of an agreement that is agreed freely by the members of the "fokonolona" (village community: the basic institution of social organization in Madagascar), or in the framework of minor tasks in the village.[158]

It seemed that, over a century, neither the nature nor the reputation of the *fokon'olona* had changed. The *fokon'olona* stood for a cooperative governmentality that had a long history and promised a prosperous future. The ICI promoted them during the colonial period because, unlike younger cooperatives in India and Indonesia, they seemed to be autochthonous and authentic. In reality, their governmental function was grounded on enforcement rather than encouragement. *Fokon'olona* were thus not a tool of liberal empowerment but the proof that colonial cooperatives were tools of repression and exploitation.

Overall, the cooperative system enforced exploitation and disguised self-exploitation as self-government. The repressive character of the allegedly liberal cooperatives revealed itself in enforced labor, wage dumping, collective punishment, additional taxation, and expropriation of land.[159] As the ILO remarked, the tight control of cooperatives allowed the colonial governments to deny credits to peasants who were not members of the cooperatives and to exclude insubordinate farmers. In this regard, they came close to the fascist and the Soviet strategy of excluding nonconformists.[160] Indeed, the cooperative turn in the 1930s was no opportunity for anti-colonial empowerment and collective action. As soon as cooperatives such as the KNPA showed signs of autonomy, let alone nationalist activity, the colonial government banned them. This restrictive policy hardly improved after World War II.

What is more, the colonial cooperatives failed to accomplish their self-declared purposes. The contribution of cooperatives to reduce poverty and bring about colonial development were not successful. In Senegal, which had allegedly established a healthy cooperative groundnut economy, Provident Societies were highly indebted. In 1933, the Kaolack cooperative owed the State 6,380,934 francs and the one in Thiès owed 9,293,296. Altogether, the debt of Provident Societies in Senegal amounted to thirty million francs.[161] In the India of the 1930s, the number of indebted workers had increased from one-third to over 50 percent of the population.[162] Right after independence, in 1962, Africa's cooperatives had 2.7 million members, a number that hardly did

---

[158] ILO, *Elimination of All Forms of Forced or Compulsory Labor*, 167.
[159] Boyer, *Les Sociétés de Prévoyance*, 102.
[160] ILO, *International Labour Conference 1930*, 16.
[161] Boyer, *Les Sociétés de Prévoyance*, 129.
[162] Qureshi, *The Future*, 1.

justice to the enormous logistic and financial effort to propagate cooperatives in the preceding colonial period. Nevertheless, development agencies and international organizations continued to regard cooperatives as a crucial tool for educating Africans in collective work. In the same year, the ILO, the Food and Agriculture Organization of the UN, UNESCO, and the Economic Commission for Africa of the UN officially recommended cooperative schemes for the "economic and social development of Africa."[163] In the era of independence, they partly remained instruments of neocolonial development policies, in which the ICI made a new name for itself.

---

[163] E/CN.14/133: United Nations Economic and Social Council: "The co-operative movement in Africa," Economic Commission for Africa Fourth Session January 15, 1962, 1.

9

"That Has Been Our Program for Fifty Years"

Sustained Development and Loyal Emancipation after 1945

When colonial internationalists met in 1947 to resurrect the ICI after the hiatus of World War II, they readily accepted decolonization. Decolonization did not necessarily equal independence, however, and endorsing it sounded more progressive than it was. This chapter shows how the ICI styled itself a progressive and pragmatic expert agency that quickly made its peace with decolonization but actually did little more than apply its fifty-year-old program of transcolonial governmentality to the entire "underdeveloped" world. While decolonization was a big step for old empires and new nation-states, the transnational ICI did not need the "motherland" and the label "colonial" anymore. It simply continued to manipulate political, administrative, social, economic, and cultural microstructures in the Global South. To be more precise, members accepted autonomy and even independence because they were well prepared to wield influence through "political and social science applied to the countries of differing civilization," as its new name stated. Inscribing the ICI's tradition of transnational governmentality into new functionalist theories of transnational governance seemed to boost the importance of the INCIDI, while making the former colonizing nations less relevant. Nation-empires had already reinvented themselves as Eurafrican and Eurasian unions that used economic functionalism to avoid democratization.

At the ICI's first meeting of October 1947, "the majority of the members favored a modification of the name to avoid any kind of allusion to the old colonial system."[1] In that period, the ICI members' understanding of decolonization was above all rhetorical. They "decolonized" their language by avoiding the term "colonial." Most importantly, they dropped the word "colony," replacing it with the allegedly uncolonial term "differing civilization." In 1949, the ICI renamed itself International Institute of Political and Social Science Applied to the Countries of Differing Civilizations, later shortened to International Institute of Differing Civilizations (INCIDI). In the members' view, using the term "civilization" and eliminating the word "colonial" was a psychological move to appease the allegedly destructive fervor

---

[1] AMAEB, D 4782, INCIDI Reunion Officieuse, October 10–11, 1947.

of radical anti-colonialists and establish a good relationship with the (post) colonial middle class along with a more subtle governmental form of dependency.[2] To de-radicalize and de-dramatize decolonization, ICI members agreed to accept autonomy and even independence, while they were more reluctant to use the term "revolution," which they banned from official statements as late as 1960, arguing that "this word ... might cause fear" and sounded "slightly brutal."[3]

At the INCIDI's meetings, new members encountered a potpourri of ICI veterans, European fascists, Catholic welfarists, utilitarian entrepreneurs, Labour party politicians, republican feminists, and moderate anti-colonialists from the Global South. The great majority of the 227 members were European and North American, and they dominated the INCIDI's meetings well into the 1960s. At the INCIDI's first General Assembly, held on March 13, 1948, these delegates decided to embrace "a world-wide scope, admit delegates not only from the Western world, but from Africa, from Asia, and from Oceania and have them consider together and on a scientific basis the ways through which the contacts between different civilizations could be rendered harmonious."[4] To do that, the INCIDI recruited delegates who had proven reliable to the colonial cause, sometimes over several generations. Their membership stood for the INCIDI's ability to portray itself as progressive, while perpetuating structures of transcolonial governmentality beyond the official end of empire. It propagated four seemingly progressive concepts for that purpose, which were new only by name: multiple civilizations, functionalism, anti-racism, and development. These concepts seemingly attested to the ICI's will to end imperial rule. However, they actually served to avoid true participation and independence. The role fascists played in shaping these concepts will illustrate their regressive character.

9.1 The Pitfalls of "Differing Civilizations"

The INCIDI's new name mattered because it acknowledged the coexistence of different civilizations and rejected the belief in a single civilizational standard to which non-Europeans needed to adjust to become independent. At the 1949 session of the INCIDI, Tracy Philipps identified five civilizations: Western Christianity, Eastern Christianity, Hinduism, Islam, and the "Extreme Orient." He and his colleagues regarded these different civilizations as "faits accomplis" to be studied "by ethnographers and ethnologists," as opposed to *the civilization*, an abstract idea to be studied by philosophers.[5]

---

[2] UCL Fonds Wigny C4, Voyage aux États-Unis, Part 2: Considerations générales.
[3] INCIDI, *Compte Rendu 1960*, 618–619.
[4] UCL Fonds Wigny C4, Voyage aux États-Unis, Speech Manuscript INCIDI, 4.
[5] INCIDI, *Compte Rendu 1949*, 22.

9.1 THE PITFALLS OF "DIFFERING CIVILIZATIONS"

More than that, Belgian expert of Bantu customary law, Antoine Sohier, reminded the INCIDI members in 1951 that "it was wrong to believe that 'civilized' means 'Europeanized,'" and that even the "Bantu race" in Congo showed signs of civilization.[6] Rejecting the civilizing standard and the civilizing mission was honorable but not new. Chailley had called it a "universal hypocrisy" and propagated the plurality of civilizations.[7] Around 1900, he and other ICI members had published the letters of the Javanese "princess" Kartini, in which she openly proclaimed: "The time has long gone by when we seriously believed that the European is the only true civilization, supreme and unsurpassed. Forgive us, if we say it, but do you yourself think the civilization of Europe perfect?"[8] "The future," ICI member Van Vollenhoven concluded, did not belong to "one civilization but to several civilizations."[9]

INCIDI members interpreted civilizations either as essentialized wholes or as flexible functional systems. Some INCIDI members followed the fascist sympathizer Tracy Philipps who equated civilization with essentialized ancient religions that provided little hope for change and progress and thus had to be analyzed by ethnologists. More progressive INCIDI members, instead, rejected essentialized definitions of civilizations, arguing that they were different from immobile "cultures," because they were potentially more dynamic.[10] At the INCIDI's meeting in 1948, the Belgian Edouard de Jonghe concluded that a civilization is a functional system, "a balanced whole, coherent, harmonious and of an individualized type" that was based on a mix of "necessities and spirituality" but above all "a manifestation of the rational activity of mankind."[11] Functionalist and rational civilizations spoke to the INCIDI's desire to combine economic development with the preservation of preexistent structures. Thus, these civilizations could potentially progress without losing their character: "Any kind of influence exerted from outside on these civilizations does not imply the destruction of this civilizations."[12]

Preserving the character of each civilization seemed honorable. Emphasizing how essentially different these civilizations were, however, served as an argument against the democratization of empires, which were about to become "multicivilizational" federations and unions after 1945. Planners of the new "Eurafrican" French Union, for example, did not want to see Africans flocking into Europe or winning a majority of votes in Eurafrican elections.[13]

---

[6] INCIDI, *Compte Rendu 1951*, 322.
[7] ICI, *Compte Rendu 1921*, 133 and 157.
[8] Kartini, *Letters*, 19–20.
[9] ICI, *Compte Rendu 1921*, 149.
[10] INCIDI, *Compte Rendu 1949*, 21 and 23.
[11] Ibid., 21, 24 and 37.
[12] Ibid., 36.
[13] Cooper, *Citizenship*, 40.

Thus, they needed an argument that justified a Eurafrican union without giving equal rights to Africans. Claiming that differing civilizations existed within Eurafrica enabled them to argue that each civilization should have its own culture, traditions, customs, legislation, and representation. Commenting on a potential Dutch-Indonesian union, Van Vollenhoven laconically put this attitude in a nutshell: "C'est leur droit, c'est leur affaire."[14] Hence, INCIDI members essentialized civilizations to keep them separate within Eurafrican and Eurasian economic federations. The preservationist argument, not to harm civilizations through the encounter of differing civilizations, had become an argument used to refuse them democratic rights.

Representatives of emerging nations saw in the concept of "civilizations" an instrument to divide their young nations. One of them was Husein Djajadiningrat, the first Indonesian to become a member of the INCIDI in 1949. He joined as a delegate of the "United Nations of Indonesia," the short-lived federal union that comprised the Netherlands and Indonesia. A year later, the union failed and Djajadiningrat represented independent Indonesia.[15] He stood for the small Indonesian elite whom the INCIDI members arrogantly believed to be loyal even beyond formal independence. He belonged to a notable Indonesian family that ICI member Snouck Hurgronje had put into important administrative positions in the Dutch Indies during the 1920s. Djajadiningrat had studied in Leiden, became a member of the Volksraad, and "reached the highest position ever held by an Indonesian during the Dutch colonial period," as director of the Department of Education and Religion.[16] At the same time, he was a member of the nationalist Sarekat Islam movement.

Although he was trained in Dutch academia, Djajadiningrat dedicated his work to reappropriating Indonesian history and writing it from a nationalist perspective.[17] Highlighting the mix of autochthonous, Muslim, and Hindu/Buddhist influences in early Indonesia, Djajadiningrat particularly rejected the idea of a "Greater Indian" civilization, which was propagated by European Indologists related to the Kern Institute in Leiden. This group had claimed that "Indic" civilization formed a unified whole and believed in the diffusion of "the Indian-Aryan civilization across the Eastern Ocean to the shores of Further India and to the islands of Indonesia."[18] Djajadiningrat exposed the errors of Dutch historians and claimed that "there are interpretations of historical facts that are incorrect" and emphasized the Muslim contribution to early Indonesian history: "It is clear that many Moors were settled here

---

[14] ICI, *Compte Rendu 1921*, 149.
[15] INCIDI, *Compte Rendu 1949*, xix.
[16] Bloembergen, "The Open Ends," 398–399.
[17] Djajadiningrat, "Local Traditions," 74–87.
[18] Thomas and Vogel, "Hendrik Kern," 174.

despite the generally limited admission of them. They brought prosperity by bringing in goods and buying products from the region."[19]

While colonial historians and some Indonesian nationalists of the 1940s embraced the diffusionist theory of "Greater India," Djajadiningrat rejected it.[20] No doubt, Djajadiningrat repudiated it in the name of Sukarno's independence government, whose minister of education and cultural affairs he became in 1952. The government was about to fight Hindu separatism in Bali that was supported and influenced from outside by India. The Muslim majority and the government saw in the "Greater Indian Civilization" theory an intellectual construct to heat the debate.

The Indian P. Kadanda Rao, who joined the INCIDI in 1952, faced a similar problem. India struggled with the partition between Hindu and Muslim parts of the country. Kadanda Rao deplored that "one of the major problems of India" was the policy of divided "linguistic states" that thoroughly "balkanized" India and territorialized the socioeconomic divide. He recommended the reconciling path of Gandhi, to unite India and recommended making reconciliation efforts also on a global level.[21]

Despite protests, the INCIDI's decade-old cultural relativism frequently degenerated into civilizational essentialism. In the eyes of members from Indonesia and India, the essentialized version of civilization seemed a way to divide their new nations and therefore delegitimize the multicommunal and multicivilizational nations they were about to build. The legacy of colonial divide-and-rule policy that had nurtured the gap between Muslims and Hindus, for example, seemed to live on in the INCIDI's civilizations.

While European INCIDI members still essentialized civilizations, nationalists in the Global South had long established sophisticated functional systems to form multicommunal and multicivilizational nations. The mastermind of multicommunal nationalism was Michel Chiha, who joined the INCIDI in 1952. A Catholic Lebanese, he had designed the Lebanese multicommunal constitution under the French mandate in 1926. He established a proportional representation that allowed Lebanon's diverse ethnic and religious communities – Sunni Muslims, Shia Muslims, Maronites, Druzes, Catholics, etc. – to each get a share of power and a position in government.

In the 1952 issue of the INCIDI's new journal *Civilisations*, Chiha celebrated the diversity of the independent Lebanese nation, arguing that

> differing civilizations have been in contact along the shores of the Eastern Mediterranean ever since ancient times …. Lebanon, at the Mediterranean crossroads of intercontinental routes, which span the

---

[19] Djajadiningrat, "Kanttekeningen," 380 and 389.
[20] Bloembergen, "The Open Ends," 398–403.
[21] Kadanda Rao, "Inde," *Civilisations* 3, no. 1 (1953), 151–156.

world, is beyond all doubt a site of unusual importance and a particularly favorable meeting-ground for civilizations .... Religions, with their own moral systems and their own particular rules, live there side by side. And civilizations interpenetrate each other here in this friendly, informal atmosphere.

With regard to the presence of a French and American University alongside a Muslim school of higher education, he concluded that "the Lebanese can claim to represent a civilization having simultaneously the face of the East and that of the West, but without confusion between the two."[22]

Chiha's multicommunalism provided a model for all independent nations who built functionalist mulitcivilizational societies. ICI members, instead, still had difficulties giving up their essentialized notion of civilization. This was partly due to the fascist legacy in the INCIDI.

9.2 Fascist Legacies: Discriminatory Eurafricas and the Legend of Anti-white Racism

The INCIDI's progressive reputation obscured its fascist legacy. Fascist ICI members who had designed a racialized and corporatist Eurafrican empire at the Volta Congress in 1938 were among those who reestablished the institute in 1949. Like the ICI of the 1930s, the INCIDI of the 1940s became a home to Italian fascists, French Vichyists, Spanish Francoists, Portuguese Estado Novoists, and German Nazis. They used the INCIDI's internationalism to rehabilitate themselves and rose in the esteem of liberals, republicans, and even Labour Party delegates in the INCIDI because of their colonial expertise.

Indeed, the fascist legacy left its mark on the INCIDI also because it was astonishingly compatible with new postwar schemes of international governance in the Global South. Corporatism remained a potential way of organizing "Eurafrican" spaces without democratizing them. Racial and ethnic categories saw a revival in segregationist policies within these Eurafrican experiments. Manipulating the psychology of the masses was as interesting for the INCIDI as creating a new malleable "middle class" in the Global South that ousted both the old aristocracy and the new communist movements. Finally, elements of the fascist organic community were compatible with the theory of functionalist societies. To be sure, these developments were not exclusively "fascist," since fascism itself was a syncretistic ideology. They had existed in the ICI long before the 1930s, but INCIDI members evoked the Volta Congress surprisingly often to frame their postwar policy.

---

[22] Chiha, "Vie Universitaire et Contacts de Civilisations des Libanais" *Civilisations* 2, no. 3 (1952), 333–338.

Italian fascists rejoined the INCIDI right after the end of World War II. One of the most active INCIDI members was the former vice governor of Mussolini's Italian East Africa, Enrico Cerulli. When he joined the INCIDI in 1949, the United Nations War Crime Commission had listed him as a suspected war criminal because of "systematic terrorism" in Ethiopia.[23] The INCIDI had accepted Cerulli's membership, knowing that he was "an advocate of the hard, if not the hardest school" of colonial domination. Before the UN War Crime Commission, his former Ethiopian interpreter, Asfäha Wäldämika'él, testified that he had "personally seen the order produced by Cerulli's department in the Ministry that called for the liquidation of the Ethiopian intelligentsia during the occupation of Addis Ababa."[24]

When the UN War Crime Commission acquitted Cerulli of Ethiopia's charges of "complicity in systemic terrorism" in the 1950s, it was largely because the Italian had activated his internationalist networks to influence the decision. His membership in the INCIDI was even more important, since the affiliation of former colonial subjects in the INCIDI seemed to give proof of the moral integrity of all members, including former colonialists and fascists. Cerulli himself referred to Léopold Sédar Senghor, who joined the INCIDI in 1954, as proof of his own dedication to reconciliation, particularly citing Senghor's suggestion that the mentalities of empire should be overcome.[25] In the 1950s, Cerulli became one of the most active INCIDI members whom conservative and liberal members admired and praised.[26]

The INCIDI also welcomed convicted antisemites such as the French Vichyist Georges Hardy with open arms. Members saw in him exclusively an expert of "native psychology," an applied science Hardy had developed since the 1920s and which INCIDI members dreamed of using to win over the "native" middle classes during decolonization. In 1949, the long-time secretary-general Octave Louwers invited the former ICI member Hardy to rejoin the INCIDI, called him "one of the biggest colonialists of our times," and "expressed the estimation and sympathy" for him "in a small report I made on the Volta Congress."[27]

Indeed, Hardy had promoted his "native psychology" at the Volta Congress in 1938, and Louwers revived it in 1949 because it also spoke to the INCIDI's idea of differing civilizations. Hardy urged colonial administrations to study the "natives' soul" and their "collective psychology" to better govern and manipulate the minds of the colonized. Inspired by racial theorist Gustave

---

[23] De Lorenzi, "The Orientalist," 165–200.
[24] Ibid., 180.
[25] Ibid., 183, 184, and 187.
[26] INCIDI, *Compte Rendu 1955*, 58.
[27] AGRB, Louwers Papers 164, Louwers to Hardy, July 7, 1949 and Hardy to Louwers, July 8, 1949.

Le Bon and the analysis of a crowd's "racial unconscious," Hardy intended to "use this psychology to win the favor of the indigenous collectivities," even though their civilization might differ from the European one. Two years after the Volta Congress, in 1940, the French Vichy regime gave Hardy the opportunity to put his theory to a test by making him rector of the university in Algiers. In Algiers, he expanded the system of primary education for Muslims but also removed 464 Jews from their posts in the education system, many of whom were deported afterwards.[28] Admitting to Louwers in 1949 that he was "free of any German tutelage" while implementing his antisemitic policy, he also went far beyond what Vichy asked for. What drove him to segregate Jews from Muslims was his essentialist belief that Muslims had "a civilization truly worth of the name" and that "the distinct psychological traits of colonized ethnic groups also required pedagogical differentiation."[29]

After he had "segregated" Muslims and Jews in the Algerian education system, the tides quickly turned. When the war was over, he wrote to Louwers that Free France under Charles de Gaulle had imposed on him a "prohibition to teach, even as a private teacher. I was placed under house arrest in Guelma and had to show up at the police office every day." Although the French acquitted Hardy, he had to retire and ran out of money. After his rehabilitation, Hardy continued to be an active writer much concerned with the fact that "the indigenous politicians are taking over" the colonies. Yet, reapplying his native psychology to the decolonization era, he claimed that "not all is lost" and that Europeans "do not have the right to abandon the natives they had come to know so well."[30] Thus, his "collective psychology" became an important inspiration for the INCIDI to win over the "hearts" of the middle classes for constructive cooperation.

With Hardy's native psychology in mind, the INCIDI ensured that no troublemakers joined the ICI, and it defined troublemakers as anti-colonial nationalists rather than procolonial ex-fascists. Among the latter was a former collaborator with Vichy, the Algerian Ahmad Ibnou Zekri who joined the INCIDI in 1951. Naturalized French, Ibnou Zekri followed in his father's footsteps, who had already provided ICI members with firsthand information about Algerian Islam around 1900. Thirty years later, Ibnou Zekri junior also worked for a gradual adaption of Islam to colonial needs, making use of his professorship at the *medersa* in Algiers. Since he opposed the anti-colonial branch of reformist Muslim leaders in Algeria, Vichy officials promoted Ibnou Zekri to head of the Consultative Commission for the Muslim Cult in the Algiers department in 1941, and he became one of four Muslim members in Vichy's central organ, the Conseil National. He met with "Maréchal" Philippe

---

[28] Singaravélou, *Professer*, 335 and 359.
[29] Segalla, *Moroccan Soul*, 91 and 97.
[30] AGRB, Louwers Papers 164, Hardy to Louwers, July 8, 1949.

Pétain, whom he publicly admired. In an interview dating from 1941, he proclaimed that

> for us, Monsieur Maréchal is a "Sid." This is Arabic and means "a seigneur" .... He is the first head of government to acknowledge the prestige of the Islamic religion next to the prestige of the Christian religion ... it is his primary desire to appeal to the spiritual values for the renovation of France; and that the beautiful Muslim religion, to which he bows, is for him one of the forces to rely on.

Ibnou Zekri's public admiration for Pétain was certainly more strategic than opportunistic. In several interviews, he proclaimed and repeated Pétain's words, knowing that this would put pressure on Vichy to incorporate Muslims into the colonial administration: "The old expression 'Franco-Muslim collaboration,'" he concluded, has to be replaced by "'Franco-Muslim fraternity.'"[31]

The INCIDI seems to have recruited Ibnou Zekri in 1951 because of his loyalty and because he launched a transcolonial initiative to train Muslim scholars whom he wanted to work for a peaceful coexistence between a moderately modernized Islam and European administration: "In our médersas in Algiers, Tlemcen, and Constantine, we prepare the lucky intermediaries between France and the Muslim populations, because we train magistrates, professors, and interpreters who go to Algeria, Morocco, and Syria. We even have delegates in Mecca."[32] His initiative to link colonial and semicolonial regions across the Mediterranean was very much to the taste of the INCIDI, which had a similar program of extending its colonial skills to postcolonial and semicolonial territories.

Time did not undo fascist legacies in the INCIDI and *Lebensraum* ideologies did not vanish. On the contrary, in 1955, the INCIDI readmitted delegates from Germany, among them former Nazis who would attend the 1961 meeting in Munich, when decolonization was well underway. Apart from using the INCIDI to whitewash themselves, they realized that its functional governance allowed them to reapply their skills. Since the INCIDI wanted a new steering and steerable middle class in the Global South, former Nazis evoked their experience in shaping a completely new middle class. They thus offered their skills to train an authoritarian and pro-European class of leaders, a *"Führungschicht* in the developing countries." This leadership group, composed of entrepreneurs and technocrats who were equally political leaders, was supposed to establish a corporate economy to oust Communist economic schemes and combat trade unionism in the so-called Third World.[33] Among

---

[31] "M. Ibnou Zekri nous declare ..." *L'Echo d'Alger* (May 23, 1941).
[32] "M. Ibnou Zekri nous declare ..." *Le Journal* (May 19, 1941)
[33] INCIDI, *Compte Rendu 1961*, 12.

the Nazis was Ernst Erdmann, head of the National Socialist Reichswirtschaftskammer from 1935 to 1945, who had aligned German companies with a corporate economy organized according to the *Führerprinzip* (leader principle). Like the internationally operating former Nazi arms producing firm Mannesmann, which sent several delegates to the INCIDI, Erdmann fought trade unions to the benefit of a corporatist company structure.[34]

Vocabulary of Nazi expansionism such as *Großraumwirtschaft* (expansive economy) and *Ergänzungsraum* (complementary space) also reappeared in the ICIDI's postwar concepts of Eurafrica.[35] They fell on fertile ground in Spain and Portugal, dictatorships that were about to consolidate their colonial Eurafricas. José Maria Cordero Torres, who represented Franco's Spain, used the INCIDI to claim "vital space" in Africa and revived ideas of *hispanidad* and Latin Africa that Spanish ICI members had already promoted in the 1890s. His chef d'oeuvre *Reivindicaciones de España* was quoted extensively by the UN's General Assembly to prove that Franco's "Spain was a fascist program."[36]

Portugal, with a huge settler community in Angola and Mozambique, used designs of Eurafrican corporatism promoted already at the Volta Congress to avoid a democratization of its Eurafrican empire. INCIDI member Marcelo Caetano stood for the political corporatism that allowed representation without democratization in Portugal. After being colonial minister between 1944 and 1947, he became president of the Portuguese Corporative Chamber, a corporative and pseudo-parliamentary body in Salazar's Estado Novo dictatorship, which had only consultative functions. Portugal's corporatism became particularly important in 1961, when Africans living in Mozambique and Angola were decreed citizens, "a status that in the authoritarian corporatism of Salazar's state brought few political rights, with little change in daily realities on the ground. Furthermore, there were no inconvenient implications of an overseas majority in representative institutions."[37] Corporatism thus contributed to the legal segregation and discrimination in the Portuguese empire as described above. This combination had its roots in the Volta Congress but lived on in the INCIDI's debates of the postwar era.

It would be oversimplified to assume that INCIDI members did not adapt and rethink their Eurafrican designs. The Italian Riccardo Astuto di Lucchesi, for example, was still emotionally attached to the fascist Eurafrica of the Volta Congress but emphasized its progressive elements. Formerly governor of Eritrea and advocate of Italy's return to Africa, he insisted that Africa's

---

[34] Monjau et al., "Informationen," 209; Kuller, *Finanzverwaltung*, 14–31.
[35] INCIDI, *Compte Rendu 1961*, 677–679.
[36] Molina Cano, "Africanismo," 81.
[37] Crawford, "Imperial Endings," in Bandeira Jerónimo and Costa Pinto, 117; INCIDI, *Compte Rendu 1957*, 62.

economic development "requires European immigration" and administration, particularly to bring capital to Africa. He thought European settlers necessary because "Africa is a de-populated country"[38] Repopulation was only possible by "including the African economy into the European one and establish[ing] a single Eurafrican economy."[39] To do so, he planned to integrate the African economy into the European Economic Community (EEC), which emerged around the same time, and create a "Eurafrican Economic Council. That is the overall goal."[40]

The idea of a corporate organization of a real Eurafrica seemed compatible with the liberal theory of functional governance that wanted public and private agencies to work together for the development of the Global South. Di Lucchesi therefore deemed Truman's "liberal" Point Four development program compatible with his corporatist Eurafrica. To prove this, he evoked "similar enterprises" of the Rockefeller Foundation in Venezuela and Brazil: the International Basic Economy Corporation and the International Association for Economic and Social Development. These private projects, he argued, had no "political purpose" and were thus accepted by the Brazilian and Venezuelan governments.[41] Di Lucchesi's way from Italian settler invasion to American corporative development was not a linear process of self-liberalization. The INCIDI was no reformatory for former fascists. Rather, Di Lucchesi tried to justify an authoritarian and settlerist Eurafrica by adding allegedly liberal elements to the scheme – without renouncing his original agenda.

9.3 From Fascist to Liberal Eurafrica

When the EEC finally incorporated former colonies into a common Eurafrican market in 1957, it was clear that INCIDI members had played an important part in this design. INCIDI secretary-general Pierre Wigny, a Belgian Christian Social Party leader interested in keeping Congo within an emerging EEC, was one of them. At first sight, his Eurafrican designs differed little from the Volta Eurafrica of 1938. Wigny claimed that "Africa is the hinterland of Europe" and naturally assumed that the exploitation of resources by former colonial powers was legitimate.[42] Like the colonies, Eurafrica "would be beneficial to Europe, which needs not only primary resources but also wants to increase its economic and human 'weight.'" His arguments became silkier

---

[38] INCIDI, *Compte Rendu 1951*, 180.
[39] Ibid., 97 and 172.
[40] Gosewinkel, *Anti-Liberal*; INCIDI, *Compte Rendu 1951*, 172.
[41] Ibid., 178.
[42] UCL Fonds Wigny, M1, vols. 1–4, 1959, Conversation with John Foster Dulles, October 8, 1958, 4.

when turning to Africans: "It would be even more useful to Africa that is on its way to development and urgently needs help .... Africa can proceed faster to real independence and economic prosperity in this [Eurafrican] framework than in isolation."[43]

What was special about the INCIDI's Eurafrica was that Wigny also promoted African political representation within the Eurafrican union, even though it was representation without democracy. Wigny advocated the idea of leaving the Council of Europe entirely to Africans in order to institutionalize Eurafrica.[44] The Council of Europe was an intergovernmental and interparliamentary body created in 1949 meant to pave the way for a common European market and political unification. The Council soon turned out to be largely inefficient because it was a consultative body only and did not manage to impose its vision of a political European Union.[45]

While the Council of Europe lost ground, other European bodies emerged that finally initiated the EEC in the Treaty of Rome in 1957, through which the "overseas territories have been enumerated in annex number five of the Treaty of the European Economic Community. There, the signatory powers have agreed that they proclaim in its preamble 'to confirm the solidarity that ties Europe and the overseas countries together and assures the development of their prosperity, in accordance with the Charter of the United Nations.'"[46] Based on this paragraph, Wigny sent a memorandum to the Council of Europe, in which he proposed to elect Africans to the Council. According to him, their presence did not entail the much-feared domination of the blacks over the whites. On the contrary. As the Council of Europe was a merely consultative body, its "absence of real power" made sure that Africans were represented but had nothing no say in matters of European policies. Hence, he concluded, it "doesn't matter if the number of Africans is equal to the Europeans or even higher."[47] Wigny continued to lobby for this political Eurafrica, which, however, never materialized. Ultimately, Wigny concluded that the functionalist governance would be a more successful strategy to maintain influence in the Congo.[48] Until the 1960s, the Council of Europe remained at the center of Eurafrican projects.[49] Africans had only nominal representation within the EEC's Eurafrica, whose makers ensured that African

---

[43] Ibid., vol. 5, 1959, Pierre Wigny: "L'Eurafrique," October 22, 1959.
[44] INCIDI, *Compte Rendu 1960*, 673.
[45] Patel, *Project Europe*, 35.
[46] UCL Fonds Wigny, M2, vol. 7, 1960, La Communauté Européenne dans le Monde, note de Pierre Wigny, 6.
[47] Ibid., vol. 5, 1959, Pierre Wigny: *L'Eurafrique*, October 22, 1959.
[48] On the context, see O'Malley, *The Diplomacy*.
[49] UN Official Records, 11th Session, 1059 Plenary Meeting, November 21, 1961, 740.

production received support only if it "complemented" the European economy and did not compete with it.[50]

In theory, hardly any Eurafrican design was more progressive than Wigny's. In practice, it did not go much beyond the Eurafrica of the Volta Congress. INCIDI member Léopold Sédar Senghor, himself at that time a delegate in the French National Assembly and a member of the Council of Europe since 1949, exposed what all the Eurafricas imagined by Europeans lacked.[51] Senghor generally thought a Eurafrica "on equal terms ... [was] necessary and possible" but remarked that a settlerist and corporatist Eurafrica that facilitated European access to African resources was doomed to fail.[52] He suggested that such a project "has to cease to be constitutional and become contractual."[53] No doubt, a mutual agreement was necessary to avoid paternalism, because, as Senghor put it, "to bring about peoples' happiness without their consent is not bringing them happiness."[54] The INCIDI's Eurafrica was neither consensual nor contractual even though African leaders such as Senghor would have accepted such a union on equal terms and even promoted it themselves.

9.4 From Multicivilizational to Multiracial Society

The membership of fascists and racialists in the 1950s and 1960s left its mark on the INCIDI. Ironically, this legacy became most visible in the INCIDI's resolution against racism. To understand this paradox, we must turn to the 1957 meeting in Lisbon, which was the most reactionary meeting in the history of the ICI/INCIDI. In Lisbon, the old fascist guard discussed with new African leaders the "Cultural and Ethnic Pluralism in Intertropical Societies." The meeting enabled Portuguese INCIDI members to show how they applied their ideology of "multiracial unity," developed in Brazil, to the new Portuguese Eurafrica.[55] At no meeting before had ethnicity and race played such an important role.

At the Lisbon meeting, Portuguese INCIDI members promoted a racialized version of multicivilizational Eurafrica by declaring a "multiracial society" the ideal way of organizing Eurafrican empires and independent nations alike. Their model was Brazil, allegedly developed by Portuguese colonialism into a harmonious "multiracial unit" that enabled the peaceful coexistence of differing races.[56] Transferring multiracialism to Portuguese Eurafrica, they

---

[50] Patel, *Project Europe*, 250.
[51] INCIDI, *Compte Rendu 1954*, 38.
[52] Montarsolo, *L'Eurafrique*, 46.
[53] INCIDI, *Compte Rendu 1960*, 150.
[54] INCIDI, *Compte Rendu 1957*, 549.
[55] INCIDI, *Compte Rendu 1957*, 68–74.
[56] Ibid.

made a strong plea that different races within Eurafrican federations should have different laws. They argued that legal duality was a result of the INCIDI's cultural relativism and a manifestation of respect for indigenous cultures. INCIDI member Marcelo Caetano promised, for example, that Portugal "will respect the secondary legal systems implied by regional and cultural differences in an ethnically plural state."[57] His compatriot Silva da Cunha claimed to pay respect to indigenous law and insisted that the INCIDI pass a resolution to "respect the cultural concepts of each people. Much more with regard to penal law than to any other law"[58]

Emphasizing different penal laws for Europeans and Africans unveiled the real purpose behind multiracial and plurilegal Eurafricas. White INCIDI members wanted legal segregation (as perfected in South Africa's apartheid system) and distinct penal laws for Europeans and "natives." Separate penal laws existed since the colonial era and were meant to protect Europeans from prosecution and ensure their privileges as a minority, which they became in most of these Eurafrican settings as well as in the independent states. Legal segregation shaped the African "provinces" of the Portuguese unitary state, for example, where Europeans fell under European law and Africans under customary law. The INCIDI's final resolution stipulated that "it is desirable to create criminal laws which are suited to each culturally autonomous group."[59] This segregated criminal law would save the colonizers from persecution in autonomous and independent territories.

African members at the 1957 meeting in Lisbon contested legal segregation. Justin-Marie Bomboko from Congo, where there was still a significant white community, proclaimed that the "natives are not in favor of a dualism of law"[60] He cautiously formulated his critique, arguing that different penal laws "risk to provoke involuntary discrimination." Immediately, the Portuguese INCIDI member Silva da Cunha rebuked him.[61] Bomboko ultimately warned the INCIDI members that "it should not be tried to oppose communities living in the same territory by creating between them impermeable partitions, but rather favor the unification of their human relations." Senghor came to his help, arguing that laws of "differing civilizations" such as Islamic law and European law were not necessarily incompatible. As an example, he mentioned that "Bourguiba in Tunisia has abolished polygamy," thereby combining Islamic and European law.[62]

---

[57] Ibid., 82.
[58] Ibid., 548.
[59] Ibid., 668.
[60] Ibid., 544.
[61] Ibid., 548.
[62] Ibid., 549.

In the same 1957 resolution, the INCIDI dismissed the biological concept of race and declared bindingly that "discrimination in any shape or form must be fought and eliminated, especially racial discrimination, which figures as the most serious obstacle to the peaceful co-existence of ethnic groups."[63] What seemed to be the INCIDI's most progressive resolution was actually its most regressive recommendation. In the context of decolonization, African conference participants unveiled, this paragraph served to maintain privileges of white people in the (ex)colonies. The INCIDI's proclaimed "anti-racism" was to protect the white community and their companies from "racial discrimination" during the transition of power to the black majority. The fear was that during decolonization, "racist" laws might collectively punish white communities in the former colonies. White INCIDI members thus used their resolution against "racial discrimination" to accuse black people of potential racism against former colonizers and white settlers, whose "security" they threatened.[64] Some white INCIDI members went as far as denouncing an "antiracist racism of Africans."[65]

Facing the allegation that anti-colonialism and decolonization were racist because they entailed the collective punishment of European colonizers, African INCIDI members had to defend themselves. Léopold Senghor felt the need to declare that "the nationalism of dependent people is not racist" and his colleague Justin-Maire Bomboko from Belgian Congo added that "the Blacks are no racists."[66]

Hence, the INCIDI's supposedly progressive respect for "differing civilizations" and its anti-racism served to perpetuate colonial situations within Eurafrican unions, as well as within autonomous and independent states. Although it seemed to be contradictory, this progressive regression can be traced back to the ICI's colonial "liberalism" of the 1890s and the Volta Congress' fascist Eurafrica alike. When independence seemed inevitable, INCIDI members continued to delegitimize anti-colonial nationalists as racists and "destructive." Against the destructive racists, it put the "constructive" nationalists.

9.5 Toward Independence: Constructive Nationalism and Postcolonial Influence

The ICI/INCIDI entered its golden years in the 1950s, not despite but because colonialism came under attack. As in the 1890s, it promised a reform to overcome the crisis of colonialism through a transnational effort of functional

---

[63] Ibid., 666.
[64] Ibid., 634.
[65] Ibid., 660.
[66] Ibid., 539 and 541.

governance by avoiding violent conflicts. INCIDI members claimed to prepare dependent peoples peacefully for self-government, a promise that colonizers had already made in 1884 and in 1919 and was not new or revolutionary at all. By the 1950s, however, independence was not at distant horizon anymore but a reality that required a reaction.

For INCIDI members, not all independences were the same and not all anti-colonial nationalisms were alike. They differentiated between acceptable and unacceptable independence based on the distinction between a constructive and a destructive nationalism among anti-colonialists. In the INCIDI's jargon, radical anti-colonialists appeared as "hypernationalists ... intoxicated by their newly won independence."[67] INCIDI members accepted decolonization if the emerging nationalist leaders were willing to engage in a constructive process of cooperation with European experts to improve the economic, social, and administrative performance of their future country. This "constructive decolonization" presupposed that nationalist leaders remained reliable and controllable after power and sovereignty had been transferred to them. In the early 1950s, constructive decolonization could mean autonomy within a federal reorganization of empire, such as the French Union, the Commonwealth, and Eurafrica. From the mid-1950s onwards, when more countries broke away from their motherlands, INCIDI members tried to ensure constructive decolonization by empowering "middle classes" that ousted the radical anti-colonialists. The latter stood for destructive independence. It was unacceptable to INCIDI members, since it originated in a destructive nationalist freedom struggle that cut all ties with the former colonizers.

Trying to delegitimize radical anti-colonialists, the INCIDI accused them of being racist and xenophobic, as we have seen above. Di Lucchesi, for example, accused the Maghreb countries of a misguided "xenophobic nationalism" when they refused to accept Eurafrican neo-empires. He traced their "racism" back to "xenophobic syndicalism." It was understood that countries that combined nationalism and socialism were likely candidates to fall under the spell of destructive nationalism.[68] Obviously, the involvement of an Italian fascist was not necessary to accuse anti-colonialists of an allegedly "destructive nationalism." The French President Charles de Gaulle showed a similar reaction when Sekou Touré's Guinea chose total independence over an autonomous status within the French Union in 1958.[69]

For allegedly different reasons, but with a similar effect, Labour politicians such as the British Colonial Secretary Arthur Creech Jones condemned "destructive" nationalism and encouraged "constructive" nationalism. As a Labour politician and INCIDI member, he saw a need to ensure democratic

[67] Ibid., 574.
[68] Ibid., 173–174.
[69] Migani, "Sékou Touré," 257–273.

participation, a potential welfare system, and the protection of workers, before proceeding to independence: "The influence of nationalism is channeled to constructive purpose and the people's representatives' share in decisions."[70] In many cases, such arguments became a strategy to delay independence, particularly because attempts to strengthen the middle class, whose members might finance a welfare state and participate in representative democracy, received little support. Creech Jones continued to introduce development programs in the remaining British colonies that benefited predominantly the metropole and not the lower and middle class in Africa, which he intended to mobilize.[71] Nevertheless, republicans, liberals, Labour Party leaders, and even modernizing fascists paid lip service to the concept of constructive autonomy and independence.

Playing constructive and destructive delegates from the Global South against each other worked quite well. Among the constructivists was Chérif Mécheri, who was also the first Algerian Muslim to make a career in higher French administration after 1945. Shortly after becoming an INCIDI member in 1951, the French president appointed him the most important functionary of the French Union, a project to associate the French colonies in a common Eurafrican federation. In his report to the INCIDI about the constructive role of the "elite" in the French colonies, Mécheri quoted the preamble of the French Union's constitution from 1946, stating that the "French Union is composed of nations and peoples who put together or coordinate their resources and efforts to *develop their respective* civilizations." By quoting the preamble, Mécheri also demonstrated his allegiance to the INCIDI's doctrine of differing civilizations. He added that nationalists had the right to develop their own local culture but should be obliged to do so "within a state that has its place in the French Union ... federalism is necessary there, where nationalism exists."[72] Such a federation, he argued, was far from being enforced by the former colonizer but by necessity and rationality: "Everyone is aware today of the obligation to constitute such big formations that have a sufficient potential of men and material." Necessity and functionality thus forced people into the French Union, as did the prospect of participation: "Thanks to an active participation, the French Union remains for the elite a political, economic, and intellectual necessity."[73]

Mécheri particularly turned against the Moroccan sultan and the freedom party (Ḥizb al-Istiqlāl) in the French protectorate. Furiously, he noted that Moroccan traditional and nationalist elites showed no intentions to join the French Union. Mécheri complained that by "refusing any kind of association

---

[70] INCIDI, *Compte Rendu 1951*, 183.
[71] INCIDI, *Compte Rendu 1949*, 109.
[72] INCIDI, *Compte Rendu 1951*, 315–317.
[73] Ibid., 317.

with France and any participation in the French Union," Moroccans displayed an "anti-French hatred" and "Islamic racism."[74] He therefore reiterated the INCIDI's idea of a destructive "xenophobic" nationalism that appeared already in Di Lucchesi's neo-fascist scheme.

Quite a few allegedly "constructivist" members of the INCIDI had proven rather destructive for their emerging nations, whose program of nation building they indeed undermined. The Indian Ramaswami Aiyer, for example, attempted to sabotage both Gandhi's and Nehru's attempt to build an Indian nation and saw in the latter a centralist and authoritarian politician to whom he preferred British rulers. Nehru instead attested that Ramaswami Aiyer had "a reputation for autocratic methods and the suppression of those of whom he does not approve."[75] During the negotiations for India's independence, Ramaswami tried to get the most he could for the princely state of Travancore, which he administered, by completely refusing to join the emerging democratic Indian Union. To do so, he declared Travancore fully independent, arguing that "I am fundamentally and intensely interested in the best features of the monarchy."[76] In 1947, he wrote to Nehru that "the special history and background of Travancore have alone inducted the Government to keep out of a Union in which her special interests may not have full scope." Travancore was not only a monarchical state but also a maritime state that produced important commodities such as coffee, tea, and rubber. To substantiate his separatist conviction, he took small monarchies such as Belgium as successful examples. His interest in the INCIDI thus certainly derived from his fascination for Belgium and his need for international support of his separatism, especially among the colonizing powers. Nehru, tired of Ramaswami Aiyer's extravagances but more concerned with the Muslim-Hindu Partition, lamented that "there are some things which are not done by any decent and patriotic individual" and claimed that Ramaswami Aiyer's "vanity" had gone "paranoiac."[77] Ramaswami quit politics after a failed assassination attempt against him and spent his time in international organizations such as the INCIDI.

Did the European INCIDI members succeed in using members from the Global South to hamper decolonization processes? They certainly tried but were only successful if their partners in crime saw their own political agenda fulfilled. This seems to have been the case with Justin Bomboko from Congo. INCIDI secretary-general and Belgian colonial minister between 1947 and 1950, Pierre Wigny had probably invited Bomboko to join the INCIDI, a cheap way to win his favor by declaring him a member of a politically

---

[74] Grosser, "Création Continue," 81.
[75] Nehru, *The Discovery of India*, 527–528.
[76] Abraham, "Rare Earth," 118.
[77] Ibid., 120.

9.5 TOWARD INDEPENDENCE

insignificant international organization. No doubt, Wigny was aware that the INCIDI might be useful to offer the Congolese superficial participation without real representation. But he was also in line with the INCIDI's strategy to accept decolonization, even claiming that the decolonization of the Belgian Congo colony was inevitable.[78]

His plan, however, was to "emancipate the Congo loyally."[79] He believed in governmentality as a means to ensure loyalty. More precisely, he argued that Belgians should persuade the Congolese to accept them voluntarily as their mentors: "We want to see the Africans chose voluntarily the continuation of a collaboration with Belgium, which is in their own interest."[80] In private letters dating from 1953, Wigny even took "real instead of nominal democracy in the colonies" into consideration, a plan that never materialized.[81] His openness about decolonization seemed to hit fertile ground in Congo. When Congolese politicians grinded out independence in 1960, Wigny indeed succeeded in co-opting members of the first government under Patrice Lumumba, especially Foreign Minister Justin-Marie Bomboko. Wigny himself became Belgium's foreign minister (1959–1961) during the decolonization process.

Bomboko, who had earned a degree from the Free University in Brussels, made wide use of Wigny and the Belgians to assert himself, especially against Lumumba. When the conflict boiled up, Bomboko was apparently involved in inviting, behind Lumumba's back, the Belgian army to intervene in the Congo to protect the Europeans. In the meantime, Wigny negotiated the "Treaty of Friendship, Assistance, and Co-operation" with Bomboko. This treaty provided for Belgium's continued influence in certain fields. Wigny was particularly keen on controlling the Congolese diplomatic service and arranged that "a *mission technique* has already been established ... which can be continued in the independent state ... to help organize its administration and to educate candidates to be ambassadors."[82] Both Lumumba and Bomboko signed the Treaty of Friendship, a seemingly "constructivist" act by INCIDI definitions. Among other provisions, this Treaty of Friendship stipulated that Belgians would advise the Congolese on how to build up a jurisdiction and further represented the Congo as diplomats and ambassadors in other European countries.[83] The treaty did not prevent the assassination of the "radical" Patrice Lumumba, while Bomboko continued to make a career as diplomat

---

[78] UCL Fonds Wigny, M1, vols. 1–4, 1959, Conversation with John Foster Dulles, October 8, 1958, 4.
[79] Ibid., Speech Wigny at Senate, April 22, 1959.
[80] Ibid., Personal note Wigny to Eyskens, June 30, 1959.
[81] AMAEB, Fonds Abeele 1, INCIDI 1953–54: Wigny to Abeele, December 3, 1953.
[82] UCL Fonds Wigny, M2, vol. 7, Première Réunion avec la Commission Politique Congolaise, March 18, 1960.
[83] UCL Fonds Wigny, M3, vols. 8–9, Notes Wigny, July 2, 1960

and foreign minister in the subsequent governments. He seemed to have used the INCIDI to strengthen his position, both within and outside the Congo.

9.6 International Development between Global and Local Functionalism

Once independence was underway, the INCIDI was ready to dissolve political dependence into a multiplicity of social micro-dependencies. INCIDI member Georges Balandier, the most important theorist of the late "colonial situation," rightly observed in 1952 that "a certain form of dependency is proper to all social realities."[84] He reframed the colonial situation, arguing that it resembled "the mise en rapport of two social beings, through which two civilizations are confronted with each other."[85] The INCIDI had excellent relationships with this "social being" that was the Global South, and relations intensified as soon as the colonies divorced from their metropoles. What is more, the INCIDI claimed to know the Global South best, since transcolonial comparison and transfer allowed it to join the dots of relationships, connections, and dependencies across the globe.

As soon as the international community realized that economic development of the world also required a global social policy, the interest in the INCIDI's (ex)colonial governmentality increased. The international community seemed to appreciate the INCIDI's holistic knowledge about the Global South and its practical work of the last fifty years. The postwar era also offered an uncolonial terminology to describe its activity. Functionalism was one of those terms, describing how different parts of a society are interdependent, and if one of them changes, the others change as well. Influential postwar sociologists, such as Talcott Parsons and Bert Hoselitz believed that global economic development could only be successful if it was functionalist, that is, is must take economic, social, psychological, cultural factors, etc. into account. Theories of modernization built on this holistic approach.[86]

More technically oriented, international organizations became interested in functional governance, defined as a joint effort of public and private international agencies to solve the social and economic problems of the world.[87] An important theorist of functional governance was the economist David Mitrany, who had been influenced by the early ICI when he was a student at the Colonial Institute in Hamburg before World War I. In the interwar period, he helped with conceptualizing the League of Nations' transnational

---

[84] Balandier, "Contribution à une Sociologie de la Dépendance," 49.
[85] Balandier, "La situation Coloniale," 44–79.
[86] Ekbladh, *The Great American Mission*, 114–152, 154; Gilman, *Mandarins*, 77.
[87] Karns and Mingst, *International Organizations*, 40–41.

governance and rose to fame among UN employees and international development agencies after 1945.[88]

Mitrany believed that functional governance would "shift the emphasis from political issues, which divide, to those social issues in which the interest of peoples is plainly akin and collective."[89] In 1948, he wanted to bring about development through need-based cooperation between international agencies (and not necessarily states). Mitrany's "functional approach to world organization" sounded like a self-description of the ICI/INCIDI: it originated in the utilitarian "needs which cut across national boundaries," required practical cooperation and an "international administration," and should include "policies of social improvement without encroaching on state sovereignty."[90] Mitrany took Eurafrica plans, as the ICI/INCIDI discussed them, as an example to illustrate functional governance: "The French, Belgian and British Governments are now working out lines of co-operations for their African territories, ranging from sanitation, irrigation and soil conversation, to the common use of communications, and other services, with a view to coordinating economic, educational, and administrative policies."[91] This list was more or less congruent with the ICI's main fields of action in the 1890s. Its early transcolonial development projects at the Congo-Matadí railway and at Buitenzorg indeed combined international cooperation and investment, multinational staff, and a will to balance social, legal, and cultural components.

Given the ICI's inclination to cultural relativism, the key question for the INCIDI was whether it was able to participate in the development of the Global South without harming preexisting cultural systems. Here, functionalist approaches equally provided a solution, yet of a different kind. The ICI's cultural relativism had not always been essentialist, and entrepreneurs such as Albert Thys had taught the ICI already in the 1890s that indigenous "cultures" were potentially functionalist societies open to the rationalism and dependencies of capitalism (see Chapter 2). Assuming that indigenous societies were functionalist enabled the ICI to start development projects in the 1890s, such as the Congo-Matadí railway. In the 1930s, ICI members saw how Malinowski further developed functionalist anthropology for indigenous societies, an approach that seemed also compatible with Eurafrica's "organic" corporatism designed at the Volta Congress. Postwar Eurafrica, allegedly comprising two or more civilizations and a distinction between European production space and African "complementary economic space" with resources, was equally imagined as being functionalist. At the same time, the

---

[88] Anderson, "David Mitrany," 577–592.
[89] Mitrany, *The Functional Approach*, 359.
[90] Ibid., 355–356.
[91] Ibid., 357.

INCIDI members saw in (differing) civilizations the perfect functionalist system, because civilizations were more adaptable than immobile cultures.

Sociological theories of modernization, which equally started from functionalist considerations, however, were less famous among INCIDI members, mostly because they intended to impose "industrialism" on the rest of the world without respecting "differing civilizations" and cultures.[92] What INCIDI members took from functionalist theories of modernization was the general argument that development projects had to be holistic and should take the interdependence of economic, social, and cultural patterns into account. This adaption was calculating, because the INCIDI's expertise lay exactly in this knowledge. After 1945, they could offer this expertise to American and European funders who were predominantly interested in economic development but who were slowly becoming aware of the social and cultural conditions it required.

American funders of development projects, however, rather adapted the functionalist approach of homegrown modernization sociologist such as Talcott Parsons.[93] Parsons had identified different "pattern variables" that described the transformation of socioeconomic systems from subsistence economies to industrialism. In Parsons' view, industrialism was not only industrialization but covered a wide range of interdependent processes in economic, political, demographic, cultural, and individual elements that made a system functional.[94] Thus, entire countries had to be "modernized" to open them for Western-style industrialization. Although they never mentioned Parsons, INCIDI members very likely rejected his simplistic dichotomies between backward and modern societies and disagreed that he practically made Western individualistic lifestyles the precondition of industrial development.[95] Despite funding options, the INCIDI never fell in love with modernization theory, claiming to know that there was more to well-being than income statistics.[96]

Rather uninterested in Parson's Western-centric functionalism, INCIDI members invited his disciple Bert Hoselitz to join their ranks. Hoselitz had applied Parsons' "pattern variables" to colonial and developing countries. INCIDI members frequently referred to Hoselitz, who reiterated Parson's idea that technical change in underdeveloped countries "requires an adaption in culture and social structure, which, in the last resort, reaches into all aspects of social life, and affects not only the outward relations between persons, but also

---

[92] Cooper, "Modernization," 33; Engermann and Unger, "Introduction," 384.
[93] Latham, *The Right Kind*, 44–47.
[94] Cooper, *Writing the History*, 14.
[95] Gilman, *Mandarins of the Future*, 76.
[96] Cullather, *Development?*, 651.

9.6 INTERNATIONAL DEVELOPMENT 337

their outlook, motivational patterns, and way of thinking."[97] But, in his report for the INCIDI on Burma and Siam, Hoselitz added that all cultures can generate economic development without outright Westernization and proletarianization. It occurred to him that there "was no single path to betterment."[98] Hence, progress could not exclusively be measured by "the growth of per capita real output."[99] His interdependent patterns were exactly what the INCIDI needed to justify its own involvement in the Global South, and INCIDI members used and reinterpreted them rather than endorsing them unconditionally.

While INCIDI members potentially capitalized on Parson's and Hoselitz's theory of modernization that needed the INCIDI's anthropological and sociological knowledge, Parsons' pattern variables seemed Eurocentric and thwarted the INCIDI's strategy to distance itself from the old colonialist narrative of backwardness versus progress.[100] Hoselitz was not free of this Europeanization narrative. Comparing Burma and Siam in his report, Hoselitz concluded that Burma had a more efficient rice production than Siam, because the Burmese had completely broken with traditional society during the colonial period and established new nationalist elites after independence, while Siam lagged behind for having failed to modernize its society.[101] Hoselitz was probably right, but the INCIDI seemed unsatisfied with the tradition-modernity divide and was also against a total exchange of elites after independence.

The INCIDI experts' capital was their ability to cope with the complexity of the (post)colonial situation, which they did not want to see washed away, neither by Western modernizers nor by radical anti-colonial modernizers. Parsons seemed to have little to say about the complex "encounter" between civilizations the INCIDI was interested in and tended to advocate a total transformation of "underdeveloped" societies to "industrialism."[102] Unlike the INCIDI, he explicitly dismissed cultural relativism, accusing its advocates to regard "the Arunta of Australia and such modern societies as the Soviet Union as equally authentic 'cultures'" by not taking into account the evolutionary status of a society.[103] That argument certainly missed the point and did not win him any sympathies among INCIDI members.

Rejecting Parsons' industrializing mission, the INCIDI remained equally skeptical toward other large-scale development programs, such as the

---

[97] INCIDI, *Comte Rendu 1957*, 370.
[98] Cooper, *Writing the History*, 6.
[99] Latham, *The Right Kind*, 51.
[100] Gilman, *Mandarins*, 87.
[101] INCIDI, *Compte Rendu 1953*, 196–207.
[102] Cooper, "Development, Modernization," 33.
[103] Gilman, *Mandarins*, 88.

American Tennessee Valley Authority (1933), which completely restructured a society living close to a new hydroelectric dam to combine economic progress with a social effort of improving living standards and agriculture.[104] Given its long history of low budget development, the INCIDI also repudiated larger state investments and the "fetishism of plans," such as the fifty billion francs Belgium planned to invest in the Congo colony, the thirty-eight million pounds that the British had spent on the Groundnut scheme in Tanganyika, the Colonial Development and Welfare Act, as well as the French FIDES development plan (all of which they regarded as inefficient because adequate local support was lacking to implement them and they predominantly benefited staff and institutions "outside the colony").[105]

9.7 The Enforcement of Sustained Development

Unlike state-financed mega-projects, whose planners wanted to impose a great leap forward on "underdeveloped" societies, the INCIDI aimed at gradual development by maintaining and using local structures and agency.[106] For example, the INCIDI highlighted the achievements of "leaders deriving their authority from traditional sources" who "are extremely effective modernizers (for example the Emperor of Ethiopia, the Sardauna of Sokoto, and the Kabaka of Buganda)."[107] Thus, the INCIDI stood for a more sustained development policy that "should be practical," "ensure the conservation of renewable resources," "raise the standard of living," respect the "mode of living," and avoid "proletarianization and unnecessary displacement of populations."[108] The INCIDI remained largely skeptical of industrialization and urbanization, a strategy that proved detrimental to its finances: the big, predominantly Belgian, mining companies who had joined after 1945 gradually lost interest in the INCIDI's work.

Given the wide interest in the ICI/INCIDI's scheme of sustained development, its members had the impression of being always a step ahead. Wigny, who became the new secretary-general of the INCIDI in 1951, endorsed Article 73 of the UN's San Francisco Charter that promised to respect the interests of the non-autonomous territories and obliged Europeans to develop them economically and guide them to self-government. "These ideas are not new," Wigny claimed at the INCIDI's inaugural session in 1949 and argued

---

[104] Mitrany, *The Functional Approach*, 355; Ekbladh, *The Great American Mission*, 190–226.
[105] INCIDI, *Compte Rendu 1949*, 13; and *Compte Rendu 1951*, 184; Ekbladh, *The Great American Mission*, 59.
[106] INCIDI, *Compte Rendu 1951*, 101–103.
[107] INCIDI, *Compte Rendu 1960*, 487.
[108] INCIDI, *Compte Rendu 1951*, 142 and 159.

that "a moral ideal has just turned into a precise legal engagement."[109] What is more, he declared that the ICI was at the origin of this transnational and governmental development policy. He referred to Harry S. Truman's Point Four Program of 1949, in which the US president urged to "win the hearts and minds" of the people of the Third World through a concerted international effort to develop their territories economically. The INCIDI cited Truman frequently.[110] Wigny both admired and qualified Truman's development program by asking rhetorically: "What does President Truman suggest in his bold Point Four for the underdeveloped areas? Financial and technical assistance. That has been our program for fifty years."[111]

Against this background, the INCIDI placed itself rather aggressively in the new market of development policies. Wigny's first official act as the INCIDI's secretary-general was to travel to the United States and offer its time-honored expertise in transcolonial functional governance to the UN; the Carnegie Foundation; the Phelps Stokes Fund, whose agents financed the education of Africans and Afro-Americans and whose chairman had joined the ICI in 1936; and the Social Science Council's Committee on World Area Research.[112] In the 1950s, the INCIDI started cooperative projects with UN-ECOSOC and UNESCO. The next step was to expand geographically.

After 1945, the INCIDI applied its activity no longer exclusively to (former) colonies but to the entire "underdeveloped territories" and underlined that it "is no more a *Colonial Institute*. From now on, what we found confirmed ... for Africa and the colonial territories is also true for those territories in which undeveloped populations live."[113] By 1955, it had invited representatives from Colombia, Cuba, Ethiopia, Haiti, Honduras, Mexico, Peru, Puerto Rico, and Trinidad to emphasize its desire to work with "underdeveloped" countries in the so-called Third World.

Small-scale rural development and self-help remained the INCIDI's preferred method for development in the late colonial period. A frequently cited "example of self-help," was the late colonial Emirate of Abrija with twenty-eight villages in Northern Nigeria. There, the ruling Emir

> has encouraged each village to increase agricultural production, to introduce cash crops, to provide a fuel plantation, to undertake contour farming against soil erosion, to build an elementary school, a dispensary and a village hall, to introduce village draining and concrete lined wells, and to improve layouts of villages and sanitation ... already in a year or

---

[109] INCIDI, *Compte Rendu 1949*, 15.
[110] INCIDI, *Compte Rendu 1951*, 163.
[111] UCL Fonds Wigny Carrière C4, Voyage aux États-Unis, MS. Colonial Policy of Belgium, 5.
[112] Ibid., Meeting March 19, 1952.
[113] INCIDI, *Compte Rendu 1951*, 105.

so, dams have been built by voluntary communal labor. Help and advice have come from the Government Departments. Last year, 250 tons of cash crops were produced ... 28 literacy classes are functioning and 200 literacy awards have been given. 6 village schools are completed and 5 medical dispensaries.[114]

Increasingly, marketing boards, often established upon agreement between the government and "a voluntary co-operative marketing association" emerged in West Africa to stabilize prices. The surplus these cooperative marketing associations made was used to finance cultural and welfare schemes.[115] The theory of such cooperative welfare schemes originated in the ICI's plans for "Social Assistance," developed in Belgium before 1914 and introduced in the Congo by ICI member Alfred Moeller de Laddersous, long before an official Belgian decree imposed indigenous cooperatives in 1949.[116]

INCIDI member and Labour politician Creech Jones added that cooperative and mutual aid societies would contribute to a feeling of independence and thus prevent radical urban anti-colonialism from spreading to the countryside. There, people could feel an "independent spirit and feeling of self-reliance" aroused by the encouragement of "voluntary and self-help movement" from the "trade union to the co-operative, the friendly society and social welfare group, the church meeting and the youth organization."[117]

The INCIDI's small-scale approach to rural development, however, was less innocent than it seemed, since it contained (neo)colonial elements and anachronistic schemes of enforced development. In 1953, the INCIDI passed a resolution stating that countries in the Third World "have an obligation" to develop their resources "in a rational manner." If they did not fulfill this task, international organizations should "advise [those] countries of their obligations." This statement resembled a right to enforce a system of neocolonial governmentality on the Third World: "The giving of international assistance by countries which have preserved a margin between their production and their needs lays an obligation on the countries aided to take measures of economic self-help to the full extent of their resources and to safeguard the capital invested."[118]

In short, the INCIDI wanted to enforce self-help on underdeveloped countries. Given its long-standing focus on agricultural development, it recom-

---

[114] Ibid., 189.
[115] INCIDI, *Compte Rendu 1951*, 195.
[116] INCIDI, *Compte Rendu 1953*, 135.
[117] INCIDI, *Compte Rendu 1951*, 183.
[118] INCIDI, *Compte Rendu 1953*, 395; AMAEB, Fonds van den Abeele 3663/198 INCIDI, Folder 1 INCIDI 1953–54, Session de la Haye, September 7–10, 1953, Séance "Économie Rurale."

mended "cooperatives and sharecropping" for that purpose.[119] Its members also deemed a "codification of customary agriculture" necessary to use and modify the customs from within to the benefit of a capitalist mode of production.[120] To achieve all these goals rapidly, "compulsory organization such as the French Provident Societies" was preferable to purely voluntary cooperative organization.[121] This system of enforced self-help through international organizations reiterated the ICI's agenda of functional governance and its (neo)colonial purpose.

Small-scale and rural development was also a legacy of the "Italian model" of peasant participation promoted at the Volta Congress and implemented again in postwar Italy. The Italian model soon came into conflict with American "Parsonian" development theory, but international experts judged it "the broadest and most attractive development plan in the world."[122] Unsurprisingly, experts of peasant participation saw in the INCIDI's 1953 meeting on rural development the triumph of the model of "community development" and the "'rural uplifting' based on the mutualist and cooperative movements."[123] Among the speakers in 1953 was Belgian-French INCIDI member Robert Delavignette who had long promoted the productive role of the "black peasant" whom the colonial administration should not regard as a potential plantation laborer anymore. Instead, he argued, black peasants should keep their own land, work traditions, rites, and established crops. Itinerant experts and administrators should then advise them how to improve within their own culture.[124]

Judging free cooperatives insufficient, experts in French Equatorial Africa introduced the so-called *paysannat* from Belgian Congo in the 1950s.[125] The idea was to oblige inhabitants of a village to cultivate "land of sufficient size and stable fertility, by integrating them into an organization that guarantees the respect of certain agronomic principles and provides them with the benefits of collective action."[126] In an unusually blunt INCIDI report full of contempt for the Congolese peasants, the Belgian head of Congo's agricultural service admitted that the *paysannat* system might resemble a Soviet "kolkhoz." While denying that the *paysannat* made use of enforced collectivization, he

---

[119] INCIDI, *Compte Rendu 1953*, 397.
[120] AMAEB, Fonds van den Abeele 3663/198 INCIDI, Folder 1 INCIDI 1953-54, "Le relèvement rural en fonction de notre connaissance de la coutume agricole par P. de Schlippé."
[121] Ibid., W. H. Beckett, General Report on Rural economy Document de travail pour la 28e session d'études de l'INDCIDI, the Hague September 7-10, 1953.
[122] Lorenzini, *Development*, 15 and 30-32.
[123] INCIDI, *Compte Rendu 1953*; Chauveau, *Enquête*, 135.
[124] Gamble, *Peasants*, 775-804.
[125] INCIDI, *Compte Rendu 1953*, 136-137.
[126] Ibid., 85.

equally justified it by describing the Congolese as "fatalist, apathetic, and insouciant" whose customary agriculture had to be "destroyed."[127] The *fokon'olona*, which became even more important as a means of strict control after the Malagasy insurrection of 1947, were augmented by *paysannat* schemes and called *Collectivités rurales autochtones modernisés* of which "some pretend that they come close to kolkhozes" and forced modernization.[128] *Paysannat* schemes were equally applied in Morocco, where "a regime of strict authority attaches them to the soil ... to break the interior resistances of the customs."[129] Finally, the famous Sociétés de Prévoyance in French Africa that the INCIDI continued to promote seemed to be "compulsory institutions" to some observers.[130]

Despite endorsing schemes of compulsory labor, the INCIDI continued to attract attention for its drive to preserve cultural integrity. It supplied huge development trusts such as the United Nations Economic and Social Council (ECOSOC) with anthropological micro-knowledge about sustainable initiatives for self-help, mutual assistance, cooperative development, low-priced housing societies, and the training of women as social and health workers. Its purpose remained to bring about soft development that was "appropriate to the native mentality."[131] For this purpose, it invited experts from the Global South to share their knowledge and offered to advise more potent and younger development organizations. The INCIDI was officially in "consultative relationship" with ECOSOC, which made use of the INCIDI's (dismissive) studies about urbanization.[132]

Its project to preserve indigenous societies and culture during the development process brought the INCIDI particularly closer to UNESCO. The purpose of UNESCO was equally preservationist and in favor of a soft development. Thus, the INCIDI's ties with UNESCO were no coincidence because they shared the same idea of combining cultural relativism and sustainable development schemes. Wigny was proud to announce in the 1950s that the "INCIDI had consultative status with UNESCO, the Economic and Social Council of the UN," and also held close ties with the International Labour Organization as well as the World Health Organization.[133] As we have seen, those organizations indeed occasionally emulated the INCIDI's governmentality in the field of development and

---

[127] Ibid., 128 and 137.
[128] Ibid., 159.
[129] Ibid., 92.
[130] Ibid., 297.
[131] Van Hove, "Social Service," *Civilisations* 1 (1951), 22–26.
[132] UN ECOSOC Expert Meeting on Social Defence, E/CN.14/SODE/6, August 18–31, 1964, 20.
[133] UCL Fonds Wigny, Speech Manuscript INCIDI, 5.

recommended, for example, to use the *fokon'olona* and Islamic craft guilds for sustained development.

Hence, the INCIDI epitomized the small-scale development schemes that the international aid industry would only adopt in the 1970s. It is thus no wonder that the directors-general of UNESCO, from Julian Huxley to Amadou-Mahtar M'Bow, became equally members of the INCIDI. As early as 1952, UNESCO funded INCIDI research projects, for example, on the preservation of the variety of local African languages in a period when independent states committed themselves to a single commercial and official language, which was often a European one.[134] Obviously, the INCIDI and UNESCO shared a drive for education, however not necessarily academic education but simply popular education, such as alphabetization and technical education to train engineers, architects, physicians, and bureaucrats.[135] Both institutions had a clear anti-communist stance, which they deemed would "destroy everything"[136]

Never innocent, the INCIDI members used UNESCO to control the cultural production and history of these independent countries. As a member of both the INCIDI and UNESCO explained: "Peoples who are in the process of acquiring, or who have nearly acquired, their independence, are unable to conduct such studies [about their own history and civilization] and are little disposed to permit other nations to undertake them, but they would frequently welcome assistance from an international agency to explore, conserve, and spread an understanding of their past."[137] The Tunisian delegate at the INCIDI protested against such attitudes, explaining that "the experience of Tunisia has shown that a foreign expert will fail in his mission if not accompanied by a sufficiently qualified autochthonous colleague."[138]

9.8 De-radicalizing Anti-colonialism with Women and the Middle Class

In the 1950s, INCIDI members spent some effort to uncover allegedly underused functional elements such as the "middle class" and women in the (former) colonies. This is why the INCIDI organized two meetings entirely dedicated to the rise of the middle class and the role of women in the colonies. The idea was to activate and integrate them both in a system of global dependencies. Making use of a new dependent middle class and women was above all an instrument to oust the supposed "racism" and "xenophobia" of

---

[134] "Chronique de l'Institut," *Civilisations*, 2, no. 1 (1952), 149–158: 153.
[135] INCIDI, *Compte Rendu 1949*, 139–140.
[136] Ibid., 157.
[137] INCIDI, *Compte Rendu 1949*, 42.
[138] INCIDI, *Compte Rendu 1960*, 566.

radical anti-colonialists, who were likely to break with the West. The middle class should prevent the rise of extremes – hyper-nationalists and communists – and women were said to have moderating effects on radical nationalists.

The meeting on the "women's role" in 1959 seemed revolutionary but its outcome was disappointing because the debate was more about women's function in late colonial societies than about their rights. It was revolutionary because former resistance fighter and feminist Marie-Hélène Lafaucheux organized it and invited almost exclusively women, two-thirds of whom came from the Global South. The INCIDI leaders had a rather "functional" interest in the issue and announced that "to neglect the education of one half of the human race is an astonishing waste of human resources"[139] Education played a an important role but rather for the purpose of production and reproduction and not higher education. Nani Sawondo from Indonesia even referred to the feminist Kartini by whom ICI members had been inspired as early as 1900: "The first primary school for girls, called 'Kartini Schools' in honor of Raden Adjeng Kartini, was established in 1913, and from then on school education for girls rapidly increased."[140] Some mentioned women's rights, others universal suffrage, but in the end, women were reduced to their role in cooperatives, market unions, hygiene, education, and reproduction. Slightly frustrated, Lafaucheux concluded that the "INCIDI is not a legislative organ and can assert itself forcefully" to demand women's rights. It did not.[141]

According to the INCIDI, training and educating the "middle class" had several positive effects. In the 1950s, focusing on the administrative and economic middle class was a way to oust the radically nationalist elites, whom the INCIDI regarded as nonrepresentative. That was hardly new, given that the ICI had always claimed to be closer to the average population than to the "alienated" nationalist elites. At the 1951 meeting, INCIDI members reiterated that an educated middle class was necessary to avoid "exposing the entire population to the tyranny of an oligarchy of intellectuals."[142] The intellectuals, of course, were the nationalist leaders and often communists, who, in the eyes of the INCIDI, had no other function than making trouble. They should be replaced with a more technocratic middle class concerned with practical questions and therefore more likely accept pragmatic solutions with the help of Europeans.[143] Through technical training, the administrators, teachers, clerks, and tradesmen would gain "importance in leadership in the building up of their nations."[144] Thus, a "social tissue" in form of a well-off and taxable

---

[139] INCIDI, *Compte Rendu 1959*, 24.
[140] Ibid., 131.
[141] Ibid., 461.
[142] INCIDI, *Compte Rendu 1951*, 75.
[143] Ibid., 76.
[144] Ibid., 81 and 130.

Figure 9.1 Opening meeting of the INCIDI's session in Palermo in 1963
© INCIDI, Les Constitutions Et Institutions Administratives Des Etats Nouveaux, Compte Rendu De La 33ème Session À Palerme 1963 (Brussels: INCIDI, 1963)

middle class would emerge, join the administrative and technical service, and work for economic progress.[145] The INCIDI thus advocated a shift from the indirect rule through traditional indigenous "elites" to the "leadership" of the new middle class.

Since the 200 members of the INCIDI were predominantly former colonial administrators, it is hardly surprising that they thought of administrators and bureaucrats as the core of the middle class. Echoing the discourse on underdevelopment, the INCIDI invented the term "under-administration," to legitimize European intervention into administrative affairs overseas.[146] After the independence of most countries in 1960, the INCIDI invited representatives from around the Third World to discuss the role of the administrative "cadres." All agreed that the new countries lacked expertise, training schools, and skilled administrators. They concluded that those who held higher positions in administration, politics, and economy should be trained in the Western world.

When faced with independence and new democracies, INCIDI members went even a step further. A member from independent Iraq generally agreed to

---

[145] Ibid., 183.
[146] INCIDI, *Compte Rendu 1961*, 620.

"produce leadership" but recommended first to "start educating everybody so as to have a broad mass of educated people for all posts." This rarely happened.[147] The INCIDI appropriated this idea for Africa: "In the African territories, we are getting away more and more from the idea of an 'elite' and are enlisting more and more the ordinary people." This fit the ICI/INCIDI's program to emphasize its bonds with these forgotten parts of the population, including those living in rural areas and women. Both "mass education" and the "higher education of women" became the INCDI's strategies to achieve this goal.[148]

In 1959, when the Congo was on its way to independence, Pierre Wigny made use of this "populist" strategy. As foreign minister, he pushed the Belgian government to keep "the extremist elements" at bay by organizing communal elections in the Congo. The organization of elections would seal independence but would also delay it and give the Belgians the opportunity to influence it. Wigny publicly announced that "we stated clearly that the definitive political status of the Congo should be determined by the Africans and we will put them into the state of choosing independence if they want it."[149] The Belgians hoped to control the process to reach a "state of choosing independence." The plan to hold general elections to oust the nationalist leaders who wanted immediate independence was in line with the ICI/INCIDI's longtime strategy to question the representativeness of more radical independence leaders. Wigny was convinced that a popular vote, steered by old collaborators with the Europeans would bring a result that was more favorable to Belgian influence in the country. He believed that "the majority of the population supports the Belgian program. Only a troublemaking minority, sometimes well organized and locally strong, oppose it."[150] When this project of governmentality failed, however, Wigny endorsed Lumumbas' assassination to find a quicker solution.[151]

At the 1963 meeting, INCIDI members nevertheless proclaimed that they were the

> prolongation of [your, the formerly colonized] preceding historical meetings, in particular the congress of Bandoeng ... which gave expression to your sense of international solidarity; the congresses of Paris and Rome, where black writers and artists from all continents engaged in memorable debates; as well as the congress recently held in Addis Ababa where the idea of the African peoples to unite was born.[152]

---

[147] INCIDI, *Compte Rendu 1951*, 87.
[148] Ibid., 77, 81, and 83.
[149] UCL Fonds Wigny, M1, vols. 1–4, 1959, Personal note Wigny to Eyskens, June 30, 1959.
[150] Ibid., M2, vol. 5, 1959, Wigny Affaires Etrangères, December 16, 1959.
[151] Witte, *The Assassination*, 23.
[152] INCIDI, *Compte Rendu 1963*, 13–14.

9.8 DE-RADICALIZING ANTI-COLONIALISM

By appropriating the famous Afro-Asian Bandung conference of 1955, which established a feeling of South-South solidarity against colonialism, the INCIDI falsely redefined itself as a trailblazer of anti-colonialism. In 1963, 160 participants from 34 countries participated in the INCIDI's meeting (see Figure 9.1). Indeed, by 1963, INCIDI's delegates came from Algeria, Congo-Léopoldville, Ivory Coast, Egypt, Ethiopia, Ghana, Upper Volta, India, Iran, Kenya, Lebanon, Libya, Morocco, Nigeria, Pakistan, the Philippines, Puerto Rico, the United Arab Republic, Madagascar, Ruanda, Senegal, Singapore, Syria, Tanganyika, Tunisia, Uganda, and Vietnam. Yet Europeans – represented by Italy, France, Belgium, Germany, and the United Kingdom – were still the main instigators. The strategy to rewrite the INCIDI's history as an anticolonial history seemed promising, but the material reality stood in the way.

In the 1960s, when delegates from the Global South came to play a more important role in the INCIDI, it seemed to lose its energy, its financial means, its exceptional expertise, and most importantly, its purpose.[153] The secretaries-general of the 1960s and 1970s, the former ILO employee Pierre de Briey and the former governor of Ruanda-Urundi Jean Paul Harroy found it increasingly difficult to raise funding. They blamed decolonization processes for making the INCIDI irrelevant, at least in the eyes of those who still thought of it as a colonial institution.[154] To overcome this crisis, the secretaries-general offered to serve as an official development organization for the Belgian state and negotiated with NATO to convert the INCIDI into an instrument to fight the Soviets in the Cold War.[155] When these initiatives failed, they offered Tunisia, Libya, Morocco, and even Congo under Mobutu to advise them in matters of economic development.[156] But, to no avail. In 1971, UNESCO suspected the INCIDI of supporting South African apartheid, but the INCIDI referred to its anti-settlerist tradition to deliver the proof that it does "not in any way countenance the doctrine of apartheid."[157] In 1973, when the oil crisis made donors retire their funding, the INCIDI had to take up a loan. It needed 579,000 francs to balance its budget and was not able to pay its employees anymore.[158] In that year, the secretary-general invited the retired Wigny to join the next session of the INCIDI, just to "assist to its decline."[159]

While the INCIDI blamed its decline on the harsh competition with more

---

[153] UCL Fonds Wigny INCIDI, Harmel (Belgian Aff Etr.) to Wigny, July 15, 1969, Annex INCIDI.
[154] Ibid., Speech Wigny for 35th Session of the INCIDI, 3–4.
[155] Ibid., Wigny to Harmel, August 9, 1969.
[156] Ibid., De Briey to Wigny, August 29, 1969.
[157] UN General Assembly, 26th session: A/8314/Add.6 (Part II), January 24, 1972, 105.
[158] UCL Fonds Wigny INCIDI, Briey to Wigny, May 15, 1973.
[159] Ibid., Briey to Wigny, June 28, 1973

potent development agencies, decolonization, and the economic crisis of the 1970s, it actually failed because of its neocolonial arrogance. In 1967, it had launched a study in several countries of the Third World to investigate the reasons for famine and the failure of agricultural development programs. It continued to blame the new independent governments of incompetence in this matter, advancing their inability to organize economic development. The INCIDI's study started from the premise that the obstacles to development of intensive agriculture did not "derive from the lack of the scientific basis or technological tools, but they came from political and economic obstacles."[160] Although the Belgian state already funded the project with 300,000 francs, the INCIDI spent as much as 600,000 francs.[161] Hence, the loan of 1973, which the INCIDI never managed to redeem. Observers complained that the study advanced too slowly and, in 1973, the INCIDI had to discontinue the project, which left the donors disappointed.[162] The INCIDI kept afloat until 1982 and then dissolved.

Nevertheless, its legacy of colonial internationalism lingered on. The journal *Civilisations*, in which INCIDI members published their research on the Third World, still exists today.[163] The ICI/INCIDI reshaped and legitimized colonialism without abandoning asymmetrical power relations. It delivered the proof that colonialism needed neither the label "colonial" nor an official government to impose itself. Thereby, the ICI and the INCIDI laid the basis for the transcolonial governmentality in the Global South that shaped the twentieth century up until the present day.

---

[160] Ibid., Harmel (Belgian Aff Etr.) to Wigny, July 15, 1969.
[161] Ibid., Note Complementaire February 21, 1973, 2.
[162] Ibid., Letter SG Harroy to Wigny, May 5, 1975.
[163] Pétit, "Éditorial," *Civilisations*, 7–8.

Conclusion

> Most of them pretend sympathy for effect, or through calculation, with some end in view. It is amusing; if one looks at the humorous side of such things, then one is not distressed. People often do such foolish things. Do not imagine that I do not see that many of those who now talk about native art, only do it to make themselves agreeable to me, and not because they have any real appreciation of it. Before me, every one is enthusiastic. Is it from conviction?[1]

In this 1902 quote, the Javanese feminist and anti-colonialist Raden Adjeng Kartini mocked her European visitors, most of whom were ICI members. Among her recent guests had been the French founder of the ICI, Joseph Chailley and the German expert of comparative colonial law and ICI member Günther Anton. Both had connected with Kartini on the recommendation of her mentor, the Dutch ICI member J. H. Abendanon, and had traveled to Djapara on Dutch Java to meet her in person. Kartini, a twenty-year-old daughter of a high-ranking Indonesian official, famous for her brilliant analysis of both traditional and colonial societies in Java, described the Europeans quite adequately: On the surface, ICI members were respectful and interested in native culture and its preservation. Yet, first-hand knowledge about native cultural and social life, as well as the personal acquaintance with an exceptional person like Kartini, was mainly for effect. They served to boost their careers as colonial experts. By visiting Kartini, whose feminism was as cautious as her anti-colonialism, ICI members did what they always did: they attempted to use the networks of colonial internationalism to portray themselves as progressive indigenophiles. When writing about Kartini in his book *Java et ses habitants*, Chailley revealed that his real interest was more mundane: "She has the merit of never turning a blind eye on the defaults of her race."[2] Knowing the strong and the weak points of this "race" provided the basis

---

[1] Kartini, *Letters*, October 27, 1902, 244.
[2] Chailley, *Java*, LXXXIV.

for manipulating and, ultimately, for governing the colonized world in a subtle way that this book calls the governmentality of empire.

The ICI's history disproves the notion of a progressive transformation and betterment of colonialism from an early violent, exploitative, and genocidal version to a late "benevolent colonialism" open to reform, participation, international cooperation, and social and economic advancement. The alleged shift from an empire of repression to an empire of opportunities is a deeply colonialist narrative. This book has shown that liberalism, reformism, and internationalism were driving forces behind colonialism from its beginning and served to legitimize it. In so doing, the narrative of internationalist and reformist colonialism enabled and camouflaged structural violence, exploitation, and the production of global inequality. Historians should thus follow the postcolonial mission to scrutinize seemingly liberal and progressive phenomena in history for underlying colonialist structures.

It is therefore the conclusion and the message of this book that colonialism is not reformable, as the ICI pretended it was, but remained pretty much the same between 1890 and 1950. The ICI is the smoking gun that proves the immobility of colonialism. To overcome colonialism and the global inequality caused by it, it needed more than a reform. As Aimé Césaire put it: "Real decolonization is revolutionary or inexistent."[3] The ICI/INCIDI did everything possible to avoid such revolutionary decolonization.

While continuity characterized the ICI, similarities in the historical contexts of 1893 and 1945 allowed the ICI to stay the same over sixty years. The ICI's self-professed progressivism, its sympathy toward the colonized, and the use of the moral language of internationalism was a strategic response to the early crisis of colonialism in the 1890s, intended to inoculate colonialism against mounting criticism. This strategy became important again in 1945.

Curiously, the colonial crisis of the 1890s resembled in many regards the crisis of colonialism after World War II. In the 1890s, the nationalist enthusiasm of the conquest era gave way to a controversy over the high costs of colonial administration and *mise en valeur*. After 1945, France, Britain, the Netherlands, Belgium, and Italy equally had to live up to their war promise to make large-scale investments in their colonies, despite the postwar financial crisis. As early as the 1890s, the international community debated the legitimacy of colonialism in face of Léopold's lethal rubber exploitation in the Congo; in a similar way, the international community debated the legitimacy of colonialism after Hitler's genocidal *Lebensraum* excesses (in both cases, by the way, people involved in the mass killings rehabilitated themselves by joining the ICI/INCIDI). Forced labor was a big topic in the 1890s, when ICI members criticized the Dutch coerced cultivation system in Java and in

---

[3] INCIDI, *Compte Rendu 1960*, 147.

1945, when the war effort had led many European empires to reintroduce forced cultivation and labor, not to speak of recruitment for the war itself.[4] Both in the 1890s and after 1945, a long history of anti-colonial movements had led the empires to rethink their colonial policy. The early ICI developed its governmental schemes explicitly to avoid conflicts such as the Sepoy war in British India (1856) and the Mokrani-Revolt in French Algeria (1870). Intellectuals such as Kartini, Casely Hayford, and Edmond Morel began to publicly criticize colonial rule around 1900, and it is no coincidence that the ICI paid special attention to them. Chailley, for example, extensively quoted and thus promulgated Kartini's criticism of colonial violence. In his book, he took the following quote from Kartini: "I have personally seen how a European – who was not among the stupid ones – flogged children, women, and young girls with a cane because they had not immediately let him past during public festivities...the horror of corporal punishment... was a humiliation for those who suffered the strokes and those who gave them."[5] While quoting Kartini did not make Chailley the Sartre of the 1890s (Sartre had written the preface to Frantz Fanon's famous anti-colonial treaty on colonial violence in 1961), he nevertheless used her to portray himself and the ICI as progressive, reformist, and internationalist. Finally, colonizers of the 1890s and the 1940s encountered similar difficulties living up to their promise of securing "moral and material well-being" of the colonized and bringing them the "blessings of civilization" (quotes from the Congo Act 1885, in which civilization meant assimilation of the economy and not yet assimilation of people). Although the comparison between the 1890s and the 1960s seems farfetched, the long history of the ICI shows that the difference was one in degree rather than in essence.

When decolonization came, the ICI was neither surprised nor unprepared. Colonizers had long held out the prospect of self-government, no doubt for too long. Yet the ICI's serenity was astonishing, given that its raison d'être was at risk. Apart from a few rhetorical charades, the ICI/INCIDI hardly addressed the dramatic changes in world history. The uttered no word about the violent conflicts that led to independence. Between 1949 and 1963, the INCIDI's conference proceedings mention the Mau Mau war in Kenya only once; conflicts in Algeria, Madagascar, and Indonesia are completely absent. The absence of liberation wars is astonishing but consequential. It followed the axiom of Bernhard Dernburg, a German ICI member and colonial reformer, who laid emphasis on the "constructive" side of colonialism, while keeping silent about the "destructive" consequences. He published his theory of constructive colonialism, probably borrowed from British Secretary of State for

---

[4] Michel, *L'appel à l'Afrique*.
[5] Chailley, *Java et ses habitants*, LXXXIV.

the Colonies Joseph Chamberlain, in 1907, while the genocide against the Herero and Nama in German South West Africa was hardly over. Like Dernburg, the ICI/INCIDI never mentioned that devastating war and genocide. Again, this was no coincidence but part of the ICI's strategy to portray colonialism as a constructive science that used a rational method to make the world better.

How could the ICI, after dedicating fifty years of its existence to becoming the biggest colonialist think tank, quietly accept decolonization in the 1950s? Answers to this question can again be found in the 1890s, when the ICI was established to portray colonialism as progressive. By declaring colonialism an international project, the ICI made it appear constructive and progressive. The ICI allegedly emancipated colonialism from selfish nationalist interests and the violent era of imperial conquest and thereby initiated a shift from emotional to rational and modern colonialism. The origins of colonialism were no longer to be found in a glorious national past but in a prosperous future. According to the ICI's view, not only the colonizing nation but all of humanity would benefit from the colonial encounter. The ICI's internationalism was thus not an end in and of itself but a means to declare colonialism more progressive. No doubt, the League of Nations and the United Nations later perpetuated the idea of a causality between internationalism and progress.

The internationalist ideal facilitated the emergence of a transnational colonial science in the metropoles. Using comparison and transfer as methods of colonial science, the ICI assembled a pool of knowledge, which was, however, structurally racist, selective, biased, and often manipulated. Unlike armchair scholars in the metropole, however, the ICI was more interested in an applied science for the colonies. Therefore, transcolonial interaction within the ICI was intended for practical application of certain technologies, such as the cultivation of higher-yielding plants and more efficient planting techniques. Transcolonial applied science was based on experience rather than theory and seemed cheaper for each empire, as Chailley put it: "Why invent if inventions already exist?" Comparison and transfer, however, often failed the self-declared technocrats of the ICI, because comparisons produced stereotypes and archetypes that stood in the way of unbiased and therefore successful prototype transfers.

The ICI aimed to see its pragmatic science applied by an international technocratic corps that laid a focus on social and economic engineering, accompanied by skills in intercultural competence. The institute considered this technocratic corps less interested in politics and the technocracy a way to depoliticize and rationalize colonialism. Technical staff for the colonies was indeed trained internationally, such as Dutch forestry experts who attended German forestry schools and Italian doctors who worked in the Congo Free State. The step to the functional governance of the League of Nations and international development agencies of the post-1945 era was a short one.

Members of the ICI were indeed among the first to apply sociological approaches to the Global South by avoiding the purely ethnographic gaze common around 1900. For the ICI members, the inhabitants of the colonies formed complex and dynamic societies and not static communities. While this was innovative and predated similar approaches by Malinowski and Balandier by forty years, it was also instrumental in manipulating the "colonial situation" to the benefit of the colonizers. Reinterpreting Islamic law, for example, started from the assumption that it was a sociological phenomenon and therefore was malleable and adoptable, especially under colonial rule. At the International Congress for Colonial Sociology, co-organized by ICI members in Paris in 1900, such sociological manipulations seemed to be well established. The will to use sociological knowledge for its governmentality distinguished the ICI from research institutions such as the International Institute of African Languages and Cultures that would not implement such strategies before the 1930s.

The ICI's transcolonial governmentality, which developed into the concept of functional governance in the 1920s, made wide use of these sociological approaches. Claiming that it wanted to govern without and beyond the state, functional governance focused on the interdependence of economy, society, and culture. According to theorists of functional governance, who were trained by members of the ICI before World War I, it needed international organizations, multinational companies, and NGOs to solve the social and economic problems of the world, without referring to nation-states that were only concerned about their sovereignty. On that point, the ICI of the 1890s and the post-1945 internationalists were congruent.

Functionalism played an increasingly important role in the ICI during the 1930s and 1940s. Malinowski's reinterpretation of "tribes" and "indigenous societies" as functionalist instead of essentialist fell on fertile ground among the utilitarians who had established the ICI and saw rationalism rule also in colonial societies with seemingly "irrational" customs. Fascists at the 1938 Volta congress saw their own theory of organic societies revived in such functionalist approaches. In practice, they tried to establish a corporatist Eurafrica that was functionalist in the sense that Africa served as a "complementary economy" to the European one. Interestingly, the Volta ideas lived on in Eurafrican unions after 1945, when republicans in France, liberals in the Netherlands, and Labour politicians in Britain tried to turn their empires into functionalist federations.

The main flaw of functionalism was that it produced (inter)dependence but prevented real democratic and legislative participation. It thus perpetuated inequality. Functionalism was the governmentality of rationality (Malinowski), of technocracy (Mitrany), and of pattern variables (Parsons). But it was not the government of the people. The kit to all these functionalist systems was (inter)dependence, often used by the ICI and others as an instrument to justify neocolonial structures.

In these functionalist imaginations, the ICI's innermost beliefs in cultural relativism retained its place. The ICI's cultural relativism aimed not only at preserving non-European cultures but also at respecting and using them for the colonial project. Cultural relativism culminated in the idea of differing civilizations that were equal but separate. Respect for differing civilizations sounds progressive at first sight but predominantly helped to maintain a segregationist order between Europeans and non-Europeans, for example, within the new Eurafrican Unions of the 1930s and the 1940s, in which Africans had a separate representative body but no real power. Starting already in 1900, the ICI had developed representative councils in the colonies in which the "natives" participated but had no majority. The ICI could reapply this strategy in the new Eurafrican Unions of the 1930s and the 1940s. In late colonialism, cultural relativism, which often resulted in a separate "native policy," as well as legal and electoral segregation between "natives" and Europeans showed its two different faces. In some cases, it was the first step to autonomy and even independence in a new nation-state. In other cases, it resulted in an apartheid state that assigned different "races" different reserved areas and denied the black population access to essential rights and social security. Cultural relativism was by no means innocent. Nevertheless, it became the reason why the ICI cooperated closely with UNESCO after 1945 and revived essentialized notions of cultures and civilizations.

As early as the 1890s, the ICI invented a holistic and functionalist concept of economic development that combined economic growth, social welfare, cultural relativism, and sustained small-scale and cooperative schemes. Rejecting large-scale modernization theories and Parson's theory that all development must result in Western-style industrialization, ICI members instead tried to encourage rural grassroots development and the revival of urban craft guilds. The ICI's theoretical purpose was to carefully teach the indigenous peoples the benefits of capitalism, by making them participate voluntarily without renouncing their culture and traditions. Through autochthonous rural cooperatives and urban crafts guilds, they were supposed to learn to appreciate the benefits of production for the market, develop "providence" by saving money, and organize schemes of mutual assistance. In theory, the ICI's scheme of sustained development resembled the more careful and respectful small-scale development schemes of the 1970s rather than the attempt of the big powers to provoke a great leap forward in the immediate postwar era. In practice, coercion was still in use to make the colonized join pseudo-autochthonous *fokon'olona* cooperative societies and Provident Societies. They continued to be coercive beyond the era of decolonization and was partly used by new states to bring about development in a governmental way.

As we have seen, the ICI readily embraced decolonization after 1945. Decolonization, however, did not mean independence. New unions, federations, and commonwealths emerged from the old empires. Even official independence did not undo dependencies, and the ICI had multiplied these social and economic dependencies on many levels below the political one. Dependence in the spheres of economy, society, administration, art, and culture made the colonial label and political domination irrelevant. Throughout its existence, the ICI had made new social groups dependent and integrated them in a functionalist system of global development. Its focus was on the "middle class," which also provided the administrations of the new nations, and women. Both had been important for colonial governmentality before 1945, when ICI members turned craft guilds into a loyal "middle class" to dominate economic, social, and political life and used women such as Kartini to establish training schools for this middle class. The ICI considered the middle class and women a stable and moderate group loyal to the Europeans that ousted radical nationalists and penetrant communists alike.

What seemed to be at first sight fundamentally different between the ICI of the 1890s and the INCIDI of the 1950s was the admission of delegates from the Global South to the INCIDI after 1945, which stood for a general policy of participation, for example, in the United Nations. However, interpreting this admission to the ICI as a revolutionary act would be falling for colonialist narratives. During the explicit colonial period, non-Europeans were never absent but supplied the ICI with information and contested and tried to influence it. Kartini was a master of this indirect influence and inversed governmentality as early as 1900. Other experts from the Global South, such as Casely Hayford, did the same. They were never absent but invisible at best, because their names were lacking on the ICI's membership lists before 1949. In addition, the colonial archives rarely mention their names. It would be a misinterpretation to assume a fundamental change when they became visible on the membership lists in 1949. Although delegates from the Global South officially joined the INCIDI in the 1950s, they did not necessarily increase their agency in a significant way.

To conclude, the ICI served as a testing ground for the internationalist effort to manipulate society and the economy in the Global South, be it before or after 1945. Analyzing it in a diachronic way reveals that colonialism was not being improved over time; instead, it was a reformers' project from the beginning that involved liberals, Social Christians, Labour politicians, republicans, fascist, and, not least, delegates from the colonized world. The ICI shows that neither being progressive nor being anti-colonial prevented people in the Global North from perpetuating colonial structures. The variety and subtlety of this colonial governmentality can be exposed by analyzing the ICI and helps to understand the continuity of colonial structures. The continuity of the ICI's agenda is striking; but rather than blaming the INCIDI of a neocolonial project, we should acknowledge that the ICI was already neocolonial in the 1890s, in the sense that it did not need the official label "colonial" and an official state who dominated the colony. The astonishing continuity in the internationalist governmentality of empire between 1893 and the 1970s reveals that colonialism was not reformable. Real decolonization, as Aimé Césaire concluded, was thus "revolutionary or inexistent."

BIBLIOGRAPHY

Archival Sources

Archives Nationales d'Outre-Mer d'Aix-en-Provence (ANOM)

ANOM FP 100APOM1-FR ANOM 100APOM719 Union Coloniale Française

100APOM61–100APOM91	Correspondance Union Coloniale
100APOM92–100APOM94	Joseph Chailley-Bert
100APOM93	Missions à Java et aux Indes Anglaises
100APOM94	Correspondance Diverse
100APOM95	Correspondance Gallieni
100APOM96	Correspondance Lyautey
100APOM222-FP 100APOM229	Institut Colonial International
100APOM222	Généralités
100APOM223	Activités de la Section Française
100APOM224–226	Sessions
100APOM227	Annuaire de Documentation Coloniale Comparée
100APOM228	Enquête sur les maladies tropicales
100APOM229	Extension des cultures indigènes dans les colonies tropicales. Régime de la main-d'oeuvre et du travail (1927/1928)
100APOM321	Copie de lettres Chailley à Lyautey
100APOM530	Colonies anglaises, allemandes coupures de presse
100APOM531	Coupures de Presse Congo Belge
100APOM532	Relations franco-espagnoles Maroc
100APOM533	Pays Étrangers, Colonies Étrangères Japon. Siam. Java. Birmanie. Indes anglaises (1894/1909)

Fonds Ministériels 50COL34–98 (MIS 34–98): Missions and Mission Requests

FM MIS//50–79,99,114	Diverse Missions to British, Dutch, Portuguese Colonies
FM MIS//63/bis	Chailley-Bert Mission aux Pays-Bas en vue d'étudier le mode de recrutement des fonctionnaires coloniaux

FM MIS//66	Colonies allemandes: mission d'études des rapports commerciaux des colonies allemandes avec l'Allemagne par Degay, publiciste (1902)
FM MIS//70	Voyage d'études de la main d'œuvre agricole au Brésil par Auguste d'Humières, ancien officier d'infanterie, ancien maire du Rivet (1906)
FM MIS//76/bis	Mission gratuite d'études des arbres à caoutchouc au Brésil et à la Trinité d'Eugène Poisson (1898/1901)
FM MIS//78	Mission d'études des chemins de fer dans les colonies africaines anglaises, portugaises, allemandes et belge d'Eugène Salesses, directeur du chemin de fer de la Guinée française à l'initiative du gouverneur général de l'Afrique occidentale française (1904/1906)
FM MIS//98	Projet de mission en Extrême-Orient de Paul Vigné, dit Vigné d'Octon (1900)

Bundesarchiv Berlin (BArch)

BArch Akten des Reichskolonialamts (R1001)

R1001/4989-5010	Eingeborenenrecht
R1001/5358-5374	Rechtspflege in fremden Ländern und Kolonien
R1001/5415	Verbesserungen des Schutzgebietsgesetzes vom 25. Juli 1900 enthält u.a.: Karl von Stengel die Entwicklung des Kongostaates
R1001/5529/1	Akten betreffend die Zusammenstellung der Resolutionen des Reichstags bezüglich der Rechtsprechung in den Schutzgebieten:
R1001/5530-5534	Rechtsprechung in den Kolonien
R1001/5557	Mohammedanisches Recht in Ostafrika
R1001/5559	Eingeborenengerichtsbarkeit
R1001/5560	Reichs-Kolonialamt betreffend Entscheidungen und Sachen der Eingeborenengerichtsbarkeit in Bezirksämtern
R1001/5561	Strafrecht in niederländischen, franz. Und englischen Kolonien
R1001/6131	Einrichtung eines Internationalen Ethnographischen Büros in Brüssel
R1001/6175	Internationales Institut für Afrikanische Sprachen und Kulturen
R1001/6186	Akten betreffend das Institut Colonial International in Brüssel vom Januar 1894 bis 31 Dezember 1906
R1001/6187	Institut Colonial International
R1001/6188-6189	Veröffentlichungen des Institut Colonial International
R1001/6190	Ostafrikanische Einheitszeit
R1001/6191, 136	Institut International pour l'étude des langues et civilisations africaines (London)

R1001/6227	Wissenschaftliche Sammlungen aus fremden Ländern und Kolonien
R1001/6288	1895-1922 Nachrichten über Arbeitsverhältnisse in fremden Ländereien und Kolonien
R1001/6289	Entwicklung der Arbeiterrekrutierung in Kolonien aus China und Java und Text der Ausarbeitung
R1001/6402	Banken und Geldinstitute in Deutschland und den Schutzgebieten Allgemeines
R1001/6410	Banken und sonstige Kreditinstitute in DOA (1891-1929)
R1001/6618-6622	Forschungsreisende in Afrika Empfehlungen
R1001/7827	Studienreise des Gouvernmentsgärtners Deistel nach Penang, Singapore, Ceylon und Java
R1001/7841	Plantagen und Eingeborenen-Kulturen in Mittel- und Südamerika. Reise des Leiters des Botanischen Gartens in Kamerun Dr. Preuss
R1001/8597-8599	Botanische Zentralstelle für die Kolonien am Botanischen Garten und Museum in Dahlem
R1001/8604-8623	Buitenzorg und Buitenzorg-Stipenium
R1001/8650	Gründung von Amani, Hebung der Einheimischen Kulturen

BArch Akten Deutsche Kolonialgesellschaft (R8023)

R8023, 109-110	Zentral-Auskunftsstelle für Auswanderer

Behörden des Deutschen Schutzgebietes Deutsch-Ostafrika (R1003 FC)

R1003/1165	Korrespondenz mit dem Kaiserlichen Landwirtschaftlichen Institut Amani (Bd. 108) 1900-1913

BArch Private Archives (N)

N2007	Nachlass Anton, Günther Karl
N2126	Nachlass Hutten-Czapski
N2345	Nachlass Zimmermann
N2303	Nachlass Stuhlmann

Hohenlohe Zentralarchiv (HZA)

Nachlass Fürst Hermann zu Hohenlohe-Langenburg

La 140 Bü 159	Gründung des Deutschen Kolonialvereins
La 140 Bü 237	Koloniale Unternehmungen in Brasilien
La 140 Bü 246	Gründung des Institut Colonial International in Brüssel

Leiden University Archives (UL)

Collection Snouck Hurgronje (ULCSH)

F.6	Congrès Mondial des Associations Internationales 1913
G. 27	Institut Colonial International Brussels
Or8952, A225	Correspondence

Archives du Ministère des Affaires Étrangères Belges/Archives Africaines Brussels (AMAEB)

Institut International des Civilisations Différentes (INCIDI)

D 4701/168	Octave Louwers: Études et Carrière Coloniales 1887–1942
D 4701/170	Publications et activité de Louwers,Folder Institut International Colonial [sic] O.L. Sécretaire Général 1926
D 4071/171	Assistance Sociale au Congo, Notes Prises dans les Papiers Louwers 1913–1949
D 4782 (also: D 89)	Institut International des Civilisations Différentes (INCIDI)

Fonds van den Abeele 3663/198 INCIDI

Folder INCIDI 1953–54
Folder INCIDI 1955–56–57

Archives Étrangères

AE I 199	Correspondence generale echangé avec les puissances etrangères Allgemagne
AE 202	Correspondance echangé avec les puissances etrangères Allemagne
AE 203	Correspondance Generale 5/1-356 Communications diverses
AE 204	Correspondance France

Archives du Palais Royal à Bruxelles (APR)

Archives du Cabinet du Roi Léopold II. Documents relatifs au dévelopement exterieur de la Belgique 56

Archives Générales du Royaume, Brussels (AGRB)

AGRB	Banque d'Outre-Mer, 16: Correspondance de la Banque d'Outremer
AGRB	Papiers Orts I 184
AGRB	Zaire, 48
AGRB	Zaire 68: Rapport d'Emil Zimmermann

BIBLIOGRAPHY 361

Archives Université Catholique de Louvain (UCL)

UCL Fonds Wigny, C1-12, Correspondance
UCL Fonds Wigny, M1-12, Mémoires
UCL Fonds Wigny, PU1-14, Publications

Archives de la famille d'Arenberg, Enghien (AFAE)

Archives Arenberg, Enghien, Carton Franz von Arenberg, Dossier "Questions Politiques"

Colonial Office Archvies, National Archives Kew (CO)

National Archives, Kew, CO 323/1043/1 Request by International Colonial Institute, Brussels for financial support from British Government, 1929.

British Library Archives (BLA)

IOR/L/E/7/1540   International Colonial Institute

Bibliothèque Nationale de France, Paris (BNF)

BNF Manuscripts,   Nouvelles Acquisitions Françaises 24327, Correspondance
                        Eugène Etienne
Bibliothèque Arsenal   Fol-JO-2431, 'L'Europe Coloniale'

Institut de France, Paris (IdF)

Fonds Auguste Terrier (Secretary General of French Africa Committee)

MS 5915   French view on Pan-Germanism
MS 5916   French view on British colonization
MS 5923-6023   Relations Colonies and Colonial Interest Groups
MS 5925, Band 1, Fol. 255f   Van Voellenhoven on League of Nations
MS 5955   Journey Lyautey to Spain

Institut für Länderkunde, Leipzig (IfL)

IfL, Nachlass Ernst Hasse   Kiste 437, Korrespondenz

Archives International Labor Organization, Geneva (ILO Archives)

N/206/1/01   Correspondence with governments, international associations and individuals on native labour 1921-1940

N/206/2/0	Committee of Experts on Native Labour, correspondence with experts
N 206/1000/15	Sessions of the International Colonial Institute 1936–1939

League of Nations Archives, Geneva (LoN)

LoN Archives	6A/4479/758
LoN Archives	R60
LoN Archives	R2295/6A
LoN Archives	R2325
LoN Archives	R4109, 6A/2639/1612

Published Sources

Adam, Leonhard. "Modern Ethnological Jurisprudence in Theory and Practice." *Journal of Comparative Legislation and International Law* 16, no. 4 (1934): 216–229.

Anonymous. "Co-operative Societies among Natives." *Annals of Public and Cooperative Economics* 11, no. 3 (1935): 356–368.

Angoulvant, Gabriel. *Les Indes Néerlandaises leur Rôle dans l'Économie Internationale*. Paris: Le Monde Nouveau, 1926.

Anton, Günther K. *Französische Agrarpolitik in Algerien*. Leipzig: Duncker & Humblot, 1893.

Antonelli, E. "Le Droit de Petition devant la Commission des Mandats." *Les Annales coloniales. Organe de la France coloniale moderne* (July 2, 1929). https://gallica.bnf.fr/ark:/12148/bpt6k6280578k.

Baccari, Eduardo. *Il Congo*. Rome: Rivista Marittima, 1908.

Baedeker, Karl, ed. *Indien: Handbuch für Reisende*. Leipzig: Baedeker, 1914.

Baden-Powell, George. "Development of Tropical Africa." *Proceedings of the Royal Colonial Institute* 27 (1895–1896): 218–254.

Balandier, Georges. "Contribution à une Sociologie de la Dépendance." *Cahiers Internationaux de Sociologie* 12 (1952): 47–69.

Balbo, Italo. "La Politica Sociale Fascista." In RAI, *CSMSA*, vol. 1, 733–749.

Barnes, J. H. "Agricultural Education in the Punjab." In *Proceedings of the Third International Congress of Tropical Agriculture*, 70–80. London: Bale, 1914.

Baty, Thomas. "Lord Reay." *Journal of the Society of Comparative Legislation* 13, no. 1 (1912): 9–10.

Becker, Carl Heinrich. *L'Islam et la Colonisation de l'Afrique: Conférence faite sous le patronage de l'Union coloniale française, le 22 janvier* Paris: Union Coloniale, 1910.

——— "Materialien zur Kenntnis des Islam in Deutsch-Ostafrika." *Der Islam* 2, no. 1 (1911): 1–48.

Bertrand, Louis. "L'Afrique Latine." In RAI, *CSMSA*, vol. 1, 202–209.
Biagi, Bruno. "Politica Sociale verso gli Indigeni. Possibilità di applicazione del sistema previdenziale." In RAI, *CSMSA*, vol. 2, 855–862.
Billiard, Albert. "Étude sur la Condition Politique et Juridique à Assigner aux Indigènes des Colonies." In *Congrès International de Sociologie Coloniale 1900*, vol. 2, 5–53. Paris: Rousseau, 1901.
Blanchard, Raphael. "L'Entomologie et la Médicine." In *Congrès international d'Entomologie, Bruxelles, 1910*, 113–123. Brussels: Hayez, 1912.
L'Insitut de Médicine Coloniale. Paris: Histoire de sa fondation, 1902.
Bohner, Theodor. *Die Woermanns*. Berlin: Ilgenfritz, 1935.
Bouvier, John, ed. *A Law Dictionary, Adapted to the Constitution and Laws of the United States of America, and of the Several States of the American Union*. Philadelphia: Childs, 1868.
Boyer, Marcel. *Les Sociétés de Prévoyance de Secours et de Prêts Mutuels Agricoles en AOF*. Paris: Domat, 1935.
Boys, Henry S. *Some Notes on Java and Its Administration by the Dutch*. Allahabad: Pioneer Press, 1892.
Brumpt, Émile. *Titres et Travaux Scientifiques*. Paris: Brumpt, 1934.
Buell, Raymond L. *The Native Problem in Africa*, 2 vols. New York: Macmillan, 1928.
Cabrera, Raimundo. *Cuba y sus Jueces*. La Habana: El Retiro, 1887.
Cahuzac, Albert. *Essai sur les Institutions et le Droit Malgaches*. Paris: Chevalier, 1900.
Casely Hayford, J. Ephraim. *Gold Coast Native Institutions: With Thoughts upon a Healthy Imperial Policy for the Gold Coast and Ashanti*. London: Sweet & Maxwell, 1903.
Cambon, Henri, ed. *Paul Cambon, Correspondance Vol. 1 1870–1898*. Paris: Grasset, 1940.
Cattier, Félicien. *Droit et Administration de l'État Indépendant du Congo*. Brussels: Larcier, 1898.
Chailley-Bert, Joseph. *Administrative Problems of British India (L'Inde britannique, engl.)*. London: Macmillan, 1910.
"Les Anglais en Birmanie." *Revue des Deux Mondes* 108 (1891): 842–881.
Les Compagnies de Colonisation sous l'Ancien Régime. Paris: A. Colin, 1898.
Dix Années de Politique Coloniale. Paris: A. Colin, 1902.
La Hollande et les fonctionnaires des Indes Néerlandaises. Paris: A. Colin, 1893.
Java et ses Habitants. Paris: A. Colin, 1900.
Java et ses Habitants. 4th ed. Paris: A. Colin, 1914. *L'Inde Britannique: Société indigène, politique indigène, les idées directrices*. Paris: A. Colin, 1910.
Chevalier, Auguste. "Alerte aux Plantations de Cacaoyers dans l'Ouest Africain." *Revue Internationale de Botanique Appliquée* 26, nos. 283–284 (1946): 161–165.
"Historique de la Revue de Botanique Appliquée et d'Agriculture Tropicale." *Revue Internationale de Botanique Appliquée* 23, no. 1 (1943): 1–6.

"La Situation des Plantations d'Hévéa dans le Monde de 1939 à 1948." *Revue Internationale de botanique* 28 (1948): 297–316.
Coster, Ch. "The Work of the West Java Research Institute in Buitenzorg." In *Science and Scientists in the Netherlands Indies*. Edited by Pieter Honig and Frans Verdoorn, 56–69. New York: Commissie voor Nederlandsch-Indië, Suriname en Curaçao, 1945.
Clozel, François. "Circulaire Relative à l'Étude des Coutumes Indigènes." In *Le pays, les peuples, les langues*. Edited by Maurice Delafosse, 18–20. Haut-Sénégal-Niger (Soudan Français). Paris: Larose, 1912.
Clozel, François, and Roger Villamur, eds. *Les Coutumes Indigènes de la Côte d'Ivoire: Documents*. Paris: A.Challamel, 1902.
Colenbrander, H. T. "Bij het aftreden van Gouverneur-Generaal De Graeff." *De Gids* 95 (1931): 373–404.
Colonial Office, ed. *Report by the Right Honourable W. G. A. Ormsby-Gore on His Visit to Malaya, Ceylon and Java during the year 1928*. London: HMSO, 1928.
Comeliau, M. L. "Hubert van Neuss." In *Biographie Coloniale Belge*, vol. 3, 653–656. Brussels: Falk, 1952.
Comité d'initiative des amis de Vollenhoven [A. Messimy and E. Roume], eds. *Une Âme de Chef. Le Gouverneur général J. van Vollenhoven*. Paris: Diéval, 1920.
Compagnie du Congo pour le Commerce et l'Industrie, ed. *Le Chemin de fer du Congo, de Matadí au Stanley-Pool*. Brussels: Bourlard, 1889.
Compagnie du Congo pour le Commerce et l'Industrie, *The Congo-Railway from Matadí to the Stanley-Pool: Results of Survey*. Brussels: Weissenbruch, 1889.
Congrès Colonial International de Paris, ed. *Congrès Colonial International de Paris*. Paris: Augustin, 1889.
Congrès International de Sociologie Coloniale, ed. *Congrès International de Sociologie Coloniale 1900*, 2 vols. Paris: A. Rousseau, 1901.
Cornet, René. *La Bataille du Rail*. Brussels: Cuypers, 1958.
Costa, Joaquín. *Reconstitución y Europeización de España: Programa para un partido nacional*. Madrid: Liga Nacional, 1900.
Costanzo, Giuseppe A. "Europe and Africa." *Eurafrica* 1, no. 1 (1953): n.p.
"L'Opera di Giuseppe Aurelio Costanzo." *Africa: Rivista trimestrale di studi e documentazione dell'Istituto italiano per l'Africa e l'Oriente* 28, no. 1 (1973): 3–10.
Costa Pinto, Antonio. *Corporatism and Fascism: The Corporatist Wave in Europe*. Florence: Taylor & Francis, 2017.
Cotta, Freppel. *Agricultural Co-Operation in Fascist Italy*. London: King, 1935.
Craggs, Ruth. "Situating the Imperial Archive: The Royal Empire Society library, 1868–1945." *Journal of Historical Geography* 34, no. 1 (2008): 48–67.
D'Agostino Orsini, Paolo. *Eurafrica: l'Europa per l'Africa, l'Africa per l'Europa*. Rome: Cremonese, 1934.
Desbordes, Jean-Gabriel. *L'Immigration libano-syrienne en Afrique occidentale française*. Poitiers: Renault, 1938.

Dammerman, K. W. "The Quinquagenary of the Foreigners' Laboratory at Buitenzorg 1884–1934." *Annales du Jardin Botanique de Buitenzorg* 45 (1935): 1–54.
Delafosse, Maurice, ed. *Haut-Sénégal-Niger (Soudan Français) vol 1. Le pays, les peuples, les langues*. Paris: Larose, 1912.
Delavignette, R. *Freedom and Authority in French West Africa*. London: Oxford University Press, 1950.
Delteil, Pierre. *Le Fokon'olona (Commune Malgache) Et Les Conventions De Fokon'olona*. Paris: Loviton, 1931.
Depont, Octave. "Aperçu sur l'Administration des Indigènes Musulmans en Algérie." In *Congrès International de Sociologie Coloniale 1900*, vol. 2. Paris: A. Rousseau, 1901.
Depont, Octave, and Xavier Coppolani, eds. *Les Confréries Religieuses Musulmanes*. Algiers: Jourdan, 1897.
Dernburg, Bernhard. *Zielpunkte des deutschen Kolonialwesens*. Berlin: Mittler, 1907.
Descamps, Édouard. *L'Afrique Nouvelle: Essai sur l'état civilisateur dans les pays neufs et sur la fondation, l'organisation et le gouvernement de l'État indépendant du Congo*. Paris: Hachette, 1903.
Deschamps, Hubert. *Roi de la Brousse*. Paris: Berger-Levrault, 1975.
Deventer, Conrad Theodor van. "De 'Eereschuld' in het Parlement." *De Gids* 64 (1900): 399–418.
——— "Drie Boeken over Indië." *De Gids* 64 (1900): 134–154.
——— "Havelaar-Voorspel: Multatuli en congé. Documents officiels inédits publiés par Joost van Vollenhoven." *De Gids* 74 (1910): 199–215.
Deventer, Conrad Theodor van, Fransen van de Putte, and Isaäc Dignus. "Ter Gedachtenis." *De Gids* 66 (1902): 128–137.
D'Haussonville, Othenin, and Joseph Chailley-Bert. *L'Émigration des Femmes aux Colonies*. Paris: A. Colin, 1897.
Dimier, Véronique. *Le Gouvernement des Colonies. Regards croisés franco-britanniques*. Paris: PUB, 2004.
——— "The Mandates Commission, international bureaucracies and the legitimacy trap: the use and misuse of expertise and comparisons." *In Experts et expertise dans les mandats de la Société des Nations: Figures, champs, outils*. Edited by P. Bourmaud, N. Neveu, and C. Verdeil, 213–227. Paris: Presses de l'INALCO, 2020..
Direction des Affaires Indigènes et du Service des Renseignements, ed. *Enquête sur les Corporations Musulmanes d'Artisans et de Commerçants du Maroc: D'après les reponses à la circulaire résidentielle du 15 novembre 1923*. Paris: Leroux, 1925.
Djajadiningrat, Achmad P. A. *Herinneringen Van Pangeran Aria Achmad Djajadiningrat*. Amsterdam: G. Kolff, 1936.
Djajadiningrat, Hoesein P. A. "Kanttekeningen bij 'Het Javaanse Rijk Tjërbon in de Eerste Eeuwen van zijn bestaan.'" *Bijdragen tot de Taal-, Land- en Volkenkunde* 4, no. 113 (1957): 380–392.

"Local Traditions and the Study of Indonesian History." In *An Introduction to Indonesian Historiography*. Edited by Soedjatmoko, 74–86. Jakarta: Equinox, 1965.

Doutté, Edmond. *Magie et Religion dans l'Afrique du Nord*. Alger: Jourdan, 1909.

Dryepondt, Gustave, and Jean E. Van Canpenhout. *Rapport sur les Travaux du Laboratoire Médical de Léopoldville en 1899-1900*. Brussels: Hayez, 1901.

Durand, Mortimer. *The Life of the Right Hon. Sir Alfred Comyn Lyall*. Edinburgh: Blackwood, 1913.

Estournelles de Constant, Paul H. B. *La Politique Française en Tunisie. Le protectorat et ses origines, 1854-1891*. Paris: Plon, 1891.

Fabié, Antonio Maria. *Don Fray Bartolomé de las Casas, Obispo de Chiapa*, 2 vols. Madrid: Ginesta, 1879.

Mi Gestión Ministerial respecto a la Isla de Cuba. Madrid: Asilo de Huérfanos, 1898.

Fairchild, David. *The World Was My Garden: Travels of a Plant Explorer*. New York: Scribner, 1939.

Fairchild, David, and Thomas Barbour. "The Crisis at Buitenzorg." *Science* 80, no. 2063 (July 13, 1934): 33–34.

Fall, Babacar. *Le Travail au Sénégal: XXe siècle*. Paris: Karthala, 2011.

Fauchère, Aimé. *Culture Pratique du Caféier et Préparation du Café*. Paris: Challamel, 1908.

La Mise en Valeur de nos Territoires Coloniaux. Paris: Challamel, 1917.

Fetter, Bruce. *The Creation of Elisabethville, 1910-1940*. Stanford: Hoover Institute, 1976.

Fontaine, L. "L'Alliance Franco-Belge dans les Colonies." *Bulletin du Syndicat des Planteurs du Caoutchouc* (October 7, 1925): 148–149.

Foucault, Michel. "Governmentality." In *The Foucault Effect*. Edited by G. Burchell et al., 87–104. Chicago: University of Chicago Press, 1991.

Froment, Georges. *Le Devoir de l'Europe en Afrique. Enquête sur la proposition de M. Lucien Hubert*. Paris: XIX, 1907.

Furnivall, John S. *Netherlands Indies: A Study of Plural Economy*. Cambridge: Cambridge University Press, 1939.

Gallieni, Joseph. *Madagascar de 1896 à 1905: Rapport du Général Gallieni (3. April 1905)*. Tananarive: Imprint Office, 1905.

Garson, John George, and Royal Anthropological Institute of Great Britain and Ireland. *Notes and Queries on Anthropology*. 2nd ed. London: Anthropological Institute, 1892.

Gelders, V. "Le Paysannat Indigène au Congo Belge." In *Congrès International et Intercolonial de la Société Indigène*, vol. 1, 90–105. Paris: Exposition Coloniale Internationale, 1931.

Girault, Arthur. "Condition des Indigènes au Point de Vue de la Législation Civile et Criminelle et de la Distribution de la Justice." In *Congrès International de Sociologie Coloniale*, 49–59 and 62–63. Paris: Rousseau 1901.

Principes de Colonisation et de Législation Coloniale, vol. 2. Paris: Larose, 1904.

Principes de Colonisation et de Legislation, vol. 2, 3rd ed. Paris: Larose, 1907.

Gorini, P. "Le Salariat et le Paysannat dans les Colonies Italiennes." In *Congrès International et Intercolonial de la Société Indigène*, vol. 1, 118–143. Paris: Exposition Coloniale Internationale, 1931.

Gouvernement Général de l'Afrique Occidentale Française. *Bulletin Hebdomadaire d'Information et de Renseignements* 9 (May 10, 1934): 16–19.

Circulaires de M. le Gouverneur Général Jules Brévié sur la Politique et l'Administration Indigènes en Afrique Occidentale Française. Gorée: Id, 1935.

Gouvernement Général de l'Algérie. *Projet de Codification du Droit Musulman: Procès-verbaux des séances de la commission. Discussion des textes de l'avant-projet concernant le statut réel immobilier et les preuves*. Alger: Fontana, 1916.

Grévisse, F. *Le Centre Extra-Coutumier d'Élisabethville. Quelques aspects de la politique indigène du Haut-Katanga industriel*. Brussels: Institut Royal, 1951.

Haarhaus, Hans. *Das Recht des Deutschen Kolonialbeamten unter Berücksichtigung. d. engl., franz. u. niederländ. Kolonialbeamtenrechts*. Karlsruhe: Braun, 1911.

Hailey, William M. *An African Survey: A Study of Problems Arising in Africa South of the Sahara*. London: Oxford University Press, 1938.

Hall, C. J. J., van. *Cocoa*. London: Macmillan, 1914.

Hartmann, Georg. "Die Mischrassen in unseren Kolonien." In *Verhandlungen des Deutschen Kolonialkongresses 1910*, 906–931. Berlin: Reimer, 1910.

Hasselmann, C. J. "De Practische Resultaten van de Recruteering van Civiele Ambtenaren uit Indie." *Tijdschrift voor het Binnenlandsch Bestuur* 31, no. 1 (1906): 155–166.

Hasskarl, Justus K. *Aanteekeningen over het Nut, door de Bewoners van Java aan Eenige Planten van dat Eiland Toegeschreven*. Amsterdam: Müller, 1845.

Heckel, Édouard, and Mandine Cyprien. *L'Enseignement Colonial en France et à l'Étranger*. Marseille: Barlatier, 1907.

Higginson, John. *A Working Class in the Making: Belgian Colonial Labor Policy, Private Enterprise, and the African Mineworker, 1907–1951*. Madison: University of Wisconsin Press, 1989.

Hill, Arthur W. "The History and Functions of Botanic Gardens." *Annals of the Missouri Botanical Garden* 2, nos. 1–2 (1915): 210–211.

Hobhouse, C. E. H et al. *Report of the Royal Commission upon Decentralization in India*. London: Darling and Son, 1908–1909.

Hobson, A. "Review of Freppel Cotta, Agricultural Co-operation in Fascist Italy (London 1935)." *American Journal of Agricultural Economics* 17, no. 3, (1935): 605–607.

Hoffmann, Stefan-Ludwig, ed. *Human Rights in the Twentieth Century*. Cambridge: Cambridge University Press, 2011.

Hough, Eleanor M. *The Co-operative Movement in India*. London: Westminster, 1932.

House of Commons, ed. *Parliamentary Debates (Offcial Report)*, 5th series, vol. 95 (June 25–July 13, 1917). London: n.p, 1917.

Hunter, William Wilson. *The Indian Musalmans*. London: Trübner, 1876.
Imperial Japanese Government Railways, ed. *An Official Guide to Eastern Asia Trans-Continental Connections between Europe and Asia: East Indies*. Tokyo: Imperial Japanese Government Railways, 1917.
Institut Colonial International, ed. *Les Chemins De Fer Aux Colonies Et Dans Les Pays Neufs*, 3 vols. Brussels: ICI, 1900. *Compte Rendu De La Session Tenue A Paris En Août 1900*. Brussels: ICI, 1900.
Compte Rendu Des Séances Tenues A Bruxelles Les 28. Et 29. Mai 1894. Brussels: ICI, 1894.
Compte Rendu De La Session Tenue A La Haye En Septembre 1895. Brussels: ICI, 1895.
Compte Rendu De La Session Tenue A Berlin Le 6 Et 7 Septembre 1897. Brussels: ICI, 1897.
Compte Rendu De La Session Tenue A Bruxelles En Mai 1899. Brussels: ICI, 1899.
Compte Rendu De La Session Tenue A La Haye En Mai 1901. Brussels: ICI, 1901.
Compte Rendu De La Session Tenue A Londres En Mai 1903. Brussels: ICI, 1903.
Compte Rendu De La Session Tenue A Wiesbaden Les 17, 18 Et 19 Mai 1904. Brussels: ICI, 1904.
Compte Rendu De La Session Tenue A Rome En Avril 1905. Brussels: ICI, 1905.
Compte Rendu De La Session Tenue A Bruxelles En Juin 1907. Brussels: ICI, 1907.
Compte Rendu De La Session Tenue A Paris En Juin 1908. Brussels: ICI, 1908.
Compte Rendu De La Session Tenue A La Haye En Juin 1909. Brussels: ICI, 1909.
Compte Rendu De La Session Tenue A Brunswick En Juin 1911, 2 vols. Brussels: ICI, 1911.
Compte Rendu De La Session Tenue A Bruxelles En Juillet 1912. Brussels: ICI, 1912.
Compte Rendu De La Session Tenue A Londres En Mai 1913. Brussels: ICI, 1913.
Compte Rendu De La Session Tenue A Bruxelles En Mai 1920. Brussels: ICI, 1920.
Compte Rendu De La Session Tenue A Paris En Juin 1921. Brussels: ICI, 1921.
Compte Rendu De La Session Tenue A Rome En Avril 1924, 2 vols. Brussels: ICI, 1924.
Compte Rendu De La Session Tenue A La Haye En Juin 1927, 2 vols. Brussels: ICI, 1927.
Compte Rendu De La Session Tenue A Bruxelles En Juin 1929. Brussels: ICI, 1929.
Compte Rendu De La Session Tenue A Paris En Mai 1931. Brussels: ICI, 1931.
Compte Rendu De La Session Tenue A Londres En Octobre 1936. Brussels: ICI, 1936.
Compte Rendu De La Session Tenue A Rome En Juin 1939. Brussels: ICI 1939.
Les Differentes Systemes D'irrigation, 3 vols. Brussels: ICI, 1906 (vol. 1); 1907 (vol. 2); 1908 (vol. 3).

Les Droits De Chasse Dans La Colonie Et La Conservation De La Faune Indigène, 2 vols. Brussels: ICI, 1911.
L'enseignement Aux Indigènes, 2 vols. Brussels: ICI, 1909; 1910.
Les Fonctionnaires Coloniaux, 3 vols. Brussels: ICI, 1897 (vols. 1 and 2); 1910 (vol. 3).
Les Lois Organiques Des Colonies, 3 vols. Brussels: ICI, 1906.
La Main D'oeuvre Aux Colonies, 3 vols. Brussels: ICI, 1895, 1897, 1898.
L'Organisation du Crédit Au Point de Vue Industriel et Comercial En Faveur des Classes Moyennes. Brussels: ICI, 1911.
Notice Institut Colonial International. Brussels: ICI, 1937.
Recueil International De Législation Coloniale, Publié Sous Le Patronage De l'Institut Colonial International. Brussels, ICI: 1911-1914.
Le Régime Des Protectorats, 2 vols. Brussels: ICI, 1899. *Le Régime Foncier Aux Colonies*, 6 vols. Brussels: ICI, 1898 (vol. 1); 1899 (vols. 2-4); 1902 (vol. 5); 1905 (vol. 6).
Le Régime Minier Aux Colonies, 3 vols. Brussels: ICI, 1902 (vol. 1); 1903 (vols. 2-3).
Le Régime Et L'Organisation Du Travail Des Indigènes Dans Les Colonies Tropicales. Paris: ICI, 1929.
Insitut International de Civilisations Différentes, ed. *Compte Rendu de la Session Tenue à Paris En Mars 1951*. Brussels: INCIDI, 1951.
Compte Rendu de la Session Tenue à La Haye En Septembre 1953: Programmes et plans de relèvement rural en pays tropicaux et sub-tropicaux. Brussels: INCIDI, 1953.
Compte Rendu de la Session Tenue à Londres En Septembre 1955: Development of a middle class in tropical and sub-tropical countries. Brussels: INCIDI, 1955.
Compte Rendu de la Session Tenue à Lisbon En Avril 1957: Pluralisme ethnique et culturel dans les sociétés intertropicales. Brussels: INCIDI, 1957.
Compte Rendu de la Session Tenue à Bruxelles En Septembre 1958: Women's role in the development of tropical and sub-tropical countries. Brussels: INCIDI, 1959.
Compte Rendu de la Session Tenue à Munich En Septembre 1960: Problème des cadres dans les pays tropicaux et sub-tropicaux. Brussels: INCIDI, 1961.
Compte Rendu de la Session Tenue à Palerme En Septembre 1963: Les Constitutions et institutions administratives des États nouveaux. Brussels: INCIDI, 1965.
Compte Rendu de la Session Tenue à Aix-en-Provence En Septembre 1967: Les agglomérations urbaines dans les pays du Tiers Mondé: leur rôle politique, social et économique. Brussels: INCIDI, 1971.
Institut International des Sciences Politiques et Sociales Appliqués aux Pays de Civilisations Differentes, ed. *Compte Rendu de la Session Tenue à Bruxelles En Novembre 1949*. Brussels: INCIDI, 1950.
Institut Royal Colonial Belge, ed. *Biographie Coloniale Belge*, 3 vols. Brussels: Falk, 1952.

International Labour Organisation, ed. *Elimination of All Forms of Forced or Compulsory Labor*. Geneva: ILO, 2001.

International Labour Conference Fourteenth Session Geneva 1930, Report of the Director, Part 1. Geneva: ILO, 1930.

International Labour Conference Twentieth Session Geneva 1936, Report of the Director c.1936 (XX)RD. Geneva: ILO 1936.

Internationale Vereinigung für vergleichende Rechtswissenschaft, ed. *Verhandlungen der Ersten Hauptversammlung*. Berlin: Vahlen, 1912.

Interracial International Program, ed. *First Universal Races Congress, University of London, July 26–29, 1911*. London: King, 1911.

Ireland, Alleyne. *Tropical Colonization*. New York: Macmillan, 1899.

Jabavu, Davidson D. T. *The Black Problem: Papers and Addresses on Various Native Problems*. Lovedale: Book Dep., 1921.

Jeffries, Charles. *The Colonial Empire and Its Civil Service*. Cambridge: Cambridge University Press, 1938.

Jonghe, Ed de. *La Politique Financière du Congo. Rapport au Comité permanent du Congrès Colonial*. Brussels: Goemaere 1925.

Kaji, Hiralal L. *Co-operation in India*. Bombay: All-India Co-operative Institutes' Association, 1932.

Karsten, G. "Paul Preuß' Expedition nach Zentral- und Südamerika 1899/1900." *Geographische Zeitschrift* 8, no. 4 (1902): 222–227.

Kartini, Raden Adjeng. *Letters of a Javanese Princess*. London: Duckworth, 1921.

Kat Angelino, A. D. *Colonial Policy*, 2 vols. The Hague: Nijhoff, 1931.

King, George. *A Manual of Cinchona Cultivation in India*. Calcutta: Government Printing, 1876.

Koningsberger, Victor J., and Albrecht Zimmermann. *De Dierlijke Vijanden der Koffiecultur op Java*. Batavia: Kolff, 1901.

Koningsveld, P. S. *Orientalism and Islam: The letters of C. Snouck Hurgronje to Th. Nöldeke; from the Tübingen Univ. Libr*. Leiden: Rijksuniv., 1985.

Kooreman, Petrus J. *De Koelie-Ordonnantie tot Regeling van de Rechtsverhouding Tusschen Werkgevers en Werklieden in de Residentie Oostkust van Sumatra*. Amsterdam: De Bussy, 1903.

Kotschnig, Walter M. "Review of the School in Colonial Expansion." *The Journal of Higher Education*, 16, no. 3 (1945): 168.

Labouret, Henri. "Le paysannat indigène en AOF." In *Congrès International et Intercolonial de la Société Indigène*, vol. 1, 18–39. Paris: Exposition Coloniale Internationale de Paris, 1931.

Lannoy, Charles De. "Le Régime et l'Organisation du Travail des Indigènes au Congo Belge." In *Compte Rendu 1929*. Edited by ICI, 85–116. Brussels: ICI, 1929.

Le Bon, Gustave. "'Algeria and the Ideas Prevailing in France concerning Colonization,' translated by Robert K. Stevenson." *Revue Scientifique* (October 2, 1887): 1–20.

——— "'The Influence of Race in History,' translated by Robert K. Stevenson." *Revue Scientifique* (April 28, 1888): 1–18.

Le Chatelier, Alfred. *Les Confréries Musulmanes du Hedjaz*. Paris: Leroux, 1887.
Le Febve de Vivy, Léon. *Documents d'Histoire Précoloniale Belge (1861-1865)*. Brussels: Acad, 1955.
Leclercq, Jules. *Un Séjour dans l'Île de Java: Le pays, les habitants, le système colonial*. Paris: Plon and Nourrit, 1898.
Leroy-Beaulieu, Paul. *De la Colonisation chez les Peuples Modernes*. Paris: Guillaumin, 1874.
Lewis, George C. *On the Government of Dependencies*. Oxford: Clarendon, 1891.
Louwers, Octave. "Camille Janssen." In *Biographie Coloniale Belge*, vol. 4. Edited by Institut Royal Colonial Belge, 437-440. Brussels: Falk, 1951.
Codes et Lois du Congo belge. Brussels: Weissenbruch, 1914.
Le Congrès Volta de 1938 et ses Travaux sur l'Afrique. Brussels: Falk, 1949.
"Orientation Actuelle des Études sur l'Afrique." In RAI, *CSMSA*, vol. 1, 60-69.
Lowell, Lawrence A. *Colonial Civil Service: The Selection and Training of Colonial Officials in England, Holland and France*. New York and London: Macmillan, 1900.
Lugard, Frederick D. *The Dual Mandate in British Tropical Africa*. Edinburgh and London: Blackwood, 1922.
Lyall, Alfred C. *Asiatic Studies, Religious and Social*. London: Murray, 1899.
The Rise of the British Dominion in India. London: Murray, 1898.
Lyautey, Pierre. "La Politique du Protectorat en Afrique Marocaine." In RAI, *CSMSA*, vol. 2, 987-1002.
Mademba Si, Fama. "Bambara, Sarakolesen usw. in den Sansading-Staaten, Westlicher Sudan." In *Rechtsverhältnisse von Eingeborenen Völkern in Afrika und Ozeanien. Beantwortung des Fragebogens der Internationalen Vereinigung für vergleichende Rechtswissenschaft und Volkswirtschaftslehre zu Berlin*. Edited by S. R. Steinmetz, 27-56. Berlin: Springer, 1903.
Malinowski, Bronislaw. *Freedom and Civilization*. London: Allen, 1947.
"Modern Anthropology and European Rule in Africa." In RAI, *CSMSA*, vol. 2, 880-901.
"Practical Anthropology." *Africa* 2, no. 1 (1929): 22-38.
"The Scientific Basis of Applied Anthropology." In RAI, *CSMSA*, vol. 1, 5-24.
Marguerat, Yves, and Tichtchékou Pelei. *Si Lomé m'était contée*, vol. 2. Lomé: Presses de l'Université de Bénin, 1993.
Massignon, Louis. "L'Artisanat Indigène dans l'Afrique du Nord." In *Congrès International et Intercolonial de la Société Indigène*, vol. 1, 165-177. Paris: Exposition Coloniale Internationale, 1931.
Écrits Mémorables, 2 vols. Paris: Laffont, 2009.
Mauss, Marcel. "Essai sur le Don: Forme et raison de l'échange dans les sociétés archaïques." *L'Année Sociologique* (1923): 30-186.
Mehta, Vaikunth L. *Co-operative Farming*. Bombay: State Co-operative Union, 1959.
Merrill, Elmer. *Report on Investigations Made in Java in the Year 1902 to the Depatment of the Interior, Forestry Bureau*. Manila: Bureau of Public Printing, 1903.

Meyer, Georg. *Die Staatsrechtliche Stellung der Deutschen Schutzgebiete.* Leipzig: Duncker & Humblot, 1888.
Milliot, Louis. *L'Association Agricole chez les Musulmans du Maghreb.* Paris: Rouseau 1911.
Mitrany, David. "The Functional Approach to Colonial Self-Government." In *Problems of Parliamentary Government in the Colonies*, 80–86. London: Hansard Society, 1953.
— "The Functional Approach to World Organization." *International Affairs* 24, no. 3 (1948): 350–363.
Money, James W. B. *Java or How to Manage a Colony: A Practical Solution Now Affecting British India.* London: Hurst and Blackett, 1861.
Morand, Marcel. *Avant-Projet de Code: Présenté à la Commission de Codification du Droit Musulman Algérien.* Alger: Jourdan, 1916.
— *Introduction à l'Étude du Droit Musulman Algérien.* Alger: Carbonel, 1921.
Moresco, Emanuel. *De la Condition des Métis et l'Attitude des Gouvernements à leur Égard.* Brussels: Mertens, 1911.
— *Les Indes Orientales Néerlandaises, Conference faite par le Dr. E. Moresco, à l'Académie Royale de Jurisprudence et de Legislation, le 11 Mai 1921, à l'Occasion de la Semaine Néerlandaise a Madrid.* Madrid: Reus, 1921.
— *De Wetgevende Raden in Britisch-Indië, Uitgegeven op last van den Minister van Koloniën.* 'S Gravenhage: Algemeene Landsdr, 1911.
Müller, Wilhelm. *Politische Geschichte der Gegenwart. Das Jahr 1885*, vol. 19. Berlin: Springer, 1886.
Multatuli. *Max Havelaar of de Koffijveilingen der Nederlandsche Handelsmaatschappij.* Amsterdam: De Ruyter, 1860.
Nehru, Jawaharlal. *The Discovery of India.* Delhi: Oxford University Press, 1985.
Netherlands Indies Government, ed. *Overzicht van de Gestie der Centraal Sarikat-Islam in het Jaar 1921 (Gedrukt ingevolge opdracht van den Gouverneur-Genoraal, gegeven bij M. G. S. van 11.8.1922–424 Geheim).* Batavia: n.p., 1922.
— *Sarekat Islam Congres. 1.-3. Nationaal Congres 1916–1918*, vol. 3. Batavia: Landsdrukkerij, 1916–1919.
Niyogi, Jitendraprasad P. *The Co-operative Movement in Bengal.* London: Macmillan, 1940.
Ortoli, Jean, and Alfred Aubert, eds. *Coutumiers Juridiques de l'Afrique occidentale française.* Paris: Larose, 1939.
Overbergh, Cyrill van. *École Mondiale. Rapport général sur les conclusions des sous-commissions Pléniére de l'École Mondiale.* Brussels: Hayez, 1907.
Paasche, Hermann. *Deutsch-Ostafrika: Wirtschaftliche Studien.* 2nd ed. Hamburg: Süd-West-Verl, 1913.
Perham, Margery, and Mary Bull, eds. *The Diaries of Lord Lugard.* Evanston: Northwestern University Press, 1959.
Pétit, Pierre. "Éditorial." *Civilisations. Revue internationale d'anthropologie et des sciences humaines* 51 (2004): 7–8.

Petit, W. L. de. *La Conquête de la Vallée d'Atchin par les Hollandais.* Paris: Baudoin, 1891.
Pettazoni, R. "Orientamenti Atuali dell'Africanistica." In RAI, *CSMSA*, vol. 1, 53–60.
Pierson, Nikolaas G. *Java en de Koloniale Questie.* Amsterdam: Funke, 1871.
Pietromarchi, Luca "Comportamento delle Strippi Camitiche verso la Civiltà Europea." In RAI, *CSMSA*, vol. 1, 610–620.
Pittaluga, Gustavo. *Elementos de Parasitologia y Nociones de Medicina Tropical.* Madrid: Casa Vidal, 1914.
Philip, André. "La Coopération aux Indes." *Revue des Études Coopératives* 34 (1930): 179–198.
Plehn, Albert. *Beiträge zur Kenntnis von Verlauf und Behandlung der Tropischen Malaria in Kamerun.* Berlin: Hirschwald, 1896.
Poisson, Eugène. *Rapport sur une Mission Scientifique au Brésil aux Antilles et au Costa-Rica.* Paris: Imprimerie Nationale, 1902.
Possoz, Émile. *Élements du Droit Coutumier Nègre.* Elisabethville: n.p., 1944.
"Polygamie." *Aequatoria* 5, no. 2 (1939): 39–53.
"Principes de Droit Nègre." *Aequatoria,* 3, no. 4 (1940): 104–109.
Post, Albert H. *Afrikanische Jurisprudenz: Ethnologisch-juristische Beiträge zur Kenntniss der einheimschen Rechte Afrikas.* Oldenburg: Schulzesche, 1887.
Post, Joannes W. *Rapport sur l'Irrigation aux Indes Orientales Néerlandaises.* Brussels: Mertens, 1904.
Preuss, Paul. *Expedition nach Central- und Südamerika 1899/1900.* Berlin: KWK, 1901.
Proceedings of the Third International Congress of Tropical Agriculture, Held at the Imperial Institute, London: Bale, 1914.
Pynaert, Léon. "Le Jardin d'Eala," *Zooleo* 37, no. 3 (1957): 211–223.
Qureshi, Anwar Iqbal. *The Future of the Co-Operative Movement in India.* Oxford: Oxford University Press, 1947.
Rathgen, Karl. *Beamtentum und Kolonialunterricht: Rede, geh. bei d. Eröffnungsfeier d. Hamburg; Kolonialinst. am 20. Okt. 1908.* Hamburg: Voss, 1908.
Reale Accademia d'Italia, ed. *Convegno di Scienze Morali e Storiche, 4–11 Ottobre 1938: Tema: l'Africa.* Rome: Reale Accademia d'Italia, 1939.
Ricard, Prosper. "Les Arts Tripolitains (Parte I)." *Rivista della Tripolitana: Rivista di Studi Orientale e Coloniali* 2, no. 4 (1926), 203–235.
Rinn, Louis. *Marabouts et Khouan Étude sur l'Islam en Algérie: Avec une carte indiquant la marche la situation et l'importance des ordris religieux musulmans.* Alger: Jourdan, 1884.
Royal Colonial Institute, ed. *A Select Bibliography of Publications on Foreign Colonization, Completed by Miss Winifred C.Hill.* London: Royal Colonial Institute, 1915.
Russel, A., and Abdullah A.-M. Suhrawardy. *First Steps in Muslim Jurisprudence Consisting of Excerpts from Bākùrat-Al-Sa'd of Ibn Abù Zayd.* London: Luzac, 1906.

Salesses, Eugène. *Les Chemins de Fer dans leur État Actuel.* Nancy: Levrault, 1914.
Sambuc, Henri. "Le Développement Économique de l'Indochine et la Culture du Riz." *Quinzaine Coloniale* (April 25, 1910): 288–289.
Santillana, David. *Code Civil et Commercial Tunisien: Avant-projet discuté et adopté au rapport.* Tunis: Picard, 1899.
Istituzioni di Diritto Musulmano Malichita: Con riguardo anche al sistema sciafiita; 1:La comunità musulmana e il suo capo. Fonti del diritto e loro ermeneutica. La legge nelle spazio e nel tempo. Rome: Oriente, 1925.
Sapieha, Léon. "Gründe für die europäsiche Solidarität." In RAI, *CSMSA*, vol. 2, 1498–1513.
Sarraut, Albert. *La Mise en Valeur des Colonies Françaises.* Paris: Payot, 1923.
Sawas, Pacha. *Le Droit Musulman Expliqué: Réponse à un article de M. Ignace Goldziher, ... paru dans le "Byzantinische Zeitschrift," II, 2, p. 317–325, 1893.* Paris: Marchal et Billard, 1896.
Say, Léon, and Joseph Chailley. *Nouveau Dictionnaire d'Économie Politique.* Paris: Guillaumin, 1900.
Schnee, Heinrich, ed. *Deutsches Koloniallexikon*, 2 vols. Berlin: Quelle & Meyer, 1920.
Si Chaïb, Aboubakr. "Note de Si Chaïb, Cadi de Tlemcen (Algérie)." In *Congrès International de Sociologie Coloniale 1900.* Edited by Congrès International de Sociologie Coloniale, vol. 2, 140–144. Paris: Rousseau, 1901.
Snouck Hurgronje, C., *The Achehnese*, 2 vols. Translated from Dutch by A. W. S. O'Sullivan. Leiden: Brill, 1906 [1893–1894].
Snouck Hurgronje, C., ed. *Ambtelijke Adviezen van C. Snouck Hurgronje 1889–1936*, 3 vols. 'S-Gravenhage: Nijhoff, 1959.
"The Holy War 'Made in Germany' (1915)." In *Verspreide Geschriften. Geschriften betreffende den Islam en zijne geschiedenis.* Edited by C. H. Snouck Hurgronje, vol. 3, 257–285. Bonn: Schroeder, 1923.
"Islam und Phonograph." In *Verspreide Geschriften. Geschriften betreffende den Islam en zijne geschiedenis.* Edited by C. H. Snouck Hurgronje, vol. 2, 419–447. Bonn: Schroeder, 1923.
Oeuvres Choisies de C. Snouck Hurgronje = Selected Works of C. Snouck Hurgronje. Leiden: Brill, 1957.
"Politique Musulmane de la Hollande: Quatre conférences." *Revue Du Monde Musulman* 14 (1911): 377–509.
Politique Musulmane de la Hollande: Quatre conférences par C. Snouck Hurgronje. Paris: Leroux, 1911.
Société des Nations, ed. *Procès-Verbal de la Onzième Session tenue à Genève, du 20 juin au 6 juillet 1927.* Geneva: SDN, 1927.
Publications de la Société des Nations III. Hygiene 10–21. Geneva: SDN, 1926.
Société Royale de Médicine Publique, ed. *Rapports Présentés au Congrès National d'Hygiène et de Climatologie Médicale de la Belgique et du Congo: Tenu à Bruxelles du 9 au 14 août 1897.* Brussels: Hayez, 1898.
Soest, Gerardus. H. von. *Geschiedenis van het Kultuurstelsel.* Rotterdam: Nijgh, 1871.

Sohier, Antoine. "Le Décret du 24 Juillet 1918 Érigeant en Infractions Certains Faits Lorsqu'ils sont Commis par des Indigènes." *Revue de Droit et Jurisprudence du Katanga* 1, no. 1 (1924): 21-67.
Mémoires et Souvenirs. www.urome.be/fr2/ouvrag/1924Sohier.pdf.
"Pour une Collaboration Juridique Intercoloniale." *Revue de Droit et Jurisprudence du Katanga* 3, no. 1 (1926): 27-28.
Pratique des Juridictions Indigènes. Brussels: Travaux Publics, 1932.
Traité Élémentaire de Droit Coutumier au Congo Belge. Brussels: Larcier, 1949.
"Un Début de Carrière Judiciaire. Souvernirs et reflexions." *Journal des Tribunaux d'outre-mer* (October 15, 1958): 145-146.
Solus, Henry. "Le Régime er l'Organisation du Travail des Indigènes dans les Colonies Francaises de l'Afrique." In *Le Régime et l'Organisation du Travail des Indigènes dans les Colonies Tropicales*. Edited by ICI, 119-176. Paris: ICI, 1929.
Soulmagnon, Georges. *La Loi Tunisienne fu 1er Juillet 1885 sur la Propriété Immobilière et le Régime des Livres Fonciers*. Paris: Sirey, 1933.
Spiller, Gustav, ed. *Papers on Inter-Racial Problems: Communicated to the First Universal Races Congress, Held at the University of London, July 26-29, 1911*. London: King, 1911.
Spire, Camille, and André Spire. *Le Caoutchouc en Indochine. Étude botanique industrielle et commerciale*. Paris: Challamel, 1906.
Steinmetz, Sebald R. ed. *Rechtsverhältnisse von Eingeborenen Völkern in Afrika und Ozeanien: Beantwortungen des Fragebogens der Internationalen Vereinigung für vergleichende Rechtswissenschaft und Volkswirtschaftslehre zu Berlin*. Berlin: Springer, 1903.
Stengel, Karl. *Der Kongostaat*. Munich: Puttkammer & Mühlbrecht, 1903.
Strachey, John. *India*. 2nd ed. London: Paul, 1894.
Strauss, Paul. *Depopulation et Puericulture*. Paris: Charpentier, 1901.
Strickland, C. F. *Confidential Report on Co-operation and Certain Aspects of the Economic Condition of Agriculture in Zanzibar to the Secretariat from May 15th, 1931* [Carbon of original typewritten draft MC: 5257989].
Co-Operation for Africa. Oxford: Oxford University Press, 1933.
"The Cooperative Movement in the East." *International Affairs* 11, no. 6 (1932): 812-832.
Stuhlmann, Franz. *Beiträge zur Kulturgeschichte von Ostafrika*. Berlin: Reimer, 1909.
Taft Commission, ed. *Reports of the Taft Philippine Commission*. Washington, DC: Government Printing Office, 1901.
Tempels, Placide Frans. *La Philosophie Bantoue*. Elisabethville: Lovania, 1945.
Tesch, Johannes. *Die Laufbahn der Deutschen Kolonialbeamten, ihre Pflichten u. Rechte*. 6th ed. Berlin: Salle, 1912.
Thillard, Robert. "La Culture du Tabac de Sumatra au Cameroun." *Agronomie Coloniale* 40 (1921): 185-194 and 227-229.

Thomas, F. W., Vogel J. Ph., and Blagden, C. O. "Hendrik Kern." *The Journal of the Royal Asiatic Society of Great Britain and Ireland* (January 1918): 173–184.

Thys, Albert. "Les Chemins de Fer aux Colonies et dans les Pays Neufs: Rapport de la commission spéciale." In *Les Chemins de Fer aux Colonies et dans les Pays Neufs*. Edited by ICI, vol. 1, 5–35. Paris: Challamel, 1900.

Au Congo et au Kassaï. Brussels: Weissenbruch, 1888.

"Devons-nous Coloniser au Congo et Comment Devons-nous le Faire." *Association des Licenciés sortis de l'Université de Liège. Bulletin trimestriel* (January 1913): 9.

Tracy Philipps, J. E. "Editorial Letter to the Journal of The Royal African Society." *Journal of the Royal African Society*, 37, no. 146 (1938): 140–142.

"The XXIVth Biennial Session of the Institut Colonial International, Rome, June 1939." *Journal of the Royal African Society* 39, no. 154 (1940): 17–21.

"The Volta Meeting in Rome." *Journal of the Royal African Society* 38, no. 150 (1939): 19–32.

Treille, Georges. *De l'Acclimatation des Européens dans les Pays Chauds*. Paris: Doin, 1888.

Organisation Sanitaire des Colonies. Progrès Réalisés – Progrès à Faire. Marseille: Barlatier, 1906.

Treub, Melchior. *Der Botanische Garten 'S' Lands Plantetarium zu Buitenzorg auf Java*. Leipzig: Engelmann, 1893.

US Department of the Treasury, Bureau of Statistics; O. P. Austin; and Library of Congress, Division of Bibliography. *Colonial Administration, 1800–1900: Methods of Government and Development Adopted by the Principal Colonizing Nations in Their Control of Tropical and Other Colonies and Dependencies*. Washington, DC: Government Printing Office, 1903.

Van der Lith, P. A. "Rechtsverhältnisse in Niederändisch-Indien." In *Jahrbuch der Internationalen Vereinigung für Vergleichende Rechtswissenschaft*. Edited by Felix Meyer and Franz Bernhöft, vol. 4, 1–21. Berlin: Hoffmann, 1898.

Van Vollenhoven, Cornelis. "Adat Guide (1910)." In *Van Vollenhoven on Indonesian Adat Law*. Edited by J. F. Holleman, 262–265. Dordrecht: Springer, 1981.

Van Vollenhoven, Cornelis. ed. *Adatrechtbundels Bezorgd door de Commissie voor het Adatrecht: Uitg. door het Koninklijk Instituut voor Taal-, Land- en Volkenkunde van Nederlandsch-Indie Adatrechtbundel bezorgd door de Commissie voor het Adatrecht*, 45 vols. 'S-Gravenhage: Nijhoff, 1911–1955.

"The Elements of Adat Law (1907)." In *Van Vollenhoven on Indonesian Adat Law*. Edited by J. F. Holleman, 7–23. Dordrecht: Springer, 1981.

"Notice Complementaire sur la Codification du Droit Musulman dans l'Afrique du Nord." In *Compte Rendu de la Session tenue en 1921*. Edited by ICI, 413–418. Brussels: ICI, 1921.

"La Politique Coloniale Par Rapport aux Us et Coutumes Indigènes." In *Compte Rendu de la Session tenue en 1921*. Edited by ICI, 363–412. Brussels: ICI, 1921.

"The Study of Adat Law (1907)." In *Van Vollenhoven on Indonesian Adat Law*. Edited by J. F. Holleman, 24–40. Dordrecht: Springer, 1981.

Vecchi, C. M. de. "Politica Sociale Verso gli Indigeni e Modi di collaborazione con essi." In RAI, *CSMSA*, vol. 1, 709–739.

Volkens, Georg. "Der Botanische Garten zu Buitenzorg und seine Bedeutung für den Plantagenbau auf Java und Sumatra." In *Verhandlungen des Deutschen Kolonialkongresses 1902*, 182–183. Berlin: Reimer, 1902.

Vries, Otto de. *Estate Rubber: Its Preparation, Properties and Testing*. Batavia: Ruygrok, 1920.

Warburg, Otto. "Über Wissenschaftliche Institute für Kolonialwirtschaft." *Verhandlungen des deutschen Kolonialkongresses 1902*, 193–207. Berlin: Reimer, 1902.

"Warum ist die Errichtung eines Wissenschaftlich-Technischen Laboratoriums in dem Botanischen Garten zu Victoria Erforderlich?" *Tropenpflanzer* 3, no. 7 (1899): 291–296.

Wauters, A. J. *Histoire Politique du Congo Belge*. Brussles: Van Fleteren, 1911.

Wildeman, Émile de. *Mission Emile Laurent (1903–1904)*. Brussels: Vandenbuggenhout, 1905.

"Ce qui devait être un Insitut Colonial et Mondial." In *Congrès International d'Expansion Économique Mondiale, Section V*, 1–5. Brussels: Hayez, 1905

Wolff, Hermann. *Die Landmesser und Kulturtechniker in Preußen*. Berlin: Maaß und Plank, 1912.

World Bank, ed. *Report No. 2898-MAG Madagascar, First Agricultural Credit Project: Staff appraisal report (7.6. 1980)*. http://documents.worldbank.org/curated/en/578491468056449509/text/multi-page.txt.

Worsfold, Basil. *A Visit to Java: With an Account of the Founding of Singapore*. London: Bentley, 1893.

Zache, Hans. *Die Ausbildung der Kolonialbeamten*. Berlin: Süsserott, 1912.

Zeijlstra, Hein H. *Melchior Treub: Pioneer of a New Era in the History of the Malay Archipelago*. Amsterdam: Koningljik Institute, 1959.

Ziemann, Hans. *Über das Bevölkerungs- und Rassenproblem in den Kolonien*. Berlin: Süsserott, 1912.

Zimmermann, Albrecht. *Der Botanische Garten zu Buitenzorg auf Java*. Berlin, Paetel 1899.

"Erster Jahresbericht des Kaiserlichen Biologisch-Landwirtschaftlichen Instituts Amani." *Berichte über die Land- und Forstwirtschaft in Deutsch-Ostafrika* 1, no. 6 (1903): 435–466.

Der Manihot-Kautschuk: Seine Kultur, Gewinnung und Präparation. Jena: Fischer, 1913.

Zimmermann, Alfred. *Die Europäischen Kolonien Schilderung ihrer Entstehung, Entwicklung, Erfolge und Aussichten*. Berlin: Mittler, 1903.

Zoli, Corrado. "The Organization of Italy's East African Empire." *Foreign Affairs* 16, no. 1 (October 1937): 80–90.

Journals

The Beira Post (Mozambique)
Biographie Coloniale Belge
Bulletin Agricole du Congo Belge
Bulletin du Comité de l'Afrique Francaise
De Gids (Batavia)
De Sumatra Post
Dépêche Coloniale
Deutsche Kolonialzeitung
Deutsche Medizinische Wochenschrift
Deutsches Kolonialblatt
Die Woche (Berlin)
Het Nieuws van den Dag voor Nederlandsch-Indië
Indian Opinion (Durban, South Africa)
La Grande Revue
L'Algérie Française
La Quinzaine Coloniale
La Verité sur le Congo
L'Europe Coloniale (Paris)
Revue algérienne, tunisienne et marocaine de législation et de jurisprudence
Revue des Deux Mondes
Staatsblad van Nederlandsch-Indië
Swakopmunder Zeitung, published as *Deutsch-Sudwestafrikanische Zeitung* (Swakopmund, Namibia)
The Gold Coast Nation. (Cape Coast, Ghana)
The Nigerian Pioneer
Tropenpflanzer
Verhandlungen des Deutschen Kolonialkongresses 1902. Berlin, 1902.

Secondary Literature

Abraham, Itty. "Rare Earths: The Cold War in the Annals of Travancore." In *Entangled Geographies: Empire and Technopolitics in the Global Cold War*. Edited by Gabrielle Hecht, 101–124. London: MIT Press, 2011.

Ageron, Charles-Robert. *France Coloniale ou Parti Colonial?* Paris: Presses universitaires de France, 1978.

Genèse de l'Algerie Algerienne. Paris: Bouchène, 2005.

"L'idée d'Eurafrique et le débat colonial franco- allemand de l'entre-deux-guerres." *Revue d'Histoire Moderne et Contemporaine* 22, no. 3 (1975): 446–475.

Aillaud, Isabelle. *Jules Charles-Roux: Le grand Marseillais de Paris.* Rennes: Marines éditions, 2004.

Alcalde, Ángel. "The Transnational Consensus: Fascism and Nazism in Current Research." *Contemporary European History* 29 (2020): 243–252.

Aldrich, Robert. *Greater France: A History of French Overseas Expansion.* New York: St. Martin's Press, 1996.
"Imperial Mise En Valeur and Mise En Scène: Recent Works on French Colonialism." *The Historical Journal* 45, no. 4 (2012): 917–936.
Ali, Tariq Omar. *A Local History of Global Capital: Jute and Peasant Life in the Bengal Delta.* Princeton: Princeton University Press, 2018.
Amaury, Lorin, and Christelle Traud, eds. *Nouvelle Histoire des Colonisations Européennes, XIXe–XXe siècles.* Paris: Presses Univ. de France, 2013.
Ames, Eric, Marcia Klotz, and Lora Wildenthal, eds. *Germany's Colonial Pasts.* Lincoln: University of Nebraska Press, 2005.
Amselle, Jean-Loup, and Emmanuelle Sibeud. *Maurice Delafosse: Entre orientalisme et ethnographie l'itinéraire d'un africaniste, 1870–1926.* Paris, Maisonneuve et Larose, 1998.
Anderson, Casper, and Andrew Cohen. *The Government and Administration of Africa, 1880–1939*, 5 vols. London: Routledge, 2013.
Anderson, David, and David Killingray, eds. *Policing the Empire: Government, Authority and Control, 1830–1940.* Manchester: Manchester University Press, 1991.
Anderson, David, and David Throup. "Africans and Agricultural Production in Colonial Kenya: The Myth of the War as a Watershed." *The Journal of African History* 26, no. 4 (1985): 327–345.
Anderson, Dorothy. "David Mitrany (1888–1975): An Appreciation of His Life and Work." *Review of International Studies*, 24, no. 4 (1998): 577–592.
Anderson, Norman. "Waqfs in East Africa." *Journal of African law Journal of African Law*, 3, no. 3 (1959): 152–164.
Anderson, Warwick. *Colonial Pathologies: American Tropical Medicine, Race, and Hygiene in the Philippines.* Durham: Duke University Press, 2006.
"Immunities of Empire: Race, Disease, and the New Tropical Medicine, 1900–1920." *Bulletin of the History of Medicine* 70, no. 1 (1996): 94–118.
Andrew, Christopher. *Théophile Delcassé and the Making of the Entente Cordiale: A Reappraisal of French Foreign policy 1898–1905.* London: Macmillan, 1968.
Andrew, Christopher M., and Alexander S. Kanya-Forstner. "The French Colonial Party: Its Composition, Aims, and Influence 1885–1914." *The Historical Journal* 14, no. 1 (1971): 99–128.
Andurain, Julie d'. "Réseaux d'Affaires et Réseaux Politiques. Le cas d'Eugène Étienne et d'Auguste d'Arenberg." In *L'Esprit Économique Impérial. Groupes de pression et réseaux du patronat colonial en France et dans l'Empire.* Edited by H. Bonin, J.-F. Klein, and C. Hodeir, 85–102. Paris: SFHOM, 2008.
Anghie, Antony. *Imperialism, Sovereignty and the Making of International Law.* Cambridge: Cambridge University Press, 2005.
Arabi, O. "Orienting the Gaze: Marcel Morand and the Codification of le droit Musulman Algerien." *Journal of Islamic Studies* 11, no. 1 (2000): 43–72.

Armitage, David, ed. *Foundations of Modern International Thought*. New York: Cambridge University Press, 2013.
Armitage, David, *Theories of Empire, 1450–1800*. Aldershot: Ashgate, 1998.
Arndt, H. W. "Economic Development: A Semantic History." *Economic Development and Cultural Change* 29, no. 3 (1981): 457–466.
Arnold, David, "Touching the Body: Perspectives on the Indian Plague, 1896–1900." In *Subaltern Studies V*. Edited by Ranajit Guha, 55–90. New Delhi: Oxford University Press, 1988.
Arnold, David, ed. *Warm Climates and Western Medicine: The Emergence of Tropical Medicine, 1500–1900*. Amsterdam: Rodopi, 1996.
Austen, Ralph A., and Jonathan Derrick, eds. *Middlemen of the Cameroons Rivers: The Dualas and Their Hinterland*. Cambridge: Cambridge University Press, 1999.
Austin, Gareth. "Capitalists and Chiefs in the Cocoa Hold-Ups in South Asante, 1927–1938." *The International Journal of African Historical Studies* 21, no. 1 (1988): 63–95.
Aydin, Cemil. *The Muslim World*. Cambridge, MA: Harvard University Press, 2017.
Baganet Cobas, Aymara et al. "Dr. Gustavo Pittaluga Fattorini: In Memoriam." *Revista Habanera de Ciencias Médicas* 13, no. 1 (2014): 11–19.
Balandier, Georges. "La Situation Coloniale: Approche théorique." *Cahiers Internationaux de Sociologie* 1 (1951): 44–79.
Baldinetti, Anna. *David Santillana, l'Uomo e il Giurista 1855–1931: Scritti inediti 1878–1920*, vol. 2. Roma: Oriente, 1995.
The Origins of the Libyan Nation: Colonial Legacy, Exile and the Emergence of a New Nation-State. London: Routledge, 2010.
Balfour, Sebastian. *The End of the Spanish Empire, 1898–1923*. Oxford: Clarendon, 1997.
Ballinger, Pamela. "Colonial Twilight: Italian Settlers and the Long Decolonization of Libya." *Journal of Contemporary History* 51, no. 4 (2016): 813–838.
Bancel, Nicolas, Pascal Blanchard, and Françoise Vergès, eds. *La République Coloniale*. Paris: Hachette, 2006.
Bandeira Jerónimo, Miguel. *The "Civilizing Mission" of Portuguese Colonialism, 1870–1930*. Basingstoke: Palgrave Macmillan, 2015.
"A League of Empires: Imperial Political Imagination and Interwar Internationalisms." In *Internationalism, Imperialism and the Formation of the Contemporary World*. Edited by M. Bandeira Jerónimo and J. P. Monteiro, 87–126. London: Palgrave Macmillan, 2018.
Barnett, Michael N. *Empire of Humanity: A History of Humanitarianism*. Ithaca: Cornell University Press, 2011.
Barth, Boris. *Die deutsche Hochfinanz und die Imperialismen: Banken und Aussenpolitik vor 1914*. Stuttgart: Steiner, 1995.
Bayly, Christopher A. *The Birth of the Modern World: Global Connections and Comparisons*. Malden: Blackwell, 2004.

Beasley, E. *Mid-Victorian Imperialists: British Gentlemen and the Empire of the Mind*. London: Taylor & Francis, 2004.
Beckert, Sven. *Empire of Cotton: A Global History*. New York: Knopf, 2014.
"From Tuskegee to Togo: The Problem of Freedom in the Empire of Cotton." *The Journal of American History* 92, no. 2 (2005): 498–526.
Bell, Duncan. *Victorian Visions of Global Order: Empire and International Relations in Nineteenth-Century Political Thought*. Cambridge: Cambridge University Press, 2007.
Belmessous, Saliha. *Native Claims: Indigenous Law against Empire, 1500–1920*. Oxford and New York: Oxford University Press, 2012.
Ben-Ghiat, Ruth, and Mia Fuller, eds. *Italian Colonialism*. New York: Palgrave Macmillan, 2005.
Bennett, Brett M., and Joseph M. Hodge. *Science and Empire: Knowledge and Networks of Science across the British Empire, 1800–1970*. Basingstoke: Palgrave Macmillan, 2011.
Benton, Lauren. *Law and Colonial Cultures: Legal Regimes in World History, 1400–1900*. Cambridge: Cambridge University Press, 2002.
Beredo, Cheryl. *Import of the Archive: U.S. Colonial Rule of the Philippines and the Making of the American Archival History*. Sacramento: Litwin Books, 2013.
Bernhard, Patrick. "Borrowing from Mussolini: Nazi Germany's Colonial Aspirations in the Shadow of Italian Expansionism." *Journal of Imperial and Commonwealth History* 41 (2019): 617–643.
Bertrand, Romain. *État Colonial, Noblesse et Nationalisme à Java*. Paris: Karthala, 2005.
"Histoire d'une 'Réforme Morale' de la Politique Coloniale des Pays-Bas: Les éthicistes et l'insulinde (vers 1880–1930)." *Revue d'Histoire Moderne et Contemporaine* 54, no. 4 (2007): 86–116.
"'Politique Éthique' des Pays-Bas à Java (1901–1926)." *Vingtième Siècle. Revue d'Histoire* 93, no. 1 (2007): 2–41.
Betts, Raymond F. *Assimilation and Association in French Colonial Theory*. New York and London: Columbia University Press, 1961.
Blackbourn, David, and Geoff Eley. *The Peculiarities of German History*. Oxford: Oxford University Press, 1984.
Blakeley, Brian L. "Pensions and Professionalism: The Colonial Governors (Pensions) Acts and the British Colonial sService, 1865–1911." *The Journal of Imperial and Commonwealth History* 4, no. 2 (2008): 138–153.
Blanchard, Pascal, Sandrine Lemaire, and Nicolas Bancel, eds. *Culture Coloniale en France de la Révolution Française à nos Jours*. Paris: CNRS, 2008.
Bloch, M. "Decision-Making in Councils among the Merina of Madagascar." In *Councils in Action*. Edited by A. Richards and A. Kuper, 29–62. Cambridge: Cambridge University Press, 1971.
Bloembergen, Marieke. "The Open Ends of the Dutch Empire and the Indonesian Past." In *The Oxford Handbook of the Ends of Empire*. Edited by Martin

Thomas and Andrew Stuart Thompson, 391–414. Oxford: Oxford University Press, 2018.

Bloembergen, Marieke, and V. Kuitenbrouwer. "A New Dutch Imperial History. Connecting Dutch and Overseas Pasts." Special issue, *BMGN – Low Countries Historical Review* 128, no. 1 (2013).

Bloembergen, Marieke, and Remco Raben, eds. *Het Koloniale Beschavingsoffensief: Wegen naar het nieuwe Indië, 1890–1950*. Leiden: KITLV, 2009.

Bonneuil, Christophe. 'Auguste Chevalier, Savant Colonial.' In *Les Sciences Coloniales, Figures et Interventions*. Edited by P. Petitjean and R. Waast, 15–36. Paris: ORSTOM, 1996.

Boomgaard, Peter. *Children of the Colonial State: Population Growth and Economic Development in Java 1795–1880*. Amsterdam: Free University Press, 1989.

——— *Empire and Science in the Making: Dutch Colonial Scholarship in Comparative Global Perspective, 1760–1830*. New York: Palgrave Macmillan, 2013.

——— "From Subsistence Crises to Business Cycle Depressions, Indonesia 1800–1940." *Itinerario* 27, nos. 3–4 (2002): 35–50.

——— "The Welfare Services in Indonesia, 1900–1942." *Itinerario* 10, no. 1 (1986): 57–81.

Booth, Anne. "Colonial Revenue Policies and the Impact of the Transition to Independence in South East Asia" *Bijdragen tot de Taal-, Land- en Volkenkunde*, 169, no. 1 (2013): 37–67.

——— "Varieties of Exploitation in Colonial Settings." In *Colonial Exploitation and Economic Development: The Belgian Congo and the Netherlands Indies Compared*. Edited by E. Frankema and F. Buelens, 60–87. London: Routledge, 2013.

Borowy, Iris. *Coming to Terms with World Health: The League of Nations Health Organisation, 1921–1946*. Frankfurt am Main and New York: Peter Lang, 2009.

Bosma, Ulbe. *Sugar Plantation in India and Indonesia: Industrial Production, 1770–2010*. Cambridge: Cambridge University Press, 2013.

Bosma, Ulbe, and Remco Raben. *Being "Dutch" in the Indies: A History of Creolisation and Empire, 1500–1920*. Honolulu: University of Hawaii Press, 2008.

Bossenbroek, Martin. "'Dickköpfe und Leichtfüße': Deutsche im niederländischen Kolonialdienst des 19. Jahrhunderts." In *Deutsche im Ausland – Fremde in Deutschland: Migration in Geschichte und Gegenwart*. Edited by Klaus Bade, 249–254. Gütersloh: Bertelsmann, 1993.

Bosworth, R. J. B. *Mussolini*. London: Arnold, 2002.

Böttger, Jan H. "Internationalismus und Kolonialismus: Ein Werkstattbericht zur Geschichte des Brüsseler Institut Colonial International (1894–1948)." *Jahrbuch für europäische Überseegeschichte* 6 (2006): 165–172.

Bouche, Denise. *Histoire de la Colonisation Française*. Paris: Fayard, 1991.

Braillon, Charlotte. "Nouvelles Perspectives sur le Droit Judiciaire du Congo Belge et les Acteurs de la Justice Coloniale: La procédure d'annulation des jugements indigènes." In *Droit et Justice en Afrique coloniale: Traditions, productions et réformes.* Edited by Bérengère Piret, 143–163. Brussels: Université Saint-Louis-Bruxelles, 2013.

Breman, Jan. *Koelies, Planters en Koloniale Politiek.* Dodrecht: Foris, 1987.

Brockway, Lucille H. *Science and Colonial Expansion: The Role of British Royal Botanic Gardens.* New York: Academic Press, 2002.

Brownlee, Jason. *Authoritarianism in an Age of Democratization.* Cambridge: Cambridge University Press, 2007.

Brückenhaus, Daniel. *Policing Transnational Protest: Liberal Imperialism and the Surveillance of Anticolonialists in Europe, 1905–1945.* New York: Oxford University Press, 2017.

Brunet La Ruche, Bénédicte, and Laurent Manière. "De 'l'exception' et du 'droit commun' en situation coloniale: L'impossible transition du code de l'indigénat vers la justice indigène en AOF. In *Droit et Justice en Afrique Colonial.* Edited by Bérengère Piret, Charlotte Braillon, Laurence Montel, and Pierre-Luc Plasmann, 117–142. Brussels: Publications de l'Université Saint-Louis, 2013.

Brunschwig, Henri. *Mythes et Réalités de l'Impérialisme colonial Français, 1871–1914.* Paris: A. Colin, 1960.

Budde, Gunilla-Friederike, Sebastian Conrad, and Oliver Janz. *Transnationale Geschichte: Themen, Tendenzen und Theorien.* Göttingen: Vandenhoeck & Ruprecht, 2006.

Buettner, Elizabeth. *Empire Families: Britons and Late Imperial India.* Oxford and New York: Oxford University Press, 2004.

Burbank, Jane, and Frederick Cooper. *Empires in World History: Power and the Politics of Difference.* Princeton: Princeton University Press, 2010.

Burke, Edmund. *The Ethnographic State: France and the Invention of Moroccan Islam.* Berkeley: University of California Press, 2014.

Burton, Antoinette M. *Gender, Sexuality and Colonial Modernities.* London and New York: Routledge, 1999.

Bynum, W. F., and Caroline Overy. *The Beast in the Mosquito: The Correspondence of Ronald Ross and Patrick Manson.* Amsterdam and Atlanta: Rodopi, 1998.

Callahan, Michael D. *Mandates and Empire: The League of Nations and Africa, 1914–1931.* Brighton: Sussex Academic, 1999.

Camilleri, Nicola. *Staatsangehörigkeit und Rassismus. Rechtsdiskurse und Verwaltungspraxis in den Kolonien Eritrea und Deutsch-Ostafrika.* Frankfurt: MPI for Legal History and Legal Theory, 2021.

Carland, J. M. *The Colonial Office and Nigeria, 1898–1914.* Stanford: Hoover Institution. 1985.

Césaire, Aimé. *Discourse on Colonialism.* New York: Monthly Review Press, 2000.

Chafer, Tony, and Amanda Sackur, eds. *Promoting the Colonial Idea: Propaganda and Visions of Empire in France.* Basingstoke: Palgrave, 2002.

Chanock, Martin. *Law, Custom and Social Order: The Colonial Experience in Malawi and Zambia.* Cambridge: Cambridge Universtiy Press, 1985.

Chatterjee, Partha. "Governmentality in the East." Talk given on April 27, 2015 at The Program in Critical Theory, UC Berkeley. http://criticaltheory.berkeley.edu/?event=governmentality-in-the-east.

Chauveau, Jean-Pierre. "Enquête sur la recurrence du theme de la 'participation paysanne' (p.p.) dans le discours et les pratiques de developpement rural depuis la colonisation." *Chroniques du Sud* 6 (1991): 129–150. www.documentation.ird.fr/hor/fdi:35375.

Chickering, Roger. *We Men Who Feel Most German: A Cultural Study of the Pan-German League, 1886–1914.* Boston: Allen and Unwin, 1984.

Christelow, A. *Muslim Law Courts and the French Colonial State in Algeria.* Princeton: Princeton Universtiy Press, 1985.

Ciarlo, David. *Advertising Empire: Race and Visual Culture in Imperial Germany.* Cambridge, MA: Harvard University Press, 2011.

Cittadino, Eugene. *Nature as the Laboratory: Darwinian Plant Ecology in the German Empire 1880–1900.* Cambridge: Cambridge Universtiy Press, 1990.

Clancy-Smith, Julia A. *Rebel and Saint: Muslim Notables, Populist Protest, Colonial Encounters (Algeria and Tunisia, 1800–1904).* Berkeley: University of California Press, 1994.

Clancy-Smith, Julia A., and Frances Gouda. *Domesticating the Empire: Race, Gender, and Family Life in French and Dutch Colonialism.* Charlottesville: University Press of Virginia, 1998.

Clarence-Smith, William G. "The Coffee Crisis in Asia, Africa, and the Pacific, 1870–1914." In *The Global Coffee Economy in Africa, Asia and Latin America, 1500–1989.* Edited by W. G. Clarence-Smith and S. Topik, 100–119. Cambridge: Cambridge University Press, 2003.

Clauzel, Jean. *La France d'Outre-mer (1930–1960): Témoignages d'administrateurs et de magistrats.* Paris: Karthala, 2003.

Clavin, Patricia. "Defining Transnationalism." *Contemporary European History* 14 no. 4 (2005): 421–439.

Clavin, Patricia, and Glenda Sluga, eds. *Internationalisms: A Twentieth-Century History.* Cambridge: Cambridge University Press, 2017.

Clerck, Louis de. "L'Administration Coloniale Belge sur le Terrain au Congo (1908–1960) et au Ruanda-Urundi (1925–1962)." *Annuaire d'Histoire Administrative Européenne* 18 (2006): 187–210.

Cohen, William B. *Rulers of Empire: The French Colonial Service in Africa.* Stanford: Hoover Institution, 1971.

Colombani, Olivier. *Mémoires Coloniales: La fin de l'empire français d'Afrique vue par les administrateurs coloniaux.* Paris: La Découverte, 1991.

Comaroff, Jean, and John L. Comaroff. *Of Revelation and Revolution*, Chicago: University of Chicago Press.

Comaroff, John L. "Governmentality, Materiality, Legality, Modernity'." In *African Modernities: Entangled Meanings in Current Debate*. Edited by Jan-Georg Deutsch et al., 107–134. Portsmouth: Heinemann, 2002.
Compagnon, Patrice, ed. *Le Caoutchouc Naturel*. Paris: Maisonneuve & Larose, 1986.
Conklin, Alice. *A Mission to Civilize: Ideology and Imperialism in French West Africa, 1895–1930*. Stanford: Stanford University Press, 1989.
Conrad, Sebastian. *Globalisation and the Nation in Imperial Germany*. Cambridge and New York: Cambridge University Press, 2010.
Conrad, Sebastian, and Jürgen Osterhammel, eds. *Das Kaiserreich Transnational: Deutschland in der Welt 1871–1914*. Göttingen: Vandenhoeck & Ruprecht, 2004.
Constantine, Stephen. *The Making of British Colonial Development Policy, 1914–1940*. London, Totowa, 1984.
Cooper, Frederick. *Citizenship between Empire and Nation: Remaking France and French Africa, 1945–1960*. Princeton: Princeton University Press, 2014.
    Colonialism in Question: Theory, Knowledge, History. Berkeley: University of California Press, 2005
    "Conflict and Connection Rethinking Colonial African History." *The American Historical Review* 99, no. 5 (1994): 1516–1545.
    Decolonization and African Society: The Labor Question in French and British Africa. Cambridge: Cambridge University Press, 1996.
    "Development, Modernization, and the Social Sciences in the Era of Decolonization: The Examples of British and French Africa." In *The Ends of European Colonial Empires*. Edited by Miguel Bandeira Jerónimo and Antónia Costa Pinto, 15–50. London: Palgrave Macmillan, 2015.
    Plantation Slavery on the East Coast of Africa. New Haven: Yale University Press, 1977.
    "Reconstructing Empire in British and French Africa." *Past & Present* 210, no. 6 (2011): 196–210.
    "Writing the History of Development." *Journal of Modern European History* 8, no. 1 (2010): 5–23.
Cooper, Frederick, and R. M. Packard, eds. *International Development and the Social Sciences: Essays on the History and Politics of Knowledge*. Berkeley: University of California Press, 1997.
Cooper, Frederick, and A. L. Stoler. *Tensions of Empire: Colonial Cultures in a Bourgeois World*. Berkeley: University of California Press, 1997.
Coquery-Vidrovitch, Catherine. *Le Congo au Temps des Grandes Compagnies Concessionnaires 1898–1930*, vol. 1. Paris: EHESS, 2001.
    "Le Financement de la 'Mise en Valeur' Coloniale. Méthode et premiers résultats." In *Études Africaines offertes à Henri Brunschwig*, 237–252. Paris: EHESS, 1982.

Condominas, George. *Fokon'olona et Collectivités Rurales en Imerina*. Bondy: ORSTOM, 1991.
Cribb, Robert. "Development Policy in the Early 20th Century." In *Development and Social Welfare: Indonesia's Experiences under the New Order*. Edited by J. P. Dirkse, F. Hüsken, and M. Rutten, 225–245. Leiden: Brill, 1993.
Crowder, Michael. "Indirect Rule: French and British Style." *Africa* 34, no. 3 (July 1964): 197–204.
Cullather, Nick. "Development? It's History." *Diplomatic History* 24 no. 4 (2000): 641–653.
Curtin, Philip D. *Death by Migration: Europe's Encounter with the Tropical World in the Nineteenth Century*. Cambridge and New York: Cambridge University Press, 1989.
  Disease and Empire: The Health of European Troops in the Conquest of Africa. Cambridge and New York: Cambridge University Press, 1998.
Dalisson, Rémi. *Paul Bert: L'inventeur de l'école laïque*. Paris: A. Colin, 2015.
Darwin, John. "Imperialism and the Victorians: The Dynamics of Territorial Expansion." *The English Historical Review* 112, no. 447 (1997): 614–642.
Daughton, James P. "Behind the Imperial Curtain: International Humanitarian Efforts and the Critique of French Colonialism in the Interwar Years" *French Historical Studies* 34, no. 3 (2011): 504–528.
  An Empire Divided: Religion, Republicanism, and the Making of French Colonialism, 1880–1914. Oxford: Oxford University Press, 2006.
Daviron, Benoit. "Mobilizing Labour in African Agriculture: The Role of the International Colonial Institute in the Elaboration of a Standard of Colonial Administration, 1895–1930." *Journal of Global History* 5 (2010): 479–501.
Davis, Clarence B., Kenneth E. Wilburn, and Ronald Robinson. *Railway Imperialism*. New York: Greenwood, 1991.
Davis, Lance E., and Robert A. Huttenback. *Mammon and the Pursuit of Empire: The Political Economy of British Imperialism, 1860–1912*. Cambridge and New York: Cambridge University Press, 1986.
Dean, Warren. *Brazil and the Struggle for Rubber: A Study in Environmental History*. Cambridge: Cambridge University Press, 1987.
Degler, Carl N. *Neither Black Nor White: Slavery and Race Relations in Brazil and the United States*. Madison: University of Wisconsin Press, 1971.
De Jong, Janny. "Kolonialisme op een Koopje: Het Internationale Koloniale Instituut, 1894–1914." *Tijdschrift voor Geschiedenis* 109 (1996): 45–72.
Dejung, Christof, David Motadel, and Jürgen Osterhammel, eds. *The Global Bourgeoisie: The Rise of the Middle Classes in the Age of Empire*. Princeton: Princeton University Press, 2019.
Del Boca, Angelo. "Caroselli, Francesco Saverio." *Dizionario Biografico degli Italiani* 34 (1988). www.treccani.it/enciclopedia/francesco-saverio-caroselli_%28Dizionario-Biografico%29/.

Deschamps, Hubert. *Roi de la Brousse: Mémoires d'autre mondes*. Paris: Berger-Levrault, 1975.
Deutsch, Jan-Georg. *Emancipation without Abolition in German East Africa, c. 1884-1914*. Oxford: Curey, 2006.
Dewey, Clive. *Anglo-Indian Attitudes: The Mind of the Indian Civil Service*. London: Hambledon, 1993.
Dibwe dia Mwembu, Donatien. *Histoire des Conditions de Vie des Travailleurs de L'Union Minière du Haut Katanga/Gécamines (1910-1999)*. Lubumbashi: Presses Universitaires de Lubumbashi, 2001.
Digby, Anne, Waltraud Ernst, and Projit B. Muhkarji. *Crossing Colonial Historiographies: Histories of Colonial and Indigenous Medicines in Transnational Perspective*. Newcastle upon Tyne: Cambridge Scholars, 2010.
Dimier, Véronique. *Le Discours Idéologique de la Méthode Coloniale chez les Français et les Britanniques de l'Entre-deux Guerres à la Décolonisation (1920-1960)*. Talence: Centre d'Étude d'Afrique Noire, 2000.
"Formation des Administrateurs Coloniaux Français et Anglais entre 1930 et 1950: Développement d'une science politique ou science administrative des colonies." PhD Diss., Université de Grenoble, 1999.
Le gouvernement des colonies, regards croisés franco-britanniques. Brussels: Éd. de l'Univ. de Bruxelles, 2004.
The Invention of a European Development Aid Bureaucracy: Recycling Empire. Basingstoke: Palgrave Macmillan, 2014.
Diouf, Mamadou, ed. *Tolerance, Democracy, and Sufis in Senegal*. New York: Columbia University Press, 2013.
Drayton, Richard H. *Nature's Government: Science, Imperial Britain, and the "Improvement" of the World*. New Haven: Yale University Press, 2000.
Eckart, Wolfgang U. *Medizin und Konolonialimperialismus: Deutschland, 1884-1945*. Paderborn: Schöningh, 1997.
Eckert, Andreas. *Grundbesitz, Landkonflikte und Kolonialer Wandel: Douala 1880 bis 1960*. Stuttgart: Steiner, 1999.
Herrschen und Verwalten: Afrikanische Bürokraten, staatliche Ordnung und Politik in Tanzania, 1920-1970. Munich: De Gruyter, 2007.
"Useful Instruments of Participation? Local Government and Cooperatives in Tanzania, 1940s to 1970s." *The International Journal of African Historical Studies* 40, no. 1 (2007): 97-118.
Eckert, Andreas, and Randeira, Shalini. *Vom Imperialismus zum Empire – Nichtwestliche Perspektiven auf die Globalisierung*. Frankfurt: Suhrkamp, 2009.
Edwards, Penny. *Cambodge: The Cultivation of a Nation, 1860-1945*. Honolulu: University of Hawai'i Press, 2007.
Ekbladh, David. *The Great American Mission: Modernization and the Construction of an American World Order*. Princeton: Princeton University Press, 2010.
El Mechat, Samia. *Coloniser, Pacifier, Administrer: XIXe-XXIe siècles*. Paris: CNRS, 2014.

"Sur les Principes de colonisation d'Arthur Girault (1895)." *Revue Historique* 657, no. 1 (2011): 119–144.
Eley, Geoff. "Empire by Land or Sea? Germany's Imperial Imaginary, 1840–1945." In *German Colonialism in a Global Age*. Edited by Bradley Naranch and Geoff Eley, 20–45. Durham: Duke University Press, 2014.
Reshaping the German Right: Radical Nationalism and Political Change after Bismarck. New Haven: Yale University Press, 1980.
Elson, Robert. E. *Village Java under the Cultivation System, 1830–1870*. Sydney: Allen and Unwin, 1994.
Javanese Peasants and the Colonial Sugar Industry: Impact and Change in an East Java Residency, 1830–1940. Singapore: Oxford University Press, 1984.
Enders, Armelle. "L'École Nationale de la France d'Outre-mer et la Formation des Administrateurs Coloniaux." *Revue d'histoire moderne et contemporaine* 40, no. 2 (1993): 272–288.
Engermann, David, and Corinna Unger. "Introduction: Towards a Global History of Modernization." *Diplomatic History* 33 no. 3 (2009): 375–385.
Erdmann, Gero. *Jenseits des Mythos: Genossenschaften zwischen Mittelklasse und Staatsverwaltung in Tanzania und Kenia*. Freiburg: Bergstraesser, 1996.
Evans, Thomas. *Algeria: France's Undeclared War*. New York: Oxford University Press, 2012.
Fabian, Johannes. *Philosophie Bantoue. Placide Tempels et son oeuvre vus dans une perspective historique*. Brussels: CRISP, 1970.
Farley, John. *To Cast out Disease: A History of the International Health Division of the Rockefeller Foundation (1913–1951)*. Oxford and New York: Oxford University Press, 2004.
Fasseur, Cornelis. *The Politics of Colonial Exploitation: Java, the Dutch and the Cultivation System*. Ithaca: Cornell University Press, 1992.
Ferguson, Niall. *Colossus: The Rise and Fall of the American Empire*. London: Penguin Books, 2005.
Ferro, Marc. *Colonization: A Global History*. London: Taylor & Francis, 2005.
Fieldhouse, David K. *Colonial Empires: A Comparative Survey from the Eighteenth Century*. London: Weidenfeld and Nicolson, 1966.
Finaldi, Giuseppe. *A History of Italian Colonialism, 1860–1907: Europe's Last Empire*. London: Taylor & Francis, 2016.
Finch, Michael P. M. *A Progressive Occupation? The Gallieni-Lyautey Method and Colonial Pacification in Tonkin and Madagascar, 1885–1900*. Oxford: Oxford University Press, 2013.
Fischer-Tiné, Harald, and Susanne Gehrmann. *Empires and Boundaries: Race, Class, and Gender in Colonial Settings*. Hoboken: Taylor & Francis, 2008.
Fitzpatrick, Matthew P. *Liberal Imperialism in Europe*. New York: Palgrave Macmillan, 2012.
Liberal Imperialism in Germany: Expansionism and Nationalism, 1848–1884. New York: Berghahn Books, 2008.

Fogarty, Richard S. *Race and War in France: Colonial Subjects in the French Army, 1914–1918.* Baltimore: Johns Hopkins University Press, 2008.
Foks, Freddy. "Bronislaw Malinowski, 'Indirect Rule,' and the Colonial Politics of Functionalist Anthropology, ca. 1925–1940." *Comparative Studies in Society and History* 60, no. 1 (2018): 35–57.
Framke, Maria. *Delhi – Rom – Berlin. Die indische Wahrnehmung von Faschismus und Nationalsozialismus 1922–1939.* Darmstadt: WBG, 2013.
Frankema, Ewout. "Colonial Taxation and Government Spending in British Africa, 1880–1940. Maximizing Revenue or Minimizing Effort?" *Explorations in Economic History* 48, no. 1 (2010): 136–149.
 "Raising Revenue in the British Empire, 1870–1940. How 'Extractive' Were Colonial Taxes?" *Journal of Global History* 5 (2010): 447–477.
Frankema, Ewout, and Frans Buelens. *Colonial Exploitation and Economic Development: The Belgian Congo and the Netherlands Indies Compared.* London: Routledge, 2013.
Fremigacci, Jean. *État, Économie et Société Coloniale à Madagascar: De la fin du XIXe siècle aux années 1940.* Paris: Karthala, 2014.
Gallon, Thomas-Peter. "Mythos oder Methode bei der Planung von Partizipation. Die verklärte 'Fokonolona'-Tradition und 'Soziale Integration' in einem madegassischen Dorf." *Africa Spectrum* 26, no. 2 (1991): 181–197.
Gamble, Harry. "Peasants of the Empire: Rural Schools and the Colonial Imaginary in 1930s French West Africa." *Études Africaines* 49, no. 195 (2005): 775–804.
Gann, Lewis H., and Peter Duignan. *African Proconsuls: European Governors in Africa.* New York: Free Press, 1978.
 The Rulers of Belgian Africa, 1884–1914. Princeton: Princeton University Press, 1979.
 The Rulers of British Africa. London: Croom Helm, 1978.
 The Rulers of German Africa. Stanford: Stanford University Press, 1977.
Gardner, Leigh A. "Fiscal Policies in the Belgian Congo in Comparative Perspective." In *Colonial Exploitation and Economic Development: The Belgian Congo and the Netherlands Indies Compared.* Edited by E. Frankema and F. Buelens, 130–152. London: Routledge, 2013.
 Taxing Colonial Africa: The Political Economy of British Imperialism. Oxford: Oxford University Press, 2012.
Garner, Reuben. "Watchdogs of Empire: The French Colonial Inspection Service in Action: 1815–1913." PhD Diss., Rochester, 1970.
Garton, Stephen. "The Dominions, Ireland, and India." In *Empires at War: 1911–1923.* Edited by Robert Gerwarth and Erez Manela, 152–178. Oxford: Oxford University Press, 2014.
Gavish, Dov. *The Survey of Palestine under the British Mandate, 1920–1948.* London and New York: Routledge Curzon, 2005.
Gayffier-Bonneville, Anne. "La Formation des Administrateurs au Soudan à l'Époque du Condominium." In *Les administrations coloniales, XIXe–XXe siècles.* Edited by Samia El Mechat, 33–44. Rennes: PU de Rennes, 2009.

Gayibor, Nicoué Lodjou. *Histoire Des Togolais*, 3 vols. Paris: Karthala, 2011.
Geertz, Clifford. *Agricultural Involution: The Process of Ecological Change in Indonesia.* Berkeley: University of California Press, 1963.
The Social History of an Indonesian Town. Cambridge, MA: MIT Press, 1965.
Gellner, Ernest. *Language and Solitude: Wittgenstein, Malinowski and the Habsburg Dilemma.* Cambridge: Cambridge University Press, 1998.
Gerwarth, Robert, and Erez Manela, eds. *Empires at War 1911-1923.* Oxford: Oxford University Press, 2014.
Geulen, Christian. *Geschichte des Rassismus.* Bonn: Bpb, 2007.
Gilmann, Nils. *Mandarins of the Future: Modernization Theory in Cold War America.* Baltimore: Johns Hopkins University Press, 2007.
Gibson, Charles. *The Black Legend: Anti-Spanish Attitudes in the Old World and the New.* New York: Knopf, 1971.
Gilmour, David. *The Ruling Caste: Imperial Lives in the Victorian Raj.* New York: Farrar 2007.
Ginio, Ruth. "Negotiating Legal Authority in French West Africa: The Colonial Administration and African Assessors, 1903-1918." In *Intermediaries, Interpreters, and Clerks.* Edited by B. N. Lawrance et al., 115-135. Madison: University of Wisconsin Press, 2006.
Gissibl, Bernhard. *The Nature of German Imperialism: Conservation and the Politics of Wildlife in Colonial East Africa.* New York: Berghahn Books, 2016.
Goebel, Michael. *Anti-Imperial Metropolis: Interwar Paris and the Seeds of Third-World Nationalism.* New York: Cambridge University Press, 2016.
Golant, William. *Image of Empire: The Early History of the Imperial Institute 1887-1925.* Exeter: University of Exeter, 1984.
Gorman, Daniel. *The Emergence of International Society in the 1920s.* New York: Cambridge University Press, 2014.
International Cooperation in the Early Twentieth Century. London: Bloomsbury, 2017.
Gosewinkel, Dieter, ed. *Anti-Liberal Europe: A Neglected Story of Europeanization.* New York: Berghahn Books, 2015.
Goss, Andrew. "Decent Colonialism? Pure Science and Colonial Ideology in the Netherlands East Indies, 1910-1929." *Journal of Southeast Asian Studies*, 40, no. 1 (2009): 187-214.
The Floracrats: State-Sponsored Science and the Failure of the Enlightenment in Indonesia. Madison: University of Wisconsin Press, 2011.
Goswami, Manu. "Imaginary Futures and Colonial Internationalisms." *The American Historical Review* 117, no. 5 (2012): 1461-1485.
Gouda, Frances. *Dutch Culture Overseas: Colonial Practice in the Netherlands Indies, 1900-1942.* Singapore: Equinox, 2008.
"Mimicry and Projection in the Colonial Encounter: The Dutch East Indies/Indonesia as Experimental Laboratory, 1900-1942." *Journal of Colonialism and Colonial History* 1, no. 2 (2000). https://muse.jhu.edu/article/7352.

Greenwood, Anna, ed. *Beyond the State: The Colonial Medical Service in British Africa*. Manchester: Manchester University Press, 2016.
Grosser, Pascal. "Une 'création continue'? L'Indochine, le Maghreb et l'Union française." *Monde(s)* 2, no. 12 (2017): 71–94.
Grupp, Peter. *Deutschland, Frankreich und die Kolonien: Der französische 'Parti Colonial' und Deutschland von 1890–1914*. Tübingen: Mohr, 1980.
——— "Eugène Etienne et la Tentative de Rapprochement Franco-Allemand en 1907." *Cahiers d'Études Africaines* 15, no. 48 (1975): 303–311.
Ha, Marie-Paule. *French Women and the Empire: The Case of Indochina*. Oxford and New York: Oxford University Press, 2014.
Hall, Catherine. *Cultures of Empire: Colonizers in Britain and the Empire in the Nineteenth and Twentieth Centuries, a Reader*. New York: Routledge, 2000.
Hallaq, Wael B. *A History of Islamic Legal Theories: An Introduction to Sunnī "uṣūl al-fiqh."* Cambridge: Cambridge University Press, 2007.
Hansen, Peo, and Stefan Jonsson. *Eurafrica: The Untold History of European Integration and Colonialism*. London: Bloomsbury, 2014.
Harries, Patrick. *Work, Culture, and Identity: Migrant Laborers in Mozambique and South Africa, c. 1860–1910*. Portsmouth: Heinemann, 1994.
Haupt, Gerhard, and Jürgen Kocka, eds. *Comparative and Transnational History: Central European Approaches and New Perspectives*. Oxford and New York: Berghahn Books, 2009.
Hausen, Karin. *Deutsche Kolonialherrschaft in Afrika: Wirtschaftsinteressen und Kolonialverwaltung in Kamerun vor 1914*. Zurich: Atlantik, 1970.
Havinden, Michael A., and David Meredith. *Colonialism and Development: Britain and Its Tropical Colonies, 1850–1960*. London and New York: Routledge, 1993.
Hée, Nadine, and Daniel Hedinger. "Transimperial History: Connectivity, Cooperation and Competition." *Journal of Modern European History* 16, no. 4 (2018): 429–452.
Headrick, Daniel R. *The Tentacles of Progress: Technology Transfer in the Age of Imperialism 1850–1940*. Oxford: Oxford University Press, 1988.
Hedinger, Daniel, and R. Hofmann. "Editorial – Axis Empires: Towards a Global History of Fascist Imperialism." *Journal of Global History*, 12, no. 2 (2017): 161–165.
Herren, Madeleine. "Fascist Internationalism." In *Internationalisms: A Twentieth-Century History*. Edited by P. Clavin and G. Sluga, 191–212. Cambridge: Cambridge University Press, 2017.
——— *Hintertüren zur Macht. Internationalismus und modernisierungsorientierte Aussenpolitik in Belgien, der Schweiz und den USA 1865–1914*. Göttingen: Oldenburg, 2000.
——— *Internationale Organisationen seit 1865: Eine Globalgeschichte der internationalen Ordnung*. Darmstadt: WBG, 2009.

Hetherington, Philippa, and Glenda Sluga, eds. "Liberal and Illiberal Internationalisms." Special issue, *Journal of World History* 31, no. 3 (2020).
Hiskett, M. *The Course of Islam in Africa*. Edinburgh: Edinburgh University Press, 1994.
Hodge, Joseph. *Triumph of the Expert: Agrarian Doctrines of Development and the Legacies of British Colonialism*. Athens: Ohio University Press, 2007.
Hoexter, Miriam. *Endowments, Rulers, and Community: Waqf Al-Haramayn in Ottoman Algiers*. Leiden: Brill, 1998.
Hopkins, Anthony G. *American Empire: A Global History*. Princeton: Princeton University Press, 2018.
——— "Economic Aspects of Political Movements in Nigeria and in the Gold Coast 1918–1939." *The Journal of African History* 7, no. 1 (1966): 133–152.
Houannou, Adrien. "Hommage à un grand écrivain: Paul Hazoumé." *Présence Africaine* 2, no. 114 (1980): 204–208.
Hough, Eleanor M. *The Co-operative Movement in India*. London: Oxford University Press, 1966.
Huetz de Lemps, Xavier. *L'Archipel des Épices. La corruption de l'administration espagnole aux Philippines*. Madrid: Vélazquez, 2006.
Hugenholtz, Wouter R. "Famine and Food Supply in Java, 1830–1914." In *Two Colonial Empires: Comparative Essays on the History of India and Indonesia in the Nineteenth Century*. Edited by C. A. Bayly and D. H. A. Kolff, 155–188. Dordrecht: Nijhoff, 1986.
Huillery, Élise. "The Black Man's Burden: The Cost of Colonization of French West Africa." *Journal of Economic History* 74, no. 1 (2014): 1–38.
Hunt, Nancy Rose. *A Nervous State: Violence, Remedies, and Reverie in Colonial Congo*. Durham: Duke University Press, 2016.
Hutchcroft, Paul D. "Colonial Masters, National Politics, and Provincial Lords: Central Authority and Local Autonomy in the American Philippines, 1900–1913." *The Journal of Asian Studies* 59, no. 2 (2000): 277–306.
Iliffe, John. *A Modern History of Tanganyika*. Cambridge: Cambridge University Press, 1978.
Irye, Akira. *Global and Transnational History: The Past, Present, and Future*. Basingstoke: Palgrave Macmillan, 2013.
Jennings, Eric T. *Curing the Colonizers: Hydrotherapy, Climatology, and French Colonial Spas*. Durham: Duke University Press, 2006.
Jiménez. I. D. "W. E. Retana y la Crítica al Modernismo: De la evolución de la literatura castellana en Filipinas." *Revista Filipina* 12, no. 1 (2008). http://revista.carayanpress.com/retana.html.
Joseph, Richard. "Un Prétendant Royal: Le prince Douala Manga Bell à Paris, 1919–1922." *Cahiers d'études africaines* 14, no. 54 (1974): 339–358.
Joseph-Gabriel, Anette. *Reimagining Liberation: How Black Women Transformed Citizenship in the French Empire*. Urbana: University of Illinois Press, 2019.
Kaiga, Sakiko. *Britain and the Intellectual Origins of the League of Nations, 1914–1919*. Cambridge: Cambridge University Press, 2021.

Kaiser, Wolfgang, and Johan Schot. *Writing the Rules for Europe: Experts, Cartels, and International Organizations*. Basingstoke: Palgrave Macmillan, 2014.
Kamel, Chachoua. *L'islam kabyle, religion, État et société enAlgérie, suivi de l'Épître (Rissala) d'IbnouZakri (Alger, 1903) Mufti de la Grande Mosquée d'Alger.* Paris: Maisonneuve & Larose, 2001.
Kaminsky, Arnold F. *The India Office 1880-1910*. New York: Greenwood, 1986.
Kamissek, Christoph, and Jonas Kreienbaum. "An Imperial Cloud? Conceptualising Interimperial Connections and Transimperial Knowledge." *Journal of Modern European History* 14, no. 2 (2016): 164-182.
Kalpagam, Uma. "Colonial Governmentality and the Public Sphere in India." *Journal of Historical Sociology* 14, no. 4 (2001): 418-440.
Karns, Margaret P., and Karen A. Mingst. *International Organizations: The Politics and Processes of Global Governance*. 2nd ed. Boulder: Lynne Rienner, 2010.
Keese, Alexander. *Living with Ambiguity: Integrating an African Elite in French and Portuguese Africa, 1930-61*. Stuttgart: Steiner, 2007.
Kesner, Richard M. *Economic Control and Colonial Development: Crown Colony Financial Management in the Age of Joseph Chamberlain*. Westport: Greenwood, 1981.
Kirchberger, Ulrike. "German Scientists in the Indian Forest Service: A German Contribution to the Raj?" *The Journal of Imperial and Commonwealth History* 29, no. 2 (2001): 1-26.
Kirk-Greene, Anthony H. M. *Britain's Imperial Administrators, 1858-1966*. New York: St. Martin's Press, 2000.
"Forging a Relationship with the Colonial Administrative Service 1921-1939." *Journal of Imperial and Commonwealth History* 19, no. 3 (1991): 62-82.
"The Progress of Pro-Consuls: Advancement and Migration among the Colonial Governors of British African Territories, 1900-1965," *The Journal of Imperial and Commonwealth History* 7, no. 2 (2008): 180-212.
Klaveren, Jan Jacob Van. *The Dutch Colonial System in the East Indies*. Rotterdam: Benedictus, 1953.
Klein, Jean F. "La Création de l'École Coloniale de Lyon: Au cœur des polémiques du parti colonial." *Outre-mers* 93, nos. 252-253 (2006): 147-170.
Koekkoek, René, Anne-Isabelle Richard, and Arthur Weststeijn. "Visions of Dutch Empire." *BMGN - Low Countries Historical Review* 132, no. 2 (2017): 79-96.
Koponen, Juhani. *Development for Exploitation: German Colonial Policies in Mainland Tanzania, 1884-1914*. Hamburg: Lit Verlag 1994.
Koskenniemi, Martti. *The Gentle Civilizer of Nations: The Rise and Fall of International Law, 1870-1960*. Cambridge and New York: Cambridge University Press, 2002.
Kott, Sandrine, and Joëlle Droux, eds. *Globalizing Social Rights: The International Labour Organization and Beyond*. Houndmills: Palgrave Macmillan, 2013.
Kott, Sandrine, and Kiran Klaus Patel, eds. *Nazism across Borders: The Social Policies of the Third Reich and Their Global Appeal*. Oxford: Oxford University Press, 2018.

Kramer, Paul A. *The Blood of Government: Race, Empire, the United States, and the Philippines.* Chapel Hill: University of North Carolina Press, 2011.
Kreike, Emmanuel. "Genocide in the Kampongs? Dutch Nineteenth Century Colonial Warfare in Aceh, Sumatra." In *Colonial Counterinsurgency and Mass Violence: The Dutch Empire in Indonesia.* Edited by Bart Littikhuis and A. Dirk Moses, 297–316. London and New York: Routledge, 2014.
Kuitenbrouwer, M. *Nederland en de Opkomst van het Moderne Imperialisme.* Amsterdam: De Bataafsche Leeuw, 1985.
Kuitenbrouwer, M., and H. A. Poeze. *Dutch Scholarship in the Age of Empire and Beyond.* Leiden: Brill, 2013.
Kuller, Christiane. *Finanzverwaltung und Judenverfolgung: Die Entziehung jüdischen Vermögens in Bayern während der NS-Zeit.* Munich: Beck, 2008.
Kundrus, Birthe."Weiblicher Kulturimperialismus: Die imperialistischen Frauenverbände des Kaiserreichs." In *Das Kaiserreich Transnational: Deutschland in der Welt 1871-1914.* Edited by Sebastian Conrad and Jürgen Osterhammel, 213–235. Göttingen: Vandenhoeck & Ruprecht, 2004.
Kwaschik, Anne. *Der Griff nach dem Weltwissen: Zur Genealogie von area studies.* Göttingen: Vandenhoeck & Ruprecht, 2018.
Lambert, David, and Alan Lester, eds. *Colonial Lives across the British Empire: Imperial Careering in the Long Nineteenth Century.* Cambridge: Cambridge University Press, 2006.
Landmeters, Romain, and Nathalie Tousignant. "Civiliser les Indigènes par le Droit: Antoine Sohier, magistrat au Congo belge (1910-1934)." *Revue interdisciplinaire d'études juridiques* 83, no. 2 (2019): 81–100.
Laqua, Daniel, *The Age of Internationalism and Belgium, 1880-1930: Peace, Progress and Prestige.* Manchester: Manchester University Press, 2013.
ed. *Internationalism Reconfigured: Transnational Ideas and Movements between the World Wars.* London: I. B. Tauris, 2011.
Laqua, Daniel, Wouter Van Acker, and Christophe Verbruggen, eds. *International Organisations and Global Civil Society: Histories of the Union of International Associations.* London: Bloomsbury, 2019.
Larmer, Miles. "Permanent Precarity: Capital and Labour in the Central African Copperbelt." *Labour History* 58, no. 2 (2017): 170–184.
Latham, Michael. *The Right Kind of Revolution: Modernization, Development, and U.S. Foreign Policy from the Cold War to the Present.* Ithaca: Cornell University Press, 2011.
Le Révérand, André, ed. *Un Lyautey Inconnu: Correspondance et journal inédits, 1874-1934.* Paris: Perrin, 1980.
Le Révérand, André, *Lyautey.* Paris: Fayard, 1983.
Legg, Stephen. "Dyarchy: Democracy, Autocracy and the Scalar Sovereignty of Interwar India." *Comparative Studies of South Asia, Africa and the Middle East* 36, no. 1: 44–65.
Leonhard, Jörn. *Der Überforderte Frieden: Versailles und die Welt 1918-1923.* Munich: C. H. Beck, 2018.

Leonhard, Jörn, and Ulrike V. Hirschhausen. *Comparing Empires: Encounters and Transfers in the Long Nineteenth Century*. Göttingen: Vandenhoeck & Ruprecht, 2012.

Empires und Nationalstaaten im 19. Jahrhundert. Göttingen: Vandenhoeck & Ruprecht, 2009.

Lev, D. S. "Colonial Law and the Genesis of the Indonesian State." *Indonesia* 40 (1985): 57-74.

Levtzion, Nehemia, and Randall L. Pouwels. *The History of Islam in Africa*. Athens: Ohio University Press, 2000.

Lezcano, V. M. *El Colonialismo Hispanofrancés en Marruecos: 1898-1927*. Madrid: Siglo Veintiuno, 1976.

Lindner, Ulrike. *Koloniale Begegnungen: Deutschland und Großbritannien als Imperialmächte in Afrika 1880-1914*. Frankfurt am Main: Campus, 2011.

"New Forms of Knowledge Exchange between Imperial Powers: The Development of the Institut Colonial International (ICI) since the End of the 19th Century." In *Imperial Co-operation and Transfer, 1870-1930: Empires and Encounters*. Edited by Roland Cvetkovski and Volker Barth, 57-78. London: Bloomsbury, 2015.

Linne, Karsten. *Deutschland Jenseits des Äquators: Die NS-Kolonialplanungen für Afrika*. Berlin: Links Verlag, 2008.

Littikhuis, Bart, and A. D. Moses, eds. *Colonial Counterinsurgency and Mass Violence: The Dutch Empire in Indonesia*. London and New York: Routledge, 2014.

Locher-Scholten, Elsbeth. *Ethiek in Fragmenten: Vijf Studies over Koliniaal Denken en Doen van Nederlanders in de Indonesische Archipel 1877-1942*. Utrecht: HES, 1981.

Women and the Colonial State: Essays on Gender and Modernity in the Netherlands Indies, 1900-1942. Amsterdam: Amsterdam University Press, 2000.

Lorcin, Patricia. *Imperial Identities: Stereotyping, Prejudice and Race in Colonial Algeria*. London: Tauris, 1995.

Lorcin, Patricia M. E., and Todd Shepard. *French Mediterraneans: Transnational and Imperial Histories: France Overseas*. Lincoln: University of Nebraska Press, 2016.

Lorenzini, Sara. *Global Development: A Cold War History*. Princeton: Princeton University Press, 2019.

Louro, Michele L., Carolien Stolte, Heather Streets-Salter, and Sana Tannoury-Karam, eds. *The League Against Imperialism: Lives and Afterlives*. Dordrecht: Leiden University Press, 2020.

Lyall, Andrew. "Early German Legal Anthropology: Albert Hermann Post and His Questionnaire." *Journal of African Law* 52, no. 1 (2008): 114-138.

Lyons, Maryinez. *The Colonial Disease: A Social History of Sleeping Sickness in Northern Zaire, 1900-1940*. New York: Cambridge University Press, 1992.

Maat, Harro. *Science Cultivating Practice: A History of Agricultural Science in the Netherlands and Its Colonies, 1863–1986*. Dordrecht: Kluwer, 2001.
Macekura, Stephen, and Erez Manela, eds. *The Development Century: A Global History*. Cambridge: Cambridge University Press, 2018.
Mackay, Allan. *A Dictionary of Scientific Quotations*. Bristol: Routledge, 1991.
MacKenzie, John. *European Empires and the People: Popular Responses to Imperialism in France, Britain, the Netherlands, Belgium, Germany and Italy*. Manchester: Manchester University Press, 2011.
MacLeod, Roy M. *Government and Expertise: Specialists, Administrators, and Professionals, 1860–1919*. New York: Cambridge University Press, 1988.
MacLeod, Roy M. ed. *Nature and Empire: Science and the Colonial Enterprise*. Chicago: University of Chicago Press, 2000.
MacLeod, Roy M., and Milton J. Lewis. *Disease, Medicine, and Empire: Perspectives on Western Medicine and the Experience of European Expansion*. London and New York: Routledge, 1988.
MacTurnan Kahin. George. *Nationalism and Revolution in Indonesia*. Ithaca: Cornell University Press, 2003 [1952].
Maier, Charles S. *Among Empires: American Ascendancy and Its Predecessors*. Cambridge, MA: Harvard University Press, 2007.
Mallat, Chibli. *Introduction to Middle Eastern Law*. London: Oxford University Press, 2007.
Mamdani, Mahmood. *Define and Rule: Native as Political Identity*. Cambridge, MA: Harvard University Press, 2002.
Manela, Erez. *The Wilsonian Moment: Self-Determination and the International Origins of Anticolonial Nationalism*. Oxford: Oxford University Press, 2007.
Mangold, S. *Eine "Weltbürgerliche Wissenschaft": Die deutsche Orientalistik im 19. Jahrhundert*. Stuttgart: F. Steiner, 2004.
Mann, Gregory. *From Empires to NGOs in the West African Sahel: The Road to Nongovernmentality*. Cambridge: Cambridge University Press, 2015.
  "What Was the Indigénat? The 'Empire of Law' in French West Africa." *The Journal of African History* 50, no. 3 (2009): 331–353.
Mann, Gregory, and J. I. Guyer. "Imposing a Guide on the Indigène: The Fifty Year Experience of the Sociétés de Prévoyance in French West and Equatorial Africa." In *Credit, Currencies and Culture: African Financial Institutions in Historical Perspective*. Edited by E. Stiansen and J. I. Guyer, 124–151. Uppsala: Nordiska Afrikainstitutet, 1999.
Mann, Kristin, and Richard L. Roberts. *Law in Colonial Africa*. Portsmouth and London: Heinemann, 1991.
Marseille, Jacques. *Empire Colonial et Capitalisme Français: Histoire d'un divorce*. Paris: Michel, 1986.
Mateos y de Cabo, Óscar I. "El pensamiento político de Joaquín Costa: Entre nacionalismo español y europeísmo." PhD Diss., Universidad Complutense de Madrid, 1996.

Maul, Daniel. *Human Rights, Development and Decolonization: The International Labour Organization, 1940-70.* New York: Palgrave Macmillan, 2012.
Mazower, Mark. *Governing the World: The History of an Idea, 1815 to the Present.* New York: Penguin Books, 2013.
——. *No Enchanted Palace: The End of Empire and the Ideological Origins of the United Nations.* Princeton: Princeton University Press, 2009.
Mbembe, Achille. "Necropolitics." *Public Culture* 15, no. 1 (2003): 11-40.
McCoy, Alfred W., Josep M. Fradera, and Stephen Jacobson. *Endless Empire: Spain's Retreat, Europe's Eclipse, America's Decline.* Madison: University of Wisconsin Press, 2012.
McNeill, John R.. *Mosquito Empires: Ecology and War in the Greater Caribbean, 1620-1914.* Cambridge: Cambridge University Press, 2010.
McVety, Amanda Kay. *The Rinderpest Campaigns: A Virus, Its Vaccines, and Global Development in the Twentieth Century.* Cambridge: Cambridge University Press, 2018.
Mehta, Uday S. *Liberalism and Empire: A Study in Nineteenth Century British Liberal Thought.* Chicago: University of Chicago Press, 1999.
Melber, Henning, ed. *The Rise of Africa's Middle Class: Myths, Realities and Critical Engagements.* London: Zed, 2016.
Mertens, Myriam, and Guillaume Lachenal. "The History of 'Belgian' Tropical Medicine from a Cross-Border Perspective." *Belgisch Tijdschrift voor Filologie en Geschiedenis* 90 (2012): 1249-1272.
Metcalf, Thomas R. *Ideologies of the Raj.* Cambridge: Cambridge University Press 1995.
Methfessel, Christian. *Kontroverse Gewalt: Die imperiale Expansion in der englischen und deutschen Presse vor dem Ersten Weltkrieg.* Cologne: Böhlau-Verlag 2019.
Michel, Marc. *L'appel à l'Afrique. Contributions et réactions à l'effort de guerre en A.O.F. (1914-1919).* Paris: Publications de la Sorbonne, 1982.
Miers, Suzanne, and Richard L. Roberts. *The End of Slavery in Africa.* Madison: University of Wisconsin Press, 1988.
Migani, Guia. "Sékou Touré et la contestation de l'ordre colonial en Afrique subsaharienne, 1958-1963." *Mondes* 2 no. 2 (2012): 257-273.
Mitchell, Timothy. *Rule of Experts: Egypt, Techno-politics, Modernity.* Berkeley: University of California Press, 2002.
Molina Cano, Jerónimo. "Africanismo y africanistas españoles (I): José María Cordero de Torres." *Empresas políticas* 7(2006): 73-100.
Monjau, Herbert, Erich Frey, and Egon Streppel. "Informationen." *Arbeit und Recht,* 20 no. 7 (1972): 208-212.
Montarsolo, Yves. *L'Eurafrique. Contrepoint de l'Idée d'Europe.* Aix-en-Provence: Publications de l'Université de Provence, 2010.
Moon, Suzanne. *Technology and Ethical Idealism: A History of Development in the Netherlands East Indies.* Leiden: CNWS, 2007.

Morales Lezcano, Víctor. *El Colonialismo Hispanofrances en Marruecos (1898–1927)*. Madrid: Siglo Veintiuno, 1976.
Moses, A. D. *Empire, Colony, Genocide: Conquest, Occupation, and Subaltern Resistance in World History*. New York: Berghahn Books, 2008.
Motadel, David. "The Global Authoritarian Moment and the Revolt against Empire." *American Historical Review*, 124, no. 3 (2019): 843–877.
  Islam and the European Empires. Oxford: Oxford University Press, 2014.
Moyn, Samuel. *The Last Utopia: Human Rights in History*. Cambridge, MA: Harvard University Press, 2012.
Mrázek, Rudolf. *Sjahrir: Politics and Exile in Indonesia*. Ithaca: Cornell University Press, 1994.
Nasson, Bill. "British Imperial Africa." In *Empires at War: 1911–1923*. Edited by Robert Gerwarth and Erez Manela, 130–151. Oxford: Oxford University Press, 2014.
Neill, Deborah J. *Networks in Tropical Medicine: Internationalism, Colonialism, and the Rise of a Medical Specialty, 1890–1930*. Stanford: Stanford University Press, 2012.
Ninkovich, Frank A. *Global Fawn: The Cultural Foundation of American Internationalism, 1865–1890*. Cambridge, MA: Harvard University Press, 2009.
Nogué, Joan, and José L. Villanova. "Spanish Colonialism in Morocco and the Sociedad Geográfica de Madrid, 1876–1956." *Journal of Historical Geography* 28, no. 1 (2002): 1–20.
Northrup, D. *Indentured Labor in the Age of Imperialism, 1834–1922*. Cambridge: Cambridge University Press, 1995.
Nugent, Paul. *Smugglers, Secessionists and Loyal Citizens on the Ghana-Toga Frontier: The Lie of the Borderlands Since 1914*. Western African Studies. Athens and Oxford: Ohio University Press and James Currey, 2002.
Nyanchoga, Samuel A. "Mutualism and Cooperative Work." In *General Labour History of Africa: Workers, Employers and Governments, 20th–21st Centuries*. Edited by Stefano Bellucci and Andreas Eckert, 585–616. Woodbridge: Currey, 2019.
O'Malley, Alanna. *The Diplomacy of Decolonisation: America, Britain and the United Nations during the Congo Crisis 1960–1964*. Manchester: Manchester University Press, 2018.
O'Malley, William J. "Plantations 1830–1940: An Overview'." In *Indonesian Economic History in the Dutch Colonial Era*. Edited by William J. O'Malley et al., 136–170. New Haven: Yale University Press, 1990.
Opinel, Annick. "The Emergence of French Medical Entomology: The Influence of Universities, the Institute Pasteur and Military Physicians (c. 1890–1938)." *Medical History* 52 (2008): 387–405.
Opinel, Annick, and G. Gachelin. "Emile Brumpt's Contribution to the Characterization of Parasitic Diseases in Brazil, 1909–1914." *Parasitologia* 47, nos. 3/4 (2005): 299–308.

Osborne, Michael A. *The Emergence of Tropical Medicine in France*. Chicago and London: University of Chicago Press, 2014.

Osterhammel, Jürgen. *The Transformation of the World: A Global History of the Nineteenth Century*. Princeton: Princeton University Press, 2014.

Padirac, Raymond de. "L'importance Économique et l'Avenir du Caoutchouc Naturel." In *Le Caoutchouc Naturel*. Edited by Patrice Compagnon, xvii. Paris: Maisonneuve & Larose, 1986.

Paillard Yvan G. "Domination coloniale et récupération des traditions autochtones. Le cas de Madagascar de 1896 à 1914." *Revue d'histoire moderne et contemporaine*, 38, no. 1 (1991): 73–104.

Paredes, Ruby R., ed. *Philippine Colonial Democracy*. New Haven: Yale University Press, 1988.

Pasetti Matteo. "Corporatist Connections: The Transnational Rise of the Fascist Model in Interwar Europe." In *Fascism without Borders: Transnational Connections and Cooperation between Movements and Regimes in Europe from 1918 to 1945*. Edited by Arnd Bauerkämper and Grzegorz Rossoliński-Liebe, 65–94. New York: Berghahn, 2017.

Passmore, Kevin. "Writing the History of Fascism and National Socialism Transnationally: The Example of France." *Bereginya* 4, no. 23 (2014): 287–304.

Patel, Klaus Kiran. "An Emperor without Clothes? The Debate about Transnational History Twenty-Five Years On." *Histoire@Politique* 26 (2015). www.histoire-politique.fr/documents/26/pistes/pdf/HP26-Pistesetdebats_Kiran_Patel_def.pdf.

——— . *Project Europe: A History*. Cambridge: Cambridge University Press, 2020.

Paulmann, Johannes, and Martin Geyer, eds. *The Mechanics of Internationalism: Culture, Society and Politics from the 1840s to the First World War*. Oxford: Oxford University Press, 2001.

Pearson, Jessica Lynne. *The Colonial Politics of Global Health: France and the United Nations in Postwar Africa*. Cambridge, MA: Harvard University Press, 2018.

Peemans, J. P. "Capital Accumulation in the Congo under Colonialism: The Role of the State." In *Colonialism in Africa*. Edited by L. H. Duignan and P. Gann, 165–212. Cambridge: Cambridge University Press, 1988.

Pedersen, Susan. *The Guardians: The League of Nations and the Crisis of Empire*. Oxford: Oxford University Press, 2015.

——— . "Samoa on the World Stage: Petitions and Peoples before the Mandates Commission of the League of Nations." *The Journal of Imperial and Commonwealth History* 40, no. 2 (2012): 231–261.

Pedraz Marcos, Azucena. "El Pensamiento Africanista hasta 1883. Cánovas, Donoso y Costa." *Anales de la fundación Joaquín Costa* 11 (1994): 31–48.

Penny, H. Glenn. "Traditions in the German Language." In *A New History of Anthropology*. Edited by H. Kuklick, 79–95. Oxford: Oxford University Press, 2007.

Penny, H. Glenn, and M. Bunzl. *Worldly Provincialism: German Anthropology in the Age of Empire*. Ann Arbor: University of Michigan Press, 2003.

Pérez, Louis A. *Cuba: Between Reform and Revolution*. New York: Oxford University Press, 2006.
Perham, Margery. *Native Administration in Nigeria*. London: Oxford University Press, 1937.
Perras, Arne. *Carl Peters and German Imperialism, 1856-1918: A Political Biography*. Oxford and New York: Clarendon, 2004.
Persell, Stuart M. *The French Colonial Lobby, 1889-1938*. Stanford: Hoover Institution, 1983.
Pesek, Michael. "Foucault Hardly Came to Africa: Some Notes on Colonial and Post-colonial Governmentality." *Comparativ* 21 (2011): 41-59.
"Sulayman b. Nasir al-Lamki and German Colonial Policies towards Muslim Communities in German East Africa." In *Islam in Africa*. Edited by Thomas Bierschenk and Georg Stauth, 211-229. Münster: Lit, 2002.
Pietsch, Tamson. *Empire of Scholars: Universities, Networks and the British Academic World, 1850-1939*. Manchester: Manchester University Press, 2013.
Pitts, Jennifer. *A Turn to Empire: The Rise of Imperial Liberalism in Britain and France*. Princeton: Princeton University Press, 2005.
Plasman, P. L. "Un État De Non-droit? L'établissement du pouvoir judiciaire au Congo léopoldien (1885-1889)." In *Droit et Justice en Afrique Coloniale: Traditions, productions et réformes*. Edited by Bérengère Piret, 27-49. Brussels: Université Saint-Louis-Bruxelles, 2013.
Podestà, Gian Luca. *Eurafrica: Vital Space, Demographic Planning and the Division of Labour in the Italian Empire*. Parma: Kriss, 2018.
Il mito dell'impero. Economia, politica e lavoro nelle colonie italiane dell'Africa orientale 1898-1941. Torino: Giappichelli, 2004.
Pogge-von Strandmann, Hartmut. *Imperialismus vom Grünen Tisch: Deutsche Kolonialpolitik zwischen wirtschaftlicher Ausbeutung und "zivilisatorischen" Bemühungen*. Berlin: Links, 2009.
Pols, Hans. "European Physicians and Botanists, Indigenous Herbal Medicine in the Dutch East Indies, and Colonial Networks of Mediation." *East Asian Science, Technology and Society* 3, nos. 2-3 (2009): 173-208.
Pommereau, Alain de. "The Invention of the Moroccan Carpet." In *After Orientalism*. Edited by F. Pouillion und J.-C. Vatin, 218-235. Leyden: Brill, 2014.
Poncelet, Marc. *L'Invention des Sciences Coloniales Belges*. Paris: Karthala, 2008.
Porter, Bernard. *The Absent-Minded Imperialists: Empire, Society, and Culture in Britain*. New York: Oxford University Press, 2004.
Porter, Roy. *The Greatest Benefit to Mankind: A Medical History of Humanity from Antiquity to the Present*. Hammersmith and London: Harper Collins, 1997.
Pouillon, François, ed. *Dictionnaire des Orientalistes de Langue Française*. Paris: Karthala, 2012.

Priestley, M. "The Gold Coast Select Committee on Estimates: 1913–1950." *The International Journal of African Historical Studies* 6, no. 4 (1973): 543–564.
Prior, Christopher. *Exporting Empire: Africa, Colonial Officials and the Construction of the British Imperial State, c. 1900–1939*. Manchester: Manchester University Press, 2013.
Quiroz, Alfonso W. "Corrupción, burocracia, colonial y veteranos separatistas en Cuba 1868–1910." *Revista de Indias* 61, no. 221 (2001): 91–111.
Raby, Megan. *American Tropics: The Caribbean Roots of Biodiversity Science*. Chapel Hill: University of North Carolina Press, 2017.
Reichardt, Sven, and Armin Nolzen, eds. *Faschismus in Italien und Deutschland: Studien zu Transfer und Vergleich*. Göttingen: Wallstein, 2005.
Renucci, Florence. "Les Magistrats dans les Colonies: Un autre apprentissage des normes juridiques." *Les Cahiers de la Justice* 4, no. 4 (2016): 687–697.
Rhodes, Rita. *Empire and Co-operation: How the British Empire Used Co-operatives in Its Development Strategies, 1900–1970*. Edinburgh: Donald, 2012.
Ribi Forclaz, Amalia. *Humanitarian Imperialism: The Politics of Anti-slavery Activism, 1880–1940*. Oxford: Oxford Universtiy Press, 2015.
Richard, Anne-Isabelle. "Between the League of Nations and Europe: Multiple Internationalism and Interwar Dutch Civil Dociety." In *Shaping the International Relations of the Netherlands, 1815–2000: A Small Country on the Global Scene*. Edited by Ruud van Dijk et al., 97–116. Milton: Taylor & Francis, 2018.
Roberts, Richard. "The Case of Faama Mademba Sy and the Ambuguities of Legal Jurisdiction in Early Colonial French Sudan." In *Law in Colonial Africa*. Edited by K. Mann and R. L. Roberts, 185–204. Portsmouth: Currey, 1991.
———. "The End of Slavery, Colonial Courts, and Social Conflict in Gumbu, 1908–1911." *Canadian Journal of African Studies* 34, no. 3 (2000): 684–713.
———. *Litigants and Households: African Disputes and Colonial Courts in the French Soudan, 1895–1912*. Portsmouth: Heinemann, 2005.
Robinson, David. *Muslim Societies in African History*. Cambridge: Cambridge University Press, 2004.
Robinson, Ronald, John Gallagher, and Alice Denny, eds. *Africa and the Victorians: The Official Mind of Imperialism*. Houndmills and Basingstoke: Macmillan, 1961.
Rodogno, Davide, Bernhard Struck, and Jakob Vogel. *Shaping the Transnational Sphere: Experts, Networks, and Issues from the 1840s to the 1930s*. New York: Berghahn, 2015.
Rogers, Susan. "The Kilimanjaro Native Planters Association: Administrative Responses to Chagga Initiatives in the 1920's." *Transafrican Journal of History* 4, nos. 1–2 (1974): 94–114.

Ross, Corey. *Ecology and Power in the Age of Empire*. Oxford: Oxford University Press, 2017.
Rousseaux, Xavier. "Introduction: Vers une histoire post-postcoloniale de la justice et du droit en sitution coloniale?" In *Droit et Justice en Afrique coloniale: Traditions, productions et réformes*. Edited by Bérengère Piret, 9–26. Brussels: Université Saint-Louis-Bruxelles, 2013.
Rumberger, Ekkehart. "Plehn, Friedrich." *Neue Deutsche Biographie* 20 (2001): 524–525.
Ruppenthal, Jens. *Kolonialismus als "Wissenschaft und Technik" das Hamburgische Kolonialinstitut 1908 bis 1919*. Stuttgart: Steiner, 2007.
Saada, Emmanuelle. "Penser le fait colonial à travers le droit en 1900." *Mil neuf cent. Revue d'histoire intellectuelle* 27, no. 1 (2009): 103–116.
Saada, Emmanuelle, and Gérard Noiriel. *Les Enfants de la Colonie: Les métis de l'empire français entre sujétion et citoyenneté*. Paris: Découverte, 2007.
Schär, Bernhard C. *Tropenliebe: Schweizer Naturforscher und niederländischer Imperialismus in Südostasien um 1900*. Frankfurt: Campus, 2015.
Schayegh, Cyrus. "The Expanding Overlap of Imperial, International, and Transnational Political Activities, 1920s–1930s: A Belgian Case Study." *International Politics* 55 (2018): 782–802.
Schilling, Britta. *Postcolonial Germany: Memories of Empire in a Decolonized Nation*. Oxford: Oxford University Press, 2014.
Schmidt-Nowara, Christopher. *The Conquest of History: Spanish Colonialism and National Histories in the Nineteenth Century*. Pittsburgh: University of Pittsburgh Press, 2006.
"Imperio y Crisis Colonial." In *Más se Perdio en Cuba. 1898 y la crisis de fin de siglo*. Edited by Juan Pan-Montojo, 31–90. Madrid: Alianza Ed., 1998.
Schmidt-Nowara, Christopher, and John M. Nieto-Phillips. *Interpreting Spanish Colonialism: Empires, Nations, and Legends*. Albuquerque: University of New Mexico Press, 2005.
Schmutzer, Eduard J. M. *Dutch Colonial Policy and the Search for Identity in Indonesia 1920–1931*. Leiden: Brill, 1977.
Schröder, Iris. *Das Wissen von der ganzen Welt. Globale Geographien und räumliche Ordnungen Afrikas und Europas 1790–1870*. Paderborn: Schöningh, 2011.
Schröder, Martin. *Prügelstrafe und Züchtigungsrecht in den deutschen Schutzgebieten Schwarzafrikas*. Münster: Lit, 1997.
Schubert, Michael. *Der schwarze Fremde: Das Bild des Schwarzafrikaners in der parlamentarischen und publizistischen Kolonialdiskussion in Deutschland von den 1870er bis in die 1930er Jahre*. Stuttgart: F. Steiner, 2003.
Schumacher, Frank. "Kulturtransfer und Empire: Britisches Vorbild und US-amerikanische Kolonialherrschaft auf den Philippinen im fruehen 20. Jahrhundert." In *Kolonialgeschichten: Regionale Perspektiven auf ein globales Phänomen*. Edited by Claudia Kraft, A. Lüdtke, and J. Martschukat, 306–327. Frankfurt and New York: Campus, 2010.

Scott, David. *Refashioning Futures: Criticism after Postcoloniality.* Princeton: Princeton University Press, 2001.
Seekings, Jeremy. "The ILO and Welfare Reform in South Africa, Latin America, and the Caribbean, 1919-1930." In *ILO Histories.* Edited by J. van Daele et al., 145-172. Bern: Peter Lang, 2010.
Segalla, Spencer D. *Moroccan Soul: French Education, Colonial Ethnology, and Muslim Resistance 1912-1956.* Lincoln: University of Nebraska Press, 2009.
Seibert, Julia. "More Continuity Than Change? New Forms of Unfree Labour in the Belgian Congo 1908-1930." In *Humanitarian Intervention and Changing Labour Relations.* Edited by M. van der Linden, 369-386. Leiden: Brill, 2011.
Serre, Jacques, ed. *Hommes et Destins - Tome XI Afrique noire.* Paris: Harmattan, 2011.
Serre-Ratsimandisa, Georges. "Théorie Et Pratique Du 'Fokonoiona' Moderne À Madagascar." *Canadian Journal of African Studies/Revue canadienne des études africaines* 12, no. 1 (1978): 37-58.
Sessions, Jennifer E. *By Sword and Plow: France and the Conquest of Algeria.* Ithaca: Cornell University Press, 2011.
Seth, Sanjay. "Foucault in India." In *Foucault and the History of Our Present.* Edited by Sophie Fuggle et al., 43-57. New York: Palgrave Macmillan, 2015.
Shaffer, Jack. *Historical Dictionary of the Cooperative Movement.* Lanham: Scarecrow, 1999.
Shaloff, Stanley. "The Income Tax, Indirect Rule, and the Depression: The Gold Coast Riots of 1931." *Cahiers d'études africaines*, 14, no. 54 (1974): 359-375.
Shepard, Todd. *The Invention of Decolonization: The Algerian War and the Remaking of France.* Ithaca: Cornell University Press, 2006.
Shipway, Martin. *Decolonization and Its Impact: A Comparative Approach to the End of the Colonial Empires.* Malden: Blackwell, 2008.
Sibeud, Emmanuelle. *Une Science Impériale pour l'Afrique? La construction des savoirs africanistes en France 1878-1930.* Paris: EHESS, 2002.
Sibeud, Emmanuelle, Claire Fredj, Hélène Blais, and Isabelle Vallee. *Sociétés Coloniales: Enquêtes et expertises.* Paris: A. Colin, 2013.
Simonis, Francis, ed. *Le Commandant en Tournée: Une administration au contact des populations en Afrique noire coloniale.* Paris: S. Arslan, 2005.
Singaravélou, Pierre. *L'Empire des Geographes: Geographie, exploration et colonisation, 19.-20. siècle.* Paris: Belin, 2008.
"L'enseignement supérieur colonial. Un état des lieux." *Histoire de l'éducation* 122 (2009): 71-92.
Professer l'Empire: Les "sciences coloniales " en France sous la IIIe République. Paris: Publications de la Sorbonne, 2011.
"Les stratégies d'internationalisation de la question coloniale et la construction transnationale d'une science de la colonisation à la fin du XIXe siècle." *Monde(s) Histoire, Espaces, Relations* 1 (2012): 135-157.

Gram-Skjoldager, Karen, and Haakon A. Ikonomou. "Making Sense of the League of Nations Secretariat – Historiographical and Conceptual Reflections on Early International Public Administration." *European History Quarterly*, 49, no. 3 (2019): 420–444.
Skovgaard-Petersen, Jakob. *Defining Islam for the Egyptian State: Muftis and Fatwas of the dār al-iftā*. Leiden: Brill, 1997.
Slight, John. *The British Empire and the Hajj: 1865–1956*. Cambridge, MA: Harvard University Press, 2015.
Slobodian, Quinn. *Globalists: The End of Empire and the Birth of Neoliberalism*. Cambridge, MA: Harvard University Press, 2018.
Sluga, Glenda. *Internationalism in the Age of Nationalism*. Philadelphia: University of Pennsylvania Press, 2013.
Spidel, Jake. "The German Colonial Service: Organization, Selection and Training." PhD Diss., Stanford, 1972.
Stengers, Jean. *Belgique et Congo. L'élaboration de la Charte coloniale*. Brussels: Renaissance, 1963.
Congo Mythes et Réalités. Brussels: Racine, 2008.
"Léopold II et le Modèle Colonial Hollandais." *Tijdschrift voor Geschiedenis* 90, no. 1 (1977): 46–71.
Stockwell, Sarah. *The British End of the British Empire*. Cambridge: Cambridge University Press, 2018.
Stoler, Ann-Laura. *Along the Archival Grain: Epistemic Anxieties and Colonial Common Sense*. Princeton: Princeton University Press, 2010.
Capitalism and Confrontation in Sumatra's Plantation Belt 1870–1979. New Haven: Yale University Press, 1995.
Carnal Knowledge and Imperial Power: Race and the Intimate in Colonial Rule. Berkeley: University of California Press, 2002.
Race and the Education of Desire: Foucault's History of Sexuality and the Colonial Order of Things. Durham: Duke University Press, 2004.
"Tense and Tender Ties: The Politics of Comparison in North American History and (Post) Colonial Studies." *The Journal of American History* 88, no. 3 (2001): 829–865.
Stoler, Ann Laura, Carole McGranahan, and Peter C. Perdue. *Imperial Formations*. Oxford: James Currey, 2007.
Streets-Salter, Heather. *World War One in Southeast Asia: Colonialism and Anticolonialism in an Era of Global Conflict*. Cambridge: Cambridge University Press, 2017.
Stuart Cohen, A. B. "Emanuel Moresco." *Jaarboek van de Maatschappij der Nederlandsche Letterkunde te Leiden, 1945–1946*, 132–141. Leiden: Maatschappij der Nederlandse Letterkunde, 1947.
Stuchtey, Benedikt. *Die Europäische Expansion und ihre Feinde: Kolonialismuskritik vom 18. bis in das 20. Jahrhundert*. Munich: Oldenburg, 2010.
Tandjigora, A. K. "Fiscalité coloniale et souffrance sociale dans les territoires protégés de la colonie du Sénégal au lendemain de la Première Guerre

mondiale." In *Histoires de la souffrance sociale XVIIe-XXe siècles*. Edited by F. Chauvaud, 213-226. Rennes: Presses Universite de Rennes: 2007.

Tetteroo, Sander. "'How They Survived the Evil Times Is a Mystery to Me': Famine in the Netherlands East Indies, c. 1900-1904." MA Thesis, University of Leiden, 2014.

Thomas, Martin, ed. *The French Colonial Mind*, vol. 1. Lincoln: University of Nebraska Press, 2011.

Thomas, Martin, *Violence and Colonial Order: Police, Workers and Protest in the European Colonial Empires, 1918-1940*. Cambridge: Cambridge University Press, 2012.

Tilley, Helen. *Africa as a Living Laboratory: Empire, Development, and the Problem of Scientific Knowledge, 1870-1950*. Chicago: University of Chicago Press, 2011.

Triaud, Jean-Louis. *La Légende Noire de la Sanûsiyya: Une confrérie musulmane saharienne sous le regard français 1840-1930*. Paris: Ed. de la MSH, 1995.

Tomlinson, B. R. "Meyer, Sir William Stevenson (1860-1922)." *Oxford Dictionary of National Biography*. Oxford: Oxford University Press, 2004. www.oxforddnb.com/view/10.1093/ref:odnb/9780198614128.001.0001/odnb-9780198614128-e-35007.

Trotha, Trutz von. *Koloniale Herrschaft. Zur soziologischen Theorie der Staatsentstehung am Beispiel des "Schutzgebietes Togo."* Tübingen: Mohr, 1994.

Trumbull, George R. *An Empire of Facts: Colonial Power, Cultural Knowledge, and Islam in Algeria, 1870-1914*. New York: Cambridge University Press, 2009.

Tully, John Andrew. *The Devil's Milk: A Social History of Rubber*. New York: Monthly Review, 2011.

Umar, Muhammad S. *Islam and Colonialism: Intellectual Response of Muslims of Northern Nigeria to British Colonial Rule*. Leiden: Brill, 2006.

Unger, Corinna R. *International Development: A Postwar History*. London: Bloomsbury, 2018.

Ureña Valerio, Lenny A. *Colonial Fantasies, Imperial Realities: Race Science and the Making of Polishness on the Fringes of the German Empire, 1840-1920*. Athens: Ohio University Press, 2019.

Vandersmissen, Jan. *Koningen van de wereld. Leopold II en de aardrijkskundige beweging*. Leuven: Acco, 2009.

Van Daele, Jasmien. "Industrial States and the Transnational Exchanges of Social Policies: Belgium and the ILO in the Interwar Period." In *Globalizing Social Rights: The International Labour Organization and Beyond*. Edited by Sandrine Kott and Joëlle Droux, 190-209. Houndmills: Palgrave Macmillan, 2013.

Van Laak, Dirk. *Imperiale Infrastruktur. Deutsche Planungen für eine Erschließung Afrikas 1880-1960*. Paderborn: Schöningh, 2004.

——— *Literatur, die Geschichte schrieb*. Göttingen: Vandenhoeck & Ruprecht, 2011.

Van Vollenhoven, C., J. F. Holleman, and H. W. J. Sonius. *Van Vollenhoven on Indonesian Adat Law: Selections from Het Adatrecht van Nederlandsch-Indië (Volume I, 1918; Volume II, 1931).* The Hague: Nijhoff, 1981.
Vanthemsche, Guy. *Belgium and the Congo 1885-1980.* Cambridge: Cambridge University Press, 2012.
Vellut, J. L. "European Medicine in the Congo Free State (1885-1908)." In *Health in Central Africa since 1885.* Edited by P. G. Janssens, 67-87. Brussels: King Baudouin Foundation, 1997.
Viaene, Vincent. "King Leopold's Imperialism and the Origins of the Belgian Colonial Party, 1860-1905." *The Journal of Modern History* 80, no. 4 (2008): 741-790.
Wagner, Florian. "Inventing Colonial Agronomy: Buitenzorg and the Transition from the Western to the Eastern Model of Colonial Agriculture." In *Environments of Empire: Networks and Agents of Ecological Change.* Edited by Ulrike Kirchberger and Brett M. Bennett, 103-128. Chapel Hill: University of North Carolina Press, 2020.
"Private Colonialism and International Co-operation in Europe, 1870-1914." In *Imperial Co-operation and Transfer, 1870-1930: Empires and Encounters.* Edited by Roland Cvetkovski and Volker Barth, 58-79. London: Bloomsbury, 2015.
Wahid, Abdul. "In the Shadow of Opium Tax Farming and the Political Economy of Colonial Extraction in Java 1807-1911." In *Colonial Exploitation and Economic Development: The Belgian Congo and the Netherlands Indies Compared.* Edited by E. Frankema and F. Buelens, 107-129. London: Routledge, 2013.
Webb, James L. A. *Humanity's Burden: A Global History of Malaria.* Cambridge: Cambridge University Press, 2009.
Weber, Andreas. "Collecting Colonial Nature: European Naturalists and the Netherland Indies in the Early Nineteenth Century," *BMGN - Low Countries Historical Review* 134, no. 3 (2019): 72-95.
Weber, Andreas, and Robert-Jan Wille, eds. "Laborious Transformations: Plants and Politics at Bogor Botanical Gardens." Special issue, *Studium* 11, no. 3 (2018).
Wedema, Steven. *"Ethiek" Und Macht: Die Niederländisch-Indische Kolonialverwaltung und Indonesische Emanzipationsbestrebungen 1901-1927.* Stuttgart: Steiner, 1998.
Weiss, Holger. *Framing a Radical African Atlantic: African American Agency, West African Intellectuals, and the International Trade Union Committee of Negro Workers.* Leiden: Brill, 2014.
Wesseling, Hendrik. L. "The Giant That Was a Dwarf, or the Strange History of Dutch Imperialism." *The Journal of Imperial and Commonwealth History* 16, no. 3 (1988): 58-70.

"Le Modèle Colonial Hollandais dans la Théorie Coloniale Française." *Revue française d'histoire d'outre-mer* 63, no. 231 (1976): 223–255.

Wheatley, Natasha. "Mandatory Interpretation: Legal Hermeneutics and the New International Order in Arab and Jewish Petitions to the League of Nations." *Past & Present*, 227, no. 1 (2015): 205–248.

Whitehead, C. *Colonial Educators: The British Indian and Colonial Education Service 1858–1983*. London: I. B. Tauris, 2003.

Wickramasinghe, Nira. "Colonial Governmentality and the Political Thinking Through '1931' in the Crown Colony of Ceylon/Sri Lanka." *Socio* 5 (2015): 99–114.

Wildenthal, Lora. *German Women for Empire, 1884–1945*. Durham: Duke University Press, 2001.

Wilder, Gary. *The French Imperial Nation-State: Negritude and Colonial Humanism between the Two World Wars*. Chicago: University of Chicago Press, 2005.

Wille, Robert-Jan. *Mannen Van De Microscoop: De laboratoriumbiologie op Veldtocht in Nederland En Indië, 1840–1910*. Nijmegen: Vantilt, 2019.

Windel, Aaron. "Cooperatives and the Technocrats; or, 'the Fabian Agony Revisited.'" In *Brave New World: Imperial and Democratic Nation Building between the Wars*. Edited by L. Beers and G. Thomas, 249–268. London: University of London Press, 2012.

"Mass Education, Cooperation, and the 'African Mind.'" In *Modernization as Spectacle in Africa*. Edited by P. Bloom et al., 89–111. Bloomington: Indiana University Press, 2014.

Witte, Ludo de. *The Assassination of Lumumba*. London: Verso, 2001.

Young, Crawford. *Politics in Congo: Decolonization and Independence*. Princeton: Princeton University Press, 2015.

Zangger, Andreas. *Koloniale Schweiz: Ein Stück Globalgeschichte zwischen Europa und Südostasien (1860–1930)*. Bielefeld: Transcript Verlag, 2014.

Zantop, Susanne. *Colonial Fantasies: Conquest, Family, and Nation in Precolonial Germany, 1770–1870*. Durham: Duke University Press, 1997.

Zimmerer, Jürgen, and Joachim Zeller. *Genocide in German South-West Africa: The Colonial War (1904–1908) in Namibia and Its Aftermath*. Monmouth: Merlin Press, 2008.

Zimmerman, Andrew. *Alabama in Africa: Booker T. Washington, the German Empire, and the Globalization of the New South*. Princeton: Princeton University Press, 2010.

Anthropology and Antihumanism in Imperial Germany. Chicago: University of Chicago Press, 2001.

"Ruling Africa. Science as Sovereignty in the German Colonial Empire and Its Aftermath." In *German Colonialism in a Global Age*. Edited by Bradley Naranch and Geoff Eley, 93–108. Durham: Duke University Press, 2014.

Zimmermann, Susan. "'Special Circumstances' in Geneva: The ILO and the World of Non-metropolitan Labour in the Interwar Years." In *ILO Histories: Essays on the Interntional Labour Organization and Its Impact on the World during the Twentieth Century.* Edited by J. van Daele et al., 221–250. Bern: Peter Lang, 2010.

Zurstrassen, Bettina. *"Ein Stück Deutscher Erde Schaffen."* Koloniale Beamte in Togo 1884–1914. Frankfurt am Main: Campus, 2008.

INDEX

'Abduh, Muḥammad 174
Abendanon, Jacques H. 78, 229, 287, 349
abolitionist movement 36–37, 42, 50, 89–91, 112, 163, 171, 189, 196, 222, 299–300, 309
Aborigines' Rights Protection Society (1897) 233–234, 245
adat law 11, 22, 100, 106, 208
Ad-Dīn al-Afghānī, Sayyid Jamāl 174
Adenauer, Konrad 12
Adjigo, family (Togo) 225–226
administration, colonial
  health insurance 17, 21, 68–69, 72, 112, 129–130, 144, 147
  old age pensions 17, 21, 111–113, 131, 138, 141, 144–147
  ousting indigenous staff 137–141
  reform of training 124–137
Afro-American returnees as transimperial agents 18, 67, 171, 196
agricultural schools, in the colonies
  Buitenzorg and Java 158–161
  French Africa 170
  German Africa 169
  India 302
  mantris 156, 158
agriculture, colonial 1, 11, 17–18, 22, 67, 81, 92, 108–109, 120, 133, 149–172, 197, 247, 275, 280, 287, 303, 309–311, 338–341, 348, 362, 396, 406
  smallholder model 22, 108, 150, 154, 160–163, 168, 170
agronomy 21, 30, 40, 112, 120, 148, 172, 341

Ahyi, Michel 171
Aiyer, Ramaswami 332
Algeciras Conference (1906) 43, 47
Almade, José d' 222
Al-Tasouli 191
Amani, Biological-Agricultural Institute 112–113, 120, 149, 158, 166–169
Amedon, Etsè 196
Ankermann, Bernhard 273
Anti-Slavery Act (1890) 89
Anton, Günther 194–195, 198, 202, 349
Arenberg, Auguste de 47
Arenberg, Franz von 37, 47, 70, 93, 209
artisanat 206–207
Asbeck, Frederick van 219
Atta, Ofori 234
Austin, Oscar Phelps 41, 108, 118
Ayirebi Acquah, Nana 234

bacteriology, colonial 71–73, 130
Bairam (Islamic scholar) 201
Balandier, Georges 20, 334, 353
Balbo, Italo 202, 259, 263, 267–269, 276, 278, 280
ban on forced labor in the colonies 244, 250–254, 305, 309
Bandung conference (1955) 18, 20, 23, 347
Bantu law 12, 103, 317
Becker, Carl Heinrich 51, 68, 174–175, 177, 181, 185, 188
Belgian Colonial Council (1908) 59
Berlin Conference 1884/5 2, 25, 213, 215, 330
Bert, Paul 28, 194
Bertrand, Louis 266

409

Biagi, Bruno 275
Bibliothèque Coloniale Internationale 14, 54, 279
Bidault, Georges 12
Bomboko, Justin-Marie 328–329, 332–333
Bonnecarrère, Paul Auguste Francois 226
botany, colonial
  applied science 149, 151, 154
  improvement of plants 150, 161, 164, 166–167, 172
  indigenous knowledge 155–157, 171–172
  transcolonial transfers 109, 113, 149, 152–153, 164–165, 167–170, 172
  transimperial 128, 134, 151–154, 156, 163–164, 169, 171
Bourguiba, Habib 328
Boyer, Marcel 288
Brévié, Jules 293, 296
Briey, Pierre de 347
British Society for Tropical Medicine and Hygiene 70
Brumpt, Émile 71
Brussels Act 1890 2, 89
Budi Utomo 229
Buell, Raymond Leslie 227, 284
Buitenzorg
  "Eastern model" 149–172
  laboratories 22, 92, 149–172
  mystification 22, 149–172
  transcolonial transfers 149–172, 335
Busse, Walter 165–166

Caetano, Marcelo 324, 328
Caix, Robert de 222
Cambon, Jules 177–178
Cambon, Paul 191
Carpentier-Alting, Johannes Hendrik 304
Casely Hayford, Joseph Ephraim 17, 211, 225–227, 238–239, 245, 284, 299, 351, 355
Castries, Henri de 174
centenaire of Algeria's conquest 253, 265
Cerulli, Enrico 321
Césaire, Aimé 11–12, 15, 350, 356

Chagga 296–297
Chailley-Bert, Joseph 1, 3, 8–9, 24, 27–32, 38–39, 47–63, 91, 96, 99, 107, 110, 117, 120–140, 143, 148, 151, 158–160, 168, 170, 175, 177, 187–188, 194, 209, 212, 216, 241, 250, 317, 349, 351–352, 356–357
Chamberlain, Austen 254
Chatterjee, Partha 4
Chevalier, Auguste 152, 170
Chiha, Michel 319
Chivapragupta 238
Christian colonialism
  abolitionism 89–91
  Catholic welfare policy 91, 93, 95, 278, 292–295, 325
  Christian internationalism 50, 262
  Christian social reform policy 21, 91, 93, 95, 278, 282, 295, 325, 355
  Dutch colonial guilt 92
  and economic development, see: ethical policy
  and free trade 91
  humanitarianism 65, 89–90, 266
  and Islam 176, 179, 181, 188, 191, 222, 257, 269–270, 278, 316, 323
  paternalism 65, 91, 93–94, 292, 294
  Protestantism, see:ethical policy
  and Roman Empire 266, 268
cinchona and quinine 70, 72, 76, 129, 131, 153, 166, 169
Civilisations (journal, INCIDI) 319, 348
cocoa 79, 164, 168–170, 243, 247, 299–300
coffee 37, 114, 116, 151, 157–158, 162, 164–165, 167, 169–170, 172, 227, 296–297, 332
Colonial Institute, Hamburg 10, 46, 121, 133, 135–136, 140, 175, 334
colonial law 15, 21, 30, 34, 54, 57–59, 94–95
  transcolonial 96–107
  transethnic 65
colonial violence 77
Committee of Experts on Native Labor (ILO) 253
concession companies 33, 80, 102, 194, 197, 246

INDEX 411

constitutionalism, colonial 102, 106, 183, 218, 228–229, 236, 240–242, 312, 319, 327, 331
Convegno Volta, *See:* Volta Congress on Africa
Cooper, Frederick ix, 15
cooperative societies, agricultural
  British West African Co-operative Association 299
  Clove Grower's Association for Zanzibar 298
  and compulsion 148, 285, 288, 290, 292, 295, 298, 302, 305, 307–309, 311, 313, 341
  cooperative world commonwealth 283
  fokon'olona 285, 305–314, 354
  in fascist Italy 258, 275–276, 281–282
  and governmentality 275, 278, 281, 283, 285, 287–288, 293–294, 296, 301, 306, 308, 311, 313, 354
  in the ICI 287
  in India 206, 283–285, 296, 302–303
  Indigenous Provident Societies (French colonies) 284, 288–292, 294–295, 313, 341, 354
  in Indochina 288
  in Indonesia 304, 312
  Kilimanjaro Natives' Planter Association (KNPA) 296–297, 313
  and marketing boards 287, 290–291, 340
  and Muslim solidarity 288–289
  and mutualism 288–289, 291, 294, 300, 307–308, 310, 340–342
  nidhis in India 300
  Pan-African 299
  and political emancipation 284, 313
  Rochdale principles 281, 284, 300
  in settler societies 285–286
  takavi loans in India 301
  as a tool for development 258, 284, 287, 292
  transimperial 206, 292–294, 312
  West African Co-operative Producers Ltd 299–300
  and women 344
Cordero Torres, José María 324
Costa, Joaquín 42

Cotta, Freppel 281–284
Council of Europe (Conseil de l'Europe) 13, 20, 326
craft guilds and corporatism
  anti-communist 205–207, 277–278, 355
  to avoid democracy 204, 277–278
  to avoid welfare state 7, 204
  and castes in India 205–206
  fascist 208, 278
  and governmentality 11, 204, 277, 287, 354
  and the ILO 206–207
  Islamic 22, 173, 204–208, 277–278, 343
  in North Africa 204–206, 277
  third way between capitalism and socialism 205, 207, 277
  tool for sustained development 173, 277, 343, 354
  transimperial 205–206, 278
credit banks 7, 19, 91–92, 95, 158, 277, 281, 286–287, 291–296, 301–304, 307, 311–313, 354
Creech Jones, Arthur 330, 340
Cremer, J. T. 116
Curzon, George 38
customary law 11, 14, 18, 22, 65, 94–107, 208, 307, 310, 317, 328, 341–342
  and adatization 208
  and Islamic law 208
  and justification of conquest 198, 289

Danckelmann, Alexander von 45
De Gaulle, Charles 322, 330
De Vecchi di Val Cismon, Cesare M 266
De Wilde, Neytzell 222
Delavignette, Robert 293–294, 341
Delcassé, Théophile 44, 46
Deli Maatschappij 116
Delteil, Pierre 307, 309, 311
Dernburg, Bernhard 3, 19, 37, 46, 48, 61, 67, 87–88, 146, 351
Descamps, Édouard 50, 60, 104
detribalization debate 18, 102–103, 231, 235, 256, 306, 344

development
  coerced 23, 100, 108, 116–118, 263, 281–314, 325, 340
  emulative 8, 16, 32, 64–65, 79, 82–84, 86–88, 109, 114–115, 118, 149, 154, 165, 168–170, 172, 188, 205, 212, 257, 264, 312, 342
  ethical 91–95, 116–117, 120, 170
  governmental 17, 20, *64–65*, *73*, 86–88, 91, 106, 109, 116, 126, 160, 220, 239, 247, 275–277, 281–314, 335, 338–342, 347, 354
  holistic 65, 336, 354
  indigenization 65, *73*, *76–77*, 88, 305–314, 336, 341, 354–355
  international agencies 4, 11, 15, *20*, *64*, *66*, 109, 325–326, 334–336, 339, 342, 347–348, 352
  late colonial 11, 19, *21*, *64*, *79*, *82*, 239, 331, 337
  mise en valeur 79, *82*, 87–88, 104, 135–136, 278, 311, 350
  origins of 10, *41*, *43*, *54–55*, 69, 71, 82, 83, 92, 116, 120, 335
  sustained 19, *21*, *23*, *58*, *65*, 89, 96, 106, 155, 204, 220, 277, 315, 317, 338–340, 342–343, 348, 354
  through colonial law 21, 54, 96–107
  transcolonial 7, 13, *21*, *64–66*, *78–79*, *82*, 101, 104–105, 107–109, 121, 149, 278, 315, 335, 339
Deventer, Conrad Theodor, van 92, 116
Diagne, Blaise 236
differing civilizations, concept 273–274, 315, 318, 321, 328–329, 331, 336, 354
dispossession 173, 194, 197–205
  ḥabūs 198–205
  inzāl 199–203
  melk and sarakat 182
  Torrens system, *see:*Torrens system
Djajadiningrat, Achmad 159, 211, 236–238
Djajadiningrat, Husein 318
Doutté, Edmond 175, 181, 190
Drummond-Shields, Thomas 222
Du Bois, W. E. B. 56, 78
Duchêne, Albert 222

empire
  Roman Empire 22, 111, 179, 200, 261, 264–268, 278–280
  État Civilisateur (Civilizing State) 50–51, 307
  ethical policy 65, 92–93, 116–117, 120, 137, 150, 160, 239, 304
  Étienne, Eugène 28–29, 31, 45, 127
  Eurafrica 3, 6, 10, 13, 20, 22–23, 257–280, 315–335, 353–354
    corporatist 278
experts
  autonomy 11, 14, 26–27, 51, 53–54, 59, 78, 109, 111, 123, 128–129, 139, 141, 146, 211, 215, 228, 230, 251, 274, 330
  experience 64, 66, 91, 95, 122, 149, 167, 172, 174, 190, 221, 231, 253, 260, 288, 292, 296, 315, 320–321, 337, 339
  from the Global South 17–18, 21, 60, 93, 112–113, 138, 149, 157, 171–172, 185, 187–188, 203–204, 206, 225–226, 281, 283, 296–297, 300–301, 303, 342–343, 345, 347, 349, 355
  knowledge 3–4, 14, 17, 24, 33, 54, 59, 61–62, 66, 83, 111–112, 171, 173–174, 179, 184, 202–203, 207–208, 211, 213, 266, 276, 310, 336, 341, 349
  professionalization 20, 53, 112, 126–128, 130, 139, 141, 144, 174, 210
  transimperial 1, 3–4, 7, 9, 17, 21, 26, 28, 32, 34, 40, 43, 51, 61, 65, 68–69, 71, 131, 140, 150, 152, 155, 170, 175, 179, 203, 205, 210, 219, 240, 257, 259–260, 270, 293, 296, 352

Fabié, Antonio Maria 3, 42, 76, 125–126
Fairchild, David 156–157
famine, in the colonies 115, 154, 158–159, 287, 290, 309–310, 348
Fanon, Frantz 351

fascism
  corporatism 208, 212, 258, 275–279, 281–284, 313, 324–325
  Eurafrica 3, 10, 13, 22, 257–280, 283, 325, 353
  in the INCIDI 320–322, 327–328
  and Islam 208, 257, 263, 268, 322
  Italian 250, 252, 257–280, 321, 324
  National Socialism 259–262, 264, 269, 323–324
  Portuguese 320, 324, 327–328
  Spanish 208, 320, 324
  transimperial 10, 15, 208, 212, 221, 248, 252, 254, 256–280, 283, 305, 316–317, 355
  Vichy 320–322
  Volta Congress 10, 22, 202, 257–280, 283, 320, 322
Federzoni, Luigi 259–260, 264
First Universal Races Congress (1911) 78
Fock, Dirk 3, 61, 135, 216, 230, 242
Food and Agriculture Organization (FAO) 314
forced labor 11, 19, 23, 68, 90, 104, 108, 116, 160, 187, 212, 227, 236, 244, 250–254, 276, 305, 309, 311–313, 340, 350
Franck, Louis 230
Franco, Francisco 324
Fransen van de Putte, Isaäc Dignus 19, 28, 91, 97, 116, 127
Freire d'Andrade, Alfredo Augusto 214
Froidevaux, Henri 61
functionalism
  anthropology 271–273, 317, 319–320, 331, 335–336, 353
  colonial law 107, 193
  economic 6, 315, 334, 336, 344, 353–355
  fascist 271
  functional governance 4, 10, 13, 21, 23, 64, 66, 111, 221, 315–316, 323, 325–326, 330, 334, 339, 341, 343, 352–354

Gallieni, Joseph 30–31, 66, 194, 279, 309
Gandhi, Mahatma 1–2, 9, 39, 107, 206, 231, 319, 332

German Colonial Society 34–35, 37, 44, 47–48, 57, 77, 99, 135, 143
German Committee for Colonial Economy (Kolonialwirtschaftliches Komitee) 109, 164, 168
Gohr, Albrecht 253
Government of India Act (1919) 218, 229, 241
governmentality, colonial 3–23, 31, 41, 56, 64–66, 73, 78, 86–87, 91–92, 95–96, 106, 109, 111–112, 148–149, 158, 172–173, 196, 204, 220, 236, 239, 247, 256, 260, 274–276, 283, 285–286, 296, 303, 308, 310–311, 313, 315–316, 333–334
Grahame, George 255
Great Depression 246, 248

Haarhaus, Hans 142, 144
$ḥabūs$, endowment under Islamic law 173, 176, 186, 189–190, 193, 198–205
Hailey, William Malcom 19, 217, 219, 284
Halewyck de Heusch, Michel-Eugène 222
Hall, C. J. J. van 81, 170
Hardy, Georges 260, 321–322
Harroy, Jean-Paul 347
Hasskarl, Justus 153, 157, 166
Hatta, Mohammed 237
Haushofer, Karl 259
Herbert, Robert 38, 146
Herero-Nama genocide 12, 109, 352
Heske, Franz 259
Heydt, Karl, von der 35–37, 60, 81, 286
hill stations, colonial 72, 112–113, 149, 166
Hill, Arthur W. 152
Hohenlohe-Langenburg, Hermann zu 34–37
Hoselitz, Bert 334, 336–337
Hubert, Lucien 44, 46, 88–89
humanitarian colonialism 89–90, 150, 172, 251, 253, 262, 266, 279–280, 295

414 INDEX

Huxley, Julian 343
hygiene, tropical *see:medicine, tropical*

Ibn Farhoun 191
Ibn Nadjim 191, 201
imperialism 10, 26–27, 43, 49, 53, 61, 63, 111, 152, 163–164, 170, 172, 213–214, 236, 238–239, 242, 253, 258, 262, 264, 266, 352
   rejected by the ICI 6, 253
indirect rule 31, 39, 41, 62, 103, 108, 128, 131–132, 177, 190–191, 194, 198, 257, 262, 264, 266, 270, 274, 277, 280, 283, 294–295, 303, 308, 345
Institut de Médicine Coloniale 70
Institute for Maritime and Tropical Diseases 70
Institute of International Law 15, 55, 85, 104
International African Association 28
International Agricultural Institute 140
International and Intercolonial Congress of Indigenous Societies (1931) 206, 305
International Colonial and Export Exhibition (1883) 32
International Colonial Congress (1889) 28, 74
International Colonial Institute (ICI)
   against settler colonialism 29, 31, 41, 53, 58, 60, 72–77, 110, 139, 194, 221
   and applied science 8, 55, 65, 71, 114, 149, 315, 321, 352
   archetype, stereotype, and prototype comparisons 111–112
   beginnings 24–63
   comparisons and transfers, *see:* internationalism, colonial:and comparisons
   and colonial science *see:* transnationalism and science
   cooperation with ILO 76, 210, 252–253
   cooperation with Institute of International Law, *see:*Institute of International Law
   cooperation with League of Nations 71, 76, 109, 111, 210, 219–222
   fascist takeover 252–256, 279
   free trade, *see:*internationalism, colonial and free trade
   friendship 44, 46–47, 51, 81, 187
   funding 8, 25–26, 53–54, 57–59, 65, 67, 120, 210, 212, 216–217, 253–255, 336, 339, 343, 347–348
   meetings 4, 14–15, 24, 28, 34, 36, 38–39, 41, 48–49, 51, 54, 56, 58, 61–62, 68–69, 75–76, 80–81, 117, 209, 216–217, 220, 236, 242, 253, 255, 315, 323, 327, 347
   membership 1–3, 7, 9, 11–12, 17–18, 21, 24–26, 28–43, 46, 48, 51–61, 71, 75–76, 79, 81, 92, 95, 109, 209, 216–217, 219–220, 236, 250, 279, 316, 318, 321, 331, 343, 347
   publications 14, 25, 41, 54, 58, 61, 75, 98, 109, 122
   and reformism 1, 3, 6, 9, 19, 30, 37, 40, 42, 61, 87, 91, 94, 109, 124–137, 142, 220–221, 258, 350–351, 355
International Congress of Colonial Sociology (1900) 19, 90, 95, 98, 185, 187, 353
International Cooperative Alliance (1895) 288
International Institute of African Languages and Cultures (IIALC) 210, 220, 255, 272, 353
International Institute of Differing Civilizations
   and independence 346–347
International Institute of Differing Civilizations (INCIDI) 20, 274
   anti-colonialism as moderate nationalism 315–348
   decline 347–348
   loyal emancipation and constructive nationalism 315–348
   members from the Global South 315–348
   middle class 344–346
   multicommunal, multiracial, and multicivilizational unions 315–348
   women 344

INDEX 415

International Institute of Political and Social Science Applied to the Countries of Differing Civilizations, see:International Institute of Differing Civilizations (INCIDI)
International Labor Organization (ILO) 15, 59, 76, 206–207, 210, 212, 220, 237–238, 244, 250–252, 288–289, 303, 305, 309, 312–314, 342, 347
International Office for the Protection of Native Races 226–227
International Society for Tropical Hygiene 70
Internationale Vereinigung für Vergleichende Rechtswissenschaft und Volkswirtschaftslehre (IVVR) 98–101, 197
internationalism
  anti-colonial 6, 13, 15, 18, 22–23, 78, 173, 198, 212, 235, 238–239, 256, 313, 316, 330, 347, 351, 355
  aristocratic 37, 46–48
  concept 5, 7, 25, 56, 62–63, 220, 238, 250, 252, 254, 258, 265, 280
  Congo 33, 35, 45, 49–50, 140, 215, 250
  continental 38, 48–50
  and development 64, 66, 82–84
  diplomacy 2, 5, 25, 43, 45–46, 56, 61, 123, 213–216, 236–237, 240, 251–252, 284, 309, 333
  fascist 15, 22, 212, 257–259, 269, 275, 279–280, 320–321, 324
  feminist 18, 56, 316, 344, 349
  and governmentality 17, 64, 66, 173, 320, 334, 339, 352, 355
  and individualism 28–29, 53
  international capital 33, 58, 60, 62, 65, 80–84, 86, 88, 92, 97, 107, 120, 196–197, 215, 221, 272, 335
  international community 116, 126, 163, 169, 206, 213, 215, 253, 296, 309, 312, 334, 350
  international law 6, 38, 45–46, 48, 50, 55–56, 60, 88, 104, 119, 213, 215, 223–225, 251
  international movements and organizations 15, 55–56, 71, 109, 202, 211–212, 219–220, 235–239, 252, 262, 280–281, 284–285, 305, 309, 312, 314, 325, 332, 334, 336, 339–343, 348, 352–353
  and knowledge 24, 31, 52, 54, 59, 62, 67–71, 99, 151, 153, 179, 203, 241, 260, 284, 288, 293, 304, 341
  marker of progress 5, 8–9, 12, 16–17, 19, 26, 53, 55, 154, 168, 208, 220, 250, 349–352
  and nationalism 6, 9, 17, 26–27, 34, 36–38, 40, 43, 51–53, 62, 86, 241, 253, 265
  Socialist 56, 236, 238–239, 258
  technocratic 111, 352
internationalism, colonial
  and colonial autonomy 6, 33, 51, 213, 215, 239–242
  and comparisons 8, 13, 15–17, 21, 40, 56, 64, 66, 68–69, 76, 82, 109–112, 120–121, 148, 198, 216, 334, 351–352
  early 28, 31–34
  and free trade 10, 21, 28, 33, 53, 65, 78–81, 87–88, 91, 97, 218
  historiography 14–15
  and science 8, 151, 153–154, 157, 172, 352
  and transfers 17, 41, 56, 67, 69, 177, 203, 217, 241
  and world wars 52, 250
internationalization
  of colonial rule 9, 25–26, 33, 209, 215, 220, 280
  of colonial staff 7, 18, 84, 111–112, 140, 155, 157, 335, 352
involution, agricultural 160
Islam in the colonies
  as a co-colonizer 175, 177–178, 263, 268, 278
  fatwa policy 178, 180, 192, 203
  Sanūsīya 176, 178, 199, 202
  Sufi brotherhoods (khouans) 176–177
  Tijāniyyah 177
Islamic law 208
Islamic law, codification and manipulation
  adatization 208

Islamic law, codification and manipulation (cont.)
  codification of Algerian law 185–191
  ḥabūs 198–205
  Inzāl 199–203
  mixing of Islamic and European law 191–194, 201
  mixing of law schools 199–203
  Muslim Code of Labor and craft guilds 203–208
  the notion of necessity in Islamic law 180, 186–188, 190–193, 203
  Ottoman Mecelle Code 199–203
  qāḍīs 179, 187
  'urf 179, 204

Jabavu, Davidson Don Tengo 299–300
Janssen, Camille 2–3, 27, 33, 35, 39, 58, 62, 94, 98, 104, 209, 216, 250
Java, model colony 22, 30, 32, 48, 51, 66–67, 71, 92, 97, 108, 114–118, 120, 126, 134, 152–153, 155–163, 165–169, 172, 229, 232, 248, 304, 349–350
Jerningham, Hubert, Sir 135
Jiménez, Saturnino 46
Jonghe, Edouard de 317
Julien, Gustave 309
Jullien, Albert 77
Jung, Karl 259

Kadanda Rao, P. 319
Kaji, Hiralal Lallubhai 206, 284
Kartini, Raden Adjeng 18, 56, 93, 138, 145, 317, 344, 349, 351, 355
Kat Angelino, Arnold, de 284
Kayer, Paul 35
Kew, Royal Botanic Gardens 152, 169
Khaled (Emir), el-Hassani ben el-Hachemi 202
Kiderlen-Wächter, Alfred von 45
Koelie-ordonnatie (Coolie-Ordinance, 1880), 116

labor migration, transcolonial 7, 18, 101, 104–106, 108, 245–246, 298
labor theory of property 198, 225
Labouret, Henri 207, 260, 288
Lafaucheux, Marie-Hélène 344

Le Neveu, Charles-Auguste 259–260
League Against Imperialism 235, 238
League of Nations 2–4, 9–11, 15, 50, 56, 59, 71, 76, 90, 109, 111, 141, 209–256, 259, 262, 268–269, 303, 309, 334, 352
Lebanese as transimperial agents 18, 88
Léopold II of Belgium 25, 27–28, 33, 35, 49–50, 71, 77, 86–87, 96–97, 102–103, 109, 115, 117, 139–140, 145, 165, 167, 169, 243, 250, 350
Lévy-Bruhl, Lucien 294
Limburg-Stirum, Johan Paul, van 230
Lith, Pieter Antonie van der 24, 27, 32, 34
Louwers, Octave 94–95, 109, 216, 222, 235, 250, 252, 254–255, 260–262, 265, 267, 272, 274, 293–294, 321–322
Lovink, H. J. 160–161
Lucchesi, Astuto Riccardo, di 324–325, 330, 332
Luciani, Jean-Dominique 185
Lugard, Frederick 3, 19, 61, 87, 108–109, 210, 217, 219–220, 250, 255, 283
Lumumba, Patrice 333, 346
Lyall, Alfred 38–39, 61, 82, 135
Lyautey, Hubert 3, 19, 30, 46, 61, 131, 174, 204, 210, 250, 263, 277–280
Lyautey, Pierre 260

M'Bow, Amadou-Mahtar 343
Maffey, John 274
Malinowski, Bronislaw 10, 20, 258, 269–275, 277, 335, 353
mandate, Lugard's dual mandate 62, 108–109
mandates (PMC)
  and civilizing mission 209–210, 220–221, 224
  and colonial autonomy 215, 224, 240
  debate in the ICI 209, 215, 219–220, 222–223
  lack of anthropological knowledge 211
  and petitions, *see:*petitions
  and political representation 219, 221, 223–225, 233, 319

practical requirements 221, 223–225, 227
redistribution 215, 219, 222, 225
theory 90, 210, 215–216, 218, 220–221, 223, 227, 240
and traditional colonies 9, 195, 210–211, 215, 218–223, 225, 227
Mangoenkoesoemo, Tjipto 230
Massignon, Louis 52, 174, 204, 206–207, 260–261, 263, 277–278
Mauss, Marcel 310
Mbanefo, Louis 298
Mécheri, Chérif 331
Mecklenburg, Henry, Prince 48
Mecklenburg, Johann Albrecht 44, 48
medicine, tropical 4, 7, 18, 21, 30, 40, 57, 60, 65, 67–73, 75–77, 112, 129–130, 134, 141, 146, 166, 295, 335, 340
Merinyo, Joseph 297
Meyer, Georg 34
Meyer, William 39, 133, 217, 241–242
middle class, in the colonies
priyayi 230, 236
Milliot, Louis 289
Milner, Alfred 214–217, 220
mise en valeur, see:development
Mitrany, David 10, 221, 334, 353
Mobutu, Sese Seku 347
Moeller de Laddersous, Alfred 340
Mokrani Revolt (Algeria) 351
Mollah Tcheragh Abi 191
Moqri, Idrīs al- 204
Morand, Marcel 174, 176, 184, 186–192
Morel, Edmond 351
Moresco, Emanuel 75–76, 119, 228–231, 249, 251
Mori, Angiolo 260
Morley, Lord 133, 229
Morley-Minto reforms (India 1909) 229
Mühlens, Peter 259
Muranjan, Sumant Khanderao 283–284
Mussolini, Benito 208, 259, 262–264, 266, 269, 275, 281–282, 321

National Socialism, *see*:fascism
native policy 15, 31, 40, 109–110, 116, 134, 178, 183, 208–209, 260, 280, 354

Nehru, Jawaharlal 332
neo-slavery (plantations) 22, 42, 117–118, 150, 162–163, 189, 307, 310
Neuss, Hubert von 194
Newton, Arthur Percival 217, 231, 255
Non-Cooperation Movement 231–232

Oemarsanoesi 161
Olivier, Marcel 260
Orestano, Francesco 259, 263–264
Ormsby-Gore, William 217, 219, 222, 254–255
Orsini, Paolo d'Agostino 259
Orts, Pierre 213–216, 219–221, 225–226, 235, 249
Orts-Milner Agreement 215

Palacios, Leopoldo 216, 219
Palestine Land Development Company 170
Pan-Africanism 56, 78, 235, 284, 299–300
Pan-Germanism 34–37, 43, 45, 53, 79
Pan-Islam 173–176, 178, 180, 184, 192, 203
Parsons, Talcott 334, 336–337, 353
Partai Nasional Indonesia 239
Patel, Vithalbhai 231
peace treaties (1919) 1–2, 9–10, 173, 202, 209, 213–215, 219, 222, 225, 240, 256, 269, 330
Penha Garcia, José Frazão, Count of 219, 251
Perhimpoenan Indonesia 238
Permanent Mandates Commission 9, 22, 109, 209–256, 266, 269, 280
Pétain, Philippe 323
Peters, Carl 35–36, 63
petitions
Paris Peace Conference 173, 202, 219
to French Parliament 198
to the British government 234
petitions (PMC)
abusive 225–227
lack of knowledge 211
and political representation 211, 224–227, 233
practical requirements 226

petitions (PMC) (cont.)
  rejection 22, 211, 224–226
  right to 90, 209, 211, 218, 225–226
Pettazzoni, Raffaele 271, 273–274
Pickens, William 238
Pietromarchi, Luca 260, 268
Piola Caselli, Eduardo 259
Pirelli, Alberto 259
Pittaluga, Gustavo 71
Pittard, Eugène 259, 274
plant engineering 22, 92–93, 149–151, 153–155, 158–159, 161, 164–169, 172, 291–292, 299, 306
Plissard, Roger 206–207
postcolonial theory 15, 350
Pouvourville, Albert de 44, 46, 48
protectionism, economic 10, 25, 33, 53, 78, 82, 85–86, 126
psychology
  colonial 315, 320–322, 334

Quashie, Léonidas 196
quinine, *see*:cinchona and quinine
Qur'an 173, 179, 184, 186, 201, 203, 207, 263
Qureshi, Anwar Iqbal 303
racism
  anti-European 23, 227, 316, 320, 322, 327, 329–330, 332, 344
  and civilizing mission 220, 274
  Hamite hypothesis 268
  ideology 4, 10, 12, 16, 23, 35–36, 75–79, 129, 220, 257, 259, 262, 273, 352
  in League of Nations 221
  medical 65, 68, 71–72, 74–75
  multi-racial society 327
  and racial degeneration 72, 74–75
  and segregation 31, 106, 221, 246–247, 269, 320, 322, 324, 328, 354

Rappard, William E. 221
Rathgen, Karl 121, 135–136, 138
Ratzel, Friedrich 35–36
Reay, Eleventh Lord Donald Mackay 28, 34, 38, 48, 60, 64, 66, 209, 216–217

Recueil International de Législation Coloniale 58, 98, 107
Rees, Daniel Fançois Willem van 219, 222–224, 227, 233, 253
regenerationist colonialism 42
representation debate
  collective responsibility and punishment 308, 313
  in the colonies 22, 132, 204, 211–212, 218, 224, 228, 234, 238–239, 299, 306–307, 312, 318–319, 323, 332–333
  corporatist representation 22, 204, 208, 248–250, 275–278, 284–286, 294, 296–297, 299, 302, 304, 306–307, 312, 318, 320, 323–324, 327
  delegitimizing indigenous representation 22, 204, 211–212, 219, 224–227, 233–235, 302, 330–331, 344, 346
  mass participation 212, 228–230, 233, 253
  multicivilizational and multicommunal representation 317, 320, 327, 329
  petitions to the PMC 218, 225–226, 233, 235
  representation of colonies in Europe 2, 19–23, 75, 151, 191, 209–213, 215, 217–219, 221, 223, 238, 251–253, 256–258, 317–318, 324, 326, 329, 333
  representatives from the Global South in International Organizations 235–239
  representatives from the Global South in the ICI 236, 316, 322, 339, 345
  representatives in the ICI 26–27, 36–39, 45–48, 52, 59–60, 241, 249–250, 267, 279–280, 316, 320–321, 347
  sovereignty vs. representativity 212
  taxation and representation 211, 242–249
representative councils in the colonies 11, 13, 22, 204, 208, 211, 218, 224,

INDEX   419

227–239, 245, 248–249, 256, 290, 312, 354
Central Legislative Assembly (India) 231
Legislative Council (Gold Coast) 229, 233–234, 239, 245
Philippine Commission and Assembly 233
Volksraad 119, 218, 228–230, 232, 236–237, 239, 248, 318
Retana, Wenceslao 43
Revue Coloniale Internationale 32
rice 86, 92, 115, 117, 151, 158–161, 290, 306–307, 337
Rockefeller Foundation 15, 71, 325
Rossetti, Carlo 260
Roume, Ernest 82, 87–89, 98, 100, 109, 219, 240, 290–291
Royal Asiatic Society 38, 57
Royal Colonial Institute 40, 50, 82, 217
rubber (caoutchouc) 12, 49, 80, 86, 88, 97, 102, 115, 154, 164–165, 167, 169–170, 215, 243, 332, 350
Ruppel, Julius 259
Ruxton, Fritz Herbert U. 260
Ryckmans, Pierre 19, 222, 260

Salazar, Antonio de Olveira 324
Salim, Hadji Agoes 237–238
sanitation, colonial, *See*:medicine, tropical
Santillana, David 191–193, 200–202
São Tomé plantations 169
Sarekat Islam 207, 229, 237, 248, 318, 372
Sartre, Jean-Paul 351
saving and savings banks, *See*:credit banks
Sawas Pasha 187–188, 191–192
Sawondo, Nani 344
Say, Jean-Baptiste 28, 79
Say, Léon 28, 55, 79
Scharlach, Julius 79–81
Schuman, Robert 12
Schweinfurth, Georg 35
Sen, Sun-Yat 238
Senghor, Léopold Sédar 13, 20, 321, 327–329

Sepoy Rebellion 1857 38, 114, 118, 351
Service of Indigenous Affairs 175, 184, 204
Service of Indigenous Arts in Morocco 205
Silva da Cunha 328
small nations 8, 27, 33, 52, 120
Smuts, Jan 216, 220
Snouck Hurgronje, Christiaan 48, 51, 117, 119, 134, 137, 174–181, 184–185, 188, 199, 221, 236, 248, 250, 318
social engineering 154, 158, 257, 293
Société de Pathologie Exotique 70
Society of Social Assistance (Belgian Congo) 95, 293–295, 340
Soejono, Pangeran Adipati 238
Sohier, Antoine 102–103, 105, 317
Sorel, François 260
Spire, Camille 167
Strickland, Claude Francis 296–298, 304
Stuhlmann, Franz 149, 164–166
Subaltern Studies 4
sugar 37, 81, 114, 117, 151, 154–155, 159, 162, 164
Sukarno 239, 319
Survey on Africa 217, 283
Swaraj 231

Taft Commission 133, 229
taxation, colonial 242–249
technocracy, colonial 10, 17, 111, 120, 211–212, 219, 274, 323, 344, 352–353
technology
  governmentality 7, 16, 53, 56
  transcolonial 7, 22, 168, 348
  transfers 7–8, 17, 22, 54, 56, 65, 156, 168, 281, 352
Tempels, Placide 12
Tervuren, Congo Museum 140, 245
Tervuren, École Mondiale 140
Tete-Ansa, Winifried 299–300
Third World, concept 11, 21, 23, 323, 339–340, 345, 348
Thiselton-Dyer, William 169
Thomas, Albert 207

Thurnwald, Richard 259
Thys, Albert 3, 24, 27, 33, 58, 60, 62, 80–91, 104, 108, 117, 130, 210, 335
Torrens system 97–98, 194–198
Touré, Sekou 330
Tracy-Philipps, James Erasmus 260, 262, 264, 267, 279–280, 316
transcolonial
  anti-colonialism, *see:* internationalism, anti-colonial
  autonomy 7
  codification and law 22, 65, 96–107, 208
  comparison 64, 83, 110–148
  concept 8
  cooperation 8, 48, 86
  development 7, 21, 64–65, 78, 82–86, 88, 92, 107–109, 275–279, 305–314
  Eurafrica 257–270
  governmentality 7, 21, 23, 64, 86, 305–314
  knowledge 7, 12, 22, 64, 66, 83, 270
  labor recruitment 7, 18, 84–85
  medicine 7, 73
  networks 6–7, 18, 48, 67, 254
  railway construction 2
  science 14, 66–68
  transfers 6–8, 13, 17, 21, 149–172
transimperialism
  anti-colonial, *see:*internationalism, anti-colonial
  concept 6
transnationalism
  aristocratic 46, 48
  concept 3–5, 7–8, 43, 48–50, 62–63, 111
  and functionalism 8, 10, 25, 53, 62, 69, 111, 329
  and governmentality 3–4, 7, 10–11, 21, 23, 64, 315, 335, 339
  in the ICI 15, 21, 26–28, 36, 40, 50, 52, 54, 56–57, 61–62, 68, 315
  and knowledge 26, 31–32, 44, 110, 203
  practice 3, 5, 7, 24–26, 33, 51, 55, 61, 65, 111, 170, 210, 257
  and reform 8, 21, 53, 63
  and science 8, 14, 17, 22, 25, 51, 55–56, 63, 68, 70, 111, 352
  and transimperialism 6
Truman, Harry S. 11, 325, 339

Ugarte, Manuel 238
Union Coloniale Française (French Colonial Union) 24, 29, 46, 49, 57, 99, 143, 168, 178, 188, 250
Union Minière du Haut Katanga 101–102, 227
Union of International Associations 56, 140
United Nations 15, 314, 321, 339, 342, 344, 352, 355
United Nations Economic and Social Council (ECOSOC) 339, 342
United Nations Educational, Scientific and Cultural Organization (UNESCO) 11, 19, 314, 339, 342, 347, 354
Universal Negro Improvement Association and African Communities League 235
Uthman, Sayyed 178

Vandervelde, Émile 56
violence, colonial 3–4, 9, 12, 16, 40, 74, 93, 109, 162, 174, 176, 227, 253, 260–261, 266, 289, 305, 321, 350–352
  British King's African Rifles 247
  Force Publique 247–248, 293
Vischer, Hanns 255, 260
Volkens, Georg 151–152, 154
Vollenhoven, Cornelis van 98, 182–183, 317–318
Volpi, Giuseppe 205
voluntariness 3, 85, 206, 281, 288–289, 307, 333, 340–341, 354

Wäldämika'él, Asfäha 321
Warburg, Otto 168–170
Weigelt, Kurt 259, 264
welfare, in the colonies 7, 11, 19, 21, 23, 65, 89, 91–92, 94, 96, 147, 159, 204, 239, 247, 262, 275, 285, 287, 307, 331, 338, 340, 354

Wigny, Pierre 325–326, 332–333, 338–339, 342, 346–347
Wilson, Woodrow 173, 202, 212, 217
Woermann, Adolph 37, 81
World Congress of International Associations (1910) 56

Yanagita, Kunio 219

Zekri, Ahmad Ibnou 322
Zekri, Mohand Said Ibnou 177, 322
Ziemann, Hans 70, 76, 143
Zimmermann, Albrecht 120, 149, 165, 167
Zimmermann, Alfred 45, 67
Zoli, Corrado 267

For EU product safety concerns, contact us at Calle de José Abascal, 56–1°, 28003 Madrid, Spain or eugpsr@cambridge.org.

www.ingramcontent.com/pod-product-compliance
Lightning Source LLC
LaVergne TN
LVHW041617060526
838200LV00040B/1315